DEFIANT PRIESTS

DEFIANT PRIESTS

DOMESTIC UNIONS, VIOLENCE, AND CLERICAL MASCULINITY IN FOURTEENTH-CENTURY CATALUNYA

MICHELLE ARMSTRONG-PARTIDA

CORNELL UNIVERSITY PRESS

Ithaca and London

First published 2017 by Cornell University Press
First paperback printing 2020

Library of Congress Cataloging-in-Publication Data

Names: Armstrong-Partida, Michelle, 1974– author.
Title: Defiant priests : domestic unions, violence, and
    clerical masculinity in fourteenth-century Catalunya /
    Michelle Armstrong-Partida.
Description: Ithaca : Cornell University Press, 2017. |
    Includes bibliographical references and index.
Identifiers: LCCN 2016050882 (print) | LCCN 2016051947
    (ebook) | ISBN 9781501707735 (cloth) |
    ISBN 9781501707810 (epub/mobi) |
    ISBN 9781501707827 (pdf) |
    ISBN 9781501748424 (pbk.)
Subjects: LCSH: Catholic Church—Clergy—Sexual
    behavior—Spain—Catalonia—History—To 1500. |
    Catholic Church—Clergy—Family relationships—
    Spain—Catalonia—History—To 1500. | Masculinity—
    Religious aspects—Catholic Church—History—To
    1500. | Marriage—Religious aspects—Catholic
    Church—History—To 1500. | Masculinity—Spain—
    Catalonia—History—To 1500. | Marriage—Spain—
    Catalonia—History—To 1500. | Catalonia
    (Spain)—Church history.
Classification: LCC BX1912.9 .A76 2017 (print) |
    LCC BX1912.9 (ebook) | DDC 262/.142467—dc23
LC record available at https://lccn.loc.gov/2016050882

Contents

Map 1. The Crown of Aragon and surrounding territories, ca. 1300.

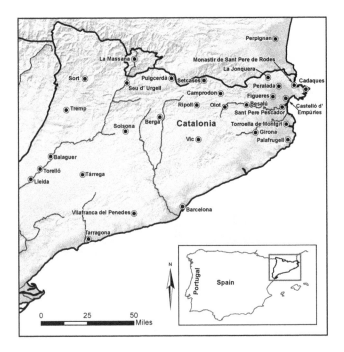

Map 2. Catalunya and surrounding territories, ca. 1300.

ACKNOWLEDGMENTS

After searching for concubinary priests and their families in the archives of Girona, Barcelona, and Vic for more than a decade, I am indebted to the generosity of family, friends, and the institutions that were critical in producing this book. I am honored to have received the University of California President's Postdoctoral Fellowship and to have been chosen as an American Council of Learned Societies New Faculty Fellow. The years I spent at the University of California, Los Angeles (UCLA) and at Emory University were indispensable to broadening my research agenda beyond the diocese of Girona and transforming my manuscript into the book I had envisioned—one that could speak more broadly to Catalan clerical culture by incorporating more archives into my study. My initial research was made possible by the University of Iowa (UI) and the support offered to graduate students by way of the UI Burke Award for International Travel and Research, the T. Anne Cleary International Dissertation Research Fellowship, and the UI Stanley Graduate Fellowship for Research Abroad. A fellowship from the American Association of University Women helped me finish writing and gave me the time to produce a more thoughtful work. Among the archives that I am most fond of and the people there whom I have received the most assistance from, I owe special thanks to Albert Serrat i Torrent at the Arxiu Diocesà de Girona, and Dr. Rafel Ginebra i Molins and Dr. Miquel Gros i Pujol at the Arxiu Episcopal de Vic. I also acknowledge the kindness shown to me by Dr. Jaume de Puig i Oliver, who from the very beginning was willing to help and share his knowledge of the Arxiu Diocesà de Girona and its staggering collection of episcopal registers.

I find myself incredibly grateful to a community of feminist scholars that sustained me during various stages of my research and writing: Allyson Poska, Dana Wessell-Lightfoot, Alexandra Guerson, Amy Livingstone, Miriam Shadis, Theresa Earenfight, Marie Kelleher, Kittiya Lee, Ray Ball, Kaja Cook, Karen Christianson, Michelle Rhoades, Dauna Kiser, and Michelle McKinley. Especially to be remembered among this group are my friends at Emory University,

Astrid Eckert, Judith Miller, Sharon Strocchia, Judith Evans Grubbs, and Brian Vick. I must also express how lucky I feel to have such dear friends at the University of Texas at El Paso. Thank you, Barbara Zimbalist, Matthew Desing, Sandy McGee-Deutsch, Marion Rohrleitner, Lowry Martin, and Andrew Fleck for your unflagging support. Since the moment we met and stupendously hit it off, we have seen each other through the highs and lows of academic life, talked incessantly about our research and writing to cheer each of us on, shared amazing meals together, and gained many pounds from our baking extravaganzas. I could not have asked for better friends and colleagues. Over the years, I have benefitted from the sage advice of my advisor, Connie Berman, and from my faculty mentors, Teófilo Ruiz at UCLA and Stephen White, emeritus, from Emory University, who were all generous with their time and kind words. Aminta Pérez and Junko Kobayashi made me feel part of a family during our years together in graduate school. I am very thankful for the mentoring that Cathy Komisaruk and Omar Valerio-Jiménez provided during their first years at the University of Iowa. My sincere appreciation goes out to Cheryl Martin, Heather Kopelson, and the many friends who read various drafts, and to Josep Maria Gironella i Granés, who shared his citations of priests' wills with me in the Arxiu Històric de Girona. I also thank Susan Webb for her gracious hospitality in Barcelona and for teaching me to cook traditional Catalan dishes. Over the years, I have spent many lovely evenings dinning al fresco in the medieval quarter of Girona with my dear friend Roser Mestre Carreras, whom I must thank for her exceptional good humor and witty stories, which are a balm for the long hours I spend in the archives each summer.

During my first research trip to Girona and the many years that have followed, the nuns of Sant Daniel have always welcomed me with warmth and affection. I will never forget the many nights I spent sleeping in the spooky Romanesque church tower and the times I made my way in the dark with a flashlight from my room in the tower across the maze of stairways, rooms, and hallways that led to the medieval cloister, where its dangerous steps and ill-placed well needed to be transversed carefully to get to my evening meal in the dining hall. This experience did much for my imagination. Although the nuns of Sant Daniel may not appreciate my association of their beautiful Romanesque cloister with the story of a slain historian, I have always thought that this would make the perfect setting for a murder mystery novel—one that I might get around to writing someday. I also wish to commemorate the memory of Dr. Josep Maria Marquès i Planagumà, the long-time archivist of the Arxiu Diocesà de Girona, who was a formidable man and scholar. Although he protected his archive and presented me with a number of challenges during my first year, I appreciate that he made me a more determined researcher when put to the test. It took years to earn a modicum of his respect, which felt like a victory. His presence in the archive is missed.

Finally, I thank my parents for their love and patience. I know they remain mystified as to how they produced an historian, especially one specializing in the Middle Ages. When my mother crossed from México illegally into this country with a third-grade education to work in a *maquiladora*, she never imagined that her daughter would one day become a *profesora* at a university. In a time when the vitriol against immigrants has peaked throughout the United States and Europe, this book is a small tribute to the hard work and sacrifices made by immigrant parents for their children and the power of education to transform a life.

Archival Abbreviations

ACG   Arxiu Comarcal de la Garrotxa
        Notarials
ACT   Arxiu Capitular de Tortosa
        Visites pastorals
ACV   Arxiu Capitular de Vic
        Visites pastorals (de Urgell)
ADB   Arxiu Diocesà de Barcelona
        Visites pastorals
        Registra Communium
        Dispensationes Apostolics
ADG   Arxiu Diocesà de Girona
        Visites pastorals
        Registres de Lletres Episcopals
        Notularum
        Processos
        Imposicions de Penes
        Obligacions de Penes
        Remissions de Penes
AEV   Arxiu Episcopal de Vic
        Visites pastorals
        Fons Notarials: Arxiu de la Cúria Fumada
AHG   Arxiu Històric de Girona
        Notarials
ASV   Archivio Segreto Vaticano
        Penitenzieria Apostolica
        Registra Avenionensia, no. 61
        Registra Vaticana, no. 151 and no. 155
        Registra matrimonialium et diversorum, no. 1 and no. 2

HMML   Hill Museum and Monastic Library
Monatic Microfilm Project, no. 31951. Visitationes, no. 1. Visitatio
diversarum
Ecclesiarum Civis et Diocesis Barcelonensis facta per Pontium Episcopum ab anno 1303 ad 1310.

A Note on Names

Although Catalan was increasingly used in writing in the later half of the fourteenth century, the diocesan registers consulted for this study were written primarily in Latin. I have rendered the names of places and people into modern Catalan, so cities such as Girona (Gerona) and Lleida (Lerida) appear in their Catalan form. Spanish forms appear when I am dealing with the Castilian church or the kingdom of Castile-León. The names of people who were not from Catalunya or Castile are in their Anglicized form.

A Note on Currency

The currency of the Crown of Aragon in the fourteenth century consisted of denars, sous, and lliures. One lliura comprised 20 sous, and 1 sou was the equivalent of 12 denars.

A Note on the Titles of Benefices

In the administrative documents of the dioceses of Barcelona, Vic, and Urgell, the title *rector* was commonly used to designate the priest who held the care of souls (*cura animarum*) in the parish. Other common titles for clergymen who were in the major orders but were not in charge of the *cura animarum* are *presbiter* and *vicarius, capellanus, diaconus*, and the ambiguous title *clericus beneficiatus*. Clerics in the minor orders were often designated *clericus tonsuratus, scolarius*, or simply *clericus*.[1]

---

1. Because the rule of celibacy applied to priests, deacons, subdeacons, canons, and monks, in other words clerics in the major orders, these were the men who were prohibited from marrying and

In the diocese of Girona, however, a different system of classification was used, and thus an explanation of parochial benefices is needed to understand the positions of clergy in the major orders in this diocese.[2] Due to a regional custom that began prior to the twelfth century, each parish church was typically assigned two *hebdomedarians* (hebdomadarii, or *domeros* in Catalan) and a *deacon*. Both hebdomedarians had the care of souls, but they alternated weekly with this charge. Over time, the responsibility for the church building was also incorporated into the duties of one of the hebdomedarians, whose title soon thereafter changed to *sacrist* (*sacrista*),[3] and the hebdomedarian likewise assumed the duties of the deacon. The titles hebdomedarian and sacrist are, in actuality, the titles of benefices that involved the care of souls, and thus these titles in large part obscure the hierarchy of clerics in parish churches because the title rector was not commonly used. Both the hebdomedarian and the sacrist were priests who could hold the care of souls, and in most parishes throughout the diocese of Girona, the care of souls was held by either one of these priests, although in very large parishes both men could hold the *cura animarum*.

Small parishes in the most mountainous areas of Catalunya were usually assigned only one priest, but larger parishes, as a rule, were staffed with a hebdomedarian, a sacrist, sometimes a deacon, a few scolares-in-training, and

are the focus of this book, while clergy in the minor orders (porters, lectors, exorcists, acolytes) could marry and are largely absent from this study of concubinary and violent clergymen.

2. For an explanation of how the system of benefices developed in the diocese of Girona, see Josep M. Marquès, "Fundaciones de beneficios en el obispado de Gerona, s. XII–XVIII," *Anthologica Annua* 36 (1989): 493–507; Josep M. Marquès, "Nuevas raíces en el antiguo suelo," in *Historia de las diócesis españolas: Barcelona, Terrassa, Sant Feliu de Llobregat, Gerona*. Vol. 2, ed. Josep M. Martí Bonet (Madrid: Biblioteca de Autores Cristianos, 2006), 491; Christian Guilleré, "Les visites pastorals en Tarraconaise à la fin du moyen âge (XIV–XV siècle). L'example du diocese de Gerone," *Mélanges de la Casa de Velazquez* 19 (1983), 145–46. A hebdomedarian was a priest who literally served for one week and alternated with another priest every other week. In large churches such as in Santa Maria de Castelló d'Empúries, up to four hebdomedarians, two sacrists (*maior* and *minor*), and four stabiliti served in the church; ADG, Visites, no. 4, 6v.–7r.v. (1329). In the earliest extant visitation registers from 1295 to 1315, the classification of the clergy is inconsistent at best. It is not uncommon to find a cleric identified in one document as simply "Petrus clericus" but to discover the same cleric labeled in other documents from the same year or in the visitation from the following year a "hebdomedarian" or "sacrist." We would expect to find terms such as *rector*, *presbiter*, and *sacerdos* used to identify the cleric who had the care of souls and to find the ranks of clerics who belonged to the major and minor orders. Yet these are terms that appear infrequently in the earliest episcopal visitation records to establish a cleric's rank. As the Girona diocesan government developed in the early fourteenth century, it took some time before the visitors and their scribes began to use standardized labels to identify the positions of parish clergy. Eventually, identifying who held the care of souls and the term *rector* appear more regularly but, even then, before 1350 this identification can be sporadic.

3. The position of sacrista should not be confused with that of the sexton found in English parishes.

anywhere from one to four *stabiliti*, depending on the size of the community. A *stabilitus* held a simple benefice that did not have the additional duties of the care of souls.[4] Clerics in the minor orders were rarely identified by rank, and more often than not appear in documents simply as a clericus, or as a sco-lar if the cleric was young. Usually, a cleric who held a benefice that required ordination into the priesthood, but who was not yet a priest, is identified as such in the visitation records. Fellow clergy and parishioners frequently re-vealed to a visitor if such a cleric had a suitable substitute in his place or if the cleric had surpassed the allotted time to receive his promotion into the holy orders.

In general, there was much fluidity in the positions of clerics and the ben-efices they held. For instance, the cleric Pere Flandin was both the rector of Matajudaica and a stabilitus in the chapel of Sant Andreu in Ullastret. The prac-tice of one cleric holding multiple benefices was widespread and meant that many parishes lacked full-time rectors. Such was the case in the parish of Santa Maria de Pineda, where the stabilitus Guillem Sabater held the care of souls in the absence of the rector Pere Turon.[5] In some parishes, the effects of this pluralism and the nonresidence of beneficed clerics resulted in a complex web of clerics employed as substitutes. In the parish of Vilacolum, the cleric Pere Vidal substituted for the sacrist Bartomeu Ferrer, who held the care of souls. A few years before, Bernat Esteve, clericus curatus in the chapel of Guàrdia, had substituted for Pere Vidal, but now he was a substitute for the stabilitus Ponç Riquer.[6] By the fourteenth century, the duties assigned to the benefices of hebdomedarian, sacrist, and even stabilitus became less clear, but all three were benefices that were held by priests. What determined the worth or sig-nificance of the benefice was its endowment and whether it was a benefice *cum cura*. Among the elite clergy, the endowment and status attached to the benefice especially mattered. Gilabert de Cruïlles, like many clerics from the nobility, was not solely a canon in the cathedral of Girona. Gilabert also served

---

4. The designation for this benefice evolved from charters in which patrons established a benefice for "stabilio locum unum sacerdotalem." J. M. Marquès explains how this benefice came to be called *stabilitus* in "Fundaciones de beneficios," 496–98. Christian Guilleré's article, "Visites pastorals en Tarraconaise," however, states that the stabilitus was one of the minor orders, contradicting Mar-quès's findings. I have found several examples in which a stabilitus had the care of souls, indicating that he was expected to be a priest. The parish of Albons is a case in point: "Castilio Roig clericus stabilitus et G<uillelmus> Vals clericus stabilitus ac regentes curam animarum in dicta ecclesiam pro Jacobo de Ville sacrista." ADG, Visites, no. 7, 88r.v.–89r. (1343). It is also common to find a stabilitus assigned to a chapel.

5. ADG, Visites, no. 4, 18r.v. (1329); ADG, Visites, no. 4, 83r. (1329).

6. ADG, Visites no. 4, 10v.–11r. (1329); ADG Notularum, no. 3, 158r. (1322); ADG Notularum, no. 6, 73r. (1326) and 140r. (1327).

as an episcopal administrator and accumulated many possessions, lands, and rents that came with the benefices he held as the hebdomedarian in the churches of Vilamalla and Fontcoberta, and as the sacrist in the church of Sant Pere de Pescador.[7]

7. Guillem de Cruïlles also held benefices in the chapels of Begur, Fonolleres, and Llambilles. The careers and benefices of numerous elite clergy are also outlined in the collection of bishops' letters transcribed by Jaume de Puig i Oliver and Josep M. Marquès i Planagumà, *Lletres del Bisbe de Girona. segle XIV*, Vol. 1 (Barcelona: Corpus Scriptorum Cataloniae, 2007), document no. 5, 79–80.

DEFIANT PRIESTS

Introduction
Understanding Priestly Masculinity

By the year 1332, the long union between the rector of Sant Romà de Sau and Elisenda des Frexe had produced three adult children and a younger son. As a paterfamilias, the rector had contracted marriages for two of his four daughters and presumably for his son Ramon since Ramon was now in possession of the rector's farmstead called Ça Frigola. The rector had given his daughter Elisenda a rural homestead where more than one house had been built, and he had given his daughter Sibil·la pastureland and a dowry of 450 sous when she married a local villager. The rector's negotiations and arrangements on behalf of his offspring—the inheritance for Ramon and the dowries for Elisenda and Sibil·la—meant that he had fulfilled his obligation as a father to provide for his children and secure their futures. The rector's role as a father and authority figure did not end there. He was also a role model and teacher, training the next generation of clergymen. Boys from the village, including his own young son, helped the rector during mass.[1] Baptisms, marriages, and feast days were likely celebrated alongside fellow villagers with his family in attendance. Clerical status and privilege distinguished the rector from the rest of his parishioners, but as a family man, he was like most adult men in his community. Integrated into the village of Sau through blood ties, marriage, and his responsibilities as pastor, the rector

---

1. AEV, Visites, no. 1200/2, 80r. (1332).

exercised both priestly authority in the parish church and paternal authority in his household. The rector, in essence, took part in the most salient characteristics of adult lay masculinity that could be found across all segments of society—he was a husband, a father, and master of his household. Neither a celibate priest nor simply a layman, he was both—a layman in priestly robes.

The parish priest, particularly as a family man in the late Middle Ages, is a little known and poorly understood figure in medieval history. Historians of the medieval church have concentrated largely on papal politics, influential religious leaders, reform movements, and the inner workings of the church as an institution. The picture of priests as husbands and fathers has been obscured by scholarship that has focused on canon law and synodal decrees that criminalized the sexuality of the clergy and thus privileged the official Church position on clerical sexuality. The actual lives of parish priests, particularly their responses to church policies that demanded they forsake the requirements of secular masculinity, have received far less attention. What is more commonly known is the plight of priests who were ordered to eschew their wives and children in the eleventh and twelfth centuries during the struggle of reformers to impose mandatory celibacy on a largely resistant clergy. The sympathetic figure of the beleaguered priest and his family in the wake of church reforms, however, is often turned into the licentious and predatory parish priest of the thirteenth and fourteenth centuries. Medievalist scholars have joyfully highlighted the examples of sexually promiscuous clergy found in medieval literature.[2] Others have focused on church legislation that repeatedly prohibited sex to illustrate that priests and regular clergy were sexually active and unrestrained in their carnal desires—all of which is used as evidence of a morally corrupt clergy. Although it is true that literary and legal sources reveal that the attempts by the Church to compel celibacy were largely ineffective in the later Middle Ages throughout western Europe, these sources tell us very little about the kinds of sexual relationships the clergy engaged in or what it meant for a parish priest to have a family two hundred years after clerical marriage had been prohibited. Recovering the personal and professional lives of late medieval parish clergy, therefore, reveals far more than the limited success of church reforms in convincing secular clergy that celibacy was an essential component to the priestly life and priestly identity: it exposes the prevalence of marriage-like unions and the importance of a woman, household, and progeny to the masculine identity of priests.

---

2. Stories of licentious priests can be found in many fabliaux. See Derek Brewer, *Medieval Comic Tales* (Cambridge, UK: St. Edmundsbury Press, 1996), 97–101, 132–33,136–39.

The personal and professional lives of lower-level clergy have received little consideration because it is so difficult to reconstruct their experiences from extant medieval sources. Still, piecing together the family life, careers, and experiences of parish priests is essential to understanding the professional and gender identities of the churchmen who made up the proletariat of the largest institution across western Europe. Secular clergy lived in a world filled with women, weapons, codes of honor, and lay ideals of masculinity. Two hundred years after the reforms of the eleventh and twelfth centuries, the comportment of parish clergy and their involvement in secular affairs remained much the same as the laity's. A multitude of evidence, from church decrees, saints' lives, pastoral manuals, medieval comic tales such as the fabliaux, and municipal laws dealing with prostitution and violence, as well as cases from both secular and ecclesiastical courts, shows that throughout the Middle Ages secular clergy continued to be influenced by the dominant male ideals of their society.[3] Many dressed as laymen and carried swords, daggers, and shields in villages, while traveling about, and even inside the parish church. They gambled in church cemeteries or streets, drank in taverns with family and friends, ate at their neighbors' houses, and wooed local women. Secular clergy enjoyed many of the same recreational sports as laymen and took part in prohibited activities, such as patronizing theatrical shows, women singers, or brothels, and attending popular forms of entertainment such as hangings and public whippings.[4] Very little differentiated parish clergymen from their parishioners because they were often raised, trained, and usually served in parishes where they had ties to family and friends. And just as priests established marital households like their parishioners, they likewise participated in a culture of violence that

---

3. See, for example, Hugh of Floreffe, *The Life of Yvette of Huy*, trans. Jo Ann McNamara (Toronto: Peregrina Publishing, 1999); Caesarius of Heisterback, *The Dialogue on Miracles*, trans. Henry von Essen Scott and C. C. Swinton Bland (Routledge: London, 1929); Robert Mannyng of Brunne, *Handlyng Synne*, ed. Idelle Sullens (Binghamton: SUNY Binghamton, Medieval and Renaissance Texts and Studies, 1983). The increasing devotion to the Virgin Mary in the twelfth and thirteenth centuries produced stories such as the *Cantigas de Santa Maria* and the *Milagros de Nuestra Señora*, in which the Virgin protects clerics from sexual temptation or demonstrates her mercy by saving the souls of fornicating clerics from the devil; *Songs of Holy Mary of Alfonso X, the Wise*, trans. Kathleen Kulp-Hill (Tempe: Arizona Center for Medieval and Renaissance Studies, 2000) Gonzalo de Berceo, *Miracles of Our Lady*, trans. Richard Terry Mount and Annette Grant Cash (Lexington: University Press of Kentucky, 1997). For humorous fables dealing with clergy, see Derek Brewer, *Medieval Comic Tales* (Cambridge, UK: Boydell & Brewer, 1996).

4. These activities were prohibited to the clergy in synodal decrees. See Jocelyn N. Hillgarth, and Giulio Silano, "A Compilation of the Diocesan Synods of Barcelona (1354): Critical Edition and Analysis." *Medieval Studies* 46 (1984), statute no. 47, 110; Tomas Noguer i Musqueras and Josep M. Pons Guri, "Constitucions sinodals de Girona de la primera compilacio," *Anales del Instituto de Estudios Gerundenses*, no. 18 (1966–1967), 67, 78, 111, 127–29, 151, 155–56. See also Robert I. Burns, "The Parish as a Frontier Institution in Thirteenth-Century Valencia," *Speculum* 37, no. 2 (1962), 248.

became one more way in which they demonstrated their masculinity in the village community. For example, the rector Romeu Capeller, who kept Elisenda and their son in his home and owned a tavern and gambling establishment, was considered a belligerent man not only because he never went "without his sword or arms" but also because he was known to physically fight with his parishioners. A similar picture emerges in the parish of Llorà, where the concubinary priest Guillem Serra was known for sporting arms while he conveyed the eucharist to sick parishioners and the poor. Villagers labeled Guillem a "pugnacious man" because he was quick to anger and cited the most recent example of Guillem slamming a gaming board into the face of a parishioner during a gambling dispute. Parish clergy employed violence to resolve disagreements, intimidate parishioners, and maintain their status and authority in the village, but clerical violence was not limited to parishioners. Clerical colleagues also fought each other to establish dominance in the clerical hierarchy of the parish; for example, the hebdomedarian Arnau and the sacrist of Sant Feliu de Beuda attacked each other with swords within the church.[5] Parish priests such as Romeu, Guillem, and the priests of Sant Feliu de Beuda, who served in village churches during the first half of the fourteenth century, represented the antithesis of what reformers had in mind when they set out to transform the comportment and customs of the secular clergy; yet in stark contrast to contemporary hopes and modern assumptions, they were in fact representative of the parish clergy in medieval Catalunya.

Based on the behaviors of the clergy that repeatedly appear in the sources, I have labeled these priests *defiant* because they defied canon law, synodal statutes, and church expectations by engaging in concubinous unions that resembled marriage and thereby compromised their vows of celibacy and obedience. Similarly, violent priests violated the principles of the Church that required secular clergy to abstain from carrying weapons and from shedding Christian blood through acts of violence. Although parish clergy conformed in varying degrees to lay culture, they rebelled against the priestly ideals of behavior delineated by the Church to reframe their profession and identity in a way that maintained their position and power in their communities. To understand how parish priests in late medieval Catalunya defined their masculinity, I examine in this book the families that priests established with women, their ties to the parish community, and their encounters with villagers and religious colleagues. Exploring the gender identity of parish priests illuminates

---

5. ADB, Visites, no. 2, 43r. (1314); ADG, Visites, no. 5, 81r.v. (1331); ADG, Remissions de Penes, no. 1, 49v. (1354). In 1345, the sacrist of Beuda was fined for saying dishonest and injurious words against the prior of Sant Tomàs de Fluvia and for having an affair with a married woman; ADG, Remissions de Penes, no. 1, 6r. (1345).

why they eschewed the very behaviors—celibacy and nonviolence—required by their profession. As Michael Kimmel and other scholars have noted, different definitions of *masculinity* exist because masculinity means "different things to different groups of people at different times."[6] Parish priests continued to have families despite the ecclesiastical prohibition of marriage because establishing a family household was central to a priest's identity as a man who was deeply connected to the community and local culture, and offered social and economic benefits as well. Although priests formed unions with women and engaged in secular behaviors associated with laymen, the gender identity of clergymen was far more complex than simply adopting elements of lay masculinity. Violence, in particular, was a part of mainstream clerical culture and integral to both the professional and gender identities of Catalan parish clergy. Clerics took part in the ritualized violence against Jews during Holy Week and followed the gendered behaviors they learned during their training as clergymen, resorting to violence to define themselves as men and dominate others. Since the vast majority of priests learned their profession from other parish clergymen, the parish became a battleground in which rivalries among clerics took place and young clerics learned from senior clergy how to establish their position in the church hierarchy. The competition for economic resources, status, and authority defined the relationships among parish clergy and often led to violent conflict. Parish priests produced a clerical masculinity that was unique to the ecclesiastical sphere because they melded the lay masculine ideals that were a part of their everyday culture with the privilege and authority of their profession.

In this study, I reconstruct the lives and careers of parish priests based on documents of practice, such as parish visitation records, ecclesiastical court cases, and the letters and registers from the bishop's curia of Girona and Barcelona. I have examined over 2,500 episcopal visitation records to parishes in the dioceses of Girona, Barcelona, Vic, Urgell, and Tortosa in the ecclesiastical province of Tarragona from 1293 through 1350.[7] These records from Catalunya are the most complete set of pastoral visitations for a given region, especially for the fourteenth century, and are without equal anywhere in western Europe.[8] Visitation records are indispensable as a source for social historians

---

6. Michael S. Kimmel, *The Gendered Society*, 3rd ed. (Oxford: Oxford University Press, 2008), 10.

7. The diocese of Lleida in Catalunya is excluded from this analysis because no visitation records exist for the fourteenth century.

8. Prior to 1350, a total of twenty-seven visitation books (made up of multiple quadernos) exist for the dioceses of Girona, Barcelona, Vic, and Urgell. Episcopal visitors in all four dioceses conducted a total of 3,876 visitations (excluding monasteries) to parish churches throughout Catalunya. After 1350, a total of eleven visitation books exist for these Catalan dioceses. For the entire fourteenth century, thirty-eight visitation books are extant. Christian Guilleré provides an overview of episcopal

because they illuminate the experiences and relationships of people that are the hardest to glimpse in historical sources—those at the lower and middling levels of medieval society. Episcopal visitations were a vehicle through which a bishop could correct the misconduct and moral lapses of parishioners and clergy, and thus they provide an unparalleled view into the lives and practices of the Catalan clergy. Each bishop or his official was expected to visit the parishes and monasteries in his diocese once a year to monitor the customs of the clergy and to watch for the defects and heresies of Christians. Visitations were meant to enforce Church ideals concerning orthodox belief, moral conduct, marriage practices, and the sexual behavior of the clergy and laity. The episcopal visitor was responsible for conducting an inquest into the state of the parish church, the moral conduct of its clergy, and, last, the conduct of the laity. When the visitor, accompanied by his entourage, arrived in the village and collected the "good men" of the parish in the church to interrogate, the "dirty laundry" of the parish emerged during the inquiry. Episcopal secretaries summarized the testimony of parishioners and parish clergy, given in Catalan, and recorded it in Latin in easy-to-carry quadernos. In all four dioceses, visitors were rarely able to visit more than half the parishes in their diocese in a year due to the difficulties of travel. The number of parishes visited in one day and the diligence of the visitor in investigating the lives of the clergy and laity during a visitation affected the amount of information and details recorded. Furthermore, the season, weather conditions, and the difficulty of accessing certain areas often determined the itinerary of the parishes visited. The most densely populated zones of the diocese, where the episcopal visitor could fit in two or more parishes in one day, were visited more often than the remote and hard-to-access mountain villages that were a challenge to reach. Thus, it is highly likely that the number of concubinous unions and violent deeds of the clergy are in actuality underreported in the extant documents.

The region of Catalunya Vella (Old Catalunya) occupies the eastern and most northern part of the Crown of Aragon, which includes the mountains

visitation records for the ecclesiastical province of Tarragona in "Les visites pastorales en Tarraconaise." The claim of exceptionalism for the medieval Catalan visitation records has been made by Noël Coulet, *Les visites pastorales* (Turnhout: Brepols, 1985), 12; Lluís Monjas, Eugeni Perea, Joaquim M. Puigvert, and Xavier Solà, "Usos historiogràfics" in *Les visites pastorals: Dels orígens medievals a l'època contemporània*, ed. Joaquim M. Puigvert i Solà, Lluís Monjas Manso, Xavier Solà Colomer, and Eugeni Perea Simon (Girona: La Biblioteca d'Història Rural, 2003), 24–25; Josep Baucells i Reig, "Visitas pastorales: Siglos XIV y XV" in *Memoria ecclesiae XV: Las visitas pastorales en el ministerio del obispo y archivos de la iglesia santoral hispano-mozárabe en las diócesis de España*, ed. Agustín Hevia Ballina, 165–294 (Oviedo: Actas del XIII Congreso de la Asociación celebrado en Sevilla, 1999). A comprehensive discussion and bibliography of visitation records throughout Europe can be found in Maria Milagros Cárcel Ortí and José Vicente Boscá Codina, *Visitas pastorales de Valencia, siglos XIV–XV* (Valencia, 1996), 2–18.

and valleys of the Pyrenees and extends as far as the Costa Brava and along the Mediterranean past the port of Barcelona to the delta of the Llobregat River. For such a small area of the Iberian Peninsula, there is a diversity of landscapes and climates: the north is characterized by rugged foothills and Pyrenean peaks that reach over 3,000 meters; in the central west, mountain ranges surround the high plateaus around Vic; to the east, the agriculturally productive river basins and the gentle mountainous area of la Garrotxa give way to the plains of the Gironès and Empordà that reach the rocky coast of the Costa Brava; and to the south, a drier and hotter climate encompasses the extensive vineyards and coastal hills of the Penedès region that extend down into Tarragona. The landscape affected the lives of priests and their families, not only because the farming, animal husbandry, and goods that could be sold and contributed to their livelihood depended on the topography of the land, but also because these families flourished, unencumbered by fines, in the more rural and remote areas of Catalunya where episcopal interference was minimal.

In the twelfth and thirteenth centuries, the growth of Mediterranean trade and the role of Catalan shipping and merchants united the diverse regions of Catalunya and its agricultural products into an important maritime power. Urban centers such as Barcelona and Girona were the economic heart of the region. Peasants in the rural areas, nevertheless, constituted the majority of the population and more commonly lived in villages established around parish churches rather than in villages attached to a castle. Many peasants in the fourteenth century, moreover, were serfs who owed labor or rents to a lord and paid substantial seigniorial dues.[9] The extant visitations undertaken in this period were made primarily to rural villages and not to the parishes in urban centers, which means that the lives of rural parish priests are more often highlighted in this study than those who lived in cities of Barcelona and Girona. For the Crown of Aragon, the fourteenth century was dominated by war with Castile, a naval campaign against the Genoese for control of Sardinia and the western Mediterranean, a rebellion organized by Aragonese nobles defending their privileges against the Crown, and a mounting intolerance for religious minorities.[10] These events affected the political culture in which the Catalan peasantry lived, particularly since seigniorial lordship became more oppressive. The meager harvests and famine that besieged the kingdom in the 1330s, before the arrival of the Black Death in 1348, took a heavy toll on the peasantry. Like the laity, the parish clergy serving in the churches of Catalunya were

9. Paul Freedman, *The Origins of Peasant Servitude in Medieval Catalonia* (Cambridge, UK: Cambridge University Press, 1991), 30–31, 152.

10. Joseph F. O'Callaghan, *A History of Medieval Spain* (Ithaca: Cornell University Press, 1975), 407–27.

also touched by the economic crisis and acted to protect their interests. Clerics pilfered food from their neighbors; sought additional means to supplement the income from their benefices; spent less on maintaining the parish church; and defended the economic benefits of their office, if necessary, through violence. There is little doubt that the economic instability and privation of the time intensified tensions at the parish level and exacerbated clerical violence. Nevertheless, the tradition of clerical unions and the use of violence among the clergy continued after the plague, which reveals that these practices were strong elements of Catalan clerical culture and that, contrary to assumptions, these behaviors were not eliminated by high medieval reforming efforts but persisted well into the sixteenth century.

A Brief History of Clerical Celibacy and Concubinage in Medieval Europe and Iberia

For the first thousand years of Christianity, parish priests lived with their wives and raised families. The Western Church campaigned to eradicate clerical marriage for over nine hundred years, beginning in the fourth century and finally prevailing in 1123 and again in 1139, when married clerics were forbidden by canon law to perform the ministry of the altar. Celibacy was imposed for the ranks of subdeacon and above, and legislation decreed any sexual relationship between a cleric and a woman to be *fornicatio*. Thereafter, clerical wives were condemned as concubines, and the children of priests were considered illegitimate. The legislation of the eleventh and twelfth centuries, during a time known as the Gregorian reform, set out to destroy the family life of the clergy. Reformers were very much aware that marriage integrated churchmen into their communities and that, more important, their marriages produced children and the desire for the hereditary succession of benefices. In the minds of Gregorian reformers, the demand for celibacy freed clerics from worldly affairs, such as marriage and the obligation to care and provide for a wife and children. The elimination of clerical marriage and simony (the buying or selling of ecclesiastical offices) required that clergy separate from their family as well as from their social networks, thereby transferring their loyalty from their kin group to the Church and their clerical community. But the campaign against clerical marriage and clerical sexuality was also fought on ideological grounds, primarily based on the idea that sex was impure and sinful. Daily celebration of the mass and the increasing complexity of the Christian liturgy demanded the cultic purity of its ministers. Priests who stood at the altar and came into contact with the sacred eucharist had to stand apart from

other men; they could not officiate at the altar and contaminate every liturgical action with their sexual impurity.[11] In response to these new ideologies, the
reform movement of the eleventh and twelfth centuries sought to fashion a
new priesthood rooted in the ideals of ascetic discipline and ritual purity. The
goal was to create a boundary separating the clergy from the laity by promoting the moral superiority of clergy, who were free from sexual pollution, as
the only men suitable to touch the eucharist and administer the sacraments.
The new ascetic discipline of the priesthood, their connection to the sacred,
and their separation from the lay world were meant to foster respect among
the laity and promote greater authority for the clergy. Through canon law and
synodal decrees, reformers changed the standards of the Church, demanding
that the men who had access to God should be identified by their celibate lifestyle, their clerical dress and tonsure, and their virtuous conduct that would
serve as an example for the laity to emulate.[12] To no surprise, implementing,
let alone enforcing, such a standard among all clergy in the major orders was
an issue that church councils continued to revisit and episcopal authorities
repeatedly dealt with throughout the medieval and early modern periods.

The demand for clerical celibacy in the twelfth century was met with great
resistance and at times outright violence. The rebellion of the clergy was such
that ecclesiastical superiors thought twice before implementing the laws on
celibacy as word spread of bishops who were attacked and nearly killed when
they attempted to separate clergy from their families.[13] At the outset of the
Gregorian reform, many clerics simply disregarded the policy on celibacy, and
it is clear that lower-level clergy continued to contract marriages and live with
their wives in spite of the momentous legislation from the Lateran Councils
of 1123 and 1139 that prohibited priestly marriage. In England and Normandy,
clerical marriage among elite clergy died out by the mid-twelfth century.[14] For

---

11. Anne Llewellyn Barstow, *Married Priests and the Reforming Papacy: The Eleventh Century Debates*
(New York: Edwin Mellen Press, 1982); Robert I. Moore, "Family, Community, and Cult on the Eve of
the Gregorian Reform," *Transactions of the Royal Historical Society* 30 (1980): 49–69; James Brundage,
Law, Sex and Christian Society in Medieval Europe (Chicago: University of Chicago Press, 1987); Peter
Brown, *The Body and Society* (New York: Columbia University Press, 1988).

12. Barstow, *Married Priests and the Reforming Papacy*, 29–32, 67–77; Maureen C. Miller, *The Formation of a Medieval Church: Ecclesiastical Change in Verona, 950–1150* (Ithaca: Cornell University Press,
1993), 55–62. See also the essays in Michael Frassetto, ed., *Medieval Purity and Piety: Essays on Medieval
Clerical Celibacy and Religious Reform* (New York: Garland Publishing, 1998).

13. Brundage, *Law, Sex, and Christian Society*, 219–20.

14. Christopher N. L. Brooke, "Gregorian Reform in Action: Clerical Marriage in England, 1050–
1200," *Cambridge Historical Journal* 12, no. 1 (1956): 1–21; Ross Williams Collins, "The Parish Priest and
His Flock as Depicted by the Councils of the Twelfth and Thirteenth Centuries," *Journal of Religion*
10, no. 3 (1930): 313–32; Julia Barrow, "Hereford Bishops and Married Clergy, c. 1130–1240," *Bulletin
of the Institute of Historical Research* 60, no. 141 (1987): 1–8; Brian Kemp, "Hereditary Benefices in the
Medieval English Church: A Herefordshire Example," *Bulletin of the Institute of Historical Research* 43,

the lower clergy, marriage seems to have remained an option for a longer period of time. Evidence from Spain, Italy, Germany, and Scandinavia shows that the practice of marriage among parish priests persisted and was not necessarily confined to remote areas distant from ecclesiastical oversight (see my discussion in the conclusion). The condemnation and prohibition of clerical unions by the Church do not mean that the attitudes of the laity and clergy toward clerical marriage immediately followed suit; the shift from clerical marriage to clerical concubinage varied according to region and proximity to enthusiastic reformers.[15] Nonetheless, the practice of clerical concubinage became a replacement for marriage and was likewise banned in canon law and synodal statutes because clergymen continued to form unions with women and to maintain households filled with their progeny. The degree to which the practice of clerical concubinage survived into the late Middle Ages, however, differed greatly, especially when we compare dioceses along the Mediterranean to those in England, northern France, and Belgium, where clerical unions were less common (see Chapter One). Particularly in urban areas such as London, York, Paris, and Dijon, far more clergymen were reported and fined for having sought out the services of prostitutes than for establishing a long-term union with a woman—so many, in fact, that there were prostitutes who catered specifically to a clerical clientele.[16] Factors such as clerical culture, ecclesiastical reforms at the local level, the prosecutorial focus of the bishop's court, and lay support for reforming programs affected the practice of clerical

---

no. 107 (1970): 1–15; C. Hugh Lawrence, "The English Parish and Its Clergy in the Thirteenth Century," in *The Medieval World*, ed. Peter Linehan and Janet Nelson (London: Routledge, 2001), 659–60; Brundage, *Law, Sex, and Christian Society*, 226, 314–18, 342–43, 401–5.

15. Maureen Miller maintains that in the diocese of Verona, Italy, there was a decline in clerical marriage because "after 1122, the wives, concubines, and sons of priests disappear from notarial documents." Although she admits that clerical concubinage was never stamped out completely, she argues that the disappearance of clerical families from documents indicates that clerics accepted the ideals of reformers; Miller, *Formation of a Medieval Church*, 55–56. See also Jennifer Thibodeaux, *The Manly Priest: Clerical Celibacy, Masculinity, and Reform in England and Normandy, 1066–1300* (Philadelphia: University of Pennsylvania Press, 2015), 111.

16. Ruth Karras, *Common Women: Prostitution and Sexuality in Medieval England* (New York: Oxford University Press, 1996), 30, 77–78; Ruth Karras and David Lorenzo Boyd, ' "Ut cum mulier': A Male Transvestite Prostitute in Fourteenth-Century London," in *Pre-Modern Sexualities*, ed. Louise Fradenburg and Carla Freccero (New York: Routledge, 1996) 101–16; Peter J. P. Goldberg, "Pigs and Prostitutes: Streetwalking in Comparative Perspective," *Young Medieval Women*, ed. Katherine Lewis, Noel James Menuge, and Kim M. Philips (New York: St. Martin's Press, 1999), 172–93; Peter J. P. Goldberg "Women in Fifteenth-Century Town Life," in *Towns and Townspeople in the Fifteenth-Century*, ed. John A. Thomson (Gloucester: Alan Sutton, 1988), 119–20; Leah L. Otis, *Prostitution in Medieval Society: The History of an Urban Institution in Languedoc* (Chicago: University of Chicago Press, 1985), 83–84; Jacques Rossiaud, *Medieval Prostitution*, trans. Lydia G. Cochrane (Oxford: Blackwell, 1988), 28, 41–42, 118, 145–48; Ruth Karras, *Unmarriages: Women, Men, and Sexual Unions in the Middle Ages* (Philadelphia: University of Pennsylvania Press, 2012), 154.

concubinage. In addition, the persistence of clerical unions in Scandinavia, central Europe, and the Baltic regions may have had more to do with the fact that they had been Christianized at a later date, like southern Iberia, and thus remained distant from the fervor of Western Church reforms of the eleventh and twelfth centuries.[17]

In the Iberian peninsula, clerical unions continued to be contracted and to flourish to such an extent that de facto marriages became a custom entrenched in clerical culture.[18] Due to the centuries-long struggle between Christians and Muslims for territory, the Iberian church had remained largely independent from Rome and the attempts of the papacy to reform and standardize religious practice among the clergy and laity. Although the location of Catalunya in the north and its connection to the Franks had protected it from the long-term occupation by Muslims in the eighth century, Al-Mansur, the caliph of Córdoba, sacked and burned Barcelona and the surrounding region in 985. Abd al-Malik, Al-Mansur's son, also plundered Barcelona and the countryside of Catalunya a number of times between 1002 and 1008. Three Catalan bishops—those of Barcelona, Girona, and Vic—lost their lives in a military campaign against the *taifa* of Córdoba in the year 1010, and other churchmen participated in a 1117 military expedition to retake Christian lands between Tarragona and the Barcelona-Vic region. The ensuing years left the Catalan church with the task of restoring its presence and reestablishing parishes throughout Catalunya. The archepiscopal city of Tarragona itself remained

---

17. For clergy and their illicit sexual activities in regions where the influence of the Christian Church was weak prior to the fourteenth century, see Anthony Perron, "Saxo Grammaticus's Heroic Chastity: A Model of Clerical Celibacy and Masculinity in Medieval Scandinavia," in *Negotiating Clerical Identities: Priests, Monks and Masculinity in the Middle Ages*, ed. Jennifer D. Thibodeaux (New York: Palgrave Macmillan, 2010), 113–35; Cameron Sutt, "Uxores, Ancillae and Dominae: Women in Thirteenth-Century Hungary in the Register of Várad," *Journal of Medieval History* 36 (2010): 142–55; Marija Karbic, "'Illicit Love' in Medieval Slavonian Cities," in *Love, Marriage and Family Ties in the Later Middle Ages*, ed. Isabel Davis, Miriam Müller, and Sarah Rees Jones (Turnhout, Belgium: Brepols, 2003), 338–39.

18. See Henry Charles Lea, *The History of Sacerdotal Celibacy in the Christian Church* (New York: Russel & Russel, 1957), 253–63, 287–99; Peter Linehan, *The Spanish Church and the Papacy in the Thirteenth Century* (Cambridge, UK: Cambridge University Press, 1971), 2–11; Peter Linehan, *Spanish Church and Society, 1150–1300* (London: Variorum Reprints, 1983), 181–84, 484–85, 496–97; O'Callaghan, *History of Medieval Spain*, 305–13; José Rodríguez Molina, "Celibato eclesiástico y discriminación de la mujer en la edad media Andaluza," *Cuadernos de estudios medievales y ciencias y técnicas historiográficas* 18–19 (1993–1994), 40, 47–49; Bernhard Schimmelpfennig, "'Ex fornicatione nati': Studies on the Position of Priests' Sons from the Twelfth to the Fourteenth Century," *Studies in Medieval and Renaissance History* 2 (1979), 38–41. See also, Ricardo García-Villoslada, ed., *Historia de la iglesia en España*, Vol. 2 (Madrid: Biblioteca de Autores Cristianos, 1979), 428–42; Reginetta Haboucha, "Clerics, Their Wives, and Their Concubines in the 'Partidas' of Alfonso El Sabio," *Acta*, Vol. 14: *Homo Carnalis: The Carnal Aspect of Medieval Human Life*, ed. Helen Rodite Lemay (Binghamton: SUNY Binghamton, Center for Medieval and Early Renaissance Studies, 1990), 85–104.

in Muslim hands until 1128, when Christians were finally able to fully recover the city and the surrounding area.[19] The role of Tarragona as the center of ecclesiastical authority for the suffragan sees of Barcelona, Girona, Vic, Lleida, and Urgell, then, was not restored until the beginning of the twelfth century, which created a disunified ecclesiastical province that held its first provincial council a hundred years later, in 1229. The need to resettle the frontier regions with a Christian population also meant that the Iberian church in the eleventh and twelfth centuries was in a period of transition marked by the necessary reorganization of dioceses and ecclesiastical provinces. Despite the attempt by the papacy to establish a closer connection to the Iberian church, the clerical customs of Iberian clergy remained largely undisturbed. The only tangible evidence of the Gregorian reform in Catalunya can be found in the papal attempts to introduce new legislation, which Iberian church leaders such as Guifré de Narbona, the archbishop of Narbona and Tarragona, refused to endorse. At the behest of papal legates in 1068, 1078, 1097, and 1101, four synods were celebrated in Girona and Besalú that passed legislation targeting the practice of simony, ordering priests to dismiss their wives, and prohibiting the sons of priests from inheriting church property.[20] These synods, however, did little to change clerical customs. In large part, indifference affected the ability of Catalan church leaders to implement and enforce reforms, and this in turn meant that standardizing Church customs in a region where episcopal oversight already faced challenges due to its diverse topography was further limited.

A clerical culture that permitted priests to keep their wives continued as before. Although the closer connection between Rome and the Iberian church in the eleventh century aided in the restoration of religious practices that were more in line with the Western Church, such as the suppression of the Mozarabic liturgy for the Roman liturgy, the appointment of bishops and abbots was still very much in the hands of secular elites who also influenced the implementation of papal reforms, such as the prohibition against the buying and selling of church offices.[21] Moreover, famous Gregorian reformers, such as Peter Damian, Humbert of Silva Candida, and Hildebrand, who targeted clerical marriage and insisted on clerical celibacy, were simply absent in the Iberian church. In fact, the vigorous reforms of the eleventh and twelfth

19. Lawrence J. McCrank, *Restoration and Reconquest in Medieval Catalonia: The Church and Principality of Tarragona, 971–1177* (PhD diss., University of Virginia, 1974), 102, 119–21, 318–20, 325.
20. Antoni Pladevall i Font, *Història de l'església a Catalunya* (Barcelona: Editorial Claret, 1989), 35, 38, 41–42, 54–57, 65, 67–71, 99.
21. Joan Bada, *Història del cristianisme a Catalunya* (Lleida: Eumo Editorial, 2003), 36–39, 54–5. See also Antonio Linage Conde, Javier Faci Lacasta, Juan Francisco Rivera Recio, and Antoni Oliver Montserrat, "Organización eclesiástica de la España cristiana," in *Historia de la iglesia en España*, Vol. 2, Pt. 1, ed. Ricardo García-Villoslada (Madrid: Biblioteca de Autores Cristianos, 1982), 227–32.

centuries seen elsewhere in Europe in many ways bypassed Spain because these Christian kingdoms were so embroiled with their fellow Christian and Muslim neighbors in a fight for territory that it consumed nearly of all their energy and resources. By the time the Iberian church was fully reintegrated into the Western Church, the enthusiasm for and commitment to such reforms had peaked. Even a century later, when the canons of Lateran IV in 1215 arrived in the Spanish kingdoms, they had minimal impact on Iberian clergy because the native-born ecclesiastical elites did not enthusiastically embrace the campaign for celibacy or, frankly, many of the reforming ideals. Indeed, only in Iberia do we find the practice of clerical concubinage to be legal in twelfth-century secular law even though it was clearly prohibited according to church law.[22] The customs of the clergy, therefore, were hardly affected by the Gregorian reform or Lateran councils that had such an impact elsewhere in western Europe. Christian rulers and the Iberian church were focused on more practical concerns, such as repopulating newly conquered Muslim areas, reestablishing episcopal sees, and appointing bishops.[23]

Given this context, the prevalence of clerical unions throughout Iberia is not astonishing. Nevertheless, the degree to which clerical unions thrived in Catalunya is surprising. Of all the ecclesiastical provinces in Iberia, it was in Catalunya in the Crown of Aragon where the reforming attempts of the papacy were considered to have had the most success, yet it is clear that clerical concubinage remained a custom among the Catalan clergy. Church authorities throughout the Iberian kingdoms did condemn clerical unions, and the clergy and laity were aware that the Church required celibacy of its clergy, but Iberian churchmen remained defiant in their determination to maintain families. The extent to which ecclesiastical officials attempted to change clerical culture and practice suggests that eliminating clerical concubinage was not considered a task of great importance in the late medieval Iberian church. The

---

22. Eukene Lacarra Lanz, "Changing Boundaries of Licit and Illicit Unions: Concubinage and Prostitution," in *Marriage and Sexuality in Medieval and Early Modern Iberia*, ed. Eukene Lacarra Lanz (New York: Routledge, 2002), 158–94; Rodríguez Molina, "Celibato eclesiàstico," 39–40.

23. José Manuel Nieto Soria, *La época medieval: Iglesia y cultura* (Madrid: Istmo, 2002), 146–47, 149; Derek W. Lomax, "The Lateran Reforms and Spanish Literature," *Iberoromania* 1 (1969): 229–313; Jocelyn N. Hillgarth, *The Spanish Kingdoms, 1250–1516* (Oxford: Clarendon Press, 1976), 1: 90–138; Odilo Engels, "Los reyes Jaime II y Alfonso IV de Aragón y los concilios provinciales de Tarragona," *VIII congreso de historia de la Corona de Aragón*, Vol. 2 (Valencia, 1970), 253–62; Peter Linehan, "Segovia: A 'Frontier' Diocese in the Thirteenth Century," *English Historical Review* 96 (1981), 483–85, 496–97; Charles Julian Bishko, "Fernando I and the Origins of the Leonese-Castilian Alliance with Cluny," in *Studies in Medieval Spanish Frontier History*, Pt. 2 (London: Variorum Reprints, 1980), 1–36, 53–68; Richard Fletcher, *The Episcopate in the Kingdom of León in the Twelfth Century* (London: Oxford University Press, 1987); Bernard Reilly, *The Kingdom of León-Castilla under King Alfonso VII, 1126–1157* (Philadelphia: University of Pennsylvania Press, 1998), 261–73; Damian J. Smith, *Innocent III and the Crown of Aragon: The Limits of Papal Authority* (Aldershot, UK: Ashgate, 2004).

renowned religious leaders of the day were not men who dedicated themselves to reforming the clergy by insisting on clerical celibacy but those who concentrated their efforts on fully Christianizing a mozarab (i.e., Christian) population that had lived too long under Muslim rule and who focused intently on converting newly conquered Muslim population now living under Christian rule. From the perspective of Iberian rulers and the church, the crusade against Islam became the center of attention. First, Christians had to deal with the appearance of the Almoravids, Muslim fundamentalists from North Africa who took advantage of the political fragmentation of Muslim Iberia in the late eleventh century to unite al-Andalus under their control and expand their territory into Christian lands. In the twelfth century, Christians battled against another fundamentalist group from the Maghreb, the Almohads, in a fight for key cities and ports such as Córdoba and Almería, that, to the disadvantage of Christians, led to the consolidation of Almohad power. Later on in thirteenth century, after the Christian victory at Las Navas de Tolosa in 1212, Christian kingdoms heavily invested their resources in the conquest and repopulation of Muslim lands, as well as the final push from Ferdinand and Isabel in 1492 to conquer the last Muslim stronghold of Granada.[24] During this reconquest period, military orders played an important role in the defensive needs of both the kingdom of Castile-León and the Crown of Aragon. The Templars and Hospitallers had made their way into Iberia in the early twelfth century, but later, strictly Iberian orders were established, such as the Order of Calatrava, the Order of Montesa, and the Order of Sant Jordi d'Alfama, which did much to masculinize a clerical culture devoted to the battling and capturing of Muslims.[25]

In the Crown of Aragon, the most influential religious leaders were Franciscans and Dominicans such as Ramon de Penyafort, Ramon Llull, and Ramon Martí, who made their marks in canon law and in writing theological treatises aimed at converting Jews and Muslims. Nicolau Eimeric and Vicente Ferrer, well-known Dominican preachers, expended much of their efforts to proselytizing and advocating the moral reform of Iberian society by insisting on the segregation of Jews and Muslims from Christians. These Catalan churchmen focused their missionizing efforts on religious minorities living in Barcelona, Girona, Lleida, Tarragona, Tortosa, Valencia, and Mallorca—important urban centers distant from the more rural areas where priests lived openly with

---

24. Richard Fletcher, *Moorish Spain* (Berkeley: University of California Press, 1992), 105–30.

25. Pladevall i Font, *Història de l'església a Catalunya*, 73–76; Alan Forey, *The Military Orders From the Twelfth to the Early Fourteenth Centuries* (Toronto: University of Toronto Press, 1992), 23–32; Paul Freedman, "Military Orders in Osona during the Twelfth and Thirteenth Centuries" in *Church, Law, and Society in Catalonia, 900–1500* (Aldershot: Variorum, 1994), 55–69.

their families.[26] We may wonder, too, how eagerly Catalan clerical elites wanted to criticize and stamp out the custom of concubinage when the kings of the Crown of Aragon had a tradition of publicly keeping their concubines at court. Jaume I of Aragon, the conqueror of the Balearic Islands and the Islamic territory of Valencia, who ruled from 1213 to 1276, was known not only for his military conquests but also for his many concubines. Pere the Ceremonious, who ruled for fifty years in the fourteenth century, married his concubine Sibil·la de Fortià after three political marriages.[27] It seems likely that the widespread practice of concubinage among the kings and the nobility of the Crown of Aragon, which was used as a strategy to provide heirs when a man was faced with none and as an alternative form of companionship to marriages forged for political reasons, must have influenced elite churchmen against vehemently attacking the custom. That concubinage was quietly accepted at the highest levels of society does much to explain why neither the kings nor the nobility actively encouraged the Catalan church to focus its efforts on targeting this practice. The lack of ardent reformers dedicated to imposing clerical celibacy suggests, moreover, that Catalan church leaders recognized the futility of trying to eradicate the tradition of concubinage among the clergy. Popular religious figures such as Ramon Llull (c. 1232–1315) and Francesc Eiximenis (c. 1327–1408), who both wrote extensively in Catalan, dedicated little of their time to addressing the issues of priestly incontinence or concubinous unions. Even at the end of the fourteenth century, Vicente Ferrer (1350–1419), the famous Valencian preacher, was still more concerned with segregating Jews and Muslims from Christians than with the penchant of priests for keeping concubines.[28] Indeed, it is striking that the topic

---

26. Robert Chazan, *Daggers of Faith: Thirteenth-Century Christian Missionizing and the Jewish Response* (Berkeley: University of California Press, 1989), 159–80; Robert I. Burns, *Muslims, Christians, and Jews in the Crusader Kingdom of Valencia: Societies in Symbiosis* (Cambridge, UK: Cambridge University Press, 1984), 80–108; John V. Tolan, *Saracens: Islam in the Medieval European Imagination* (New York: Columbia University Press, 2002), 234–42.

27. For the concubines of Jaume I of Aragon, see Robert I. Burns, "The Spiritual Life of James the Conqueror King of Arago-Catalonia, 1208–1276: Portrait and Self-Portrait," *Catholic Historical Review* 62, no. 1 (1976); 26; Cynthia L. Chamberlin, "The 'Sainted Queen' and the 'Sin of Berenguela': Teresa Gil de Viduare and Berenguela Alfonso in the Documents of the Crown of Aragon, 1225–1272," in *Iberia and the Mediterranean World of the Middle Ages; Studies in Honor of Robert I. Burns*, ed. Larry J. Simon (Leiden: Brill, 1995), 303–21; Miriam Shadis, "'Received as a Woman': Rethinking the Concubinage of Aurenbiaix of Urgell," *Journal of Medieval Iberian Studies* 8, no. 1 (2016): 38–54. For King Pere the Ceremonious (r. 1337–1387), see Núria Silleras-Fernández, "Money Isn't Everything: Concubinage, Class, and the Rise and Fall of Sibil·la de Fortià, Queen of Aragon (1377–87)" in *Women, Wealth, and Power in Medieval Europe*, ed. Theresa Earenfight (New York: Palgrave, 2010), 67–88.

28. A summary of the religious content in the works of Ramon Llull, Francesc Eiximenis, and Vicente Ferrer can be found in David J. Viera, *Medieval Catalan Literature: Prose and Drama* (Boston: Twayne Publishers, 1988). See also Núria Silleras-Fernández, *Chariots of Ladies: Francesc Eiximenis and the Court Culture of Medieval and Early Modern Iberia* (Ithaca: Cornell University Press, 2015); Anthony

of priestly sexuality is mostly absent from the writings of these celebrated Catalan authors, indicating that clerical concubinage was not a priority for reforming Catalan society. The defiant practices of Catalan priests, then, meant that the family life of parish clergyman continued unabated into the late medieval period and was not an impediment to ordination or promotion; indeed, maintaining a woman and children remained key to the definition of priestly masculinity. Overall, ecclesiastical officials and lay society throughout Catalunya tolerated the long-held practice of clerical unions during the Gregorian reform, after Lateran IV in 1215, and well into the seventeenth century.

Studies on Clerical Masculinity and Priestly Identity

Throughout the medieval period, secular and regular clergy struggled with, contested, and negotiated their own ideas of manliness and the demands of the Church. Terms such as *manliness, manhood,* and *masculinity* are used to refer to the behaviors, abilities, traits, and physical and moral qualities that were considered socially acceptable for men to achieve masculine status in medieval society. Simply existing as a biological male did not make one a man. To gain status as a man, men performed activities and exhibited traits that were coded as masculine. For example, Catalina de Erauso, a Basque nun, escaped her convent and traveled to the Americas dressed as a man, where she wooed women, fought in military battles, and initiated duels to defend her honor. No one suspected that she was a woman because her behavior, dress, and actions were such that society perceived her to be man.[29] Judith Butler's theory that gender is performative is important here for understanding the choices that priests made in repeatedly engaging in a set of behaviors and activities that were meant to be perceived as masculine in their social milieu. According to Butler, gender is constructed and inscribed on the surface of bodies so that its performance has social meaning and its repetition becomes a form of legitimation.[30] Parish priests chose to reproduce certain gender norms by performing their masculinity in such a way that medieval culture registered this

Bonner, *Doctur Illuminatus: A Ramon Llull Reader* (Princeton: Princeton University Press, 1985); Amador Vega, *Ramon Llull and the Secret of Life,* trans. James W. Heisig (New York: Crossroad Publishing, 2003).

    29. Catalina de Erauso, *Lieutenant Nun: Memoir of a Basque Transvestite in the New World,* trans. Michele Stepto and Grabriel Stepto (Boston: Beacon Press, 1996).

    30. Judith Butler, *Gender Trouble: Feminism and the Subversion of Identity* (New York: Routledge, 1999), xv–xvi, 185–87, 190–92.

behavior as masculine. In medieval society, social and cultural trends that focused on marriage, fatherhood, and displays of patriarchal authority shaped how many men understood and reacted to gendered ideals that ultimately affected how they formed their own masculine identity. Because masculinities are constructed and measured in relation to other men (and women), the religious ideals of churchmen, the military ethic of the nobility, and the ever-important role of paterfamilias influenced masculine ideals in the greater medieval cultural sphere. Clergy received the gendered messages of their environment, and some conformed, modified, or challenged gendered prescriptions in creating their masculinity. Depending on their social status, education, and clerical rank, clergymen expressed their masculine identity in a variety of ways that included, but were not limited to, celibacy, active sexuality, models of spirituality, pious devotion, intellectual prowess, abstinence from manual labor, military skill, and violence.[31]

Much of the scholarship on clerical masculinity in the Middle Ages has focused on the crisis of masculinity wrought during the Gregorian reform of the eleventh and twelfth centuries, or on the immediate challenges that clerics faced when confronting and adopting the secular ideals of manliness in the century after the reform. Studies on clerical masculinity have exposed how the monasticization of parish priests and the obligation of celibacy triggered a crisis of gender identity that left the Church and clergy struggling to redefine clerical masculinity. Having already separated the clergy from their wives and children, church legislation further sought to disconnect the clergy from the secular world, denying them even the most common features of lay masculinity—weapons, secular apparel, social drinking, and hunting. Jo Ann McNamara's groundbreaking article on the impact of the Gregorian reform in restructuring the gender system has established that, once churchmen were barred from sex, marriage, procreation, and the markers of secular manhood, anxieties concerning gender roles and gender differences between men and women reverberated throughout medieval society. Deprived of their

---

31. For the numerous ways in which clergy defined their own masculine ideal, see P.H. Cullum and Katherine J. Lewis, eds., *Holiness and Masculinity in the Middle Ages* (Toronto: University of Toronto Press, 2004); Jennifer D. Thibodeau, ed., *Negotiating Clerical Identities: Priests, Monks and Masculinity in the Middle Ages* (New York: Palgrave Macmillan, 2010); Katherine J. Lewis, "Male Saints and Devotional Masculinity in Late Medieval England," *Gender & History* 24, no. 1 (2012): 112–33; Sharon Farmer, "Manual Labor, Begging, and Conflicting Gender Expectations in Thirteenth-Century Paris," in *Gender and Difference in the Middle Ages*, ed. Sharon Farmer and Carol Braun Pasternack (Minneapolis: University of Minnesota Press, 2003), 261–87; Frassetto, *Medieval Purity and Piety*. See also the essays on clergy and masculinity in Dawn M. Hadley, ed., *Masculinity in Medieval Europe* (London: Longman Press, 1999); Mathew Kuefler, *The Manly Eunuch: Masculinity, Gender Ambiguity, and Christian Ideology in Late Antiquity* (Chicago: University of Chicago Press, 2001).

sexuality, clerics had to find a new way to prove their manhood—one that prized celibacy as a manly virtue and eschewed any contact with women.[32]

In response to McNamara's argument on the impact of this watershed reform movement on gender roles in medieval society, early scholarship on clerical masculinity placed celibacy at the center of clerical gender identity. A number of scholars have focused on the effects of reform at the top of the ecclesiastical hierarchy, showing that elite clergymen employed the strength of their celibate conviction as a sign of manliness.[33] Maureen Miller has brought to light how educated Ottonian and northern Italian clergymen who embraced the Gregorian reform ideals constructed their own version of clerical manhood in an attempt to mark their masculinity as superior to elite lay masculinity. The revisions of saints' *vitae* from the eleventh century represent these early efforts, which pitted clerical manliness against lay manliness and worked to denigrate the manhood of laymen to elevate the masculinity, power, and authority of clergymen. Thus, the writings of the reformers portrayed secular men as weak and morally corrupt in their desire to usurp church lands and benefices. These clergymen, by comparison, were shown as "manly" and powerful when they defended their churches and people against greedy and violent laymen. Still, what truly underscored clerical manliness, according to these reform writers, and set the clergy apart from laymen was their physical and spiritual separation from women.[34] During the same period, Anglo-Norman reformers promoted a similar message about celibacy in their religious texts. These religious writers characterized priests as effeminate and their bodies as disorderly when dominated by their lust for women. They promoted the idea that absolute sexual self-control defined clerical manliness.[35] In an altogether different approach to clerical gender identity, Robert Swanson has argued that celibate clergy could be considered a third gender because, in their renunciation of male sexuality, they placed themselves in an ambiguous position somewhere between masculinity and femininity. Such a theory has been difficult to prove for the reason that the sources do not show that clergymen were ever

---

32. Jo Ann McNamara, "The Herrenfrage: The Restructuring of the Gender System, 1050–1150," in *Medieval Masculinities: Regarding Men in the Middle Ages*, ed. Clare A. Lees (Minneapolis: University of Minnesota Press, 1994), 3–29.

33. Monastic masculinity similarly focused on celibacy during this period, but I have limited my discussion here to secular clergy. See important work by Jacqueline Murray, "Masculinizing Religious Life: Sexual Prowess, the Battle for Chastity and Monastic Identity," in Cullum and Lewis, *Holiness and Masculinity in the Middle Ages*, 24–37, and other essays dealing with regular clergy in Cullum and Lewis, *Holiness and Masculinity in the Middle Ages* and in Thibodeaux, *Negotiating Clerical Identities*.

34. Maureen C. Miller, "Masculinity, Reform, and Clerical Culture: Narratives of Episcopal Holiness in the Gregorian Era," *Church History* 72 (2003): 25–52.

35. Thibodeaux, *Manly Priest*, 27, 40.

categorized as neither man nor woman; in addition, there is little evidence that clergy after the Gregorian reform existed "in a state of gender limbo."[36] The work of Megan McLaughlin, however, shows that alternative images of religious masculinity emerged in the wake of the Gregorian reform movement as clerics struggled to renounce contemporary ideals of manhood. Reformers such as Peter Damian tried to redirect clerics, who were now cut off from the "culturally powerful and emotionally very resonant masculine role of father," to replace biological fatherhood with spiritual fatherhood. Spiritual fathers could still be fertile and "propagate" children in the faith by performing the sacraments and holding ecclesiastical office. According to McLaughlin, reformers were attempting to find a substitute for a cleric's marriage or family, and employed the allegory of a bishop married to his church, symbolized by the ring given to the bishop at his consecration as a sign of Christ's marriage to the Church.[37] Despite the importance of celibacy to these new forms of clerical manliness, it is evident that clergymen wanted to convince their religious colleagues that they could still attain the hallmarks of adult masculinity in medieval society, albeit through avenues that continued to mirror the centrality of marriage and procreation to secular manhood.

The reality of the crisis of masculinity brought about by the Gregorian reforms, however, is that the attempts to create new clerical identities with celibacy as a core characteristic worked only for a small number of clergymen, especially for those who were among the clerical elites of their day. The letters, hagiographies, and treatises of this select group exist precisely because of the reputation, fame, and influence these men exerted in their elite circles. These ecclesiastical leaders and role models were able to develop alternative masculinities as spiritual fathers, bridegrooms, and warriors because they associated predominantly with men who shared their views, goals, and elite backgrounds. Yet the masculine ideals defined by this group of clergymen cannot be thought to represent the typical parish priest, who, as the working class of an international institution, functioned in a very different environment. Although bishops may have promoted the idea that they represented a father with spiritual authority, it is doubtful that parish clergy or even the lower classes saw themselves as the spiritual sons or children of bishops and priests. Rather,

---

36. Robert N. Swanson, "Angels Incarnate: Clergy and Masculinity from Gregorian Reform to Reformation," in Hadley, *Masculinity in Medieval Europe*, 174, 160–77.

37. Megan McLaughlin, "Secular and Spiritual Fatherhood in the Eleventh Century," in *Conflicted Identities and Multiple Masculinities*, ed. Jacqueline Murray (New York: Garland Publishing, 1999), 25–43 at 27; Megan McLaughlin, "The Bishop as Bridegroom: Marital Imagery and Clerical Celibacy in the Eleventh and Early Twelfth Centuries," in *Medieval Purity and Piety: Essays on Medieval Clerical Celibacy and Religious Reform*, ed. Michael Frassetto (New York: Garland Publishing, 1998), 209–38.

the people of the village knew their parish priest in the capacity of a brother, son, cousin, nephew, friend, and even enemy, as well as a father to his biological children. Moreover, a priest who attempted to underscore his manliness with an aggressive spirituality that shunned women and denigrated the manhood of laymen was not likely to receive the support of female parishioners, let alone the men of the village. Such a masculine identity seems not only impractical for the typical parish priest but also one guaranteed to alienate the laity and undermine the priest's position in the community. In actuality, parish clergy could relate more to the laymen in their village than with elite clergymen because they shared the common markers and practices that their social milieu considered manly. The degree to which Gregorian models of clerical masculinity influenced parish clergymen who were in constant contact with the normative ideals of lay masculinity seems minimal at best, especially in the rural parishes of fourteenth-century Catalunya. In addition, we must take into consideration that two hundred years after the era of reforms in the eleventh and twelfth centuries, the passion to reform the clergy and remake the masculine identity of priestly clerics had not only waned but also had not filtered equally throughout all parts of Europe. The Western Church never abandoned its ideals of celibacy and its belief that marriage and procreation should not define the priestly caste; yet, there is little evidence that Catalan clergy were exposed to Gregorian models of clerical masculinity to draw on in their own formation. As we will see in the following chapters, some of the most salient characteristics of adult manhood—being the head of a household composed of a woman and children, providing for the family, protecting oneself and one's family from harm or dishonor, dominating socially inferior men, and socializing with male peers to validate one's male status—were also markers of masculinity among parish clergy.

The reasons that the parish clergy in Catalunya adopted values that defined manhood in secular society are not hard to deduce. Clerics accepted many of the precepts of lay masculinity because they often had no other life experience to fall back on to shape their gender identities. Most came from humble backgrounds without the experience of university life and had little, if any, contact with the religious leaders of their day. Many failed to live according to the unfamiliar clerical gender ideals promoted by the Church—which centered on celibacy, spiritual marriage, spiritual fatherhood, spiritual prowess, nonviolence, and a submissiveness based on filial obedience to the Church and God—because it was not easily assimilated into their formative experiences. Even though medieval society esteemed such lofty ideals and some secular clergy did strive to live by them, the Church standards of priestly behavior were not the preeminent values that mattered most in a parochial setting. Above all else, the clergy's experiences growing up as laymen and the segment of society in which they had originated determined how they perceived and measured themselves as men. Although a career in the Church as a secular clergyman was one of the few professions that admitted young boys and men from a vast array of socioeconomic backgrounds, the reality was that a gulf existed between the parish clergy and the bishops, archdeacons, and their administrators that was based not only on clerical rank but also had very much to do with social status. The diversity of the secular clergy's experiences and backgrounds explains why a coherent model of clerical masculinity is simply not found at all levels of the ecclesiastical hierarchy. Whereas the writings of elite clergymen document the ways in which the ecclesiastical hierarchy dealt with these challenges, I focus here on the records of the behaviors and actions of parish clergy to make sense of the ideals of masculine conduct they followed and, by extension, to show how priests reconciled the mandates of their clerical profession with the notion of manhood instilled in them from childhood.

Parish priests in Catalunya constructed a clerical masculinity that adopted hegemonic patterns of masculinity in late medieval society, functioned best in a parochial setting, and promoted their status and authority as priests. The masculinity that priests created was one that could suitably operate in an environment that laymen could recognize, bond with, and respect without the risk of being considered unmanly. In fourteenth-century Catalunya, parish priests and other clergymen in the major orders achieved social adulthood because they formed marriage-like unions, produced children, and established a household to provide for the well-being of their families. In their communities, they performed the masculine roles of husband, father, patriarch, provider, and householder like the laymen they lived among. A multiplicity of masculinities existed during the medieval period, and yet secular society generally defined adult male masculinity, as Ruth Karras has noted, by the performance of heterosexual desire, dominance over women and inferior men, and the acquisition of a household to govern over dependents.[38] By the standards of late medieval society, Catalan priests were masculine. There is no denying that the proclivity of parish priests to engage in sexual behaviors means that they adopted elements of secular masculinity that were in opposition to Church models of clerical masculinity. Therefore, given that concubinary clerics dominated the clerical landscape in Catalunya, it is erroneous to continue to maintain that celibacy was the defining feature of priestly

---

38. Ruth Karras, *From Boys to Men: Formations of Masculinity in Late Medieval Europe* (Philadelphia: University of Pennsylvania Press, 2003), 151–59.

masculinity when the evidence proves otherwise.[39] Even if we discount the number of clergymen in the major orders who established long-term relationships and went out of their way to publicly display their women and children, a significant number were still involved in casual, short-term affairs. For parish priests, sexually active men were real men, especially when they took on the adult responsibilities that came with forming a union.

To push the point further—parish priests openly rejected celibacy and, instead, incorporated sexuality into their own clerical identity. By *sexuality*, I mean the broadest definition of the term, defined best by Anna Clark as "the desire, relationships, acts, and identities concerned with sexual behavior."[40] These priests were concerned with exposing their relationships with women and engaging in procreative sex acts to father children as part of their masculine identity. Just as parish priests acted like laymen and adopted the key secular norms of masculinity, such as the performance of heterosexual desire, parish clergy in the late medieval villages of Catalunya forged their own version of a clerical masculinity that included an active and public sexuality commonly characterized by, although not limited to, a long-term union with a woman.

Yet as much as sexuality and marriage-like unions were crucial to the masculine identity of parish priests in Catalunya, sexuality in and of itself should not be considered the most significant aspect of clerical manhood. Nor should it be assumed that, because clergymen engaged in heterosexual sex and biological fatherhood, that they were heterosexual. Coitus and performing heterosexual desire before other men and society did not preclude a man from feeling same-sex love or having a preference for male sexual partners.[41] It is worth mentioning that the initial scope of this study was not limited to heterosexual relations among the clergy; however, there is only a single account of same-sex relations in the visitation records.[42] The absence of same-sex sexual activity in the records is certainly significant, but based on the questions put to parishioners, it is clear that visitors were not soliciting this type of

---

39. Janelle Werner has reached a similar conclusion and notes that scholars should not assume that celibacy was a given for the masculine identity of the clergy; "Promiscuous Priests and Vicarage Children: Clerical Sexuality and Masculinity in Late Medieval England," in Thibodeaux, *Negotiating Clerical Identities*, 162–63. Ruth Karras has also noted that "university authorities did not enforce, much less the students adopt, the teachings of the church about celibacy and chastity as part of their model of masculinity." Karras, *From Boys to Men*, 80.

40. Anna Clark, *Desire: A History of European Sexuality* (New York: Routledge, 2008), 3.

41. James A. Schultz, "Heterosexuality as a Threat to Medieval Studies," *Journal of the History of Sexuality* 15, no. 1 (2006): 14–29. See also Kim M. Phillips and Barry Reay, *Sex before Sexuality: A Premodern History* (Cambridge, UK: Polity Press, 2011).

42. ACV, Calaix 31 / 43, Visites, no. 4, 32r.–34r.v. (1315).

information from witnesses. It appears, then, that ecclesiastical officials were not concerned with parish clergy engaging in same-sex relations. That witnesses did not report incidents of same-sex acts to ecclesiastical authorities or make these charges against their clergy and neighbors similarly suggests that this was not a concern for parishioners. But to assume that Catalan clergy were simply not engaging in same-sex sexual relations because such behavior went unreported would be a naïve and faulty conclusion to make. The very clerics who had sex with women and produced children could have also been involved with men.

Just as priests formed unions with women and fathered children to prove their adherence to a masculine ideal prevalent in their parish communities, they also appropriated violence into their clerical masculinity. The topic of violence regularly enters into discussions of masculinity, especially because historians and sociologists have identified an obvious link between masculinity and violence in cultures across both historical time and geographical space. The connection between male violence and masculinity, however, is not culturally universal since gender identities are created and are specific to particular social groups, races, ethnicities, places, regions, and times. Studies based on this social constructionist approach to gender have found that in societies where gender inequality is a key feature and where masculine bravado, physical strength, and prowess are defining attributes of masculinity, the level of male violence is also higher. In such societies, men use aggressive acts to assert or maintain control over others, which in turn reaffirms their masculinity, enhances their self-esteem, and, in cases of interpersonal conflict, reclaims interpersonal power.[43] This holds true for medieval society: violence was perceived to be gendered in that aggressive acts were considered something "that men do, not women."[44] Masculine culture, particularly among elites, glorified the masculine values of toughness, force, competition, and dominance—even if most men and boys did not fully live up to this ideal. But these masculine values do not suddenly appear in adulthood. They are learned traits that are taught and sustained in cultures that institutionalize male dominance and patriarchy. The masculinization of control teaches children that boys should strive for power and that aggression is a means of achieving their goals. Granted, not all masculinities demonstrate the same degree of aggression, domination,

---

43. Kimmel, *Gendered Society*, 315–18; Suzanne E. Hatty, ed., *Masculinities, Violence, and Culture* (Thousand Oaks: Sage Publications, 2000), 55–59. See also Robert W. Connell, "The Social Organization of Masculinity," in *Masculinities*, 2nd ed. (Berkeley, University of California Press, 2005), chap. 3.

44. Ross Balzaretti, "'These Are Things That Men Do, Not Women': The Social Regulation of Female Violence in Langobard Italy," in *Violence and Society in the Early Medieval West*, ed. Guy Halsall (Woodbridge, UK: Boydell Press, 1998), 186–89.

or competitiveness, but in so far as these behaviors were salient characteristics of more socially admired medieval masculinities, which many men strove to emulate, these dominant masculine values infiltrated the clerical identity of parish priests.[45]

Priests used violence not only because they were influenced by secular manhood but also to maintain their status and authority in the masculine hierarchy of village society. Unlike the disorderly behaviors of biologically adult clergymen stuck in adolescence, parish priests in Catalunya exercised violence as a form of power: to correct the behavior of parishioners they deemed offensive, to enact retribution, to demonstrate control over laymen and women, to show their superiority by taking the women of village men, and to subjugate their male parishioners. Such behavior was not abnormal in medieval society, especially when we consider that interpersonal violence and intrasocietal violence are widespread in societies where definitions of masculinity and femininity are highly differentiated and where the epitome of manhood is associated with dominance over both men and women.[46] These parish priests not only established a masculine hierarchy between themselves and the laymen of the village, but they also created a hierarchy among their clerical colleagues to compete for prestige, authority in the parish church, and economic resources. The training of clerics under the supervision of parish priests even inculcated the acceptance of violence in that it was used to discipline and put lower-level clergy in their place, and was part of the professionalizing process during Holy Week, when clerics participated in the ritualized violence against Jews. Clerics-in-training also witnessed senior clergymen competing with clerical rivals to safeguard their positions in the clerical hierarchy of the parish, which means that younger clerics learned that violence was a component of their professional identity. Violence, then, need not fall within the purview of clergymen trapped in a state of adolescence but could also be employed by adult priests seeking to dominate the men and women in their parish. And before we assume that priestly violence was out of the ordinary or only a marker of a youthful masculinity, it is worth keeping in mind that violence was permissible and even acceptable between husbands and wives, parents and children, feudal lords and peasants, and masters and

---

45. For a discussion of how violence is gendered and learned through socialization, see Lee H. Bowker, "On the Difficulty of Eradicating Masculine Violence," in *Masculinities and Violence*, ed. Lee H. Bowker (Thousand Oaks: Sage Publications, 1998), 1–14; Martha K. Huggins and Mika Haritos-Fatouros, "Bureaucratizing Masculinities Among Brazilian Torturers and Murderers," in *Masculinities and Violence*, ed. Lee H. Bowker (Thousand Oaks: Sage Publications, 1998), 29–54. See also Suzanne E. Hatty, "Engendering Violence: Starting Points," in *Masculinities, Violence, and Culture*, 1–22.

46. Kimmel, *Gendered Society*, 317; Karras, *From Boys to Men*, 10–11.

servants or apprentices as long as it was not excessive. The experience, training, and socialization of younger clerics who became priests reinforced gendered stereotypes and produced a clerical gender identity that accepted sexual activity and violence as significant elements of clerical manhood.

Decoding Priestly Masculinity

In this book, I revise the standard portrayal of medieval parish priests as promiscuous men constrained primarily to casual affairs or the services of prostitutes to include those who chose a marriage-like union. Chapter One demonstrates the pervasiveness of clerical unions and the proclivity of parish priests to form de facto marriages with women. I trace a number of clerical families over a sixty-year period to show that these were enduring unions in which clerics were fully committed to their women and children. Maintaining a family, moreover, did not hinder the careers of priests since many clerics were promoted from the minor to major orders, and even to the position of rector, in spite of their unions and households of children. The omnipresence of long-term unions and sexual affairs among the clergy illustrates that forming a sexual relationship with a woman became an element of clerical manliness in medieval Catalunya. Visitation records show that episcopal officials worked not to eradicate clerical unions among the clergy but to prevent the clergy from flagrantly displaying their families in public. The administration of clerical fines for concubinage was not an outright de facto licensing fee. The fines were certainly used to increase episcopal revenues, but at the same time, monetary fines functioned to regulate these illicit unions and curtail their outright pervasiveness. The dioceses of Girona and Barcelona profited most from the administration of fines because these two dioceses developed a more systematic method to track and fine concubinary clergy than did the dioceses of Urgell and Vic. Tracking the families and the fines paid to episcopal visitors for their concubinous unions reveals that many clerics refused to set aside their families in the face of repeated pecuniary punishment, indicating that economic hardship was preferable to losing their families. Chapter Two ties the sexuality of parish clergy to their masculine identity and explores why priests were involved in relationships that were, for all intents and purposes, marriages. Indiscriminate sex alone was not enough to prove manliness; marriage and progeny were central attributes of the dominant forms of masculinity in medieval society. In addition, priests were invested in their children and in their role as paterfamilias beyond the practical economic reasons for having a family.

In Chapter Three, I address the extent to which parish clergy were embedded in their local community and consider how familial, social, and economic factors firmly bound clerics to a life that very much mirrored that of their parishioners. In fact, the people of the parish were often connected to their priests through ties of kinship and affinity. Clerics lived out their lives as more than just priests; they were also the sons, brothers, uncles, and nephews of the people in the parish. The economic disparity between parish priests and elite clergy, moreover, underscores the differences not only in the lived experience but also in the gender identity that parish clergy attained because they were born, raised, grew to adulthood, and served the church among the very peasantry and lower strata of medieval society they belonged to. Priests, in effect, behaved like laymen because they were laymen in the priestly profession. Indeed, parish clergy represented an amalgamation of both the clerical and secular worlds. The clerical profession provided them with a priestly identity, and their experience as men of the village, in turn, influenced how they interacted with parishioners as priests.

My focus in the last three chapters shifts to the preponderance of clerical violence among men whose lives were, in theory, to be dominated by prayer, celebrating the divine office, administering the sacraments, and providing moral guidance to their parishioners. In Chapter Four, I show that employing violence to resolve disputes, uphold authority, and exert male privilege in a patriarchal culture was key for clergy to demonstrate their masculinity in the parish community. Much of this clerical violence centered on the public nature of personal honor, which dictated that men had to avenge and restore their reputations. The conflict-ridden interactions between parishioners and their priests was a product of how fully integrated clerics were into village life, particularly when these hostile interactions were based on personal animosities and hatreds. Furthermore, a great number of priests were reported to be belligerent, quarrelsome men who acted violently against parish villagers. Priests used violence to intimidate parishioners, a strategy that worked to bolster their control over villagers and parish affairs. To be sure, parish clergy used their status and clerical authority to establish a hierarchy in the parish that allowed them to subordinate their parishioners. Dominating socially inferior laymen in the parish village, however, was only one component of the gender identity of parish clergymen. The masculinity and professional identity of parish clergy were also shaped and defined by their interactions with their clerical colleagues.

In Chapter Five, I demonstrate that clerics learned early on in their clerical training that violence, conflict, dominance, and sexual unions were not only accepted social norms for clergy but needed to be publicly exercised in front of other men. The manner in which tonsured children acquired the knowledge for their future livelihood is important because of the connection between gender identity and professional identity. Perhaps the most convincing evidence of how clerical masculinity became instilled in clerics from an early age comes from the lives of priests and their sons. The sons of priests witnessed a model of clerical masculinity in which their fathers engaged in concubinous unions, carried weapons, fought, and socialized with their male peers; they too followed this pattern of behavior. Evidence that priests trained their sons for a clerical career reveals that tonsured boys learned a model of clerical behavior from their fathers that incorporated characteristics of lay masculinity. As a result, the clerical education and training of priests' sons and the influence of senior clergy as role models all coalesced to produce a unique clerical identity, very different from that of ecclesiastical elites—one in which the violent acts of parish clergy can be connected to their professional identity as clerics and to their personal identity as men. Chapter Six focuses on priests, priors, and monks who wielded swords against their religious colleagues to carve out status and privilege and to gain prestige within the hierarchy of the parish and greater access to economic resources. To subordinate their co-workers and demean their rivals, clerics insulted, sabotaged, and orchestrated petty acts of revenge and violence on their rivals. Performative acts of intimidation as well as verbal and physical violence functioned not only to humiliate a clerical opponent professionally but also challenged the authority and influence of the colleague by making him look weak. The economic crisis of the 1330s in Catalunya intensified the competition among the parish clergy struggling to survive in a time of famine, deprivation, and inflation. Clerics frequently quarreled over the customary gifts obtained when they officiated at baptisms and marriages, celebrated special masses, and buried the dead. They became more aggressive in defending the privileges connected to their status and the rights attached to their benefices. A clerical culture existed in Catalunya that countenanced verbal and physical aggression as a way for clerics to compete for primacy and improve their professional and masculine standing amid their colleagues.

At its core, this book is a regional study of Catalan clergy in which I show how clerics negotiated their familial ties, integrated the priestly profession with their diverse roles in the parish, and constructed a masculine identity that functioned to their advantage in a predominantly rural setting. This project highlights the conflict inherent in the ideal model of clerical behavior as expounded in canon law, Lateran councils, and synodal decrees with the lived reality of parish clergy embedded in their communities through ties of kinship, friendship, business, and occupation. My hope is that it offers a complex view of parish clergy that situates them in a more realistic environment and complicates the image of the lecherous and debauched priest so fondly depicted in the histories of the medieval church. I cannot, unfortunately, fully answer the extent to which clerical families and priestly masculinity in Catalunya differed elsewhere in Europe during the first half of the fourteenth century. Although it seems likely that Iberian clergy, and in particular Catalan clergy, practiced concubinage at an exceptional level compared to England and France, studies in other areas of the Mediterranean and northwestern Europe suggest that clerical unions were also common in these regions. In place of a definitive answer, I offer a study of how clerical culture, professional privilege, episcopal policies and administrative structures, as well as social mores and customs, such as the acceptance of informal unions among the clergy and laity, shaped the masculine identity of parish priests. Finally, the appendix to this book contains tables listing the numbers of concubinary clergy charged in the visitation records from each diocese, numerous examples of clerical families and priestly violence, and evidence of family relations in the parish that could not all be integrated into my narrative. The many examples are included not only to illustrate the widespread practice of concubinage but also to show how common it was for clerics to have family ties in the parish. In providing these tables, I hope to demonstrate that the examples of clerical violence I discuss were far from isolated cases or incidents but can be considered to have been commonplace and to be evidence of a shared clerical culture in late medieval Catalunya.

CHAPTER 1

Marriage Defines the Parish Priest

Hail fell from the sky and pounded the parish of
Sant Christòfol de Cogolls in 1329. Unable to explain this bizarre weather, parishioners blamed the rector, claiming that "on account of his sin the whole
parish was struck by hail." Looking to root out the sins of their clergy, the
members of the community forced the rector's concubine Maria and his two
daughters from their home and expelled them from the parish. But parishioners did not stop there; Maria Cigario and her three sons by the deacon Guillem were also ousted. The priest Pere de Font, Maria de Prat, and their two
daughters were spared, presumably because they lived on the family's manse
outside the parish. After parishioners drove out the women and children from
the parish, both the rector and the deacon left to live with their families in another village, and the priest Pere's family continued to live on their manse.[1]

When a community experienced bad weather, failing crops, or epidemics,
people looked to their neighbors seeking evidence of immorality to explain
God's wrath.[2] Examples of parishioners condemning the sexual lives of their

---

1. ADG, Visites, no. 4, 113v.–114r.v. (1329).
2. The belief in divine punishment, especially in the form of a disease in which the body was
thought to mirror the illness or corruption of the soul, such as leprosy or the plague, was often used
to justify violence against lepers, Jews, Muslims, and even clerics. Many people also believed that the
plague was a direct result of the sexual licentiousness of Christian society. David Nirenberg, "Conversion, Sex, and Segregation: Jews and Christians in Medieval Spain," *American Historical Review* 107

clergy and driving clerical families out of the parish are exactly the kind of evidence we would expect to find considering the vast amount of literature that denounced clerical marriage and clerical wives. The belief that the sexual sins of the clergy could provoke divine punishment is found in saints' lives and exempla written during the Gregorian reform, when the church was battling to end clerical marriage and impose clerical celibacy. In these didactic stories, a priest might be stricken with a painful disease or be consumed by the fire of his own lust, and under exceptional circumstances, a woman and cleric fornicating in a church could be fused together like dogs until the community prayed for the sinners to be released.[3] Such stories were meant to discourage clerics from sexual temptation and convey the importance of a sexually pure clergy; pastoral manuals and synodal legislation, however, offered more practical advice on how to deal with clerical couples. Moralists advised parishioners to refuse to attend mass celebrated by a priest who "remains in the arms of his concubine" because an unchaste priest defiled sacred objects with his corrupted touch. Parishioners were directed not only to socially ostracize the concubines of priests but also to prohibit them from entering the church or, at the very least, to deny these women the kiss of peace during mass.[4]

(2002): 1076–78; Rafael Narbona Vizcaíno, *Pueblo, poder, y sexo: València medieval, 1306–1420* (Valencia: Diputació de València, 1992), 75; David Herlihy, *The Black Death and the Transformation of the West*, ed. Samuel K. Cohn, Jr. (Cambridge: Harvard University Press, 1997); Robert I. Moore, *The Formation of a Persecuting Society* (Oxford: Basil Blackwell, 1987), 60–65; Guido Ruggiero, "Sexual Criminality in the Early Renaissance: Venice, 1338–1358," *Journal of Social History* 8 (1974): 24–25; J. Romeu Figueras, "Folklore de la lluvia y de las tempestades en el Pirineo catalán," *Revista de dialectología y tradiciones populares* 7 (1951): 292–326.

3. Dyan Elliot, "Sex in Holy Places," in *Fallen Bodies: Pollution, Sexuality, and Demonology in the Middle Ages* (Philadelphia: University of Pennsylvania Press, 1999), 63–68. See also Dawn Marie Hayes, "Mundane Uses of Sacred Places in the Central and Later Middle Ages, with a Focus on Chartres Cathedral," *Comitatus: A Journal of Medieval and Renaissance Studies* 30 (1999): 11–37; Phyllis G. Jestice, "Why Celibacy? Odo of Cluny and the Development of a New Sexual Morality," in *Medieval Purity and Piety: Essays on Medieval Clerical Celibacy and Religious Reform*, ed. Michael Frassetto (New York: Garland Publishing, 1998), 81–116. Examples of clerics or monks punished for their sexual indiscretions in didactic literature are far too numerous to list here, but it is worth mentioning a few. Hugh of Floreffe, *Life of Yvette of Huy*; Caesarius of Heisterback, *Dialogue on Miracles*; Robert Mannyng of Brunne, *Handlyng Synne*. The increasing devotion to the Virgin Mary in the twelfth and thirteenth centuries produced stories such as the *Cantigas de Santa Maria* and the *Milagros de Nuestra Señora* where the Virgin protects clerics from sexual temptation or demonstrates her mercy by saving the souls of fornicating clerics from the devil. See *Songs of Holy Mary of Alfonso X*; Gonzalo de Berceo, *Miracles of Our Lady*.

4. Pastoral manuals and handbooks were written to guide priests in their pastoral duties, but these works also filtered into popular literature. Thomas of Chobham's *Summa confessorum* ("De continentia clericorum," "De pena concubinarum," and "Sacerdos incenstuosus punitur per suspensionem,") in *Analecta mediaevalia namurcensia*, ed. F. Broomfield (Paris: Beatrice-Nauwelaerts, 1968), 376–86. Chobham classified concubinage as incest due to the priest's corruption of a spiritual daughter. He believed that women who accepted penance from priests were their penitential and, often, their baptismal daughters; therefore, priests should avoid their spiritual daughters as if they were their own

Yet before we point to the expulsion of clerics and their families from Cogolls as evidence that parishioners expected a celibate clergy and took Church teachings to heart, a closer analysis of this event reveals that parishioners had quarreled with their rector about his concubine Maria. The reason the villagers disliked Maria is not revealed, but it is clear that both the rector and Maria were considered strangers who had no familial ties to the community. In the previous year, the rector had exchanged his rectorship in the parish of Sant Mateu de Montnegre for the one in Cogolls.[5] Problems seem to have arisen because the rector was frequently absent. In fact, the rector held another benefice in his native parish and had entrusted the service of his benefice in Cogolls, without the bishop's consent, to the priest Pere de Font, who was serving in the nearby castle of Hostoles. Parishioners most likely resented that they were left without a priest residing full-time in the parish who could administer the sacraments without great delay. The rector may have also created more conflict when he became involved with Graïda Sacosta, a woman from the parish with whom he had a child. The community did not look favorably on a cleric who already had a family and dallied with single women without the promise of a committed relationship. That parishioners also targeted the deacon Guillem's family seems to have been more a consequence of the impetus to dismiss the rector than anything else. The priest Pere and his family in large part remained unaffected because he continued to serve in Hostoles, and Maria de Prat and their children remained on their family manse.

To what extent then should we consider the actions of the parishioners of Sant Christòfol de Cogolls against their concubinary priests as characteristic of the medieval populace in Catalunya? In the roughly sixty-year time span of this study, this is the only reported incident in which parishioners expelled the families of churchmen because of their perceived sinfulness. Similar episodes may have occurred elsewhere, but in the dioceses of Girona, Vic, Urgell, and Barcelona, this event is an anomaly in pastoral visitation records. Certainly the reaction of the parishioners suggests that the laity connected clerical sexuality with sin and sin with natural disaster, but these documents also reveal that medieval people in general expressed very little shock or outrage when their priests formed unions with women or established households with a family. After all, the parishioners of Cogolls could hardly claim ignorance of the sexual sins of their clergy when, in fact, the deacon Guillem and his family, and

---

carnal daughters. See also John W. Baldwin, *Masters, Princes and Merchants: The Social Views of Peter the Chanter and His Circle* (Princeton: Princeton University Press, 1970); Brundage, *Law, Sex, and Christian Society*, 405, 476.

5. ADG, Notularum, no. 6, 153v. (1328). Pere de Terrades, who held the care of souls, exchanged his benefice in Sant Mateu de Montnegre with Joan Morell, rector of Cogolls.

the priest Pere de Font and his two daughters had been living in or near the village for more than fifteen years.

This study of episcopal visitation records allows us to trace the history of some of these families, such as that of the deacon Guillem and his concubine Maria de Cigario from the parish of Cogolls. They already appear as a family in 1314, as does the priest Pere and his concubine Maria de Prat in 1315 when their children were still "infantes."[6] Their unions had endured for at least sixteen years, if not longer, when the clerics and their families were expelled in 1329. Pere de Font served both in Cogolls and in the chapel of the castle of Hostolets, but he spent the remaining part of his career in Hostolets, where he and Maria de Prat had another child. Pere bought a manse called ça Fabrega located near Cogolls for his family, and he and Maria lived together there for thirty years.[7] Based on the long residence of these couples in both the villages of Cogolls and Hostolets, we can surmise that many parishioners spent a good part of their life interacting with these families, perhaps even seeing their children playing and growing up together.

Unfortunately, the records disclose little else about the relations between the parish clergy and their parishioners; however, the visitation of 1329 exposes a profoundly significant detail: the rector and the deacon chose to follow their expelled families rather than stay and minister to their flock. The fact that these clergymen were unwilling to be separated from their families attests to the greater allegiance they felt to their families than to their parish church. In making this choice, these clerics, as husbands and fathers, were indistinguishable from their lay counterparts, further indicating that many clerics did not forsake marriage—even if their relationship was marriage in all but name. Although the image of the promiscuous and randy priest (and monk) was common in medieval literature, sermons, and in devotional texts, documents of practice show that a great many were family men who formed long-term unions with women and found ways to preserve their families when faced with ecclesiastical punishment. Based on an analysis of episcopal visitation records and Catalan diocesan policies that dealt with clerical incontinence, in this chapter I show that two hundred years after canon law had prohibited clerical marriage long-standing clerical unions were ubiquitous throughout Catalunya. What is more, episcopal officials were lenient in their policies of tolerating and punishing concubinage, and repeat offenders were not removed from their benefice or deprived of their clerical status. As long as a cleric paid the fine,

---

6. ADG, Visites, no. 1, 20v. (1314); Visites, no. 2, 34v.–35r. (1315). In the visitation of 1329, the priest Pere de Font claimed that he had received a letter of dispensation three years earlier for his relationship with Maria de Prat.

7. ADG, Imposicions de Penes, no. 1, 55r. (1344).

he could keep his family as before. The examples of concubinous unions I use in this chapter and others are limited primarily to couples whose relationship is documented in more than one visitation, fined on more than one occasion, described as a long-term union, or are at least recorded as a union that produced numerous children to indicate its longevity. My goal is not only to illustrate the pervasive practice of clerical concubinage but also to show that priests were choosing to enter into marriage-like unions and establish a family household despite repeated fines that could prove to be a financial hardship. While church law deemed such unions to be concubinary, I use terms such as *de facto marriage* and *marriage-like union* or *relationship* because both the clergy and laity often perceived these unions to be marital partnerships. That clerics started out their careers in a union with a woman and then progressed through the holy orders to the priesthood also indicates that they believed it possible to be in the priestly profession and still enjoy a marriage-like union and a family. For these men, forming a long-term union with a woman and supporting a family was such an important part of their life course that it became a marker of manhood in spite of their priestly profession.

The three clerical families found in the parish of Sant Christòfol de Cogolls are representative of the widespread practice of clerical concubinage throughout Catalunya. Not only were parish clergy sexually active but, more important, a significant number of these clerics chose to establish long-term unions with women and supported their children in a family household. In the parishes of late medieval Catalunya, episcopal visitation records from the dioceses of Barcelona, Girona, Vic, and Urgell reveal that clerical unions were de facto marriages. The rector Pere de Quintana lived in the same house with Ermesenda de Comba in the parish of Sant Vicenç de Maià. The couple had so many offspring that parishioners were unsure whether they had seven or eight children. The eldest was around twenty years old and the youngest was ten.[8] Clerical families could be prosperous and quite large, and many clergymen bought additional houses or manses for their families, as did the rector of Sant Martí de Bas, who bought Guillema a farmstead called Funaya. The couple had raised their seven children there, but only four of their children now lived at home, and Guillema was expecting their eighth child.[9] A number of couples lived jointly for twenty or thirty years, such as the priest Guillem Mul and Ferrara who spent more than twenty-five years together, and some were considered so elderly that parishioners doubted whether they could "join together

---

8. ADG, Visites fragmentaris, 1303–1305, 15 r.v., 18 r.v. (1303).
9. AEV, Visites, no. 1200/2, 64v. (1330–1332).

carnally."[10] The longevity of such unions underscores the marital nature of these relationships, especially when we consider the extent to which parish priests worked to preserve their families in the face of punitive fines.

Clerical unions were exceedingly common in small, rural and mountainous parishes; however, clerical households could also be found, albeit in smaller numbers, throughout the larger towns and cities of Catalunya, such as Barcelona and Girona.[11] In 1331, the large town of Cervera in the diocese of Vic had twenty-six clerics in the major orders who were cited for publicly keeping women and children. A smaller town such as Santa Coloma de Queralt in the hills between the towns of Cervera and Manresa had five clerical couples with a total of thirteen children. Local priests such as Pere Muntayola, who had three children with Maria, and Jaume Ferrer, who had two daughters with Gondieta, also worked in the town *scribania* as notaries. Considering the visibility of these priests and their offspring, it is hard to imagine that the townspeople in Queralt were unaware of their families.[12] Further to the south of Barcelona in Vilafranca del Penedès, ten clerics in the major orders and three rectors from nearby parishes were charged with concubinage.[13] Nearly every parish in Catalunya had a concubinary priest, and numerous parishes had more than one clerical family. Given that small parishes housed two to three clergymen in the major orders and larger parishes had four to five clerics, the presence of concubinary clergy across the parishes of the region is significant. What is more, evidence that secular and regular clergy maintained families at all social levels can be found. In the episcopal seat of Urgell, it was public knowledge that four canons in the cathedral publicly kept their families in their homes. The canon and magister Ramon was known for keeping a "wife"

---

10. ADG, Visites fragmentaris, 22r. (1305). A number of elderly couples whose relationships had lasted more than twenty years are noted in visitation records. I list a few here. In the diocese of Girona: ADG, Visites fragmentaris, 12v. (1305); ADG, Visites, no. 1, 88v. (1315); ADG, Visites, no. 6, 95r.v. (1340); ADG, Visites, no. 7, 19r.v.–20r. (1341). In the diocese of Vic: AEV, Visites, no. 1200/2, 64v. (1330–1332). In the diocese of Urgell: ACV, Visites, Calaix 31/43, no. 7, 35r. (1313); ACV, Visites, Calaix 31/43, no. 1, 34v. (1312). In the diocese of Barcelona: ADB, Visites, no. 2, 75r. (1315); ADB, Visites, no. 4, 20v., 32r., 48v., 60r. (1336) and 79v. (1337). See also Susanna Vela Palomares, "Visites pastorals a la diòcesi d'Urgell. L'Example de les Valls d'Andorra. (1312–1314)," *Annals* (1990): 59–103; Jocelyn N. Hillgarth and Giulio Silano, eds., *The Register Notule Communium 14 of the Diocese of Barcelona (1345–1348): A Calendar with Selected Documents* (Toronto: Pontifical Institute of Mediaeval Studies, 1983), nos. 266, 305.

11. Episcopal visitors made few visitations to parish churches in cathedral cities such as Barcelona, Girona, and Vic; thus, the visitations overwhelming represent clergy living in the countryside.

12. For the towns of Cervera and Santa Coloma de Queralt, see AEV, Visites, no. 1200/2, 6r.v.–10r., 40v.–41r.v. (1331). Gregory Milton, in his work on the economic significance of Santa Coloma de Queralt, has identified the priests Pere Muntayola, Jaume Ferrer, and Bernat Esteve as men who also worked regularly in the town scribania: *Market Power: Lordship, Society, and Economy in Medieval Catalonia, 1276–1313* (New York: Palgrave Macmillan, 2012), 45–49.

13. Josep Maria Martí Bonet, "Las visitas pastorales y los 'communes' del primer año del pontificado del Obispo de Barcelona, Ponç de Gualba (1303)," *Anthologica Annua* 28–29 (1981–1982): 672–75.

in Montepesullano. The canon Bernat de Condamina financially supported two families. He lived with Saurina and their three children in his home in Urgell; at the same time, he also provided for Na Rosa and their children, who lived in Berga. Other clerical elites were also noted for their public involvement with women, but the nature of their unions is difficult to determine. The archdeacon of Urgell, Bartomeu de Garriga, had a relationship with Maria Romana, sister to the canon Ramon de Villautar.[14] The bishop of Urgell, during an inquest into whether he had obtained his office through simony, reportedly had kept a woman whom he later endowed with church funds and married to another man.[15] Guillem de Soccarrats, an episcopal visitor and a monk at Sant Pere de Galligans, who punished parish clergy for concubinage, was himself found guilty of incontinence.[16] Given the high-profile careers of clerics such as the archdeacon and bishop of Urgell, it was probably more difficult for such men to maintain a long-term union, particularly a public one, yet many clergymen in the upper echelons of the ecclesiastical hierarchy reportedly kept women and cared for their offspring.

Clerical unions were so prevalent throughout Catalunya that they can be found among both priests and regular clergy. In the monastery of Santa Maria de Ullà, Pere Arnau, a canon and priest, had three children with Guillema Jafera from 1322 to 1341; the canon Berenguer Sartor had two sons with Gerarda Peregrina, both of whom stayed with him in the monastery.[17] Some women lived in the monastery or frequently visited their clergymen there, for example, Guillema de Mansbarano, who lived with the prior Ramon de Soler. Likewise, the prior of Sant Joan de les Fonts also kept his woman, Ermesenda, in the monastery and had even refused to comply with the bishop's order to expel her. According to the monks of Sant Joan de les Fonts, the elderly couple spent much of their time in the kitchen, where Ermesenda read books and the prior said the hours.[18] Not all, however, were bold enough to live with their

---

14. ACV, Calaix 31/43, Visites, no. 1, 4v.–6v. (1312).
15. ACV, Calaix 31/43, Visites, no. 7, 1v. (1313).
16. ADG, Lletres, no. 2, 166r.v. (1326). Guillem de Soccarrats appears as an episcopal visitor in Visites, no. 2 and no. 3.
17. ADG, Imposicions de Penes, no. 1, 4v. (1336); ADG, Visites, no. 5, 31r.v., 33r., 122r.v.–123r.v. (1331); ADG, Visites, no. 6, 118v.–122r.v. (1341); ADG, Imposicions de Penes, no., 1, 4r. (1335), 20v. (1338), 34r. (1340), and 39v. (1342). In the diocese of Vic, Pere Cariera, a canon and vicar in the monastery of Santa Maria de Manlleu, kept his son in the monastery; AEV, Visites, no. 1200/1, 25v. (1330). Similarly, a monk kept Elisenda de Correla and their three children in the village of Granollers de la Plana; AEV, Visites, no. 1200/1, 26v. (1330). A great number of canons in the cathedral see of Tortosa, including the archdeacon, were charged with keeping concubines in ACT, Visites, 3r.v.–12r.v. (1387).
18. ADG, Visites, no. 1, 26r.v. (1315). The prior of Sant Esteve de Caneres, Bartomeu Sabater, also kept his concubine Raimunda in the priory, and the prior Ferrar de Palau keep his concubine in the priory of Sant Ponç de Corbera; ADG, Visites, no. 3, 7v.–8r. (1321); ADB, Visites, no. 5, 100v. (1342).

women in the monastery. The prior of the monastery Santa Maria de Lluçà kept Na Paschala, the daughter of En Juglares, on his manse, called des Vilars in Cantacorps. The couple apparently spent their time both at the monastery and at their farmstead.[19] In other examples, the *"amasia"* of the canon Berenguer Cervera frequently visited the monastery of Rocarrosa and left with items of food. The family of the monk Bernat de Miars similarly visited him in the monastery of Sant Miquel de Cruïlles and his ten-year old daughter was reported to frequently carry away foodstuff to take back to her mother. Bernat's longtime partner, Anglesa, and their children were also seen staying in his private residence in the village of Cruïlles.[20] In his study of fourteenth-century Dominican friars in the Crown of Aragon, Michael Vargas notes that the order had such a problem with friars who disappeared from the convent to socialize with women and visit their families that provincial chapter statutes had to address the issue. The order viewed the unsupervised entrance and exiting of friars, women, and boys to be so widespread that statutes prohibited friars from "creating passages through bedchamber walls by which they might have unlicensed exit."[21] While the Dominicans were attempting to impose a stricter discipline in their Order, the gates of other monastic orders were something of a revolving door for monks and their families. The monks Berenguer Falgons and Ramon Falgons regularly left the monastery of Santa Maria de Cervià to visit their women and children. Episcopal visits to monasteries show that many monks not only left without license from the abbot or prior but also rarely resided full-time in the monastery. Like the canon Guillem Lloret of Rocarossa, who kept Ermesenda Riera and their four children in Hostalric, a number of regular clergy owned houses outside the monastery and found it

---

19. AEV, Visites, no. 1200/2, 65r. (1331). There are other examples in the diocese of Vic. The canon and sacrist Jaume ÇaConomina of the monastery of Santa Maria de Manlleu kept Margarida in the town of Manlleu. The relationship between the canon and Margarida began during her marriage and continued after she became a widow; AEV, Visites, no. 1200/1, 24r. (1330). The monk Pere Vendrel kept Maria in the village of Santa Maria de Folgaroles and, according to parishioners, she "frequently enters and exits the house of that monk." AEV, Visites, no. 1200/1, 23r. (1300). In the diocese of Barcelona, the monk and priest Guillem de Rippis kept Guillema ÇaSerra and his two daughters. Parishioners in the village of Sant Esteve de la Garriga mention that the monk brought Guillema and the girls to the church when he served there; ADB, Visites, no. 2, 89r. (1315). The monks living in the priory of Sant Sebastià in the diocese of Barcelona did not live together in a monastery but, rather, in a few homes associated with the priory because their building with the communal dormitory and chapel were falling apart; ADB, Visites, no. 5, 46v. (1342); Martí Bonet, "Visitas pastorales," 670–71.

20. ADG, Imposicions de Penes, no. 1, 7v. (1336); ADG, Visites, no. 7, 68r. (1343); ADG, Visites, no. 8, 12v.–13r. (1345). In the monastery of Sant Feliu de Guíxols, two monks and two priests serving in the monastery were involved with women and had children. The chaplain Arnau de Font had kept Cecília for twenty years. The priest Bernat Loret had two daughters with Na Catalina and kept one of his daughters at the monastery; ADG, Processos, no. 40, 1v.–2r. (1320).

21. Michael A. Vargas, *Taming a Brood of Vipers: Conflict and Change in Fourteenth-Century Dominican Convents* (Leiden: Brill, 2011), 141, 153.

easier to keep their families in nearby villages.[22] The extent to which clerical unions can be found among both the regular and secular clergy points to a clerical culture that accepted clerical de facto marriages as not only a norm but also as a custom entrenched in Iberian society.[23] Such a practice among parish priests, elite clergy, monks, and friars speaks to a clerical culture that did not view maintaining a family as an impediment to a profession in the church, and it is evidence that establishing a sexual relationship with a woman had become important to the gender identity of clergymen (see Chapter Two). To get a sense of the pervasiveness of the custom of clerical unions, a statistical analysis of episcopal visitation records reveals the extent to which marriage-like unions or clerical concubinage was a common practice among secular clergy in the four dioceses of northern Catalunya. Because priests, deacons, and subdeacons were bound to the rule of celibacy, the statistics apply only to parish clergy in the major orders. Tables 1.1, 1.2, and 1.3 (see appendix for all tables) show the breakdown of the number of parishes visited by year, the number of clergy accused of concubinage, and the total number of clerics charged with incontinence. In the diocese of Girona, an examination of the records shows that in the 1,391 visitations to parish churches carried out from 1303 to 1346, episcopal visitors charged anywhere from 50 to 83 percent of incontinent clergy with having a concubinary relationship. In the more remote and mountainous Pyrenean dioceses of Catalunya, however, the rate of concubinage was higher, ranging from 73 to 96 percent depending on the year. In the diocese of Urgell, the 975 visitations undertaken during a three-year period (from 1312 to 1315), found 528 incontinent clergymen, and 492 of these clerics (93 percent) were cited for concubinage. In the 461 visitations to parish churches in the diocese of Vic from 1330 to 1339, 331 clerics were accused of incontinence, and 279 of these clerics (84 percent) were charged with concubinage. A similar pattern emerges in the diocese of Barcelona. In visitation records from 1303 to 1343, 880 clerics were cited for incontinence,

---

22. ADG, Visites, no. 5, 29v. (1331); ADG, Imposicions de Penes, no. 1, 62v., 66r. (1346); ADG, Visites fragmentaris, 23r.v.–24r.v. (1320). It was not uncommon for monasteries to receive visitors. A visit to the monastery of Sant Pere d'Arquells in the diocese of Vic reveals that the nephews and relatives of the monks frequently visited. A monk serving in the church of Sant Esteve de Granollers de la Plana kept Elisenda and their three children in the village; AEV, Visites, no. 1200/2, 35r. (1331); AEV, Visites, no. 1200/1, 26v. (1330). In the monastery of Sant Martí de Sacosta, the chaplain Arnau de Planes's concubine, Dolça, frequently visited and on one occasion brought a basket of apples and pears to Arnau; ADG, Processos, no. 55, 2r., 8r. (1322). Three monks from Sant Cugat des Valles kept their women and children in neighboring parishes; ADB, Visites, no. 4, 38r.v.–39r.v. (1336).

23. Michelle Armstrong-Partida, "Priestly Marriage: The Tradition of Clerical Concubinage in the Spanish Church," *Viator* 40, no. 2 (2009): 221–53. Marie Kelleher has also addressed the high incidence of clerical concubinage in visitation records in "'Like Man and Wife': Clerics' Concubines in the Diocese of Barcelona," *Journal of Medieval History* 28 (2002): 349–60.

and 786 (89 percent) of them were charged with concubinage.[24] South of Barcelona, in the diocese of Tortosa, the extant visitation records show that clerical concubinage was just as prevalent in this agricultural region as in the northern region of Catalunya.[25] The total number of clergy accused of concubinage in the dioceses Girona, Barcelona, Urgell, and Vic from 1303 to 1346 amounts to 2,148 (85 percent) out of 2,526 charged with incontinence in 3,877 parish visitations. These figures point to clerical concubinage, or de facto marriage, being the norm in Catalan society. Even what little evidence exists after the 1348 plague in the diocese of Girona—a series of visitations carried out in 1350, and a book detailing the fines imposed on clergy from 1335 to 1363—indicates that the prevalence of clerical unions continued unabated among the surviving clergymen.[26]

It is more than likely, however, that the number of clerical unions in the major orders is underrepresented in this analysis of visitation records. The visitations from the dioceses of Vic and Urgell, moreover, indicate that episcopal authorities were not as interested in the sexual activities of clergy because such activities do not receive the same attention as the incontinent clergymen in the visitations from the dioceses of Girona and Barcelona. Furthermore, the extant visitations for the region of northern Catalunya during the preplague years permit only a rough estimate of the sexual activities of clergy because visitors were rarely able to cover more than one-half or one-quarter of a diocese at a time. Many of the visitations to parishes were perfunctory and carried out so quickly that some episcopal visitors managed to visit more than four parishes in one day, resulting in highly abbreviated accounts that

---

24. Josep Baucells i Reig, *Vivir en la edad media: Barcelona y su etorno en los siglos XIII y XIV (1200–1344)* (Barcelona: Consejo Superior de Investigaciones Científicas, Institución Milá y Fontanals, Departamento de Estudios Medievales, 2006), 3: 2494–97. Out of these 786, 55 percent (488 clerics) are recorded as having confessed to keeping women, and only 6 percent denied the charge. In 38 percent of these cases, there was no documentation of the cleric's response to the charge.

25. Although far fewer visitation records exist for the dioceses of Tortosa, they nevertheless show that clerical unions were also common. The earliest set of visitation records, which cover a two-year period from 1314 to 1316, reveal that in the 82 parishes visited 59 clergymen in the major orders (72 percent) were accused of keeping concubines. This figure is based on my counting of concubinary clergy from published visitations records. See Maria Teresa García Egea, *La visita pastoral a la diocesis de Tortosa del Obispo Paholac, 1314* (Diputacío de Castelló, 1993). I have also studied the visitation records for 1337 and 1387 in the ACT. Although I did not undertake a statistical analysis of the clerics accused of sexual transgressions, I can confirm the prevalence of clerical concubinage in these records. The visitations for 1337 are in a poor state and are mostly loose quadernos and folios that have not been bound together; ACT, Llibres de Visites Pastorals, 1337 and 1387.

26. ADG, Visites, no. 9 (1350); ADG, Obligacions de Penes, no. 1 (1335–1363). Post-plague visitation records for the fourteenth century are sparse in all the Catalan dioceses. A resumption of episcopal visits to parishes does not begin until the 1360s for dioceses of Girona and Barcelona, and until 1391 for the diocese of Vic; no visitations exist for the remainder of the fourteenth and fifteenth centuries for the diocese of Urgell.

simply state, "all is well," and suggest, moreover, a less than thorough investigation into parish affairs. How meticulous a visitor was in carrying out his duties, therefore, affected the number of incontinent clergy recorded in the visitations. Particularly in the mountainous villages of the dioceses of Urgell and Girona, the numbers of clerics engaged in sex is underrepresented because it was not uncommon for the visitor to arrive and find no one in the parish to interrogate or to record that, due to inclement weather, the parish could not be reached.[27] Despite the difficulties of carrying out yearly visitations, the real burden lay with the parishioners, who were obligated to pay the procuration fee for the visitor's expenses.[28] The payment could prove difficult for parishioners to amass. Letters from episcopal registers show that some rectors would ask for their parish to be exempted due to extreme poverty and that parishes could be placed under interdict for failing to pay. At times, a visitor's intrusion prompted hostility on the part of both the clergy and the laity, particularly when there was a sense that the visitor visited the parish simply to charge the procuration fee. On a number of occasions in the diocese of Urgell, rectors protested against paying the procuration fee, and parishioners refused to participate in the inquiry and declared that they would not be "corrected" by the visitor.[29] Although parishioners used a visitor's probe into parish matters to complain about their clergy or fellow villagers, the visitations also reveal that the people of the parish were not always keen on the imposition of episcopal authority into their affairs. How much this attitude affected the testimony of parishioners is hard to determine.

It is also worth noting that episcopal officials did not indiscriminately charge parish clergy with concubinage. An effort was made to distinguish a concubinary relationship based on financial support and publicly establishing a household with a woman from clerics who were reported as only sinning carnally (*peccat carnaliter*) or those who were defamed by associating with

---

27. In the 1312 to 1316 visitations for the diocese of Urgell, visitors arrived to find neither clergy nor parishioners present in 59 parishes. Furthermore, in 65 parishes, no parishioners were questioned, and in 27 parishes, the cleric was either absent or refused to testify. In the diocese of Girona, when poor weather conditions impeded a visitor from making it up to mountainous parishes, the visitor usually sent a messenger to bring the priest and a parishioner or two to the visitor. In many of these cases, only the priest appeared before the visitor. It is interesting that, in all the cases in which the visitor was unable to conduct a visitation in the parish itself, neither the priest nor the witnesses offered testimony about the sexually illicit affairs of the clergy or laity.

28. It was not uncommon for a number of neighboring parishes to contribute a portion to the procuration fee. Since the procuration fee was meant to cover the food and lodging of the episcopal visitor and his entourage, including shelter for the horses of the visitor's traveling party, the amount was too much for one parish to pay.

29. ACV, Calaix, 31/43, Visites, no. 2, 25v., 28v., 57r.v. (1313); ACV, Visites, no. 3, 24v., 28r. (1313); Visites, no. 4, 2v., 3r., 5r., 10v., 13r. (1314); ACV, Visites, no. 5, 12v., 18v. (1315); ACV, Visites, no. 6, 8v. (1315).

certain a woman (*diffamatus de quadam muliere*). Particularly in the diocese of Girona, a greater attempt was made to document concubinary relationships so that these clerics could be subjected to a greater fine when the next visitation was made.[30] And although it is likely that not every cleric charged with breaking his vow of chastity was guilty, one way that authorities determined guilt was to note the number of children the cleric had sired with a woman or women, and this explains why offspring were recorded in the visitations. Admittedly, my figures are far from ideal because the total number of concubinary clergy should be divided by the total number of clergy in the major orders throughout an entire diocese, but based on the extant documents, it is impossible to determine these numbers. Nevertheless, this analysis shows that an overwhelming number of clerics charged with sexual incontinence chose to enter into a marriage-like relationship. Parish clergy wanted more than to simply engage in sex with a woman; they sought to establish relationships with women that were socially acceptable. The high incidence of clerical unions suggests not only that clerical couples and families were the standard in this society but also that Catalan clergy engaged in the social practice of marriage.

Comparing the prevalence of clerical unions in Catalunya with other regions in Europe is difficult because finding comparable data is a challenge. No other quantitative study of clerical concubinage from the first half of the fourteenth century exists. In addition, the few studies that look at the sexual activity of the clergy do not single out clerical unions when undertaking a general count of clerical incontinence. Nevertheless, it is worth the effort to draw some comparisons with these studies from France, England, and Belgium and to note a marked difference between Catalunya and northern Europe. A study of visitations undertaken by the bishop Odo of Rigaldus from 1248 to 1258 shows that the sexual indiscretions of Norman priests ranged between 9 and 28 percent of the clerical population in the diocese of Rouen, indicating that the campaign of the Church to eradicate clerical marriage and impose

---

30. In the diocese of Girona, the visitor typically asked questions that dealt with the public nature of the relationship and a cleric's financial investment in the union: Did the cleric publicly eat and drink with the woman? Where did the cleric or concubine reside? What were the duration of the union and the number of children? (The age of the youngest child was often noted as of way of determining the last time the couple had sex, specifically if the cleric had been previously fined for concubinage.) Finally, did the cleric provide his concubine and children with food and clothing? Visitation records from Urgell tend to be more abbreviated and provide less detail about clerical couples than visitations from Girona, Barcelona, and Vic. The sporadic and meager fines for concubinage (anywhere between 5 and 20 sous) are a further indication that episcopal officials in Urgell had a limited interest in clerical concubinage. Instead, visitors were focused on obtaining the procuration fee for the visitation and for fining clerics who celebrated mass while excommunicated, or for fining clerics who continued to say mass and administer the sacraments while the parish was under interdict.

celibacy after Lateran IV had a serious effect on the sexual behavior of the Norman clergy.[31] By the last decade of the thirteenth century in the diocese of Canterbury in England, a mere fourteen clerics in the major orders were charged with incontinence in fifty-two parish churches, and only four of these for keeping a concubine. Near the English-Welsh border, in the diocese of Hereford, Janelle Werner's study of visitations from the year 1397 finds that 14 percent of 470 priests were charged with sexual misconduct, and only 19 parishes out of 260 were reported to have priests who kept concubines.[32] Considering the numbers of concubinary clergy in the major order reported in the dioceses of Girona, Barcelona, Vic, and Urgell, the concubinary priests in the dioceses of Canterbury and Hereford seem almost negligible. Further to the east on the Continent, accounts of fines leveled in the episcopal court of Tournai in Belgium from 1446 to 1462 show that 161 of 263 clerics (61 percent) charged in the secular priesthood were found guilty of incontinence, but how many of these clerics were involved in concubinage is not noted. Between 1420 and 1470, the episcopal court of Troyes in northern France prosecuted 311 clergymen in the major orders out of 859 cases (36 percent) dealing with sexual offences among both the clergy and laity.[33] Although these statistics from the

---

31. I have extrapolated the percentages of sexually incontinent priests in the diocese of Rouen from the numbers reported in Jennifer D. Thibodeaux, *"Man of the Church or Man of the Village": The Conflict of Masculinities among Priests in the Thirteenth-Century Diocese of Rouen* (PhD diss., University of Kansas, 2004), 316–21. I arrived at the following percentages: 32 out of 308 priests (10 percent) charged with sexual incontinence in the archdeaconries of the Petit Caux and French Vexin in 1248–1249; 15 out of 139 priests (11 percent) charged with a sexual offense in the archdeaconry of Norman Vexin in 1249; 31 out of 225 priests (14 percent) charged with sexual incontinence in the archdeaconry of the Grand Caux in 1252; 74 out of 261 priests (28 percent) in 1248 and 24 out of 261 priests (9 percent) in 1258 were charged with a sexual offense in the archdeaconry of Eu. Thibodeaux does not differentiate between clerics who engaged in concubinage and those who had short-term affairs.

32. For Canterbury, nine clerics were charged with fornication and five with concubinage (one in the minor orders) in fifty-two parish churches and two chapels; Eveleigh Woodruff, "Some Early Visitation Rolls Preserved at Canterbury," *Archaelogia Cantiana* 32 (1917): 143–80. For the diocese of Hereford, see Werner, "Promiscuous Priests and Vicarage Children." A very small number of clerics who engaged in sex can also be found in the visitation records for the region of Cheshire and the archdeaconry of Sudbury in the diocese of Norwich; Antonia Gransden, "Some Late Thirteenth-Century Records of an Ecclesiastical Court in the Archdeaconry of Sudbury," *Bulletin of the Institute of Historical Research* 22 (1959): 62–69; Nigel J. Tringham, "The Parochial Visitation of Tarvin (Cheshire) in 1317," *Northern History* 38, no. 2 (2001): 197–220. See also Christopher Robert Cheney, "The Diocese of Grenoble in the Fourteenth Century," *Speculum* 10, no. 2 (1935): 162–77.

33. From 1470 to 1481, 243 out of 356 clerics (68 percent) in the secular priesthood were found guilty of incontinence; Monique Vleeschouwers-Van Melkebeek, "Mandatory Celibacy and Priestly Ministry in the Diocese of Tournai at the End of the Middle Ages," in *Peasants & Townsmen in Medieval Europe: Studia in Honorem Adriaan Verhulst*, ed. Jean Mari Duvosquel and Erik Thoen (Leuven: Belgisch Centrum voor Landelijke Geschiedenis, 1995), 681–92. For the diocese of Troyes, 166 priests, 68 curates, 61 chaplains, and 16 vicars were charged with incontinence, in addition to 69 friars, 57 priors, and 12 monks. Sara McDougall concludes that the officiality court of Troyes made a greater

dioceses of Tournai and Troyes indicate that a significant number of clerics in the major orders were involved in illicit sexual activities, the percentage of concubinary clerics remains a mystery. Neither study remarks on the procliv-ity of clerics to be in engaged in concubinous relationships, suggesting that such a practice was not common.

Most recently, Ruth Karras's study of 1,656 cases of sexual offenses in the criminal registers of the archdeacon of Paris during a twenty-two year pe-riod, from 1483 to 1505, finds that 299 priests were charged. Of these, about 30 percent may have been involved in a concubinous or long-term relation-ship, which is greater than the numbers reported in England but still difficult to compare with the numbers of incontinent clergy reported in Tournai and Troyes. The inconsistency of the archdeacon's court in labeling unions as concubinous, as well as using terms such as "maintaining" or "frequenting" a woman to indicate a domestic partnership or stable relationship, makes it dif-ficult to determine how many of the 299 priests charged with sexual inconti-nence were actually engaged in concubinage. The fact that ecclesiastical officials were not very concerned with determining the nature of the relation-ship reveals that officials did not believe the practice of clerical concubinage to be widespread. The infrequent use of terms dealing with concubinage in these ecclesiastical legal records, produced by church authorities familiar with canon law and the decrees of Lateran councils, further suggests that such unions were not as common in Paris. Karras also notes the infrequent use of phrases that describe a priest's sexual partner as a wife or a relationship as one of marriage, further showing that the laity did not perceive many of these unions to be like marriages.[34] The practice of concubinage in Paris stands in stark contrast to Catalunya, where over 80 percent of the clergy in the coun-tryside were charged with concubinage, and long-term domestic partnerships were so common that parishioners described these unions as marriage-like. What is more, the Catalan laity did not consider priests' concubines to be

---

effort to prosecute the sexual offences of the clergy than the laity; "The Prosecution of Sex in Late Medieval Troyes" in *Sexuality in the Middle Ages and Early Modern Times: New Approaches to a Fundamen-tal Cultural-Historical and Literary-Anthropological Theme*, ed. Albrecht Classen (New York: Walter de Gruyter, 2008), 706–8.

34. Karras breaks down the sexual offenses of priests into eleven categories based on the language used by ecclesiastical officials, such as *adultery, defloration, paternity,* and *scandal.* I have combined the categories that are most closely related to a long-term union—concubinage (18), maintaining (37), and maintaining with carnal knowledge (30)—to arrive at 85 cases (28 percent) that probably involved concubinage. Clearly, there is a possibility of underestimating or overestimating the number of unions brought before officials because, as Karras notes, either the court was not careful to record the exact offence or the defendants were pleading to a lesser charge; Karras, *Unmarriages,* 153–60.

women of ill repute simply because they cohabited with a local cleric. The label *priest whore* and the association of a priest's companion with a prostitute were more commonly found in large cities and towns such as London, York, and Dijon, where prostitution and brothels were far more visible and likely to cause social commentary. As Ruth Karras has observed, religious authorities in England did not "distinguish between prostitutes who had sex with priests and women who lived with priests as wives."[35] It makes sense that this attitude would be more prevalent in urban areas where people were less likely to encounter a "wife" and more likely to see prostitutes servicing clergy.

In addition, such a hostile view of clerics' concubines is generally not found in Iberia or Italy, suggesting that the prevalence of clerical unions in the Mediterranean affected how people viewed and labeled priests' concubines. Even medieval Iberian literary texts, such as the *Debate de Elena y María*, in which two sisters debate the merits of becoming the concubine of a priest or a poor knight, confirm the acceptance of clerical concubinage as commonplace.[36] The *Debate* is also noteworthy because it does not portray a priest's woman as sinful or treat her with disdain. In fact, in the debate between the two women, María, the concubine of the priest, is unrepentant and shows no shame in her role as concubine. María, furthermore, portrays her man as a "model minister, healthy, well-to-do, respected in the community, and . . . adept at seeing to her needs." The poem ends, according to Kevin Reilly, with the final judgment in favor of the priest as the better lover and provider, and with the impression that the author is more sympathetic to the concubine of the priest.[37]

---

35. Karras, *Common Women*, 108. In the visitation records from the diocese of Lincoln in England, Ruth Karras finds that parishioners called the priest's woman a *meretrix*, meaning something along the lines of concubine. Therefore, Karras asserts, women who cohabited with clergymen were simply considered "loose women" and were often called a "comon preste hure" or a "munkhore and frerehore." Ruth Karras, "The Latin Vocabulary of Illicit Sex in English Ecclesiastical Court Records," *Journal of Medieval Latin* 2 (1992): 1–17. See also Karras and Boyd, ' "Ut cum mulier' "; Goldberg, "Pigs and Prostitutes"; Goldberg, "Women in Fifteenth-Century Town Life," 119–20; Rossiaud, *Medieval Prostitution*, 28, 41–42, 118, 145–48. Studies on prostitution in Spain and Languedoc do not identify *priest whore* as an insult or label used for prostitutes; M. Carmen Peris, "La prostitución Valenciana en la segunda mitad del siglo XIV," *Revista de història medieval* 1 (1990): 179–99; María Eugenia Lacarra, "La evolución de la prostitución en la Castilla del siglo XV y la mancebía de Salamanca en tiempos de Fernando de Rojas," in *Fernando de Rojas and Celestina Approaching the Fifth Century. Proceedings of an International Conference in Commemoration of the 450th Anniversary of the Death of Fernando de Rojas*, ed. Ivy A. Corfis and Joseph T. Snow (Madison: Hispanic Seminary of Medieval Studies, 1993), 33–77; Otis, *Prostitution in Medieval Society*, xii, 16–17, 71–72.

36. Ramon Menéndez Pidal, "Elena y María (disputa del clérigo y el caballero). Poesía leonesa inédita del siglo XIII." *Revista de Filología Española* 1 (1914): 52–96.

37. Kevin C. Reilly, "The Conclusion of Elena y María: A Reconsideration," *Kentucky Romance Quarterly* 30, no. 3 (1983): 252, 256.

The fourteenth-century *Libro de Buen Amor*, which focuses on the sexual escapades of the archpriest of Huita to show that love has many virtues,[38] has the priest admit that one must experience carnal love to embrace *buen amor* (good love), which is the love of God.[39] The *Libro* is famous for the archpriest Juan Ruiz's honest and brazen desire not only for sexual fulfillment but also for his need for female companionship, especially because he approves of marriage as a weapon against incontinence.[40] In the *Libro*, the archpriest engages in a number of amorous affairs with women of various social classes, including young virgins, widows, peasant women, a Muslim woman, a bakergirl, and a noblewoman. He promises to marry only two women—both *serranas* (wild mountain women)—in an attempt to secure their help as he travels through the mountains of the Sierra de Guardarrama near Segovia. In one encounter, the archpriest is lost and is found by Mengua, a *serrana*, who asks him what he is looking for in the mountains. Juan Ruiz answers that he is seeking a mate, to which she replies that he cannot go wrong marrying a mountain woman who will please him. Believing him to be a "pastor," which in Castilian can literally mean both a shepherd and a priest, Mengua offers to marry him if he can list his good qualities as a husband. Mengua then reassures the archpriest that he can have a marriage that suits his needs and asks for jewelry, clothing, and trinkets; to this, Juan Ruiz promises to gift her with everything she has asked for and tells her to invite her family to the wedding.[41] In another encounter by the archpriest with a *serrana* named Alda, she too offers to marry the archpriest in return for jewels and clothing, and he promises to return with these gifts.[42] There is little doubt that the *serranas*

---

38. Juan Ruiz, *The Book of Good Love,* trans. Rigo Mignani and Mario A. di Cesare (Albany: SUNY Press, 1970), 22–23.

39. Connie L. Scarborough, "'The Rape of Men and Other 'Lessons' about Sex in the *Libro de Buen Amor*," in *Sexuality in the Middle Ages and Early Modern Times: New Approaches to a Fundamental Cultural-Historical and Literary-Anthropological Theme,* ed. Albrecht Classen (Berlin: Walter de Gruyter, 2008), 565–77.

40. After witnessing various weddings and their joyful celebrations, the archpriest comments that, "A los que eran solteros, entonces ya casados, los vi con sus esposas andar acompañados; me propuse gozar también tales agrados pues, si el hombre está solo, tiene muchos cuidados. Llamé a Trotaconventos . . . le pedí me buscase alguna tal guarida para mi, porque, solo, era triste mi vida." Juan Ruiz, *Libro de buen amor,* trans. María Brey Mariño (Madrid: Editorial Castalia, 1995), 228. See also Francisco Márquez Villanueva, "Juan Ruiz y el celibato eclesiástico," in *Juan Ruiz, Arcipreste de Hita, y el "Libro de Buen Amor": Congreso Internacional del Centro para la Edición de los clásicos españoles* (Alcalá La Real: Centro para la Edición de los Clásicos Españoles, 2004), 26–27.

41. "Qué buscas por esta tierra? ¿Como andas descaminado? Dije: «Ando por esta sierra do casaría de grado.» Ella dijo: «Pues no yerra quien es por aquí casado; busca y hallarás tu agrado.» [. . .] «Aquí tendrás casamiento tal como lo apetecieres. Casaréme a mi contento contigo; si algo me dieres, tendràs buen entendimiento.» [. . .] Dije: «Te daré esas cosas y aún más . . . A tus parientes convides; hagamos luego las bodas . . . »". Ruiz, *Libro de buen amor,* 184–86.

42. Ibid., 189–90.

know Juan Ruiz to be a cleric since other characters in the *Libro* readily identify him as a priest. The archpriest's adventures with the *serranas* indicate that
people were aware that priests established de facto marriages with peasant
women in the mountains and that clergymen were believed to be good providers. Mengua's statement that they can have the kind of marriage that he
desires is telling—a sign that she is willing to accommodate his profession as
long as he financially supports her like a wife. The *Libro* ends with the reactions of the priestly community in Talavera to the news that the pope has
decreed that no cleric can keep a concubine. The churchmen cry, become
enraged, and decide to appeal to the king of Castile against the pope because
the king knows that they are "all made of flesh" and will take pity on them.[43]
This reference to the king was, more than likely, meant to remind the audience of the kings of Castile and their long history of royal concubinage, including the contemporary King Alfonso XI (1312–1350), who was known for
keeping his long-time partner, Leonor de Guzmán, as his official concubine.[44]
It is also noteworthy that the priests of Talavera, who express their great con-
tentment with their domestic partners, threaten that they will renounce their
benefices and stipends rather than forsake their women, showing once again
that the laity were not only familiar with the dedication of the clergy to their
concubines but also had a sense of humor about it.[45] When we consider these
literary texts and the widespread practice of concubinage among the nobility,
laity, and clergy, in addition to the lenient ecclesiastical policies on concubinous unions, we see that Iberian society showed an understanding of, if not
sympathy for, clerical sexuality and, in particular, an extraordinary tolerance
for the practice of concubinage and clerical concubines.

It is likely that a similar culture of acceptance existed in Italy. Daniel Bornstein's work on the episcopal visitations of the diocese of Cortona and Roisin
Cossar's examination of priests' wills in the diocese of Bergamo both note the
omnipresence of clerical concubinage in Italy during the fourteenth century,
indicating that the preponderance of clerical unions may have been more of
a Mediterranean phenomenon.[46] Although neither of these studies presents
a statistical analysis of clerical incontinence or clerical concubinage in Italy,
they reveal a common element in the clerical cultures of Iberia and Italy, and a

---

43. Ibid., 284–85.
44. Silleras-Fernández, "Money Isn't Everything," 71.
45. Márquez Villanueva, "Juan Ruiz y el celibato eclesiástico," 28.
46. See Daniel Bornstein, "Parish Priests in Late Medieval Cortona: The Urban and Rural
Clergy," *Quaderni di Storia Religiosa* 4 (1997): 165–93; Daniel Bornstein, "Priests and Villagers in the
Diocese of Cortona," *Richerche Storiche* 27 (1997): 93–106; Roisin Cossar, "Clerical 'Concubines' in
Northern Italy during the Fourteenth Century," *Journal of Women's History* 23, no. 1 (2011): 110–31.

more tolerant attitude toward concubinary clergymen and their domestic partners. In her study of clerics' concubines in northern Italy, Cossar makes the point that, when ecclesiastical sources identify these women as a group, the term *mulieres inhonestas* is used to describe and censure them. These same sources, however, refer to the women, as individuals, kept by priests as *concubina, amasia* (lover), *ancilla* (domestic servant), and *foccaria* (hearth mate)— terms that are more benign than *meretrix* and even *mulier inhonesta*. Yet the labels employed by the church differ from those of the Italian priests who in their last will and testament addressed their domestic partner as "the woman who lives with me."[47] The experiences and treatment of clerics' concubines in the Mediterranean differed from northern Europe in large part because the familial and social ties that a clerical couple had in the community greatly affected their acceptance in the parish. The danger, therefore, lies in assuming that medieval people across the spectrum of society and across Europe had a uniform perception of clerical unions or of the women who lived out their lives with clergymen.

The prevalence of clerical unions in Catalunya undoubtedly influenced how people understood these unions. As an institution, the Church sought to undermine the unions between priests and their partners, and labeled these relationships concubinage rather than marriage, but the evidence shows that the laity and priests themselves viewed these relationships in a different light.[48] Parishioners employed the phrase "like man and wife" to describe clerical unions, particularly when they witnessed the signs of a domestic partnership and marital affection between the two individuals. Moreover, when parishioners testified in Catalan, it is likely that they referred to the cleric's partner in more neutral terms than *concubine*. For example, a court record from 1328 reveals that it was well known in the neighborhood of Sant Feliu in Girona that the beneficed cleric Ramon Fererr kept Venguda, whom people called "la dona den Ramon Ferrar"; the term *dona*, coincidentally, also meant "wife."[49] Notaries routinely translated the Catalan testimonies of parishioners into Latin

47. Cossar, "Clerical 'Concubines' in Northern Italy," 111–13.

48. According to María Asunción Esteban Recio and María Jesús Izquierdo García, the ubiquity of clerical union underscores "la aceptacíon de tal costumbre por el conjunto de la sociedad." "Pecado y marginación. Mujeres públicas en Valladolid y Palencia durante los siglos XV y XVI," in *La ciudad medieval: Aspectos de la vida urbana en la Castilla bajomedieval*, ed. Juan A Bonachía Hernando (Valladolid: Universidad de Valladolid, 1996), 155. Clerical concubinage was legal in secular law and tolerated in the kingdom of Castile until the fifteenth century, when royal and municipal legislation, under the influence of the church, set out to punish these unions more harshly (156–60). See also Ricardo Córdoba de la Llave, "Las relaciones extraconjugales en la sociedad castellana bajomedieval," *Anuario de Estudios Medievales* 16 (1986): 604–11; Lacarra Lanz, "Changing Boundaries of Licit and Illicit Unions," 164–70.

49. ADG, Processos, no. 100, 16v. (1328).

when recording the results of a visitation in a quaderno and could filter the words of witnesses by choosing what terms to use. Since episcopal notaries knew that the cleric's woman in question could not be his wife, they could have easily substituted the term *concubina* for the more natural descriptors parishioners' used, such as the cleric's *muller, dona*, or *fembra*. If church officials were going to fine the clergymen for their sexual failings, they needed to identify the offense and label the culprits.

Furthermore, it is significant that neither Catalan episcopal officials nor the Catalan laity used the terms *meretrix* and *concubina* interchangeably to identify a cleric's woman. Even though terms such as *vilis mulier, bagassa*, and *puta* were used to indicate a woman's sexual promiscuity in Catalan society, such language is largely absent in the visitation records in describing priests' partners. Marie Kelleher has observed that legal authorities in the Crown of Aragon "recognized a separate category of unmarried women who may have engaged in sexual activity without being branded prostitutes," further indicating that the laity's perception of these women did not reduce them to sexually promiscuous women.[50] That church authorities in Catalunya primarily used the term *concubina*, rather than the more inflammatory labels *meretrix, mulier inhonesta*, and *lupa* (she-wolf) to refer to priest's partners, indicates not only that they were using the term in a legal context to punish clergymen for keeping a woman but may also suggest a strategy of employing a more benign label that granted some measure of legitimacy to these women. Considering that so many clergymen across the ecclesiastical spectrum of the Catalan church had established relationships with women and were invested in raising their children, they too may have preferred and conscientiously used a more socially acceptable term. The word *concubine*, after all, was a term that church officials used in labeling women who similarly engaged in domestic partnerships with laymen; therefore, its use for relationships with clergy shows that these officials did not choose a more pejorative term for the women who lived out their lives with clergymen.

When we compare clerical unions in Catalunya to those in England and northern Europe, the extensive practice in Catalunya points not only to a custom entrenched in clerical culture but also to a lived reality for parishioners who were accustomed to living with a clerical family in their midst. Catalan villagers did not commonly express contempt for their parish priest specifically for forming unions with women and establishing families that resembled marriages. Derek Neal's assertion that priests who broke their vows of celibacy

---

were perceived to be "false" in English society and endangered their social identity by placing their moral worth in question seems more applicable to England where clerical concubinage was less common than in the Mediterranean. Neal argues that "a cleric had more to lose, as a man, by breaking his vows of celibacy than by remaining chaste."[51] This may be the case in England, where there seems to have been a greater expectation among the laity that a priest would honor his vow of celibacy; in contrast, given that so many parish clergy in Catalunya chose to be sexually active and established households with women, such behaviors suggest that clerics were not concerned with the perception that they were not "true men" because they broke their vows of celibacy. It is more likely that the clerics who abandoned their women and children, and those who neglected their patriarchal duties as husbands and fathers, were considered less than "true men."

The marriage-like behavior that defined so many clerical unions also explains why the community did not censure these couples. Parishioners recognized that a stable, long-term relationship caused less trouble than a promiscuous priest preying on village women or leaving the parish in search of a sexual gratification.[52] The people of the village acknowledged that parish priests, such as the rector of Salomó, who kept Romia at his table and in his home as a man keeps a wife (*"tenet eam in mensa et in loco sicut vir uxor"*), were involved in marriage-like unions that mimicked their own.[53] Equally important, these unions were public relationships recognized by the parties involved, the cleric and the woman, as well as by parishioners, who viewed them as established unions that were permanent if not long lasting. Considering the pervasiveness of clerical couples and their children, the laity would have been accustomed to having at least one, if not more, clerical families in their midst and most likely knew someone who had a cleric for a parent. Visitation records, moreover, indicate that among the laity adultery and leaving a spouse to form a new union were not uncommon. In the diocese of Vic, the visitations show that, from 1331 to 1332, 160 lay couples in 179 villages were accused of concubinage, and that 51 of these 160 (32 percent) involved couples in which one or both were already married. From 1332 to 1333, 116 couples in 132 villages were accused of concubinage, 69 (60 percent) of these couples were single and 47 (40 percent) were involved with someone who

---

51. Derek G. Neal, *The Masculine Self in Late Medieval England* (Chicago: University of Chicago Press, 2008), at 111, 100–101, 112.

52. Daniel Bornstein has made a similar argument in "Parish Priests in Late Medieval Cortona" and "Priests and Villagers in the Diocese of Cortona." Anthony Perron has also noted that the Danish "were not so favorably disposed" to a celibate clergy. "Saxo Grammaticus's Heroic Chastity," 113.

53. ADB, Visites, no. 2, 69r. (1314).

was married.[54] These numbers show that premarital sex and concubinary unions were a common occurrence among the peasantry. Peasant villagers, then, were accustomed to having clerical families and other variations of informal families in their communities, and they were much more tolerant of sexual permissiveness than were church authorities. In addition, the familial and social ties a clerical couple had in the community greatly affected their acceptance in the parish. Villagers often knew the intimate details and the family histories of clerical couples. Of the three concubinary priests serving in the village of Santa Maria de Granyena, two were related to their concubines within the four degrees of consanguinity. Similarly, the parishioners of Sant Feliu d'Areu testified that their rector Miquel Bonfil was related to his concubine Blanca but added that the two were so old they did not believe the couple engaged in sex.[55] These examples and others (see Chapter Three) illustrate that clerical couples often had familial ties to their parish and explains why communities were so tolerant of these unions.

If the priest was an unknown figure in the community, it was the woman who brought legitimacy to the union. Parishioners were familiar with these women and their families in that they describe them as the daughters and sisters of villagers they knew. Berengaria, who had children with the priest Guillem Ros in the parish of Sant Vicenç de Lançà, is identified as the daughter of Pere de Guarriguela of Lançà, not only by the people of Llançà but also by the villagers in the neighboring parish of Sant Miquel de Colera. Agnes, who had a child and lived with the hebdomedarian Guillem de Sola in the parish of Montagut, was the daughter of Bernat, a weaver in the village. In the parish of Sant Pedor, villagers testified that the beneficed cleric Bernat de Mans had "many children" (*plures filios*) with the daughter of Na Gentil who also lived in the parish.[56] When thinking about the acceptance of these unions among the peasantry, we must keep in mind that the concubine's

---

54. Out of the fifty-one couples engaged in concubinage and committing adultery, thirty-three were men and twelve were women, and in six cases, both the man and woman were married. Three instances of adultery that did not involve concubinage, as well as two cases of bigamy, were also reported. For 1332–1333, out of the forty-seven couples engaged in concubinage and committing adultery, forty-one were men, four were women, and two involved both a married man and woman. The sexually illicit behavior of the laity in the diocese of Vic is comparable to that found in visitation records from the diocese of Barcelona. Over a period of forty-one years, from 1303 to 1344, Baucells counted a total of 771 accusations of sexual misconduct among the laity: 455 of fornication, 308 of adultery, and 8 of incest; *Vivir en la edad media*, 3: 1916–18.
55. AEV, Visites, no. 1200/2, 21v. (1331); ACV, Visites, no. 5, 18r. (1315).
56. ADG, Visites, no. 1, 98v.–99r. (1315); ADG, Remissions de Penes, no. 1, 31v. (1352); AEV, Visites, no. 1200/2, 61v. (1331). The identity of the woman, particularly in terms of family relations and place of origin, appears in visitation records, but in some cases, more information is provided in the Remissions de Penes.

brothers, sisters, parents, aunts, uncles, and cousins were a part of the community and that her sons and daughters married fellow villagers. Certainly the four children of the priest Guillem Teyes and Elisenda Vergera—Guillem, Pere, Alamanda, and Francesca—grew up in the parish of Sant Pere dels Vilars among their mother's relatives and probably married into local families that had a connection to their village and were aware of this priestly family's history.[57] A clerical family would have been part of the community like any other family in the village or town.

Scholarship that overemphasizes the rigid medieval attitudes of the elite in respect to sexual behavior has obscured the practices of a vast segment of the medieval population. Social status affected medieval people's views of what were considered acceptable and unacceptable sexual relationships; therefore, we should not assume that the position of a priest's partner or their children meant that they were automatically ostracized or objects of contempt in the community. Shame and dishonor may not have been an issue, considering that concubinage among both the peasant clergy and laity was so pervasive. Allyson Poska's study of early modern peasant women in the predominantly rural and mountainous region of Galicia, which is similar to Catalunya, underscores how the importance of sexual purity and honor of women was not a notion accepted at all levels of Spanish society but one that was very much tied to class.[58] Informal unions and the illegitimate children produced from such unions were omnipresent among the lower levels of society. Even at the highest levels of the royal court and nobility in the Crown of Aragon, Núria Silleras-Fernández has noted that, "The kings of the Barcelona dynasty were anything but chaste—the chronicles of the Crown are peopled by a parade of royal bastards." The illegitimate children of kings and magnates born from these elite concubinous unions, Silleras-Fernández asserts, "carried their pedigree with pride."[59] It is quite possible that the children of priests also found pride in their parentage because of the respect, status, and authority connected to the profession of their father, especially if the mother's family were serfs or among the greatly impoverished peasantry of rural Catalunya. Considering that parish clergy were often among the wealthiest peasants in the village, parents who could not afford to bestow the customary dowry of money or

---

57. The cleric Guillem Teyes served in the parish of Sant Pere dels Vilars, where he had four children with Elisenda Vergera in 1340. By 1351, Guillem was the rector of Sant Christòfol dels Horts, a parish very close to Sant Pere dels Vilars, and the couple had yet another child; ADG, Visites, no. 6, 60v. (1340); ADG, Imposicions de Penes, no. 1, 37r. (1342) and 108v. (1356); ADG, Remissions de Penes, no. 1, 23v. (1351).

58. Allyson M. Poska, *Women and Authority in Early Modern Spain: The Peasants of Galicia* (Oxford: Oxford University Press, 2005), 83, 6–9, 107–11.

59. Silleras-Fernández, "Money Isn't Everything," 69–70.

land may have encouraged clerics to form unions with their daughters, particularly because they knew that such unions could be enduring ones. Parents who could ill afford to marry off their daughters had little to lose but much to gain financially by encouraging clerics to form unions with their daughters. Certainly a union with a cleric was a risky venture for a woman that could result in abandonment, but it could also offer a dowryless woman a de facto marriage and a path to social mobility for her family and children. Moreover, whether the village considered the priest's partner a woman of disrepute depended not on her concubinous relationship but on her conduct. As long as a cleric's concubine behaved with decorum and was not a source of conflict in the community, her union with the cleric warranted little commentary.[60] Indeed, many of these women enjoyed stable unions in which they were recognized as a priest's long-standing and faithful partner.

Clerical Unions: A Custom Entrenched in the Iberian Church

As far as the universal Church was concerned, the stability or transitory nature of a relationship between a clergyman and woman was of little consequence. In an attempt to delegitimize clerical marriage, the Church classified these unions as concubinous, labeling priests' women concubines and their children bastards. With the decrees of the first and second Lateran councils in 1123 and 1139, clerical marriage was made illegal for subdeacons and above. These two councils and the third and fourth Lateran councils in 1179 and 1215 recognized that priests could substitute a concubine for a wife and thus banned clerical concubinage as an alternative to marriage. The Church, in effect, criminalized the sexuality of the clergy and considered any sexual relationship between a cleric and a woman to be illicit. The Lateran decrees outlined the penalty for concubinary clergy in the holy orders: deprivation of ecclesiastical office and loss of benefice.[61] The official position of the Church on clerical sexuality was universal, in so far as every pope, cardinal, bishop, and ecclesiastical official parroted its condemnation and commitment to punishing such misconduct.

---

60. Michelle Armstrong-Partida, "Priestly Wives: The Role and Acceptance of Clerics' Concubines in the Parishes of Late Medieval Catalunya," *Speculum* 88, no. 1 (2013): 166–214.
61. Lateran I, canon 7; Lateran II, canon 6; Lateran III, canon 11, Lateran IV, canon 14; Norman P. Tanner, ed., *Decrees of the Ecumenical Councils*, Vol. 1 (Washington, DC: Georgetown University Press, 1990), 191, 198, 217, 242. See also Helen Parish, *Clerical Celibacy in the West: c. 1100–1700* (Farnham, UK: Ashgate, 2010), 99–104.

Yet the Iberian church is a good example of the incongruous reality between Church policies and clerical practice. A number of Spanish scholars, among them Federico Aznar Gil, José Sánchez Herrero, José Rodríguez Molina, and Roldàn Jimeno Aranguren, have noted that canon law was blatantly ignored with little consequence well into the fifteenth century in that synodal legislation in the regions of Castile, León, Andalucía, and Navarre continued to prohibit clergy in the major orders from contracting marriage. Concubinage, too, was such a collective practice among Iberian clergy in the thirteenth and fourteenth centuries that clerics were not concerned with hiding or keeping their families secret. Priests were known to include their families in public acts such as the selling and buying of property, and bequeathed their wealth to their concubines and children. Despite church decrees that prohibited the children of beneficed clerics from inheriting private or church property, ecclesiastical charters reveal this practice continued regardless of canon law.[62] In fact, clerical concubinage, or *barraganía,* as it was called in Castile-León, was legal under secular law until the thirteenth century. Although King Alfonso X of Castile incorporated into his secular legal code, *Las Siete Partidas,* the decrees of Lateran IV depriving concubinary clerics of their office and ecclesiastical benefice, his support for Church regulations was less than consistent. In the same legal codex, Alfonso authorized bishops to grant a dispensation to a priest "to retain his office if he should marry a virgin," as long as the priest did penance and separated from his wife.[63] He further disregarded the Church prohibition against clerics' children inheriting when he granted

---

62. Federico R. Aznar Gil, "Penas y sanciones contra los clérigos concubinarios en la Península Ibérica (ss. XIII–XVI)" *Studia Gratiana* 29 (1998): 501–20; Federico R. Aznar Gil, *La institución matrimonial en la Hispania cristiana bajomedieval, 1215–1563* (Salamanca: Universidad Pontificia de Salamanca, 1989), 137–49; José Sánchez Herrero, "Los sínodos de la diócesis de León en los siglos XII al XV," in *León y su historia,* vol. 3 (León: Centro de Estudios e Investigación "San Isidoro," 1975), 165–262; José Sánchez Herrero, *Las diócesis del Reino de León. Siglos XIV y XV* (León: Centro de Estudios e Investigación "San Isidoro," 1978), 157–66; Roldàn Jimeno Aranguren, "Concubinato, matrimonio y adulterio de los clérigos: Notas sobre la regulación jurídica y praxis en la Navarra medieval," *Anuario de Historia del Derecho Español,* no. 71 (2011): 554–58; Rodríguez Molina, "Celibato eclesiástico," 40, 47–49; José Rodríguez Molina, *El obispade Baeza-Jaén (siglos XIII–XVI): Organización y economia diocesanas* (Jaén: Diputación Provincial de Jaén, Instituto de Cultura, 1986), 129–30. Evidence of clerics in the major orders including their children in charters also dates to the first half of the fifteenth century.

63. "He has the power to grant a dispensation to a priest who has received the higher orders, to retain his office if he should marry a virgin; and this after he has performed penance." The same code allows prelates to grant dispensations to priests who have committed adultery. Robert I. Burns, ed., *Las Siete Partidas,* trans. Samuel Parsons Scott (Philadelphia 2001) 1: 79, 102–3. Title V. Law LXIII. In What Way Prelates Can Grant Dispensations to the Priests of Their Bishopric. For the decrees of Lateran IV, see Tanner, *Decrees of the Ecumenical Councils,* 198. This thirteenth-century legal code was far more influential in the fourteenth century under Alfonso XI when it had more legal force and "gradually supplanted other sources as the principal body of law in the kingdom of Castile;" O'Callaghan, *A History of Medieval Spain,* 451.

the clergy of the diocese of Salamanca and those of Guadalajara the privilege of naming their children as their legitimate heirs.[64] The kings of Navarre also protected the privileges of married clergy in the major orders into the fourteenth century, allowing them to maintain their benefices and often permitting their children to inherit.[65] The custom of clergymen maintaining a family, then, was reinforced in secular law and royal policies that favored clerics. Even at the close of the fourteenth century, Vicente Ferrer, a famous Valencian Dominican friar, recognized the propensity of priests to keep women and establish families in their communities as he traveled throughout Castile and the Crown of Aragon. In Ferrer's sermons, however, the sin of clerical concubinage receives far less attention than his opposition to the acceptance of Jews in medieval Iberian society.[66]

The custom of clerical unions is reflected not only in the tolerance for this practice in the Iberian church and society but also in the acceptance by the papacy that Iberian clergy could not be expected to conform to the Church laws on celibacy. That so many bishops in the thirteenth century failed to convene and clergy neglected to attend provincial councils and diocesan synods throughout Iberia certainly remained an impediment to implementing reforms of clerical discipline and education. Yet, although synods and councils presented bishops with the opportunity to educate clergy and present new policies of reform, the effectiveness of such events should not be overstated. Delivering clerical instruction and informing clergy of reforming decrees promulgated by greater Church councils did not immediately translate into changes in clerical behavior. Indeed, the decrees of Lateran councils had such a minimal impact in Navarre, Castile, León, and the Crown of Aragon, that Pope Gregory IX sent John of Abbeville, a legate and cardinal bishop, to reform the Iberian clergy in 1228. According to Peter Linehan, John of Abbeville's attempts to enforce the penalties for concubinage excommunicated so many clergymen that there was a severe shortage of church personnel. Because there were not enough priests to say mass or administer the sacraments, Pope Innocent IV was forced to revoke Abbeville's sentences of excommunication in 1243 for the clergy of Burgos, in 1246 for the clergy of León and Tarragona, and in 1251 for the clergy of Valladolid, Lleida, and Vic. Initially, Pope

---

64. Rodríguez Molina, "Celibato Eclesiástico," 39; Haboucha, "Clerics, Their Wives, and Their Concubines," 92–94. Rodríguez Molina has also shown that, despite the legislation of the Cortes of Soria in 1380 that prohibited clerics' children from inheriting, the custom continued unabated; *El obispado de Baeza-Jaén*, 128–30.

65. Aranguren, "Concubinato, matrimonio y adulterio," 550, 552–58.

66. Francisco M. Gimeno Blay and María Luz Mandingorra Llavata, eds., *Sermonario de San Vicente Ferrer*, trans. Francisco Calero Calero (Valencia: Ajunatament de Valencia, 2002), 107, 181, 245.

Innocent absolved concubinary clerics in return for a monetary contribution to papal funds for the Holy Land, but the papacy later allowed individual prelates in their communities to replace the penalty of suspension or excommunication with a fine. The concession of the papacy that a monetary fine could replace excommunication and removal from office for the crime of concubinage is evidence, Linehan argues, that even the papacy accepted that Iberian clergy could not be expected to conform to the law of celibacy.[67] The ecclesiastical province of Tarragona embraced the commutation of this standard penalty for a system of fines in its 1251 council, a policy that was subsequently adopted in the dioceses of Barcelona, Girona, Vic, Urgell, and Tortosa.[68] In addition, visitors in all Catalan dioceses seem to have used a definition of concubinage that the cardinal Abbeville outlined as a guideline to determine concubinous relationships: "whoever in his own home or in another's, in his own parish or in another [parish], to a woman with which he has sinned and has provided in food, or dress, or in the joining of houses, or if he sins publicly with anyone in which scandal arises in his own parish, he shall be judged as one who keeps a concubine."[69]

Sanctions against concubinage were not unknown in Iberia, yet the enforcement of clerical celibacy remained haphazard and ineffective throughout the thirteenth and fourteenth centuries. Examples of Iberian clergy resisting and flouting the ban on concubinage are numerous. As late as 1246, priests in Córdoba claimed ignorance of the law that prohibited them from keeping concubines.[70] Bishops who attempted to implement the reforms of Lateran IV

67. Linehan, *Spanish Church and The Papacy*, 2–4, 20–34, 50–53; Linehan, *Spanish Church and Society*, 484–85, 496–97. See also Fletcher, *Episcopate in the Kingdom of León*, 204–8, 227; Lomax, "Lateran Reforms and Spanish Literature."

68. Josep María Pons i Guri, ed. "Constitucions conciliars tarraconenses (1229–1330)," *Annalecta Sacra Tarraconensia* 48 (1975): 250, 254–55. Although the diocese of Girona maintained the punishment of excommunication, loss of benefice, and suspension in its synodal decrees for concubinage and did not specifically commute the penalty to a fine, visitation records and episcopal letters indicate that fines were assigned to concubinary clerics, at least by 1296, the date when Girona's Notularum and Lletres begin. For the diocese of Barcelona, the bishop Bernat Peregrí was the first to commute the punishment for concubinage to a monetary fine in 1289; Baucells i Reig, *Vivir en la edad media*, 3: 2473–77. In 1336, the provincial council took an even more lenient approach to clerics who publicly kept women. It eliminated the penalty of fines and decreed that a form of penance should be imposed in its place. It is not surprising that many dioceses did not eliminate the fine despite this new decree because the system of fines was an important source of revenue. See also Santiago Bueno Salinas, *El derecho canónico catalán en la baja edad media: La diócesis de Gerona en los siglos XIII y XIV* (Barcelona: Facultat de Teologia de Catalunya, 2000), 280–83.

69. Noguer i Musqueras and Pons Guri, "Constitucións sinodals de Girona," 55. "Concubinatu sic declaravit dominus Sabinensis: Ut quicumque in domo propria vel aliena in parrochia sua vel alia, mulieri cum qua peccaverit provideret in victu, vel veste, vel conductu domorum vel etiam si ita publice peccaret cum aliqua quod in sua parrochia scandalum oriretur, concubinarius judicetur."

70. Lea, *History of Sacerdotal Celibacy*, 259.

suffered defeat at the hands of their diocesan clergy, who were not afraid to simply reject the bishop's mandate. When the bishop Giraldo of Segovia banned concubinage in his diocese, the clergy united against him. Clerics from the town of Sepúlveda and surrounding rural villages formed a pact to oppose the bishop, fining and ostracizing any cleric who broke his oath to the group. In the end, bishop Giraldo yielded to diocesan clergy. He did not address clerical concubinage in his synodal decrees of 1216—an issue that no bishop of Segovia tackled until 1325.[71] When in 1342 Pope Benedict XII sent a letter to the archbishops and bishops of Spain exhorting them to address the vice of incontinence among the clergy, the bishop of Toledo proved unwilling to enforce the punishment for concubinage; he simply banned the ecclesiastical burial of priests' concubines and punished any priest who permitted the burial with a fine. As Henry Ansgar Kelly notes, the bishop was obviously averse to attacking the practice of concubinage head on and so focused instead on "frightening and shaming the women into desisting."[72] In the northern Iberian kingdom of Navarre, synodal legislation prohibiting priests from publicly keeping concubines in Pamplona made its debut in 1330, more than one-hundred years after the ban in canon law, but due to the protests of elite clergymen, a bishop later modified the synodal decree in 1349 to substitute a monetary fine for the loss of one year's salary. The move to penalize priests in the diocese of Pamplona was new despite an earlier attempt that had failed. In 1298, the archbishop of Pamplona carried out visitations to a small portion of the diocese and found more than four hundred concubinary priests, but when the archbishop handed over the task of punishing these concubinary clerics to the bishop of Pamplona, he ignored the mandate.[73]

In Catalunya, episcopal officials made a greater effort than their Iberian brethren to address clerical concubinage in synodal legislation, but this energy rarely went beyond the law in the thirteenth century. Scholars who point to the synods convened in Catalunya during the eleventh century as evidence of the impact of the Gregorian reform and who use later synods from the thirteenth century that incorporated the canons of Lateran IV into diocesan legislation as confirmation of reforming policies taking root in Catalunya often make the mistake of seeing these imposed legal norms as evidence of changing attitudes among the clergy.[74] To the contrary, synodal legislation reveals

71. Linehan, "Segovia," 483–85, 496–97.

72. Henry Ansgar Kelly, *Canon Law and the Archpriest of Hita* (Binghamton: SUNY Binghamton, Medieval and Renaissance Texts and Studies, 1984), 87–88.

73. Aranguren, "Concubinato, matrimonio y adulterio," 565–66.

74. See the works of Josep Martí Bonet, Josep M. Marquès, Antoni Pladevall, Santiago Bueno Salinas, Josep Baucells i Reig, and Lluís Monjas Manso cited in this chapter and in the bibliography.

only limited reform in that clerical authorities were attempting to impose Church standards and cannot be used as evidence of significant social change among the proletariat of the Catalan church. Although it is true that synods attempting to refashion the life of the clergy were held more frequently in Catalunya during the thirteenth and fourteenth centuries than in Castile and Navarre, reforming legislation did not translate into aggressive episcopal action. Extant episcopal registers from the dioceses of Barcelona and Girona reveal that clergy were punished infrequently for their sexual transgressions in the thirteenth century. It was not until fourteenth century that episcopal officials in Catalunya made any real attempt to discipline the clergy for their concubinous unions. Particularly in the dioceses of Vic, Urgell, and Tortosa, episcopal authorities did not consistently punish clergy for having illicit sex, whereas officials in the dioceses of Barcelona and Girona did attempt to penalize clergy for their sexual misdeeds to generate a source of revenue. Even though episcopal visitations could be used as a platform to implement reforms, the records show that attempts to punish and fine concubinary clergy over the course of a century did not result in a priestly population that accepted celibacy and rejected concubinage. These visitation records indicate that the primary motive for episcopal officials to carry out the visitations was not the instruction of the clergy and laity on issues of Christian morality but economics—the procurement of the visitation fee that every visitor collected from parishes during the visit.[75]

Certainly diocesan legislation from Barcelona and Girona confirms the efforts made by bishops to deal with the established practice of clerical concubinage in Catalunya, but when understood in the context of a regional tradition, this legislation is evidence of episcopal attempts to curtail the public nature of clerical unions, not of a strident campaign to wipe out clerical concubinage. Consider that the convention of clergy setting up family households was so prevalent that the bishop Arnau Mont-rodon of Girona in 1339 had to prohibit clerics from buying homes for their concubines within the limits of the parishes where they served. The decree, however, did not ban clergy outright from buying homes *outside* the limits of their parish, which many did do for their families. Mont-rodon also passed legislation that banned clerics from entering their concubines' home (and these women were likewise banned from entering the clerics' homes), in addition to including the 1336 provincial council decree that prohibited priests' sons from assisting with the

---

75. Josep M. Palau i Baduell has come to the same conclusion in his work, *La moralitat dels clergues i laics als comtats de Pallars a través de les visites pastorals de 1314 i 1315* (Màster de Cultures Medievals, Universitat de Barcelona, 2009), 26.

mass and forbade priests from keeping their children in the church or in their own homes.[76] In spite of the monetary fine of 50 sous he assigned to both of these decrees, neither decree was seriously enforced. On the surface these decrees appear to deal harshly with the practice of concubinage, but this legislation was never enforced vigorously. Rather than severely punishing the clergy for their unions, the bishop Mont-rodon's decrees were designed to limit clerics from parading their women and children before their parishioners. Consider too that in the diocese of Barcelona, the subject of clerical concubinage in synodal legislation remained untouched in the fourteenth century after the bishop Bernat Peregrí, in 1289, commuted the punishment for concubinage to a fine based on one year's loss of income from the offending cleric's benefice. Episcopal records indicate, moreover, that officials understood the financial burden of losing a year's worth of salary because they imposed smaller fines ranging from 20 to 50 sous on the concubinous clerics of Barcelona.[77]

It is telling that Catalan episcopal officials did not put into practice John of Abbeville's harsh punishment for concubines: excommunication and burial in a "grave of asses."[78] Even more interesting, the synodal decrees of Girona do not outline the punishment for concubines, and episcopal authorities in the diocese of Barcelona disregarded their own statute that punished concubines with a fine of 10 maravedis.[79] Although visitation records sometimes refer to a concubine receiving a dispensation along with the cleric, the absence of dispensations granted to concubines in the episcopal registers of Girona indicates that the excommunication of these women was uncommon. It is significant that episcopal officials could have used synodal legislation that targeted the concubines of priests to create a greater burden for clergymen and their

---

76. Noguer i Musqueras and Pons Guri, "Constitucións sinodals de Girona," 133. Visitation records attest that clergy frequently bought their women and children a home separate from the one that came with their benefice. Arnau de Mont-rodon added the statute on priests and their sons to Girona's sinodal constitution c. 1339, after the archbishop Arnau Sescomes decreed it in the provincial council of Tarragona in 1336. "Quod filii presbiterorum non deserviant in divinis. Item quia ex eo quod filii clericorum patribus deserviunt in divinis, inter laicos contra ipsos clericos scandalum generetur, et quia tales filios et filias publice in propriis vel ecclesie secum tenent, statuimus ne aliquis sacerdos teneat secum filium vel filiam quem vel quam procreaverit ex quo fuerit ad sacros ordines promotus, nec talis filius eidem deserviat in divinis. Qui vero contrarium fecerit, penam quinquagintorum solidorum Barchinone incurrat, nostro erario aplicandum" (128).

77. The visitations from 1336 to 1338 show that most clerics were fined 30 or 50 sous for concubinage; Hillgarth and Silano, "Compilation of the Diocesan Synods, 81, 119–22; Martí Bonet, "Visitas pastorales." Repeat offenders often promised to pay a large sum, for example, 200–300 sous, if found guilty again; Hillgarth and Silano, *Register Notule Communium*. See also Richard Francis Gyug, *The Diocese of Barcelona during the Black Death. The Register Notule Communium 15, 1348–1349* (Toronto: Pontificial Institute of Mediaeval Studies, 1994).

78. Pons i Guri, "Constitucions conciliars tarraconenses," 79; Salinas, *Derecho canónico catalán*, 59–66, 286–87; Noguer i Musqueras and Pons Guri, "Constitucións sinodals de Girona," 55.

79. Hillgarth and Silano, "Compilation of the Diocesan Synods," 121–22.

women if they persisted in their unions but they chose not to. When evaluating diocesan synodal legislation, then, we must be careful not to assume that reforming decrees were enthusiastically put into practice but consider that bishops may have been motivated to give the appearance of reforming the clergy while maintaining the status quo.

By adopting a monetary fine to punish clergy for concubinage and focusing on clergymen who publicly acknowledged their children in their homes and parish churches, the Catalan church seems to have been content with restricting the clergy from openly flouting church law. In the day-to-day administration of their dioceses, episcopal officials must have known that enforcing celibacy among their diocesan clergy was not only an impractical policy but also a futile one. Although the episcopal registers during Mont-rodon's episcopate confirm a greater effort to punish clerics for their illicit relationships, the very same documents show that his administration applied these edicts with leniency. Clerics regularly paid much smaller fines than the mandated 50 sous and were on occasion absolved without penalty for incontinence.[80] Moreover, the fines could vary drastically, and priests with large families were not the ones who were most harshly punished. For example, the hebdomedarian Bernat Guillem, who had a child with Elisenda, was charged 15 sous; the priest Jaume Mager, who kept Beatriu and their two daughters, was fined 25 sous; the rector Pere Penocars, who kept Maçana and his four children in the village of Capsec, was fined 50 sous; and the priest Guillem de Tor, who had only one child with Margarida, was fined 50 sous.[81] In a number of cases, priests who were involved with multiple women were punished more severely than

---

80. A survey of volume 7 of the Lletres, dating from 1339 to 1344, revealed fifty-two dispensations for clerical incontinence. The typical fine in the Lletres is recorded as 10 sous or 22 sous. Fines administered for concubinage can also be found in two registers that cover the years 1335–1363 and 1336–1338: the Imposicions de Penes and the Obligacions de Penes. The register Obligacions de Penes shows that fines less than the mandated 50 sous were frequently administered. The Imposicions de Penes provides more information as to why a cleric was found guilty of the crime of incontinence or concubinage, and records what penalty the cleric would suffer if found guilty a second time. A register of letters of remissions for 1345–1367 also exists, but the Remissions de Penes does not note the amount of the fine. Considering that clerics who appear in the Remissions de Penes do not appear in either the Imposicions or Obligacions and that a cleric recorded in the Imposicions does not show up in the Obligacions and vice versa, it appears that, although officials were attempting to keep better track of the fines administered to the clergy, the fines were not consistently recorded. Another peculiarity is that in certain years authorities recorded a large number of fines and in other years they recorded very few fines. In contrast to the diocese of Girona, the bishop of Tortosa imposed fines of 100 to 200 sous to concubinous clergymen, but in many cases, local authorities received half of the amount of the fine; García Egea, Visita pastoral a la diocesis de Tortosa, 56.

81. For Bernat Guillem, the sacrist of Espinavesa, see ADG, Obligacions de Penes, no. 1, 5v. (1337); ADG, Imposicions de Penes, no. 1, 13v. (1337). For the stabilitus Jaume Mager, see Obligacions de Penes, no. 1, 3v. (1336); ADG, Imposicions de Penes, no. 1, 11v. (1336). For the rector Pere Penocars, see ADG, Obligacions de Penes, no. 1, 27v. (1343); ADG, Imposicions de Penes, no. 1, 40r. (1343).

those who had stable unions. The sacrist Andreu Moner, who kept Berengaria in his home and had dalliances with two other women, was fined 150 sous, but the sacrist Bernat Carbó, a two-time offender who had three children with Maria, was fined 100 sous.[82] The wide range of fines applied to concubinary and promiscuous clergymen shows that officials exercised some discretion in administering punishment and took into account a cleric's ability to pay, as well as the stability of a union, punishing more harshly those who brought disorder to the community with their polyamorous affairs.

Catalan prelates and reformers such as the bishop Arnau Mont-rodon must have realized that prescribing stricter punishments for concubinage and adhering doggedly to synodal legislation was not a viable solution; otherwise, they would have faced the same problem encountered after the cardinal legate John of Abbeville's visit in 1228—a large population of excommunicated and suspended clergymen who could not carry out their pastoral duties. Authorities were already aware that many clerics could not pay the fine because some had to set up payment plans, which must have influenced the decision to assign fines that were less than the mandated 50 sous. It also became a problem when some clerics opted to commute their fine to time in the bishop's jail because the diocese lost a source of revenue and risked large numbers of family men spending months in jail, clogging up the bishop's prison.[83] Furthermore, harsh penalties could provoke clerics into simply leaving their ministry. A militant approach to separating clergymen from their women would have affected episcopal officials as well since many among them were known to keep women and provide for their children. The policies of the bishop Mont-rodon's successor, Berenguer de Cruïlles, further underscores the leniency with which officials dealt with clerical concubinage and how the guidelines could be adjusted to the circumstances at hand. In 1351, Berenguer de Cruïlles amended the penalty of fines established by the bishop Arnau Mont-rodon and ordered that a fine could only be imposed at

---

For the priest Guillem de Tor in the parish of Bordils, see ADG, Obligacions de Penes, no. 1, 25v. (1342); ADG, Imposicions de Penes, no. 1, 39r. (1342).

82. The sacrist Moner was threatened with a fine of 150 sous if he continued to have a relationship with Berengaria and keep her in his home, and another fine of 100 sous if he sinned again with Elisenda and Na Giradora; ADG, Obligacions de Penes, no. 1, 13v. (1339); ADG, Imposicions de Penes, no. 1, 25r. (1340). For another example of a priest charged 150 sous for his involvement with multiple women, see the sacrist Arnau Famada in ADG, Obligacions de Penes, no. 1, 10v. (1339); ADG, Imposicions de Penes, no. 1, 22r. (1339). For the sacrist Bernat Carbó, see ADG, Obligacions de Penes, no. 1, 22v. (1342); ADG, Imposicions de Penes, no. 1, 36v. (1342). The sacrist Bernat was also fined in 1336 for keeping the same woman; ADG, Imposicions de Penes, no. 1, 3r. (1336).

83. Although this was never a popular option among clerics, the alternative of spending time in jail in lieu of paying a pecuniary fine seems to have disappeared in the mid-1340s.

his discretion.[84] Berenguer de Cruïlles was responding to a crisis. Earlier
in the fourteenth century, bad harvests and famine had left the population
vulnerable, but when the Black Death appeared in Catalunya in 1348, it deci-
mated the populace and left parishioners, clergymen, and the Church impoverished. The bishop had little choice. Cruïlles could neither extract money
the clergy did not possess nor impose sentences of excommunication when
there were so few clerics to staff his churches. No doubt the lack of clergy
was a profound concern, and Cruïlles's response was to annul all sentences
of suspension and excommunication.[85]

Neither the manner in which episcopal officials throughout Catalunya enforced the decrees prohibiting clerical unions nor the extant synodal legislation points to an aggressive campaign against concubinous clerics. The aim
was not eradicate a practice entrenched in clerical society. The objective behind
the legislation of the diocese of Girona, as we have seen, was primarily to con-
strain the clergy from living with their families publicly and, at the same time,
significantly augment the bishops' coffers. Mont-rodon's synodal decrees specifically targeted clergymen who publicly acknowledged their children in their
homes and parish churches. In the dioceses of Girona and Barcelona, there
was clearly an effort to regulate the punishment for concubinage, but episcopal
officials carried out the policy in a flexible and practical manner meant to
limit the widespread practice of concubinage while profiting from the revenues
it generated. For example, in the diocese of Barcelona, the bishop appointed
the deans of Penedès and Vallès, as well as their episcopal procurators, in

84. Salinas, *Derecho canónico catalán*, 287–88; Noguer i Musqueras and Pons Guri, "Constitucións
sinodals de Girona," 104–5. As outlined in his decree, the bishop Berenguer de Cruïlles's reason for
rescinding the sentence of excommunication and penalty of fines is dubious. Cruïlles explains that
many clerics, on account of the envy of their enemies, are accused of concubinage. Thus, they suffer
the punishment of suspension and do not obtain absolution, causing harm to their souls because they
continue to participate in the divine office. Although unjust accusations were certainly a problem,
this rationale is suspect because the motives of the witnesses who accused clerics of any crime were
considered by the bishop's official during his visitation of the parish. And in court cases, witnesses
were asked if they harbored any "*odio*" for the accused cleric. Moreover, the possibility of malicious
accusations was certainly not a new concern at this time.

85. Clerics found guilty of gambling were the only exception. Despite the shortage of clergy
after the Black Death, Cruïlles's practical approach to dealing with concubinary clerics may have gone
too far in suspending all punishments for incontinence. Cruïlles backpedaled in 1354. In what appears
to be an effort to prove he was not indulging the sexual sins of the clergy, Cruïlles adopted a harsh
stance that punished concubinary clerics with a fine of 100 sous. He decreed that clerics could no
longer keep women with whom they carnally sinned in their homes. Clerics were given one month
to expel their concubines from their homes; otherwise, after three warnings to comply, they not only
would have to pay the fine but would incur a sentence of excommunication. Perhaps Cruïlles now
understood the significance of following the example of his predecessors—keeping up the appearance of reproving and disciplining concubinary clerics was a necessary ploy in conforming to Church
policy; Noguer i Musqueras and Pons Guri, "Constitucións sinodals de Girona," 157–58.

1346 to investigate "crimes of incontinence and other excesses committed by the clergy" in their jurisdictions and authorized that the deans take 4 sous and the procurators 2 sous for every 20 sous exacted in fines.[86] Such an organized effort to administer and collect fines is not seen at the same level in the dioceses of Vic and Urgell. Visitation records from these two northern dioceses reveal that episcopal officials were even more lenient and imposed fines ranging anywhere from 4 to 100 sous, if they imposed fines at all. Particularly in the diocese of Urgell where the canon Galceran de Sacosta served as a visitor for the archbishop of Tarragona from 1312 to 1316, officials were more concerned with obtaining the fee for the visitation than with punishing and fining clerics for concubinage. For instance, the parish of Sant Miquel de Segu owed the visitor 40 sous for the visitation, yet the priest Guillem Dorceu owed only 5 sous for publicly keeping his domestic partner and child. Similarly, in the parishes of Santa Maria de Mont-ros and Sant Sadurní de Gramenet, a priest and chaplain owed 6 sous each for concubinage, but the procuration fee for both parishes was just shy of 15 sous.[87] The rector Arnau Curer apparently did not pay a fine because he managed to obtain a license from the bishop of Urgell to keep his concubine in his home on account of his "infirmity."[88] Punishing concubinary clergy was not a priority in the more mountainous and rural dioceses of Urgell or Vic. There is evidence, moreover, that priests ignored the penalty for concubinage, just as they similarly failed to pay the procuration fee, which resulted in their parishes being placed under interdict. The visitor Galceran de Sacosta excommunicated a number of recalcitrant clergy who had failed to appear at the bishop's court to confess their sin of concubinage and pay the assigned fine, and even letters ordering clergy to pay their fine for concubinage under penalty of excommunication admitted that many of the named clerics had already been already excommunicated for other "irregularities."[89] That so many clergymen disregarded their sentences of excommunication indicates a certain level of defiance, further suggesting that these clerics knew there were real limits to the authority of officials.

---

86. Hillgarth and Silano, *Register notule comunium*, 130–31.

87. ACV, Calaix 31/43, Visites, no. 4, 5r., 9r., 14r., 15r. (1314). The wide spectrum of fines assigned to clergy for concubinage can also be seen in the lists of assigned fines found in ACV, Calaix 31/43, Visites, no. 3, note inserted in Visites, 55r. (1315); ACV, Calaix 31/43, Visites, no. 4, 47r.–48r.v. (1315); ACV, Calaix 31/43, Visites, no. 7, letter, 8r., 10r (1313); ACV, Calaix 31/43, Visites, no. 8, 15r. (1314).

88. ACV, Calaix 31/43, Visites, no. 6, 12v.–13r. (1315). Apparently the rector's sickness had to do with urinating.

89. The visitor Galceran de Sacosta excommunicated the rector of Canillo, the capellan of Encamp and Massana, and the priest of Lòria. The fines for concubinage assigned in these letters also varied. It is also evident that the visitor Galceran took a stronger stance against concubinary priests in the cathedral city of Urgell than in rural areas; ACV, Calaix 31/43, Visites, no. 1, 10r.v., 12r. (1312); ACV, Calaix 31/43, Visites, no. 7, 14r.v.–15r. (1314), 16r. (1313), and 47r. (1313).

62   CHAPTER ONE

In practice, therefore, there appears to have been no standardized fine or treatment of clergymen who kept concubines in the dioceses of Vic and Urgell, even though an effort was made to punish these clerics. The visitation records are incredibly brief compared to those produced in the diocese of Girona and Barcelona, showing that visitors in general exerted a minimal amount of effort inquiring into the lives of the clergy and laity. Considering the brevity of the visitations and that visitors visited up to four to seven parishes in one day in these dioceses, where the terrain was difficult to transverse, it is evident that visitors spent little time examining witnesses.[90] Even when a visitor arrived at a parish to find neither the clergy nor the laity to question, he still insisted on the payment of the visitation fee. The records reveal a far greater effort to acquire the procuration fee with the threat of excommunication and ecclesiastical interdict than a far-reaching policy to punish clerics and their domestic partners.[91] In fact, in the visitations of 1312–1313 in Urgell, the number of clerics fined for concubinage was much fewer than the number of clerics fined at a sum rarely seen in the records, 100 sous, for celebrating the mass while excommunicated because these priests had failed to pay the procuration fee.[92] The actions of both the clergy and laity make it clear that they resented the visitor's inquiry into parish affairs and his demand for payment. The parishioners of d'Espinalbet, Querol, Loseles, and Castelltort refused to testify in the visitor's inquest, and the parishioners of Sorba declined to admit the visitor into their church. A number of clerics, such as the rector and vicar of Sant Andreu de Calcibros, the capellan of Besant and the capellan of Mercadel, rebelled against paying the procuration fee. The capellan of Sant Sadurní d'Aos was not polite when refusing to pay for the visitation. He called the visitor and his men "liars" and "deceivers" and attacked them with his sword.[93] This

---

90. Visiting four parishes in one day was not uncommon, but visiting eight was certainly rare. In 1312, the visitor Galceran de Sacosta visited seven parishes on the second nonas of January; ACV, Calaix 31/3, Visites, no. 1, 31r.v. (1312).
91. See ACV, Calaix 31/43, Visites, no. 3, 50r.v., 53r., 55r. (1315); Visites, no. 4, written inside the cover of this visitation book, 10r., 17r., 26r.v., 27v., 47r.v.–48r.v. (1314); Visites, no. 5, 1r.v.–3r.v., 16r., 19r.v.–20r.v. (1315). Galceran Sacosta, the archbishop's visitor, frequently delegated his duty to Ramon de Sant Sadurní (rector of Begano), the canon Nicolau de Nelios, Arnau de Mans (rector de Berga), Pere Graner, the canon Guillem de Viver, and the monk Joan Dençes.
92. ACV, Calaix 31/43, Visites, no. 2, 26r., 35r., 36r., 40r.–42r., 44r.–46r., 48r., 50r., 51r.–56r., 61r., 63r.–64r., 66v.–67r., 73r., 74r. (1313).
93. ACV, Calaix 31/43, Visites, no. 2, 13v., 28v., 39v. (1313); ACV, Visites, no. 3, 23r., 24v., 39v., 40v. (1313); ACV, Visites, no. 4, 2v., 3r., 5r. (1314); ACV, Visites, no. 5, 7r., 14r., 18r. (1315); ACV, Visites, no. 6, 4r. (1312); ACV, Visites, no. 7, 33v. (1313). According to the document, the capellan of Aos verbally abused (vituperavit) the visitor, notary, and others in the visitor's entourage before he "voluit iruere contra ipsos ponendo manum ad gladium etiam clamando male voce viafors et morantur quia non sunt nisi falsarii et deceptores." ACV, Calaix 31/43, Visites, no. 8, 11v. (1314). The capellan of Sant Sadurní de Castelleviy refused to appear before the visitor to answer questions about keeping a

is the only account of a cleric attacking a visitor, but it illustrates that clerics believed the archbishop's visitations were merely an excuse to collect money. Parishioners, too, may have felt less hostile about gathering what little means they had as a parish to pay their own bishop during a visitation, but being required to pay the archbishop's procuration fee was an added burden that they begrudged. This may also explain why a number of rectors and priests were indifferent to the authority of the archbishop's visitor and disregarded sentences of excommunication by continuing to celebrate the mass in their parish churches. These rectors were excommunicated and their parishes placed under interdict because they were simply too impoverished to pay the full amount of the procuration fee.[94] It is striking that just as these clergymen flagrantly ignored their vows of celibacy and the ban on marriage, they equally disregarded the archbishop's sentence of excommunication. There was clearly a disconnect between the punishment and enforcement of provincial and diocesan church statutes, one that clergymen used to their benefit to show their disdain for the authority of their superiors. It is quite possible that parish clergy gained some sense of satisfaction in demonstrating their contempt for canon law and the ecclesiastical hierarchy.

More than anything, the punishment meted out to first offenders and recidivists throughout Catalunya denotes a policy of tolerance. Prior to the fourteenth century, there is little evidence in the episcopal registers that clergy were punished harshly for concubinage. In the diocese of Girona, the extant visitations from 1314, 1315, and 1321 record very few fines. The same is true for the diocese of Barcelona from 1303 to 1326, the diocese of Vic from 1330 to 1332, and the diocese of Urgell from 1312 to 1316. Given that visitors in the diocese of Urgell had such a difficult time compelling parish clergy to pay the procuration fee even after they were excommunicated and their parishes placed under interdict, it is unlikely that they would have had any great success in collecting large fines for clerical incontinence. While the procuration fee was an amount that the community as a whole remunerated, the fee for incontinence was paid only by the cleric. Although many parish communities and clergy were extremely poor and lacked the monetary resources to pay, from the perspective of episcopal administrators the chances of the community's pooling its resources to pay the procuration fee was greater than the cleric's forfeiting a significant portion of his salary. Moreover, when assigning

---

concubine; ACV, Calaix 31/43, Visites, no. 4, 11v. (1314). For more examples of parishioners refusing to speak with the visitor, see ACV, Calaix 31/43, Visites, no. 2, 18r., 21v., 57r., 71v. (1313); ACV, Visites, no. 5, 5v., 12v. (1314); ACV, Visites, no. 6, 11v. (1316).

94. ACV, Calaix 31/43, Visites, no. 2, 27r., 35r.–36r., 44r.–46r., 50r., 52r.–56r., 61r., 64r., 73r.–74r. (1313); ACV, Visites, no 3, 32r., 34r., 45r. (1313); ACV, Visites, no. 5, 4v., 10v. (1315).

fines, the archbishop's visitors seem to have taken into account a cleric's economic standing. Clerics were charged what they could afford, which explains why the rector of Castells, who had four children with Simona, was fined 10 sous, and the rector of Sant Esteve de Luç, who had multiple children with Teresa, was fined 100 sous. A few clergymen were fined 45 libras or 10 aureos, but these were most likely assigned to men who could afford to pay such an exorbitant amount.[95]

On the surface, it might appear that a policy of fines for clerical incontinence was a de facto licensing fee so that the episcopal bureaucracy could benefit from such an income and the clergymen could to continue in their relationships. But the inconsistency with which officials recorded and collected fines, not to mention the clerics who were absolved of paying any penalty, points, if anything, to an ineffective system of punishment just as much as a fiscally driven policy to regulate clerical concubinage. There is no doubt that episcopal coffers increased due to the fines administered for concubinage, but officials ultimately could not extract money that the clergy did not possess. For instance, when the episcopal visitor found the elderly priest of Agullana living with his domestic partner in 1329, he assigned a small fine of 10 sous on account of his poverty and old age.[96] Reducing fines to a more reasonable quantity allowed episcopal officials to collect more money over the long run.

Consider, too, the example of the priest Bernat Mola and Berengaria Rotlana, who over the course of sixteen years were punished by episcopal officials on at least on five occasions. Bernat never paid the maximum fine for the crime of incontinence. In 1329, a visitation to the parish of Calonge revealed that the couple had one daughter. Along with three other priests in the parish who were found guilty of keeping concubines, Bernat, like all the men, promised not to return to his concubine under penalty of a fine of 50 sous. Twelve years later, in 1341, Bernat still lived with Berengaria, who according to parishioners was at least fifty years old. The couple had two daughters, which should have compounded the fine. Yet Bernat paid a fine of 50 sous and promised to expel Berengaria and their children from his home or incur a fine of 100 sous. He did not keep his promise, and, in 1343, Bernat paid a 30 sous fine and once again took an oath to eject Berengaria and his daughters from his home, this time under penalty of a fine of 200 sous. Either Bernat was not concerned with paying a fine of 100 or 200 sous, or he knew it was a threat that officials rarely carried out. The latter seems to have been the case. Bernat

95. ACV, Calaix 31/43, Visites, no. 1, 31v., 43r., 50r. (1312); ACV, Visites, no. 4, 3v., 8v., 22r (1314); ACV, Visites, no. 5, 17r. (1315); ACV, Visites, no. 6, 2r. (1315).

96. ADG, Visites, no. 4, 204v. (1329).

paid a smaller fine than the mandated 50 sous and the promised 200 sous when he failed to comply (for the third time) and extricate himself completely from his family. The accumulation of fines over the years, however, must have taken a toll on the family. By all accounts Bernat and Berengaria were still a couple in 1345, but the family had made changes to their living arrangements to avoid further trouble. Berengaria now lived in a separate house in the parish, and one of their daughters remained in Bernat's house to look after him. Notes in the margin of the visitation record disclose that Bernat was absolved of his fine, a sign of clemency on the part of the visitor, who most likely thought that nights of carnal passion no longer occurred for this elderly couple.[97] It is a challenge, nevertheless, to ascertain whether clerics could pay such exorbitant penalties and whether officials actually required them to do so.

Although clerical couples such as Bernat and Berengaria were willing to risk the economic hardship of repeated fines, they also employed strategies to conceal their families to avoid punishment. Given that the average yearly income for many poor beneficed clergy amounted to 100 sous, a fine of 20, 50, or 100 sous could be devastating. Some clerics removed themselves or their families prior to the visitor's arrival. Since visitors typically sent a messenger announcing their visit to the parish, these clerics hoped to persuade the visitor that they had dismissed their concubines by claiming they had recently expelled them.[98] Other strategies included moving the family to a separate home or a neighboring village to circumvent detection, with the hope of convincing officials that the sexual and familial relationship had been severed. In many cases, this tactic worked only for a short time because the parishioners were quick to notice the telling behavior of couples. In spite of living separately, the frequent comings and goings of the woman and children was definitely suspect, especially if the woman continued to wash the cleric's clothes and take care of his affairs. Equally telling was the continued financial support of the woman and children. Nevertheless, clerics knew that their family's living in the same house compounded the penalty and that at least living in separate homes meant a lesser fine. Clerics were also aware that confessing their crime to the visitor usually resulted in the reduction of the penalty and sometimes even in the absolution of the fine for elderly priests. Clerics who kept their families

97. ADG, Visites, no. 4, 71v.–72r.v. (1329); ADG, Imposicions de Penes, no. 1, 35r. (1341) and 44v. (1343); ADG, Visites, no. 7, 35r.v. (1341); ADG, Obligacions de Penes, no. 1, 30v.–31r. (1343); ADG, Lletres, no. 7, 106r. (1344); ADG, Visites, no. 8, 17v.–18r. (1345). Bernat Mola held the benefice of claviger in Calonge, but it is clear that he was a priest because he served as a substitute for the sacrist Pere de Plana in 1329.

98. ADG, Visites, no. 2, 34v.–35r. (1315); ADG, Visites, no. 4, 116v., 120r.v.–121r.v. (1329); ADG, Visites, no. 1, 84r.v., 98r.v. (1315).

in a separate home were in the minority compared to those who lived in a single household, however, more chose this option after 1339 when the bishop Mont-rodon implemented an effective policy of fines. Living in separate household would have distinguished clerical families from other, lay families, but it is significant that these clergymen persisted in preserving their families and took on the burden of paying for two households to keep their woman and children.

It is difficult to imagine that these clerics believed that their parishioners would fail to notice that a relationship existed between two households or that a cleric's family frequently came to visit him. The point of the strategy of maintaining separate homes, nevertheless, was to convince the episcopal visitor that the relationship had been severed and to incur a smaller fine or no penalty at all. The tactics used to cover up their illicit relationship could also have undermined the testimony of parishioners, who would have fewer incriminating details to provide to visitors. In answering questions about the sexual activities of parish clergy, some parishioners clearly did not wish to cause trouble for their clerics. When the bishop of Girona questioned the parishioners of Falgars about their rector's "way of life" (*conversatio*) in 1340, they revealed that the rector Ferrar was defamed for having a daughter with Na Farnera and two sons with Na Alma. These parishioners added that "they do not have hatred for the rector nor do they believe that anyone in the parish wishes him ill."[99] Others characterized their clergymen as living "rightly," as did the villagers of Sant Quirze de la Coma, who told the visitor in 1313 that their rector "lived honestly" even though he kept a concubine and son. Similarly, when the parishioners of Sant Martí de Cost admitted that the rector had six children with Guillema, they nevertheless declared that the rector was "a good man."[100] These statements suggest that parishioners reported the sexual activities of their priest not because they had problems with the sexual lives of their parish clergy but because officials sought this information. The visitor solicited the information from the witnesses, and the line of questioning

---

99. ADG, Visites, no. 6, 76r.v. (1340).

100. ACV, Calaix, 31/ 43, Visites, no. 2 (1313); ACV, Calaix 31/41, Visites, no. 1, 17v. (1312). The villagers of Sant Martí de Cost responded that "ipsum esse probum virum tamen tenet publice concubinam Guillelmam ex qua VI filios habet." In Santa Maria de Valls, parishioners stated that their chaplain "bene vivit" even though he kept Arsena de Valls. ACV, Calaix 31/43, Visites, no. 2, 71v. (1313). Likewise, the parishioners of Montfalc reported that, although their chaplain celebrated mass with his son, he still "bene eum vivere." ACV, Calaix 31/43, Visites, no. 3, 46r. (1315). The villagers of Sant Hilari de Sacalm stated that the clerics in their parish "honesti sunt et bone vite," even though the rector had a three-year-old child with Tomasia. AEV, Visites, no. 1200/2, 81r. (1332). In the village of Santa Eulàlia de Pardines, parishioners testified that their rector performed his office well despite the fact that he kept Elisenda and many children; AEV, Visites, no. 1200/2, 66r. (1331).

influenced their responses. The questions asked during a visitation were structured in such a way as to highlight the defects of the parish church, the inadequacy of its clergy, and, last, the shortcomings of the laity. Scribes also used formulaic language when recording testimony, indicating that witnesses' statements were first filtered through the scribe, who often summarized their testimony.

Although the acceptance of clerical unions depended on the familial and friendship ties that the couples had to their community, unhappy parishioners could use the opportunity to retaliate against a priest—a finding that Daniel Bornstein and Roisin Cossar also observe in their studies of Italian episcopal visitation records.[101] It is highly probable that disgruntled Catalan parishioners gleefully reported the sexual misdeeds of their parish priest to episcopal visitors, but it also just as likely that, based on past experience, they would have known that neither the priest nor the woman would be removed from the parish. The illicit nature of these relationships, nevertheless, meant that the couple was vulnerable and could easily be condemned when villagers felt the need to be less accommodating to clerical couples. Reports that the laity boycotted the mass performed by a concubinary priest or comments that the women were a source of pollution to their partners, however, are completely absent from visitation records. On the whole, the testimonies of witnesses reveal that the presence of clerical unions throughout the villages of Catalunya was normal and unremarkable enough to warrant few negative comments.

The impermanence of some clerical unions, however, was one consequence of the burdensome fines. Whereas some clerical couples modified their lifestyles to evade punishment and parish clergy put themselves at risk to keep their families, not all clerics clung to their women and children so steadfastly. Some priests chose to end a relationship when their sexual partner was with child. This was the case when Francesca became pregnant and the sacrist Bartomeu de Ter expelled her from his home. In another example, the priest Bernat confessed to impregnating Alisenda, but he claimed that once she had given birth he no longer knew her carnally or accepted her in his home.[102] Similarly, after Berengaria and Geralda had both given birth to his children, the sacrist Ramon Raditor "no longer provided for these women."[103] It is worth noting that in some of these cases the women are not identified as concubines in the documents, suggesting that these relationships were not perceived to

101. Bornstein, "Priests and Villagers in the Diocese of Cortona," 98–100; Bornstein, "Parish Priests in Late Medieval Cortona," 174; Cossar, "Clerical 'Concubines' in Northern Italy," 116–17.
102. ADG, Visites, no. 4, 58v.–59r. (1329); ADG, Visites, no. 4, 113r.v. (1329).
103. ADG, Visites, no. 3, 19v.–20r. (1321). The testimonies of parishioners do not reveal whether Ramon publicly kept both women at the same time or they were in serial relationships.

be unions.[104] Knowing that a pregnant woman or a woman and child in their home would be seen as evidence of guilt, a number of clerics banished their sexual partners when they became pregnant as a way to avoid punishment. After being punished or threatened with a fine, certain clerics found it easier to move on to a different relationship that was equally short-lived and less likely to incur the more substantial fines that could accumulate over time for an established union. If they were caught, paying a fine of 20 or 30 sous may have been preferable to some clerics, unlike the sacrist Pere Rovira, who was fined twice and paid a total of 80 sous in three years for his relationship with Francesca.[105] Moving from one short-term affair to another may have been a more economical strategy for some clerics, but it fostered resentment in the parish and was not a strategy that guaranteed an absence of ecclesiastical fines. Church officials were just as likely to punish a cleric for sexual promiscuity as they were for his having a long-standing union with a woman, although officials tended to administer a heftier fine when a cleric was involved with more than one woman at the same time.[106] In other cases, a promiscuous cleric later established a domestic partnership that proved to be more stable and was therefore prepared to pay the consequences. It is also possible that some clerics simply did not want the responsibility of providing for a family. Even though the role of paterfamilias governing over a household was an important marker of masculinity, these men were still able to demonstrate their virility by fathering children because the production and ejaculation of semen, according to Patricia Simons, was seen as one facet of manhood.[107]

These short-term affairs, nevertheless, underscore how easily a cleric could dissolve his ties to a woman and his offspring. The transient nature of some clerical relationships could leave women and children in a precarious financial situation, although a surprising number of clergy maintained ties to their

---

104. Similar examples can be found in the testimonies of both parishioners and the accused priest, who acknowledged a carnal relationship and the child produced from such an affair; however, neither the parishioners nor the priest used the term *concubina;* ADB, Visites, no. 2, 40v.–41r.v. (1314).

105. In 1340, the sacrist Pere Rovira, who served in the parish of Vilamari, was fined 60 sous under penalty of 100 sous if he continued his relationship with Francesca. By 1343, Pere had two infants with Francesca. He was fined 20 sous under penalty of 100 sous; ADG, Obligacions de Penes, no. 1, 18r. (1340) and 29v. (1343); ADG, Imposicions de Penes, no. 1, 30r. (1340) and 42v. (1343).

106. For example, the deacon Guillem Oliver was fined 20 sous under penalty of 50 sous for his relationship with Guillema Susqueda that had produced a child. In comparison, the hebdomedarian Guillem Fuster was fined 100 sous for his involvement with Raimunda and Garsenda, a married woman; ADG, Obligacions de Penes, no. 1, 5v., 6v. (1337). The register Imposicions de Penes shows that clerics who were involved with more than one woman at a time were threatened with higher fines; ADG, Imposicions de Penes, no. 1, 6r. (1336); 13r. (1336); 21r. (1339); 23r. (1339); 29v. (1340); 30v. (1340); 44r. (1343).

107. Patricia Simons, *The Sex of Men in Premodern Europe: A Cultural History* (Cambridge, UK: Cambridge University Press, 2011), 37.

children and provided for them even when their relationship to the mother had ended (see Chapter Two). That clerics continued to support their children and that the family of the woman and the village community expected a cleric who initiated a relationship, particularly with a woman who was a virgin, to provide for her and any resulting offspring also suggest that this obligation was seen as part of a man's responsibility when entering into a recognized union with a woman. In his sermons to priests, Vicente Ferrer even acknowledged how difficult it was for a priest to leave his children and his concubine, particularly if the woman had been a virgin.[108] The evidence of priests providing dowries and husbands for their former concubines so they could enter into marriage with a layman further indicates not only that there was an expectation that a cleric would ensure the future of his partner but also that carrying out such a duty was another facet of what it meant to be a man. And, although women who attached themselves to priests lived an insecure existence because their illicit union could easily be dissolved, we should also take into account that in many cases the sacrament of marriage did not protect peasant women from being deserted by their husbands. The vulnerable position of clerics' concubines was in many respects no better and no worse than that of other peasant women who could not afford to enforce their marriages in court. The visitation records are filled with complaints about husbands who abandoned or dismissed their wives for another woman, practiced bigamy, or kept both a wife and a concubine.[109]

For parish priests who chose to establish a family, however, the documents are unambiguous on one point: the threat of fines did not deter a significant number of clergymen from forming long-term unions with women. The union of Berenguer de Conill, the hebdomedarian of Aro, and Beatriu, sister to Guillem de Pagès de Calonge, is cited five times in the Girona episcopal records from 1329 to 1344. Despite a prior fine for his relationship with Beatriu, Berenguer confessed in 1329 that Beatriu and his two daughters continued to live in his home. If caught again Berenguer promised to pay the penalty sum of 100 sous for failing to dismiss Beatriu, but there is no evidence in the registers that he did so. Six years later in 1335, Berenguer was found guilty of keeping Berengaria as his concubine for a third time. An entry in the bishop's Notularium in March 1335 records that Berenguer was fined 20 sous under penalty of a fine of 200 sous for the "crime of incontinence." The stakes were

---

108. In the village of Lorca, before an audience of priests, Vicente Ferrer preached, "ad tercium, propter se ipsum est grave tenere concubinam propter dificultatem dimitendi eam, quia forte habuit eam virginem, vel habet filios de ea. Et ita est forte exire de tali peccato." Gimeno Blay and Mandingorra Llavata, *Sermonario de San Vicente Ferrer*, 107–8.

109. Armstrong-Partida, "Priestly Wives," 205–12.

higher now, yet Berenguer remained with Beatriu. Two years later in a visitation to the parish of Aro in September of 1338, the visitor found that Beatriu
had recently given birth to a fourth daughter. Berenguer was ordered to pay
100 sous rather than the 200 sous previously assigned in 1335. The penalty for
being caught, however, had changed. Berenguer pledged to surrender his benefice and spend one year in the bishop's jail if he returned to Beatriu or in any
way provided for his children. Nevertheless, the threat of losing his position
and livelihood did not persuade Berenguer to abandon his family. A year later
in November 1339, Berenguer was fined another 100 sous and he pledged once
again that he would lose his benefice if caught a sixth time. Nonetheless in
1344, Berenguer was found still living in the same home with Beatriu and their
children. He was fined 30 sous for incontinence and for gambling; no mention is made of Berenguer's pledge to renounce his benefice and serve time in
jail.[110] Clearly for Berenguer, the pledges, fines, and harassment by episcopal
officials was worth keeping his family.

That episcopal officials often failed to follow through on their threats of
increased fines for repeat offenders underscores not only the mediocre implementation of synodal decrees and inefficient strategy for increasing episcopal
revenues but also a guiding principle of moderation. A policy that translated
a fine into a de facto licensing fee would require a more organized system of
recording monetary penalties as well as a standardized approach to assessing
and collecting fines—a strategy that is simply not evident in the extant records. The Catalan episcopal authorities were attempting to both regulate and
discourage clerical sexuality without waging a draconian campaign to put an
end to the outright pervasiveness of concubinage. Berenguer de Conill's case
also shows that, despite the threat of hefty fines, officials were willing to negotiate or reduce the amount to a fine that the cleric could presumably pay.
While a cleric might somehow manage to pay 50 to 100 sous, officials knew
that 200 or 300 sous was far more than the typical parish clergyman could for-
feit, which is why these exorbitant fines were frequently reduced. Episcopal
authorities were practical in dealing with the inordinate number of clerics
breaking their vows of celibacy; officials maintained the possibility of disciplining clerics and benefited from the revenues while tolerating a certain level
of clerics' illicit sexuality. This was certainly the case in the diocese of Barcelona, where, to continue construction of the new cathedral and avoid further
debt to his Jewish lenders, the bishop Ponç de Gualba imposed pecuniary fines

---

110. ADG, Visites, no. 4, 73r.–74v. (1329); ADG, Notularum, no. 10, 14r. (1335); ADG, Visites,
no. 6, 3r.v. (1338); ADG, Imposicions de Penes, no. 1, 4v.–5r. (1336), 18r. (1338), and 25v. (1340); ADG,
Obligacions de Penes, no. 1, 9v. (1338) and 14r. (1339); ADG, Lletres, no. 7, 162v. (1344).

on the clergy in lieu of penance. Thus, the 1303 Barcelona visitation records document that the bishop ordered incontinent clerics to pay their fines "for the building of the church."[111] Similarly, the building of a new gothic cathedral in Girona began in 1312 and continued steadily until 1347. Although the ultimate use of the fines imposed on the clergy is not specified in the Girona visitation records, it is difficult to imagine that the construction of the cathedral was financed solely on pious donations and rents belonging to the cathedral canons.[112]

The lenient approach to the sexual activity of clerics is best seen in the cases of fornication or concubinage brought before the bishop's court in Girona from 1282 to 1350. A total of seventy-nine criminal cases exist for this period. Of the sixty cases dealing with clerical offenses, such as murder, theft, and physically assaulting a parishioner or fellow clergyman, only seven cases were prosecuted exclusively for clerical incontinence.[113] In some instances, clerics in the other cases were also accused of illicit sex, but this charge was one among a long list of crimes and was not the focus of the trial or investigation. The fact that few clerics were brought before the court for their sexual misconduct reveals that officials were more concerned with clerical violence than with the sexual offences of the clergy. The diocese of Girona was not unique in this respect. Of the 2,000 extant cases for the diocese of Barcelona from the fourteenth and fifteenth centuries, only eleven deal with clerical concubinage. Instead, the bishop's court spent most of its time adjudicating disputes over ecclesiastical benefices.[114] The small number of clergymen and laity prosecuted

---

111. See José Maria Martí Bonet, Puigvert, L. Niqui, and F. Miquel Mascort, eds. *Las Series "Visitas Pastorales," Registros "Communium" y "Gratiarum" y los "Procesos" del Archivo Diocesano de Barcelona. Aportacion Archivística a la Historia Eclesiástica de la Diócesis de Barcelona* (Barcelona: Archivo Diocesano, 1978), 648–51, 686.

112. From 1312 to 1347, nine chapels and a new sanctuary were built. Construction apparently continued through the plague years but did not accelerate until the 1360s; Josep M. Martí Bonet, ed., *Historia de las diócesis españolas: Barcelona, Terrassa, Sant Feliu de Llobregat, Gerona*, Vol. 2 (Madrid: Biblioteca de Autores Cristianos, 2006), 528–29; Christian Guilleré, *Girona al segle XIV*, Vol. 1 (Barcelona: Publicacions de l'Abadia de Montserrat, 1993), 484–87; Antoni Pladevall i Font, "Arnau i Bertran de Mont-rodon, dos grans bisbes gironins del segle XIV," *Annals de l'Institut d'Estudis Gironins* 34 (1994): 395–426.

113. Josep M. Marquès, "Processos anteriors al 1500 de l'arxiu diocesà de Girona," *Annals de l'Institut d'Estudis Gironins* 44 (2003): 145–77; Josep M. Marquès, *Arxiu diocesà de Girona. Processos medievals* (Girona: Arxiu Diocesà de Girona, 1999), 14, 15. From 1351 to 1450, only two cases dealing with illicit sex were brought before the court.

114. Jaume Codina i Vilà, "Els processos dels segles XIV i XV" in *Processos de l'arxiu diocesà de Barcelona*, ed. Josep M. Martí Bonet, Leandre Niqui i Puigvert, and F. Miquel i Mascort (Barcelona: Department de Cultura de la Generalitat de Catalunya, 1984), 165, 178, 191–94. After we subtract the 36 cases from the fourteenth century, the 1,964 processos are from the fifteenth century. Jaume Codina estimates that 40 percent of these processos deal with benefices. Twenty-four of the thirty-six cases from the fourteenth century deal with disputes among clerics concerning benefices. The cases dealing

solely for sex offences is in stark contrast to the number of prosecutions for sexual crimes found in the ecclesiastical courts of England, Normandy, and Troyes.[115] Just as telling are the lack of public penances assigned to the guilty individuals. Rarely is there any mention in visitation or court records of ecclesiastical officials in Catalunya imposing whippings around the church, penitential pilgrimages, or other forms of public humiliation—punishments that were far more common in England and on the Continent.[116] As long as a cleric paid the fine, he was absolved of the crime of incontinence. Even repeat offenders were not removed from their benefices or deprived of their clerical status. Such a moderate treatment of offenders stands in contrast to the bishop of Rouen's disciplinary methods in Normandy, which entailed removing errant clerics from office, forcing those involved in concubinous unions or affairs with married women to serve in another parish or diocese, or mandating that a sexual incontinent priest embark on a pilgrimage to Rome as penance.[117]

It is significant, moreover, that clerics in the minor orders who had families were still permitted to progress through the major orders to become priests. For example, the tonsured cleric Pere Sartor had two children with Marta in the parish of Sant Joan de Aïguaviva in 1320. By 1329, Pere was a priest and Marta had recently given birth to a son, their third child. Prior to the birth of his son, Pere had been cited for incontinence, suggesting that sometime

with concubinage are from the fifteenth century, although a few processos are incorporated into the visitation records of 1303. See also Yolanda Serrano Seoane, "El sistema penal del Tribunal Eclesiàstico de la diócesis en la baja edad media. Primera parte. Estudio," *Clio & Crimen*, no. 3 (2006): 360, 379.

115. A significant number of cases in the church courts in England and France involved the sexual crimes of the clergy and the laity. See Andrew Finch, "Sexual Morality and Canon Law: The Evidence of the Rochester Consistory Court," *Journal of Medieval History* 20 (1994): 261–75; Andrew Finch, "Sexual Relations and Marriage in Later Medieval Normandy," *Journal of Ecclesiastical History* 47 no. 2 (1996): 236–56; Andrew Finch, "Women and Violence in the Later Middle Ages: The Evidence of the Officiality of Cerisy," *Continuity and Change* 7 no. 1 (1992): 30–34; McDougall, "Prosecution of Sex." See also Sandra Lee Parker and Lawrence R. Poos, "A Consistory Court from the Diocese of Rochester, 1363–4," *English Historical Review* 106 no. 420 (1991) 652–65; Richard H. Helmholz, "Crime, Compurgation and the Courts of the Medieval Church," *Law and History Review* 1 no. 1 (1983) 1–26; Robert N. Swanson, *Church and Society in Late Medieval England* (Oxford: Oxford University Press, 1989), 106–7. Henry Ansgar Kelly's survey of the prosecution of sex offenses in secular and ecclesiastical courts throughout Europe shows that Italy, like Catalunya, did not enthusiastically prosecute adultery, fornication, or sodomy. He also notes that the prosecution of sexual offenses in Normandy tailed off after 1370; "Law and Nonmarital Sex in the Middle Ages," *Conflict in Medieval Europe: Changing Perspectives on Society and Culture*, ed. Warren C. Brown and Piotr Górecki (Aldershot, UK: Ashgate, 2003), 175–93.

116. Tringham, "Parochial Visitation of Tarvin," 197–220; Finch, "Sexual Morality and Canon Law," 265–67; Swanson, *Church and Society*, 178–79.

117. Thibodeaux, *Manly Priest*, 129–30.

between his status as a tonsured cleric and ordination as a priest, he was twice found guilty of financially providing for a woman and children.[118] Likewise, Joan Fresc and Michaela were a couple when Joan was a tonsured cleric in the parish of Sant Vicenç de Vilamala in 1329. Seven years later, Joan was a priest in parish of Sant Miquel de Garrigàs and the couple had three children.[119] It appears that having a family did not impede clerics from obtaining the priestly order, nor did it prevent them from obtaining promotions. Numerous examples indicate that, despite the repeated appearance of these clergymen in the episcopal records, the recurring fines for concubinage did not hinder their priestly careers. In 1329, the priest Besalú Guerau was fined for having a five-year relationship with Sibil·la Sacosta, yet a visit to the parish of Santa Maria de Bolòs in 1331 found that she continued to reside in his home. Thirteen years later in 1342, Besalú had moved up the ecclesiastical hierarchy to become rector of the parish of Sant Valentí d'Arcs. Apparently Besalú did not see a need to end his relationship with Sibil·la when he assumed his new position of rector;

---

118. ADG, Visites fragmentaris, 30v. (1320); ADG, Visites, no. 4, 100v.–101r. (1329); ADG, Visites, no. 5, 82r.v. (1331). A visitation to the parish in 1331 found that Pere and Marta were still together. In another example, Joan Galceran was the sacrist of Sant Joan de Bellcaire in 1329, when he was fined 25 sous for keeping Francesca Savanera and a son in his home. In 1342, Joan was the rector of Sant Silvestre and was still with Francesca; ADG, Visites, no. 4, 12v.–13r. (1329); ADG, Imposicions de Penes, no. 1, 36v. (1342).

119. ADG, Visites, no. 4, 11r. (1329); ADG, Imposicions de Penes, no. 1, 5v. (1336). Other examples include Nicolau Sunyer, who started out as a tonsured cleric and had a child with Na Esmengartz in the parish of Santa Eulàlia de Vilanova in 1323. By 1329, Nicolau is identified as a stabilitus who had two sons with Esmengartz. In a visitation to the parish in 1341, Nicolau was now serving as a stabilitus in the monastery of Sant Joan de Croses and had four children with Esmengartz. The cleric Arnau Codina kept Constancia in his home as his "focaria" in 1341 while he served as a substitute deacon in the parish of Llofriu, but by 1344, Arnau was a priest serving in the nearby parish of Palafrugell and continued to keep Constancia and his child. In 1347, Arnau and Constancia appear together in the parish of Vilaromà. The parishioners of Sant Martí de Foix testified that the priest Berenguer Calabuig had had his concubine before his ordination to the priesthood and that he continued to keep her publicly in his home. In 1336, the cleric Bernat Carbó served in the parish of Palafruguell and kept Maria in the parish of Armentera. By 1342, Bernat was a sacrist serving in the parish of Garrigoles and his family with Maria, daughter of Pere Llorenç from Armentera, now included two sons and one daughter. Bonanat Pagès served as a cleric in Aïguaviva in 1336 and kept Sibil·la, who was from the village of Canavels. Six years later in 1342, the couple was still together and had two children; Bonanat Pagès now served in the parish of Santa Eulàlia de Noves as an hebdomedarian. For Nicolau Sunyer, see ADG, Visites fragmentaris, 10r. (1323); ADG, Visites, no. 6, 6v. (1329); ADG, Imposicions de Penes, no. 1, 2v. (1336) and 38v. (1342); ADG, Visites, no. 6, 156v. (1341); ADG, Obligacions de Penes, no. 1, 24v. (1342) and 33v. (1344). For Arnau Codina, see ADG, Visites, no. 7, 32r. (1341); ADG, Remissions de Penes, no. 1, 2r. (1345); ADG, Imposicions de Penes, no. 1, 71r. (1347). For the priest Berenguer Calabuig, see ADB, Visites, no. 4, 89v. (1337). For Bernat Carbó, see ADG, Imposicions de Penes, no. 1, 3r. (1336) and 36v. (1342). For Bonanat Pagès, see ADG, Imposicions de Penes, no. 1, 9v. (1336) and 40r. (1342).

she was still at his side in 1346.[120] The example of the subdeacon Berenguer
Puyola further illustrates that clerics did not view marriage and a priestly
career as mutually exclusive. Berenguer reportedly planned on taking a "wife"
even though he anticipated becoming a priest in the near future, and he intended, nonetheless, to keep the priestly benefice he had obtained while still
in the minor orders.[121]

The duration of these unions, whether the couple lived together or apart,
is evidence that Catalan clergymen engaged in the social practice of marriage
and underscores the marital quality of these relationships. Certainly the financial and emotional strain that clerical families were willing to undergo in the
face of episcopal interference suggests that these couples were committed to
one another. While canon law barred clergy in the major orders from marrying and the Church labeled these illicit relationships concubinage, it is clear
that clergymen and their women viewed their unions differently and may have
even believed them to be legitimate. The rector Jaume Ferrer and Jaçmeta not
only behaved like a married couple but also considered themselves to be married. The two had exchanged promises of commitment to each other at the
altar of Jaume's church before Jaçmeta's mother, brother, and a family friend.
Jaume swore "over the four holy gospels of God that he would never forsake
Jaçmeta" and would "always provide for her expenses." Jaçmeta, in turn,
pledged that, "she would never dismiss him for another."[122] Jaçmeta promised
to be faithful, confirming a husband's expectation that his wife be a respectable and honorable woman, and Jaume's vow not to physically and financially abandon Jaçmeta confirmed his responsibility as a man expected to take
care of his family. That the couple professed their vows to one another in
Jaume's church before family and friends indicates that everyone involved believed this to be the equivalent of a marriage ceremony. Indeed, according to
Jaçmeta's brother, his sister had told him "it was true that they performed

---

120. ADG, Visites, no. 4, 141r. (1329); ADG, Visites, no. 5, 68v. (1331); ADG, Obligacions de Penes, no. 1, 26r. (1342); ADG, Imposicions de Penes, no. 1, 39r. (1343) and 66v. (1346). In another example, the cleric Guillem Teyes served in the parish of Sant Pere dels Vilars where he had four
children with Elisenda Vergera in 1340. By 1356, Guillem was the rector of Sords, and Elisenda and
their youngest child continued to live with him; ADG, Visites, no. 6, 60v. (1340); ADG, Imposicions de
Penes, no. 1, 37r. (1342) and 108v. (1356); ADG, Obligacions de Penes, no. 1, 22v. (1342); ADG, Remissions de Penes, no. 1, 23v. (1351).

121. ADG, Visites, no. 3, 5v. (1321). Berenguer Puyola held the benefice of sacrist, which required
that he be a priest. In his defense, Berenguer told the visitor that he had a dispensation from the
bishop Guillem that permitted Berenguer to wait four years, preferably to study, before obtaining the
rank of priest.

122. Pere Benito i Monclús, *Les parròquies del maresm a la baixa edat mitjana. Una aproximació des de
les visites pastorals, 1305–1447* (Mataró: Caixa d'Estalvis Laietana, 1992), no. 18, 284–87, at 287.

the sacrament."[123] There are doubtless many more couples like Jaume and Jaçmeta who wanted to validate their unions and undergo some kind of formal process before their kin, modeled after marriage rituals of the laity, to underscore their commitment to each other. It is possible that such a commitment ceremony might have taken place between the vicar En Juliol and the sister of Jaume de Puig in the village of Gurb. According to parishioners, the vicar was "wanting to marry" Jaume de Puig's sister and presumably left the parish with her and their child to do so.[124] Such evidence reveals that some clerical couples wanted to authenticate their union with the sacrament of marriage, albeit privately to avoid punishment. Moreover, it is an indication that clerical marriage was still taking place in the fourteenth century—more than a century after historians have claimed that clerical marriage had died out.[125] Even though episcopal sources labeled these unions concubinous, it is quite possible that a good number of these couples had their relationship validated in a discreet ceremony at which the sacrament of marriage was performed by the groom or by a trusted priestly colleague.

Taking into account the stability of so many clerical unions, it is likely that many clerical couples had, at the very least, a mutual understanding or verbal agreement between them. Couples such as Jaume and Jaçmeta, backed by their families, may have entered into a contract of sorts that specified a cleric's responsibilities to his concubine and in which the woman promised, in addition to her pledge of fidelity, any surplus grain, harvest, or farm animals that the family could offer as a token dowry.[126] There is no way of knowing how many clerical couples made private commitments to each other because the information on courtship and marriage customs of nonelites comes primarily from suits brought before the church courts to enforce or dissolve marriage contracts. Unlike secular marriages, in which marriage contracts specified the dowry and dower arrangements, clerical unions did not produce such legal contracts. The illicit nature of clerical concubinage meant that it was an

---

123. Ibid., 287.

124. AEV, Visites, 1200/1, no. 1, 27r. (1330).

125. In 1956, Christopher N. L. Brooke claimed that clerical marriage had died out among elite clergy in England in the mid-twelfth century; "Gregorian Reform in Action," 18. Jennifer Thibodeaux, in 2015, followed suit, asserting that: "clerical marriage died out among the elite clergy probably by the mid-twelfth century but certainly by the beginning of the thirteenth century." *Manly Priest*, 153. Both authors skirt the issue of when parish clergy stopped contracting marriage, but explanations that priests at all levels of society substituted clerical concubinage for clerical marriage follow this time line.

126. It is also possible that a cleric would provide surplus grains or foodstuff to a woman's family or that he might sell land at a favorable price to her relatives. The rector of Sallent sold a piece of land belonging to the parish church to Ermesenda de na Font, who may have been a relative of his concubine, Berengaria de na Font; ADG, Visites, no. 4, 155v.–156r. (1329).

informal relationship in which neither party had any legal standing to make a claim in court. As a result, we are left without documents that could offer insight into the arrangements and perhaps even rituals involved in the formation of clerical unions. The example of Jaume and Jaçmeta suggests that clerical couples may have planned a private commitment ceremony that validated their relationship to their family and friends. Although church authorities would have viewed such a ceremony as a sacrilege and violation of canon law, we cannot dismiss the possibility that this promise of commitment had meaning for the couple and other people involved or that they did not view it as significant as the sacrament of marriage. I am not arguing that clerical couples were not aware that their illicit union was considered substandard by some in medieval society or that they did not recognize that their union engendered many legal disadvantages; nevertheless, it does not seem out of the realm of possibility that these couples viewed such a vow of commitment as one way to legitimize their union—even if it lacked the legal formality and recognition of a Church sanctioned marriage. That priests and their partners recognized their unions as something akin to marriage is evidenced by the longevity of the unions and the commitment to maintaining and supporting these union in the face of ecclesiastical harassment and opprobrium.

Other evidence can be gleaned from sources that suggest parish clergy followed the same practices as their lay counterparts when entering into marriage. According to the villagers of Sant Pere Pescador, the priest Pere Fresc was betrothed to Stella, the daughter of Pere Respland, and the couple had three children together. The testimony of parishioners does not reveal whether the priest Pere had become engaged to Stella prior to his ordination, but they nonetheless explained that Pere keeps Stella "as if she were his wife." Pere and Stella were not the only "engaged" clerical couple in the village; the priest Ramon Perpinyà was similarly betrothed to Dolça Monda, who lived in his home and looked after their child.[127] In both cases, the verb *desponsare* was used to describe the relationship between these clerics and the women. Although in the classical sense *desponsare* meant "to betroth," it was also used in medieval

---

127. ". . . dixerunt quod R\<aymundus\> Perpinyani clericus stabilitus [. . .] tenet secum publice in domo Dulciam Mondam et procreavit prolem ex ea et [. . .] dicitur desponsavit eandem. [. . .] Item dixerunt quod P\<etrus\> Fresch clericus stabilitus [. . .] desponsavit Stella filia Petri Resplandi et procreavit ex ea tres infantes quorum minor non dum est amplius et tenet dictam mulierem ac si esset eius uxor et fuit penitus iam per episcopum et nondum est correctus." ADG, Visites fragmentaris, 5v. (1304). In another example, the priest Ramon de Vila serving in the monastery of Sant Feliu de Guíxols was reportedly engaged "per verba de presenti" to Na Matevina before he was ordained. Ramon was no longer involved with Na Matevina but, instead, kept Constancia, the daughter of Berenguer Blanc, as his concubine and had children by her. Na Matevina was now the concubine of the brother Arnau de Mont; ADG, Processos, no. 40, 2r. (1320).

Latin to refer to marriage.[128] Whether or not these couples exchanged future or present consent to contract a marriage or solemnized their union before the face of the parish church is unknown. Nevertheless, the use of the word *desponsare* suggests that the couples had entered into some kind of financial agreement that outlined what each party brought to the relationship. The example of Jaçmeta and Jaume also reveals that some women, backed by their families, entered into a contract of sorts that specified the cleric's responsibilities. We have no way of knowing whether the cleric compensated the woman's family by providing foodstuff and moveable goods or whether he sold a piece of land at a favorable price to her relatives, but it seems likely that clerical couples would have negotiated the terms of their relationship.

It is not a surprise that clerical couples may have privately contracted marriage or even skipped over the public solemnization of their union at the church. Lay couples frequently neglected to publicize the banns and solemnize their marriages before a priest or publicly at the church for fear that an impediment to their union would be discovered. Others failed to ensure the presence of witnesses during the formal exchange of present consent as a strategy that would allow the couple to dissolve their marriage or even provide one partner with an escape if they regretted their decision. Clandestine marriages constituted a considerable portion of the marriage suits brought before church courts, suggesting that many, especially among the lower classes, were not concerned with the formalities of marriage required by canon law.[129] Nevertheless, it is obvious that the criminal status of clerical unions most likely prompted couples to perform their ceremonies in secret to protect them from ecclesiastical punishment. For a cleric, keeping a concubine was a crime, but taking part in the sacrament of marriage elevated the crime to an entirely different level—one of sacrilege. Family members who knew what was at stake for the couple would most likely keep it a secret. And, if the event did come to light, witnesses denied their involvement in the ceremony or suffered from amnesia, as did Jaçmeta's brother, who claimed that he "did not recall that he was present."[130] We can imagine that a many a couple sat around the table of a parent's farmhouse negotiating a financial agreement, perhaps discussing

---

128. Edwin Hall, *The Arnolfini Betrothal: Medieval Marriage and the Enigma of Van Eyck's Double Portrait* (Berkeley: University of California Press, 1994), 49–51.

129. Michael M. Sheehan, "The Formation and Stability of Marriage in Fourteenth-Century England: Evidence of an Ely Register," in *Marriage, Family, and Law in Medieval Europe: Collected Studies*, ed. James K. Farge (Toronto: University of Toronto Press, 1996), 38–76; Brundage, *Law, Sex, and Christian Society*, 499–501.

130. Benito i Monclús, *Parròquies del maresm*, no. 18, 287.

when the priest and his future wife would exchange promises to each other before their prospective families and planning a celebratory feast.

Conclusion

When in 1867 Henry Charles Lea first published his controversial book, *The History of Sacerdotal Celibacy in the Christian Church*, which chronicles the long struggle by the Church to impose priestly celibacy, he declared that "the question of sacerdotal celibacy seems to have been virtually ignored in Spain. . . . It is very evident that the pontiffs who so energetically enforced the rule of celibacy throughout the rest of Europe were content to offer little opposition to the obstinacy of the Iberian priesthood." Lea further assessed the situation in Spain by concluding that "wild and insubordinate as was a large portion of the European clergy, the ecclesiastics of Spain were even wilder and more insubordinate."[131] Like Lea's appraisal of the Spanish clergy, Peter Linehan's work on the Iberian church has highlighted the rebelliousness of these clergymen and their fondness for entering into unions with women. Indeed, Linehan's characterization of the clergy is often emphasized in general histories of medieval Iberia, in particular when he declares that "all Spanish churchmen were frontiersmen, to some extent. They differed in degree, not in kind. In matters of ecclesiastical discipline they expressed the frontier-spirit by their contempt for distant authority—papal authority included—and their rejection of any reforms which threatened their peculiar institutions, the most ineffectively threatened if not the most peculiar of which was clerical concubinage."[132] The repeated denunciations of clerical unions and clerical offspring in synodal legislation throughout Iberia in the thirteenth and fourteenth centuries certainly corroborates this image of defiant priests persisting in unions that were by all accounts marriage. The carnal appetite of the Iberian clergy and their predilection for concubines are further documented in the late medieval literature of Iberia. Literary texts such as the *Debate de Elena y María* and the *Libro de Buen Amor* underscore that Iberian culture accepted and even had a sense of humor about the fact that clergymen flagrantly broke their vows of celibacy and formed unions with women.

My own study of the episcopal records from the dioceses of Girona, Barcelona, Vic, Urgell, and Tortosa confirms Lea's and Linehan's evaluations of

131. Lea, *History of Sacerdotal Celibacy*, 253, 258–59. The earliest publications date from 1867 and 1907.

132. Linehan, *Spanish Church and the Papacy*, 2–4, 20–34, 50–53, quotation p. 3. See also Linehan, *Spanish Church and Society*, 484–85, 496–97; Linehan, "Segovia," 483–85.

the scope of clergy's nonconformity to the law regarding celibacy and shows that clerical couples and families were very much a widespread phenomenon throughout Catalunya. Focusing exclusively on papal reforms, synodal legislation, and the clergy's predilection for sex in literature, however, is not very helpful in determining why the practice of clerical marriage and concubinage continued to exist or why clerical unions appear to have been more widespread in Iberia than in other regions of Europe, such as England and France. It is more useful to consider various factors—clerical culture, regional reforms, the lack of royal interference, and the Church and royal focus on the conversion of Jews and Muslims—in explaining why clerical marriage and clerical families survived and even flourished in Iberia. As I have argued, the omnipresent practice of clerical unions and its acceptance was due in large part to its having been a tradition among Catalan clergy—a custom that prevailed and remained largely unaffected by the Gregorian reform and the fourth Lateran council of 1215. Certainly the reform movement of the eleventh century and the impact of Lateran IV are watershed moments in the history of the medieval Church; the former eradicated clerical marriage, and the latter ordered bishops to carry out more diligently the enforcement of clerical celibacy and punishment of concubinary clerics. Yet these watershed moments did not play out in the same way throughout Europe, nor did parish clergy experience papal and episcopal attempts of reform in the same manner. Given that the zeal to eradicate clerical marriage was in short supply at the diocesan level and the greater medieval populace did not fervently insist on a celibate clergy, we can hardly expect a widespread popular movement in which the parish clergy voluntarily accepted the Church mandate on celibacy. Ecclesiastical sources, by and large, favor religious leaders, moralists, canon lawyers, and the papacy; consequently, we tend to forget that lower clergy were not passive receptacles but active agents in this process called reform. That the evidence thus far points to clerical unions flourishing to a greater extent in Iberia and parts of Italy than in England and France may simply reflect the vitality of clerical culture in opposing changes that affected the very fabric of clerics' lives.

The widespread practice of clerical unions reflects the tolerant policies of Catalan church officials. Despite synodal legislation that prohibited concubinage and the number of episcopal visitations undertaken in the fourteenth century that punished the clergy for their unions, these very sources do not reveal that the Catalan church waged an aggressive and all-out comprehensive campaign to eradicate clerical concubinage. In fact, episcopal authorities worked not to eradicate concubinage among the clergy but to prevent clerics from flagrantly displaying their families in public and at the same time to augment episcopal coffers. Pecuniary fines were meant to discourage clerics from forming unions with women, but clerics continued to be promoted to the priesthood and attain benefices in spite of maintaining a family. The administration of fines for concubinage lies somewhere between regulating sexuality, as in cases of prostitution with de facto licensing, and attempts to put an end to the outright pervasiveness of concubinage. Synodal decrees and their mediocre implementation were ineffective in combating clerical fornication and concubinage because episcopal authorities were careful not to apply draconian measures or exorbitant fees that would result in a large number of clerics being suspended from office. What is more, episcopal officials recognized that clerical unions were a custom entrenched in Iberian society, and they most likely appreciated the limited revenue that came with tolerating such relationships. Nevertheless, clerics endured ecclesiastical harassment and multiple fines to keep their families. A de facto marriage must have benefitted clergy in important ways to be worth the hassle and economic strain; otherwise, clerics would have opted for short-term relationships in far greater numbers.

The prevalence of clerical unions throughout Catalunya, moreover, reveals two important details about the lives of clergymen: first, the practice of marriage had not died out among the clergy even as late as the fourteenth century; second, the Church campaign to criminalize sexuality and eradicate clerical marriage had not been successful in changing the mentalité of clerics so they would accept celibacy in lieu of the roles of husband and father. Documents of practice such as the parish visitation records, registers of fines, and letters from the bishop's curia point to a custom among clerics that favored a stable union rather than sexual promiscuity. Visitation records allow us to the track the careers of clerics and their families, not only highlighting the high incidence of clerical unions throughout the dioceses of Catalunya but also establishing that they were the norm in this society. The preponderance of evidence reveals that parish clergy preferred to enter into marriage-like relationships that involved a family and a household, and points to the social practice of marriage having continued to be a significant measure of clerical manliness. Indeed, it was a clerical union, not celibacy, that marked the Catalan priest as a man.

The ubiquity of these de facto marriages similarly reveals that parishioners were accustomed to living with clerics and their families and that they in many respects would have considered it normal. The prevalence of informal unions among the Catalan laity likely helped foster an acceptance of these relationships. Moreover, the marital quality of these clerical unions greatly promoted their acceptance among the laity. Too often historians have relied on prescriptive church sources to infer that the attitude of the laity toward clerical marriage and sexual indiscretions corresponded to the Church's message. That the general medieval populace fully accepted the Church views on clerical celibacy and contempt for clerical partners is questionable. The evidence from Catalunya points to a familiarity with and even tolerance for clerical unions that imitated marriage. Given that parish clergy were among the wealthiest in the village, poor families may have encouraged a union between their daughter and a priest. The fate of a dowryless daughter was usually concubinage. Becoming the concubine of a priest held the promise of financial gain for the family and was just as respectable, if not more so, than becoming the concubine of a layman. That the laity and the couples involved could perceive their union to be one of marriage is underscored in the terms that parishioners used to describe these relationships, especially because the couples seem to have entered into verbal contracts that made clear promises of financial support and fidelity. Clearly, forming a long-term union with a woman offered far more than just a sexual outlet. As I discuss in Chapter Two, keeping a woman and maintaining children was important to a cleric's identity as a man, and establishing a family household offered social and economic benefits that made the risk worthwhile.

CHAPTER 2

Proof of Manhood

Priests as Husbands and Fathers

Catalan clerics did not forsake marriage—their relationships were marriage in all but name. In fact, many went to great lengths to engage in a relationship that could offer them a sexual outlet, companionship, and perhaps even love. Yet if we look beyond the sexual needs of the body and the emotional attachments that humans form, a question still remains: Why did these clerics disregard their vows of celibacy and defy canon law to imitate the social and cultural practice of marriage among the laity?

Marriage, quite simply, was normative in medieval society. For much of medieval society, the nuclear family household, which consisted of parents and children, was the basic unit of social organization. Among the peasantry, the household economy was structured around the labor of a husband, wife, and children.[1] Although the number of single men and single women grew during the late medieval period, most of the male and female population still married and had children. For both men and women, marriage was a rite of passage that signaled their attainment of adult status in society. For men and women, both marital status and the single, unmarried state had serious implications for their gender identity.[2] Marriage offered women the respectable

1. Judith M. Bennett, *A Medieval Life: Cecilia Penifader of Brigstock, c. 1295–1344* (Boston: McGraw-Hill College, 1999), 88–91.

2. Karras, *From Boys to Men*, 144–50; Susan Mosher Stuard, "Burdens of Matrimony: Husbanding and Gender in Medieval Italy," in *Medieval Masculinities: Regarding Men in the Middle Ages*, ed. Clare A.

role of wife and mother; for men, it was the cornerstone of a patriarchy that was maintained and reinforced male authority in law and social customs. Masculine identity was intricately tied to the marital state not only in providing men access to social adulthood but also in the role of paterfamilias. Becoming the head of a household was as an important public display of male governance over wives, children, servants, and slaves—an authority that servants, slaves, and apprentices did not exercise. It also meant the responsibility of managing the family's finances, protecting the family's reputation, and participating in civic culture.[3]

It is easy to see that clerics who formed unions with women were following the norms of medieval society. However, acquiring adult male status and attaining the role of paterfamilias was more than just a way for clerics to take part in a common social practice. Although clerical unions would never be on par with lay marriages because they lacked legal recognition and the ceremonial trappings of a relationship sanctioned in the eyes of the Church, these marriage-like relationships nevertheless afforded clerics important social and familial roles as husbands and fathers. What is more, the role of husband and father allowed clerics to participate in the culture of lay masculinity. If marriage was a vehicle through which laymen exhibited their masculinity, paternal authority, and privilege in medieval society, why would parish clergy not seek to do the same?

For parish clergy, who often originated from the well-to-do peasantry or the middling level of medieval society, there was very little to differentiate them from their parishioners. They spent their lives embedded in lay society and in many ways lived according to the masculine ideals of laymen. Even prior to their promotion to the priesthood or major orders, secular clergy were socialized to live like their male peers through social interactions and expectations. Participation in male culture inculcated the masculine behaviors prevalent among laymen. In theory, becoming a priest meant that a man renounced his existing masculine identity for a new gender identity centered

Lees (Minneapolis: University of Minnesota Press, 1994), 61–72; Stanley Chojnacki, "Subaltern Patriarchs: Patrician Bachelors in Renaissance Venice," in *Medieval Masculinities: Regarding Men in the Middle Ages*, ed. Clare A. Lees (Minneapolis: University of Minnesota Press, 1994), 73–90; Janet L. Nelson, "Monks, Secular Men, and Masculinity, c. 900," in *Masculinity in Medieval Europe*, ed. Dawn M. Hadley (London: Longman, 1999), 121–42. See also Sharon Farmer, *Surviving Poverty in Medieval Paris: Gender, Ideology, and the Daily Lives of the Poor* (Ithaca: Cornell University Press, 2002), 25–28; Judith M. Bennett and Amy M. Froide, eds., *Singlewomen in the European Past, 1250–1800* (Philadelphia: University of Pennsylvania Press, 1999).

    3. David Herlihy, *Medieval Households* (Cambridge, MA: Harvard University Press, 1985), 116–17, 129; Shannon McSheffrey, "Men and Masculinity in Late Medieval London Civic Culture: Governance, Patriarchy, and Reputation," in *Conflicted Identities and Multiple Masculinities*, ed. Jacqueline Murray (New York: Garland Press, 1999), 243–78. See also Neal, *Masculine Self*, 72–73.

on celibacy. Yet the demand for celibacy ran counter to societal norms as well as clerics' experiences and notions of masculinity. Hence, it was not a failure to understand the Church expectation that led many parish clergy to not practice celibacy. It was perhaps simply easier and more a matter of habit that clerics continued to follow the more familiar ideals of lay masculinity found in the villages in which they had grown up and where they served in local churches. Parish clerics, then, negotiated their own gender identity among the demands of their profession, parish life, and the ingrained notions of masculinity learned in childhood. The result was the inclusion of sexuality into their definition of manhood, typified by marriage-like unions with women that produced a marital household with children.

That medieval churchmen observed secular values and engaged in many of the same social and cultural practices as laymen was not, by any means, new. The need to separate the clergy from the secular world and emphasize their distinctiveness from the laity was, after all, one of the reasons for prohibiting clerical marriage.[4] Reformers understood that marriage integrated clergymen as husbands and fathers into the community to a greater extent and that a man's responsibility to his family could present a considerable distraction from his priestly office. The insistence on clerical celibacy and the dissolution of clerical families was also meant to prevent the alienation of church property to the sons and daughters of priests, especially the hereditary succession of the office from father to son. This is why church law in the late eleventh and twelfth centuries evolved to exclude the sons of clergy from ecclesiastical office.[5] Nevertheless, the eleventh-century religious reforms that sought to disengage clerics from these worldly concerns had the unintended consequence of destabilizing the gender system. The mandate for clerical celibacy meant that a significant portion of the male population could no longer prove their manhood by way of marriage. Furthermore, the children of clergy were considered illegitimate and thus prohibited from inheriting from their fathers. According to Vern Bullough, clerics, then, were stripped of the three most important markers of masculinity in medieval society: "impregnating women, protecting dependents, and serving as provider to one's family."[6]

The medieval Church of the eleventh and twelfth centuries endeavored to redefine clerical masculinity and offer alternative models that excluded women and biological children to convince married clergy to eschew contemporary

---

4. Paul Beaudette, ' "In the World but Not of It': Clerical Celibacy as a Symbol of the Medieval Church," in Frassetto, *Medieval Purity and Piety*, 23–46.

5. Schimmelpfennig, " 'Ex fornicatione nati.' "

6. Vern L. Bullough, "On Being Male in the Middle Ages," in *Medieval Masculinities: Regarding Men in the Middle Ages*, ed. Clare A. Lees (Minneapolis: University of Minnesota Press, 1994), 34.

ideas of masculinity. The new priestly ideal promoted priestly functions, in particular access to the eucharist, as an important characteristic that separated priests from the laity, while at the same time, emphasizing the manliness of those who could radically distance themselves from female impurity and familial entanglements. Clerical elites endorsed messages that emphasized the substitution of traditional marriage with spiritual marriage to the parish church and the substitution of biological fatherhood with the pastoral care of "spiritual children."[7] These reformers were in essence challenging the hegemonic ideals of secular masculinity that up until twelfth century could be found among both clergymen and laymen. This reconstruction of clerical manhood, however, was counterintuitive to an ideal that connected marriage closely with an adult male gender identity. These new models of clerical masculinity were ultimately unsuccessful for secular clergy because the ideals of lay masculinity continued to dominate the societal perception of what it meant to be man. The importance of marriage for men and the privileged status of paterfamilias in medieval society could not be so easily replaced with spiritual fatherhood and spiritual marriage to the Church.

In fact, the exposure of Catalan clergymen to these models of clerical masculinity propagated by Gregorian reformers and found among intellectual elites is difficult to find anywhere outside of synodal legislation. There is not one example to be found in the Crown of Aragon of a Catalan bishop or a Catalan male saint whose vita was written to celebrate the new priestly ideals of the Gregorian reform. Such an absence of hagiographical texts produced or even circulated in Catalunya promoting priestly celibacy and the ideas of spiritual fatherhood is telling and further underscores the extent to which the reforms of the Gregorian era bypassed Iberia. If parish clergy were exposed to these clerical models of manhood espoused in clerical literature, then it is apparent that they rejected these alternatives to marriage and biological fatherhood. The situation in Catalunya reveals that clergy were not exposed to a clerical culture that greatly valued celibacy, considering that concubinage and sexual incontinence among parish clergy, clerical elites, and regular clergy was so omnipresent. It is difficult, moreover, to pinpoint a flourishing intellectual culture that permeated all levels of the clerical population. The cathedral library in Girona owned various juridical texts and only one theological treatise by the fifteenth century. Although libraries in Barcelona as well as libraries housed in Dominican and Franciscan communities had a greater collection of books, there appears to have been a preference for legal and theological texts

7. Miller, "Masculinity, Reform, and Clerical Culture," 49–50; McLaughlin, "Secular and Spiritual Fatherhood"; Thibodeaux, *Manly Priest*, 120–21.

because hagiographical texts are largely missing from their inventories.[8] The books that parish clergy had access to are unknown. It is unlikely, however, that clerics serving in predominantly rural areas and small towns would have read juridical and theological texts, or known the lives of male saints known for their chastity and spiritual prowess that were popular among clerical elites and monastic intellectuals across Europe.[9] Episcopal registers from the dioceses of Barcelona and Girona, moreover, reveal that an incredibly small minority of the parish clergy had received a university education in the fourteenth century.[10] Some among the bishops, canons, and jurists centered in cathedral cities had had a university education, usually from Bologna, but the vast majority of secular clergy serving in parishes missed out on this experience. Neither Barcelona nor Girona, and certainly not Vic or Urgell, was known to be a vibrant intellectual center in late medieval Europe. In addition, the university of Lleida, founded circa 1300, did not have the same reputation or prestige in the academic world that nearby university centers such as Paris, Bologna, and Montpellier enjoyed. Ramon Peñafort, Ramon Martí, and Nicolau Eimeric, famous Dominicans, as well as the Franciscans Ramon Llull and Arnau de Vilanova, after all, had all been educated outside of Catalunya, in Bologna, Montpellier, and Paris.[11]

The Dominican Order, which was known throughout Europe for its high level of education, had only a small presence in the Crown of Aragon compared to the number of convents established in France and Germany. The influence of Dominicans on the clerical intellectual culture in Catalunya was not profound, especially at the parish level, because they were closely connected to the king and the royal court. Robin Vose notes that "Given the

---

8. Marquès, "La iglesia de Gerona," in Martí Bonet, *Historia de las diócesis españolas,* 537; Baucells i Reig, *Vivir en la edad media,* 1: 442. Dominican convents in the Crown of Aragon, according to Robin Vose, were quite conservative in their holdings because their libraries consisted mostly of theological treatises and canon law texts; *Dominicans, Muslims and Jews in the Medieval Crown of Aragon* (Cambridge, UK: University of Cambridge Press, 2009), 116–17. For the Franciscans, see Jill R. Webster, *Els Menorets: The Franciscans in the Realms of Aragon from St. Francis to the Black Death* (Toronto: Pontifical Institute of Mediaeval Studies, 1993), 265–68.

9. See the essays based on the saints' lives and personal writings of clergy in Cullum and Lewis, *Holinesss and Masculinity in the Middle Ages*; Thibodeaux, *Negotiating Clerical Identities*; Dyan Elliot, "Pollution, Illusion, and Masculine Disarray," in *Constructing Medieval Sexuality,* ed. Karma Lochrie, Peggy McCracken, and James A. Schultz (Minneapolis: University of Minnesota Press, 1997), 1–23.

10. Josep Baucells has located ninety-two licenses for university study in the episcopal registers of Barcelona for the fourteenth century. For the fourteenth and fifteenth centuries, Josep Marquès has counted only thirty-eight licenses for study in the episcopal registers of Girona. Baucells i Reig, *Vivir en la edad media,* 1: 458; Marquès, "Iglesia de Gerona," 538.

11. Webster, *Els Menorets,* 262, 264–66. See also, Antonio Oliver, "Teólogos y hombres de ciencia," in *Historia de la Iglesia en España,* Vol. 2, ed. Javier Fernández Conde (Madrid: Biblioteca de Autores Cristianos, 1982), 218–39.

small numbers of friars in the Crown of Aragon, and the various demands for their time and services both within the convent itself and at the highest levels of lay and ecclesiastical society, the Dominican Order was limited in the extent to which it could minister effectively to less exalted individual members of the local populace—and it could not do so in regions where it had no regular presence."[12] The Franciscans, however, were present in greater numbers than the Dominicans in Catalunya. Many of the friars came from the merchant class or from noble origins and were strongly tied to urban centers where much of their support came from wealthy citizens.[13] The cultural impact of the Franciscans in Catalunya, according to Jill Webster, was more significant in their contribution to the development of Gothic architecture and art seen in the churches and convents constructed in the thirteenth and fourteenth centuries throughout the Iberian Peninsula. The Franciscan contribution to a scholastic environment, in contrast, was subtle and felt more in the latter half of the fourteenth century, after the Black Death, when the writings of Francesc Eiximenis, considered a more successful Catalan writer than Ramon Llull, influenced the intellectual scene in Catalunya.[14] The extent to which parish clergy outside the cathedral cities of Barcelona and Girona came into contact and were influenced by the mendicants is hard to know, but it is doubtful that they a great impact on the model of clerical behavior that parish clergy followed. Given that the Dominicans in the Crown of Aragon also had issues with celibacy, as Michael Vargas has observed,[15] it seems unlikely that the parish priests used the Dominicans as an alternative model to an active sexuality.

The reality is that an educational, social, and economic chasm existed between clergymen serving in parishes and privileged clergymen who secured lucrative benefices and important offices in the administration of the diocese or served in positions of authority in the mendicant orders. It is hard to imagine, therefore, that the model of masculinity valued by the high-powered and highly educated clergy was the same model followed by parish clergy. Although it is clear that there was a variance of masculine ideals and practice at all levels of the ecclesiastical hierarchy, it is significant that so many parish clerics in Catalunya modeled their family life after the example of the laity and chose to be husbands and fathers. The personal writings of parish clergy do not exist to allow us to examine the language and imagery of how they conceptualized

---

12. Vose, *Dominicans, Muslims and Jews*, 88, 75–77, 84–93. See also Vargas, *Taming a Brood of Vipers*, 78–79, 102.

13. Webster, *Els Menorets*, 39, 106–13, 137–48.

14. Ibid., 260, 264–66, 268–74.

15. Vargas, *Taming a Brood of Vipers*, 141, 153.

their own masculinity, but the voices and experiences of lower-level clergy can be recovered from visitation and church court records. Their actions and testimony provide evidence of how these men responded to the social and economic situations in their environment. Their behaviors, in effect, reveal how clerics negotiated their masculine identity when caught between the Church standards for clerical behavior and the more pervasive secular notions of manhood. The ubiquitous presence of clerical unions suggests that clerics needed families precisely because having a family was proof of manhood in their social milieu. Like a lay union, a clerical union announced a man's adult status in society and the establishment of a household indicated his role as provider and master of his domain. Fatherhood, too, was a sure sign of virility.

What follows here is an attempt to reconstruct the lives of parish clergy to show that their unions with women and their role as paterfamilias were intricately tied to their identity as men. To best understand how clerics carried out their roles as husband and fathers, it is necessary to demonstrate that clerics fashioned their relationships along the same lines as the laity. The similarity between lay and clerical relationships was, in one sense, a result of socialization in which couples, regardless of their religious or lay status, imitated what they knew. If clerics were emulating laymen and their roles as husbands, providers, and fathers, then my first task is to show clerics performing these roles. Documents of practice, such as episcopal visitations, indicate that the practice of marriage had not died out among the Catalan clergy. Evidence that parishioners considered clerical unions to be like marriages and that clerics treated their companions as de facto wives can be seen in the terms used to describe these unions: *tenet eam ut uxorem, tenet eam in domo ut uxor, in uxorem, sicut vir uxori* and *tanquam vir cum uxore*.[16] Parishioners in the small village of Horta, for instance, admitted to calling Durera the wife of the priest Romeo.[17] Parishioners employed phrases such as *like man and wife* because they identified the manner in which the couple performed the duties of a husband and wife. It is important to note that simply bearing a cleric's child did not make the woman his de facto wife or concubine. Because temporary sexual escapades could result in pregnancy, parishioners and episcopal officials identified signs of domesticity in which the woman performed wifely tasks as evidence of concubinage. As a cleric's chief helper, women cleaned, bought and prepared food, did laundry, and took care of their partner's "affairs." These women frequently lived in the cleric's home under the pretext that they were only a

---

16. Josep Baucells i Reig has found similar descriptions of the relationships between clerics and their partners in *Vivir en la edad media*, 3: 2575–76.

17. AEV, Visites, no. 1200/2, 58v. (1331).

servant (ancilla or pedisseca), but in reality they functioned as so much more. They bore children, acted as nursemaids, and contributed to the family household through their labor. Quite simply, a cleric's partner acted as a lover, wife, and mother. While episcopal visitors considered a cleric and a woman eating, drinking, and sleeping together to be a sign of concubinage, it was also a sign of domesticity in that the cleric and woman were perceived to be establishing a household and maintaining a family.

As far as episcopal officials and parishioners were concerned, financial support was an important indication of a cleric's investment in the relationship and was often connected to parishioners' perceptions of how a cleric treated his woman. In the town of Castelló d'Empúries in 1329, neighbors described the priest Bernat Serena as providing Ermesenda, the mother of his two children, with food and clothing "as if she were his wife." Indeed, according to many, Ermesenda was dressed more "splendidly and richly" than other wives in the parish. In the opinion of one man, Bernat abided by the wishes of Ermesenda "in so much or more than if he were her husband." Similarly, the villagers of Sant Feliu de Cabrera in 1310 described their rector Jaume Ferrer, who publicly kept Jaçmeta and their five children, as "providing for her at the table and in bed as a man for his wife." The community considered the rector and Jaçmeta to hold their goods in common, given that Jaume had bought a house belonging to the church and had given it to Jaçmeta. She had then converted the house into a place that sold bread and wine to supplement the family's income.[18] Even when couples tried to avoid an episcopal fine by living in separate houses, a cleric's providing food and clothing for a woman and child was still seen as a sign of concubinage. For instance, the priest Ramon did not keep Maria Almara in his home (although she freely entered his), but because he provided for the majority of her "necessities," parishioners still labeled this a relationship in which Ramon "publicly kept" Maria.[19] In the eyes of parishioners and the couples involved, sex alone did not define these unions. For example, the priest Guillem and Saurina were still seen as a couple despite the fact that they were considered too old to have sex. Not only did the couple have many children, but Guillem also brought foodstuffs to Saurina's house, and it was their son who prepared Guillem's food.[20] Because the role of a husband was to provide for his wife and children, medieval people recognized that many clergymen performed the same role for their own families.

---

18. ADG, Processos, no. 103, 7r., 24r.v., 27r.v. (1329); Benito i Monclús, *Parroquies del maresm*, no. 18 (1310), 284.

19. ADG, Visites, no. 1, 3r. (1314).

20. ADG, Visites, no. 3, 11r. (1321); ADG, Visites, no. 4, 32v.–33r. (1329).

Signs of affection between clerical couples were also evident to the community. Parishioners noted when women tended to ailing partners during
times of bad health or when clerics such as the vicar Arnau Martell cared for
the mother of his four children during her multiple illnesses. For five years,
the chaplain Guillem Oliba had looked after his woman even though it was
evident to parishioners that the couple could no longer have sex.[21] Elderly
couples tended to one another even when they had adult children to care for
them. Some clerics explained that they remained with their elderly (*vetula*) partner out of poverty or necessity, but it seems likely that more than a sense of
obligation motivated the priest de Santa Maria de Palautordera to watch over
his blind spouse.[22] Some actions, such as that of the deacon Guillem, suggest
deep emotional ties. The deacon was so distraught when Maria de Casis ended
their relationship and evicted him from their home that he committed one of
the gravest sins of all—he took his own life. Passion and violent emotion can
also be seen in the case of the priest Berenguer Molar and Mercera, who left
her husband for Berenguer. The two men not only came to blows over Mercera, but Berenguer was also suspected of later killing her husband. And
whether neighbors or family considered it a youthful indiscretion or simply
an infatuation, some women went against the wishes of their parents and
eloped, or left their husband to form a new union with a priest.[23] Risking dis-
inheritance and possible banishment from one's family for love of a cleric was
a daring move indeed. Yet we need not rely on extreme cases of suicide, homicide, and elopement to see these emotional bonds.

Although forthright declarations of love and affection do not appear in the
sources, people advertised their emotional relationships by performing acts
that were interpreted as meaningful and signaled love, friendship, or goodwill.
In studying the emotional sociology of social hatred in the medieval Mediterranean city of Marseille, Daniel Lord Smail notes that emotional states were
"never seen as internal states of minds"; rather, "emotions of love and hatred

21. ADG, Visites, no. 4, 92v. (1329). See also ADG, Visites, no. 3, 21r. (1321); ADG, Processos,
no. 78, 6r. (1324); AEV, Visites, no. 1200/2, 31r. (1331); ACV, no. 2, Calaix 31/43, 7v. (1313).

22. Baucells i Reig, *Vivir en la edad media*, 3: 2576–77. Other examples of elderly couples appear in
AEV, Visites, no. 1200/1, 13r. (1300); AEV, Visites, no. 1200/2, 64v. (1331); ACV, Visites, no. 1, Calaix
31/43, 34r. (1312); ACV, Visites, no. 3, 22r. (1313); ACV, Visites, no. 5, Calaix 31/43, 17v. (1315); ACV,
Visites, no. 7, Calaix 31/43, 35r. (1314); ACV, Visites, no. 8, Calaix 31/43, 26r. (1315); ACV, Visites,
no. 8, Calaix 31/43, 27r. (1315); ADG, Visites, no. 1, 72r.v., 88v. (1315); ADB, Visites, no. 2, 75r. (1315);
ADB, Visites, no. 4, 60r. (1336).

23. ADG, Visites, no. 5, 145v. (1333). In another example, the father Guillem Caradells also had
plans to marry his daughter, but the rector Guillem Coma had removed her from his home before
Caradells's daughter could have a "virum." The rector's action was a source of enmity between the
rector and her family members; AEV, Visites, no. 1200/2, 68v. (1331).

were seen as patterned behaviors and performances." Smail observes that love and affection were demonstrated when two people are described as "conversing frequently, sharing food and wine, sleeping in the same house or the same bed, and generally acting as housemates."[24] The signs of domesticity and descriptions of priests who lived like man and wife with their female companions indicate that these unions were more than just social and economic but were based on affection, if not love. That so many clergymen continued to keep their families in the face of repeated episcopal fines underscores their importance to these men. Over a period of twenty-three-plus years, the priest Mateu Carbó repeatedly dealt with the intrusions of episcopal officials but refused to be separated from Sibil·la and their seven children.[25] The priority given to the family is evident when clerics faced a choice between their parish or their women and children. The clerics serving in the previously mentioned parish of Cogolls were not the only ones who left the ministry of their church in favor of their family when discord within the community threatened their loved ones. According to the parishioners of Campllong, when relations with a certain villager soured, the priest Arnau Riparia left the parish and took Na Doucha and his child with him, presumably to protect his family.[26] Indeed, we can infer from the stability of these relationships, the provision of food and clothing for a lover and offspring, and the hardships clerical families faced when living in separate homes or in neighboring towns that affection was at least a factor in keeping families together.

Setting up a household and financially supporting one's family was certainly a marker of adult masculinity in medieval society, but it was also important for clerics to create a union that functioned as an economic unit. Barbara Hanawalt has described peasant marriages as "based firmly on the partnership of husband and wife, each contributing their separate skills and their separate domains of labor." Medieval marriage was certainly not a partnership of equals, but the labor of women, especially peasant women, was crucial to the survival of the household. A woman and children were indispensable to a clergyman whose benefice included land that had to be farmed or who bought

24. Daniel Lord Smail, *The Consumption of Justice: Emotions, Publicity, and Legal Culture in Marseille, 1264–1423* (Ithaca: Cornell University Press, 2003), 100–101.

25. ADG, Visites, no. 1, 85r. (1315); ADG, Visites, no. 3, 32r.v. (1321); ADG, Visites, no. 4, 22v. (1329); ADG, Obligationes de Penes, no. 1, 3r. (1336). In 1315, Sibil·la and Mateu reportedly had two children; in 1329, six children; and by 1336, a total of seven children. In 1336, Mateu was ordered, under penalty of a fine of 200 sous, to expel Sibil·la and their seven children from his home. It is likely that the couple continued their relationship after 1336.

26. ADG, Visites, no. 2, 41v.–42v. (1315); ADG, Visites no. 6, 60v. (1339); ADG, Visites, no. 4, 92r.v. (1329).

land to supplement his income.[27] Even the episcopal visitor in a visit to the parish of Begur in 1347 understood the role of women in helping with the farmstead when he banned Guillema not only from entering the rector Mateu Duran's house but also from working in Mateu's vineyard, gardens, and other lands. Considering the rector's extensive holdings, Guillema and their children were most likely responsible for managing these properties.[28] Occasionally we catch other glimpses of how a cleric's domestic partner and children contributed to the family household. Berengaria worked the priest Bernat's land, growing flax, and Guillema and her six children with the rector of Sant Esteve de Peladaries assisted in harvesting crops. Sança collected saffron, a valuable commodity, for the priest Guillem Ferriol, and Guillema Bosc gathered olives for the rector of Bigues and extracted oil from the olives.[29] These women were clearly working to produce products that were profitable in a local market economy.[30] Some women even helped with clerical duties as a way of ensuring the family's livelihood. Dolça made the hosts to assist her clerical partner and frequently rang the church bells, lighted candles, and attended to other things in the church.[31] The children of the priest Berenguer in Montfullà rang the bells for mass and did "many things in the church" to help their father.[32] Although we can imagine these children playing in the nave of the church, it is likely that they were also responsible for tidying, sweeping, and aiding their father with small tasks to care for their parish church.

The economic partnership of clerical couples is further illustrated in the relationship between the sacrist Bernat Sabater and Guillema in the parish of

---

27. Barbara A. Hanawalt, "Peasant Women's Contributions to the Home Economy in Late Medieval England," in *Women and Work in Pre-Industrial Europe*, ed. Barbara A. Hanawalt (Bloomington: Indiana University Press, 1986), 17; Barbara A. Hanawalt, *The Ties That Bound: Peasant Families in Medieval England* (New York: Oxford University Press, 1986), 141–55, 158–61. See also Cristina Segura Graiño, "La sociedad feudal," in *Historia de las mujures en España*, ed. Elisa Garrido González (Madrid: Editorial Síntesis, 1991), 166–69.

28. ADG, Imposicions de Penes, no. 1, 70r.v. (1347). Women mostly did the raising of sheep, pigs, and chickens, including the making of cheese; Thomas N. Bisson, *Tormented Voices: Power, Crisis, and Humanity in Rural Catalonia, 1140–1200* (Cambridge, MA: Harvard University Press, 1998), 43.

29. ADG, Visites, no. 3, 22r. (1321); Visitatio diversarum ecclesiarum civis et diocesis Barcelonensis facta per Pontium episcopum ab anno 1303 ad 1310, HMML, microfilm no. 31951, Visites, no. 1, 76v. (1307), 84v. (1307), and 127v. (1310). Bonanata Caçabascera and her three children helped the priest Pere Falines during the harvest; ADG, Visites, no. 1, 7r. (1314).

30. Saffron was quite valuable. Gregory Milton observes that the local production of saffron in the area around Santa Coloma de Queralt was increasing in the fourteenth century. Olive oil, wine, and saffron were important for local consumption as well as for international trade; Milton, *Market Power*, 13, 102–3.

31. ADG, Visites, no. 6, 71v.–72r. (1340). In another example, Guillema de Bosc, the mother of his two children, helped the priest Guerau make the holy oil for the church; ADB, Visites, no. 2, 26v. (1313).

32. ADG, Visites fragmentaris, 31r.v. (1320).

Sant Martí de la Vajol. The priest Berenguer Polverell testified that one day in May the sacrist Bernat had called on him to deliver mass for the burial of a parishioner. Berenguer recounted that, while reciting the gospel for the funeral, he was in need of hosts and was unable to proceed with the mass "until Guillema, the concubine of the sacrist, sent the key to the sacristy where the hosts were." Evidently the sacrist Bernat was out of town, and he had entrusted the keys to the sacristy not to his colleague Berenguer but to his concubine. Guillema was also entrusted with preparing the dough and helped Bernat make the holy hosts. Bernat, in turn, helped Guillema, who kept a tavern in her home where she sold bread and wine. He frequently managed the tavern in her absence.[33]

Clerics who could afford to buy property purchased houses and farmsteads to support their families. The priest Berenguer bought a home with enough land for Beatriu to look after cows, pigs, and fowl. It seems likely that their four children would have aided in the care of the domestic animals.[34] The rector of Querós and Guillema CesFrabrages needed a new home for their three sons and three daughters. The couple built the house across the street from the church, and Guillema directed its construction "at the rector's expense."[35] Purchasing property and building a home, of course, was just one way that a cleric could boldly publicize both his wealth and his family. Arnau Mora, the rector of Sant Pere de Sanborns, could afford to buy more than one home. According to the rector Arnau, he had purchased one home for his son and

---

33. ADG, Visites, no. 1, 75v.–76r. (1315). The sacrist Guillem de Maliver in the parish of Siurana also entrusted the keys of the church to the Raimunda Saura, the mother of his children; ADG, Imposicions de Penes, no. 1, 99v. (1355).

34. ADG, Visites, no. 6, 3v. (1338); ADG, Visites, no. 4, 73r. (1329). Other examples include Guillem Arnau, the capellan of Palol de Vila-robau, who bought a manse outside the parish for his domestic partner and three children; ADG, Visites, no. 9, 30v.–31r. (1350). Parishioners reported that the capellan lived mostly with his family on the manse and infrequently stayed at the house that belonged to his benefice. The beneficed cleric En Ripoll çaFabrega, who served in the chapel of Gurb in the diocese of Vic, kept his woman and children on his manse called Pou des Coyl; AEV, Visites, no. 1200/1, 27r. (1330). Beatriu, the concubine of the rector of Sant Pere de Pla, lived on the rector's manse with their two children—a manse that he "tenet ad laborationem"; AEV, Visites, no. 1200/3, 24v. (1332). In the diocese of Barcelona, examples of clerics buying property or farmsteads for their families are just as numerous; Baucells i Reig, Vivir en la edad media, 3: 2555nn. 103, 105, 106.

35. "Item quod idem rector tenet concubinam vocatam Guillelmam cesFrarages a qua habet tres filios et tres filias et comedunt omnes in domo rectoris et dicta mulier construxit hospicium coram dicta ecclesia ad expensas rectoris." AEV, Visites, no. 1200/2, 82v. (1332). For more examples of clerics who bought homes for their families, see ADG, Visites, no. 4, 144r.v. The cleric Pere, serving in the parish of Capsec, bought Mateva and his two children a house in the nearby parish of Socarrats. The rector of Sobremont, in the diocese of Vic, bought his woman, the daughter of Pere Salort, a house in the parish; AEV, Visites, no. 1200/1, 9r. (1330). Likewise, the rector of Santa Eulàlia d'Ahuri bought a home for Maria de ÇaVila and their children in the diocese of Urgell, as did the chaplain of Sant Martí de çaCorriu, who bought a house for his woman and child in a nearby village; ACV, Calaix 31/43, Visites, no. 1, 24r. (1312); ACV, Calaix 31/43, Visites, no. 3, 36v. (1314).

another for Maria, the mother of his three children from "his own goods."[36] Considering the number of parish clergy who managed to buy additional homes and land to care for their families, it is clear that they were quite often among the wealthiest in their village. Their relative prosperity is evident in the frequency with which parishioners accused clergymen of engaging in usury or charging higher prices for grain, most likely because they had easier access to cash than many of their neighbors. In some cases, lending money at interest was a family affair. The son of the capellan of Pabruna used his father's income to loan money, and not only did the rector of Santa Maria d'Enuey charge interest when he leased land and vineyards to his parishioners but his concubine was also involved in these "usurious contracts."[37]

It is difficult to locate the last wills and testaments that show clergymen passing on their property and goods to their women and biological children because canon law prohibited the illegitimate sons and daughters of priests from inheriting from their fathers.[38] Nevertheless, there is some evidence from a small number of extant wills that clerics were able to provide for their families from the hereafter. The priest Guillem de Bruguera in 1362 entrusted a fellow priest from the parish of Sant Julià de Beuda with ensuring that his concubine Raimunda Dolça received the movable goods from his home. Raimunda most likely received her portion since the vicar general approved the execution of the will.[39] Episcopal officials may have looked the other way, especially for clerics of high status in the church. In his testament, the archdeacon of Besalú, Arnau de Soler, founded the Benedictine monastery Vilanera for his daughter Felipa, which he placed under the direction of his sister Fresca, then prioress of Pedardell. The archdeacon wisely chose to make his sister Fresca and the monastery his universal heirs with the stipulation that, when his daughter Felipa reached the proper age, she would become abbess of Vilanera.[40] Other, less well-to-do clerical families may have had some difficulty receiving their inheritance. When the episcopal visitor learned that the 1327 last will and testament of the priest Guillem de Pedrinyà outlined that his

36. ADB, Visites, no. 2, 74v. (1315).

37. ACV, Calaix 31/43, Visites, no. 5, 8r. (1315); ACV, Calaix 31/43, Visites, no. 4, 18v. (1314). In the diocese of Urgell, the son of the priest Bernat de Casis and Na Borda den Gual was involved in usury; AEV, Visites, no. 1200/2, 4r. (1331). The son of the priest of Cubelles in the diocese of Barcelona also engaged in usury; Martí Bonet, "Visitas pastorales," 703.

38. Brundage, Law, Sex, and Christian Society, 20.

39. ADG, D 161, 73v.–74r. (1362). Guillem de Bruguera also left 420 sous and two pieces of silver to the poor and ordered his executor to pay off his debts.

40. Josep M. Marquès, "Set cenobis femenins de l'empordà," in Estudis del Baix Empordà no. 15 (1996), 84–89. For the many misadventures of Felipa de Soler, see ADG, Visites, no. 6, 125v.–137r.v. (1340); Puig i Oliver and Marquès i Planagumà, Lletres del bisbe de Girona, document no. 395, no. 406, no. 417, no. 418, no. 421, no. 506.

concubine Guillema Strader and her son Francesc were to receive "many goods" from Guillem's estate, the visitor ordered the executor to refrain from carrying out the will until he received approval from the bishop.[41] Conversely, unless relatives contested a cleric's bequest to his children or "concubine," ecclesiastical authorities may have been none the wiser and inheritors would have received their legacies without complication.

Although clergymen were not legally permitted to bequeath property to a woman who held the legal status of concubine, some made bequests to these women without revealing their status.[42] References to women as concubines per se rarely appear in the wills of clerics. Instead, the woman is identified as a servant (ancilla) who receives similar treatment as other family members or stands out because of the significance of the bequest. For instance, the rector Guillem Marrell bequeathed to his "ancilla" Guillema Figueres the right to live out the rest of her life in his house, in addition to 5 lliures, a bed, clothing, and other goods in the home. Likewise, the jurist Pere de Fontclara from Girona, outlined in his will that his "ancilla" Ermesenda should for the duration of her life receive a farmstead that he owned in the parish of Campllong, along with the rents and rights that pertained to the land, as well as a small piece of terraced land with vines that produced wine.[43] Pere's gift to Ermesenda was quite substantial given that she appears only as a servant in this document. In other examples, the cleric Ramon gave his ancilla Elisenda the largest sum of money bestowed on anyone in his will, 5 lliures; the rector Ponç Selvà was more circumspect when he granted Dolça, the woman "who stays with me," a small sum of money. Dolça is not identified as an ancilla because Ponç employed Elisenda as his actual servant—indicated by the granting of a much smaller sum of money to Elisenda than he gifted to Dolça.[44] The rector Ponç's

41. ADG, Visites, no. 1, 30v. (1315); Visites fragmentaris, quaderno no. 2, 27r. (1323). Guillem and Guillema first appear in a 1315 visitation, in which the couple and their sons and daughters lived next to the church in Santa Eulàlia de Noves.

42. Ruth Mazo Karras, "Marriage, Concubinage, and the Law" in *Law and the Illicit in Medieval Europe*, ed. Ruth Mazo Karras, Joel Kaye, and E. Ann Matter (Philadelphia: University of Pennsylvania Press, 2008), 122–27.

43. The testament of the jurist Pere de Fontclara is transcribed in Anna Gironella i Delgà, "L'hospital de Na Clara de Girona: Nous documents per a la història de l'assistència als pobres en època medieval," in *Miscel·lània en Honor de Josep Maria Marquès*, ed. Narcís Figueras i Pep Vila (Montserrat: Abadia de Montserrat, 2010), 145.

44. ADG, Notularum, no. 3, 172v.–173r. (1322) and no. 20, 112r. (1348); AEV, Testaments, ACF-3509 (1319–1324), 9r. (1319). The term *friend (amicae)* may have been used in a similar fashion. Although a woman designated as *friend* might simply have been nothing more than a friend, it is likely that this term could mean something more. The cleric Bernat Martí gave his "friend" Celia and his "friend" Berengaria Martí in Girona the sum of 25 sous. It is possible that Bernat had a sexual history with both women or that Celia, a single woman, was his concubine and Berengaria Martí was his daughter because the two shared the same last name; ADG, Notularum, no. 15, 4r.v. (1340).

testament underscores that, while the term *ancilla* could be code for a domestic partner in clerics' wills, it could also signify what it was meant to signify—a servant. It is likely that clergymen used this ambiguity to their advantage when they wanted to include their women in their wills.

In some last will and testaments, the relationship between a cleric and a woman is also suggestive of something more. Consider the will of the capellan Lancelot Bertran, who bestowed a significant sum on money, 40 lliures, and various items from his home on Raimunda, the daughter of Joan Sardina. To Raimunda's children, Maria, Englentina, Bartomeva, and Berenguer Bertran (her son), the capellan granted clothing, cloth, household items, money, and small pieces of property. The will, on its own, does not reveal the relationship between the capellan Lancelot Bertran and Raimunda, but Lancelot's concubinous union with Raimunda is confirmed in episcopal registers in which he was fined for keeping En Sardina's daughter and supporting their children.[45] In other cases, it is harder to confirm the relationship presented in a last will and testament. For instance, the priest Pere d'Espinal donated an unspecified amount of money to his servant Anna Espriu, who is identified as the mother and guardian of Guillema, possibly Pere's daughter. Arnau de Planes, the sacrist of Sant Feliu de Girona, left Maria de Riba of Pallerols money so that she could marry off her daughter. Although there is no evidence that confirms that Anna Espriu was the concubine of Pere d'Espinal, and that Guillema was his daughter, or proof that Maria de Riba had a sexual relationship with Arnau de Planes that produced a daughter, it is quite possible that beyond the vague ties presented in wills, a far more intimate bond existed among these men, women, and children.[46] Also, a woman who was not related to a cleric and who was granted a substantial amount of money raises questions about the nature of their relationship.[47] It is entirely possible these bequests were made to women on the basis of friendship rather than a past sexual

---

45. The capellan Lancelot Bertran's testament is recorded in AHG, Llibre de Testaments, no. 215, Figueres, 6 ides of April (1347). His relationship with Raimunda (aka Moneta), the daughter of En Sardina, is documented in ADG, Imposicions de Penes, no. 1, 48r. (1343); ADG, Obligacions de Penes, no. 1, 33v. (1344); ADG, Lletres, no. 8, 49v. (1344).

46. Arxiu Municipal de Girona, *Catàleg de pergamins del fons de l'Ajuntament de Girona (1144–182)*, Diplomataris 32, Vol. 1 (Barcelona: Fundació Noguera, 2005): no. 124 (1301), 112; no. 424 (1348), 338–39.

47. The beneficed cleric Jaume Molar gave 2.5 lliures to Celia, the wife of Bernat Albert—the exact sum that he bequeathed to his mother and sister. The fact that Celia is identified as a married woman does not mean that Jaume was not involved with her because a number of married women left their husbands for priests; ADG, Notularum, no. 9, 34v. (1334). See also ADG, Notularum, no. 20, 48v., 133v. (1348); ADG, Notularum, no. 21, 30r.v. (1348). In another example, the hebdomedarian Arnau Pont left "some houses and a garden" to Elisenda Gilaberta in his will that were to revert back to the "poor of Jesus Christ" after her death; Hillgarth and Silano, *Register "Notule Communium,"* 111.

relationship, but considering the prevalence of clerical unions, we have to consider that clerics purposefully used imprecise terms to disguise their intimate connection to these women. When a cleric obscured the relationships between him and a woman and her children in his will, he could then make bequests without openly acknowledging his union and progeny. Moreover, this practice is also found in the wills of priests in fourteenth-century Bergamo who likewise were able to overcome the issue of legal inheritance for their children by transferring property to their concubines prior to their death or bequeathing property to women who are identified as their domestic servants.[48] The scarcity of references to concubines and their children in the wills of priest is most likely due to the fact that including such references would leave a cleric's woman and children at the mercy of episcopal officials and was not a foolproof plan to ensure the financial security of his family. As Guillem de Pedrinya's example illustrates, when a cleric named his woman and son as inheriting a portion of his estate attempts to contravene these legalities were not always successful. What is more, clerical testators who openly acknowledged their biological heirs or concubine also took the risk that their kinfolk could easily contest the will.

Catalan clergy, however, did manage to buy land and homes for their de facto wives and children that would have remained in the family's hands after their death. During more than thirty-five years with Berengaria, the rector Berenguer had "sold" land, a homestead with a garden, to Berengaria, who in turn passed it along to their daughter. The rector also established a small piece of farmland belonging to his benefice, in return for a rent, to his son Arnau de Puigolo, who built a home there.[49] Other clerics chose to give their children money prior to their deaths, most likely to contract marriages, acquire land, or to start a business.[50] To ensure that domestic partners were taken care of and that their children could inherit, clerics purchased land and properties and then handed them over to a family member. The rector of Vilamilanys, who had one daughter and two sons with Elisenda Riudescelles, confessed to the visitor that he had purchased two homes for his family in the nearby parish of Sant Cugat. Although he lived with Elisenda in one home, he gave both houses

---

48. Cossar, "Clerical 'Concubines' in Northern Italy," 122–25; Roisin Cossar, "Defining Roles in the Clerical Household in Trecento Venice," *Viator* 45, no. 2 (2014): 237–45.

49. ADG, Visites, no. 3, 45r.v. (1321); Visites, no. 4, 155v.–156r. (1329). The rector Berenguer also sold land belonging to the church to Ermesenda dena Ferrara, a relative of his concubine Berengaria dena Ferrara. In another example, the rector Arnau Mora bought a number of homes from "his own goods." He gave one to his son in Vilafranca and another to the mother of his three children, Maria de Sobirats; ADB, Visites, no. 2, 74v. (1315).

50. ACV, Visites, Calaix 31/43, no. 5, 11r. (1314). It does not appear that the 1,000 sous were for a dowry because typically it would be identified as such in the documents.

to his daughter on the occasion of her marriage, including a small piece of land and 7.5 lliures (150 sous) for her dowry. The total dowry was worth 50 lliures (1,000 sous), suggesting that the rector had contracted a very good marriage for his only daughter.[51] Similarly, in an effort to provide for all of his six children, the rector Jaume de Veger bought a manse (farmstead) with diverse lands called Çes Pujades and had the title deed put in the name of his domestic partner Elisenda Cirada and their children.[52] Likewise, the rector of Sant Feliu d'Estiula bought a manse for Sibil·la and his three daughters and son. According to parishioners, the rector had transferred the property to Sibil·la, and she was in possession of the deed.[53] Sibil·la was now the owner of the property, and therefore she could ensure the succession of the farmstead to her children. As Roisin Cossar has noted in her study of clerical concubinage in northern Italy, the concern of both parents to provide for the future welfare of their children underscores the marital quality of clerical unions.[54] In the same vein, the extent to which clerics protected the financial well-being of their women and children highlights how seriously they took their role as husband and father.

What is noteworthy about the number of clerics who provided legacies for their families is that, unlike synodal legislation in France and Germany that prohibited priests from purchasing property with the intent to pass it on to their offspring as a legacy and that prohibited bequeathing church goods or property obtained from church resources to children, concubine, or relatives, Catalan synodal statutes did not specifically address clerics and their inheritors.[55] Provincial and synodal legislation, of course, mimicked canon law, which banned the bastard sons (*spurii*) of clergymen from entering clerical orders and from inheriting their fathers' ecclesiastical benefices.[56] Yet the only

---

51. Visitatio diversarum, HMML, microfilm no. 31951, Visites, no. 1, 9v. (1304). Similarly, the sacrist Guillem in Requesens gave his daughter a *mansatum* (lands pertaining to a rural homestead) as a dowry; ADG, Visites, no. 3, 11r. (1321).

52. AEV, Visites, no. 1200/2, 77v. (1330–1332).

53. AEV, Visites, no. 1200/3, 21v. (1332).

54. Cossar, "Clerical 'Concubines' in Northern Italy," 121.

55. See Schimmelpfennig, "'Ex fornicatione nati,'" 32–33; Kathryn Ann Taglia, '"On Account of Scandal . . .': Priests, Their Children, and the Ecclesiastical Demand for Celibacy," *Florilegium* 14 (1995–1996): 64–65.

56. For Church legislation dealing with the children of clergy, see Constance M. Rousseau, "Pope Innocent III and Familial Relationships of Clergy and Religious," *Studies in Medieval and Renaissance History* 14 (1933): 107–48; Laura Wertheimer, "Children of Disorder: Clerical Parentage, Illegitimacy, and Reform in the Middle Ages," *Journal of the History of Sexuality* 15, no. 3 (2006): 382–407. For Catalunya, see Pons i Guri, "Constitucions conciliars tarraconenses," 79. Also, synodal statutes from the diocese of Barcelona, such as "De Possessionibus Ecclesiarum," do not address clerics passing on church property or their own personal property to their children; Hillgarth and Silano, "Compilation of the Diocesan Synods," 115–16.

statute that could have affected inheritance is from the 1339 Girona synod; it prohibited clerics from buying homes for their women within the limits of the parish where they served, regardless of whether a cleric used his own funds or resources belonging to the church to purchase the home.[57] The aim of such a statute (as I argue in chapter 1) was to limit clerics from the more flagrant and public display of maintaining families, particularly in that the decree is vague concerning a cleric buying a home outside of his parish. If the issue was property that could potentially end up in the hands of the children, then we would expect to see language in the decree that specifically forbid clergy from buying homes or assets for their children. Taking into account the prevalence of clerical couples and the large number of children produced from such unions, it is doubtful that episcopal officials would not have expected clergymen to provide inheritances for their offspring. That such provincial and synodal legislation is nonexistent further suggests that church officials accepted or at least were resigned to the reality that clerics maintained families. Evidence that clerics provided for their families can certainly be found; for example, the priest Arnau provided a home for Mateva and his three children with the resources from his benefice, and the capellan of Santa Gracià used church goods to buy property for his children.[58] It is remarkable, however, that parishioners made this allegation infrequently to visitors, considering the prevalence of clerical families and their offspring throughout Catalunya. Given that alienating the property or rents belonging to their benefice would eventually bring about the attention of episcopal officials, clerics knew that doing so put their families at risk. Indeed, they may have been cautious about selling the lands or rents attached to their benefice precisely because such action fostered resentment among parishioners, which would in turn prompt the episcopal visitor to look into the matter. Although episcopal authorities tolerated the custom of clerics keeping families, they would not have been inclined to allow clerics to alienate church property. A widespread practice of

---

57. ". . . statuimus quod decetero nullus clericus qui beneficio ecclesiastico sustentetur, alicui mulieri cum qua publice peccat, vel de qua sit graviter diffamatus, emat domum aliquam infra terminos sue parrochie constitutam, vel domum in qua ipsa mulier habitat, intret sine iusta causa et per canones approbata, vel eam ad domum quam ipse clericus habitat venire seu intrare faciat seu permittat. Qui vero contrarium fecerit, penam quinquaginta solidorum per nos piis usibus applicandum ipse pro vice qualibet se noverit incurrisse." Noguer i Musqueras and Pons Guri, "Constitucions sinodals de Girona," 133.

58. AEV, Visites, no. 1200/2, 21v. (1331). In another example, the chaplain of Santa Gracià used Church goods to buy property for his children; ACV, Visites, Calaix 31/43, no. 4, 6r. (1314). A visitor to the parish of Santa Gracià in 1315 also reported that the capellan celebrated mass with his son; ACV, Visites, no. 5, Calaix 31/43, 4r. (1315).

bequeathing church resources to family members would have caused officials to respond with stringent synodal legislation.

Communities expected, nevertheless, that clerics would support their
children and looked unfavorably on those who abandoned their families. For
instance, a parishioner found the rector Pere Granata's behavior so distasteful
that he informed the visitor that a three-year-old child belonging to Pere had
died from starvation because the rector had refused to support his daughter.
Taking advantage of a virgin was also seen as reprehensible. After deflowering, impregnating, and abandoning Brunissenda, the sacrist of Sant Sadurní de
Garrigoles left the village because he feared her family and friends.[59] Societal
norms dictated that men had an obligation to feed, clothe, and care for their
children. According to Debra Blumental, masters in fifteenth-century Valencia
who impregnated their slave women were also expected to financially support their offspring.[60] Providing for one's children, however, was not simply a
societal obligation but a sign of adult manhood. The cleric Bonanat Pagès, who
claimed to have renounced his family but was later accused of providing food
to them, implored the visitor to understand that he had given "sustenance for
life" to Sibil·la and his two sons to ease their poverty. Similarly, the vicar Arnau
of Vallfogona insisted that he continued to provide for Berengaria "for the
love of God" because of her enduring sickness.[61] Many families relied on the
financial support of a cleric and without it, found themselves in dire straits.

Considering that clerical fathers employed strategies to conceal family
members in their wills, it is remarkable that so many Catalan clergymen lived
openly with their domestic partners and children. Some certainly tried to circumvent ecclesiastical punishment by living in separate homes or by residing
in different parishes, but as parishioners' testimonies reveal, it was difficult to
keep their relationships hidden from the community. The extent to which clerics and their women publicly demonstrated their couplehood suggests that
they were, for the most part, unconcerned with revealing the relationship to
their friends and neighbors, and even publicized their unions. Take, for example, the sacrist Bernat, who sold wine and bread to his parishioners from the

59. Kelleher, '"Like Man and Wife,"' 355; ADG, Visites, no. 1, 84v. (1315). Other examples in-
clude the sacrist Bartomeu de Ter, who ejected the pregnant Francesca from his home, and the sacrist
Ramon Raditor who impregnated two women but did not provide for either one or for their infants;
ADG, Visites, no. 4, 59r. (1329); ADG, Visites, no. 3, 19v.–20r. (1321).

60. Debra Blumenthal, *Enemies and Familiars: Slavery and Mastery in Fifteenth-Century Valencia*
(Ithaca: Cornell University Press, 2009), 188–89.

61. ADG, Visites, no. 6, 98r. (1340); AEV, Visites, no. 1200/2, 31r. (1331). Although the vicar Arnau Martell kept Berengaria in his home, he stated that "non tenet eam in concubinaris sed amore dei
providet ei cum sicut et fuerit diu infirma qua III infirmitate." The couple shows up as having two
children in a visitation from 1339; AEV, Visites, no. 1200/3, 57v. (1339).

home of Guillema. There was little doubt as to the nature of their relationship since Bernat's clothes could be seen hanging on a rod next to Guillema's
bed. Similarly, there could be no uncertainty about the paternity and extended
family of the priest Berenguer in the parish of la Vajol because he publicly celebrated mass with his eight-year-old son and small nephew.[62]

Clerical couples acted and behaved like other couples. Some quarreled, and
others demonstrated their unhappiness with their partners before their neighbors. The hebdomedarian Joan de Apilia beat the mother of his children, Na
Saura, publicly in the marketplace of Hostalric; the hebdomedarian Guillem
Vidal was known for beating his concubine, Raimunda Pava, on a daily basis.[63]
Even though the rector Bonanat de Rippa had kept Dolça Sala "as a wife" for
more than ten years, Dolça was known for her fits of jealousy and on one occasion threw stones at the rector's head.[64] The lack of discretion among clerical families also implies a sense of normalcy. The sacrist Guillem and Maria
Rosa from the village of Montcal often invited friends over to his home for a
meal. Maria Rosa and their child may have lived next door to the sacrist, but
their relationship was evident to all because Maria Rosa played the part of the
hostess and ate with their guests. The people of the parish knew of their relationships because clerical couples were open about them. In the village of Vilafranca del Penedès, the rector and his family had invited parishioners to eat in
their home and had likewise dined in the homes of their neighbors for the previous eighteen years.[65] When the sacrist of Requesens held a "great banquet"
in 1321 to celebrate his daughter's marriage, parishioners knew about the event
because they participated in the celebration or heard of it from neighbors.[66]
These are not the actions of people practicing subterfuge. If anything, these
clerics and women were not censoring their behavior in public but advertising their couplehood and family to the parish. The open nature of these relationships stands in sharp contrast to the rector of Castellgalí's attempt to keep

---

62. ADG, Visites, no. 1, 75v.–76r. (1315).
63. ADG, Visites fragmentaris, 20r. (1320). Nine years later, in 1329, the hebdomedarian and Na
Saura were still together and now had four children; ADG, Visites, no. 4, 88r. (1329). For the hebdomedarian Guillem Vidal and Raimunda Pava, see ADG, Visites, no. 4, 55v. (1329). Other examples
include the priest Andreu Majoll, who beat his pregnant concubine so severely that she miscarried,
and the hebdomedarian Ponç de Pla, who similarly beat his pregnant concubine, Brussendis Moner,
to such an extent that both she and the child died during labor. The rector Galceran de Queralt was
fined 30 sous for beating his "ancilla," and the hebdomedarian Pere Ferrar, who served in the parish
of Riudellots de la Selva, was fined for returning to his concubine Caterina in addition to beating her;
ADB, Registrum Communium, no. 4, 162r. (1328); ADG, Lletres, no. 3, 55r.v. (1328); ADB, Registrum
Communium, no. 9, 141r. (1341); ADG, Imposicions de Penes, no. 1, 19v.–20r. (1340).
64. Visitatio diversarum, HMML, microfilm no. 31951, Visites, no. 1, 74r. (1307).
65. ADG, Visites, no. 2, 76r. (1315); Martí Bonet, "Visitas pastorales," 674.
66. ADG, Visites, no. 3, 11v.–12r. (1321).

Na Grassa "hidden" in his home for days at a time. Given the close-knit ties of village parishes, it is clear that parishioners knew about the relationship, especially because they described the rector taking mulberries to Na Grassa when he visited her in a neighboring village.[67] The difference is that the rector did not publicly proclaim his relationship to villagers by openly showing that he kept Na Grassa as his woman, and the two did not engage in behaviors that labeled them a couple. In fact, it is clear that parishioners, clerics, and episcopal officials made a distinction between a sexual relationship and one in which the couple made their relationship known to the community. For example, the rector of Calders admitted to "carnally knowing" the wife of Berenguer Oler but specified that he had "never kept her publicly." Similarly, the priest Jaume Rossell confessed to a sexual affair with Gaya but specified that he "did not publicly participate with her" ("sed dixit quod non participavit publice cum ea").[68] Acknowledging a woman publicly and broadcasting the marital nature of the relationship to the community affected how people perceived and categorized the relationship. Temporary sexual encounters were usually discreet, but a man who publicized that he "kept" a woman not only signaled that he wanted others to recognize the relationship but also made public that the woman belonged to him.

Although very few clergy were prosecuted in the bishop's court for clerical incontinence, the case against the cleric Bernat Ferrer further reveals the public nature of such relationships. For more than nine years, neighbors in the city of Girona were accustomed to seeing Bernat and Elisenda de Vernet together. Elisenda was a former prostitute and was also known by the name of Na Dolor. Remarkably, very few women involved with clerics were identified as "common women" or prostitutes, but it is likely that Elisenda's past profession triggered the interest of parishioners.[69] Initially the couple lived in

---

67. AEV, Visites, no. 1200/2, 75v. (1331).

68. Josep M. Martí Bonet, Leandre Niqui i Puigvert, and F. Miquel i Mascort, eds., *Processos de l'arxiu diocesà de Barcelona* (Barcelona: Department de Cultura de la Generalitat de Catalunya, 1984), 72, 90. In another example, the parishioners of Sant Policarp de Cortàs revealed that they believed their chaplain kept a concubine but not "publicly"; ACV, Calaix 31/43, no. 7, 39v. (1313).

69. Contrary to findings in England, where parishioners labeled the priest's woman a *meretrix*, and the women who cohabited with clergymen were considered "loose women" and called a "comon preste hure," or a "munkhore and frerehore," this attitude toward clerics' concubines is not present in visitation records from Catalunya in which parishioners did not associate a priest's concubine as a woman of ill repute; Karras, "Latin Vocabulary," 1–17. The prevalence of clerical unions in northern Europe and the Mediterranean may have affected how people viewed and labeled clerics' concubines. For a discussion of the terms used to describe concubines in the Mediterranean and elsewhere in Europe, see Armstrong-Partida, "Priestly Wives," 184–86. Although Emlyn Eisenach does not address the concubines of clergymen specifically, she does note that in sixteenth-century Verona the word *concubine* did not "necessarily imply a loose woman. . . . villagers recognized that these were long-term relationships, most over a decade old, in which the women were monogamous." Emlyn

the same home, but at some point after Bernat's first punishment for keeping Na Dolor, she moved out and made her residence elsewhere. Nevertheless, various wives and daughters of neighboring families testified that Na Dolor frequently entered Bernat's home by night and day, and that they regularly saw her preparing food and buying bread, wine, figs, meat, and other necessities for the cleric. Na Dolor, moreover, helped Bernat make the sacred oil for his "work." The woman next door to the priest had observed Na Dolor with a key to Bernat's house and related that, while Bernat had been out of town, Na Dolor had stayed in his home until his return. On numerous occasions, people reported seeing the couple sitting together on the doorstep to his house "solus cum sola" or the cleric sitting on his windowsill as he talked to Na Dolor. From time to time, Bernat and Na Dolor were also seen sharing a cup of wine and some bread together while sitting before his home. Far from a casual affair, Bernat clearly depended on Na Dolor for more than just sex. Na Dolor, in turn, showed the depth of her concern when she nursed Bernat, suffering from fever and ulcers, for a period of six months.[70]

Bernat and Na Dolor may have lived apart, but their public behavior suggests that they were not trying to be discreet. The very act of sitting in doorways and windows was one way in which people socialized and observed the goings-on of their neighbors. Like many clerics who kept their concubines "publicly," Bernat continually exposed his relationship with Na Dolor to his community. These attempts to both conceal and make known a sexual liaison were contradictory, suggesting how torn clerics could be between a financial penalty and the need to demonstrate their manhood by publicly displaying their women. Couples such as Bernat and Na Dolor, living in cathedral cities, likely had to be more circumspect about their relationships to avoid the attention of episcopal officials. The gamble of getting caught and fined for sexual incontinence or concubinage definitely made some clerics poorer, but they were rarely removed from office. Nonetheless, episcopal harassment and financial punishment were an ever-present aggravation and a greater burden for clerics who were poverty-stricken. Why, then, would clerics go to the trouble to advertise their roles as husbands and fathers, and increase their chances

Eisenach, *Husbands, Wives, and Concubines: Marriage, Family, and Social Order in Sixteenth-Century Verona* (Kirksville, MO: Truman State University Press, 2004), 162.

70. ADG, Visites, no. 1, 27r.v. (1315); ADG, Processos, no. 78, 1r.v.–14r. (1324). The risk to Bernat's career because of his illicit relationship with Na Dolor turned out to be minimal. He was not removed from his office and remained in his parish for at least another two years; ADG, Notularum, no. 6, 39v. (1326). Na Nicola, the concubine of the rector of Cenguyeles, who lived in Vilafranca, took care of the rector's home and goods when he traveled to Barcelona; ADB, Visites, no. 2, 73r. (1314).

of getting caught? Or perhaps the better question is, what did clerics have to gain by publicly flaunting their families?

Clergy were involved in stable, long-term unions and provided a home, food, and clothing for their women and children because having a family was an important marker of masculinity for priests. The normativity of marriage in medieval society fashioned people's perceptions of what the relationship between a man and woman should be like. Masculine identity, moreover, was intricately tied to the marital state. Thus far, we have seen that clerics benefitted economically, sexually, and even emotionally from forming long-standing relationships with women. For women who had very little prospect for marriage because they lacked dowries and were already predisposed to accepting informal unions, clerical concubinage was a favorable option. Practically speaking, an informal union with a cleric did not provide any more security than one with a layman. And although perhaps "having a priest for a husband was preferable to having no husband at all,"[71] a surprising number of married women left their husbands for clergymen, indicating that their choice of partner was motivated by more than just the religiously sanctioned title of "wife."[72]

For men, the role of husband, father, and provider was closely linked to the public role of paterfamilias. In medieval society, men demonstrated their manhood by dominating a woman, generating offspring, and using their male authority as a paterfamilias to discipline, guide, and financially support their family.[73] Clerics, as we have seen, formed unions that resembled lay marriages. They set up households and provided for their families during their lifetime and after their death. Clergymen achieved the social markers of adult manhood by imitating many of the secular behaviors practiced by married laymen. It was important, therefore, for clerics to publicly keep their women and children to make their adult status and masculinity known. Engaging in routine, everyday behaviors, such as eating and sleeping together, performing household chores, and managing financial resources to take care of children,

---

71. Marjorie Ratcliffe, "Adulteresses, Mistresses, and Prostitutes: Extramarital Relationships in Medieval Castile," *Hispania* 67, no. 3 (1984), 348.

72. For example, Brunissenda left her husband for the sacrist of Monells, and together the couple had three children; ADG, Visites, no. 4, 61r. (1330). Although women who aligned themselves with clerics were always financially vulnerable, there were benefits to a union with a cleric that made the risk worthwhile for many women. See also Armstrong-Partida, "Priestly Wives," 207–9.

73. Bullough, "On Being a Male," 34; Joan Cadden, *Meanings of Sex Difference in the Middle Ages: Medicine, Science, and Culture* (Cambridge, UK: Cambridge University Press, 1993), 133, 178, 192–93; Jennifer Thibodeaux, "Man of the Church, or Man of the Village? Gender and the Parish Clergy in Medieval Normandy," *Gender and History* 18, no. 2 (2006): 387–89. Derek Neal sees "husbandry," which entailed the "prudent and honorable management of property and household dependents," as an important dimension of medieval masculinity. *Masculine Self*, 58–62, 140–43.

revealed their relationship as one of marriage to the community. But sharing a meal with friends, sitting together outside the home, openly quarreling before friends and neighbors, and even having your woman clean the church exposed the union on an entirely different level. If indiscriminate sex and promiscuity alone could have signaled what it meant to be a man in medieval society, then clerics would have had no need for marriage-like unions and the formation of a marital household. The greater number of clerics in the holy orders who chose to enter into de facto marriages rather than short-term affairs means that husbandhood and fatherhood were symbols of masculinity for these men. Parish clergy sought to be manly in the same manner as their male parishioners. Manliness, then, was not demonstrated by the act of sex alone. A cleric's promiscuous behavior negatively affected his reputation, and visitation records show that clerics received the opprobrium of their community when they seduced and abandoned local women. In contrast, it is striking how few condemnations of clerics who established de facto marital unions are found in the testimony of parishioners.

The importance of having a "wife" and children to a cleric is best seen in the 1315 case of the deacon Guillem and Maria de Cases in the village of Bescanó. From all reports, the couple had a stormy relationship, and they were known to quarrel in the presence of others. On a number of occasions, Guillem had publicly blamed Maria for miscarrying three infants. Guillem was so aggrieved by the loss of his children that he had shown male parishioners where the infants were buried. By the time villagers reported this information to the visitor, however, Guillem was already dead. According to witnesses, Guillem became "crazed" when Maria refused to admit him into her home, table, or her bed, and he began gnawing on tiles with his teeth. So distraught was Guillem by Maria's rejection that he later threw himself into the river and drowned.[74] Decoding the behaviors of Guillem and Maria in this account is certainly difficult, but it gives us insight into the value a cleric could place on having a domestic partner and progeny. Guillem's insistence on showing his male peers where his offspring were laid to rest suggests that he wanted to prove that he was capable of fathering children. Proof of physical potency, penile erection, and the production of sperm were important characteristics according to medieval medical theories that defined the male body, and they

---

74. "ex hoc fuit ita turbatus dictus clericus quod accipiebat tegulas et cum dentibus rodebat fortiter et taliter etiam insanivit quod proiecit se in aqua supra molendinum in tantum quod nec fuissent aliqui qui ipsum juvarunt suffocatus fuisset in aqua et hoc faciebat quia ipsa mulier eiecerat ipsum de domo ut ipse clericus dicebat. [. . .] Et etiam dixit dictus clericus eidem mulieri pluries quando ritxabantur secum publice presentibus predictis testibus et aliis pluribus quod ipsa abortivit bis vel ter et quod ipse hostenderet loca ubi iacebant abortivi sui." ADG, Visites, no. 2, 41v.–42v. (1315).

served as the "basis for the conceptualization of the masculine" that Joyce Salisbury, Joan Cadden, and Jacqueline Murray have shown shaped beliefs about
men's bodies in medieval society.[75] In showing evidence of his ability to generate offspring, Guillem wanted to prove he was capable of performing sexually and perhaps wanted to dispel any doubts that he was impotent and
responsible for his childlessness. If anything, Guillem's actions speak more
broadly to his anger at being denied the role of a father and to the affection
and need, however twisted, he felt for his spouse.

A man deprived of a wife and dependents was a man deprived of his natural role as a ruler of his household. Outside the domestic sphere, husbandhood also opened up avenues, especially for a senior and respectable older man,
to governance over social relationships in the community and even involvement in civic politics that placed unmarried men at a disadvantage.[76] For clergy
who lived among the laity in villages, hamlets, and towns, the benefit of keeping a woman and children was that a family provided evidence not only of
virility but also an ability to provide for and govern dependents. Maintaining a
stable union and managing a household conferred a respectability that would
have affected a cleric's relationship with his parishioners. Domestically settled
clerics who had familial ties to the parish were also more likely to be good
members of the village community. Moreover, a cleric who understood the
trials of family life could bond over these experiences with his parishioners,
and undoubtedly parishioners would have preferred the priest who gave the
nuptial blessing at their children's weddings or officiated at the baptism of their
children or grandchildren to be a man they esteemed. A relationship of mutual respect, we imagine, had to be present when parents asked a priest to act
as a godparent to their child. Personal ties were important, but amicable business and social relationships in the community were equally vital to a cleric's
professional and even financial well-being.[77]

---

75. Joyce E. Salisbury, "Gendered Sexuality," in *Handbook of Medieval Sexuality*, ed. Vern L.
Bullough and James A. Brundage (New York: Garland Publishing, 1996), 85, 88–89, 91; Cadden, *Mean-
ings of Sex Difference*, 105–17, 131–34, 178, 197–98; Jacqueline Murray, "Hiding behind the Universal
Male: Male Sexuality in the Middle Ages," in *Handbook of Medieval Sexuality*, ed. Vern L. Bullough and
James A. Brundage (New York: Garland Publishing, 1996), 129, 139.

76. McSheffrey, "Men and Masculinity," 243–78; Chojnacki, "Subaltern Patriarchs," 75–77; Neal,
Masculine Self, 82–87.

77. Bornstein, "Parish Priests in Late Medieval Cortona," 173–75; Neal, *Masculine Self*, 92–95;
Derek Neal, "What Can Historians do with Clerical Masculinity? Lessons from Medieval Europe," in
Thibodeaux, *Negotiating Clerical Identities*, 26–27. Considering the familial ties clerics commonly en-
joyed in their parish or surrounding villages, many would have acted as godparents, which is why the
Girona synod dealt with the issue in 1354; Noguer i Musqueras and Pons Guri, "Constitucions sinod-
als de Girona," 162.

Conversely, clerics who brought shame to their household and conflict to the parish because of their multiple sexual affairs or their involvement with married women were not respectable figures. The villagers of Sant Martí de Maçanet, for example, considered the priest Joan de Molar to be disreputable for having fathered three children by three different women. Parishioners could easily accept a cleric who established a family household that conformed to social mores, but it was quite another matter entirely to have three bastards and their unattached mothers in the community due to the parish priest's sexual misconduct.[78] Similarly, parishioners condemned the rector Andreu for having a "shameful affair" with the wife of Pere Textor, who also happened to be his "step-son."[79] As fathers, clerics were likewise expected to guard the reputation of their household and, in particular, to oversee the relationships of their female dependents. Since a man's honor was connected to the reputation of his women, a paterfamilias monitored the sexual behavior of the women in his household. Parishioners, therefore, thought it unseemly and a poor reflection on the rector Guillem de Boix that he allowed his daughter Margarida to admit "disreputable lovers" into his home.[80] As Shannon McSheffrey has shown in her study of patriarchy in medieval London, good husbandry and responsible paternity earned men respectability and cemented their status as paterfamilias, and any behavior to the contrary marked them as men who lacked discipline in themselves and their household.[81] Promiscuous behavior affected a priest's reputation, particularly when his sexual affairs caused discord in the community and left women and their families dishonored because the relationship did not meet the hallmarks of respectability—a stable union in which the priest maintained and governed over his dependents as a proper paterfamilias.

Whether they were involved in a short-term affair or a long-standing union, a great number of parish clerics experienced fatherhood. Visitation records

---

78. Examples of clergymen that parishioners held in contempt for bringing scandal and chaos to the parish can be found in ADG, Processos, no. 136 (1335); ADG, Visites, no. 1, 10r. (1314); ADG, Visites, no. 4, 111r.v.–112r., 150v. (1329). ADG, Visites, no. 6, 60r.v. (1339); ADG, Visites, no. 8, 17v.–18r.v. (1345); ACV, Visites, no. 6, Calaix 31/43, 20v. (1315).

79. ADG, Visites, no. 4, 167v.–168r. (1329). In another example, the hebdomedarian Joan de Apilia caused "great scandal" in the parish when he had an affair with the wife of Pere Gentiles. Considering that Joan had four children with Na Saura, the havoc caused to two households most likely fueled the negative comments against him; ADG, Visites, no. 4, 87r., 88r. (1329). After committing adultery with the wife of Guillem de Bolera, the chaplain left his church because he was threatened by the husband and the feudal lord of the village; ACV, Visites, no. 5, Calaix 31/43, 12r. (1314). See also ADG, Visites fragmentaris, 8r. (1320); ACV, Visites, Calaix 31/43, no. 4, 18r. (1314).

80. ADG, Visites, no. 4, 141r. (1329). Guillem de Boix had five children with Saurina and was known to celebrate mass with his son Pere.

81. McSheffrey, "Men and Masculinity," 263–66. See also Neal, *Masculine Self*, 69–72.

reveal that clerical offspring made up a significant portion of the population—
the majority of Catalan villages could count at least one clerical couple and
two children among its inhabitants (see tables 1.1, 1.2, and 1.3). Consider that
in the diocese of Girona, from 1303 to 1305, 64 clerics in 49 villages fathered
at least 120 children and that, in 1321, 66 clerics in 76 villages fathered 109 plus
children. A similar trend is apparent in the diocese of Vic, where in the visitations from 1331 to 1332, 149 clerics in 179 parish communities fathered more
than 205 children.[82] Given these numbers, villagers in these regions most likely
knew someone who had a cleric for a parent. Indeed, the number of clerics'
children is likely to be higher because the figures presented in tables 1.1, 1.2,
and 1.3 are a conservative tally based on the somewhat vague terms employed
for children in the visitation records. The scribes were not consistent about
recording actual numbers but often used the plural form of the word *child* or
infant (*proles* and *infantes*) to indicate more than one child. Terms such as *multos infantes* and *plures filios* were used to denote many children, but it is impossible to determine how many children constituted "many" (*multos* or *plures*).
The scribes tended to use actual numbers when they recorded clerical couples
who had a significant number of children; for example, the rector Pere de Ca-
sacamela and Guillema had seven children, and the deacon Bernat de Cerrar
and his partner had ten children.[83] Tables 2.1, 2.2, and 2.3 show that clerics
had a significant number of children. The survival of seven or ten children was
certainly noteworthy given the infant mortality among the urban and rural
poor throughout the Middle Ages and would have caught the attention of the
episcopal visitor and scribe. Based on these imprecise terms, unless the scribe
noted the number of children, I counted an "infantem" or "prolem" as one
child, "proles" and "infantes" as two children, and "multos infantes" or "plures
filios" as three children. The potential of underestimating the number of
children, then, is quite high considering that the term *many children* could represent any number of children greater than three.

82. The number of clerical offspring is the diocese of Urgell, however, is much less from 1312
to 1313. Sixty-six clergymen fathered seventy-five children in 149 villages, and from 1315 to 1316,
seventy-three clerics fathered twenty-seven children in 91 villages. The fewer numbers of children
reported in the visitation records for the diocese of Urgell is not a sign that clerics were less engaged
in sex but a reflection of the visitor's interest in recording this information. The visitations, in their
brevity, simply note the clerics who were engaged in a concubinous relationship. Episcopal scribes in
the diocese of Urgell infrequently recorded the name of a cleric's concubine or the number of
children these unions produced. Thus, the number of clerical offspring in the visitations for Urgell is
far from an accurate picture.
83. AEV, Visites, no. 1200/2, 64v. (1331); Visites, no. 1200/3, 29v. (1333); ADG, Visites fragmentaris, 4r. (1305).

Even though such a tally of clerical offspring is an underestimation of re-production among clerical couples, a far from comprehensive series of visita-tions to the parishes of the dioceses of Girona and Vic show that clerics fathered a considerable number of children—385 and 359 children, respectively, in a ten-year period. Clerics in the diocese of Urgell produced at the very least 267 children over a span of four years. These numbers are striking when we con-sider that most of the extant visitation records cover at most only a quarter of each diocese.[84] Perhaps a better approach to determining the number of cleri-cal offspring in a generation (forty years) is to analyze the visitations of 1329–1330 in the diocese of Girona—the most complete episcopal investigation of diocesan parish affairs in that 391 parish churches out of 414 parishes were visited. The 248 clerics accused of incontinence during this period (the majority—207—were accused of concubinage) produced at least 287 children. Peasant women in the preplague years of the fourteenth century could give birth to three to six children in their lifetime, depending on the economic prosperity of the household.[85] The potential number of children produced in one generation in one diocese could range anywhere from 708 to 1,418, which is not an insignificant contribution to the population. In the diocese of Barcelona, Josep Baucells estimated there were a minimum of 1,019 children

84. From 1330 to 1339, 386 children were counted for the diocese of Vic. In the diocese of Urgell, 267 children were counted for the years 1312 to 1316. Considering that in the mountain parishes of Urgell the visitor arrived to find neither the clergy nor parishioners present in fifty-nine parishes and that in sixty-five parishes no parishioners were questioned, information on clerical children went un-reported in these visits. In the diocese of Girona, 754 children were counted from the scattered visitation records of 1303–1305, 1312, 1318, 1320, and 1323 and from the visitation books dated 1315–1316, 1321, and 1329. One hundred sixty-three children were counted in the visitations for 1331, 1339–1341, and 1341–1344. The total number of children reported in the visitations from 1303 to 1344 is 841. Preg-nant women and children reported dead are included in these numbers.

85. Studies on birth rates and the fertility of women have found that poverty reduced fertility. In central England before the Black Death, Zvi Razi estimated that, on average, each family had three children; wealthier families had on average five children, and poor families had two children; Zvi Razi, *Life, Marriage, and Death in a Medieval Parish. Economy, Society, and Demography in Halesowen, 1270–1400* (Cambridge, UK: Cambridge University Press, 1980), 83–87; Philip R. Schofield, *Peasant and Community in Medieval England, 1200–1500* (New York: Palgrave Macmillan, 2003), 83–84. In the high plains of the diocese of Vic, around the area of Collsacabra (150 km squared, encompassing twenty-six villages), Assumpta Serra i Clota estimates that in this agropastoral society families had four to six children; *La comunitat rural a la Catalunya medieval: Collsacabra (s. XIII–XVI)* (Vic: Eumo Editorial, 1990), 32–33. Similarly, prior to the plague years in Florence, women bore four to six children; David Herlihy, *Medieval and Renaissance Pistoia. The Social History of an Italian Town, 1200–1430* (New Haven: Yale University Press, 1967), 96–99. Based on the 1427 Catasto, David Herlihy finds that in Pistoia, It-aly, women in rural communities "were producing four children for every three born to a like number of women in the city."; Herlihy and Christiane Klapisch-Zuber, *Tuscans and Their Families: A Study of the Florentine Catasto of 1427* (New Haven: Yale University Press, 1985), 81–82.

belonging to clergymen from 1303 to 1344.[86] Considering that the population
in Catalunya before 1348 is estimated at 500,000 and half of it was overwhelm-
ingly peasant,[87] it is entirely possible that the number of clerical children in
the five dioceses (Barcelona, Girona, Lleida, Vic, and Urgell) that made up Old
Catalunya could easily amount to 1 percent of the population in the first half
of the fourteenth century.

Such a significant population of clerical offspring underscores the reproductive capabilities of clergymen, but medieval culture defined fatherhood as
more than simply impregnating a woman. Virility was a sign of masculinity,
but for a man to be considered a respectable adult male—a paterfamilias—he
had to do more than father children. A paterfamilias protected and raised his
sons and daughters, and ensured their future by providing them with an inheritance. There was an expectation that a father should work to improve the
lot of his children so that he would be remembered for the inheritance he
passed on to his heirs. The future welfare of his children was tied to his own.
The comforts to be found in old age came with the knowledge that his children
would care for him, they would pray for his soul, and he could see his likeness
in the faces of his grandchildren.[88] The idea that fatherhood encompassed
more than just the act of procreation and that men had paternal responsibilities can be seen in the writings of the fourteenth-century Catalan Franciscan
Francesc Eiximenis. Fathers, according to Eiximenis, are disposed "by nature"
to love their children, to provide for them, and to be concerned with their spiritual and moral upbringing. Eiximenis also comments on the obligations of
fatherly love and the biological need for men to become fathers: "a son is the
natural product of the father and, by nature, every producer loves what he
has produced, and just as nature drives man to beget, so also it drives him to
love what he has begotten." He further explains that a man is obliged to create his own likeness before "death draws near"; thus fathers "perpetuate themselves through their sons."[89] Eiximenis's guide to educating children reflects
the social expectation that fatherhood entailed the masculine duties of foster-
ing, guiding, teaching, and maintaining progeny to ensure their welfare. He
emphasizes, moreover, that the laws of nature compel men to reproduce,

86. Baucells i Reig, *Vivir en la edad media*, 3: 2530–32. Baucells counted 863 children, then added
156 instances in which the cleric reportedly had "many children" to arrive at 1,019 children. Needless
to say, this figure underestimates the number of clerical children.

87. Thomas N. Bisson, *The Medieval Crown of Aragon* (Oxford: Clarendon Press, 1986), 163–64.

88. Shulamith Shahar, *Childhood in the Middle Ages* (London: Routledge, 1990), 13, 166–70; Danièl
Alexandre-Bidon and Didier Lett, *Children in the Middle Ages: Fifth–Fifteenth Centuries*, trans. Jody Gladding (Notre Dame: University of Notre Dame Press, 1999), 58–59, 62–64.

89. Xavier Renedo and David Guixeras, eds., *Francesc Eiximenis: An Anthology*, trans. Robert D.
Hughes (Barcelona: Tamesis, 2008), 67–68.

suggesting that medieval Catalan society at large may have understood the need for priests to seek out fatherhood.

Like laymen, parish clerics experienced fatherhood as a rite of passage. Clerics who baptized their children, celebrated mass with their sons, and married off their sons and daughters, not only announced their paternity to the community but also signaled their position as the patriarch of the family. The rector Jaume Ferrer is a good example of a cleric performing the role of paterfamilias. When the rector baptized his own son, the baptism was not a secret event. Jaume secured Elisenda, one of his parishioners, as a godparent to present his son at the sacred font. The rector had another one of his sons stand next to the altar and assist him with the pitcher and sacred vessels. Jaume's five children with Jaçmeta signaled his virility, but baptizing one son and displaying another next to the altar allowed Jaume to publicly proclaim his offspring.[90] Similarly, the rector of Torelles baptized many of his children by Geralda. He had his eldest son Bernat and a female parishioner serve as godparents when baptizing his son Arnau. Although the rector's son Bernat was already married with children, the rector nonetheless celebrated mass with Bernat on Sundays and feast days, with Bernat's sons and daughters in attendance. Every Sunday, then, parish members observed their rector fill the church with his children and grandchildren.[91] It is unlikely, therefore, that village members did not see their clerics as fathers and as family men who exerted power over their children and parishioners. What is more, clerics extended the paternal authority of their household to include the parish church. The priest Bartomeu Monju ruled his church as he would his home: he did not permit his parishioners to receive the kiss of peace unless they obtained it first from his son.[92] Bartomeu, in essence, was demanding that the community acknowledge the status and position of his son. The priest directed his parishioners and determined what occurred in his church while he said the mass with his son, just as he would govern his household and dependents.

Because sons often followed their father's profession, fatherhood meant that many clerics could take pride in the social identity they passed on to their sons. Like the peasant men who took their sons to the fields and taught them the agricultural skills they would need as adults, clerics trained their sons for a priestly career.[93] Indeed, the very act of training a son advertised the cleric's

---

90. Benito i Monclús, *Parroquies del maresm,* 284–86.
91. Martí Bonet, "Visitas pastorales," 720–25.
92. ACV, Visites, no. 4, Calaix 31/43, 37v. (1315).
93. Barbara A. Hanawalt, "Medievalists and the Study of Childhood," *Speculum* 77, no. 2 (2002), 449–50; Hanawalt, *Ties That Bound,* 183–84; Alexandre-Bidon and Lett, *Children in the Middle Ages,* 75–77, 79–82.

role as a father. Parishioners certainly knew the parentage of the two boys who celebrated mass with the rector of Pax and of the two sons of the rector Berenguer, in the parish of Albà, who aided their father while he chanted the mass.[94] Clerical fathers, like many lay fathers, sought to tonsure their sons so that they could benefit from the legal privilege of clerical status, which protected clerics from personal inviolability and the jurisdiction of secular courts (clerics could be tried only in an ecclesiastical court). Nevertheless, the sons of priests could not be admitted into the clergy because their illegitimacy made them ineligible. This obstacle could be removed by obtaining a papal dispensation for illegitimate birth (*defectus natalium*) to enter into holy orders and receive the tonsure.[95] Traveling to Rome and applying to the papal curia for a dispensation was a time-consuming and costly affair, which is why many did not bother with the process. The rector of Foix slyly took his son Jaume Torres to another village, where people were less likely to know of his parentage, to have the bishop tonsure him. Evidently the rector's relationship to the boy was discovered because the notary noted that Jaume was tonsured *"per fraudem."* It seems likely that a number of clergymen found ways to tonsure their sons without a dispensation, and some of these clerical sons entered into the major orders. A visitation to the parish of Cubelles uncovered that the priest Berenguer Boschet was the son of a priest and had been ordained without a dispensation for the circumstances of his birth.[96] It is striking, moreover, that so many of the sons of priests seeking a career in the Church bore the surname and even the given name of their father, suggesting that these men not only wanted to claim their sons publicly but proudly passed on their paternal surnames.[97]

---

94. Martí Bonet, "Visitas pastorales," 678, 690. Other examples of clerics celebrating mass with their sons in the diocese of Barcelona include the rector of Fontrubí, the rector of Calafell, the rector of Bellvei, and the rector of Torelles; Martí Bonet, "Visitas pastorales," 685, 696, 709. For the diocese of Tortosa, see García Egea, *La visita pastoral a la diocesis de Tortosa del Obispo Paholac*, 196, 229, 237. For the dioceses of Girona, Vic, and Urgell, see the Tables 4.1, 4.2, 4.3.

95. Schimmelpfennig, "'Ex fornicatione nati,'" 20–26, 36–41; Laura Wertheimer, "Illegitimate Birth and the English Clergy, 1198–1348," *Journal of Medieval History* 31 (2005): 211–29.

96. Martí Bonet, "Visitas pastorales," 678, 686, 703. The rector Pere Joan was also ordained "falsely" because he did not obtain the correct dispensation that identified him as the son of a priest; ACV, Calaix 31/43, Visites, no. 1, 25r. (1312). The rector Pere Arnau had his twelve-year-old son Ramon tonsured, but he was still fined 50 sous for celebrating mass with his son Ramon; ADG, Visites, no. 4, 53v.–54r.v. (1329).

97. The dispensations for *deffectus natalium* in the diocesan archive of Barcelona contain the testimonies of witnesses who often identify both the father and mother by name, and these documents reveal that the son bore his father's last name; ADB, Dispensationes Apostolics, 1.r.v. (1331); 16v. (1331); 22v.–23r. (1333); 44r.v.–45r.v. (1337); 73r.v.–75r. (1342); 76r.v.–78r. (1342); 79r.v.–80r.v. (1343). See also the examples in tables 4.1, 4.2, and 4.3 that deal with clerical fathers and sons.

As the family patriarch, a father was involved in arranging his children's marriages. Visitation records show clerics acting with paternal authority in this capacity by contracting marriages and providing dowries for daughters or inheritances for sons. The parishioners of Cantallops described their priest Pere Marcinal as "giving a wife to his son," indicating that, as a father, Pere had arranged the marriage.[98] Other fathers did what they could to ensure the future prosperity of their children. The rector of Vilaramó had eight children. He explained to the visitor that he had married off all but two of his daughters but that their mother had provided their dowries. Considering the couple had so many children, it is not surprising that the dowry of the latest daughter to be married was worth only 350 sous (17.5 lliures). It is noteworthy, however, that this clerical couple could provide dowries for all their daughters. In comparison, the priest Guillem Ferran could afford to give his only daughter (he also had three sons) a modest dowry worth 1,000 sous (the equivalent of 50 lliures).[99] For the middling strata, marriage contracts ranged between 150 and 200 lliures, and a dowry of less than 1,000 sous (50 lliures) indicated a family from the lower strata of society, suggesting that many clerical families belonged to the upper echelon of the peasantry and a few were part of the middling level of society.[100] Still, some fathers struggled to find the resources to arrange advantageous marriages for their offspring. For instance, the sacrist of Camprodon promised his future son-in-law in a public document that he would hand over all the rents from his benefice for a term of four years as a dowry for his daughter Elisenda.[101] Apparently the sacrist had no land and little cash for his daughter's dowry, so he resorted to promising the future earnings of his benefice to contract the marriage.

---

98. ADG, Visites, no. 3, 11r. (1321). For the important role of fathers in contracting the marriages of their sons, see Rachel E. Moss, "An Orchard, a Love Letter and Three Bastards: The Formation of Adult Male Identity in a Fifteenth-Century Family" in *What Is Masculinity?: Historical Dynamics from Antiquity to the Contemporary World*, ed. John H. Arnold and Sean Brady (New York: Palgrave Macmillan, 2011), 231–33, 237–38.

99. AEV, Visites, no. 1200/2, 69r. (1331); AEV, Visites, no. 1200/2, 5r. (1300). In one exceptional case, Francesc de Villar, a priest and beneficed cleric in the church of Manresa, was said to have endowed his daughter with 3,000 sous (150 lliures); AEV, Visites, no. 1200/3, 66r. (1339).

100. A number of marriage contracts can be found in Arxiu Municipal de Girona, *Catàleg de pergamins*. See also Teresa-Maria Vinyoles i Vidal, *La vida quotidiana a Barcelona vers 1400* (Barcelona, 1985), 180–82.

101. ADG, Visites, no. 5, 67r. (1331). The priest Arnau of Llanars also had eight children and had married off two daughters and one son. Arnau was fortunate to have the funds to contract marriages for three of his children; ADG, Visites fragmentaris, 22v.–23r. (1305). The hebdomedarian Ramon Llorenç struggled to provide a dowry for his daughter. Ramon had six children with Bernarda, and when arranging a marriage for one of his daughters, he promised a total of 500 sous for her dowry. Parishioners noted, however, that the rents and possessions belonging to Ramon were worth only 200 sous; ADG, Visites fragmentaris, 8v. (1303).

As fathers, clerics also took an interest in the important details of the wedding, which advertised the family's status and wealth in the community. The
sacrist of Requesens gave such a "great banquet" to celebrate his daughter's
marriage that the event brought people from surrounding villages. In another
example, the rector of Vilamilanys must have made his daughter happy
when he traveled to Barcelona to buy her nuptial clothing.[102] The novelty of
purchasing clothing in the city of Barcelona certainly made an impression
on the villagers, and the expense of the trip and bridal clothing most likely
impressed the groom's family. Fathers were expected to finance a wedding
celebration and contribute, along with the mother, to their daughter's trousseau. The marriage feast, quality of the nuptial clothing, and value of the dowry
and trousseau were indicative of the family's wealth and status, but such
markers also demonstrated a cleric's role as paterfamilias in arranging, financ-
ing, and publicly performing his role as the father of the bride. No one could
mistake the role of the rector Bernat when he presided over the nuptials of
his daughter Ermesenda at the door of his parish church.[103] That parishioners
viewed clerics as husbands and fathers acting as patriarchs is evident in the
description of the chaplain Pere's household: "Pere Rubey cleric of the chapel of Santa Maria de Bell·lloc de Vilaromà lives on a manse with his concubine Ermesenda from whom he has children . . . [and] this year the said cleric
gave the manse to his son Bernat at the time when Bernat contracted marriage. And the said cleric [Pere] lives on the said manse with all the above said
people as a paterfamilias with his family."[104]

Fatherhood, then, was a responsibility that clerics took seriously. Even
though the sources infrequently reveal the day-to-day relations between
clerics and offspring, we can catch glimpses of their involvement in their
children's lives. After the birth of his son, Ferrar Barbarano, a canon at the
cathedral of Urgell, hired a nurse to care for the infant because Alisendis had
not recovered from the delivery. The rector of the chapel of Sant Salvador
had taken Na Gaurdia to the home of his mother to care for her during the

102. ADG, Visites, no. 3, 11v.–12r. (1321); no. 3, 11r. (1321); Visitatio diversarum, HMML, microfilm no. 31951, 9v. (1304).

103. Visitatio diversarum, HMML, microfilm no. 31951, Visites, no. 1, 19r. (1305). Baucells notes
that four priestly fathers are recorded as the priest who presided over the marriage ceremony of their
daughters; Baucells i Reig, *Vivir en la edad media*, 3: 2540n. 347.

104. ADG, Visites, no. 1, 10v. (1315). Similarly, the rector Guillem of Sant Martí de Capsec kept
Saurina, his son, and daughter-in-law on his manse called Noguer; ADG, Visites, no. 1, 47v. (1315).
The rector of Cases also kept his daughter-in-law in his home. It appears that his son was no longer in
the picture because his daughter-in-law was now involved with another man, and the couple apparently lived in the rector's house; ACT, Visites, 3v. (1337).

pregnancy.[105] The attention to pregnant partners and the care of offspring to ensure their survival was one way that clerics acknowledged their paternity. When a cleric's woman gave birth in his home, this was not an event unnoticed by neighbors. The midwife and a woman's female family members and friends would have gathered together to assist in the birth. The community, therefore, assumed the cleric to be the father when such an event took place in his home.[106] Knowing this, clerics used birthing events to proclaim their fatherhood. Even sad incidents such as the death of a child, a stillbirth, and a miscarriage[107] prompted clerics to recognize their offspring and act like fathers when they baptized their child, buried the child in the parish cemetery, and said a mass for the child's soul. Furthermore, it was the responsibility of the father to choose the godparents and assemble them in the church for the baptism because post-partum women could not enter sacred spaces for six weeks.[108] Clerical fathers announced their fatherhood to the village community and publicly recognized their offspring when they took part in the religious rituals of birth and death.

Clerics, moreover, protected their children from harm and used their paternal influence to intervene on their behalf. In 1331, during a time of meager harvests, the rector of Boixadors reportedly made himself a "pauper" because he gave whatever wheat he had to his sons. Likewise, the vicar of Tavèrnoles also provided wheat to his son during the beginning years of the

---

105. ACV, Visites, Calaix 31/43, no. 1, 5r. (1312); Visitatio aliquarum ecclesiarum facta per epsicopum anno 1323–1326, et 1327. Sunt alique Collationes et alia usque ad anno 1328. Visitationes no. 3. HMML, microfilm no. 31953, 3r. (1321).

106. AEV, Visites, no. 1200/1, 7v. (1330); ADG, Visites, no. 1, 84r.v., 78r. (1315); ADG, Visites, no. 3, 29v. (1321).

107. For children who died in infancy or young adulthood, there are the following examples. The child of the priest Bernat Jover and Alamanda Valenta died at the age of ten; ADG, Visites, no. 7, 9r. (1341). The second child of the cleric Berenguer and Guillema Cardona died shortly after his birth; ADG, Visites, no. 3, 3v. (1321). After the death of their daughter, the rector Ramon de Villa and Bonanata Barbera split up; ADG, Visites, no. 5, 24v. (1331). The hebdomedarian Bernat Rocha and Saurina lost one of their daughters; ADG, Visites, no. 4, 38r. (1329). The first-born child of the priest Pere Caragoll and Barchinona de Garriga died, but the couple later had a son; ADG, Visites, no. 5, 101v. (1331). The cleric from Adrí and his woman lost an infant shortly after its birth; ADG, Visites, no. 5, 156r. (1332). At the age of four, the child of Pere Camallera and Berengaria de Ulmà died; ADG, Visites, no. 7, 142v. (1341). The rector of Sant Vicenç de Torelló had a daughter with Venguda, but their son died; AEV, Visites, no. 1200/1, 10r.v. (1330). Romia and the rector of Salomó had two sons who died; ADB, Visites, no. 2, 69r. (1314). For infants who were miscarried or stillborn, see ACV, Calaix 31/43, Visites, no. 5, 12r. (1314); Martí Bonet, "Visitas pastorales," 677. The rector of Vulpellac buried his child, which had been born prematurely, in the parish cemetery; ADG, Lletres, no. 3, 55r.v. (1328).

108. Barbara A. Hanawalt, Growing Up in Medieval London: The Experience of Childhood in History (New York: Oxford University Press, 1993), 42–44.

famine in the Crown of Aragon.[109] It seems likely that these clerics were not
the only clerical fathers to sacrifice comfort and profits to ensure the survival,
if not the prosperity, of their offspring. Concern for the happiness and perhaps security of daughters can also be seen. Rather than insist that his
daughter Guillema return to her husband, the rector of Aristot allowed his
unhappy daughter to remain in his home because she no longer wished to
live with her husband.[110] As the paterfamilias, the rector could have forcibly
delivered Guillema into her husband's custody, but he chose instead to offer
her the protection of his home. The chaplain of Sant Cebrià d'Ordino acted
similarly when his son-in-law came to collect his daughter Maria. According
to villagers, the chaplain "did not permit" the husband to remain with Maria
and closed the door of his home in the face of his son-in-law. For whatever
reason, the chaplain no longer approved of Maria's husband. He, instead, promoted a new union between his daughter Maria and the deacon Berenguer
Joan, and the couple now had a son together. In this case, the chaplain not
only extended his protection to his daughter, but he also, by all accounts, intervened to keep Maria separated from her husband and knowingly gave his
consent to the deacon to pursue a relationship with his daughter.[111] While
some clerics intervened in the marriages of their daughters, others intervened to protect their sons from ecclesiastical punishment. The majordomo
to the bishop of Girona, Pere des Puig, officially pardoned his son Marc des
Puig for what appears to be a youthful indiscretion of stealing a lance and
firewood. Marc des Puig had most likely been tonsured so that his father, the
majordomo, had the authority to pardon him for a crime brought before an
ecclesiastical official. The archdeacon of Vic likewise used his influence to
intercede on his son Francesc's behalf when he had the tonsured Francesc
transferred from the jail of the bishop of Barcelona to his own custody to
await a trail for his "crimes."[112] These clerical fathers found ways to support
their children and secure their futures. Bertran Mont-rodon, rector of Caldes
de Montbui and capellan of Taravaus, the bishop of Girona's own brother,
had a daughter he financially supported. And it was most likely Bertran's son,

109. AEV, Visites, no. 1200/2, 53v. (1331); Visites, no. 1200/3, 8r. (1332). Famine besieged the
kingdom in 1333, which Catalans later remembered as *el mal any primer* ("the first bad year").

110. ACV, Visites, no. 1, Calaix 31/43, 34r. (1312). The visitor ordered Guillema to return to her
husband, Guillem Forn, or face excommunication. Likewise, all those who housed Guillema in their
home or provided assistance were threatened with excommunication.

111. ACV, Visites, no. 1, Calaix 31/43, 21v. (1312). In 1313, the deacon Berenguer Joan was now
rector of Canillo, and he still kept Maria as his concubine in the village of Ordino; ACV, Visites, no. 7,
16r. (1313).

112. Puig i Oliver, and Marquès i Planagumà, *Lletres del Bisbe de Girona,* 116–17n. 105; Hillgarth
and Silano, *Register "Notule Communium,"* no. 319, 219.

with the family name of Mont-rodon, who received a dispensation for illegitimate birth from his own uncle, the bishop, to enter into clerical orders.[113] We can imagine Bertran asking his brother Arnau, the bishop, to secure a clerical career for his son. Like lay fathers, the role of a clerical father did not end at providing food, shelter, and clothing or after the children reached adulthood. Clerics did what they could to help their offspring during hard economic times, during troubled marriages, and when faced with punishment for their unlawful activities, and they acted to secure their children's futures to ensure that they were taken care of and had a livelihood.

The clergymen who were single parents and cared for their offspring further underscore a devotion to family. Despite the difficulties of looking after children without a domestic partner to feed, clothe, supervise their activities during work and play, and protect them from accidents, clerics nonetheless chose to keep their children by their side. Presumably these children could have been left in the custody of the cleric's or mother's family, the grandparents or possible even aunts or uncles, so it is surprising that they remained in their natal household. For example, the priest Guillem Pellicer kept his ten-year-old daughter in his home despite the death of her mother.[114] The affair between the sacrist Mateu de Valls and the married woman Laufrera resulted in a daughter. Mateu and Laufrera had parted ways some years before, but the daughter Mateva remained with the sacrist.[115] In another example, the priest Guillem deç Peresols looked after his two small children without the aid of another woman in the home (whether the mother of his children had died or simply left is not mentioned).[116] Clerics tended to live near their families in

---

113. Hillgarth and Silano, *Register "Notule Communium,"* 92–95n. 55.

114. ADG, Visites, no. 4, 124v.–125r. (1329). Similar examples include the cleric of Torroella de Montràs, who was left with two children when his domestic partner died, and the deacon Arnau de Ermedans in the parish of Santa Coloma de Fitor, who was also left with two children, a daughter and son, after the death of his concubine. Ramon de Sala, the rector of Ginestar, kept his son when his concubine Ermesenda de Camps died; ADG, Visites, no. 4, 69v.–70r. (1329); ADG, Visites, no. 4, 202r. (1329).

115. ADG, Visites, no. 6, 123v.–124 r. (1341); ADG, Imposicions de Penes, no. 1, 34r. (1341). When the priest Pere Batlle's concubine married a man in the town of Bisbal, their daughter remained with Pere in the parish of Santa Eulàlia de Cruïlles; ADG, Visites, no. 8, 16r.v. (1345). The hebdomedarian Bernat Maçanet fathered two sons from Maria Ramis, a married woman. After the couple split, Bernat's sons continued to visit him in the parish of Colonge. The sacrist Pere Canal kept his five-year-old son in his home, but the mother appears to have stayed in Girona; ADG, Visites, no. 5, 18v., 37v. (1331). Although no mention is made of the rector of Sant Pere de Valldeneu's relationship that resulted in a child, he nevertheless kept his daughter in his home; AEV, Visites, no. 1200/1, 16r. (1330).

116. ADG, Visites, no. 4, 159v. (1329). Other examples include the rector Pere de Camp, who kept his two daughters in his home in the parish of Sant Iscle de Vallalta, despite the fact that their mother lived in Barcelona, and the rector of Santa Coloma de Cervelló, who kept his son and two daughters in his home in the absence of their mother; ADG, Visites, no. 4, 84r. (1329); ADB, Visites, no. 5, 96r. (1342).

the same parish or in a neighboring village, hence it is possible that relatives helped care for the children. These single fathers, however, did not always remain single. The chaplain Ramon had a daughter with Sibil·la, a woman who either died or left the parish of Albanyà. Ramon continued to raise (*nutrit*) his daughter in his home after he formed a new relationship with Clara de Morer.[117] In another example, for nine years the rector Pere ces Planta had kept the married woman Elisenda Monera as his concubine, but one of his two sons from a past relationship also lived in his home.[118] Although it is impossible to know what happened to all the children of the couples who separated, these examples are evidence that clerics did not abdicate their parental responsibility. Mothers, moreover, were not always the primary caregivers. Couples may have negotiated custody depending on the age and gender of their children.

Even clerics who had children with more than one woman maintained ties to their offspring and continued to financially support them. The chaplain Guillem de Areis in the village of Riumors had "infantes" with a woman from Figueres as well as with a woman who lived in a nearby parish. Villagers reported that both women and their children visited the chaplain and left his home "burdened" with flour, meat, and cabbages.[119] Years had passed since Ermesenda had left the priest Perpinyà Clergue to marry Ferrar de Beuda, but it was the priest who married off their daughter and frequently ate in the daughter's home with her new husband.[120] Similarly, the capellan of Castellar had a new daughter with Ermesenda cesCases, but his son from Maria Ovela came by his home on a daily basis.[121] In spite of the difficulties of dissolved parental unions and separate households, clerics sustained the bonds with

---

117. ADG, Visites, no. 4, 166r. (1339). No information is provided on whether Sibil·la Gorgueta died or abandoned her daughter with the chaplain Ramon de Gordiola because she apparently no longer lived in the village. The rector also had another daughter with Na Vinyals de Llorona, but this daughter lived with her mother in Albanyà. Similarly, January, the rector of Salomó, raised his son and daughter after the death of their mother with Romia, the rector's new domestic partner. The rector of Santa Maria de la Bisbal also raised his two daughters from two different women who had died with his current domestic spouse, Na Balestera, with whom he had a two-year-old son; ADB, Visites, no. 2, 69r. (1314); ADB, Visites, no. 2, 67r. (1314). In another example, the sacrist of Mieres, Bernat Augustí was ordered to expel his daughter Agnes from his home and was warned not to carnally sin with three women or pay a fine of 200 sous. Despite Bernat's promiscuous behavior, he chose to raise his daughter Agnes; ADG, Imposicions de Penes, no. 1, 30v. (1340).

118. AEV, Visites, no. 1200/2, 83r. (1332). Prior to his relationship with Elisenda Monera, the rector Pere ces Planta had two sons with a married woman from the parish of Sant Martí de Sacalm.

119. ADG, Visites, no. 3, 22v.–23r. (1321).

120. ADG, Visites fragmentaris, 16r. (1303). Even though the relationship had ended between the hebdomedarian Arnau de Costabela and the mother of his daughter, he still provided for the girl when she came to visit him. ADG, Visites, no. 4, 205r. (1329).

121. ACV, Calaix 31/43, Visites, no. 3, 4r. (1313).

their children into adulthood and could be a part of their everyday lives. The daughters who looked after their elderly priestly fathers also point to the strong ties between clerics and their children. Eight years had passed since the deacon Arnau's concubine had died, and now sickly and hard of hearing, he was cared for by his thirty-five-year-old daughter. So, too, did Guillema, who was single and about 20 years old, look after her father, the cleric Ponç de Plano.[122] Whether married or single, the daughters of clergymen watched over their elderly parents. And clerics may very well have understood that a woman and children, especially a daughter, would be a source of comfort to them in their old age. Sons were also known to aid their fathers. When the rector of Brunyola was sick and could no longer perform his duties in the church, his son reportedly stayed in his home and looked after him. Likewise, the rector of Sant Esteve de Vinyoles was "old," "weak," and "incapable" of performing serving in the church, so his two sons took over his duties and the youngest served in the church for him.[123]

This rosy picture of clerics as fathers must also be balanced by the cases of clerics who abandoned their women and children or dismissed their pregnant concubines. Unfortunately, the sources rarely reveal what happened to a concubine and her offspring when the relationship with a cleric dissolved, but the voices of these women sometimes appear in the records. Sibil·la de Pont told the visitor to her parish of Esponellà that the hebdomedarian Guillem de Bell·lloc, who now lived in the parish of Serinyà, refused to provide for their son and three-year-old daughter. Sibil·la declared that she did not have anything with which she could support them, adding that she "implores" Guillem

122. ADG, Visites, no. 4, 209r. (1329); ADG, Imposicions de Penes, no. 1, 3r. (1335) and 96v. (1354). The deacon Arnau is described as *"senectutem infirmitate et surditate."* Guillema was most likely the daughter of Ermesenda. Ponç had been fined for keeping Ermesenda and their children in 1335, which means that in 1354 Guillema was probably around twenty years old. The rector Berenguer of Sant Vicenç de Sallent lived separately from his long-time partner Berengaria, but their twenty-five-year-old daughter lived with Berenguer and cooked his food; ADG, Visites, no. 3, 45r.v. (1321). Margarida, the daughter of the hebdomedarian Bernat, also looked after her father because her mother lived part-time in Girona; ADG, Visites, no. 4, 92v. (1329). So, too, did the daughter of the priest Bernat Mola, who was ten years old; according to parishioners, Bernat and his long-time partner Berengaria Rotlana lived separately, but their daughter lived with Bernat as his *"pedisseca"*; ADG, Visites, no. 8, 17v. (1345). The rector of Santa Maria d'Oló kept his young daughter in his home while his concubine Mateva lived in the city of Manresa; AEV, Visites, no. 1200/2, 67r. (1331). The ties between clerics and their daughters were not broken when the daughters married. In the parish of Rupià, Bernat d'Ullà's daughter and her husband visited the cleric in his home. The rector of Vilagrassa had a married daughter in Cervera who frequently came to visit; ADG, Lletres, no. 11, 4v.–5r. (1347); AEV, Visites, 1200/2, 22v. (1331). The canon Arnau de Castelló was ordered to expel his daughter Romia from his home; ADB, Registrum Communium, no. 1 44v. (1315).
123. ADG, Visites, fragmentaris, 29r.v. (1320); AEV, Visites, no. 1200/ 1, 13r. (1330). In another example, the son who lived with the rector of Fillol was described as *"managing"* (*gubernat*) his home; AEV, Visites, no. 1200/2, 45v. (1331).

to provide for their children. Similarly, the priest Bartomeu Juià abandoned Na Ugueta and their children after a second warning by episcopal officials to terminate his relationship. Villagers reported that Na Ugueta frequently complained and wept about her circumstances.[124] The transient nature of some clerical unions undoubtedly left these women in a precarious financial situation. Those who were desperate enough and had little recourse because their families could not or would not provide assistance may have left their children in foundling hospitals.[125] The widow Elisenda had a child with her husband's brother Ramon, who also happened to be the rector of the parish of Cans. She and the rector Ramon de Sant Pere traveled to Cervera and left the infant at a hospital there.[126] It is impossible to know whether her husband was dead or whether she could not count on the rector's support, but the situation drove Elisenda to leave her baby at a foundling hospital.

The forsaken women and children of parish clergy, however, stand out in the records because there are so few reports of deadbeat fathers. It is likely that the clerics who abandoned their families are underreported in the visitations, but the actions of these clerics must be weighed against those who continued to provide for and live with their children after the mother died or had moved on to another relationship. That Catalan clerics kept and housed their children under these circumstances stands in contrast to Philippa Maddern's findings that the children of English clergymen were not raised in their father's household but were sent to a boarding school in a monastery or convent, or were expelled from the home with their mothers when the clergymen were faced with ecclesiastical punishment for sexual incontinence.[127] On the whole, it appears that Catalan clerics felt a responsibility to care for their offspring and were not overly concerned with the appearance of a celibate household. Indeed, the clerics who established separate residences for their

---

124. ADG, Visites, no. 5, 14r. (1331); ADG, Visites, no. 3, 15v.–16r.v. (1321).

125. For a remarkable case in which a woman abandoned her baby in a hospital in Barcelona and later changed her mind and returned to retrieve her child, see Benito i Monclús, *Parroquies del maresm*, document no. 18; ADB, Visites, no. 1 bis, 136v.–139r. (1310), 284–85. Evidence from the fifteenth century shows that, in addition to impoverished couples who could not care for their children, some women involved with clerics gave their children to hospitals; Teresa-Maria Vinyoles i Vidal and Margarida González i Betlinski, "Els infants abandonats a les portes de l'hospital de Barcelona (anys 1426–1439)," in *La pobreza y la asistencia a los pobres en la Cataluña medieval*, ed. Manuel Riu (Barcelona: C.S.I.C., 1981–1982), 191–285. It is also likely that in situations where the mother died or refused to care for the child, the cleric made the decision to leave his offspring at a foundling hospital because he had no one to care for such a young child. This may have been the case for the hebdomedarian Ramon Eimeric, who promised a significant sum of money to a hospital in Torroella de Montgrí to clothe and feed his young son for a period of three years; ADG, Notularum, no. 6, 57r.v. (1326).

126. AEV, Visites, no. 1200/2, 55v.–56r. (1331).

127. Philippa Maddern, "Between Households: Children in Blended and Transitional Households in Late-Medieval England," *Journal of the History of Childhood and Youth* 3, no. 1 (2010): 79–78.

families and kept their sons in their home as young male students (*scolares*) to help with church duties suggests not only that clerics benefitted from their assistance but also that, as fathers, clerics wanted to display their male children to the parish.[128] The pressure of the village community, the stigma of callously casting off a woman and children, and the standards of lay manhood that expected a man to provide for his offspring may have also influenced clergymen to acknowledge their paternity and look after their progeny. A cleric who deserted a woman and child was likely to face the censure of the community and lose the respect of his parishioners. For Catalan clergy, then, achieving social manhood and fatherhood entailed more than simply impregnating a woman; it involved establishing a union with a woman; publicly acknowledging their offspring; and financially supporting, training, educating (if possible), and marrying off a son or daughter.

Conclusion

Legitimate marriage was not an option for clerical couples. Nevertheless, it is remarkable that so many Catalan clerics in the holy orders chose to enter into marriage-like unions. These unions resembled lay marriage as it was commonly practiced in medieval society. Clerics and their women not only emulated what they observed in their own communities but also strove to acquire the roles of husband and wife, and the status that these roles conferred. Marriage offered both sexes a socially recognized transition from youth to adulthood. A woman left her father's home and became the mistress of her own home. Her duties as a wife and mother signified that she had achieved what society considered to be the most respectable and appropriate function for a woman. A man went from being a dependent in the household of another man to becoming independent and establishing his own household. Like marriage, a clerical union provided a home and children, and at least the trappings of marriage. The women who allied themselves to clergymen may not have had the legitimate title of wife, but they still assumed the roles of wife and mother. For men, simply possessing a penis did not confer manhood in medieval society. Men's bodies—at least in the production and emission of sperm and the ability to generate offspring—mattered in the formation of masculinity. For clerics, a stable union with a woman meant that they became the head of a household in which they governed over their dependents, proved their virility through fathering children, and provided for their family. It also allowed

---

128. See, for example, ADG, Visites, no. 5, 18v. (1331).

clerics to acquire the roles of husband and father in their community—the social markers of adult lay manhood found throughout medieval society. P.H. Cullum's argument that clerics remained in a juvenile state while in the minor orders and became adult men only when they were ordained as priests and acquired a church benefice seems to better fit the clergy in England than in Catalunya, where clerics openly established marital households prior to their ordination.[129] The conferral of priestly authority certainly bolstered the standing of a cleric in his community, but ordination itself did not bestow social adulthood. For Catalan clerics, admission to the priesthood was not the equivalent of marriage and not the ultimate sign of achieving adult manhood; many had already assumed the role of husband and father as they progressed from the minor to major orders.

Gender historians have often pointed out that the obligation of celibacy deprived clerics of the most visible indicators of masculinity—wives and children. Yet numerous clerics disregarded the obligation of celibacy and continued to adopt these markers of lay masculinity well after the eleventh and twelfth century reforms.[130] The notion that clerics were manly because they eschewed the company of women and could substitute spiritual marriage and spiritual fatherhood for wives and children failed to penetrate the lower ranks of the Catalan clergy. The evidence that Catalan parish clerics engaged in stable, long-term unions to a far greater extent than short-term affairs or casual sex suggests that establishing a household and producing a family were important to their identity as men. These priests chose to enter into domestic partnerships that afforded them the social and economic benefits of marriage that indiscriminate sexuality could not offer. Although it is true that promiscuous behavior affected the reputation of clergymen, the marriage-like unions of priests did not undermine their priestly authority in the community. The views of Gregorian reformers, who believed that sexual impurity and the lack of bodily self-control marked these priests as unmanly and thus unable to lead in their parishes, is simply not found in the documents of practice or synodal legislation from Catalunya.[131] On the contrary, the de facto marriages and the adult responsibilities of husbandhood and fatherhood that accompanied such unions probably strengthened the convergence of clerics' priestly and

---

129. Pat H. Cullum, "Life Cycle and Life-Course in a Clerical and Celibate Milieu: Northern England in the Later Middle Ages," in *Time and Eternity: The Medieval Discourse*, ed. Gerhard Jaritz and Gerson Moreno-Riano (Turnhout, Belgium: Brepols, 2003), 274; P.H. Cullum, "Boy / Man into Clerk/ Priest: The Making of the Late Medieval Clergy," in *Rites of Passage: Cultures of Transition in the Fourteenth Century*, ed. Nicola McDonald and William Mark Ormrod (York, UK: York Medieval Press, 2004), 52, 58.

130. Werner, "Promiscuous Priests and Vicarage Children," 170–71.

131. Thibodeaux, *Manly Priest*, 140.

patriarchal authority in the parishes. The choice not to abide by their vow of celibacy indicates that priests did not accept a clerical gender identity that prohibited any expression of male sexuality and that marriage-like unions conferred what celibacy could not in these villages—adult masculinity. By the fourteenth century, the Western Church had spent the preceding nine hundred years promoting and insisting on the sexual abstinence of its clergy, yet it remained unsuccessful in convincing a large number of parish clergy in Iberia to equate celibacy with manliness and to reject the benefits of marriage; this suggests that, at the very least, the proletariat of the Catalan church rebuffed, if not disdained, the prescribed behaviors and religious masculinity of the reforming efforts that had been in effect throughout Europe for the previous three hundred years.[132]

Medieval society, moreover, had not changed its general perception of male sexuality. Sex was seen as a masculine activity in which men were the initiators and the aggressors; women were sexually passive.[133] Medical theories about the production of sperm as a sign of a man's virility and potency, in addition to fears about impotence, show that there was a link in the minds of medieval people between sexual ability and masculine identity. The late medieval medical treatise, *The Mirror of Coitus (Speculum al foderi)*, dedicated exclusively to coitus and sexual hygiene, insists on the benefits of sex. Written in Catalan, the text advices that "when men are healthy they should copulate to reduce the amount of sperm, to excite the mind, and to cool hot vapors," and it declares that "the body cannot be healthy if it does not rid itself of excess semen."[134] Since the text was written in the vernacular, it is possible that the medical views espoused in the *Mirror of Coitus* were known to Catalan men. The works of Galen were also present in the Crown of Aragon in the early fourteenth century by way of Arnau de Vilanova, the renowned Aragonese physician. A great number of medical texts were available to readers in Iberia in the fourteenth and fifteenth centuries and became popular guides for nonprofessionals.[135] At the very least, the advice found in the *Mirror of Coitus* may have resonated with Catalan churchmen, especially the passage in the text that warns that men who "for religious reasons" do not engage in coitus become

132. Miller, "Masculinity, Reform, and Clerical Culture"; Thibodeaux, "Man of the Church?" 384–85.

133. Salisbury, "Gendered Sexuality," 94; Murray, "Hiding behind the Universal Male," 130–36.

134. *The Mirror of Coitus. A Translation and Edition of the Fifteenth-Century Speculum al foderi*, trans. and ed. Michael Solomon (Madison: Hispanic Seminary of Medieval Studies, 1990), 14.

135. Michael Solomon, *Fictions of Well-Being: Sickly Readers and Vernacular Medical Writing in Late Medieval and Early Modern Spain* (Philadelphia: University of Pennsylvania Press, 2010), xii, 1–3, 16–17.

depressed, show signs of insanity, and lose their appetites.[136] Clerics may have used this warning as a way to justify their sexual activity. Scholars such as Jacqueline Murray and Edward Behrend-Martínez have argued that a sexually dysfunctional man in the premodern period was considered effeminate and "less than a real man."[137] The guidance offered in the *Mirror of Coitus* indicates that the desire and ability to perform sex, and even the arousal of a female sexual partner, was important to men. Chapters in the *Mirror of Coitus* that address the treatment of impotence, how to generate greater sperm production, medicines that arouse the desire for coitus, and tips on foreplay to prepare a woman for sexual coupling indicate that men were concerned with these issues. Although Derek Neal makes the valid point that masculinity for priests or even laymen was not "solely defined by genital sex acts," generating and supporting children seems to have been key to the masculine identity of Catalan priests. Moreover, Neal's claim that the overt sexuality of a clergyman could make him effeminate in the eyes of the laity is not a view that I have found in these Catalan sources.[138] Such overwhelming evidence of clerical sexuality and the high rates of clerical offspring would not exist if the parish clergy had embraced celibacy. In the peasant communities of Catalunya where informal unions were more common and acceptable, fatherhood and the maintenance of a patrilineal lineage was a sign of masculine status—not feminization.

Understanding why clerics needed families is important to understanding how clerics defined themselves as men. Certainly there were practical reasons for having a family. Clerical de facto wives provided certain services that a parish cleric needed, such as buying and preparing food, doing laundry, taking care of the home, and even helping with church duties. In addition, these women contributed to the household economy through their labor. They tended the cleric's small plot of land, watched over his animals, and helped with the harvest. Children also played an important role and could assist their parents with various tasks and errands needed on the family farm. In particular, boys could help their fathers by taking the place of a scolaris and assisting

---

136. *Mirror of Coitus*, 13. The anonymous author of *Mirror* claims that "I myself have seen men with a great amount of sperm who for religious reasons delay coitus. These men lose their body, suffer paralysis, become greatly depressed without cause, show signs of insanity, and lose their desire to eat." As Michael Solomon has noted, the author of *Mirror* ignores the "impropriety of his counsel and left his readers with no clear imperative for reconciling his advice on sexual intercourse with Christian ethics."

137. Murray, "Hiding behind the Universal Male," 139; Edward Behrend-Martínez, "Manhood and the Neutered Body in Early Modern Spain," *Journal of Social History* 38, no. 4 (2005): 1076–77, 1080.

138. Neal, *Masculine Self*, 91, 108–9.

with the celebration of the mass. But deeply connected to the benefits of family life was the opportunity for the parish clergy to demonstrate their masculinity. Secular clergy were entangled in lay society by way of their pastoral work, ties to friends and family, and relationships with their women and children. They were not impervious to the lay masculine ideals present all around them. On the contrary, they were influenced by the culture of lay masculinity and participated in the arena of masculinity with the rest of the men in their parishes.

The prevalence of clerical unions in Catalunya indicates not only that clerics were demonstrating their sexuality but also that for many Catalan clerics being a man included having a family, setting up a household, and supporting a woman and children. Parish clergy may have practiced secular manhood to avoid accusations of effeminacy. This would correspond with Ruth Karras's observation that "if men vie to prove to each other that they are more manly, then they prove at the same time that they are not womanly, and this rejection of the feminine is implicit if not explicit in all understandings of masculinity."[139] If this is the case, secular clerics who adhered to the Church standards of celibacy would have been emasculated figures in their communities. The tradition of clergy keeping a family, therefore, was not simply a way for clergy to fit in with male peers or medieval society at large but a means to express their masculinity. Clerics failed to conceal their relationships to such an extent that, in effect, they advertised their connection to their spouses and children; they treated their domestic partner as a wife and nurtured, raised, baptized, and married off their sons and daughters and displayed them in the parish church. Public knowledge about their relationships alleviated any doubts about their manhood and their ability to engage in procreative sex. Ecclesiastical officials recognized this problem, which is why they inquired whether the cleric kept his concubine and children "publicly." Husbandhood and fatherhood, therefore, were proof of manhood in a village community.

---

139. Karras, *From Boys to Men*, 153.

CHAPTER 3

Laymen in Priestly Robes

The lives of parish clergy were rooted both in the ecclesiastical and secular world. The priestly profession separated clergymen from the laity in their access to sacred space, sacred mysteries (i.e., the eucharist), and their sacred duty to administer the sacraments. Yet these men were more than priests in their communities—they were the neighbors, sons, brothers, friends, and even the enemies of the people of the parish. A de facto wife and children, and the concerns over family that went hand in hand with fatherhood and husbandhood meant that clerics were fully enmeshed in the lay world. The connection to family and friends remained strong despite the expectation of the Church that a priest's commitment to God and the Church take precedence over his biological family. In Catalunya, parish priests often grew up near the villages where they served or had familial ties to their parish. Affection, if not loyalty, bound clergymen to their parents and siblings, who in turn were important supporters in times of need. Furthermore, a priest's union with a village woman forged ties to the community because he acquired a father- and mother-in-law and brothers- and sisters-in-law. Through the birth of his children, he cultivated these ties as family friends and fellow villagers were chosen as godparents. The marriages of his children further cemented these relationships to the community as he welcomed a son- or daughter-in-law into the family. In many instances, the people of the parish were connected to their parish priest through ties of kinship or affinity. The priestly profession was only one marker, one identity, among many.

The boundary separating the clergy from the laity was thin and permeable. In disconnecting the clergy from their families and the concerns of the secular world, reformers of the eleventh and twelfth centuries intended that clerics place their loyalty, affection, and obedience to the Mother Church (*mater eccle-sia*) above their kin group.[1] The parish clergy, however, did not replace their relationship to their natal and marital households with their relationship to the household of God. The choices clerics made to preserve and secure the survival and prosperity of their kin shows that family concerns, when pitted against duty to the Church and the precepts of their profession, often won out. These strong bonds of kinship meant that clerics were protective of the social status and economic security of their family members. Family loyalty and the opportunities for social and economic gain could, however, lead to clashes with fellow villagers. It is hard to imagine that clerics such as the priest Pere Pol, who lived in the parish of Estanyol for more than thirty years with Berengaria Giberta and his "many children," and who spent much of his time socializing at the local tavern with parishioners and his coworker, the hebdomedarian Ramon, did not benefit from the support of his family or forge lasting friendships.[2]

In this chapter, I address the extent to which parish clergy were embedded in their local community. I consider how familial, social, and economic factors firmly bound clerics to a life that very much mirrored that of their parishio-ners. For many clerics who originated in the lower strata of medieval society, very little differentiated them from their fellow villagers. Clergy and laity shared many of the same experiences in their rural communities when they ploughed fields, tended to farm animals, and harvested their crops. On feast days, the vicar Guillem was known to work on his land rather than take a day of rest. In the case of the villagers of Verges, they recalled that the beneficed cleric Dalmau d'Auresols, as a young boy of five, had helped his father and brother look after the family's animals and played with their sons while running through the streets of the village.[3] Since many clerics who served in rural

---

1. See Megan McLaughlin, "The Mother of the Faithful," *Sex, Gender, and Episcopal Authority in an Age of Reform, 1000–1122* (Cambridge, UK: Cambridge University Press, 2010), 123–59. See also Moore, "Family, Community and Cult."

2. ADG, Visites fragmentaris, 6v. (1320). Parishioners commented on the socializing activities of the priest Pere Pol and the hebdomedarian Ramon while relating the story that an inebriated Pere Pol left the tavern of Arnau Bigues one night, and fell into a pond and nearly drowned. Pere was fined 10 sous for his disorderly conduct.

3. AEV, Visites, no. 1200/2, 69v. (1331). The vicar Guillem ÇaConamina supported a concubine and two children. For the beneficed cleric Dalmau d'Auresols, see ADG, Processos, no. 273, 2r.v.–3v. (1353).

villages belonged to the well-to-do peasantry, they shared a similar social background with their parishioners. Family security, social advancement, and economic prosperity were of interest to both clergymen and laymen. Clerics sought to maintain any social or economic privilege that could elevate their status in the community, including dabbling in side businesses such as moneylending, tavern-owning, shopkeeping, and working as a *batlle* (bailiff) to supplement their income. It was not the desire to improve their lot that separated the clergy from the laity; the difference lay in the opportunity and means for clerics to exploit their position to their benefit.

Parish records, on occasion, disclose how clerics' social and familial networks in the villages they served placed them firmly in the lay world. Tables 3.1, 3.2, and 3.3 show that many clerics worked in an environment that was not free from personal ties of kinship and friendship. These clergymen, therefore, could not easily separate their role as a parish priest from their roles in the family. Take, for instance, the sacrist Pere Camallera, who served in the parish of Garrigàs where his brother Ramon Pere and Ramon's wife Guillema, his sister Raimunda, and his father Bernat Camallera, as well as his partner Berengaria d'Olm and their two children, lived. The sacrist Pere interacted daily in the village with various family members, and on the feast of Sant Miquel, he traveled to the town of Castelló d'Empúries with his father and brother to sell a large amount of wax.[4] Pere was not only a priest in his community but also a father, a son, a brother, a brother-in-law, and uncle to the people who attended his church.

Although the visitation records do not consistently reveal the family ties between clergy and parishioners, it is likely that a great number of clerics were related to the people of their parish. The information on a cleric's ties to kin appears randomly in the visitations because episcopal visitors were not interested in recording such matters. Usually these personal details were noted when a complaint, crime, or violation of canon law was investigated. For example, the visitor had to dismiss the testimony of witnesses who claimed that the capellan of ça Coma performed his office well and no longer sinned with his domestic partner because it was revealed by other villagers that the witnesses were related to the cleric.[5] Similarly, we know that the hebdomedarian Ramon Bartomeu, his sister Sibil·la, and uncle Berenguer Cunyl all lived in the village of Esponellà because the visitor looked into a complaint that Ramon had broken into the house of Jaume de Costa to have an amorous encounter with Jaume's wife. The testimony of parishioners disclosed that

4. ADG, Visites, no. 7, 142v.–150r. (1343).
5. ACV, Calaix 31/43, Visites, no. 3, 36r. (1314).

the hebdomedarian Ramon's uncle owned a tavern in the village; his sister was married to a fellow villager; and Ramon had at one time been sexually involved with Pere Guerau's wife, who also happened to be related to Ramon. In the same visitation, we learn that the sacrist Guillem d'Anglada's brother also lived in Esponellà because the two brothers were involved in a fistfight with a fellow parishioner.[6] The overlapping role of clerics who lived among their family means that they had a support network in place and could count on the backing of family when relationships with their fellow villagers soured. Notarial documents also reveal the ties of a cleric and his family to a parish. In the village of Vilatenim, the stabilitus Pere Ferrar gave the lands attached to his benefice to his nephew, Pere Ferrar, to farm for half the profits produced from these possessions. The priest Jaume de Sant Pol made a similar agreement with his brother Guillem, who also received half of the profits for farming the land belonging to his brother's benefice in Vilatenim.[7] Clerics frequently relied on their family members to make advantageous business deals that benefitted everyone involved and trusted that their siblings and nephews would look out for their greater interests.

That more than just parents and siblings could be counted among a cleric's relatives in his parish is not unexpected. Considering the close-knit communities and limited mobility of the peasantry who lived in the small villages in the mountains or foothills of the Pyrenees, many people were related to each other by blood, marriage, or spiritual affinity. Indeed, a number of clerics were sexually involved with women who were related to them within the prohibited four degrees of consanguinity and affinity.[8] The rector of Sant Pere de Colls kept Anglesa, who was both his parishioner and relative (*consanguinea*).

---

6. ADG, Visites, no. 5, 8v.–16v. (1331). Another account that reveals family ties is quite disturbing. The rector Pere Granada lived in the same parish as his married sister Ferrara and a female cousin, Maria Romesgosa. According to the testimony of Ferrara's husband, Pere Galceran, cousin Maria arranged for the rector Pere to "deflower" Galceran's sister, Elisenda, who then became pregnant; ADB, Visites, no. 2, 73v. (1315).

7. AHG, Notorials, Peratallada, no. 1044, 6v. (1333).

8. For example, the priest Berenguer Folc had four children with Saurina, his "consanguinea" (relative). The bishop of Barcelona charged the beneficed cleric Bernat de Fabrica with committing incest with Ermesenda, who was related to him "in quarto gradu consanguinitatis." The priest Andreu Maioll was charged with committing adultery and incest with the wife of his kinsman and with violently raping the daughter of another family member. The priest Pere Bons in the parish of Sant Vicenç de Sarrià was accused of impregnating Elisenda, the daughter of Pere Bons (same name as the priest), who was related to the priest Pere within three degrees of consanguinity; ADB, Registrum Communium, no. 3, 6r. (1314); ADB, Registrum Communium, no. 9, 182v. (1341); ADB, Registrum Communium, no. 4, 162r. (1328); ADB, Visites, no. 2, 77v. (1315). Other examples for the dioceses of Girona, Vic, and Urgell are listed in tables 3.1, 3.2, and 3.3. Baucells found thirty-two cases mentioned in visitation records in the diocese of Barcelona in which clerics were related by blood to their concubines and sixteen cases in which a cleric and his partner transgressed the ties of affinity through baptism or marriage; *Vivir en la edad media*, 3: 2523–24.

Parishioners mentioned that Anglesa had recently died due to a difficult child-birth and that it was rumored in the neighboring parish of Muntayola that she had done so without confession. Yet the rector admitted to the visitor that he had heard Anglesa's final confession because the capellan of Muntayola had not arrived in time. The rector, then, had committed incest with a blood rela-tive and spiritual incest with a woman to whom he had administered last rites.[9] In the case of the rector of Santa Maria de Montcuyl, he too was related to his concubine's husband within the second degree of consanguinity.[10]

The intricate ties of kinship between a cleric and his domestic partner are best seen in the small parish of Ordino, a village nestled in the mountains of the Pyrenees in Andorra. The deacon Berenguer had a child with Maria, the daughter of the chaplain of Ordino. As it turned out, Maria's mother, the chap-lain's concubine, was a first cousin to the deacon Berenguer.[11] Thus, Maria and Berenguer were second cousins, and their son was both a grandson and nephew to Maria's mother. Therefore, it is more than likely that Berenguer's immediate family and Maria's grandparents lived in Ordino or in the surround-ing area. Serving in the parish of Ordino, Berenguer could hardly help that many of the people gathered in the parish church were related to him in some degree.

That the laity and the clergy were married to or carnally involved with people who were also their kin is not remarkable. Studies of marriage con-tracts in Catalunya have shown that peasant families strategically practiced en-dogamy. Over 50 percent of men and women married someone from the same parish, and 20 percent married someone who lived within 20 kilometer of their village.[12] In these small and sometimes isolated rural villages, finding

---

9. ACV, Calaix 31/43, Visites, no. 5, 6r. (1315). The rector of Sords also administered last rites to his concubine Na Crespina when she was sick. She later died and left him with two children; ADG, Processos, no. 49, 1r.v. (1321); ADG, Visites, no. 5, 23r. (1331). Thomas of Chobham classified clerical concubinage as incest because a priest corrupted his spiritual daughter through sex. A woman who accepted penance from a priest was both his penitential and baptismal daughter. Priests, therefore, should avoid their spiritual daughters as if they were their own carnal daughters; Thomas of Chob-ham, *Summa confessorum* ("De penitentia iniungenda ei qui filiam spirutualem corrumpit"), 383–84.

10. ACV, Calaix, 31/43, Visites, no. 5, 11v. (1315).

11. ACV, Calaix 31/43, Visites, no. 1, 21v. (1312). In another example, the rector Bernat report-edly married off his daughter Ermesenda to Andreu, a distant cousin; Visitatio diversarum, HMML, microfilm no. 31951, Visites, no. 1, 19r. (1305).

12. Jaume Codina, *Contractes de matrimoni al delta del Llobregat (segles XIV a XIX)* (Barcelona: Fun-dació Noguera, 1997), 33–36. Christian Guilleré also finds that the peasantry around the city of Gi-rona had a high rate of endogamy. In fact, Guilleré estimates that in 87 percent of the cases (ninety-seven contracts) both the groom- and bride-to-be came from the same parish; *Girona al segle XIV*, 413–14. See also Josep Fernández i Trabal, *Una família catalana medieval: Els Bell·lloc de Girona, 1267–1533* (Barcelona: Publicacions de l'Abadia de Montserrat, 1995), 184–86.

a potential spouse who was not related by blood or affinity must have presented a challenge.

Additional details haphazardly recorded during visitations show the close-knit ties between clerics and their families. The priest Guillem serving in the parish of Santa Maria de Gremp kept his concubine in the home of his father; the priest Miquel in the parish of Cervelló kept Guillemona Fabrica and their child in the home of his mother.[13] When clerics could not afford to rent or buy a separate home for their family, or were intent on avoiding an episcopal fine for living with their wives and children, they turned to their father or mother for assistance. Some parents continued to aid their clerical sons into adulthood and were willing to welcome a son's family into their household. Not all parents, however, were pleased with their son's choice of partner. A villager reported in the parish of Sant Feliu de Rahona that it was known that the parents of the priest Bernat d'Orts did not approve of their son's three-year relationship with La Garnava, a woman that the entire parish considered to be "common" and "very wicked."[14] The fact that villagers knew that the priest's family objected to his relationship further reveals that clerics were a part of the community.

Just as parents looked after their children, it is clear that clerics and their partners felt a responsibility to look after family members in need. The elderly father of the rector Francesc de Aparia lived with Na Serra and their three children. According to the rector, Na Serra "pampered and served" (*fovet et deservit*) his decrepit father. Similarly, Guillemona, the rector Jaume Mateo's concubine, took care of his sister who was "infirma."[15] It is not surprising that a cleric's partner was the primary caregiver. The domestic role of women as nurses and healers further underscores how a cleric benefitted from the labor and expertise of his domestic partner.[16] For parish clergy, the ties to family were not severed when they entered into clerical orders but remained an integral part of their natal family unit. Cultural norms, moreover, dictated that children honor their parents and support them in their old age. Just as the parents of clergymen assisted their sons and family, so too did these clerical sons

---

13. ACV, Calaix 31/43, Visites, no. 4, 1r. (1314); Visitatio diversarum, HMML, microfilm no. 31951, Visites, no. 1, 7r. (1304). Similarly, the rector of Cantabella kept his concubine, daughter, and mother in his home; AEV, no. 1200/2, 8r. (1331). The priest Mateu Colomer kept his concubine and child in the home of his father, and the cleric Guillem Arbort kept his concubine and daughter in the home of his mother; Martí Bonet, "Visitas pastorals," 93, 113.

14. ADB, Visites, no. 4, 71v.–72r. (1337).

15. Visitatio diversarum, HMML, microfilm no. 31951, Visites, no. 1, 43v. (1305); Visites, no. 1, 74v. (1307).

16. Montserrat Cabré, "Women or Healers? Household Practices and the Categories of Health Care in Late Medieval Iberia," *Bulletin of the History of Medicine* 82, no. 1 (2008): 18–51.

and their women care for elderly parents. Although the structure of clerical families typically revolved around a nuclear household, consisting of parents and their children, examples of stem or extended family households that contained grandparents, parents, and grandchildren can also be found.[17]

The example of the cleric Simó Alenyà, serving in the parish of Serro de Daró, who kept Sibil·la and their two children in the home of his mother in the parish of Fonolleres, tells us a lot about the extent to which clerics tried to stay close to their families.[18] Many gravitated to benefices that were in parishes near their natal household, where they continued to live in communities that had known them from childhood and were familiar with their family history. This is not unusual considering that patrons of presentative (i.e., simple) benefices could present their own candidate for the bishop's approval and conferral. Patrons were more likely to present a local candidate whom they knew rather than a stranger. Indeed, a study of simple benefices endowed by the laity in the diocese of Girona, particularly among the middling level of society, has found that parishioners established benefices for the clerical members of their families.[19] In addition, the high numbers of clerics who exchanged their benefices in episcopal registers may reflect clerics who were trying to obtain benefices closer to home.[20] In 1314, Simó Alenyà started out as a tonsured cleric in the parish of Sant Juià de Corçà, which was 6 kilometers from his home, or about a walking distance of an hour and a half. At this time, Simó had "infantes" with Simoneta, the daughter of another Simó from the parish of Serra de Daró, which was the village adjacent to Fonolleres and less than 2 kilometers away. Corçà, then, was close enough that Simó could visit his

---

17. For a discussion on how inheritance norms, marriage patterns, and the family lives of the elderly affected household formation in the Iberia and Italy, see David I. Kertzer and Caroline Brettell, "Advances in Italian and Iberian Family History," *Journal of Family History* 12, no. 1 (1987): 87–120. José Enrique Ruiz Doménec has argued that, from the eighth to tenth centuries, Catalan peasant families practiced cognatic inheritance and formed extended households, but that an increase in population and a need to protect family property meant that family structure and inheritance in the eleventh century and after were based on an agnatic or patrilineal model; "Las estructuras familiares catalanas en la alta edad media," *Cuadernos de Arqueología i Història de la Ciutat* 16 (1975): 90–108. That a diversity of family structures was still present in fourteenth-century Catalunya is discussed in Montserrat Richou i Llimona, "El baix maresme a l'època baix medieval," *Butlletí de la Societat Catalana d'Estudis Històrics* 19 (2008): 153–66. See also Herlihy, *Medieval Households*, 136–44.

18. ADG, Visites fragmentaris, 2r. (1318).

19. Marquès, "Fundaciones de beneficios." Gregory Milton also finds that the nonnoble elite in the community of Santa Coloma de Queralt filled both the local secular and clerical administrative offices with their sons. Many rectors of the area churches, including priests and notarial scribes came from this middling-level class; Milton, *Market Power*, 45–49, 141–42. For a discussion of presentative benefices, see Kristine T. Utterback, *Pastoral Care and Administration in Mid-Fourteenth Century Barcelona: Exercising the "Art of Arts"* (Lewiston: Edwin Mellen Press, 1993), 87–89.

20. See Josep M. Marquès, *Una història de la diòcesi de Girona* (Barcelona: Abadia de Montserrat, 2007), 90–91; Utterback, *Pastoral Care*, 99–101.

family regularly in Fonollores. Simoneta, who at the time lived in Fonolleres with Simó's mother and visited him regularly in Corçà, could easily visit her parents in Serra from both villages. In 1318, Simó Alenyà obtained the benefice of stabilitus in Serra de Daró and then served as the hebdomedarian of Serra until the end of his career.[21] Years later when Simó was an elderly man, another Simó Alenyà, probably his son, served as sacrist and then rector of Fonollores from 1341 to the mid-1350s.[22] Throughout his clerical career, Simó senior served in parishes close to his home village where parishioners knew his immediate family and relatives, which explains why the villagers of Corçà were familiar with the personal details of Simó's and Simoneta's family histories. What is more, the villagers of Corçà, Daró, and Fonolleres would have known Simó and Simoneta as adolescents, young parents, and as grandparents.

While clerics such as the two Alenyàs obtained benefices near their natal village, other clerical families managed to hold positions in the parish church for two or more generations. In the village of Sant Llorenç de la Muga, three priests with the last name of Roure served in the parish for over forty years, and it is very possible that these were fathers and sons.[23] The same is probably true for the hebdomedarian Pere de Quintana, who served in the parish of Sant Vicenç de Maià de Montcal in 1303 and had numerous children (reportedly eight). Thirty years later, a Ramon de Quintana served as hebdomedarian in 1331, and he could have been Pere's son or grandson.[24] Fathers and uncles also renounced their benefices for their younger sons and nephews. The priest Bartomeu Roig relinquished his position of deacon so that Anton Roig, a cleric in the minor orders, could assume his benefice. In the parish of Rupià, the priest Arnau de Guardia arranged for his nephew Joan de Guardia to serve in

21. ADG, Visites, no. 1, 2v. (1314); ADG, Visites, no. 2, 7r.v. (1315); ADG, Visites fragmentaris, 1r., 2r. (1318); ADG, Notularum, no. 6, 125v. (1327).
22. ADG, Visites, no. 7, 18r. (1341); ADG, Notularum, no. 23, 21r.–26v. (1349); ADG, Lletres, no. 6, 134v. (1343); ADG, Visites, no. 9, 3v. (1350); ADG, Lletres, no. 21, 211v.–212r. (1353).
23. Guillem de Roure appears as a hebdomedarian in 1315 and was still a hebdomedarian in 1329. In the 1315 visitation, he is noted as having a son with a woman from the village. Fifteen years later, in 1329, a cleric by the name of Bartomeu de Roure is identified as the deacon of the church. Bartomeu had numerous children with Simona and was brought to the bishop's court in 1332 for beating a parishioner who disciplined his son. He served in the church until at least 1352, when he is identified as a stabilitus. In 1352, a beneficed cleric, Guillem de Roure, also served in the church and was fined for his participation with Bartomeu Roure against the hebdomedarian of the parish. In 1355, Guillem was fined for an affair with a married woman; ADG, Visites, no. 1, 65r. (1315); ADG, Visites, no. 4, 41r.v. (1329); ADG, Visites, no. 6, 58v. (1340); ADG, Imposicions de Penes, no. 1, 4v. (1336); ADG, Remissions de Penes, no. 1, 40r., 41r. (1352); ADG, Obligacions de Penes, no. 1, 98v. (1355).
24. ADG, Visites fragmentaris, 14r.v.–15r. (1303); ADG, Visites, no. 5, 104r.v. (1331). By 1340, Ramon served as a rector in the parish of Palera, which is 6.5 kilometers from Maià de Montcal; ADG, Obligacions de Penes, no. 1, 17v. (1340); ADG, Imposicions de Penes, no. 1, 29v. (1340) and 73v. (1347).

his absence.[25] Siblings also worked together in the same parish or exchanged benefices with one another. The brothers Joan Simó and Guillem Simó took turns holding the same benefice in the parish church of Santa Maria de Centenys in the early 1320s. In the 1330s, the priests Pere Simó and Berenguer Simó served together in the church of Centenys, and a generation later, Bernat Simó also served as a priest there.[26] Although it is often unclear how these clerics were related, when the last name of a clergyman matches that of parishioners living in the village, it is likely that some family relationship existed. In the village of Vilatenim, prior to his retirement in 1324, the sacrist Guillem Albert instituted a benefice in the parish church of Sant Joan, which Bernat Albert shortly thereafter obtained as a stabilitus. During his twenty-year tenure as sacrist, Guillem Albert had also served with the cleric Ramon Albert, who was probably his cousin or nephew. The Albert family had a strong presence in Vilatenim because Guillem and Ramon Albert attended to the parish church beginning in the early 1300s, and Bernat Albert later followed in their footsteps in 1328 when he was eighteen years old. Notarial documents reveal that Ramon and Bernat Albert were related, and Bernat's mother, brother, sister, nieces and nephews, in addition to various uncles and cousins, lived in Vilatenim.[27] In the parish of Llançà, the Corts family held positions in the parish church for over twenty years. The sacrist Pere de Corts and the stabilitus Bernat de Corts served there during the 1330s and 1340s.[28] When clerics in the same generation shared the same last name, they were most likely cousins or brothers.[29] In

---

25. AHG, Peratallada, no. 199, 44r.v. (1332); ADG, Visites, no. 4, 15v.–16r. (1329).

26. ADG, Visites, no. 5, 7r.v. (1331); ADG, Notularum, no. 4, 59r. (1323); ADG, Notularum, no. 5, 65r. (1325): ADG, Imposicions de Penes, no. 1, 89r. (1353).

27. AHG, Notarials, Peralada, no. 1044, 3r. 9r., 11v., 20r., 24r., 71v., 73r., 96r. (1331–1336). See also, ADG, Notularum, no. 2, 65r., 68r. (1306); ADG, Notularum, no. 4, 127r. (1324); ADG, Notularum, no. 6, 188v., 195v. (1328); Lletres, no. 3, 138r.v. (1328).

28. ADG, Visites, no. 4, 36v.–37r. (1329); ADG, Visites, no. 7, 126r.v. (1343); ADG, Obligacions de Penes, no. 1, 23v., 37v. (1342); ADG, Imposicions de Penes, no. 1, 33v. (1341) and 47v. (1343); ADG, Lletres, no. 7, 128r. (1344); ADG, Remissions de Penes, no. 1, 6v. (1347) and 14r. (1349). Both Bernat and Pere de Corts maintained relationships with women who were from the parish. The sacrist Pere had three children with Sibil·la, the daughter of Pere Simó. The stabilitus Bernat de Corts had a son with Martina, who was also from Llançà. Two male parishioners with the last name of Corts appear as lay witnesses in the visitations to the parish in 1321 and 1343. It is also likely that the hebdomedarian Pere de Banc and the sacrist Ramon de Banc, who served in the village of Sant Pere de Pescador, were related to each other; ADG, Visites fragmentaris, 5r.v.–6r. (1304). In another example, in the village of Vilatenim, Guillem Albert served as the sacrist and retired prior until 1330 and a Bernat Albert served as a beneficed cleric in the 1330s. Joan Albert, probably a related to Guillem and Bernat, also appears in the notarial records for the village of Vilatenim; AHG, Notorials, Peralada, no. 1044, 3r. (1332), 20r. (1334), 24r. (1334), 73r. (1335); ADG, Obligacions de Penes, no. 1, 71v. (1347).

29. In the appendix, see the parishes of Aro, Bellcaire, Centenys, Farners, Maçanet, Sant Pere de Pescador, Camprodon, Vilatenim, and Sant Iscle d'Empordà for clerics who served in the same parish and shared the same last name.

the parish of Sant Juià de Fortià, the deacon Berenguer Escuder and the married cleric Bernat Escuder are identified as brothers. Similarly, the deacon Arnau de Bosso serving in the parish of Sant Feliu de la Garriga had brothers who lived in the parish, and it is likely that the priest Guillem de Basso was his brother, if not his cousin.[30] In a visit to the parish of Llambilles, the hebdomedarian Guillem Ferrer was fined for keeping his two sons in his own home. The same visitation reveals that two tonsured clerics, Guillem Ferrer and Berenguer Ferrer, were brothers who served in the parish church and were very likely the sons of the hebdomedarian.[31] Indeed, the lists of scolares tonsured during visitations show the same surname among parishioners, clergy, and newly tonsured clerics.[32] As clerics-in-training, many nephews, sons, and cousins started out in their home parish before acquiring benefices elsewhere as they progressed from the minor to major orders, and some were fortunate enough to receive a benefice in their home village.

The draw of living close to his family had an effect on a cleric's career. Full-time residency was a problem for those who were not fortunate enough to obtain a benefice close to home. The parishioners of Vilarig complained that their rector was frequently absent from the parish because he left to visit his parents. Similarly, the priest Bernat Juner, serving in the parish of Riumors, was from Castelló d'Empúries and left for three or four days at a time to return home.[33] Clerics who kept their women and children in distant villages also triggered complaints that they could not be located when they were needed to administer last rites or to baptize a child. The rector Guillem Salvador barely resided in his parish of Llabià; he stayed in Fonolleres where his concubine and child lived. Both the hebdomedarian and deacon of Sant Llorenç d'Adri were frequently absent because they kept their families in Girona.[34] Given the problems with nonresidency and the poor ministry of an absent priest,

---

30. Arnau de Basso appears in a case before the episcopal court for a fight that occurred between Arnau and the sacrist Guillem Agustini. The sacrist reportedly threatened and later injured Arnau and his brothers; ADG, Processos, no. 23 (1315); ADG, Visites, no. 1, 36r.v. (1315). For the Escuder brothers, see ADG, Obligacions de Penes, no. 1, 9r. (1338).

31. ADG, Visites, no. 4, 75v.–76r. (1330).

32. See, for example, the names of scolares tonsured in the parishes of Segúries and Sant Joan de las Abadesses who have the same last name as clergy serving in the parish as well as the parishioners who participated in the visitation; AEV, Visites, no. 3, 48r.v. (1336).

33. ADG, Visites, no. 3, 7r. (1321); ADG, Visites, no. 3, 22v. (1321). See also, ACV, Calaix 31/43, Visites, no. 1, 33r., 40r., 54v. (1312).

34. ADG, Visites, no. 4, 120r.v. (1329). Further examples include the parishioners of Sant Christòfol de Masons, who similarly complained that their chaplain did not remain in the parish but, instead, resided in Castelaç with his concubine and child; the rector of Sant Esteve d'Areu, who kept a concubine from Cerdanya and was called "vagabundus"; and the rector of Santa Maria de Martorelles, who did not reside in the parish but lived in Barcelona with Na Serra; ACV, Calaix 21/43, Visites, no. 5, 14v. (1315); ACV, Calaix 31/43, Visites, no. 8, 4v. (1314); ADB, Visites, no. 2, 29r. (1314).

parishioners may have preferred their clergy to be "local" men who could establish their families in the village or surrounding area. Villagers tended to be suspicious of strangers, and having a cleric whose parents and kin they knew personally or by reputation could be seen as an advantage rather than a detriment. The idiom—"better the devil you know than the devil you don't"— comes to mind. In the diocese of Cortona in Italy, Daniel Bornstein has also found that villagers did not object to a cleric keeping a concubine because domestically settled clerics were "a dependable presence in the village" and "good member[s] of the village community."[35] Domestically settled clerics were also more likely to establish roots in the community and feel a greater responsibility to the parish church and its members.

The advantage of maintaining ties to and living near family can be seen in the more mundane interactions of notarial documents. Joan, the deacon Bonanat's brother, had paid off the deacon's debt to a Jew in Girona during a time that the deacon supported Elisenda and their two children.[36] The sacrist Pere de Puteo, serving in the village of Ultramort, ceded to his brother's son, Pere, a family home in the village of Parlavà in return for rents that his nephew owned.[37] Close to the castle of Peralada, the beneficed cleric Bernat Albert, serving in the parish of Vilatenim, appears in a notarial document borrowing money along with his son, Berenguer Albert, and a female relative, Brunisendis Albert.[38] For clerics, economics, just as much as affection for family, may have motivated them to stay closer to home. The previously mentioned rector Guillem Salvador in Llabià owned rents in his home village of Fonolleres that were probably not connected to his benefice. Other examples include the vicar of Sant Quirze de Muntanyola, who resided for the greater part of the year in Ripoll because he farmed land there that was part of his ancestral inheritance (hereditatem paternam), and the cleric Ponç d'Om, who had an incentive to stay in his home village of Vilanova de la Muga where his father and presumably other family members lived. Ponç's father cultivated his land and

35. Bornstein, "Priests and Villagers," 98.

36. AHG, Notorials, Monells, no. 161, 28r. (1333). The document records the deacon Bonanat, who served in the parish Sant Cebrià de Lledó, paying a debt of 100 sous owed to his brother Joan for a loan. Joan lived in the neighboring village of Santa Pellaia. In the Girona visitation records of 1329 and 1331, the episcopal visitor noted that Bonanat kept Elisenda de Tapiols and their two children in his home.

37. AHG, Notorials, Rupia, no. 559, 34r.v.–35r. (1318). The priest Pere de Puteo served in the church of Santa Eulalià de Ultramort, but both Bernat, his brother, and Pere, his nephew, lived in Parlavà, which is 2.3 kilometers from Ultramort.

38. AHG, Notorials, Peratallada, no. 1044, 3r. (1333). The hebdomedarian Pere Papini, who also served in Vilatenim, appears as a witness to Bernat's loan document.

looked after the beasts that belonged to Ponç.[39] Whether the land belonged to Ponç's benefice or was passed down by his father is impossible to determine. What is clear, however, is that Ponç needed the help of his family to work the farm. Living in a community with family members provided both emotional and economic support that entailed not only collaboration but also a kind of insurance that, should something go wrong, family was there to help.[40] Clerics were also unwilling to forgo the extra income from rents and inherited land, especially if they held a benefice of little worth. The income and land assigned to a benefice could vary greatly, and many clerics needed the extra income to get by. Some, such as the rector of Albalat, spent more time cultivating their land than tending to the people of the parish. The parishioners of Albalat complained that the rector was "sufficiently adequate" at celebrating the divine office but that he was often too "busy" farming his land and looking after his animals to celebrate the mass regularly.[41] Farming, then, was a priority that could supersede priestly duties. It is likely that the rector invested heavily in his farm because it was more profitable than the income from his benefice. (The paltry value of benefices is a topic that I return to later in the chapter.)

Certainly, ambition and the lure of a higher paid benefice encouraged many clerics to relocate. Berenguer Barners progressed from a sacrist in the small village of Santa Margarida to become the sacrista maior of Santa Maria de Castelló d'Empúries, the largest and most important church in a town that was the seat of power for the Counts of Empúries. In the space of fifteen years, Berenguer obtained five benefices and served in four parishes all within 15 kilometers of Castelló d'Empúries.[42] It is difficult to establish precisely where Berenguer was from, but considering that he remained in a concentrated geographical area, it is likely that he was a native of the comital town of Empúries.

A mobile lifestyle, however, did not appeal to all clergymen. Some managed to stay in one or two parishes their entire careers, and others may not have had much of a choice when they sought better-paying benefices that were

---

39. AEV, Visites, no. 1200/3, 6v. (1332); ADG, Visites, no. 6, 157r. (1341). Ponç appears as hebdomedarian of Vilanova de la Muga in 1349.

40. Bisson, *Tormented Voices,* 120–21. Judith Bennett outlines how the Penifader family aided each other in working the land in *Medieval Life,* 79–82.

41. Cárcel Ortí and Boscá Codina, eds., *Visitas pastorales de Valencia,* 120. The parishioners of Sant Pere de Mieres also described their hebdomedarian Joan Ferrer as a dedicated farmer who woke early to tend his fields before going to the church to perform the divine office; ADG, Visites, no. 3, 46r.v. (1321).

42. ADG, Visites, no. 3, 34r.v. (1321); ADG, Notularum, no. 6, 128v.–130r. (1327) and 179r. (1328); ADG, Lletres, no. 3, 26r. (1328); ADG, Visites, no. 5, 88r.v. (1331); ADG, Lletres, no. 5, 63r. (1333); ADG, Notularum, no. 9, 127v. (1335); ADG, Lletres, no. 6, 148v. (1343). Josep M. Marquès notes the high number of clergymen in the fourteenth and fifteenth centuries who renounced or exchanged their benefice for another in *Història de la diòcesi de Girona,* 90–91.

farther from home. Moving around did take its toll. While in Santa Margarida, Berenguer had at least three children with Bartomeva, but as he moved from Sant Miquel de Fluvià to Vilamacolum, to Palau Saverdera, and back to Castelló d'Empúries, the relationship ended and Bartomeva presumably returned to her home village. Uprooting a family more than once would place a strain on any relationship, particularly because the peasantry tended to remain in the same parish for generations and generations—even when faced with an oppressive seigniorial regime.[43] Obtaining a benefice in a new parish could be an opportunity for a fresh start, and some started new families. In other cases, it is clear that, as some clerics moved around and limited themselves to a specific geographical area, they kept their families in a particular village where either the cleric or the woman could remain close to their kin.[44] The family could therefore avoid being relocated, and if they had a business or assets of land, their work could continue uninterrupted. The families that stayed behind would explain why a cleric's woman and children disappeared and reappeared in the records as he moved from parish to parish. When families did follow clerics and moved to a new location, the long-distance commute between parish and family must have influenced their decision. For example, Elisenda followed Ramon de Costa to the French border, some 60–70 kilometers from her home parish of Pineda in la Garrotxa, when he became rector of Sant Martí de Curçavell. The couple had three children in Curçavell, and years later Ramon served in the parish of Santa Maria d'Escales, nearly 50 kilometers south of Curçavell in the Costa Brava, with Elisenda and the children in tow.[45]

---

43. Freedman, *Origins of Peasant Servitude*, 144–45.

44. See, for example, the stabilitus Pere Çaragoll, who served in the parish of Cabanelles but kept Barchiona and their children in Crespià; ADG, Visites, no. 5, 101v. (1331) and 129v. (1332). The rector and capellan of Sant Pere de Palau-sator kept Ermesenda, who was from Vulpellac, in the parish of Peratallada, which was located mid-way between Vulpellac and Palau-sator; ADG, Visites, no. 1, 10r. (1315). While serving in the parish of Taravaus, the cleric Guillem Negre established a relationship with a woman from the parish, Sibil·la Roura, and had a child with her. Five years later, Guillem was serving in the parish of Vilanant, which was less than 2 kilometers from Taravaus; ADG, Imposicions de Penes, no. 1, 50r. (1343) and 82v. (1348). Bernat Rocha, the rector of Sant Miquel de Colera, kept Na Comes and their three daughters in Banyoles. According to parishioners, the family kept a residence both in Colera and Banyoles, and parishioners complained that the rector was frequently absent from the parish of Colera; ADG, Visites, no. 9, 22v. (1350).

45. ADG, Imposicions de Penes, no. 1, 17r. (1337) and 68r. (1347); ADG, Processos, no. 201, 1r.v. (1338). The sacrist Bartomeu Sabater moved Raimunda and their children some 13 kilometers from Terrades to Caneres (near Darnius) when he became prior of Sant Esteve de Caneres; ADG, Visites, no. 1, 65v. (1315); ADG, Visites, no. 3, 7v.–8r. (1321). Maria de Taravaus initially followed Berenguer Feliu from the parish of Colomers to Estanyet, but she appears to eventually return to Colomers; ADG, Visites, no. 4, 13v. (1329); ADG, Imposicions de Penes, no. 1, 10v. (1336) and 24v. (1338). The sacrist Francesc Alagotz established a relationship with a village woman, Raimunda Rega, in the parish of Matajudaica, and the couple had a son, named Joan. Three years later, Francesc had moved his family to Siurana, 250 kilometers from Raimunda's home village of Taravaus, where the couple was

Clerics employed different strategies to ensure that they stayed close to their kin. Exchanging benefices or serving as a substitute were common tactics. Mateu Carbó held the benefice of hebdomedarian in the church of Sant Martí de Empúries, but both Mateu and Sibil·la Martorell, the mother of his seven children, were from Armentera. Mateu must have been unable to exchange a benefice of equal value in Empúries for one in Armentera because Castelló d'Empúries was a far more prosperous town. Nevertheless, Mateu managed to stay in L'Armentera by substituting for the beneficed priest Guillem Çaragall in Armentera while Guillem substituted for Mateu in Empúries. For more than twenty years, Mateu preferred to trade his superior benefice of hebdomedarian so that he could stay in the village where both he and Sibil·la had roots. Sibil·la's mother, Na Berengaria Martorell; Mateu's father, Guillem Carbó; and probably other family relatives lived in Armentera. These family connections must have aided Mateu's business as a public scribe because Mateu and Sibil·la were a relatively prosperous family. Not only could Mateu afford to provide for a large family of seven children, but he also promised to buy a chalice for the church of Armentera.[46]

When a cleric was a new presence in a village, forming a union with a local woman was one way to become part of the community. Establishing a household and joining village society through a woman's family connections could result in losing the status of outsider. It probably took some time to court the woman and set up an arrangement with her family, but once the couple's union received the family's endorsement, a cleric would have acquired not only a new set of kin but also a support group in the parish. Take, for example, the rector of Colls, who used a farming tool belonging to his concubine's father.[47] Welcomed into the family, a cleric could count on the assistance of the woman's family members. Conversely, a woman's family most likely recognized the advantage that a union with a priest offered and looked to benefit from his

expecting their second child; ADG, Imposicions de Penes, no. 1, 64r. (1346) and 83r. (1349). In another example, Elisenda Vergera followed Guillem Teyes from the parish of Sant Pere dels Vilars, near the French border, to Sant Christófol dels Horts, and finally to Sords, near the city of Girona. The couple were together for at least twenty years, since in 1340 Guillem and Elisenda had four children and had at least one more child by 1351; ADG, Visites, no. 6, 60v. (1340); ADG, Imposicions de Penes, no. 1, 37r. (1342) and 108v. (1356); ADG, Remissions de Penes, no. 1, 23v. (1351).

46. Mateu Carbó and Guillem Çaragall received approval from the bishop's curia to substitute for each other; ADG, Visites, no. 1, 85r.v. (1315); ADG, Visites, no. 3, 32r.v., 34r. (1321); ADG, Visites, no. 4, 21v., 22v. (1329); ADG, Imposicions de Penes, no. 1, 3r. (1336); ADG, Notularum, no. 6, 10r. (1326); ADG, Lletres, no. 2, 29v. (1326); ADG, Notularum, no. 10, 25r. (1335); ADG, Obligacions de Penes, no. 1, 3r. (1336).

47. ACV, Calaix 31/43, Visites, no. 5, 6v. (1315). After the death of the concubine Anglesa, the tool had not been returned to her father Salvador, and Salvador asked the visitor for the rector to return his tool, which was worth 40 sous.

influence and power in the community. The baptism of the couple's children also brought a cleric closer to his parishioners. Parents were banned from choosing family members as godparents for their children, which meant that the choice of friends and fellow villagers extended the ties a couple had to their community. Although Church policy was to minimize the number of godparents to two or three because the greater number of ties of spiritual kinship in a person's geographical area limited the number of people available for marriage, it was not uncommon for three godparents to sponsor a child at the sacred font—usually two men and one woman for a male child and two women and one man for a female child.[48] The rectors of Malanyeu and Vallcebre received three and four godparents, respectively, for each of their two children.[49] Both men were then connected through ties of affinity to six or eight people among their friends and villagers. The complaint that these rectors had a large number of godparents for their children could be a sign that parishioners were vying to be connected to the rector or that the rector wanted to extend this connection to a greater number of people. Either way, the sacrament of baptism integrated the cleric and his family into the parish community.

Marriage further reinforced the bonds of kinship and friendship between a cleric's family and the villagers. Marriages among the peasantry were contracted from a small pool of potential mates from a limited geographical area, so it is likely that the two families were at least acquainted, if not friends, or distantly related. Peasant communities were small and intimate, and marriages solidified these ties. The marriages of clerical children were no different in this respect. Guillem, the son of Berenguer, the former rector of Segúries, married a woman whom his father had baptized as a child.[50] Berenguer was no longer rector of the parish church, but his son had been raised in Segúries, chosen a woman from the village as his bride, and settled in the parish to start

---

48. Baucells i Reig, *Vivir en la edad media*, I, 641–42; Elisheva Baumgarten, *Mothers and Children: Jewish Family Life in Medieval Europe* (Princeton: Princeton University Press, 2004), 57–59, 79–83; John Bossy, "Blood and Baptism: Kinship, Community, and Christianity in Western Europe from the Fourteenth to the Seventeenth Centuries," in *Sanctity and Secularity: The Church and the World*, ed. Derek Baker (Oxford: Basil Blackwell, 1973), 129–43.

49. ACV, Calaix, 31/43, Visites, no. 3, 12v.–13r. (1313). The rector Nicolau had his children baptized by his colleague, the priest Jaume Cot, in the parish church where they both served; ADB, Visites, no. 2, 87r. (1315). It is likely that some clergymen also sought to baptize their children outside the parish where they served. The parishioners of Vilanova de la Muga mentioned that the sacrist Pere de Mans and Serdana baptized their first child in Castelló d'Empúries and the second child in the village of Peralada. The couple may have chosen these other villages because they had connections there; still, it is noteworthy that villagers knew where the couple chose to baptize their children; ADG, Visites, no. 1, 101v. (1315). Pere and Serdana appear in 1315 with two children, and the couple was together at least until 1341 when they disappear from the records; ADG, Visites, no. 4, 184v. (1329); ADG, Obligacions de Penes, no. 1, 2v. (1335); ADG, Visites, no. 6, 156r. (1341).

50. AEV, Visites, no. 1200/3, 48r. (1336).

LAYMEN IN PRIESTLY ROBES

his own family. Marriage sometimes resulted in newlyweds joining the paternal household. Three of the rector Ramon's five children with Na Maniars lived
at home with the rector, including his son and daughter-in-law.[51] It is telling
that the eldest son of a priest brought his wife to live in the home that would
one day belong to them. The incorporation of the daughter-in-law into the
family home and the son-in-law into the family network would have strengthened the relationship between the cleric and the people of the parish, who
were also his in-laws. When a cleric formed a union with the daughter of another cleric in the village, the ties of kinship and profession were even stronger. Fastening himself to the daughter of the canon of Santa Maria de Tolo
integrated the sacrist Joan Denesel into the parish and most likely aided his
priestly career. Clerical fathers could create clerical dynasties through their sons
and grandsons, as well as through their daughters who tied themselves to other
clergymen and produced more grandsons that could one day enter into holy
orders.[52]

During its campaign to impose celibacy on the clergy, the Church delegiti-
mized the offspring of clergymen and made them a source of moral pollution. Synodal legislation and church literature declared these children an
anathema to the Christian community. Kathryn Ann Taglia, in her study of
French synodal legislation, has claimed that the offspring of priests were considered pariahs not only by the Church but also by medieval society.[53] Relying
on synodal legislation as a barometer for social attitudes, however, is problematic in that it reveals only the attitudes of church leaders and possibly
the elite of society. Similarly, Laura Wertheimer has argued that the reformers of the eleventh century created an image of clerics' children as a symbol
of their fathers' failure to remain chaste and preserve cultic purity. These
children, according to Wertheimer, became objects of pollution for both the
clergy and laity.[54] In contrast, comments that the children of clergymen pol-
luted sacred space or represented a priest's sin in violating his vow of chastity
are completely absent from the testimony of Catalan witnesses in the documents. The reality is that the writings of Gregorian reformers seemed to have
had little effect on the acceptance of priests' children in Catalunya. Bernhard
Schimmelpfennig's study of the position of priests' sons in the Church notes
that some parishioners accepted the presence of a priest's children because
they preferred to have a priest who had a stable relationship with one woman

---

51. AEV, Visites, no. 1200/2, 31r. (1331). In the parish of Cantallops, the stabilitus Pere Marcinal
also kept his son and daughter-in-law in his home; ADG, Visites, no. 3, 11r. (1321).
52. ACV, Calaix 31/43, Visites, no. 8, 30r. (1315); ADG, Imposicions de Penes, no. 1, 7v. (1336).
53. Taglia, '"On Account of Scandal,'" 57–70.
54. Wertheimer, "Children of Disorder," 393–96.

rather than a priest who had liaisons with several women of the parish.[55] My own study of the visitation records reveals little evidence that priests' children were stigmatized or shunned in medieval Catalan peasant society. Many Catalan clerical families were from the well-to-do peasantry, so it seems unlikely that the village community treated these clerical children as outcasts. Barbara Hanawalt's and Zvi Razi's studies on the late medieval English peasantry have pointed out that illegitimacy was not a great stigma when the labor of every able-bodied child and adult had value.[56] What is more, the marriages of clerics' children raises questions about the extent to which medieval people held such views. Evidence that clergymen provided dowries for their daughters and inheritances for their sons illustrates not only that they could find marriage partners for their illegitimate children but also that fellow villagers may have seen an advantage in marrying into a clerical family that could boast of some affluence and influence in the community.

Given the clergymen who could afford to build houses for their family and purchased farmsteads and lands that were passed on to their offspring, marrying into a prosperous clerical family may have overshadowed any concerns over the social stigma of illegitimacy, especially because illegitimate births and informal unions were not uncommon among the peasantry. Ermesenda, the daughter of the capellan Romeo of Gósols, was a married woman who left her marriage for Guillem Graner, a fellow villager. Bernat, the son of the capellan Romeo, kept a local woman as his concubine. Illegitimate by birth, both Ermesenda and Bernat entered into formal and informal unions that produced a subsequent generation of illegitimate children. Whether in a legitimate marriage or in a concubinous union, the children of clerics were involved with people who were familiar with their family history and did not find their illegitimate status an impediment to establishing a relationship. In fact, it is possible that marrying into a clerical family was seen as an advantage—one that brought an elevation in social and economic status if the father's benefice was prestigious and his family was prominent in the community. The marriages of Margarida and Pere, the children of the sacrist Ramon de Torrent, are another case in point. Early in his career, Ramon had a daughter named Margarida with Maria Burga, his long-time partner, and a son named Pere with Guillema Burga, Maria's sister; both women were from the parish of Caçà de

55. Schimmelpfennig, "'Ex fornicatione nati,'" 32–36.
56. Hanawalt, *Ties That Bound*, 156; Razi, *Life, Marriage, and Death*, 64–71. In the peasant community of Halesowen in Central England, Zvi Razi has estimated that, for every 1.9 people married, one woman gave birth to a child out of wedlock.

Pelràs.[57] Despite the scandal that must have occurred from Ramon impregnating two sisters and producing two illegitimate offspring who were both
siblings and cousins, Margarida and Pere were successful in contracting marriages to local people. As a beneficed cleric and scribe of the village, the inheritance that Ramon could provide for his children was sufficient to attract
marriage partners.

Although the range of wealth among parish clergy varied, they could still
be among the most prosperous of the peasantry in the rural villages of Catalunya. Church rectors, in particular, often held control over the property surrounding the church itself, as well as other pieces of land within the limits of
the parish that were meant to supplement their income.[58] They could make a
profit from renting out or illegally selling church land to parishioners, which
apparently they did with frequency. A rector could exploit the land and revenues from the property attached to his benefice, but because owning a manse
(a house with a substantial amount of arable property) characterized the well-
to-do peasant, any priest who could afford to purchase a large manse for his
family was among the wealthiest of the village.[59] A few priests were even able
to support two families. The sacrist Guillem Vidal in the parish of Santa Maria d'Anglès kept Na Rega and their children in the nearby parish of Sant Juià
de Llers, in addition to Na Cortessa and two other children in the parish of
Anglès. Likewise, the rector Pere Subihes housed one family in the village of
Amer and kept another in his home in the parish of Montcal.[60] Although these
clerics must have had the financial means to support two households, it appears that few parish clergy had the resources to do so. Priestly status and clerical privilege, as we will see, afforded clergymen plenty of opportunity to

57. ADG, Visites fragmentaris, 10v., 13r. (1320). The priest Pere de Triles also had children with
two sisters—Marieta and Maria. The pregnant Maria had two children with the priest while the sister
Marieta was also pregnant; ADB, Visites, no. 4, 58v. (1336). Other examples of clerics marrying their
children to people in the parish where they served include the sacrist Pere Blanc, who married his
daughter in the village Palausator where he kept his family; the sacrist of Sant Iscle d'Empordà, who
also married a daughter; and the sacrist of Empúries married off one of his daughters in the village
of Sant Feliu de Garriga; ADG, Visites, no. 9, 1r.v., 3r. (1350); ADG, Visites fragmentaris, 3r. (1303).
58. For a discussion on land in the control of Church rectors, see Milton, Market Power, 27–29.
59. Freedman, Origins of Peasant Servitude, 36–37. Freedman notes that "the manse was looked
upon as the average holding of a moderately well-established peasant. . . . In fact the more significant
difference was between peasants who cultivated a full manse and those who held less, who attempted
to survive on mere slivers of land" (37).
60. ADG, Visites, no. 4, 106r.v. (1329); ADG, Visites, no. 4, 121v.–122r.v. (1329). In the visitations
for 1329, only six clerics in the major orders kept two concubines simultaneously; ADG, Visites, no. 4,
13v., 69v.–70r., 114v., 126v., 150v.–151r., 184r. (1329). In the visitations for 1331, only the deacon of
Centenys kept two concubines simultaneously, and in the visitations for 1341, two clerics in the major
orders from the parish of Vilanova likewise kept two women. The priest Ferrar Rubey was also
charged with keeping and impregnating two women, Manda and Romia, in the diocese of Barcelona;
ADB, Registrum Communium, no. 10, 88r. (1341).

exploit their position in the community to their economic benefit, but these parish clergymen could not rival the prosperity of clerics from the middling level or nobility who were appointed to more lucrative benefices. Clerical elites, for instance, could afford to support financially more than one family at a time. Four cathedral canons and one archdeacon in Urgell managed to keep multiple households with women and children, and appear to have supported past concubines by relocating these women to homes outside the cathedral see. The canon Bernat Condamina kept Saurina and their three children in his home in Urgell and another concubine, whom he had had "for a long time," in the village of Berga in a home that housed various children and a son-in-law.[61] The high rents and multiple benefices that elite clergy held meant that they had the wealth not only to buy property to house their families but also to provide dowries and inheritances that would place their progeny in a higher socioeconomic strata than the children of the parish clergy. Fathers such as the archdeacon of Besalú could establish a religious house solely for his illegitimate daughter, Felipa de Soler, and arrange to have her appointed abbess of Santa Maria de Vilanera when she reached the proper age.[62]

As the proletariat of the diocesan church, parish clergy were not appointed to the most well-paid benefices and held a status below that of elite and university-educated clerics working in the bishop's curia.[63] The benefices they received in the small villages distantly located from commercial areas such as Girona, Besalú, La Bisbal, Peralada, and Castelló d'Empúries could not compete with the prestige and lucrative benefices assigned to cathedral canons, priors, and archdeacons, who generally came from the nobility. These elite clerics commonly held more than one benefice and the income from these benefices could be worth more than 500 lliures. Even a cleric such as Antoni Major, who originated from the middling strata of society and became a procurator for the bishop of Girona and eventually a judge, earned more than 150

---

61. The canon Guillem de Apilia kept Rosa and their newborn child in his home in Urgell and another concubine that he had had "for a long time" when he was a "prepositus" in a distant village. The canon Ferrar de Barbarano was reported to have supported three concubines and more than five children. The archdeacon Bartomeo de Garriga kept Maria, the sister of the canon Ramon de Villautar, as his concubine. The canon Guillem Bernat kept both Abeylana and Andorana in Urgell, and was accused of committing adultery with a married woman. In a rare visitation to the cathedral church in Urgell, numerous clerical and lay witnesses exposed the relationships of the cathedral canons; ACV, Calaix 31/43, Visites, no. 1, 4r.v.–6r.v. (1312). Two priests testified that the archdeacon maior of Urgell, Bernat de Costis, kept an undisclosed number of women from whom he had both sons and daughters; ACV, Calaix 31/43, Visites, no. 7, 11r. (c.1313).
62. Marquès, "Set cenobis femenins de l'empordà," 84–89. See also ADG, Notularum, no. 35, 129v.–130r. (1359). Felipa de Soler received a dispensation for her illegitimate birth in 1359 and is confirmed as abbess in the same document.
63. Marquès, Història de la diòcesi de Girona, 102–3; Utterback, Pastoral Care, 128–31, 134–36.

lliures from the rights and possessions attached to his benefice—an amount that clearly set him apart from the majority of parish clergy.[64] By comparison, 10–20 lliures was a modest income for a rector, and anything above 40 lliures would have been an exceptional income for a peasant priest.[65] To put these salaries into perspective, an average merchant family in Barcelona spent 10 lliures per year per person on food and clothing. Furthermore, benefices worth 4–5 lliures (80–100 sous) were considered quite poor, especially in light of the fact that the annual salary of a male servant in Girona amounted to 3.75 lliures (75 sous).[66] The sheer numbers of clergy in both the dioceses of Barcelona and Girona, moreover, exacerbated the issue of inadequate incomes. Josep Martí Bonet estimates more than 10,000 clergymen served in the diocese of Barcelona, of which at least 2,500 were in the major orders.[67] Indeed, historians of the Catalan church have emphasized not only the sizable clerical population in the region but also the contentious disputes among parish clergy over the rights attached to their benefice that affected their incomes.[68] Adding further distress to the livelihood of the clergy was the disappearance for some of the tithe provided by parishioners for the upkeep of the parish church

---

64. Xavier Soldevila i Temporal, "Un clergue Vilatà del segle XIV. Antoni Major, de Torroella de Montgrí," in *Miscel·lània en honor de Josep Maria Marquès*, ed. Narcís Figueras i Pep Vila (Montserrat: Abadia de Montserrat, 2010), 192–96.

65. ACV, Calaix 31/43, Visites, no. 1 (1312–1313); Visites, no. 2 (1312–1313). For the diocese of Urgell, only in the first two visitation books does the visitor note the value of the rents attached to a rector's, vicar's, or capellan's benefice. The incomes for 201 benefices were reported. Of these 201, 144 benefices were valued at 20 lliures or less, and 52 benefices were valued at 21–50 lliures. (Only twelve benefices reached the 40 lliures mark, and two benefices were valued at 45 and 50 lliures). The remaining 6 of the 201 reported benefices received a certain amount of grain, rather than cash, as their income. For the diocese of Girona, the visitations from 1303 and 1305 report the value of clerics' benefices. Fifteen benefices assigned to rectors were valued at 10 lliures and below, and eighteen rectors' benefices ranged between 12.5 and 20 lliures. None were reported as being over 20 lliures. The benefice of a hebdomedarian or sacrist without the care of souls ranged from 10 to 15 lliures and was always less than that of the rector. The income attached to the benefice of a capellan varied the most—5–40 lliures. The benefice of a stabilitus rarely received an income more than 10 lliures. Deacons were the poorest of the clergy—their benefices were worth less than 5 lliures. The visitations for the diocese of Vic do not report the value of clerics' benefices. See also Josep Baucells i Reig, "L'església de Catalunya a la baixa edat mitjana," *Acta Historica et Archaelogica Mediaevalia* 13 (1992), 437; Josep Maria Gironella i Granés, *Viure en una parròquia catalana baixmedieval: Pedret i Marzà, 1285–1348* (Girona: Ajuntament de Pedret i Marzà, 2015), 74–75.

66. Vinyoles i Vidal, *Vida quotidiana a Barcelona*, 185–86; Guilleré, *Girona al segle XIV*, 316.

67. Josep M. Martí Bonet, "La Iglesia de Barcelona," in *Historia de las diócesis españolas: Barcelona, Terrasa, Sant Feliu de llobregat, y Gerona*, ed. Josep M. Marquès Planagumà and Josep M. Martí Bonet (Madrid: Biblioteca de Autores Cristianos, 2006), 162. Martí estimates that for every one hundred men, eight served the church. He also notes that the majority of the 10,000 plus clerics were either simply tonsured or married clergy.

68. Codina i Vilà, "Els processos dels segles XIV i XV," 170, 176–77. Codina finds that 40 percent of the *processos* in the diocese of Barcelona during these two centuries dealt with disputes concerning ecclesiastical benefices. See also Marquès, *Arxiu diocesà de Girona*, 13, 16–17.

and the rector. In his study of the rural economy in the community of Santa Coloma de Queralt in the diocese of Vic, Gregory Milton finds that secular lords often appropriated the tithes meant to support the parish churches.[69] In the diocese of Girona, Christian Guilleré estimates that for the region of la Selva, 83 percent of the rectors in sixty-six parishes shared the tithe with the laity.[70] Parish clerics, therefore, could not always depend on the tithe as a significant source of income. This explains why parish clergy came to rely so much on the collection of the *primicias*,[71] as well as the customary, yet voluntary, donations by parishioners for administering the sacraments during baptisms, marriages, extreme illness, and burials. Thus, the evidence points to a population of parish clergy who were struggling to support themselves solely on the income from a benefice and tithes owed to the parish church.

The inflation that resulted from the famine in the early fourteenth century also affected the monetary value of benefices. Simple benefices endowed by the laity were commonly based on rents that did not increase to match the rise in the prices for food or goods during the preplague years. The insufficient income from a benefice meant that parish clergy attempted to obtain more than one benefice, which contributed to the problem of absenteeism or clergy who were willing to substitute for an even smaller income.[72] Such meager salaries also left some clerics to find alternative places to live because they could not afford to reside in their parish nor afford to pay for a substitute if they had to reside elsewhere. The deacon of Matajudaica, "on account of the poverty of his benefice," lived in a nearby village with his father. The stabilitus Guillem Sartor lived in a monastery close by and returned to his parish to celebrate the divine office. In the parish of Avinyonet, no one resided for the absent sacrist because the fruits of his benefice did not exceed 5 lliures.[73] These

---

69. Milton, *Market Power*, 28.

70. Guilleré, *Girona al segle XIV*, 346–47.

71. Gironella i Granés, *Viure en una parròquia catalana*, 65–69. Parishioners could also refuse to pay the tithe or primicias; ADB, Registrum Communium, no. 4, 176v., 220v.–221r. (1328).

72. Marquès, *Història de la diòcesi de Girona*, 90–91. Gregory Milton discusses the example of Pere Piquer, from a nonelite family in the town of Santa Coloma de Queralt, who held two benefices and was also employed as a scribe; *Market Power*, 46–47.

73. Guillem Sartor claimed that, "he was not able to live from his benefice since its rents did not exceed 100 sous." The deacons of Santa Maria de Daró and Santa Maria de Requesens did not reside in their parishes because their benefices were not worth more than 40 and 60 sous, respectively. In the parish of Viladamí, the deacon's benefice was valued at 30 sous. The twelve villagers of Sant Genís de Sprach could not attract a cleric to serve in their church because the benefice was worth only 80 sous. According to a fellow cleric, the capellan of Sant Jaume de la Garriga was "very poor." In the parish of Bausitges, a cleric from a nearby monastery was commissioned by the bishop to serve that parish because the income from the benefice did not amount to 50 sous. Clerics in the parish of Esponellà testified that the parish did not have a sacrist or a deacon because the rents for such benefices were of such little value. In the parish of Cantallops, the rector did not reside there because the benefice was

priestly incomes worth 5 lliures or less during the hardest years of economic
hardship, from 1329 to 1334, when the price of wheat rose from 8 sous to nearly
1 lliure, mean that clerics must have struggled to survive during this period.[74]
What is more, despite the fact that many benefices came with a small house
for the cleric's use, some were so dilapidated that they were uninhabitable.
After forty years of service to the church of Cistella, the cleric Pere Garriguis
died in a home that was in such ruin that the bishop ordered any remaining
funds from Pere's estate be used to make repairs since it had been Pere's duty
to maintain the house attached to his benefice. Similarly, the capellan of Santa
Eulàlia apparently did not even have a home in the village because he committed all kinds of "indecencies," such as cooking inside the church.[75] Impoverished clerics were visible enough that hospitals such as the Poor Clerics in
Urgell were established for the old and infirm since many benefices failed to
provide adequate pensions for retired clerics.[76] Considering that a career in the
Church was not a sure path to financial prosperity for clergy from the lower
level of society, a cleric's affluence must have depended on more than the monetary value of his benefice.

For many, the income from their benefice did not ward off economic hardship, and thus it is not surprising that clergymen looked for additional means
to supplement their income. Working as a scribe or notary in the local *scribania* was a popular option because it augmented a cleric's respectability and authority.[77] Parish clergy also frequently dabbled in other types of occupations

---

of "modici valoris"; ADG, Visites, no. 3, 5r. (1321); ADG, Visites, no. 4, 17v., 19v.–20r., 32v., 34r.v., 38r.,
44v., 49r. (1329); ADG, Visites, no. 5, 17r. (1331); ADG, Visites, no. 6, 113v.–114r., 114v.–115r. (1340);
ADG, Visites, no. 7, 113v. bis, 115v., 116v., 121r.v. (1343). Similar examples can be found in the diocese
of Urgell. The capellan of Santa Maria de Valls did not reside in his parish due to the "poverty" of his
benefice, and the rector of Castllanç and the capellan of Figols also could not live on the rents of their
benefices; ACV, Calaix 31/43, Visites, no. 1, 31r. (1312); ACV,Calaix 31/43, Visites, no. 2, 11r., 71v.
(1313); ACV, Calaix 31/43, Visites, no. 7, 22r. (1313); ACV, Calaix 31/43, Visites, no. 8, 10v., 11r. (1315).
P. H. Cullum addresses the poverty of clerics in "Life Cycle and Life-Course." See also Simon Townley, "Unbeneficed Clergy in the Thirteenth-Century: Two English Dioceses" in *Studies in Clergy and
Ministry in Medieval England*, ed. David M. Smith (York, UK: University of York, 1991), 38–64. For the
disparity between the incomes of higher clergy, such as cathedral canons, and the average parish
priest, see Peter Linehan, "A Survey of the Diocese of Segovia (1246–47)," *Spanish Church and Society*
(London: Variorum Reprints, 1983), 163–206; Jorge Díaz Ibáñez, *Iglesia, sociedad y poder en Castilla: El
obispado de Cuenca en la edad media, siglos XII–XV* (Cuenca: Editorial Alfonsípolis, 2003), 237–39.
  74. Guilleré, *Girona al segle XIV*, 298–99.
  75. ADG, Lletres, no. 6, 132v. (1343); ACV, Calaix 31/43, Visites, no. 11v. (1315). The sacrist of
Sant Feliu de Beuda is another example. The home attached to the benefice was falling apart, and
parishioners blamed the sacrist for not repairing it and for choosing to reside elsewhere; ADG, Visites,
no. 2, 77v. (1315). A similar example can be found in ADB, Visites, no. 5, 68r. (1342).
  76. James William Brodman, *Charity and Welfare: Hospitals and the Poor in Medieval Catalonia* (Philadelphia: University of Pennsylvania Press, 1998), 37. See also, ADG, Visites, no. 6, 78v. (1340).
  77. Milton, *Market Power*, 45–49.

such as a tavern-owning, moneylending, shopkeeping, or working as bailiffs, even though synodal statutes prohibited these activities.[78] The capellan of Castellar kept a tavern in the church, and the beneficed cleric Ferrar Mata ran a tavern out of his home. These sites were popular for gambling, and clerics, like other tavern keepers, provided gaming boards for their customers. Other priests sold wine and bread out of their homes or bought a small building that functioned as both a shop and tavern of sorts.[79] Some invested in joint business ventures with local farmers to raise sheep and pigs, or sold wine and oil from their farmsteads to neighbors,[80] while others had business dealings that required them to leave the parish. The deacon Arnau Luper was absent for extended periods of time because he traveled to Barcelona and Valencia for "trade."[81] Despite the numerous bans against the buying or exchanging of currency, or selling of wine or grain for profit, such activities were common among clerics needing to find a way to support themselves or their households. The priest Bartomeu Roig is a good example of how clerics could be involved in a number of activities not limited to the priestly profession. Parishioners

78. The rectors of Sant Pere de Valldeneu, Santa Maria de Vilagrassa, and Sant Vicenç de Malvehy and the priest Pere Ermengard held the position of bailiff; AEV, Visites, no. 1200/1, 16r. (1330); AEV, Visites, no. 1200/3, 11r. (1331); AEV, Visites, no. 1200/2, 3v. (1331); ACV, Calaix 31/43, Visites, no. 5, 14r. (1315). In the diocese of Girona, the hebdomedarian of Sant Pere de Albanyà, the capellan of Pallerols, and the cleric Martí de Vinçano held the office of batlle; ADG, Visites, no. 1, 61v.–62r. (1315); Visites, no. 4, 203v. (1329); Visites, no. 3, 30r.v. (1321). For the diocese of Barcelona, see ADB, Registrum Communium, no. 3, 13v. (1314); *Visitatio diversarum,* HMML, microfilm no. 31951, Visites, no. 1, 92r. (1308); Martí Bonet, "Visitas pastorals," 710, 721; Baucells i Reig, *Vivir en la edad media,* 4: 2664–70.

79. Reports of clerics who operated taverns can be found in ACV, Calaix 31/43, Visites, no. 3, 4r. (1313); ACV, Visites, no. 8, 1v. (1314); ADG, Visites, no. 1, 4v.–5r. (1314); ADG, Visites, no. 4, 111r.–112r. (1329); ADG, Visites, no. 6, 47v.–51v. (1339); ADG, Imposicions de Penes, no. 1, 28v. (1340). Guillema, the concubine of the sacrist Bernat in the parish of Agullana, owned a business for selling bread and wine; ADG, Visites, no. 1, 76r. (1314). In the parish of Cabrera, the rector Jaume had bought a building for Jaçmeta to sell bread and wine. The beneficed cleric Ferrar Mata was accused multiple times of owning a tavern and gaming board, but he denied the charge; ADB, Visites, no. 4 bis, 5r., 6r. (1337). The parishioners of Sant Sadurní de Subirats complained that their rector was always armed with a sword, owned a tavern, and allowed clerics and scolares to gamble in the church; ADB, Visites, no. 2, 43r. (1314). See also Benito i Monclús, *Parroquies del maresm,* 284–87. For the prohibition of money-making activities outside of their clerical profession, see Noguer i Musqueras and Pons Guri, "Constitucions sinodals de Girona," 105, 132; Hillgarth and Silano, "Compilation of the Diocesan Synods," 141, 150–51.

80. ACG, Notarials, Besalú, no. 3, 37r., 39r. (1315); ACG, Notarials, Besalú, no. 5, 26v., 63v. (1333–1334).

81. ADG, Visites fragmentaris, 18v.–19r. (c. 1312–1313). The vicar Bernat Ricart often left the village of Santa Coloma de Ter to take care of his "business" and purchase goods for the church. The rector of Sant Feliu de Bruguera was known for buying and selling land, as well as buying rents from his parish that belonged to the monks of Ripoll. Both the sacrist and hebdomedarian of Sant Pere de Llorà were known to leave the parish and travel to Girona for "their business"; ACV, Calaix 31/43, Visites, no. 6, 13r. (c. 1315–1316); ACV, Calaix 31/43, Visites, no. 1, 57r. (1313): ADG, Visites, no. 4, 118r. (1329).

described Bartomeu as a "merchant" because he sold grain at a higher price and had recently established a "corrupt custom" that required anyone who removed ground meal from the mill to pay the lord of the castle 12 dinars. Bartomeu personally benefited from this payment because the lord granted him a portion of the mill tax.[82] The added earnings to Bartomeu's income would have placed him in much higher economic bracket than many of the villagers he taxed, which clearly fostered resentment.

Given the number of complaints that clerics were involved in usury or over-charged when selling their crops, parish clergy had more access to cash than many of their parishioners.[83] Bernat de Bass, the deacon of Paret-Rufí, was considered so successful in his side business of lending money that rumor had it he made nearly 1,000 sous.[84] A decent portion of a cleric's income could come from the tithes that parishioners paid in cash or with foodstuff, so they had more disposable income to lend money or invest in a business or trade. Moneylending could also be a family affair because the sons of clerics and sometimes their concubines were involved in making "usurious contracts."[85] Parish clerics, therefore, were more than just priests to their parishioners when they farmed land, owned a small business, or lent money at interest. They re-sembled the laity in that they were involved in a number of economic activi-ties to maximize their income.

Finding additional means to supplement an income could make a cleric wealthier, but it could also foster a great deal of resentment in the parish. When a parishioner entrusted the clerics of Viladasens with a valuable piece of cloth to pay for the burial of his father, the hebdomedarian sold the cloth and re-fused to give the parishioner what money remained after the burial costs had been deducted. The parishioner undoubtedly felt cheated and accused the

---

82. ADG, Processos, no. 244, 7v.–8r. (1347). Bartomeu Roig paid his fine because he received a letter of remission in 1347; ADG, Remissions de Penes, no. 1, 6v. (1347).

83. See, for example, ACV, Calaix 31/43, Visites, no. 1, 34r. (1312) and 54v. (1313); ACV, Calaix 31/43, Visites, no. 4, 1r., 15v., 22r., 24r. (1314); AEV, Visites, no. 1200/2, 8r. (1331); AEV, Visites, no. 1200/3, 9r. (1332) and 31r. (1333); ADG, Visites fragmentaris, 7r.v. (1303); ADG, Visites, no. 1, 8v.–9r., 23r., 82v.–83r. (1315); ADG, Visites fragmentaris, 19v. (1320); ADG, Visites, no. 3, 3v., 4v. (1321); ADG, Visites, no. 4, 13r., 37r., 122v., 126v. (1329); ADG, Remissions de Penes, no. 1, 7v. (1347) and 11v., 12v. (1348). The beneficed cleric Bernat Serena was brought before the bishop's court for usury; produc-ing false documents; accusing people of false crimes; stealing ducks; and various other crimes, such as concubinage, rape, and violence; ADG, Processos, no. 103, 1v.–3v. (1329).

84. ADG, Visites, no. 4, 125r. (1329). Reports of the deacon's wealth also reached the parishes of Montcal and Sant Joan de Montbó. When the visitor asked parishes how they knew the deacon had amassed so much money, the villagers replied that he could not have such wealth from his benefice because it was worth no more than 50 sous; ADG, Visites, no. 4, 121v.–122r.v. (1329).

85. ACV, Calaix 31/43, Visites, no. 4, 18v. (1314); Visites, no. 5, 8r. (1315); Martí Bonet, "Visitas pastorales," 703. The wives of laymen were also involved in moneylending; ADG, Visites, no. 1, 3r. (1314); ADG, Visites, no. 2, 103r. (1315); ADG, Lletres, no. 10, 184v. (1346).

hebdomedarian of committing a sacrilege by selling the cloth and keeping the remaining money with the excuse that the dead man was obligated to pay as a penance for his sins.[86] Some clerics were able to take advantage of an entire community, not just an individual parishioner. The *obrers* (churchwardens) of Sant Vicenç de Maià de Montcal denounced the sacrist Guillem de Ferrar to the episcopal visitor for fraudulently removing grain belonging to church. According to their testimony, the sacrist had sought to buy the grain and had offered a price of 100 sous, which the obrers had initially rejected as too small a sum. When the parish finally agreed to the sacrist's price, the obrers insisted that the sacrist should pay before taking the grain. But when neither party reached an agreement on this detail, they left the church, only to discover later that in their absence the sacrist had "deceptively" removed the grain and that he subsequently refused to pay the 100 sous.[87]

The actions of the hebdomedarian Guillem of Viladasens and the sacrist Guillem of Montcal show how easy it was for some clerics to appropriate parish resources because of their access to the church and their position in the community. Villagers most likely knew they had little recourse in requiring the clergyman to pay, especially because the community had to expend the time and money to take its case to episcopal officials. In cases in which parish clergy appropriated church funds, not only did the loss of revenues affect the parish's ability to care for their church but it inevitably made parishioners resent the payment of church tithes because they knew that neither their church nor their community—but only their priest and his superiors—would benefit.[88] It is worth noting, however, that such blatant attempts to steal from the church and its parishioners appear infrequently in the visitation records; evidence that many parishes were so impoverished that they could barely maintain the upkeep of their church, let alone raise additional funds to replace the parish's lost revenues, is far more common. The number of parishes that were placed under interdict because they could not afford to pay the procuration fee or provide the most basic of necessities to their clergy—capes, surplice, or liturgical books—highlight the general poverty of many parishes.[89] Rather than stealing outright from the church or parishioners, clerics were more apt

86. ADG, Visites, no. 4, 63v. (1329).

87. ADG, Visites, no. 2, 74r.v. (1315). In the parish of Centeny, villagers complained to the visitor that the priest Bernat, who now served in another parish, had failed to pay them 30 sous for a sale of wheat before he left; ADG, Visites, no. 4, 7v. (1329). The parishioners of Santa Maria de Castrobó called their rector "greedy"; ACV, Calaix 31/43, Visites, no. 1, 32r. (1313).

88. Swanson, *Church and Society*, 209–25. See also, ACV, Calaix 31/43, Visites, no. 2, 48v. (1313).

89. ADG, Lletres, no. 2, 169r., 171v.–171r. bis (1326); ADG, Lletres, no. 6, 100v.–101r., 104r., 135r., 175v. (1343); ADG, Lletres, no. 7, 36r.v. (1340) and 135v., 155v., 160r., 165r. (1344); ADG, Lletres, no. 8, 15r., 131r. (1344); ADG, Lletres, no. 10, 144r. bis, 140v. (1346) and 165v. (1347).

to skimp on providing goods such as wax for the candles, consecrated oil (chrism), and wine. And as complaints show, parish clergy were less than diligent in lighting the candles at the altars in their attempt to conserve wax.[90] Although these actions could be seen as defrauding the church, they were more a means to save money. What might at first glance appear as greediness in actuality simply helped a cleric spend less on church resources and keep the money in his pocket.

In the fourteenth century, Catalunya, like the rest of Europe, suffered from overpopulation and an economy reduced to subsistence level. Prior to the plague, the Crown of Aragon had been beset with a number of economic and political problems. The reconquest of Mallorca, the war with Castile, and the crop failures and famines that began in 1333, all took their toll on the population and economy.[91] A greater number of people struggled to survive, and so too did the parish clergy. Given the inadequate income from benefices and the diversity of economic activities the clergy engaged in to supplement their earnings, reports that clerics stole from their parish church and pilfered food from their neighbors indicate that the clergy were grappling with the same difficulties as the peasantry. Parish churches, like their parishioners, were in poor condition—roofs leaked, the church bells and baptismal fonts needed repair, and many lacked the proper liturgical ornaments and books. Parishes were so poor that when a cleric stole liturgical books, chalices, and vestments and moved to another parish, the church would be placed under interdict because the community could not raise the funds to replace the objects.[92] The pitiful yield of cultivated crops further affected community relations when parish clergy abused their positions. The clerics of Vilabertran were placed under ecclesiastical censure for stealing fruit and produce from their parishioners' vineyards and gardens; and in the parish of Vilamacolum, the deacon and several other clerics were fined for pasturing animals in their parishioners' fields.[93] The poverty of some clerics is seen in the example of the young

90. ADG, Visites fragmentaris, 2v. (1312); ADG, Visites fragmentaris, 24v. (1323); ADG, Visites, no. 4, 3r.v., 91r.v., 139r.v., 142r. (1329); Visites, no. 7, 155r., 157v., 168r. (1344); ADG, Visites, no. 8, 53r.v. (1346).

91. Carmen Batlle Gallart, *La crisis social y económica de Barcelona a mediados del siglo XV* (Barcelona: Consejo Superior de Investigaciones Científicas, 1973), 1: 44–57; Bisson, *Medieval Crown of Aragon*, 104–32, 162–73; Hillgarth, *Spanish Kingdoms*, 1: 233–86. For the economic burdens of peasants and the difficulties of holding land tenure, see Freedman, *Origins of Peasant Servitude*.

92. ACV, Calaix 31/43, Visites, no. 3, 27v. (1313); ADG, Visites, no. 3, 42r.v. (1321). AEV, Visites, 1200/2, 85v. (1332). ADG, Visites, no. 4, 36v., 91r.v., 142r., 201v.–202r. (1329). Baucells i Reig also addresses the condition of parish churches in *Vivir en la edad media*, 3: 1195–272.

93. ADG, Lletres, no. 7, 31v.–32r. (1340) and 53v.–54r. (1341). In another example, unidentified clerics from the parish of Montagut were caught stealing oil and other goods from the sacristy; ADG, Lletres, no. 7, 108r. (1344).

priest Simó Giró who was brought before the bishop's court not only for stealing money and a tunic but also for pilfering cabbage and fruits from the gardens of village people.[94]

When committing agrarian offences in their communities, clerics had the upper hand because they were rarely prosecuted for such crimes and their status in the community was such that they felt entitled to disregard the rights of those inferior to them.[95] No doubt many of these instances went unreported, but sources indicate that clerics repeatedly and brazenly trespassed on parishioners' lands for their own gain. Furthermore, letters from the bishop's curia show that clerics believed their clerical privilege would shield them from their disregard for secular authority. Church officials frequently dealt with clerics who claimed clerical privilege to avoid paying secular fines for their crimes or who failed to abide by the banns imposed by secular authorities. Such was the case when the bishop of Girona ordered the bailiff of Castelló to punish the "many clerics, tonsured as much as married as even those constituted in the sacred order," throughout the villages and parishes of Castelló, Vilanova, and Fortià because they "seize, consume, or carry off the produce" from lands in these parishes and, "claiming [the excuse of] clerical privilege, assert that they are not to be held to pay the said fine."[96]

Despite the hard economic times and shortage of grain and food, we cannot dismiss the possibility that clerics were motivated to commit these crimes to accumulate wealth. Nevertheless, while it is easy to label clergymen as "greedy" based on the complaints that they used church resources to enrich themselves, their meager incomes could have driven them to purloin goods that belonged to the church.[97] We must also keep in mind that parishioners

94. ADG, Processos, no. 30, 2v.–3r. (1319). Simó was also charged with keeping a concubine and carrying weapons at night in the town of Castelló d'Empúries. Clerics accused of stealing fruits and vegetables in the diocese of Tortosa can be found in ACT, Visites, 4r. (1337); García Egea, *La visita pastoral a la diocesis de Tortosa del Obispo Paholac*, 114.

95. Flocel Sabaté, "L'esglésa secular catalana al segle XIV: La conflictive relació social," *Anuario de Estudios Medievales* 28 (1998): 757–88. See also Warren O. Ault, "The Village Church and the Village Community in Medieval England," *Speculum* 45, no. 2 (1970): 199–204; H. G. Richardson, "The Parish Clergy of the Thirteenth and Fourteenth Centuries," *Transactions of the Royal Historical Society* 6 (1912): 89–128.

96. ADG, Lletres, no. 6, 95v. (1343). In 1339, the bishop of Girona, Arnau de Mont-rodon, decreed that if clerics failed to pay the fine imposed by secular authorities for the protection of crops, then the clergy, like the laity, would incur a monetary penalty. The exception was, of course, that the penalty was paid to the bishop and not to secular authorities; Salinas, *Derecho canónico catalán*, 99, 305–6.

97. The rector of Avellanacorba was punished for selling a pile of stones belonging to the church and for appropriating 10 migerias of oil for his own use. Likewise, the rector of Sant Miquel de la Torre used 10 migerias of oil that had been intended to light the lamps in the church. The rector of Sant Cugat de Salt was accused of selling wax that belonged to the church and lending his right to the mill at interest; ADG, Visites, no. 4, 126v., 142r., 201v.–202r. (1329). The capellan of Vallfogona

resented paying the tithe and, during times of economic insecurity, defaulted on their payments, which in turn affected the financial stability of the clergy.[98] Parish clerics were not immune to the economic crisis, and they were more than willing to use their status and clerical privilege to improve their situation.

The last wills and testaments of clergymen provide further information on the diversity of wealth found among the ecclesiastical hierarchy and parish clergy. Although the wills of elite clergymen and beneficed clerics working in the bishop's curia appear more frequently, far fewer extant wills for parish clergy can be found. I have located nearly thirty last wills and testaments for nonelite clerics in the diocese of Girona and twenty-one for the diocese of Vic. The surviving wills of parish clergy in the bishop's registers of Girona and the notarial registers of Vic seem to reflect the clerics who had more disposable income to bequeath to local churches, religious orders, and family members. It seems likely that truly impoverished clerics are not represented in the existing documents. The disparity of wealth even among parish clergy is striking. The hebdomedarian of Salt bestowed sums of 2–5 sous to his church and fellow clerics, 5 sous for candle wax, 10 sous for the executors of his will, and the largest sum, 5 lliures, for the celebration of masses for his soul. Considering that the hebdomedarian had more clothing than money to bequeath, it is clear that he had little to leave to family and friends.[99] Others donated similar amounts to their parish church but appear to have been better off than the hebdomedarian of Salt. The rector of Sant Pere de Torelló bequeathed a small house with a garden to his brother, and the rector of Sant Vicenç de Medalia Groni allotted 2 lliures (40 sous) for the dowries of each of his three nieces. The beneficed cleric Berenguer Erumir left 10 sous to his mother and 5 lliures (100 sous) for his sister's dowry.[100] In her study of the peasantry near Barcelona, Montserrat Richou notes that the majority of peasants left between 5 and 10 lliures (100–200 sous) in pious donations. Some clerics donated in this range as well, but others donated much less. A number of clerics did not even own any property that they could hand over to family members and, at most, could afford very small donations of 5 and 10 sous for anniversary masses. The

collected a rent of 2 denars worth of wheat that he used for his own purposes rather than for the church, and he allowed trees on the land that belonged to his benefice to be cut down for a price; AEV, Visites, no. 1200/3, 57v. (1339).

98. For example, in the parish of Rexach, seventeen parishioners refused to pay their dues for the upkeep of the church; ADB, Visites, no. 5, 93r. (1342). See also Hillgarth and Silano, Register "Notule Communium," 93.

99. ADG, Notularum, no. 20, 129r.v. (1348). Testaments for other impoverished clerics appear in ADG, Notularum, no. 9, 34r. (1334); ADG, Notularum, no. 13, 11r.v. (1338); ADG, Notularum, no. 21, 28v.–29v., 64r.v.–65r. (1348).

100. AEV, Testaments, ACF-3506 (1296–1308), 28v. (c. 1300), 49v. (1303), 73r. (1298).

sacrist Nicolau had only an insignificant amount of money to bequeath, but he left various household items to his ancilla Boneta, including a bed.[101] These clergymen had little property and cash to bestow for the salvation of their souls, and they left what remained of their wealth to their family.[102] That only a handful of clergy had the means to erect an altar or establish a priestly benefice in their parish church is further proof that many could not leave behind tangible evidence that would commemorate their service and memory in a community where they spent the better part of their lives.[103]

Those clerics who owned properties, such as a farmstead or vineyard; owned a liturgical book; owned a number of rents; and bestowed 2.5 lliures (50 sous) or more to family members were most likely to be among the well-to-do peasantry,[104] but they were still not part of the middling strata of society, as was the cleric Anton Major. Property and goods that were not attached to Anton's benefice included two large properties, a number of rents and privileges, barrels of wine, 15 migerias of wheat, a variety of other foodstuff, a fur cloak, and books. The settlement of Anton's estate must have been a sizable amount because the portion received by the bishop of Girona amounted to 523 lliures.[105] By comparison, the affluence of Gispert Fulcarà, professor of law and episcopal vicar of the diocese of Girona, who also held the position

---

101. AHG, Llibre de Testaments, no. 215, Figueres, 10 kalendas August (1347); AHG, Llibre de Testaments, no. 2091, Castelló, 8 kalendas Augusti (1303); AHG, Llibre de Testaments, no. 187, Castelló, 17 kalendas July (1348).

102. Richou i Llimona, "Baix maresme," 163–64.

103. ADG, Lletres, no. 8, 146r.v., 149r., 179r.v. (1344); ADG, Lletres, no. 18, 6v. (1351). See also Hillgarth and Silano, Register "Notule Communium," no. 177, 82.

104. Bernat Crus, the sacrist of Vilamalla, can be considered a cleric of moderate means. He bestowed money for the Franciscans and Dominicans, the redemption of Christian captives, and the new hospital in Girona, and he allotted 50 sous for the executors of his will. In addition, the sacrist bequeathed 15 lliures and a breviary to a nephew, and 50–100 sous to a number of friends and family members. The sacrist of Sant Gregori owned a vineyard. In the case of the rector of Quart, Ponç Silvar, the fact that his brother Bonanat was a bailiff and that he owned rights to a mill, and the level of donations to the church and family members (5 lliures and above), indicate that he was well-off. The deacon Joan de Vilar died intestate according to a fellow cleric, who also valued the deacon's goods at 300 sous (15 lliures); ADG, Notularum, no. 20, 133r.v. (1348); ADG, Notularum, no. 17, 139v.–140r. (1344); ADG, Notularum, no. 20, 111v.–112r. (1348); ADG, Visites, no. 2, 27v. (1316). The rector of the altar of Sant Joan owned houses in Vic and lands and a garden in the surrounding area. Another beneficed cleric from Vic donated 5 lliures for anniversary masses and 10 pounds of wax for candles, and he bequeathed his sister 10 lliures. The cleric Bernat Hort owned houses in Vic and provided 10 sous to a nephew, niece, godson, and goddaughter; AEV, Testaments, ACF-3509 (1319–1324), 91v. (c. 1319–1324); AEV, Testaments, ACF-3509 (1319–1324), 42v.–43r. (1319); AEV, Testaments, ACF-3509 (1319–1324), 3r. (1319). See also AHG, Llibre de Testaments, no. 215, Figueres, 6 ides April (1347); AHG, Llibre de Testaments, no. 215, Figueres, 3 kalendas May (1348).

105. Soldevila i Temporal, "Clergue Vilatà del segle XIV," 195–96. Anton Major received a letter of dispensation for keeping a concubine in 1352; ADG, Remissions de Penes, no. 1, 33r. (1352). The canon Berenguer de Medalia was probably also from the middling strata of society. He bestowed 15 lliures to his mother, sister, and niece. Berenguer also bequeathed 1,000 lliures to the cathedral canons

of deacon in the cathedral of Lleida, illustrates the disproportionate wealth between middling-level and elite clergymen. In his last will and testament,
Gispert left more than 200 lliures to various monasteries, chapels, and parish
churches for the celebration of mass for his soul and building restorations,
in addition to 600 lliures total to seven nieces as a contribution to their dowries, 420 lliures total to five nephews, and 35 lliures total to his three man
servants.[106] The financial chasm between a peasant priest and his clerical colleagues from the middling-level and elite ecclesiastical hierarchy was truly in-
surmountable. Consider, too, that peasant priests borrowed money and entered
into *comanda* contracts to buy simple household items or animals needed for
farming, which higher-strata clergymen could purchase outright due to their
income level. For example, the rector Berenguer de Mans entered into a *comanda* contract with the cleric Ferrar Bonet, who invested 85 sous in the rector's animal business, to purchase five cows. Likewise, the rector of Castelltersol
needed a *comanda* contract to purchase a mule and, at the same time, he also
borrowed 65 sous to buy a blanket and a saddle. Other clerics, such as the rector Berenguer de Roure and the rector Arnau Borrat, purchased such small plots
of land from their neighbors that they were worth 40 sous or less, which could
still qualify as a significant purchase considering that, depending on the worth
of their benefice, the price could amount to a quarter, if not half, of their yearly
salary.[107] Given the economic constraints that peasant priests experienced,
these men had little more than their profession in common with privileged
churchmen—their social and economic statuses set them worlds apart from
each other. Indeed, parish clergy had more in common with their village parishioners than with fellow clergymen like Anton Major and Gispert Fulcarà.

The property and dowries that parish priests provided for their children are
yet another indication of the financial resources found among this group of
clergymen. The value of the houses, fields, gardens, and manses that clerics
bought for their families and passed on to their sons and daughters is impossible to determine from the extant records. It is rare in the notarial records to
find parish priests purchasing land or entering into contracts at a level of 50
lliures or above. Nevertheless, that the rector of Sant Romà de Sau gave his
son Ramon a manse called Ça Frigola, his daughter Elisenda a parcel of land
to build a house, his daughter Sibil·la pasture land, and another two daughters
cash for their dowries illustrates that he had the resources to endow five

of Vic for anniversary masses on the day of his death, gave 5 lliures for the repairs of the cloister, and
donated his breviary to the choir; AEV, Testaments, ACF-3509 (1319–1324), 6v.–7r. (1319).
    106. ADG, Notularum, no. 20, 54r.v. (1348).
    107. AEV, Notarials, ACF-35 (1300–1301), 30v., 51r.v., 64v., 109v., 110r.

children, even though the value of the property is unspecified.[108] In fact, a cleric
in possession of a farmstead known as a manse was considered to be among
the wealthy peasantry. Recall that a manse was a sizable piece of property (6–12
hectares) that contained a house or two, lands for the cultivation of cereal or
a vineyard, pastureland, and in some cases rights to the forest. Peasants who
cultivated a full manse were considered superior to those who cultivated an
assortment of land.[109] Clerics who prospered from a decent benefice and side
business probably sought to gain possession of a manse. Indications that parish clergy (or their concubines and sons) had manses are scattered throughout the documents, but such possessions went unreported in the visitation
records because officials were not concerned with property that did not belong to the Church.[110] The same principle applies to the information on dowries in the visitation records. Although limited, the reported worth of cash
dowries gives us a sense of the economic position of the parish clergy. Merchant families in the town of Bell-lloc endowed their daughters with sums anywhere from 150 to 300 lliures, while the lower strata of society, particularly
the peasantry, typically gave dowries less than 50 lliures (1,000 sous). Four out
of ten clerics endowed their daughters with 50 lliures, and a fifth was rumored
to have given his daughter 200 lliures. Another cleric reportedly provided 40
lliures, while the remaining four provided an amount between 15 and 22.5
lliures.[111] A dowry less than 25 lliures was meager indeed and stands in contrast

108. AEV, Visites, no. 1200/2, 80r. (1332). For other clerics who bought properties and possessed
manses, see AEV, Visites, no. 1200/1, 27r. (1330); AEV, Visites, no. 1200/2, 64v., 65r., 77v. (1331) and
82v., 85r., 85v. (1332); AEV, Visites, no. 1200/3, 8v., 11v., 21v., 24v. (1332). ACV, Calaix 31/43, Visites,
no. 1, 57r. (1313); ACV, Calaix 31/43, Visites, no. 3, 36v. (1314); ACV, Calaix 31/43, Visites, no. 4, 6v.
(1314). ADG, Visites, no. 1, 47v. (1315); ADG, Visites, no. 2, 10v. (1315); ADG, Visites, no. 3, 11r.
(1321); ADG, Visites, no. 4, 155v. (1329); ADG, Visites, no. 6, 3v. (1338).
109. Rosa Congost Colomer, "La Catalunya del mas, és a dir, la Catalunya Vella," in L'organització
de l'espai rural a l'europa mediterrània, ed. Rosa Congost Colomer, Gabriel Jover, Giuliana Biagioli
(Girona: Associació d'Història Rural de les Comarques Gironines, Centre de Recerca d'Història Rural
de la Universitat de Girona, 2003), 24–26, 31–32; Rosa Lluch Bramon and Elvis Mallorquí, "Els masos
a l'època medieval. Orígens i evolució," in L'organització de l'espai rural a l'europa mediterrània, ed. Rosa
Congost Colomer, Gabriel Jover, Giuliana Biagioli (Girona: Associació d'Història Rural de les Comarques Gironines, Centre de Recerca d'Història Rural de la Universitat de Girona, 2003), 38, 47–52;
Freedman, Origins of Peasant Servitude, 36–37; Serra i Clota, Comunitat rural a la Catalunya medieval,
171, 193–99; Víctor Farías Zurita, El mas i la vila a la Catalunya medieval. Els fonaments d'una societat senyorialitzada, segles XI–XIV (València: Universitat de València, 2009), 25–26, 173–76; Lluís To Figueras
"La diferenciació pagesa a la diòcesi de Girona (segle XIV): Una nota metodològica," in El feudalisme
comptat i debatut. Formació i expansió del feudalisme català, ed. Miquel Barceló, Gaspar Feliu, Antoni
Furió, M. Miquel, and Jaume Sobrequés (València: Universitat de València, 2003), 441–63.
110. Notarial documents in the Girona city archive show that priests owned and sold property
like the laity; AHG, Calonge no. 194, 14v. (1321); AHG, Toroella no. 567, 12r., 95r., 106r. (1341); AHG,
Monells no. 161, 29r. (1333); AHG, Peratallada no. 199, 75r. (1332); AHG, Rupià no. 559, 34r.v. (1318).
111. AEV, Visites, no. 1200/1, 4r. (1330); AEV, Visites, no. 1200/2, 5r., 7r., 16v., 69r. (1331) and 80r.
(1332); AEV, Visites, no. 1200/3, 1v. (1332) and 66r. (1339); ACV, Visites, Calaix 31/43, no. 5, 11r.

to the dowries of Estefania, worth 200 lliures, who was to marry a scribe, and Ermesenda, worth 50 lliures, who was engaged to a mason from Girona. A statistical analysis of marriage contracts reveals that the average dowry amount before the plague in the delta de Llobregat, a region southwest of Barcelona, was 45.8 lliures.[112] Even though it is likely that a great many of parish clergy were of modest means, it is clear that some were able to do quite well within their social class and provide a dowry greater than 25 lliures.

Conclusion

Thus far, we have seen that parish clergy were integrated into the parish community. Parishioners were related to their clergy through ties of kinship or spiritual affinity, or knew them as members of the rural community who had lived in the area for generations. The extended networks of support established when a man set up a household with a woman, as well as through important life events such as the baptism and marriage of their children, further cemented these relationships. Far from the clergy's filling only the singular function of a pastor who administered the sacraments, the laity knew their clergy in their roles as husband, father, uncle, brother, and son. The de facto marriages between the clergymen and women were also accepted because so many among the laity also took part in informal unions. Parishioners were unperturbed by cohabiting couples who lived as if they were married—in a predominantly monogamous relationship that emulated a marital household. They may even have found some comfort or reassurance in the example of their parish priest and his family. What is more, clerics could relate to their male parishioners as husbands and fathers, and they formed bonds of friendship with their neighbors and parishioners.

(1312). For the dowries of the merchant class in Bell-lloc, see Fernández i Trabal, *Família catalana medieval*, 55–56.

112. A number of marriage contracts can be found in the Arxiu Municipal de Girona, *Catàleg de pergamins*. Concerns about providing daughters with dowries can also be seen in deeds of inheritance and in the wills and last testaments of parents similarly located in this collection; documents no. 87, no. 359, no. 86, no. 108, no. 164, no. 394. Jaume Codina found only 7 out of 441 fourteenth-century marriage contracts in which women's dowries amounted to less than 10 lliures; *Contractes de matrimoni*, 77, 255–56. In fifteenth-century Barcelona, dowries ranged from 40 to 600 lliures and could reach 1,500 lliures or more for women among the bourgeoisie; Teresa-María Vinyoles i Vidal, *Història de les dones a la Catalunya medieval* (Lleida: Pagès editors, 2005), 162–63; Vinyoles, *Vida quotidiana a Barcelona*, 180–82. For the dowries and marriage contracts of laboring-status women in Valencia, see Dana Wessell Lightfoot, "The Projects of Marriage: Spousal Choice, Dowries, and Domestic Service in Early Fifteenth-Century Valencia," *Viator* 40, no. 1 (2009): 333–53. Dowries and the assistance available to poor women are discussed in Brodman, *Charity and Welfare*, 100–110.

A cleric's economic endeavors likewise incorporated him into the village and surrounding area when he sold grain, wine, and other goods to his parishioners; lent money; and collected rents and taxes when acting as a landlord or bailiff. Whether a cleric was prosperous or struggled financially to support his family, providing an income, a home, and future security for a domestic partner and their offspring were concerns that parish priests shared with the men of their village. Nevertheless, the social and economic disparity between the parish clergy, particularly in rural areas, and the well-to-do clergy of the middle and upper strata of society underscores the differences not only in the lived experience but also in the gender identity that parish clergy attained as they were born, raised, grew to adulthood, and served the church among the very peasantry and lower strata of medieval society to which they belonged. When a parish cleric encountered the bishop, his vicar general, or the episcopal visitor and his attendants, notaries, and other episcopal officials, there is little doubt they did not have much in common beyond their vows to God and the tonsure. Even their clerical habits were not cut from the same cloth. The shabbily dressed parish priest, who spent his free time farming the land or running a tavern, was in the eyes of clerical elites a different being altogether. A chasm of education, wealth, dress, manners, rank, and degree of authority separated them. It is hard to imagine that the vast majority of parish clergy identified with these privileged clergymen more than they did with the laymen in their own communities. Nevertheless, parish clergy represent an amalgamation of both the clerical and secular worlds. They had access to the divine and administered the sacraments, but they defined themselves as men using some of the very same traits their fathers, uncles, brothers, and friends used to measure manhood—they had a profession, supported a woman and children as husband and father, and socialized with their male peers like any other man. Being a cleric provided them with a professional identity, and their experience as men of the village provided them with a masculine identity that mirrored many of the characteristics of their fellow laymen. Although we might anticipate that the expectations of church leaders, which focused on devotion to God and the priestly office, meant that the clerical lifestyle collided with the secular one, parish clergymen were able to accommodate and merge the two worlds.

The merging of profession and lay customs can also be seen during holidays and local feast days, funerals, and the celebration of marriages and baptisms, when clerics were not only integral to but also part of the village community. The role of the parish priest in meting out the sacraments was indispensable, but his participation in such celebrations as a father, brother, uncle, and friend forged a deeper connection to his parishioners. Gambling and drinking at the local tavern were social events that marked the cleric as a fel-low villager. The man who wore a clerical habit and joined the group of local men gathered in the main street of the village, the church cemetery, or the church itself to play dice and place bets was joining his friends and kin in a game just like the other village men.[113] Even the fistfights between clerics and parishioners, and the family members who came to a cleric's defense or the detractors who stood against him, reveal the extent to which parish clergy were integrated into the male community. Like laymen, clerics also took part in the same recreational activities, patronizing brothels and attending popular forms of entertainment such as hangings, the burnings of heretics, and public whip-pings and beatings.[114] Some were even known for playing musical instruments while wandering about the village at night in hopes of wooing local women.[115] In these instances, the laymen of the village most likely viewed the man in the clerical habit as family, friend, or foe, as well as a man in the holy orders. These social occasions blurred the lines between the identity of a parish cleric as a clergyman and his identity as a layman. Indeed, the two were often inseparable.

113. For clerics who used the church or the cemetery as a gambling hall, see ADB, Visites, no. 2, 43r. (1314).

114. Burns, "Parish as a Frontier Institution," 248; Utterback, *Pastoral Care*, 54–56. These activities were prohibited to the clergy in synodal decrees; see statute no. 47 in Hillgarth and Silano, "Compilation of the Diocesan Synods," 110; Noguer i Musqueras and Pons Guri, "Constitucions sinodals de Girona," 79, 80, 103, 107.

115. The chaplain Nicolau in the parish of Palausator was known to frequently sit in the doorway of Geralda, the priest Pere's sister, and strum his instrument, presumably to sing love songs to her. The stabilitus Bernat Gener in the parish of Castelló d'Empúries reportedly played his instrument by night and day: "tangit instrumenta musica per villa Castilionis de nocte et de die"; ADG, Visites, no. 10r. (1314); Visites fragmentaris, 5r., 6r. (1323).

CHAPTER 4

"Quarrelsome" Men

Violence and Clerical Masculinity

The sacrist Bernat Batlle and Jaume Moner, a layman, were well-known enemies. It was common knowledge that the two men had on many occasions exchanged insults and come to blows with their swords. The final straw occurred in the church of Verges when, in the presence of many local men, Jaume spit in the sacrist Bernat's face. A few days afterward, Jaume was attacked near the town mill and subsequently died from his wounds. Before his passing, Jaume identified his attackers, the sacrist and his two fellow clerical friends, to the town bailiff. Witnesses testified that on the day Jaume was assaulted the sacrist was seen leaving the castle of Verges armed with a crossbow and sword (*ballistam et ensem*) in the company of his two friends, who were clerics from neighboring villages.[1]

Using violence to resolve disputes and enact revenge may appear at odds with men whose profession centered on the care of souls. The priestly profession was not intended to be a life focused on physical action, passion, or arms but a life dedicated to saving souls through the chanting of the mass, preaching, prayer, and the administration of the sacraments. Synodal statutes like the 1319 Barcelona decree ordered clergy to bear spiritual arms, specifically the

---

1. ADG, Processos, no. 25, 2v.–5r., 15v.–16r.v. (1318). The sacrist Bernat Batlle first appears in the parish of Verges in a visitation from 1303, in which he was cited for having a child with Bernarda Ciborg; ADG, Visites fragmentaris, 2r. (1303).

weapons of prayers and tears, rather than physical arms.[2] Fighting and killing in service to the Church was acceptable for those monks professed in the military orders battling against the infidel or in times of war, when the wielding of weapons was permissible. Shedding Christian blood, however, was sinful and morally repugnant for parish priests, who mediated God's grace through the sacraments. Thus, violence against fellow Christians was forbidden, and clerical discipline banned churchmen from fighting and drawing blood except in cases of self-defense.[3] Yet priestly violence—aimed at enemies, parishioners, or strangers—was unexceptional in Catalunya. The sacrist Bernat's case illustrates what many people would have known was commonplace behavior for their clergymen. Clerics were armed and carried daggers, swords, and shields while inside the parish church and when traveling about. A verbal or physical insult could not pass without incident, and clerics wielded their weapons to preserve their pride and reputation.

Parish priests habitually lived and behaved like members of the laity, and they were prone to the same vices and moral failings as their parishioners. Like the laity, they were capable of feeling resentment, dislike, and even hatred toward any individual in their community, and they could act accordingly by holding grudges. Parish clergy, moreover, were affected by many of the same economic concerns, social tensions, power relations, and feuding factions as the lay people they lived among. The conflict-ridden relationships between the clergy and their parishioners is a telling indicator of just how embroiled secular clerics were in the lay world. Scholars have attributed the anticlerical sentiment of the medieval populace to a high level of discontent with a negligent and uneducated clergy, but what is frequently overlooked are the personal histories between parish clergy and their parishioners. Priests committed acts of violence against their parishioners that had little to do with professional defects and more do with personal relationships and past history. The incidence of robbery, kidnapping, and ganglike behavior ranked a far distant second compared to interpersonal violence. Clergymen were bound by the very same codes of honor as laymen in medieval society; these could mean the loss of status and reputation, and therefore they carried weapons and sought revenge to restore their honor just like laymen. As Hannah Skoda has noted in her study

2. Hillgarth and Silano, "Compilation of the Diocesan Synods," 142.

3. Peter Clarke, "The Medieval Clergy and Violence: An Historiographical Introduction" in *Violence and the Medieval Clergy*, ed. Gerhard Jaritz and Ana Marinkovic (Budapest: Central European University Press, 2011), 3–16. See also Lawrence G. Duggan, *Armsbearing and the Clergy in the History and Canon Law of Western Christianity* (Woodbridge, UK: Boydell Press, 2013), 98–101; Ranulph Higden, *Speculum Curatorum: A Mirror for Curates, Book I: The Commandments*, ed. and trans. Eugene Cook and Margaret Jennings (Paris: Peeters, 2012), 261–63.

of medieval violence, the function and mechanisms of violence "were rooted in cultural paradigms which shaped its perpetration, and its motivations were deeply embedded in socio-cultural contexts," so that "the perpetrators of interpersonal violence were, even at an unconscious level, influenced by the norms of their society."[4]

Employing violence to resolve disputes, uphold authority, and exert male privilege in a patriarchal culture was key to demonstrating masculinity in medieval society. Ruth Mazo Karras has argued that violence was a key component of medieval masculinity that cut across social lines and became "the fundamental measure of a man because it was a way of exerting dominance over men of one's own social stratum as well as over women and other social inferiors."[5] In her study of men's efforts to create a masculine identity, Megan McLaughlin has posited that, "men's struggle to create and maintain their identities as men inevitably involves doing violence to other men."[6] Failure to defend one's honor or seek revenge was a sign of shame and personal weakness. Failure to exert masculine privilege and use aggression when provoked emasculated a man and left his manhood in question. Christopher Fletcher has made the case that honor, strength, and steadfastness, above all other traits, characterized medieval manhood because it appears as a culturally valued form of behavior in several kinds of literary texts in the Middle Ages.[7] Whether the protection of personal honor was one of *the* defining traits of manhood in the Middle Ages has yet to be proven, but it certainly was a characteristic that seems to have been present across the spectrum of society. Indeed, historians of medieval violence have observed that, at all levels of society, violence was employed as a "form of social discourse utilized not just by kings, knights, inquisitors, and mobs to oppress and abuse others, but by artisans and peasants, and men and women of whatever religions, to lay claim to honor and integrity, and to establish and defend a place for themselves and their families in local society."[8] In his study of rural Catalunya, Thomas Bisson has also shown that the peasantry experienced honor and shame and that they not only complained of the unjust seizures and exactions

---

4. Hannah Skoda, *Medieval Violence: Physical Brutality in Northern France, 1270–1330* (Oxford: Oxford University Press, 2013), 3.

5. Karras, *From Boys to Men*, 21, 60.

6. McLaughlin, "Secular and Spiritual Fatherhood," 40.

7. Christopher Fletcher, "The Whig Interpretation of Masculinity? Honour and Sexuality in Late Medieval Manhood," in *What is Masculinity?: Historical Dynamics from Antiquity to the Contemporary World*, ed. John H. Arnold and Sean Brady (Hampshire: Palgrave Macmillan, 2011), 57–75.

8. Meyerson, Mark D., Daniel Thiery, and Oren Falk, "Introduction," in *"A Great Effusion of Blood"?: Interpreting Medieval Violence*, ed. Mark D. Meyerson (Toronto: University of Toronto Press, 2004), 5–6.

of their oppressive lords but also were indignant and humiliated by the insults, striking, beatings, and pulling or shaving of beards that "dishonored"
them.[9] As we will see, the people in the villages and towns of late medieval
Catalunya understood that there were specific words and actions that were
meant to cause offense and to which people expected a reactive response from
the injured party in the face of shame. Many of these people experienced firsthand that, just like the castellans, bailiffs, and count's men who abused their
power and public authority to subordinate the peasantry for greater revenues, the parish clergy also used their status and clerical authority to establish a hierarchy in the parish that allowed them to subordinate their
parishioners. The domination of villagers allowed parish clergy to establish
their superiority in the parish and was a means by which they demonstrated
their manliness to the community.

It seems clear that, just as parish clergy did not abjure sex, marriage, and
family, they also did not abjure violence to establish their masculine identity
in their communities. The amount of violence that parish clergy enacted
against male and female parishioners, as well as fellow clergymen, indicates
that secular clergy engaged in violent behavior to display their masculinity to
male society. Judith Butler's theory that gender is performative is useful here
in understanding why and under what circumstances parish clergy chose to
take part in violence.[10] Manhood is proven in a public arena where verbal insults lead to retaliatory violence to defend masculine honor. Performing medieval manhood, and in this case doing violence to others, required the presence
and interaction of men (and sometimes women) so that the clergyman could
subordinate a male or usurp the patriarchal authority of the man responsible
for the female the cleric was targeting. Ultimately these violent interactions
functioned to preserve male honor as much as they served to establish and
secure masculine identity before the community. Indeed, parish clergy used
violence to sustain their dominance. I argue, therefore, that secular clerics in
the major orders who lived in the lay world produced a clerical masculinity
that melded the lay masculine ideals that were a part of their everyday culture with the privilege and authority of their profession. Clerics resorted to
violence to defend their honor and reputation, and they also reacted violently
when a layman or clergyman challenged their status and position in the community. In this chapter and in Chapters Five and Six, I explore the ways in which
violent behavior was an integral part of parish clergy's masculinity, showing

---

9. Bisson, *Tormented Voices*, 127–36. See also Flocel Sabaté, *La feudalización de la sociedad Catalana*
(Granada: Universidad de Granada, 2007), 133–34.

10. Butler, *Gender Trouble*, xv–xvi, 185–86, 191–93.

that clerics frequently upheld their identity as men by doing violence to men as well as to women.

In this chapter, in particular, I connect the lay ideals of masculinity with those of clerical masculinity to show that parish clergy were still very much influenced by standards of masculine behavior set in their society. Nevertheless, parish clerics were not simply laymen. They may have shared the common role of paterfamilias with the men in their village, but their profession and leadership position meant that their standing in the parish was above most of their parishioners, who were predominantly villagers and peasants, along with some artisans and merchants of small means. A cleric's identities as a priest and as a man were not mutually exclusive; his identity was an amalgamation of both. Neither identity could be divorced from the other. Similarly, knights were both warriors and noblemen, and artisans were both skilled craftsmen and men representative of the middling strata of society. Social status, profession, education, holding public office, membership in a confraternity or guild, expressions of devotional piety, and even manners and dress are all factors that affected how men constructed their identities.[11] Profession was just one identity among many that medieval men possessed. Although his occupation mattered greatly in the formation of a man's identity, profession did not solely define the parish clergy. This would be a far too simplistic a view of clerical masculinity and precludes other significant factors or influences. If we think about the multiplicity of roles and identities that people maintained and performed depending on the circumstance and audience, then a man garbed in priestly robes could be dedicated to his priestly duties and yet still abide by a male code of conduct that resonated with his fellow villagers. As we have seen in the previous chapters, clerics carried out a number of familial roles that were not limited by their profession—husband, father, son, brother, and uncle. Parish clergy could never fully disconnect from family and friends because they often grew up in the villages neighboring the parishes they served or had familial ties in their parishes. Even though they had gained a professional identity as clergymen, their relationships with family and friends changed very little. These real-life roles meant that clerics shared more common ground with their male contemporaries than with clerical elites.

---

11. See Lewis, "Male Saints"; Steven Bednarski and Andrée Courtemanche, "Learning to Be a Man: Public Schooling and Apprenticeship in Late Medieval Manosque" *Journal of Medieval History* 35 (2009): 113–35; Kim M. Phillips, "Masculinities and the Medieval English Sumptuary Laws" *Gender & History* 19, no. 1 (2007): 22–42; Sharon Wells, "Manners Maketh Man: Living, Dining and Becoming a Man in the Later Middle Ages," in *Rites of Passage: Cultures of Transition in the Fourteenth Century*, ed. Nicola F. McDonald and William Mark Ormrod (York, UK: York Medieval Press, 2004), 67–81; Mark Johnston, "Gender as Conduct in the Courtesy Guides for Aristocratic Boys and Girls of Amanieu de Sescás" *Essays in Medieval Studies* 20 (2003): 75–85.

It is noteworthy that men in the priesthood could be just as violent as tonsured or married clerics, and even laymen. The priests studied here did not engage in violence simply because they were stuck in a state of adolescence due to their not having achieved the social markers of adulthood—marriage and biological fatherhood.[12] Moreover, the argument that medieval priests engaged in brawling to combat slurs against their virility and questions about their sexual prowess is not convincing for Catalan clergymen considering that the evidence of heterosexual normativity among clerics was everywhere in Catalan society.[13] It is also important to keep in mind that violent acts were not limited to youths or groups of young men. Limiting the connection between masculinity and violence to an adolescent stage of life misrepresents the great number of reasons why men, and people in general, enacted violence. Acts of brutality could be perpetrated by men of all ages, and as Hannah Skoda has determined in her study of violence in northern France, men in the artisanal and mercantile professions, who were established members of the local community, also used violence to defend their personal and familial honor as well as to establish a hierarchy of social relationships. Skoda further emphasizes that tavern violence, particularly outside of Paris, was not limited to youths and social outcasts but involved respectable folk such as doctors, clothmakers, tailors, butchers, and burghers.[14] In addition, the perception that clerical violence was mostly limited to tonsured or married clerics continues to persist and, indeed, an examination of the diocesan registers of Barcelona and Girona confirms that violent acts among clergy in the minor orders was widespread. Yet it is problematic to assume that clergy in the minor orders were more inclined to violence because they could marry and live like laymen, and thus more easily adhere to the principles of lay manhood and that in contrast, clergy in the major orders were less inclined to violent or criminal behavior because their education, dedication to office, and the pressure to serve as role models to the laity caused them to shun violence. Such an assumption ignores the conditions under which priestly formation and training took place—the same environment that influenced clergy in the minor orders and in which clerical mentors kept women and participated in violence. What is more, claims that adult men sought the tonsure and that parents tonsured their children so that they could enjoy the legal privilege and

12. Thibodeaux makes this argument in "From Boys to Priests," in *Negotiating Clerical Identities: Priests, Monks and Masculinity in the Middle Ages,* 136–58.

13. Thibodeaux asserts that, "clerics engaged in brawls to defend themselves against questions of their sexual prowess." *Manly Priest,* 144–45.

14. See Skoda, *Medieval Violence,* 62–63, 68, 97–98, 110.

protection of clerical status are not entirely convincing.[15] It seems doubtful that men who were criminals had the forethought to receive the tonsure before starting their criminal careers to shield themselves from secular jurisdiction or that these men became violent or criminals while in the service of the Church. This view fails to consider that armed men and violence were omnipresent in a society in which masculinity was intimately tied to honor, reputation, bravado, and physical strength. A more likely explanation involves the increase in the number of men in minor orders throughout the fourteenth and fifteenth centuries who decided not to proceed to the major orders because their clerical educations afforded them other employment opportunities—it is these clerks (*clerici*) who made up a greater portion of the clerical population that frequently show up as the perpetrators of violence.[16] All the same, secular clerics, whether in the minor or major orders, were deeply embedded in society, and the fact that both groups of clergymen participated in violent acts, particularly to recapture their honor, exact retribution, and dominate social inferiors, suggests that they were imbued with the same cultural norms as were laymen across the whole spectrum of medieval society.

Whether people respected the man in the priestly robes was not the same as their respecting the rights that came with belonging to a privileged caste in medieval society. Contact with the divine and the protection of clerical privilege, more than anything else, marked the difference between clergy and laity. Church law, specifically the canon known as *privilegium canonis*, dictated excommunication for anyone who lay violent hands on a cleric or monk. Assaulting a cleric was a serious transgression that required papal absolution. The Catalan legal code, the *Usatges de Barcelona*, reinforced canon law and punished those who killed a bishop, monk, priest, deacon, or subdeacon with stiff fines

---

15. Bronislaw Geremek, *The Margins of Society in Late Medieval Paris* (Cambridge, UK: Cambridge University Press, 1987), 136–47; James Buchanan Given, *Society and Homicide in Thirteenth-Century England* (Stanford: Stanford University Press, 1977), 82–86; Barbara Hanawalt, *Crime and Conflict in English Communities, 1300–1348* (Cambridge, MA: Harvard University Press, 1979), 136–37, 264; Trevor Dean, *Crime in Medieval Europe; 1200–1500* (London: Longman, 2001), 108–11; David Nirenberg, *Communities of Violence: Persecution of Minorities in the Middle Ages* (Princeton: Princeton University Press, 1996), 223–24. Swanson has also addressed this common view in *Church and Society*, 151–52.

16. The large number of tonsured clerics in the diocese of Barcelona is discussed in Josep M. Martí Bonet, "El ministerio pastoral del Obispo Ponç de Gualba en sus visitas (a. 1303–1330)," *Memoria Ecclesiae* 4 (1993): 39–41; Martí Bonet, *Historia de las diócesis Españolas*, 162–64. Martí calculates that in the fourteenth century there were 10,000 clergymen in the diocese of Barcelona, many of whom were tonsured or married clerics. He further estimates that out of the sizable population of tonsured clerics, only twelve out of one hundred reached the level of deacon or priest. See also Swanson, *Church and Society*, 40–44, 150–52; P.H. Cullum, "Learning to Be a Man, Learning to Be a Priest in Late Medieval England," in *Learning and Literacy in Medieval England and Abroad*, ed. Sarah Rees Jones (Turnhout, Belgium: Brepols, 2003), 134–53; Cullum, "Boy/Man into Clerk/Priest."

that ranged from 15 to 45 lliures.[17] Clergy were also afforded another protection, the *privilegium fori*, which meant they could not be tried in a secular court or punished by secular authorities. When clerics engaged in illicit activities or committed crimes against their parishioners, they had the advantage of being tried in an ecclesiastical court and were likely to receive more lenient treatment. The protection that clerical privilege afforded clergymen gave them leeway to behave more assertively, even violently, toward their enemies. Although profession and clerical privilege set them apart from the laity, their behaviors did not.

That late-medieval clergymen could be just as violent as the laity is attested to in the letters of absolution and dispensation located in the registers of the Apostolic Penitentiary, where criminal and violent clerks sought to be free of their excommunicated and irregular status. A cleric who committed or took part in violence, particularly a homicide, became "irregular" because he was suspended from service to the altar and removed from his office, as well as being denied the income from his benefice. Although the systematic documentation of Penitentiary petitions did not begin until the mid-fifteenth century, the fact that such petitions arrived from all over Christendom (Spain, Portugal, Italy, France, Germany, the British Isles, and eastern and northern Europe) in the late medieval and early modern period suggests that clerical violence was not limited to a geographical place or time. Clearly this international assortment of clergymen were not all bloodthirsty killers, but these documents show that clerics were willing to employ violence to address a perceived wrong or to express their anger and hatred. Consider that during the six-year pontificate of Pius II (1458 to 1464), 1,305 supplications to the Apostolic Penitentiary dealt with violent behavior that often resulted from quarrels in which knives, swords, sticks, metal objects, and fists were used to injure an opponent. The majority of these petitions involved clerics, not laymen, as the perpetrators or victims of violence. Yet, before concluding that priests were exceptionally violent, we must keep in mind that any study of petitions to the Penitentiary cannot accurately portray the frequency of violence between clergymen, laymen, or both. The Penitentiary did not deal with violent acts between laymen because the local bishop could absolve such acts.[18] Furthermore, although all

---

17. *The Usatges of Barcelona: The Fundamental Law of Catalonia*, trans. Donald Kagay (Philadelphia: University of Pennsylvania Press, 1994), 98.

18. For example, focusing exclusively on Finland in the registers of the Penitentiary from 1450 to 1521, Kirsi Salonen finds that the number of priests (thirty) who perpetrated a killing or assault was far higher than that of laymen (four); Kirsi Salonen and Ludwig Schmugge, *A Sip from the "Well of Grace": Medieval Texts from the Apostolic Penitentiary* (Washington, DC: Catholic University of America Press, 2009), 28–31, 48; Kirsi Salonen, "Violence in Finland in the Middle Ages and the Sixteenth Century in the Light of Source Material from the Vatican Archives" in *Manslaughter, Fornication and*

Christians who laid violent hands on a cleric were in theory required to seek absolution from the pope, lay petitioners appear far less frequently than clergymen because they too could also appeal to their local bishop.[19] This is not surprising given that the long-distance travel to Rome was prohibitively expensive for many. Plus, the laity did not have the same need to obtain absolution as clergymen who wanted to keep their benefice and income. Therefore, the petitions to the Penitentiary reveal that clerics throughout Europe were capable of assault, manslaughter, homicide, rape, and self-defense in the face of injury or death, but the nature of the sources distorts the level of violence among the clergy compared to the laity.

How common clerical violence was during the late Middle Ages is still a question that remains to be investigated. It is likely that the cases brought to the Penitentiary represent only a fraction of clerics involved in violence, murder, or warfare. The registers of the Penitentiary indicate that the more populated European territories as well as the dioceses closest to the Apostolic See made up the greatest number of petitions, whereas the number of petitions from northern and eastern Europe are far fewer. Historians of the Penitentiary are not certain that all petitions handled by the office were copied into the registers, meaning that those petitions that were rejected are likely absent from the records.[20] The registered dispensations, therefore, do not adequately represent clerical violence across Europe. Nevertheless, Lawrence Duggan notes in his study of arms-bearing among the medieval clergy that the "fighting cleric became even more prominent in the fourteenth century" because the "level of ordinary and organized warfare in Europe rose." The increased participation of the clergy in times of war was bolstered by changes in canon law during the twelfth and thirteenth centuries that justified "the right of every cleric to defend himself against attack and even to kill or wound if necessary to preserve his own life without fear of irregularity, much less sin."[21] Duggan argues that the extent to which clergy could use arms in their defense was decided on the diocesan level by bishops. The most frequently conceded exception to the prohibition against bearing arms in Iberia and other European dioceses was while a cleric was traveling, but other exceptions were allowed.

Sectarianism: Norm-Breaking in Finland and the Baltic Area from Mediaeval to Modern Times, ed. Anu Koskivirta and Sari Forsström (Saarijärvi: Annales Academiae Scientiarum Fennicae, 2002), 100–120. Kirsi Salonen provides the number of supplications dealing with violence from 1458 to 1464 in "The Apostolic Penitentiary and Violence in the Roman Curia" in *Violence and the Medieval Clergy*, ed. Gerhard Jaritz and Ana Marinković (Budapest: Central European University Press, 2011), 20n. 7.

    19. See ADB, Registrum Communium, no. 2, 9v. (1311); ADG, Notularum, no. 30, 126r.v.–131r.v. (1352).

    20. Salonen and Schmugge, *Sip from the "Well of Grace,"* 18–21.

    21. Duggan, *Armsbearing and the Clergy*, 29, 142.

In the diocese of Girona, despite a generic ban on clergy carrying weapons, thirteenth-century synodal statutes permitted clerics to bear weapons for their defense or in the case of "just cause for fear."[22] In the diocese of Barcelona, a fourteenth-century synodal statute banned all clerics from carrying swords, javelins, spears, crossbows, and armor both within and outside the city, *unless* a cleric had a license from the bishop. This same statute also permitted, without the need for a license, a cleric to carry a weapon within the city if there was "a reasonable cause."[23] Because few clergy appear to have petitioned the bishop for a license, the latitude of the "reasonable cause" statute essentially allowed diocesan clergy to decide for themselves when to carry a weapon. What is more, episcopal registers indicate that clerics were rarely punished for bearing arms. Considering the widespread use of swords and daggers among the clergy, an armed cleric was the norm in Catalunya, which reveals that parish clergy may have been more inclined to use their weapons and further suggests that the bearing of arms was a trait associated with manliness.

Nevertheless, the actual rates of clerical violence in Iberia are difficult to determine because church court records and episcopal registers vary from diocese to diocese, and these sources are not always the most reliable in revealing acts of violence that did not involve homicide or seriously maiming an individual. For example, clerics who were accused of beating their parishioners in the fourteenth-century Girona visitation records do not appear in the court records of the diocese. It is possible that these court cases were lost over the centuries, but it is more likely that episcopal officials did not want to clog up the court with what might have been viewed as less severe acts of violence. Determining whether the clergy were more violent than the laity is also a challenge since so few studies have attempted to quantify violence among the laity over time and space to be able to draw any kind of comparison, let alone well-founded conclusions.[24] No qualitative study of lay violence in Barcelona, Girona, or elsewhere in Catalunya exists to determine whether Catalan clergy participated in violence at a greater rate than the common layperson.

Parish visitation records, episcopal registers, and ecclesiastical court documents from the dioceses of Barcelona and Girona, however, reveal a surprising level of violence among clergymen, considering that cases of minor violence usually went unreported (See Table 4.1). Josep Baucells counted 161

22. Noguer i Musqueras and Pons Guri, "Constitucions sinodals de Girona," 67. See also ibid., 158.

23. Hillgarth and Silano, "Compilation of the Diocesan Synods," 142.

24. Given, *Society and Homicide*, 82–86; Hanawalt, *Crime and Conflict in English Communities*, 136–37, 264; Geremek, *Margins of Society*, 136–47; Dean, *Crime in Medieval Europe*, 108–11; Finch, "Women and Violence."

rectors, priests, and beneficed clerics involved in physical violence in the diocese of Barcelona from 1303 to 1344. In comparison, twenty-three laymen
were accused of wounding and seven of killing a cleric. A study of the Barcelona ecclesiastical court records for the fifteenth century finds that 40 percent
of the total number of criminal cases (157) dealt with clerics committing acts
of physical violence.[25] For the diocese of Girona, of the 265 court cases extant from 1282 to 1350, 30 percent (79) dealt with criminal cases, and of these
79 cases, 14 percent (30) involved clerical violence.[26] Once again, it is doubtful
that such numbers represent the actual level of violence among Catalan clergymen, especially in light of the fact that these ecclesiastical courts were in-
undated with disputes over ecclesiastical benefices, privileges, tithes, and
matrimonial litigation. It is also problematic to find meaning in these numbers with such variant data sets, but the cases themselves tell us a lot about
the motivations and justifications for violence presented by clerics before episcopal officials. To summarize here, sources point to a significant amount of
violence among the clergy throughout medieval Europe and, in particular,
in Catalunya, but it is difficult to say whether the level or degree of violence
among Catalan clergy was exceptional or ordinary.

A far easier question to address is, under what circumstances did clerics use
violence? The accounts of clerical violence in Catalan episcopal sources indicate that churchmen used violence not only to resolve conflict but also to exert their power and authority in their parishes. Like the lay people they lived
among, Catalan clergymen engaged in poor neighborly behavior; disputes over
land and goods; and petty, retaliatory acts. Many were known for their abra-
sive personalities and were described not as peacemakers but as belligerent
men ready to fight with anyone in the village. Indeed, parishioners frequently
described their parish cleric as a "quarrelsome man"—a *homo ritxosus* or *homo
brichosus,* terms that described clergymen who not only verbally insulted clerics and parishioners alike but also were known for physically assaulting others.
Although clerics were especially prone to creating conflict because of their
central role in the community and the potential for abuse in carrying out
their religious duties, the antagonistic interactions between the clergy and laity
were more often than not the result of personal animosities that developed

---

25. Baucells i Reig did not include the fourteenth-century Barcelona ecclesiastical court records
in his study because so few criminal cases have survived from this period; *Vivir en la edad media,* 3:
2430–40, 2445–49, 2460. For an excellent study of the fifteenth-century Barcelona church court records, see Serrano Seoane, "Sistema penal. Primera parte."
26. The bishop's registers, in which the fines imposed for concubinage and "excesses" appear,
indicate that clerics on occasion were fined for violence; ADG, Obligacions de Penes, no. 1 (1336–
1386) and Remissions de Penes, no. 1 (1345–1367). These two registers simply state the cleric's name,
parish, crime, and fine, but they do not identify the reason behind the violence.

due to the day-to-day interactions of living in a small community. What follows is not a catalog of clerical misdeeds to illustrate the defects of the clergy.
Rather, in providing a context for the violent behaviors of clerics, my goal is to
illustrate not only the extent to which clerics were a part of the parish community but also to show how clerical identity embodied characteristics that
similarly defined laymen: the need to avenge public humiliation and employ
violence to protect or defend themselves, their families, and their friends. The
meaning of honor is deeply gendered and defined by culture, and honor is
acutely tied to the experience of shame and humiliation, as well as the desire
to shame and humiliate those who have claimed the honor for themselves.[27]
The honor of parish clergy was tied to their status in the village, their profession as clerics, their reputation and the reputation of their family members,
the ability to defend kith and kin, and the domination of other men. Honor
was contested and maintained through violence, and in doing so, clerics not
only engaged in a socially sanctioned form of male expression but also affirmed
their masculinity. Moreover, a cleric's willingness to act aggressively further
worked to bolster his standing and became one way of defining difference and
hierarchy in the in the community.

The defense of honor, through violence if necessary, was a deeply established cultural practice in medieval society. In his study on *Violence in Medieval
Europe*, Warren Brown has explored how medieval Europeans understood different forms of violence and whether they believed such violence to be justified or worthy of condemnation. He observes that, of the two most important
norms of violence found in medieval sources from different centuries and
regions, a violent response to an injury or insult was considered a legitimate
one, a wrong that needed to be made right to avoid shame, isolation, and
possible victimization by others. Brown notes that the aristocracy, townspeople, and the peasantry alike shared some of the same ideas about violence,
rights, and honor.[28] Medieval attitudes toward violence and personal affronts
can be seen in legal codes from the Crown of Aragon that punished offenders for physical injuries and slander. The fundamental law code in Catalunya,
the *Usatges of Barcelona*, outlines the fines for violent acts that would cause
a count, knight, or any man dishonor: slapping and spitting in a man's face,
pulling or shaving his beard, shoving and pushing him to the ground, and striking him with blows, using a fist, stone, rock, or club, that caused blood to be

27. David D. Gilmore, "Honor, Honesty, Shame: Male Status in Contemporary Andalusia," in
Honor and Shame and the Unity of the Mediterranean, ed. David D. Gilmore (Washington, DC: American
Anthropological Association, 1987), 90–91.
28. Warren C. Brown, *Violence in Medieval Europe* (London: Pearson, 2011), 12, 13, 39–41, 113–15,
159, 288–89.

shed.[29] Even though counts and knights received far greater compensation for their "serious dishonor" at the hands of their enemies, it is telling that the common man should also be compensated for the wrong done to him. Municipal law codes, such as the *Fuero de Jaca* and the *Fuero de Calatayud* in the Crown of Aragon also evolved to include penalties for verbal "injuries," described as "dishonored through words" (*denostado por palavras*). Strangely enough, the specific injurious words that incurred the penalty equivalent to half the fine for homicide, 1,000 maravedís, are not outlined.[30] This suggests that everyone culturally shared the same basic vocabulary concerning insults to know what *denostado por palavras* meant. Visitation and court records reveal the most common verbal insults for men: whoreson, *cuguç* (cuckold), *arlot* (a man who was financially supported by a prostitute), *bacallar* (an imbecile or uncivilized man who was socially inferior to a peasant), traitor, and thief.[31] In Barcelona, the records of the royal bailiff document the fines administered to citizens such as milliners, bakers, sailors, slaves, Jews, and women for insulting others with "injurious words" and for slapping or fighting with adversaries.[32] Hence, across social and economic lines, and even religious ones, the entire spectrum of society understood that verbal and physical insults could elicit a violent response.

Although the use of violence to defend one's honor was a socially prescribed behavior, historians such as David Nirenberg and Daniel Lord Smail have shown that physical violence could be channeled through litigation when people chose to pursue their enmity in the courts. Pursuing an enemy, business competitor, annoying neighbor, or even a creditor or debtor through the courts was a popular option for medieval people in the fourteenth century, particularly in urban centers. These same studies find, however, that assaults and vengeance killings were still numerous among prominent families and the lower classes. As Smail points out for the city of Marseille, "the culture of vengeance and violent retribution was in a flourishing condition."[33] In the Crown of Aragon and elsewhere in Spain, disputes were frequently settled with fists

29. *Usatges of Barcelona*, 65–68. See also Rafael Serra Ruiz, *Honor, honra, e injuria en el derecho medieval español* (Murcia: Sucesores de Nogués, 1969).

30. Alfonso Guallart de Viala, *El derecho penal histórico de Aragón* (Zaragoza: Excma. Diputación Provincial, Institución Fernando el Católico, D. L. 1977), 191–93.

31. A discussion of verbal insults can also be found in Baucells i Reig, *Vivir en la edad media*, 3: 2353–54, 2356; Serrano Seoane, "Sistema penal. Primera parte," 377–78.

32. *Llibre del Batlle Reial de Barcelona, Berenguer Morey (1375–1378)*, ed. Josep Maria Casas Homs (Barcelona: Fundacio Salvador Vives Casajuana, 1976). Here, too, people are fined for "pauraules injurioses," but the precise words used to cause offense are not listed.

33. Smail, *Consumption of Justice*, 8.

and swords rather than opting for the courts.[34] Even among Jews in the kingdom of Valencia, royal officials and the leaders of the *aljama* (a self-governing Jewish community) were bypassed because the violent defense of individual or family honor was a common and expected response. Jews not only used violence to respond to verbal and physical affronts but also resorted to violence to degrade their enemies and compete for status in the Jewish community. Acts of retribution allowed Jewish men to earn or preserve the respect of fellow Jews, and by participating in feuds, they made an "honorable showing" that elevated a family's reputation.[35] Muslim communities in the kingdom of Valencia were likewise marked by intracommunal violence that involved family honor in the competition for material wealth, status, and power. According to Mark Meyerson, "the plethora of official truces between rival Mudejar families, the numerous acts of violence in which agnates were implicated, and the importance of vengeance as a motive for such violence all indicate that the feud was so pervasive as to constitute a primary determinant of Mudejar social relations."[36] Although Mudejars used the courts to settle their economic disputes, issues of honor for which societal norms demanded vengeance were contested publicly in the community. Across Christian, Jewish, and Muslim societies in the Crown of Aragon, then, questions of honor, whether in defense of the individual or family, were more apt to be settled through violence than the courts.

Secular clergymen were no different in this respect. Even though clerics and villagers of northern Catalunya had access to municipal courts or the bishop's court,[37] it is not surprising that they too chose to settle their disputes publicly in the parish. Indeed, many of the reported conflicts were resolved through public violence before a host of witnesses. The point of public violence was exactly that it was public—an act done in private and in secret gave the deed an aura of cowardice that could also taint it as unwarranted.[38] In

34. Nirenberg, *Communities of Violence*, 30; Blumenthal, *Enemies and Familiars*, 156–69; Marta Madero, *Manos violentas, palabras vedadas: La injuria en Castilla y León, siglos XIII–XV* (Madrid: Taurus Humanidades, 1992), 22–23, 45–48, 159–81, 188–93; Fernando Lojo Piñiero, *A violencia na Galicia do século XV* (Santiago de Compostela: Universidad de Santiago de Compostela, 1991), 73–91.
35. Mark D. Meyerson, *A Jewish Renaissance in Fifteenth-Century Spain* (Princeton: Princeton University Press, 2004), 167, 175–79.
36. Mark D. Meyerson, *The Muslims of Valencia in the Age of Fernando and Isabel: Between Coexistence and Crusade* (Berkeley: University of California Press, 1991), 244, 232–54. See also Brian Catlos, "The de Reys (1220–1501): The Evolution of a 'Middle-Class' Muslim Family in Christian Aragon," *Viator* 40 (2009): 197–219; Nirenberg, *Communities of Violence*, 133–39, 160–63.
37. For example, the hebdomedarian Bernat Badot took his wounded reputation over "injurious words" to the secular court and won; ADG, Visites, no. 5, 38r. (1331).
38. Paul R. Hyams, *Rancor and Reconciliation in Medieval England* (Ithaca: Cornell University Press, 2003), 11.

most cases, the violence enacted on the victim was not life threatening, but in the eyes of the perpetrator, the victim received his due while at the same time the perpetrator made a public declaration that a personal affront would not be tolerated. Consider that the canon Joan claimed that he beat his female neighbor on a public street because the woman had publicly criticized his behavior and had said "injurious words" to him. Similarly, when a gambling dispute prompted an angry exchange of words and a rock thrown at his head, the beneficed cleric Guillem de Tor attacked his opponent with a sword in the presence of, according to one witness, one hundred men. Such a high number of witnesses seems exaggerated, but for Guillem, the "loss of face," whether before ten or one hundred men, meant that he had to respond accordingly to the insult.[39]

Gambling among men was an activity that frequently led to violence; it is what Scott Taylor has labeled "aggressive male sociability" because it centered on "competition, risk, public performance, and material gain and loss." Since gaming and gambling took place before other men who could criticize or mock the players and always ended with a defined loser, it is no surprise that male honor and reputation were at risk in the public performance of competitive gaming sports among men.[40] The honor and reputation of public officials were also at stake when local men challenged their authority publicly and, in doing so, disregarded the official's power and failed to demonstrate the proper deference. After "many injurious words" between Bernat Batlle, a minor royal official, and his brother, the priest Pere Batlle, Bernat attacked his brother the priest with a sword before many clerics and servants of the abbot of Sant Miquel de Fluvià. According to Bernat Battle, his priestly brother was a "brawler and quarrelsome" man ("rixosus et bricosus") whom he beat to "correct."[41] Despite the ties of kinship, Bernat felt that he needed to teach his brother a lesson publicly about respecting his position as a royal official and

---

39. ADG, Processos, no. 66, 1v., 2v. (1323); ADG, Processos, no. 73, 2r., 4v., 8r.v.–9r.v. (1323). Other examples include the cleric Bernat Gener, who after having a "dispute and insulting words" ("rixam et verba contumeliosa") with Joan Alaó, drew a large knife and wounded Joan in the head, and the cleric Berenguer Collel, who beat the married woman Guillema with a club on the main street of the village of Maçanet before ten or more villagers for insulting his sister. Berenguer added further insult to injury when he impugned her reputation by stating that Guillema, a married woman, was frequently in the company of "common" men; See ADG, Processos, no. 33, 1r.v.–2r.v. (c. 1320); ADG, Processos, no. 106, 1r.v. (1330).

40. Scott Taylor, *Honor and Violence in Golden Age Spain* (New Haven: Yale University Press, 2008), 140–50. See also Dwayne E. Carpenter, "Fickle Fortune: Gambling in Medieval Spain," *Studies in Philology* 85, no. 3 (1998): 267–78.

41. ADG, Processos, no. 125, 1v. (1333). In another example, the beneficed cleric Bernat Gener of Castelló d'Empúries attacked the layman Joan Alaó with a large knife over "contumelious" words; ADG, Processos, no. 33 (c. 1320).

to shame his brother in front of fellow clergymen. It is not a coincidence that, when men sought to redeem their reputations and return the insult, they chose to do so before witnesses who could then publicize that they had reclaimed their honor.

By far, more than any other type of violence, interpersonal violence appears most frequently. Parish clergy were not immune to suffering disgrace or feeling the need to vindicate their honor and recover their personal dignity. Indeed, the maintenance of the honor and reputation of a cleric or his family was at the center of much clerical violence in Catalunya, particularly when it meant protecting the honor of family members. The layman Joan Gibern lost his left hand to the cleric Ponç de Roca's sword for punching Ponç's father in the parish church of Llançà and causing a "great amount of blood" to flow from his nose. At the time that Joan Gibern had punched Ponç's father, Ponç was studying at a grammar school in Peralada and news of the beating found its way to Ponç there. Three years went by before Ponç encountered Joan Gibern, and according to his confession in the bishop's court, he considered himself greatly offended and insulted by what had transpired. Ponç explained that he had wanted to "avenge the injury to his father," so he attacked Joan with his sword.[42] For three years, Ponç's humiliation at his father's dishonor seems to have festered, until he took advantage of the opportunity for retribution. Ponç's return to his home village of Llançà probably made the need to restore his family's honor more pressing particularly because he was no longer a boy but a young man. Punishing Joan Gibern was important to Ponç, but just as important was announcing to the community that he would retaliate against an offense to himself or his family.

Episcopal officials were not strangers to hearing a cleric defend his actions in response to a personal affront that began with offensive words and escalated to violence. The bishop's curia had also investigated Ponç de Roca (previously mentioned) for the death of a fellow cleric, Bernat Vives, in a sword fight that started when Bernat called Ponç a "bleating centaur" and a "filthy pimp." Similarly, the beneficed cleric Bernat Gener was brought before the court for "gravely" wounding the layman Joan Alaó in the head with his knife after an exchange of insults. Yet these disputes involved more than just insulting words. In the bishop's palace of Girona, a sword fight ensued between a jurist and scribe working in the curia that began when the scribe criticized the jurist for the way in which he had carried out his duties.[43] It was much more than the

---

42. ADG, Processos, no. 16, letter of confession (1309). Other examples include a cleric defending his father; García Egea, *Visita pastoral*, 133, 207.

43. ADG, Processos, no. 16, 5v.–7v. (1308); ADG, Processos, no. 33, 1r.v.–2r. (c. 1320); ADG, Processos, no. 129, 1v.–2r. (1334). The scribe criticized the jurist over a decision made concerning a case.

exchange of disparaging words that had prompted the confrontation; the scribe had called into question the jurist's competence and performance of his duties, thereby attacking his reputation as a professional. Clerics were not unique in their violent reactions to personal affronts that impugned their familial or professional honor; laymen likewise fought over "injurious words" that challenged their honor. For example, when the sacrist Guillem Mata had gone to the local sheriff's home to recover a sword belonging to his nephew, he called the sheriff a "false son of a whore" who came "from a line of bastards," which resulted in the sheriff's grabbing the sacrist by his frock and punching him in the face. There is no doubt that the sacrist had offended the sheriff by insulting his parentage, but he had also questioned the sheriff's authority to take the sword and had failed to show the expected deference to a town official.[44] Royal officials were likewise concerned with their reputations and the respect that their position entitled them to. When the abbot of San Feliu de Guíxols claimed that he had beaten Pere de Climent while Pere was carrying out his official business as a royal police officer, Pere responded by violently kidnapping the abbot and holding him in a tower outside the city of Girona until he personally returned the abbot to the bishop's palace.[45] Pere's actions suggest that he was attempting to salvage his reputation and humiliate the abbot for boasting that he had bested Pere. Such behavior indicates that men across the social spectrum of town and parish village, regardless of clerical robes, were bound by similar codes of honor that called for action, if not retaliation.

Ricardo Córdoba de la Llave has noted in his study of violence in Castile that medieval people made a distinction between violence that resulted from quarrels or provocation, which they found far more excusable, and premeditated violence committed in cold blood (*a sangre fría*).[46] Provoked violence, such as the exchange of insults that led to a violent act, however, was usually not a singular incident but a consequence of a deep-seated hatred or longstanding animosity that exploded into a physical assault. Think back to the

---

The sword fight took place before various officials, and the jurist received injuries to his arm, hand, and nose.

44. ADG, Processos, no. 134, 12ff. (1334–1335). In another example of laymen entering into disputes concerning honor and reputation, Bernat Bonet and Bonanat de Camps exchanged "irate words" when Bernat accused Bonanat of having stolen chickens and grain; this led to slaps in the face and ended with Bernat dragging Bonanat "by the hairs" before fourteen village men after Sunday mass in front of the church; ADG, Processos, no. 261, 20ff. (c. 1350). In one more example, the sword fight between Pere Gifreu, a draper, and two laymen reportedly started over "injurious words"; ADG, Processos, no. 264, 7ff. (c. 1350). See also ADG, Notularum, no. 2, 5r. (1304).

45. ADB, Dispensationes Apostolics, 6r.v.–12r.v. (1332).

46. Ricardo Córdoba de la Llave, "Violencia cotidiana en Castilla a fines de la edad media" in *Conflictos sociales, políticos y intellectuales en la España de los siglos XIV y XV*, ed. José Ignacio de la Iglesia Duarte (Logroño: Instituto de Estudios Riojanos, 2004), 418.

opening example in this chapter, in which the sacrist Bernat Batlle and Jaume
Moner, a layman, had a history of insults and sword fighting long before the
sacrist mortally wounded Jaume after a face-spitting incident.[47] Similarly, a
nasty exchange of words that led to a sword fight between the rector Ramon
Bernat and Bord de Foixà was based on a deeply rooted hostility from more
than simply insults. According to Bord de Foixà and many witnesses, the rector became angry when Bord reproached Ramon for committing adultery with
a local married woman, particularly since the rector already had a family with
Englentina, his concubine of eight years. Yet, according to Ramon, who was
the rector of the chapel located in the castle of Foixà, Bord de Foixà was re-
taliating against him because Bord, his brother, the nobleman Bernat Guillem
de Foixà, and his wife Ermesenda were "angry" and "indignant" that the rector
had dined with the "swines" of the village of Rupià, who were the "enemies"
of the nobleman Bernat Guillem. In fact, both men had reportedly called each
other "false" and "traitor," but the rector blamed Bord de Foixà for accusing
him, before an episcopal official, of personally damaging a water mill that
belonged to the Foixà family.[48] On the surface, the sword fight appears to
have been about a local nobleman criticizing a rector for his sexual indiscretion, but the bad blood stemmed from more than just the rector's sexual affair and was more likely the result of what the Foixà family perceived to be
the disloyalty of their own rector. Physically violent encounters such as the
one between rector Ramon and Bord de Foixà were often the result of protracted hostilities. From the point of view of the Foixà family, the rector
Ramon's actions were a betrayal. Friendship in medieval society could be
constructed along the line of a common enemy; therefore, the rector had
associated with the enemy and thus had become "the friend of my enemy is
my enemy."[49] Far from being excluded from contentious issues in the community they served, parish clerics were known to side with certain factions

47. ADG, Processos, no. 25, 4r. (1317).
48. ADG, Processos, no. 188, 83ff. (1337). The rector Ramon Bernat also testified that the lady
Ermesenda had stated that the men of the village of Ultramort had broken the mill and that she became angry when he disagreed and claimed that the men of Fonayeres and Sant Iscle had done the
damage. Another example can be found in a clash that started over an exchange of insults between
the beneficed clerics Ramon Ferrer and Arnau Vic when Ramon charged Arnau with his sword, calling him "a pimp, a dishonest man, and a thief." In actuality the controversy centered on Ramon's
keeping Venguda, Arnau's sister, as his concubine for more than two years, which explains why Ramon boasted before Arnau and other clerics that it was "no wonder that I have already had your
sister." Arnau's rancor stemmed from his disapproval of Ramon's relationship with his sister, and
Ramon's malice stemmed from Arnau's efforts to disparage Ramon's reputation, including his likely
attempts to obstruct the relationship. It appears that Ramon Ferrer was a beneficed cleric serving at
the church of Sant Feliu, where Arnau de Vic was also serving, but it is unclear what benefice, if any,
Arnau had; ADG, Processos, no. 100, 5v.–6r., 9r.v., 16v., 22r. (1328).
49. Hyams, *Rancor and Reconciliation in Medieval England*, 22, 27, 31.

and participate in feuds. Consider also the canon Francesc Calvet and the sacrist Pere Dalmau, who were imprisoned for resisting arrest and causing public disorder in the city of Girona. The two friends defended their violent rebellion against the bailiff and his sheriff because they had taken away their swords, which they claimed had been done "unjustly" since the weapons were needed "for the defense of their person" on account of "certain enemies."[50] These men expected their enemies to seek them out and do them harm, and this justified their need to carry swords for self-defense. Enemies could be real threats, and as Paul Hyams has noted in his study of vengeance, "the notion of mortal enmities was pervasive in medieval society."[51] Considering the familial ties and friendships that parish clergymen were bound to have in the parish, it is not a surprise that they became involved in feuding. The point is that parish clergy cultivated enemies and took part in the cycle of retribution like everyone else.

Clerics spent years serving in a community where personal animosities and conflicts were bound to develop. Participating in a personal vendetta and becoming involved in local politics were not the only reasons that clergymen behaved violently. Indeed, the confrontational and belligerent personality of some clergymen created discord in the community. The visitations reveal that these contentious personalities fostered much resentment among parishioners, particularly when they used their clerical position to retaliate against their opponents. After the priest Berenguer Pagès reported his fellow villager Pere to the local curia, Pere showed up on the priest's doorstop spouting "many reproaches" and "many words" that led both men to draw their swords. Parishioners reported that this same priest had recently punched another parishioner, Guillem de Sigario, in the face in church during a quarrel, and three years before in a separate incident, he had clashed swords with the same Guillem.[52] Although it is evident that parishioners considered the priest Berenguer a troublemaker in the village, a history of personal ill will caused these men to come to blows. The underlying cause of the violent quarrels between clergymen and villagers is frequently unexplained in the records, yet the fact that the parties knew each other suggests that these were not random acts of violence but conflicts that stemmed from personal hostilities.[53] The participation of

---

50. ADG, Processos, no. 275, 2r.v., 5r. (1354).

51. Hyams, *Rancor and Reconciliation in Medieval England*, 59.

52. ADG, Visites, no. 4, 103v.–104r.v. (1329). Although the cause behind some cases of violence between clergymen and villagers is unclear, the dispute and the violence itself indicate that it was motivated by personal animosity rather than impersonal violence.

53. See ADG, Visites fragmentaris, 5r. (1312–1313); ADG, Visites, no. 3, 38r. (1321); ADG, Notularum, no. 4, 153r. (1327); ADB, Registrum Communium, no. 4, 162r. (1328); ADB, Registrum Communium, no. 7, 113v. (1337); ADB, Registrum Communium, no. 7, 211r. (1338).

parish clergy in inimical relationships is also proof of their integration into village society. Even though their profession and clerical privilege set them apart from the laity, the fact that they could hold grudges and seek retribution did not. Indeed, clerics' personal conflicts and high-handed tactics explain why so many parishioners did not hold their parish clergy in high esteem.

Clashes with neighbors over inconsiderate and unneighborly behavior also fostered acrimonious relations between a cleric and his parish. The rector Guillem Bosc fought "excessively" with his parishioners because he allowed his beasts to pasture on their lands and did not mind his animals when they wandered onto parishioners' planted fields. The hebdomedarian Berenguer Cunyl and Beatriu were unpopular because the couple let their cows and pigs inflict damage in the neighborhood. In another case, the neighbors of the beneficed cleric Bernat de Fabrica accused him of stealing their chickens.[54] Some clerics, such as the sacrist Pere Vidal, were physically aggressive when dealing with their inconsiderate neighbors. The sacrist Pere had to deal with the poor manners of his neighbor Guillem who used the building next to Pere's property as a shelter for his pigs and cows. Guillem and his wife lived elsewhere and did not have to deal with the smells, noises, and droppings of the animals that so troubled the sacrist Pere. In retaliation, Pere sent his neighbor a clear message: when Guillem arrived home one day, he found cow manure on the door and lock of his home. On a separate occasion, Pere had thrown a rock at Guillem's head when he had come on his daily routine to care for his animals.[55] The final straw between neighbors occurred when the sacrist Pere had killed one of Guillem's pigs during a confrontation. An exchange of insults in which Guillem called the sacrist Pere a *bacallar* (uncivilized man), a false thief, and a deceiver of women resulted in Pere and his brother-in-law Francesc beating the layman Guillem until he lay prostate and "half-dead" on the ground. The sacrist Pere's status and position in the village of Verges most likely had much to do with the assault and humiliation of Guillem. The sacrist was not an outsider but had family ties to the parish, such as the support of his sister and

54. Visitatio diversarum, HMML, microfilm no. 31951, Visites, no. 1, 79v. (1307); ADG, Visites, no. 6, 3v. (1338); ADB, Registrum Communium, no. 9, 182v. (1341).

55. It was not unusual for people to express their discontent by throwing stones at the king's palace, as well as at official buildings and neighbors' houses. The laws in some Catalan towns specifically prohibited people from throwing rocks at the doors and houses of their enemies, although this was regularly used as a form of ritual violence against Jews during Holy Week throughout Catalunya. In Barcelona, people showed their anger by throwing rocks at the king's palace. In general, stone throwing in medieval Catalunya functioned as way to mock one's enemy and publicly advertised the perpetrator's disdain for his victim. David Nirenberg addresses some of the meanings of stone throwing and explains that it was an essential part of the ritualized violence against Jews throughout Catalunya, in *Communities of Violence*, 201–14. See also *El Fuero de Teruel*, ed. José Castañé Llinás (Teruel, 1991), no. 284, 220.

brother-in-law Francesc. As sacrist of the village for more than twelve years, parishioners knew him in more than one capacity—certainly as a clergyman but also as an angry neighbor, brother, brother-in-law, and a lover to two village women.[56] When clerics violently lashed out against their parishioners, these were more often than not personal conflicts in which they reacted in a violent fashion that bolstered their status and authority in the community. In the majority of these cases, the priest had the upper hand in the situation and gained a certain amount of capital in the village that showed off his privilege, allowing him place his rights and needs above those of his neighbors.

Particularly when a cleric served in a village where he had family ties, the support and participation of family and friends exacerbated conflicts. Take, for example, the deacon Arnau de Bosso and his known enemy, Guillem Agustí, in the parish of Sant Feliu de la Garriga. Hostilities between the two men erupted in a sword fight that embroiled the deacon Arnau and his brothers, on one side, and Guillem Agustí, Guillem's fifteen-year-old brother Berenguer Agustí, and Guillem's friend, the sacrist of la Garriga, and the sacrist's nephew Pere and his two cousins, on the other side. The cause for such hatred between the deacon Arnau and Guillem, and the deacon and the sacrist, is not identified in this incomplete court record, but witnesses refer to the existence of a general animosity, resulting in a number of previous standoffs and both parties threatening the other with violence.[57] The professions of the deacon Arnau and the sacrist seem to have mattered little to the three men and their family and friends, who were natives of the same village and probably grew up together. Profession made a difference in so far that episcopal officials investigated the fight because clergymen were involved, but the rivalry between these men stemmed from a past history of enmity, the details of which are now lost to us. Many of the cases dealing with clerical violence refer to the existence of bad blood between the parties but provide little information as to its cause. An enduring public relationship of hatred between two adversaries,

---

56. ADG, Processos, no. 198, 1r.v.–2r.v., 7v. (1338); ADG, Lletres, no. 2, 94r., 168r. (1326); ADG, Obligacions de Penes, no. 1, 12r. (1336) and 27r. (1339). Elizabeth S. Cohen has coined *house-scorning* for the practice of assaulting a house with stones, vials of ink, blood, mud, or excrement. House-scorning was a form of revenge that demonstrated public contempt for an enemy and was considered an affront to the victim's honor; Elizabeth S. Cohen, "Honor and Gender in the Streets of Early Modern Rome," *Journal of Interdisciplinary History* 22, no. 4 (1992): 597–625.

57. ADG, Processos, no. 23, 10ff. (1315). Despite the enmity between the two parties, the deacon Arnau de Basso continued living in the parish and is present in visitation records from 1315 and 1321; ADG, Visites, no. 1, 36r.v. (1315); ADG, Visites, no. 3, 38r.v. (1321). In another example, the priest Francesc Guilabert from the parish of Vilafranca was reprimanded for fighting and injuring the rector Guillem de Busquets and his brother Bartomeu de Busquets from the parish of Granada, as well as the laymen Jaume Pagès and his sons, who were also from Granada; ADB, Registrum Communium, no. 9, 32r. (1339).

for which Daniel Lord Smail has coined the term *social institution of hatred*, aptly describes the actions of clerics who expressed their hatred by means of assaults, insults, and threats against their enemies. Although the pursuit of honor was an important element for engaging in a public relationship of enmity, social hatred was also a way to recruit family and friends into vendettas and to reinforce friendships "to the point where a group of friends would avenge one of their own."[58] Evidence that parish clergy engaged in public relationships of hatred can be seen in the example of the hebdomedarian Bernat Rourich, who helped friends exact vengeance on a fellow villager on account of the "odio capitalis" they felt for their enemy.[59] Similarly, when the priest Arnau de Juvinyà attacked two men from the nearby village of Banyoles, a witness explained that the priest felt hatred (*odio*) for the men, especially because they were "the friends of the bailiff of Banyoles," whom the priest Arnau also hated. The source for such hatred is undisclosed in the case, but its intensity is clear in the description of the priest Arnau chasing and fighting the two men (one of whom later died from his wounds) with his sword in the church cemetery.[60] The testimony of witnesses may not reveal the origins of the conflict or the precise motivation of the aggressor(s), but they do reveal the extent to which clerics were integrated into parish life, in that a personal conflict could lead to a cycle of retribution in which the people of the parish took sides and actively took part in the process of feuding. Far from engaging in impersonal or senseless violence, clerics participated in public disputes and feuds that involved their families and friends, and acted out of personal hatred. The response of these clergymen, however, seems disproportionate to the supposed affronts and suggests that their action was more than retaliatory but a way to dominate other men and also ensure that others in the community recognized their masculinity.

As we have seen, the ties to family and bonds of friendship integrated a cleric into his community and could be a source of support in clashes, but these very same loyalties could also be a source of conflict. When the local butcher pushed his son off a table, the deacon Bartomeu de Roure slapped and punched him, which resulted in the butcher reporting the assault to episcopal officials. It is not a surprise that a father defended his son or that brothers protected

58. Daniel Lord Smail, "Hatred as a Social Institution in Late Medieval Society," *Speculum* 76, no. 1 (2001): 107.

59. ADG, Processos, no. 259, 3r., 9r.v. (c. 1350). Paul Hyams also makes the point that relationships of enmity were "more than the business of an individual" and that the principle "the friend of my friend is my friend too" governed many male relationships. Hyams, *Rancor and Reconciliation in Medieval England*, 23. The language of enmity, such as the terms *inimicus, inimicitia,* and *odium capitale,* is also discussed in Smail, *Consumption of Justice*, 105.

60. ADG, Processos, no. 5, 4v. (1299).

each other, as when the sacrist Guillem d'Anglada and his sword came to the defense of his brother Berenguer during a gambling dispute with a parishioner.[61] Clerics also protected their daughters, sisters, nieces, and cousins from predatory males. The priest Pere Ferrar fought with the chaplain Nicolau when Nicolau made amorous advances toward his sister Geralda, who happened to be married. Thereafter, relations between the two clerics deteriorated.[62] The stabilitus Joan Escuder, and his brother Bernat, came to blows with the cleric Ponç Tina for defaming Joan's daughter and their widowed niece Adalayde, whom he called a whore. It appears that, when Adalayde rejected the enamored (*filocaptus*) Ponç, he broke into her home, beat her, and later threatened to kill her if she revealed what had occurred. Ponç's troubles over his pursuit of Adalayde were not limited to his fellow clergyman Joan Escuder but also involved Joan's nephews and friends, who had warned Ponç to leave the two women alone.[63] The priest Joan's connections in the parish meant that he could marshal a contingent of family and friends to defend the honor of his daughter and niece, but it also involved him in a messy family affair that created a scandal in the village. These ties of kinship complicated relationships with fellow clerics or parishioners who were not family, and it is unlikely that parishioners expected these clergymen to be impartial or independent actors in the community. The people of the parish understood that their local cleric could also be an angry and vengeful father, brother, uncle, or cousin. Honor also dictated that a man defend his female kin, particularly against accusations of sexual misconduct. That clerics responded aggressively to insults that impugned the sexual honor of the women in their families indicates that their reputation and the reputation of their family mattered to their masculine identity.

Such protective behavior of family members could create tensions in the parish, but much of the resentment aimed at clergy stemmed from the highhanded abuse of their position when they set out to blatantly take what they wanted. The possession of women, especially married ones, could be a great source of controversy when clerics poached the daughters or wives of laymen. Although the misogynistic writings of churchmen frequently placed the blame on the women for seducing and tempting clerics into sexual sin, parishioners

---

61. ADG, Processos, no. 124, 4ff. (1332); ADG, Visites, no. 5, 15r.v. (1331).

62. ADG, Visites, no. 1, 10r. (1315). In another example, there was great discord between the sacrist Arnau de Terrades and the hebdomedarian Arnau de Comellis because the hebdomedarian reportedly had an affair with the sacrist's married sister; ADG, Visites, no. 3, 31r.v. (1321).

63. ADG, Processos, no. 185,1v., 11r.v., 12v., 14r.v.–16r.v. (1337). In 1337, Joan Escuder appears in an episcopal register of fines and was fined 24 sous for "excesses"; ADG, Obligacions de Penes, no. 1, 9r. (1337).

were more likely to blame the cleric.[64] These parish clerics are depicted as the aggressors in their manner and method of obtaining women. For example, villagers reported that the rector of Caradells had "forcibly removed" Guillem's daughter from her paternal home to keep her as his concubine.[65] When the bishop of Girona visited the parish of Albons, Bernat Llorenç, a layman, informed him that the sacrist Joan Feliu had impregnated his daughter Marsela and kept her "hidden" in another village. Bernat's testimony reveals that he did not approve of the sacrist's relationship with Marsela because he made a point of telling the bishop that "he hoped to marry [off] his daughter in the present year."[66] The sacrist's tactics appear quite cavalier in removing Marsela from her parent's home and preventing Marsela from contacting her parents. These clerics are presented as men who took a daughter without the approval or consent of the father; the women themselves are portrayed as passive participants, without any mention of any assent or opposition they may have voiced about being removed from their family, friends, and parish. Despite the women's complicity or lack thereof, what matters here is that the people of the parish viewed these clerics as the active agents behind the deflowering of young women and their removal from their natal household. The fathers appear to be unable to protect their daughters when faced with a cleric who takes any woman he wants. Caroline Dunn, in her study of abducted women in England, has noted that members of the clergy were falsely accused of abducting women when the family or community disapproved of a relationship between a cleric and local woman.[67] It is possible that such allegations of

---

64. For studies that address medieval views on women's sexuality, see Josep-Ignasi Saranyana, *La discussion medieval sobre la condición femenina, siglos VIII al XIII* (Salamanca: Universidad Pontificia Salamanca, 1997); Michael Solomon, *The Literature of Misogyny in Medieval Spain: The Arcipreste de Talavera and the Spill* (Cambridge, UK: Cambridge University Press, 1997); R. Howard Bloch, *Medieval Misogyny and the Invention of Western Romantic Love* (Chicago: University of Chicago Press, 1991); Karras, *Common Women*, 108–11; Salisbury, "Gendered Sexuality," 81–102; Cadden, *Meanings of Sex Difference*; John W. Baldwin, *The Language of Sex: Five Voices from Northern France around 1200* (Chicago: University of Chicago Press, 1994).

65. AEV, Visites, no. 1200/2, 68v. (1331). According to parishioners, the daughter of Guillem Taradels would have had a husband if it were not for the rector taking the daughter. In another example, the canon Guillem de Apilia was also reported to have forcibly taken the wife of a man in the village of Muntala; ACV, Calaix 31/43, Visites, no. 8, 26r. (1316).

66. ADG, Visites, no. 5, 145v. (1333). The sacrist was fined 500 sous, and he swore, under penalty of a fine of 1,000 sous, that he would not keep Marsela in his home or return to her. Rather than leave his parish church in fear of Bernat's retribution, the sacrist must have felt secure enough to continue to serve in the same parish. In a similar fashion, the sacrist of Navata removed Elisenda to the parish of Vilacolum to live with his father after having "violated and impregnated" her. According to the parishioners of Vilacolum, the sacrist feared the reprisal of her parents and took her to another location, essentially keeping Elisenda away from her family; ADG, Visites, no. 3, 28r. (1321).

67. Caroline Dunn, *Stolen Women in Medieval England: Rape, Abduction, and Adultery, 1100–1500* (Cambridge, UK: Cambridge University Press, 2013), 162, 186–89.

ravishment are a reflection of a community condemning a cleric's sexual affair and could be used as a tactic of revenge when preexisting animosities existed between the cleric and parishioners. Nevertheless, it is equally possible that some clergymen felt entitled to take a woman, especially if she was his social inferior. As much as anticlerical sentiment may have influenced the negative and aggressive portrayal of these clergymen, the bottom line for the affected parents, family, and parish was that they perceived the cleric to be at fault.

In some cases, it is clear that families feared confronting the cleric who had taken their daughter, particularly because it was not unknown for a cleric to retaliate against the family of a woman for disparaging him. There was a "great fight" between the stabilitus Guillem Jaffer and his friends, and the family of the virgin woman whom he "violated," "forcibly removed" from the village of Armentera, and then took to another village because her family spoke "against him." The fight resulted in the death of a cleric, one of Guillem's friends.[68] Accounts such as that of the priest Guillem in the parish of Berga and the rector of Susqueda, who were both involved in fights with the brothers of the women they had deflowered and kept as concubines, reveal not only that the family objected to a relationship they did not sanction but also that there was little they could do when a cleric set out to woo or claim a woman as his own.[69] In most of these cases, the cleric is mentioned as continuing the relationship. It is not unexpected that such unsanctioned relationships caused great enmity between the cleric and the woman's family;[70] what is surprising are the few accounts of families that retaliated with violence against the cleric. In addition, a woman who left a cleric or the people who sheltered a cleric's concubine could also be at risk. The armed priest Bernat broke into the home of Pere deç Quer, where his concubine Bernardona was staying, or perhaps hiding, and violently beat her.[71] Considering that so few clerics who took advantage of local women are mentioned as fleeing the parish in fear of retribution, villagers may have been apprehensive about seeking vengeance against

68. ADG, Visites, no. 3, 31r. (1321). An account is also given in the visitation to l'Armentera in ADG, Visites, no. 3, 32v. (1321). One of Guillem's friends may have injured the girl's father. After this event, Guillem was in a sword fight with Ramon Pere, but no reason is specified for this violent encounter.

69. AEV, Visites, no. 1200/3, 5v. (1332); AEV, Visites, no. 1200/2, 82r. (1332); ADG, Visites, no. 8, 25r. (1345); ADB, Visites, no. 5, 40v. (1341).

70. AEV, Visites no. 1200/2, 68v. (1331). There was great "enmity" between the rector of Caradells and the family and friends of the woman he took from her father's home to keep as his concubine.

71. ADB, Registrum Communium, no. 4, 49r. (1326). The priest Bernat Coucellar from Vilafranca confessed to these actions and received absolution from the bishop's curia.

a cleric. The threat of punishment, fines, and excommunication for laying violent hands on a clergyman must have dissuaded some from seeking to do
bodily harm to the cleric.[72] Moreover, people may not have had confidence in
ecclesiastical officials because parishioners such as the "good men" of the
town of Castelló d'Empúries protested that clerics had committed "many
homicides" and went unpunished for their crimes.[73] They understood that
clergymen had the advantage when perpetrating violence against the laity and
may not have had much hope that denouncing a cleric for taking one's daughter
without permission would cause authorities to react.

Parish clerics who appropriated the wives of laymen were likewise seen as
intimidating figures who audaciously went against the marital authority of
other men to claim women. It is not a surprise that a union between a priest
and woman that caused a husband to leave his wife troubled parishioners.
What is noteworthy is that the local populace held the priest, not the woman,
responsible for the dissolution of the marriage.[74] The testimonies of witnesses
are telling. Parish priests are presented as aggressors, who stole or took away
(*abstulit*) the women of married men while the women are attributed little to
no agency in choosing the cleric over their husband. For example, the chaplain Pere of Bellcaire was reported to have "stolen" Maria, a married woman,
from her husband and taken her to the village of Ullà, and the rector Berenguer of Sant Vicenç de Torelló reportedly had "violently" taken Venguda from
her husband. The sacrist of Fontcoberta, according to the husband of Sibil·la,
had taken his wife and kept her "enclosed" in his home. To add insult to injury,
the sacrist and Sibil·la had stolen some of his belongings.[75] It is impossible to
determine with any certainty whether these are accounts of forced abductions

---

72. The example of five laymen who attacked and injured the sacrist Bernat Provinçal of Palau
de Tor indicates that the fines could be quite exorbitant for the peasantry. The men were found guilty
and ordered to pay the sacrist 200 sous for his injuries and 90 sous each to the church for committing
the sacrilege of placing violent hands on a priest. The five men were excommunicated for their failure
to pay both fines; ADG, Notularum, no. 30, 126r.v.–131r.v. (1352). In another example, when five parishioners wounded the sacrist Pere Soguert during a dispute, the men received a sentence of excommunication for eight years; ADG, Visites, no. 3, 38r. (1321).
73. ADG, Visites fragmentaris, quaderno no. 1, 7r. (1323).
74. See for example, ACV, Visites, no. 4, 18r. (1314); ADG, Visites, no. 1, 67v. (1315); ADG, Visites,
no. 2, 80r. (1315); ADG, Visites fragmentaris, 8r. (1320); ADG, Visites, no. 3, 4r.v. (1321); ADG, Visites,
no. 4, 87r., 88r., 116r.v. (1329); ADG, Visites, no. 5, 38r., 96r. (1331); ADG, Visites, no. 6, 80v.–81r.,
107r.v. (1340); ADG, Visites, no. 8, 17v., 18v.–19r. (1345).
75. ADG, Visites, no. 3, 39r.v. (1321); AEV, Visites, no. 1200/ 1, 10v. (1330); ADG, Visites, no. 4,
49v. (1329). In the parish of Toroella de Montgrí, the sacrist Guillem Amanller and the stabilitus Pere
Pich were said to have "taken away" married women to be their concubines ("eam abstulit viro suo").
The sacrist Dalmau in the parish of Sant Pere Pescador "removed" the married woman Francesca
from her husband's home, as did the cleric en Niol, from Castelló, who reportedly beat the husband
of the woman he abducted. In the parish of Sant Esteve de Mata, the rector Pere Barboni reportedly
"violently and against the will of the husband and the woman's father" "abstraxit" Dolça from her

or in actuality fictitious abductions in which a wife deserted her husband by staging her removal from the household. Although it seems likely that some of these accusations conceal a consensual relationship between the cleric and married woman, parishioners' accounts frequently underscore the role of the cleric in forcefully stealing away a married woman.[76] Indeed, the husbands are portrayed as helpless bystanders when faced with the determination of a parish priest to keep their wife. Consider the example of Bernat, the rector of Palera, who was said to keep the married woman Maria against "the will" of her husband. Apparently Maria was not free to choose her husband, and any resistance on the part of the husband was in vain. In another example, the hebdomedarian Ramon Eimeric is described as keeping the married woman Na Bundia in his home, and his control over the situation was such that he "did not permit her to live with her husband."[77] The parish priest is the dominating figure in these accounts, highlighting that parishioners viewed them as men who imposed their will on others, especially if their acquisition of a woman went against the wishes of her husband.

Attempting to reclaim one's wife, however, could be dangerous. Parishioners suspected the priest Berenguer Molar of killing the husband of his concubine Mercera. After a fight between the husband and priest, Mercera's husband was subsequently attacked and killed in Girona, allegedly at the priest's request.[78] Mercera's husband had clearly objected to the desertion of his wife, but it mattered little to the priest Berenguer, who may or may not

---

marital home; ADG, Visites, no. 4, 21r. (1329); ADG, Visites, no. 9, 6v., 16v., 20r. (1350). The priest Pere Textor is also said to have "abstulit" the wife of a parishioner; ACV, Visites, no. 3, 28r. (1313).

76. Dunn, Stolen Women in Medieval England, 184, 188. Dunn has found that clerics in England were more likely to be accused of wife-theft than of the abduction of maidens or widows. She points out that, in some cases, charges of ravishment actually reveal an adulterous relationship. Only one account suggests that the woman played a part in leaving her husband. When the rector Pere Barboni violently took the married woman Dolça from her home to Castelló to keep her as his concubine, the couple reportedly arranged to have her husband beaten, which resulted in the husband, Guillem Janer, losing his hearing and becoming deaf; ADG, Visites, no. 9, 20r.v. (1350). These accounts of women "taken" from the conjugal household by a priest are different than those of priests who are reported to have carnally known a woman through violence (violenter carnaliter). For example, the hebdomedarian Pere Rielli of Besalú appears to have been a serial rapist. He was fined for breaking into three separate homes and raping or attempting to rape both married and single women; ADG, Remissions de Penes, no. 1, 54v. (1354).

77. ADG, Visites, no. 1, 71r. (1315). For the hebdomedarian Ramon Eimeric, see ADG, Visites, no. 4, 73v.–74r. (1329). Ramon Eimeric caused a lot of controversy in the parish of Aro because he was infamous for his various quarrels and fights with fellow parish clergymen; see Table 4.1, page 481, for more information on his relationships with clerics. In another example, the monk Pere Cavall kept Raimunda, the daughter of Bernat de Banc and wife of Ramon de Font, whom he "did not permit to stay with her husband"; ADG, Visites, no. 3, 31r.v. (1321). In the case of the rector of Pierola, he "abstulit" Geralda from her husband, and the husband left the parish and "vadit per mundum vagabundo discurrendo." ADB, Visites, no. 4, 7v. (1336).

78. ADG, Visites, no. 6, 60v. (1339).

have caused the husband's demise. In the parish of Sant Vicenç de Horts, the priest Andreu de Maioll was accused of attempting to kill the husband of his lover with a crossbow.[79] Getting rid of a bothersome spouse was not an option many clerics pursued; yet, it is remarkable that so few violent confrontations are reported between clerics and cuckolded husbands. In fact, there is no report of a husband reasserting his marital authority over his wife and forcibly removing her from the priest's control or home—or at least episcopal documents did not record such events. Some husbands may have been resigned to losing their spouse to a clergyman, especially because people believed that the wealth of the priest had prompted a wife to desert her marriage. Many, however, attempted to save face by publicly dismissing their adulterous wife and leaving the village. Given the protected status of clerics under canon law and the wealth, connections, and position of clergy in the community, they could be formidable adversaries, and any violent encounter could very likely mean greater repercussions for the layman than the clergyman. Moreover, winning over and taking the wife of another man elevated the status of the cleric. Men performed and were on display for other men, and by dominating the woman of another man, proved their superiority in the competition for women.[80] Clergymen who appropriated the wives and daughters of village men certainly created conflict and went against the ideal of masculine self-restraint important to patrician men; however, it is possible that these clerics cultivated an aggressive masculinity to demonstrate the privilege of their position and status in the community. Such behavior might have aided their placement at the top of the hierarchy of village men. What is more, sexually assertive behavior was considered manly. Accounts of transgendered women who seduced women as men were reported to have "manly will" when they were described initiating sexual relations, and these transgendered individuals revealed their male desire by instigating physical contact through grabbing, hugging, and kissing "just like a man."[81] Although sexually aggressive behavior had the potential to bring men before secular or ecclesiastical authorities, it is clear that this sexual activism was coded as masculine.

That clergymen used their clerical standing and authority in the parish to their advantage is further evident in their interactions with parishioners, particularly in their high-handed behavior when disciplining children and

79. ADB, Registrum Communium, no. 4, 162r. (1328).
80. Karras, From Boys to Men, 25, 60–61, 152–53.
81. Helmet Puff, "Female Sodomy: The Trial of Katherina Hetzeldorfer (1477)," Journal of Medieval and Early Modern Studies 30, no. 1 (2000): 60. See also Simons, Sex of Men, 35–36; Judith Bennett, ' "Lesbian-Like' and the Social History of Lesbianisms," Journal of the History of Sexuality 9 (2000): 18–19.

beating village women. Guillema, the daughter of Pere Celi, was struck in the face and neck when the priest Bernat Serena found her sleeping in the chapel of Santa Margarida with the sheep in her care. Similarly, the young boys Simó and Castelló received injuries to their heads when beaten by the bad-tempered cleric Ramon.[82] Rather than taking his anger and complaint to the husband, the rector of Porqueroles beat the wife of Arnau and broke her arm, and the capellan Arnau Marenes, in a fit of anger, reportedly injured and mutilated the sister of his concubine.[83] Indeed, a number of domestic servants and married women were the targets of clerical violence.[84] Even pregnant women did not escape brutal beatings. The pregnant wife of Guillem Matamala was beaten so severely that she miscarried.[85] Such mistreatment infringed on a parent's and a husband's right to discipline his family, and these reports suggest that parishioners believed the cleric acted out of personal anger rather than out of a responsibility to moderately chastise a parishioner for his or her spiritual welfare. It is noteworthy that such clergymen disregarded the authority of parents and husbands to punish these women and children, indicating that they believed their own authority surpassed that of others. Usurping the role of a husband or parent showed that the cleric had ultimate control and reinforced his role and his supremacy in the village. Priests who meted out this kind of disciplinary violence to punish and humiliate parishioners reiterated the privilege of their gender and status in the community. Administering physical correction became an act of manliness, an act that conferred patriarchal authority and denied it to others. It is also significant that many of these extreme cases of priestly reprimand came to the attention of episcopal officials during an inquest into the criminal behavior of a cleric brought before the bishop's court for other charges, suggesting that the actions of priests who exceeded the acceptable bounds of chastisement frequently went unreported.

Single women of low status who lacked the protection of a male family member were also the easy targets of clerical violence. The beneficed cleric Guillem de Tor savagely beat Francesca, a servant to the lady Ricolesse, for

---

82. ADG, Processos, no. 103, 5v. (1329); ADG, Visites, no. 1, 100r.v. (1315).

83. AEV, Visites, no. 1200/1, 10v. (1330); ADG, Visites fragmentaris, 7v. (1320).

84. During a dispute with Na Pascala, the rector of Torelló physically injured the woman, and the priest Simó Giró beat a woman named Adelayde for refusing to help him take care of the cemetery; AEV, Visites, no. 1200/2, 44r. (1331); ADG, Processos, no. 30, 13r. (1319). Other examples of women who were beaten by parish priests include the Berenguera, the pedisseca of Na Coloma in the village of Banyoles; Castellà, the wife of Guillem Mercadell who was injured during a fight the sacrist of Aguyana had with her husband and other parishioners; the daughter of En Frigola de Seguer, who lived with the deacon Pere Cloper as an ancilla and was beaten by the sacrist Arnau de Quera in the parish of Sant Feliu de Beuda; and Brunissenda, the wife of Bernat Matí, who was beaten by the hebdomedarian Bonanat Bonet; ADG, Remissions de Penes, no. 1, 5v. (1346) and 32r., 35r., 38v. (1352).

85. ADG, Remissions de Penes, no. 1, 37r. (1352).

reporting to her employer that he had entered the home of Romia in her husband's absence. The lady Ricolesse was most likely an influential patron of the church in the parish, and Guillem feared that such gossip had jeopardized his reputation in the eyes of a possible benefactor. The prior Pere de Vic beat the "intemperate" Guillema Blanc for "disparaging" him. The canon Baldrà de Soler and his servants sliced the face and nose of Astruga, a servant to the lady Cilia de Gornallo, to keep her from revealing his sexual affair with a married woman.[86] These clerics made clear that they were not going to endure the gossip, interference, or disapproval of women who were their social inferiors. The canon Baldrà, in particular, saw fit to threaten and mutilate a servant who could expose his clandestine love affair. Moreover, single women such as Na Oliva, who rebuffed the sexual advances of a cleric, could also find themselves in serious danger. The canon Pere de Pahols was charged with threatening Na Oliva and setting fire to her door. Pere reportedly had "hatred" for Na Oliva because "she did not want to sin with him carnally," and in retaliation, he wanted to burn her body.[87] The same Na Oliva was brutally beaten by the canon Joan Oliver. Joan had reportedly beaten two other women in surrounding villages, but he was brought before the bishop's court for nearly killing the laywoman Na Oliva. Joan had entered Na Oliva's home and had accused her mother of killing his chicken, punched the elderly woman, and rubbed the dead chicken in her face. Na Oliva had become enraged by the attack on her mother and cursed the canon loudly enough that Joan returned to beat her with his staff. He hit Oliva in the head so forcefully that the baby in her arms fell to the ground, and he continued to beat her until she remained prostrate and "semi-dead."[88] Clerics may not have believed their

---

86. ADG, Processos, no. 73, 11r.v. (1323); ADG, Visites, no. 6, 38r.v. (1338); ADG, Processos, no. 89, 2r.v.–3r.v. (1325). In another incident in which a servant was beaten, the cleric Pere Guillem, who served in the monastery of Sant Esteve de Banyoles, received a letter of remission for his "excesses," which included beating Berengaria, the pedisseca of Na Coloma in the village of Banyoles; ADG, Remissions de Penes, no. 1, 5r. (1346).

87. ADG, Processos, no. 18, 4v. (1328). The canon Pere de Pohols was also charged with carrying weapons, gambling, and creating disorder in the monastery. Only a list of charges to be investigated by the judge Guillem de Socarrats exists for this case. The *processo* has been dated circa 1310, but the charges mention the case of Joan Oliver and Na Oliva, which dates to 1323. Also, there are two documents in the registers dating from 1328 that deal with transferring Pere de Pohols to the bishop's prison and a letter sent out to various parish rectors announcing an inquest into Pere's crimes; ADG, Notularum, no. 6, 171v.–172r. (1328); ADG, Lletres, no. 3, 95v.–96r. (1328). In the latter document, it is mentioned that Pere de Pohols had previously been excommunicated for nonresidence and for carrying weapons.

88. ADG, Processos, no. 66, 25r.v.–26r.v., 66v. (1323). Joan Oliver's list of crimes is extensive and includes carrying various arms, gambling, assaulting multiple people, and engaging in rebellious activities against the prior of the monastery of Lledó, whom he considered to be his "enemy." He reportedly boasted around the local area of the beating he had administered to Na Oliva.

actions to be extreme when punishing errant children or meddling women. On the contrary, they may have felt their actions were warranted. Francesc Eiximenis's work advises men that, to save women from "wickedness," it is best to "keep them in a state of fear" to prevent them from "saying or doing evil things."[89] Because these women were husbandless, clerics may have felt they had the authority to discipline women who were not subject to the control of a patriarch. Although publicly reprimanding an ill-behaved woman or child before the parish community was considered within the purview of a priest guiding his flock, administering a beating out of personal anger and retaliation was not within a cleric's pastoral mandate. Nevertheless, a parish priest may have felt entirely justified because of his position. The beating of social inferiors seems to have been a way to enforce respect for his standing in the village. Such violence, however, did not change the fact that it only bolstered the reputation of the cleric as a quarrelsome figure.

Parishioners resented a cleric who felt entitled to punish their children or used excessive force against women; moreover, striking an adult, particularly a male parishioner, was an equally important display of power and male authority. The rector of Santa Margarida not only beat the layman Berenguer for insulting him but also, in the process of punishing such behavior, shamed the man before others.[90] Indeed, clerics enforced their status as well as their authority when they humiliated and beat parishioners before the parish community. As clergymen who exercised spiritual authority over their flock, their profession and clerical status gave them a sense of superiority, which is often seen in the manner clerics treated their parishioners. In the village of Sant Pere de Llorà, the sacrist Guillem de Serra was described as "a fighting man who daily bears arms and says abusive words to parishioners and their wives."[91] But the sacrist's vituperative words were not the only problem. He struck a man in the face with a game board in a gambling dispute and, in a separate incident, beat another man with his staff. Similarly, the parishioners of Cadaqués reported to the episcopal visitor that the capellan Arnau Ferrar was such a belligerent man that there was "scarcely a man in the entire parish who has not quarreled with him." The capellan did more than quarrel; he

---

89. Renedo and Guixeras, *Francesc Eiximenis*, 100.

90. Visitatio diversarum, HMML, microfilm no. 31951, Visites, no. 1, 35r. (1305). In another example, the rector of Sant Sadurní de Sobirats was accused of always being armed with a sword, slapping the laymen Bernat Prohensall, and fighting with another parishioner; ADB, Visites, no. 2, 42v. (1314).

91. ADG, Visites no. 5, 81r.v. (1331). In another example, the capellan Bernat, in the parish of Santa Maria de Merola, is described as daily creating great discord among his parishioners. The capellan was known for travelling about armed, and on one occasion, he beat and stabbed a parishioner, as well as a woman who subsequently died from her wounds; ACV, Calaix 31/43, Visites, no. 3, 15r. (1313).

reported parishioners to the local curia and beat multiple villagers with his staff.[92] Similar examples abound. The prior of Sant Tomàs dragged a male parishioner by his hair before villagers for creating a filthy mess in the courtyard before the cemetery. The beneficed cleric Francesc Caluet grabbed a peasant (*rusticus*) by the throat and threatened him with his sword when he objected to the price of a pair of shoes the peasant was trying to sell him. And when a villager failed to give a portion of his grape harvest to the local priest, the priest beat him in the face with a candlestick.[93] The priest Berenguer Pagès also had a history of violence against several men in the village, including an attempt to kill a fellow cleric. According to villagers, his latest conflict involved a sword fight with a villager for reporting the man to the local curia. Denouncing a foe to local authorities seems to have been one strategy that clerics used when dealing with the parishioners they had problems with.[94] Although a certain level of discord between people and their clergymen was not uncommon, especially when it centered on the administration of the sacraments or the care of the parish church, the extent of the friction reported is significant. That so many parishes complained of a belligerent cleric suggests that parish clergy used threats and violence to instill fear, if not to control the people of the village, with little or no risk to themselves. And given that the priest Berenguer Pagès engaged in a number of brawls and sword fights, it is telling that the episcopal visitor saw fit to fine him for a sexual indiscretion and for failing to show up regularly to say the divine office rather than punishing him for employing violence against parishioners. The priest Berenguer's actions did not cause him to appear in the bishop's court, which might indicate that episcopal visitors viewed this type of behavior as normal.

Accounts that parish clergy insulted, threatened, and beat people with their fists, a staff, or a sword can be found throughout the visitation records, as seen in table 4.1. Very few clerics, however, were accused of outright murder.[95] Nevertheless, there is little doubt that these clergymen were seen as bullies who instilled a certain level of fear in the populace. The people of Sant Juià de

---

92. ADG, Visites, no. 3, 17r.v.–18r.v. (1321).

93. ADG, Visites, no. 6, 37v.–38r. (1338); ADG, Processos, no. 276 (1354); AEV, Visites, no. 1200/3, 3v. (1332).

94. The rector of Sant Vicenç de Torelló and the priest Berenguer Pagès reported fellow parishioners to the local curia. In the parish of Rupià, the beneficed cleric Arnau de Guardiola was charged with falsely accusing a female parishioner of stealing wheat, for which she was punished with a public beating in the village; AEV, Visites, no. 1, 10v. (1330); ADG, Remissions de Penes, no. 1, 25v. (1351). See also ADB, Visites, no. 4, 49r. (1336); ADG, Visites, no. 3, 18v.–19r. (1321); ADG, Visites, no. 4, 103v.–104r.v. (1329); ADG, Processos, no. 244, 3v. (1347); ADG, Processos, no. 103, 2v. (1329).

95. See, for example, AEV, Visites, no. 1200/2, 51r. (1331); ACV, Calaix 31/43, Visites, no. 7, 35r. (1314).

Corçà feared being attacked by their deacon, who frequently went about the parish armed. The parishioners of Vilamilanys informed their visitor that "fearing and abhorring the violent quarrels and abuses" of their rector, they no longer attended church services.[96] In a visit to the parish of Marata, the verbally abusive language aimed at parishioners was so extreme that the bishop threatened the rector with a fine of 10 lliures if he did not stop terrorizing people with his "illicit, vituperative, and otherwise dishonest" words that fostered "rancor and hatred."[97] Such aggression between a cleric and parishioners frequently resulted from a dispute or quarrel, whose cause is often unspecified, but in some instances, it appears that the cleric felt disrespected and needed to put the offender in his place. For example, the rector of Torelles slapped a male parishioner in the face, and the rector's son defended his father in such a way that the man "did not dare to speak." Such a violent response was most likely intended to demean the man but also meant to intimidate others from challenging the rector's authority. Described as a "homo rixosus," the rector was a daunting figure, particularly because he had fought and injured two other men on separate occasions and had even punched a fellow priest in the parish church for insulting him.[98] The priest Pere Alda likewise appears to have terrorized his community. He was charged with threatening villagers with arms and "inflicting abuse on whomever he wished." Although he was found guilty of attacking a parishioner's home with rocks and weapons in his parish of Caldes de Mont Buí, of beating a female parishioner with a staff, of using arms against three men who had fought with a family member, and of wounding a tonsured cleric in the head with his sword, he received absolution and a letter of dispensation from the bishop's curia.[99] Men such as the rector of Torelles and the priest Pere Alda were not known for an exceptional, singular episode of violence but were repeat offenders who created an atmosphere of fear and intimidation.

Conclusion

The extent to which these clergymen insulted, brawled, and beat their parishioners speaks to more than a few clerics with bad tempers or vile

---

96. ADG, Visites, no. 1, 2v. (1314); Visitatio diversarum, HMML, microfilm no. 31951, Visites, no. 1, 9v. (1303).

97. Visitatio diversarum, HMML, microfilm no. 31951, Visites, no. 1, 73v. (1307).

98. Martí Bonet, "Visitas pastorals," 709–11, 720–27; Visitatio diversarum, HMML, microfilm no. 31951, Visites, no. 1, 92r. (1308).

99. ADB, Registrum Communium, no. 4, 161v. (1328).

personalities that alienated people. The verbal and physical violence that clergymen inflicted on parishioners set them apart from other laymen in the village and helped them maintain a level of dominance that only the authority of a feudal lord and his officials could surpass. In addition to these violent confrontations, the degree to which clerics insulted and verbally abused parishioners is a sign that they believed themselves to be of a higher social rank and status. Parish priests probably felt entitled to correct the behavior of their parishioners, particularly when they expected but did not receive the deference due to their position. Although churchmen such as Thomas of Chobham believed anger to be sinful because it brought spiritual harm to the sinner and could lead to physical violence, blows that stemmed from anger were permissible if administered as a "punishment or correction," such as when a teacher corrected his students or when a priest imposed physical discipline on his penitents.[100] If parish priests were not familiar with Chobham's work on penance, they could find that pastoral manuals, such as the popular fourteenth-century *Handbook for Curates* written in the Crown of Aragon, could be interpreted as supporting their use of physical violence. The *Handbook for Curates* instructs priests to teach their parishioners that physically harming one's neighbors is a sin, but the manual also concedes that "anger is virtuous and not a sin, namely, when the desire for vengeance is according to the due order of justice and with charity, as when one seeks the correction of sin and not one's own vindication . . . but only seeks vindication for the guilt of the offense." The *Handbook for Curates* further explains that "it is not permitted for one to take such vengeance, unless one has the authority."[101] It is easy to see how, in spite of the overarching message that anger, hatred, and retribution endangered the soul, parish priests could justify their violent deeds against their parishioners. In their view, the physical correction they administered was appropriate because they had the authority to chastise penitents. The physical violence aimed at parishioners not only reveals an attitude of entitlement to discipline and punish but also shows that clerics did not fear

---

100. Thomas of Chobham, *Summa confessorum*, 420.
101. Guido of Monte Rochen, *Handbook for Curates: A Late Medieval Manual on Pastoral Ministry*, Anne T. Thayer and Katherine J. Lualdi, trans. Anne T. Thayer (Washington, DC: Catholic University of America Press, 2011), 224–25. In England, Ranulph Higden's revision of the *Speculum curatorum*, sometime in 1350, also supports (although to a lesser extent) the use of violence for those who have authority over others. In chapter 33, "About Striking," he writes, "Another kind of striking is corporeal, which can happen when one administers a beating without authority or, if one does have authority, one exacts revenge because of anger or envy or even, because of pride, desires to cause more fear. This is sin. If, however, striking occurs in order to achieve a modicum of correction, it is lawful for those who have jurisdiction over subordinates." Nevertheless, Ranulph concludes "that a clerical striker living under holy orders ought to be corrected; if he does not amend his ways, he ought to be removed." Higden, *Speculum curatorum*, 267, 269.

reprisals or, at least, believed their clerical privilege would protect them from parishioners' aggression. It is significant that reports of resentful laymen accosting parish priests, mutilating their priestly garments, or disrupting the performance of the mass to protest the bullying behavior of parish clergy are largely absent from the episcopal registers, suggesting that parishioners did fear retribution. Moreover, given that so few cases of clerical violence and abuse found in the visitation records reached the bishop's court and that episcopal visitors seem to have done little more than exhort clergymen to get along with their parishioners, it is unlikely that clerics feared the punishment of episcopal officials. Ultimately such impunity strengthened the authority of parish clergy and gave greater license for clergymen to act violently against their parishioners.

Far from being depicted as mediators who brought peace and reconciliation to their community, parish clergy were seen as contentious figures who sowed discord and fostered resentment for their high-handed tactics. Yet the conflict-ridden interactions between parishioners and their priests were the product of how fully integrated the clerics were into village life. Like their lay counterparts, they experienced a full range of human emotions, including personal animosities and hatreds. And like their fellow villagers, clerics could be bad neighbors, ill-tempered, and spiteful, in addition to exploiting their position to the disadvantage of others.

They also participated in the culture of honor and were concerned with acquiring, maintaining, and, above all, not losing their reputation as men. As we have seen, clerics employed violence to preserve their honor, participated in feuds, defended family members and friends, and at the same time protected their property, rights, and privilege, often to the detriment of their fellow villagers. The violent acts that clergymen performed, therefore, were not meaningless and had the added effect of validating a cleric's manhood. Medieval culture lauded male fierceness and virility; any man—cleric or layman—who failed to defend his reputation, protect his family, maintain loyalty to his friends, and secure his privilege was emasculated and considered weak. As Scott Taylor has noted in his study of Castilian honor, men at all levels of the social spectrum used the language of honor to publicly demonstrate not only that they were dangerous men who were capable of defending themselves but also that their opponents were weak, disreputable, and morally flawed. By using the rhetoric of honor, these men "articulated a vision of themselves as fully moral, integrated into their community, and wholly in control of their lives."[102] Parish clergymen, then, responded to such provocations in a manner that society

---

102. Taylor, *Honor and Violence*, 152.

and the male community understood, if not expected. Resorting to violence in the name of honor and reputation allowed clerics to show not only that they took part in male culture but also that they knew how to negotiate the demands of manhood through a performative process that marked them as men.

In addition to these retaliatory acts, which were considered a legitimate use of violence by a society that highly valued honor, clerics used violence for another purpose, more often than not, in a disproportionate manner. A great number of clerics were reported to be belligerent, quarrelsome men who acted violently against parish villagers. These reports indicate that parish clergy used verbal insults and violence to intimidate parishioners—a strategy that bolstered their control over villagers and parish affairs, and at the same time confirmed their masculinity. It is clear that clergymen were especially prone to creating conflict because of their central role in the community; in addition, the potential for abuse lay not only in carrying out their religious duties but also in maintaining their standing and wielding power over their parishioners. Violence, then, was used to dominate and exert authority. In the same vein, clerics who appropriated the married women and unmarried daughters of their male parishioners point to another way that clergymen could claim superiority over other men. To brazenly disregard patriarchal authority and control the wife or daughter of a village man was a means of exercising power over men and of simultaneously proclaiming the cleric's status as a man who dominated others. Such actions suggest that clergymen, although from the very same socioeconomic background as the peasant farmers and villagers they ministered to, were at the top of the parish social hierarchy and felt secure in their status and position to treat parishioners they saw as their social inferiors so harshly. Whether male or female, parishioners were subordinate to the parish priest. Thus, it is no surprise that so many people in the town and villages of Catalunya characterized their clerics as combatative men who beat men, women, and children indifferently.

Parish priests cultivated and performed a type of manhood that not only positioned them within an acceptable spectrum of medieval manliness but also placed them at the uppermost level of the masculine hierarchy that existed in these villages. Michael Kimmel has argued that institutions in our society are gendered and shape the gender identity of individuals.[103] And we have seen that the parish church was a gendered institution that likewise influenced the masculine identity of its clerics. It created a gender order of hierarchy and power in which priests, and in particular the rector, occupied the top position in the church and often in the village. This emphasized their superior status

---

103. Kimmel, *Gendered Society*, 110–12.

because they were the men who administered the sacraments through God's grace and they also had a right to demand the respect of the laity because they were God's intermediaries. The church as a gendered institution cultivated an attitude among its clergy that they had the spiritual authority to impose penance, if not punishment, on those who failed to show them deference. It is possible that the parish church created gendered normative standards among its clergy that emphasized aggressive traits in the protection of their status, authority, and right to instruct and correct the laity. Although church authorities did not encourage the parish clergy to physically and verbally abuse their parishioners, evidence from diocesan registers reflect a lack of concern over their violent treatment, suggesting that on some level such behavior was accepted and implicitly condoned.

Episcopal officials rarely punished these violent clerics by removing them from a parish or stripping them of their benefice; therefore, parish priests received the message that violence aimed at rural parishioners was tolerated. Officials also reinforced the role of the authoritative parish priest, which meant that many communities had to endure living in conflict with their priest until the cleric died or found a new benefice in a different parish. We might expect, then, that in such a violent society there would be numerous reports or cases brought before the bishop's court of villagers, who fed up with the abuse of their clergymen, had retaliated. Yet evidence that the Catalan laity injured or killed their clergymen is far less than we might imagine, or at least these incidences went largely unreported in the visitations and rarely made their way to the church courts. Instead, complaints about aggressive, confrontational, and violent clergy stand out compared to other complaints, especially about the poverty of the parish church or the negligence of the clergy. Certainly clerical privilege afforded clergymen protection from physical harm, but the reasons that peasants and villagers tolerated clerical abuse may have stemmed from the experience and long history of bad customs (*mals usos*) and violence endured by those under seigniorial dominion. The oppression and humiliation that parish clergy meted out to their parishioners, although less extreme, is reminiscent of Paul Freedman's description of the "seigniorial terrorism" of peasants in Catalunya that often took the form of "symbolic degradation, such as yoking peasants together, shaving their beards, or threatening mutilation."[104]

---

104. It is likely that a great many in the parishes in rural areas and in the mountains that were visited were under seigniorial control. According to Freedman, "it appears that in the diocese of Girona, where by 1300 servile tenure was extremely widespread . . . a majority, consisting of peasants of middling economic condition, were legally serfs." Freedman, *Origins of Peasant Servitude*, at 152, 111.

The association between masculinity and violence is not unexpected when we consider that medieval society in large part idealized knighthood, battle, and physical prowess and defined male leadership as dominating other men. The convergence of clerical masculinity with violence is undeniable when we consider that parish clergy fashioned a masculinity that was built on the lay masculine ideals of their society, combining them with the position and privilege of their clerical profession. Reputation, fear of being emasculated, and dominating the parish community played an important part in the use of violence to prove manhood. The fear of being thought effeminate may even have affected clergymen on some level, although arguments that men in the priesthood were considered "womanly" and never fully masculine fall by the wayside in the face of such widespread sexuality and bellicosity.

Yet, violence was more than just a response to an affront, an attempt to regain honor, or another means to dominate or demonstrate conformity to masculine ideals. As we will see in Chapter Five, violence played an important role in mainstream clerical culture and was an integral part of the gender identity of Catalan clergymen. Clerics employed violence not only as a means to dominate laymen but also as a way to dominate their own clerical competitors in the parish church.

CHAPTER 5

Becoming a Priest
Clerical Role Models and Clerics-in-Training

On a November evening in 1329, parishioners from Sant Vicenç de Maià de Montcal and villagers from neighboring parishes gathered around the local church. Summoned by the ringing of bells that signaled an emergency throughout the land, people traveled to the parish for two days—to arrive only to find that there was no real crisis or danger. Rather, two tonsured scolares, who had been locked inside the church all day, had sounded the cry of alarm. The testimonies of parishioners revealed that many believed that this was no accident but that the boys, Guillem and Pere, were simply victims of a long-standing feud between two parish priests—their uncle, the hebdomedarian Guillem Jaubert, and the sacrist Guillem Ferrer.

Events had unfolded earlier on that November morning when the two tonsured boys, Guillem and Pere, were in the church reading the books the sacrist had given them from a locked chest. Just before lunch, the sacrist locked up the church with the two boys inside, left, and took the key to his home. The hours passed until vespers, when the boys could no longer wait. Hungry and in need of relieving their bladders, the boys rang the church bell and sounded the alarm. Soon people began congregating around the church as they learned what had transpired that day. The boys, Guillem and Pere, and the hebdomedarian accused the sacrist of intentionally locking the boys in the church and hiding the key. The sacrist, to the contrary, claimed that the boys

had been unwilling to leave the church. He, in turn, accused the hebdomedarian of ordering his nephews to sound the alarm.[1]

The hebdomedarian Guillem and the sacrist Guillem had a history of violent conflict. For more than fourteen years, these two priests exchanged abusive and insulting words on a daily basis. The parishioners of Sant Vicenç de
Maià had complained during several episcopal visitations to their parish that
the rancor and hatred between their priests affected the service of the mass
and divine office. In fact, the two clerics performed their offices fully armed
with swords, lances, shields, and crossbows.[2] Years earlier, the sacrist had attacked the hebdomedarian with a dagger after the hebdomedarian had offended him by celebrating mass at a side altar at exactly the same time the
sacrist was performing the mass at the high altar. A scuffle had ensued when
the sacrist then "violently" removed a candle from the side altar and prevented
the hebdomedarian from concluding the mass. Days later, the sacrist lured the
hebdomedarian out one night by throwing rocks at his house. When the hebdomedarian ran out of his home with a shield, the sacrist, hiding by the door,
jumped out with his dagger and struck such a blow that the shield broke.[3]
Thereafter the sacrist celebrated the mass first, before the hebdomedarian, but
relations between the two clerics clearly had not improved years later. Despite
an order from the bishop's vicar general for the two priests to find "peace and
agreement," both men apparently found it too difficult to generate goodwill
after such prolonged hostility. The hebdomedarian left the parish two years
after the scandal involving his tonsured nephews. His absence, however, did
not stop the sacrist from reporting to an episcopal official that the hebdomedarian owed the bishop money for a penance imposed during a past visitation.
The sacrist further complained that, before leaving, the hebdomedarian
had seized the offerings from Easter mass, which by right, he argued, belonged to him.[4]

The case of the sacrist Guillem Ferrer and hebdomedarian Guillem Jaubert
is just one of many examples of parish clergy who engaged in a battle of wills
that established a pecking order of clergymen in the village. Relations between
parish clerics were fraught with economic and social tensions that had much
to do with power, status, and wealth. This dispute began, as far as we know,

---

1. ADG, Visites, no. 4, 170v.–171r.v. (1329). Guillem and Pere denied that their uncle had in-
structed them, but the parishioners were divided, and some believed that the boys had sounded the
alarm on the advice and instruction of their uncle.

2. ADG, Visites, no. 4, 170v. (1329). The flames of the sacrist's resentment were further fanned
when he discovered that the hebdomedarian had absolved some parishioners who had been excommunicated by the bishop's officials for debts without collecting the money they owed.

3. ADG, Visites, no. 2, 74r.v.–77r. (1315).

4. ADG, Visites, no. 5, 104r.v. (1331).

at the time the hebdomedarian failed to respect the sacrist. Because the heb-domedarian had the care of souls, the sacrist may have resented the hebdome-darian's higher rank as the rector of the church. When the hebdomedarian decided to say mass and read the gospels at the same time as the sacrist, who was celebrating the mass at the main altar, he was in essence competing with the sacrist for the attention of their parishioners. The sacrist's initial reaction was to stop his rival. According to one parishioner, the sacrist hastened to fin-ish the mass so quickly that he omitted the kiss of peace, and he at once ap-proached the altar where the hebdomedarian was celebrating mass and "violently removed" one of the candles when the hebdomedarian prevented the sacrist from seizing the other candle. The end result of the skirmish over the candles was the humiliation of hebdomedarian when he could no longer continue with the mass.[5] Days later, the sacrist repaid the insult with his sur-prise assault on the hebdomedarian's house and person.

By the two men displaying such aggression, the whole community under-stood that the sacrist and hebdomedarian were trying to establish a hierarchy in the church. In truth, the sacrist had much to gain by humiliating the heb-domedarian, who stood to lose face by failing to enforce the clerical hierar-chy. Respect, status, and honor were hanging in the balance for both men. The sacrist seemed to be winning this competition. Even the sacrist's behavior toward his parish community reveals his forceful personality and confidence in doing whatever he pleased. And the sacrist did do as he pleased when he removed grain belonging to the church without the permission of the church-wardens and refused to pay the agreed-on price for the grain.[6] Rounding out this image of the sacrist are the fines for his "wanton affairs" with two mar-ried women in the parish and the details of his concubinary relationship with Maria Rosa, who with the sacrist dined as a couple with their friends. In fact, parishioners were accustomed to seeing Maria and his child living in the sac-rist's home, where Maria made bread, cooked, and took care of his affairs.[7] By all accounts and actions, Guillem Ferrer used violence to ensure the re-spect of his rank in the clerical hierarchy, and he was not afraid of competing with and dominating a rival. He was a priest and an adult man, who formed a union with a woman, produced a child, provided for his family, and demon-strated his capacity to forcefully deal with any competition or threat to his sta-tus. In essence, the sacrist embodied many of the characteristics of a masculine

---

5. ADG, Visites, no. 2, 74v.–75r. (1315). The hebdomedarian Guillem Jaubert appears as the rec-tor of Maià in 1328; ADG, Lletres, no. 3, 157r. (1328).

6. ADG, Visites, no. 2, 74r.v. (1315).

7. ADG, Visites, no. 2, 75r.v. (1315); ADG, Visites, no. 4, 192v.–193r. (1329).

ideal that men at all levels of medieval society embraced and attempted to attain.

Considering what we know of the sacrist and the hebdomedarian of Sant Vicenç de Maià de Montcal, we can only speculate about how their behavior affected the development of the tonsured boys, Guillem and Pere. What message did they receive when they saw their uncle and the sacrist celebrating the mass and performing the divine office fully armed, or when they witnessed the verbal insults, antagonism, and even hostile violence between the two clerics? Did the image of the sacrist and his family, or even the sacrist and his promiscuous affairs, penetrate their conception of manhood and the priesthood? Surely Guillem and Pere would have assimilated such behaviors of aggression, competition, and sexuality into their gender and professional identities. Moreover, they would have learned from an early age in their clerical training that violence, conflict, dominance, and sexual unions were not only accepted social norms for clergy but behaviors that must be publicly exercised in front of other men.[8]

In this chapter, I argue that violence was a component of clerical identity among Catalan clergy. There is little doubt that the characteristics of lay masculinity influenced the development and training of clergymen as they progressed from boyhood to male adulthood. Children who grew up with lay ideals and were socialized as laymen found it incredibly difficult as clergymen not to blur the line between the lay and clerical estates. In her study of English clerics, P.H. Cullum sees an erosion of clerical identity in which clerical masculinity more and more frequently came to mirror that of laymen, to the extent that "by the fifteenth century learning to be a priest was increasingly like learning to be a man, and vice-versa."[9] She posits that once clerics began to share life experiences similar to those their lay counterparts, clerical identity was no longer as distinctive as it had once been. In earlier centuries, literacy had been the most obvious characteristic that distinguished the clergy from the laity, but by the fourteenth and fifteenth centuries, several nontraditional clerical occupations were open to minor clergy, who could work as notaries, clerks employed by guilds or the royal chancery, estate administrators, and ecclesiastical lawyers. By the fourteenth century, the older tradition of advancing through the orders according to age and maturity fell out of practice as clerics bided their time in deciding whether to choose a secular or an ecclesiastical career. Added to this phenomenon was the increasing number of

8. See Marilyn Thomson, "Boys Will Be Boys: Addressing the Social Construction of Gender," in *Masculinities Matter! Men, Gender and Development*, ed. Frances Cleaver (London: Zed Books, 2002), 171–75.

9. Cullum, "Learning to Be a Man," 135–53.

clerics who chose to marry and not progress to the priesthood, coupled with the practice of local elites and urban gentry sending their sons to be educated in cathedral schools. The result, according to Cullum, was that the sum of these changes and the diversity of career options available during the fourteenth century produced a fragile clerical gender identity because such a clerical identity was acquired later in life by young men rather than boys.[10] She reasons that clerical gender identity was weakly embedded in the minds and subconscious of clerics because it was contrary to their life experience and was, in fact, "a conscious ideological creation of the eleventh and twelfth centuries which had itself to be consciously learned in opposition to conventional lay masculinity."[11]

Yet clerical gender identity need not have been fragile simply because many young men chose to take a vow of celibacy later in life. Cullum's theory assumes that, once young clerics progressed to the major orders, their training and the influence of their senior colleagues would fall in line with the ideological creation of clerical masculinity. And, as a result, this imposed clerical masculinity meant that clerics knew what was expected of them but simply strayed from this model because it did not come naturally to them. Moreover, the gender anxiety it triggered meant that clerics opted to prove their masculinity by carrying weapons, engaging in physical conflicts, and promiscuous sexuality to counteract any doubts regarding their manhood. I do not believe the gender identity of Catalan clerics was tenuous; based on the evidence from episcopal archives, I consider that the socialization of clerics and their training at the parish level had a greater impact than the Church vision of clerical masculinity. Senior clergymen who were taking part in lay culture and living according to the masculine ideals of laymen trained and educated tonsured boys and young clerics. Clerics, then, did not arm themselves, engage in violence, keep women, and establish households because they were intent only on demonstrating they were not effeminate men; they partook in such behaviors because this is how they defined themselves as both men and clerics in their local communities. In my view, the actual and real-life clerical masculinity of Catalan clergy had deviated so far from the Church ideological model that it simply incorporated the social practice of marriage and the aggressive characteristics of lay masculinities. More to the point, clerical education and training, and the influence of the senior clergy as role models coalesced to produce a clerical gender identity that had behavioral

10. Cullum, "Boy/Man into Clerk/Priest," 52–53. See also ibid.
11. Cullum, "Learning to Be a Man," 136; P.H. Cullum, "Clergy, Masculinity, and Transgression in Late Medieval England," in *Masculinity in Medieval Europe*, ed. Dawn M. Hadley (New York: Longman, 1999), 195–96.

characteristics that were very similar to those of lay masculinity: exercising power and authority in front of other men, behaving aggressively when circumstances dictated it, socializing with men while drinking and gambling, sexually dominating women, and generating offspring. Although a deficient education may have left many clerics without a solid foundation of essential Christian doctrine or a profound theological knowledge of their office, clerics still learned their profession in informal ways—by observation and imitation. And herein lies the answer as to how violence, sexuality, clerical gender identity, and professional identity converged.

The Molding of Clerics-in-Training

The Church was unable to instill its ideological model of clerical masculinity, in part, due to the very manner in which education, training, and ordination were set up to quickly advance candidates from the minor to major orders. By the fourteenth century clerics rarely progressed through the seven ranks of holy orders according to the traditional method of yearly intervals to receive their priestly offices. In fact, in many cases candidates received licenses to all four minor orders of porter, lector, exorcist, and acolyte in one day. Sometimes licenses for the major orders were also issued together, which suggests that clerics spent little time learning the duties for each rank and that their training was most likely insufficient.[12] Attempts to improve the education and quality of those in charge of the care of souls abound in the canons of provincial and diocesan synods throughout western Europe in the thirteenth and fourteenth centuries. The provincial statutes for Tarragona, which included the dioceses of Barcelona, Girona, Lleida, Vic, Tortosa, and Urgell, dictated that no one should be promoted to holy orders unless he could speak Latin competently and that no priest could celebrate his first mass until he had been examined on the canon of the mass by the bishop or his vicar. The theory and practice of pastoral care, however, were worlds apart. The visitation records reveal that some priests did not know enough Latin to celebrate the mass correctly or even know when to make the sign of the cross during the mass. This reality is reflected in educational mandates, such as the decree in the 1354 Barcelona synodal statutes that required only those competent in Latin to be ordained as deacons and above.[13]

---

12. Utterback, *Pastoral Care,* 117–20. See also Cullum, "Boy/Man into Clerk/Priest," 52–55.

13. Utterback, *Pastoral Care,* 49–50, 117–18. The synodal decrees for the diocese of Girona express a similar concern for the need to educate clerics and reflect much of the same requirements for clerical education as the Barcelona synodal decrees. Although there are deviations and additions for each

The manner in which tonsured children acquired the knowledge they needed for their future livelihood is important here because of the connection between gender identity and professional identity. In England and elsewhere throughout Europe, basic instruction for a career in the minor or major orders began in an elementary or song school, where children learned rudimentary Latin, basic prayers, and also chanted hymns and responses to the liturgy. The more fortunate and wealthier boys could continue their education at a grammar school to further develop their Latin skills, but few of these were able to attend a university. Josep Baucells i Reig estimates that only 8–10 percent of the clerical population in Barcelona learned to read and write during the first half of the fourteenth century.[14] Even in the Dominican Order, undereducated novices were a problem in the Crown of Aragon. In 1328, the Provincial Chapter ordered that remedial Latin instruction be provided to all friars who needed it.[15] The number of grammar students taught in the order, however, seems to have been quite small because, according to Michael Vargas, twelve of the eighteen convents in the Crown of Aragon received fifty-seven students in 1347. Furthermore, provincial statutes from the first half of the fourteenth century for the Order also reveal a concern that Dominicans did not have the necessary training to be sent out as preachers and confessors among the Catalan laity. Although by 1353 the Dominicans could boast of twelve convents that offered training at a level above that of a grammar school,[16] it is unlikely that the training of future Dominican preachers at these convents greatly improved the learning of parish priests. A general survey of episcopal administrative documents for the dioceses of Barcelona and Girona further reveals a limited number of grammar schools outside of the cathedral cities of Catalunya, and only a small number of clerics received licenses to

---

diocese, all dioceses used the provincial statutes for Tarragona as a template for their own. Pope Gregory IX sent John of Abbeville, the cardinal bishop of Sabina, to bring the reforms of Lateran IV to the Spanish kingdoms. Under Abbeville's supervision the provincial council for Tarragona met in Lleida in 1229 and essentially adopted the canons of Lateran IV verbatim into their own statues. For a discussion of John of Abbeville's mission to Spain, see Linehan, *Spanish Church and the Papacy*. For a comparison of the 1229 Tarragona statutes with the fourteenth-century Girona synodal decrees, see Noguer i Musqueras and Pons Guri, "Constitucions sinodals de Girona," 49–212.

14. Baucells i Reig, *Vivir en la edad media*, 1: 439.

15. Vose, *Dominicans, Muslims and Jews*, 102.

16. Vargas, *Taming a Brood of Vipers*, 182, 193, 197. There appear to have been few grammar schools in the diocese of Girona during the fourteenth century. The city of Girona had two grammar and song schools, one sponsored by the cathedral canons and the other by the church of Sant Feliu. Grammar schools have also been documented in the towns of Peralada, Castelló de Empúries (1338), and la Bisbal (1367). In the fifteenth century, grammar schools appear in Banyoles, Camprodon, Olot, and San Feliu de Guíxols; Marquès, "Iglesia de Gerona," 537–38. For grammar schools in the diocese of Barcelona, see Baucellsi Reig, *Vivir en la edad media*, 1: 446–49.

study at universities in Spain or elsewhere.[17] Many clerics, especially those destined to serve at the parish level, reached the limits of their formal education in an elementary school, and by far the most conventional way in which tonsured children and young clerics learned their profession was by assisting parish clergy in their duties.[18]

It was not uncommon for a young man or boy to enter a clerical household for training, an arrangement from which both the priest and the apprentice benefited. The priest could supplement his income by charging a fee or, at least, could rely on the labor of his apprentice, while his apprentice learned how to perform the mass and administer the sacraments.[19] The fourteenth century Girona synodal decrees recognized this important custom and outlined the duty of senior clerics in educating novice priests: "that any cleric is held to prepare and instruct novice priests holding benefices in their church, and in and about what words are performed for the body and blood of Jesus Christ, and [how] baptism is bestowed and conferred, and what prayers for the above-said and other ecclesiastical sacraments must be performed. . . ."[20] This statute highlights the role of parish clergy in training the next generation

---

17. As for clerics who received a university education, an examination of various volumes of the bishops' Lletres and Notularum in the diocesan archive of Girona uncovered a small number of licenses for study. Marquès has counted the extant number of licenses for university study for both the fourteenth and fifteenth centuries in the diocese of Girona. He finds that thirty-eight clerics received licenses to study in Lérida, six at Montpellier, four at Tolosa, and two for each of the universities in Paris, Bolonia, and Perpiñan; Marquès, "Iglesia de Gerona," 538. Josep Baucells counted ninety-two permissions granted to clergy in the diocese of Barcelona for study; Vivir en la edad media, 1: 458. Kristine Utterback has found a similar trend in the Barcelona episcopal documents, which is also confirmed in Baucells's study; Pastoral Care, 128–29.

18. John Shinners and William J. Dohar, Pastors and the Care of Souls in Medieval England (Notre Dame: University of Notre Dame Press, 1998), 33–37. Even with the proliferation of universities in urban areas during the High Middle Ages, very few clerics would have received an advanced education at a university. Not until the Council of Trent did the Catholic Church mandate that students entering the priesthood receive their training in seminaries; prior to 1545, the Church had no universally available education for training its priests.

19. Cullum, "Boy/Man into Clerk/Priest," 61–64; Cullum, "Learning to Be a Man," 138–40; Cullum, "Life Cycle and Life-Course," 276–78. Examinations of English clerics and their families has revealed that, especially among those who dominated royal administration, and some at more junior levels of the church, they created clerical dynasties in which nephews (or perhaps their sons) were adopted and brought up in a clerical household to promote their clerical careers. Cullum points out that this pattern may have been a deliberate attempt on clergymen's parts to imitate the families of laypeople and provided these senior clergymen with the opportunity to be heads of their households. See also Julia Barrow, The Clergy in the Medieval World: Secular Clerics, Their Families and Careers in North-Western Europe, c. 800–c. 1200 (Cambridge, UK: Cambridge University Press, 2015), 117–47; J. L. Garssi, "Royal Clerks from the Archdiocese of York in the Fourteenth Century," Northern History no. 5 (1970): 12–33. Paul Freedman has shown that several castellan families dominated both the membership and the administration of the cathedral chapter of Vic; The Diocese of Vic: Tradition and Regeneration in Medieval Catalonia (New Jersey: Rutgers University Press, 1983), 48–61.

20. Noguer i Musqueras and Pons Guri, "Constitucions sinodals de Girona," 76.

of clerics and indicates that clerics who had the opportunity to attend a grammar school and acquire the basic education necessary to become a priest were most likely in the minority. That the training of clergymen took place primarily at the parish level is further seen in another bishop's directive that any cleric teaching young boys to read should also teach them the Ten Commandments, the Seven Deadly Sins, the Seven Works of Mercy, the Fourteen Articles of Faith, and the Seven Canonical Sacraments. Although this decree was meant to improve the education of the laity in general, it was also an attempt to set in motion the education of future clerics, or at least instill the most rudimentary knowledge needed for an ecclesiastical career. These fundamentals were clearly important because every priest in the ecclesiastical province of Tarragona was required to own a copy of the diocesan and provincial statutes that enumerated Church law as well as the Articles of Faith, the Commandments, and the Sacraments of the Church. This was yet another means to teach the clergy what they needed to know for the pastoral care of the laity.[21]

Like many of their contemporaries entering into apprenticeships—whether agricultural, artisanal, or scholastic—boys began their clerical training during early adolescence. Preparation for a clerical career inculcated a professional identity, and in this case a gendered identity, that significantly influenced the clerics' way of life. Keeping in mind that, as apprentices, young clerics were trained to follow the example of senior clergy and that children from a young age learned from their society what was considered appropriate behavior for a boy or a girl, it follows that the demeanor, behavior, and actions of their role models reinforced the gender identity of the young clerics as well as their understanding of acceptable professional behavior.[22] Because socialization and everyday interactions signaled to children the gendered behavior that was expected of them, we should consider the behaviors that tonsured children and young clerics would have learned from these senior clergymen.

Episcopal records allow us a glimpse of the types of actions and conduct that would have molded and influenced younger clerics. From an early age, the brawling and sexual relationships of parish clergy would have shaped the expectations of children as to what it meant to behave as a cleric. Consider

---

21. In 1354, the bishop Berenguer de Cruïlles added this statute to the Girona synodal legislation; ibid., 114, 144–46. John, Patriarch of Alexandria, wrote the treatise that every cleric in the diocese of Barcelona was required to obtain; Utterback, *Pastoral Care,* 27–28.

22. Steven Bednarski and Andrée Courtemanche have also argued that lessons about gender were not only learned at home but also reinforced at school and during an internship that inculcated a particular type of masculinity—in this case, a masculinity that accommodated the values of the burgher class in Provençal, France; "Learning to Be a Man."

that the rector Pere de Fontanella, who was responsible for teaching the "science of letters and grammar" to parish children, was reprimanded by episcopal officials for his excessive "habit of fighting" and joining in feuds, both inside and outside the parish. The monk Francesc de Pallerols, who was in charge of teaching scolares, was punished for keeping a concubine and injuring fellow monks but was permitted to continue his teaching responsibilities. In addition, the boys attending the school in Apiaria were exposed to the serious quarrels between the parish priest Pere Bons and the schoolteacher (magister), as well as the priest Pere's fighting with the local bailiff, suggesting that these boys might have perceived clerics to be combative figures.[23] Similarly, the scolares of Sant Juià d'Ordis witnessed the constant brawling of the sacrist and the hebdomedarian, which often took place in the church and contaminated its sacred space with their blood.[24]

It is possible that these children would have viewed such bellicose behavior as normal for clergymen, especially in view of the fact that young scolares and tonsured clerics did more than just witness the behavior of their parish clergy. They, too, participated in violent deeds, perhaps indicating that they were imitating the clerical deportment they found familiar. For example, in the previously mentioned town of Apiaria with the quarrelsome clerics, a fight among nine young tonsured clerics resulted in the death of one. The conflict seems to have been divided along family lines because three tonsured brothers from the Droch family fought against two Claramont brothers, two Corts brothers, and a couple of other friends.[25] In other examples, the beneficed cleric Bernat Nogera, who had lived with the priest Pere Vert and his concubine Elisenda as a scolaris for six years, attacked and wounded the priest in the head and arm after a severe reprimand by his priestly mentor. Also, Guillem de Oliver and Jaume de Vic, two tonsured clerics who resided with the rector Jaume Ricard in Barcelona, were found culpable in the death of a young

23. Hillgarth and Silano, Register "Notule Communium," 47–48; ADG, Lletres, no. 7, 129v.–130r., 147v.–148r. (1344); ADB, Registrum Communium, no. 1, 2r. (1309); ADB, Registrum Communium, no. 4, 227v. (1328).

24. ADG, Visites, no. 6, 25v. (1338). From 1338 to 1336, parishioners mentioned to visitors the conflict between these two clerics. See also ADG, Visites, no. 8, 47r. (1346).

25. ADB, Registrum Communium, no. 4, 191r.v., 194v., 214v. (1328). Guillem and Jaume Claramont, as well as their friend Bernat Guilabert, were found responsible for the death of Laurenç Droch and the injuries to his brothers Guillem and Bernat Droch, and to the father Arnau Droch. The brothers Gaufred and Ramon Corts, both tonsured clerics, and their friend Bartomeu Martí, also participated in the fight against the Droch brothers. I identify these clerics as "young" because they are identified as the sons of village men. Tonsured clerics who are not identified as the sons of their fathers were most likely no longer under their patriarchal authority and had reached a mature age at which they were considered responsible for themselves. Evidence of boys fighting, not necessarily scolares, can also be found in ADG, Lletres, no. 7, 154v. (1344); ADG, Lletres, no. 8, 12v–13r., 117r. (1344).

man from Aragon.[26] My point here is not that violent clergy caused young clerics to be violent but that a culture of violence among churchmen existed in which young clerics received the message that aggression was an acceptable and appropriate response to conflict.

Even from a young age, clerics in the minor orders were taught that it was acceptable to fight and participate in feuds. Take, for example, the young tonsured cleric Guillem Claper. Guillem's father was the rector of Santa Fe de Penedès, and Guillem and his brother regularly helped their father with the divine service. During an episcopal visitation to the parish of Santa Fe in 1337, the rector revealed that his eldest son Guillem was permitted to serve in the minor and major orders because he had received a papal dispensation for his illegitimate birth.[27] By 1342, Guillem de Claper now served with the priest Bartomeu Guarner in the castle of Granada. Both men were involved in at least two fights with the rector of the parish church of Granada, Guillem de Busquets, and the rector of Sant Christòfol de Mont Cugat, Bartomeu Busquets, his brother, that resulted in injuries for everyone involved.[28] Earlier that year, Guillem and his father, the rector of Santa Fe, were fined a hefty sum, 7 lliures, for inflicting injuries on members of the Busquets and Servarnes families. Guillem, then, served as a young cleric in a parish where he witnessed and participated (alongside his father and his mentor, Bartomeu Guarner) in a feud against the Busquets. These clerical Busquets siblings were also involved in another conflict with a priest from Vilafranca, indicating that the multiple fights with the priest Berenguer Guarner, Guillem Claper, and the rector of Santa Fe were not the only occasions in which they resorted to violence.[29] At

26. ADB, Registrum Communium, no. 1, 21v.–22r. (1304); ADB, Registrum Communium, no. 4, 39v., 42r. (1326).

27. The rector's claim of a dispensation for his son, Guillem Claper, to the minor and major orders is confirmed in the registers of Pope Clemens VI; ASV, Registra Vaticana, no. 151, 210r. (1342–1343); Registra Avenionensia, no. 61, 163r. (1342–1343). Guillem's dispensation for promotion to the minor orders is also registered in ADB, Dispensationes Apostolics, 22v.–23r.v. (1333); ADB, Visites, no. 5, 113v.–114r. (1342). The rector acknowledged being pardoned for one of his sons in a visitation to the parish of Sant Fe in 1336. Parishioners testified that the rector had a sixteen-year-old son serving in the parish of Sant Pere de Riudebitlles and a thirteen-year-old son also serving in a church; ADB, Visites, no. 4, 88v., 90r. (1336).

28. The conflict between the Busquets and Guarner families dates back to at least 1327. The bishop of Barcelona punished Guillem Busquets, the rector of Granada, and Ponç Busquets, a family member, along with Ferrar Guarner, for fighting and causing a great scandal in the village of Granada. Under penalty of a fine of 100 morabatins, the men were ordered to make amends; ADB, Registrum Communium, no. 4, 98r. (1327).

29. In 1337, parishioners reported that the rector of Santa Fe de Penedès had a sixteen-year-old and thirteen-year-old son—meaning that Guillem, by 1342, was either age eighteen or twenty-one; ADB, Visites, no. 4, 88v., 90r. (1337); ADB, Registrum Communium, no. 10, 128v., 138r., 170v. (1342); ADB, Registrum Communium, no. 11, 7v.–8r.v., 13r.v. (1342); ADB, Registrum Communium, no. 9, 32r. (1339); ADB, Visites, no. 5, 110v (1342). The Claper family might have had some relations in the

a minimum, we know that Guillem's clerical upbringing meant that he was surrounded by senior clergymen in the major orders who used violence and aggression in clashes with other clerics. As the son of a priest, he was raised, acknowledged, supported, and trained by a father who influenced his gender identity as a man and his professional identity as a cleric. Although these are the only documented experiences of the cleric Guillem Claper, such information reveals at least a facet of the climate in which Guillem grew up in and an environment that perhaps affected his future career as a priest.

That the lifestyle of the senior clergy greatly influenced young priests cannot be discounted, particularly when so many clerics were trained not in cathedral schools but in the parish church. Examples of clerics from the village of Siurana show how the actions of senior clerics may have affected younger clergy. In a 1321 visitation to the parish, villagers complained that the hebdomedarian Pere Messeguer and the stabilitus Guillem de Garrigàs neglected their priestly duties "on account of their youth." The hebdomedarian and stabilitus were clearly not students, but already as young priests they had acquired the characteristic markers of clerical masculinity. Both men had concubines, and both, as far as we know from the few documents that survive, were involved at some point in their careers in violent confrontations and threatening behavior. Sometime in 1319, the stabilitus Guillem de Garrigàs had "deflowered" Ramona, the daughter of Joan Barrera, whom he reportedly kept in the parish of Riumors. Parishioners also claimed that he kept another woman, a widow by the name of Na Priora, with whom he had a daughter. Six years before this visitation, the hebdomedarian Pere Messeguer had had a child with a woman from Siurana called Celia, but recently he had been in trouble for kidnapping a small girl from the village of Peralada, whom he refused to release until the men of the Count of Empúries broke into his home and removed the girl.[30] Already at an early stage in their clerical careers, *juvenes* such as Pere and Guillem would have learned the importance of keeping women to their gender identity as parish clergymen. They had two examples to follow that we know of with certainty. The elderly hebdomedarian Ramon Roig had kept a concubine in past years, and the sacrist

---

parish of Granada because a Berenguer Claper appears as a lay witness in a visitation to the parish in 1314; ADB, Visites, no. 2, 56v. (1314). In another example, the tonsured clerics and brothers Pere and Arnau Pinyol participated in a family feud with their father Guillem Pinyol, a married cleric, against Berenguer Marmer. The two tonsured clerics were under the guardianship of the priest Jaume Colello, who promised the bishop's officials that he would turn them into the court; Hillgarth and Silano, *Register "Notule Communium,"* no. 3, no. 6, no. 7, no. 28, no. 31 (1345), 22, 23, 31, 32.

30. ADG, Visites, no. 3, 25r.v. (1321).

Arnau de Truil kept his concubine and children in the parish.[31] We know that the sacrist Arnau was an established priest in the parish when Guillem and Pere appeared because he is mentioned in a 1315 visitation. In 1315, Guillem de Garrigàs was simply a cleric assisting the sacrist Arnau and not yet in the major orders.[32] For young scolares who advanced to the priesthood, the physical maturity of their bodies and the ability to engage in sex would have been important markers of adulthood. Along with physical strength, facial hair, and the capacity to produce semen, male maturity was linked to virility in medieval culture and medical theories about the male body.[33] Promotion to the priesthood, as well as important indicators such as evidence of sexual activity, the formation of a union with a woman, and the production of progeny were markers that a cleric had attained adult male status. Just as Ruth Karras has pointed out that university students displayed an aggressive heterosexuality and used prostitutes and servants to "demonstrate their assimilation into manhood,"[34] clerics-in-training likewise used sexual activity to demonstrate their qualifications for manhood. The eventual establishment of a marriage-like union by so many parish clerics further indicates that young priests adopted a model of masculinity that was founded on the ideal of a conjugal union and governing a household. As youths, clerics learned a masculinity that accepted sexual activity, and as they progressed to full adulthood, they transitioned to marriage-like unions that mimicked the marriages of adult laymen.

Adulthood also influenced how men used violence to navigate their social relations with other men. Violence was linked to manhood, particularly when it was employed to defend a man's status and to establish and regulate a hierarchy among men, which may explain why so many parish clergy engaged in interpersonal violence with their fellow clergymen. As in so many villages throughout Catalunya, in Siurana aggressive confrontations and rivalries existed among the parish clergy. Nearly a decade after the 1321 visitation, the hebdomedarian Guillem de Garrigàs had established himself in the parish, and there was now discord between Guillem and the newly appointed hebdomedarian Pere Bernat. According to parishioners, both men brought arms to the church and said prayers with swords in their hands. Recently they had

31. The hebdomedarian Ramon Roig appears in the ADG index of the bishop's Lletres and Notularum, http://www.arxiuadg.org/index-de-llocs-i-persones (accessed August 12, 2013): ADG, Notularum, no. 1, 56r. (1297). For the sacrist Arnau Truil, see ADG, Visites, no. 3, 25r. (1321).

32. ADG, Visites, no. 1, 90r. (1315); ADG, Notularum, no. 19, 6r.v. (1346); ADG, Lletres, no. 5, 59r. (1332) and 120r. (1333). By 1329, the sacrist Arnau disappears from visitation records, but the stabilitus Pere Messeguer remained in his benefice until his death in 1346, and the hebdomedarian Guillem de Garrigàs remained at least until 1333.

33. Cadden, Meanings of Sex Difference, 158, 171–72, 181.

34. Karras, From Boys to Men, 80.

had a dispute in the church during which both men had unsheathed their swords during Guillem's celebration of the mass. When Guillem had read from the gospel, Pere Bernat had objected and had threatened the young boy who was helping with the water and wine. Pere's violent outburst contaminated the ceremony so that "the said en Garrigàs [Guillem] remained still for a long pause because he could not proceed with the mass on account of the defect in the water and wine." Pere Bernat, it seems, wanted to correct Guillem because he ordered, "from now on, if you touch this [missal] you should carry the missal from the altar yourself." In response, Guillem seized the missal and declared, "I will see who shall bring this book to me."[35] The verbal and armed confrontation was a power struggle between two men. Pere Bernat's interruption of the mass was an attempt to humiliate and control Guillem. Guillem resisted Pere Bernat's attempts to dominate him, not only by arming himself and having a standoff before the alter but also by defying Pere's order and insisting that he would control how he performed the mass.

Five years later, in 1341, Pere was serving as the hebdomedarian in the village of Vilanova de la Muga, where he was known as a quarrelsome man who fought with clerics and villagers. Pere had injured a parishioner with his sword and had refused to give the young cleric, Joan Escuder, the key to the chest where the chalices were kept for mass. Parishioners also complained that, out of negligence, and sometimes drunkenness, he failed to celebrate mass. In addition, Pere kept a concubine, Garssenda, and had a son who served as a cleric in the parish of Siurana.[36] It is likely that Pere's son grew up in both Siurana and Vilanova, where he was exposed to at least five concubinary priests and his father's belligerent acts. Certainly the tonsured clerics Nicolau Sunyer and (fifteen-year-old) Joan Escuder were trained under the tutelage of Pere Bernat and the rector. Both senior clerics kept families in the village and had troubled relationships with their parishioners due to the laxity with which they carried out their priestly duties.[37] Ten years later, both Nicolau Sunyer and

---

35. ADG, Visites, no. 4, 9v.–10r. (1329). Confirmed by the bishop as a hebdomedarian of Siurana in 1328, Pere Bernat replaced the hebdomedarian Ramon Roig, who died that same year. By 1334, Pere Bernat had renounced his benefice to become the hebdomedarian of Vilanant. That same year Bernat Guasch became the sacrist of Siurana; ADG, Notularum, no. 6, 156v. (1328); ADG, Lletres, no. 3, 65v.–66r. (1328); ADG, Lletres, no. 5, 133r.v. (1334).

36. ADG, Visites, no. 6, 155v.–157r. (1341). In 1334, Pere Bernat renounced his benefice in Siurana to become a hebdomedarian in Vilanova de la Muga. A summary of the documents concerning the new appointment can be found in ADG index of the bishop's Lletres and Notularum: ADG, Notularum, no. 6, 156v. (1328); ADG, Lletres, no. 3, 65v.–66r. (1328); ADG, Lletres, no. 5, 133r.v. (1334).

37. ADG, Visites, no. 6, 156r.v. (1341). In this same visitation, the rector of Vilanova was accused of threatening the parishioners who had complained of his negligence to the bishop. Joan Escuder received a dispensation for his age when he obtained his benefice in Vilanova in 1328; ADG, Lletres, no. 3, 79v. (1328).

Joan Escuder were priests in the village of Vilanova. Nicolau served in the nearby monastery of Sant Joan de Croses, but he kept his four children with Na Mingartz in Vilanova. Joan held the benefice of stabilitus and had come to blows with the cleric Ponç de Tina when Ponç had made unwanted sexual advances to Joan's daughter and niece.[38] Joan, then, had grown up to father a daughter and had engaged in combat against a fellow priest with a sword and shield.

What does this limited view of the clerics from Siurana and Vilanova tell us about how both the professional and gender identity of clerics were influenced by the clerical culture found in parishes? We know that from a young age both Guillem de Garrigàs and Pere Messeguer behaved as did many of their senior colleagues, engaging in sex, keeping a woman, and fathering children. The stabilitus Pere Messeguer had been involved in the kidnapping and, presumably, rape of a young girl. The hebdomedarian Guillem had been in verbal and physical altercations with the hebdomedarian Pere Bernat to establish who dominated the parish church while saying the mass. Pere Bernat was a combative and armed priest who fought with fellow clerics in Siurana and Vilanova. It is likely that he trained at least three young clerics—his son, the cleric Nicolau Sunyer, and the fifteen-year-old cleric Joan Escuder. The youth of clerics such as Joan, Nicolau, and of young clerics such as twelve-year-old Berenguer Fuster, who received a dispensation to obtain a priestly benefice, underscores the impact that senior clerics had on their younger counterparts as they worked with and trained the next generation.[39] Indeed, both Nicolau Sunyer and Joan Escuder became priests, established a relationship with a woman, and fathered children; in addition, we know that at least Joan proved that he was willing to engage in violence to defend family members and put a lower-level cleric in his place when he allowed a tonsured cleric to take part in the assault against the cleric Ponç de Tina.

What is more, despite Pere Bernat's apparent pugnacious personality, his harsh treatment of younger clergy may not have been unusual. Tonsured clerics who were mentored by senior clerics may have been subjected to punitive treatment. Consider that the rector Martí de Coll was excommunicated for causing injury and placing "violent hands" on the scolaris who lived with him. Likewise, the priest Berenguer de Olivella was punished for his violence against

---

38. ADG, Visites fragmentaris, no. 9v. (1323); ADG, Visites, no. 4, 6v. (1329); ADG, Visites, no. 6, 156v. (1341); ADG, Processos, no. 185, 1v. (1337); ADG, Obligacions de Penes, no. 1, 9r. (1337).

39. ADG, Lletres, no. 7, 54r. (1341). The age most commonly found in dispensations to obtain a benefice is fourteen years old, although one nine-year-old was given a dispensation to obtain a benefice without the cura. See also ADG, Lletres, no. 6, 94r. (1343); ADG, Lletres, no. 7, 117v. (1344); ADG, Lletres, no. 8, 160r., 179r. (1344); ADG, Lletres, no. 10, 102v. (1346).

"tonsured boys" that caused an "effusion of blood." And the priest Pere de Alda was punished for, among other things, the slapping, beating, and dragging of the tonsured cleric Francesc de Pont by his hair to a chapel in the church of Montbuí.[40] In addition to observing armed clerics performing their duties in the church and the violent deeds of senior clergy against fellow clerics, younger clerics may have experienced firsthand that violence was used to reprimand and put lower-level clergy in their place. Disciplinary violence was considered a legitimate form of violence as long as it was not excessive. The priests mentioned here more than likely had crossed the line, which is why these accounts appear in diocesan records, and it seems likely that senior clergy used many forms of violent correction to discipline and humiliate young clerics-in-training. Medieval society condoned the beating of children and adolescents to deter wickedness and instill virtuous habits, so young clerics may have expected that their training would involve some form of physical discipline. Indeed, Francesc Eiximenis, the influential Catalan writer, warns adults that they "must reprimand the young," and that the young must accept "correction" to prevent a "damnable and immoral" life.[41] The fourteenth-century manual of instruction for parish clergy, the *Speculum Curatorum* (*A Mirror for Curates*), also sanctions the beating of one cleric by another if the beating is done to correct an "incorrigible" cleric and cites Ramon of Peñafort as an authority who condoned the beating of secular clergy in the major and minor orders for their "faults."[42] Disciplinary violence among the clergy, moreover, upheld the hierarchies of age and rank, and would have been seen as maintaining the patriarchal principle of order.[43]

The connections among sexual relationships with women, violence, and clerical identity, therefore, can be found in the experiences of scolares and young clerics. That they witnessed a clerical culture that used violence to compete with and gain status over rivals was only one part of their education, and enduring the physical correction that reiterated the power of senior clerics was another. Junior clergy learned that discipline in the form of violence accorded status and deprived others of it. These clerics-in-training followed the examples of senior clergy who were involved with women and used violence to settle disputes and enforce their authority over their clerical colleagues.

---

40. ADG, Notularum, no. 1, 4v. (1310?); ADB, Registrum Communium, no. 4, 123r. (1327) and 161v. (1328). In a separate incident, the priest Pere de Alda had attacked the tonsured cleric Francesc de Pont with his sword while Francesc was standing before the altar of Sant Maria.

41. Renedo and Guixeras, *Francesc Eiximenis,* 77–79.

42. Higden, *Speculum curatorum,* 267–69.

43. Alexandra Shepard, *Meanings of Manhood in Early Modern England* (Oxford: Oxford University Press), 130–39; Bednarski and Courtemanche, "Learning to Be a Man," 123–24, 134.

It is difficult to determine, however, the age at which senior clergymen refrained from using violence to exert their authority. Gender definitions change over the course of a person's lifetime, and thus it is likely that at an advanced age, marked by physical decline, clergymen reached a point when violence was no longer a component of their gender identity. Unfortunately, the visitation records rarely mention elderly and decrepit priests or their activities, particularly those that merited commentary because of their violent nature. This suggests that these clerics had transitioned to a different stage of life at which physical aggression was not needed or even possible.

Perhaps the most convincing evidence of how clerical masculinity incorporated lay ideals that had been imbued in clerics from an early age comes from the lives of priests and their sons. The succession of priests' sons into the clerical profession did not die out with the abolition of clerical marriage in the twelfth century. Bernhard Schimmelpfenig, in his study of fourteenth-century dispensations, finds that more than two-thirds of the sons of clerics mentioned in papal registers were the sons of priests.[44] Ludwig Schmugge's study of the papal Penitentiary records from 1449 to 1533 counts 37,916 petitions from illegitimate children, and 60 percent of these petitions belonged to the children of clerical fathers. The prevalence of papal dispensations for "natural" sons from dioceses throughout Europe in the late medieval and early modern period indicates that many of these sons followed in their fathers' footsteps.[45] The argument that priests' sons were marginalized as a result of their bastard status, and even had their own manliness questioned as the sons of men feminized for their sexual conduct, is not supported by the evidence in Catalunya.[46] Tables 5.1, 5.2, and 5.3 illustrate that a career in the Church could be a family profession shared by fathers and sons, brothers, and uncles and nephews in Catalan communities. Any survey of the Catalan visitation records reveals that it was not uncommon for priests to employ their sons to help them celebrate the mass and carry out their duties, nor was it uncommon for these sons to pursue a clerical career. Take, for example, the case of Ramon Ricart, who became the rector of Sant Vicenç d'Oveç, the church where his father had once been rector.[47] Unlike the sons of Anglo-Norman priests, who disappeared but reappeared as "nephews" in the twelfth century,

44. Schimmelpfennig, "'Ex fornicatione nati,'" 37–38.

45. Ludwig Schmugge, "'Cleansing on Consciences': Some Observations Regarding the Fifteenth–Century Registers of the Papal Penitentiary," *Viator* 29 (1998), 359; Salonen and Schmugge, *Sip from the "Well of Grace,"* 19–20, 58–59. See also Brundage, *Law, Sex, and Christian Society,* 315; Martí Bonet, *Visitas Pastorales,* 703.

46. The marginalization argument is made by Thibodeaux in *Manly Priest,* 75, 85.

47. ACV, Visites, Calaix 31 / 43, no. 4, 20v. (1314).

Catalan priests are frequently identified with their sons and not their nephews, or in some cases with both their sons and their nephews, indicating
once again that the Church could be a family profession.[48] Moreover, the
prevalence of clerical fathers and sons was unlikely to shock parishioners in
the rural villages and towns of Catalunya. Medieval society in general expected that a son would be inclined to take up his father's profession. The
Franciscan Francesc Eiximenis notes not only that nature compels men to
beget sons but also that men seek to have their likeness reproduced in their
sons—an excuse that priests may have used to justify encouraging and training
their sons for a clerical career. According to Eiximenis, fathers love their sons
because they "resemble their fathers in nature," and he further explains that it
is the responsibility of the father "to teach his son a worthy profession." Furthermore, it is the right of a son to reproach his father for teaching him an
unprofitable way of life and denying him the acknowledgement and privileges
of a son.[49] Given this common view of fatherhood and the belief that the
priesthood could be a noble profession, it is possible that many in these small
communities thought that priestly fathers were doing right by their sons.

When we consider the reproductive capabilities of clergymen and the ten-
dency for priestly sons to follow in their father's footsteps, it is surprising that
there are so few dispensations for illegitimate birth (*defectus natalium*) from
Catalan dioceses, or any dioceses from Iberia, in the papal registers for the
fourteenth century. What is more, a survey of the first Apostolic Penitentiary
register for the years 1409 to 1411 reveals that it does not contain many petitions from the ecclesiastical province of Tarragona that granted a dispensation for illegitimate birth, suggesting that the practice of obtaining a papal
dispensation was largely disregarded by Catalan clergymen.[50] By the middle
of the fifteenth century, however, when the bureaucracy of the Penitentiary
had expanded to meet the needs of Christians requiring apostolic dispensation and the process had become more routine, Spain and Portugal together
represented 24 percent of the petitions for *defectus natalium* that the Penitentiary handled, while France and Germany represented 17 and 36 percent, respectively.[51] Particularly from 1314 to 1334, only a small number of papal
dispensations, among hundreds, were granted to clerics from the ecclesiastical province of Tarragona.[52] And, out of more than 1,000 dispensations for

48. Thibodeaux, *Manly Priest*, 82.
49. Renedo and Guixera, *Francesc Eiximenis*, 67–69.
50. ASV, Penitenzieria Apostolica, Registra matrimonialium et diversorum, no. 1 (1409).
51. Salonen and Schmugge, *Sip from the "Well of Grace*," 61.
52. Guillaume Mollat, *Lettres Communes des Papes d'Avignon. Jean XXII (1316–1334)*, Vols. 1–4 (Paris:
Albert Fontemoing, 1904), 3: 279, 4: 73.

defectus natalium issued from 1342 to 1343 under Pope Clemens VI, only twenty-eight clerics from the province of Tarragona appear in these regis-ters.[53] Even among the extensive diocesan registers of Girona and Barcelona, few dispensations for illegitimate birth administered by the papacy and granted by the bishop are recorded. This stands in stark contrast to England. Laura Wertheimer's study of dispensations granted to illegitimate clergy in the thirteenth and fourteenth centuries in five English dioceses shows that there are far more dispensations recorded in the episcopal registers than are recorded in the papal records for England as a whole because applicants had to pay extra for their dispensation to be noted in papal records.[54] Such a differ-ence between the English and Catalan episcopal registers might suggest that the episcopal authorities in England were far more insistent that the illegiti-mate sons of priests obtain dispensations than were the Catalan episcopal authorities. Furthermore, given that the Catalan provincial and synodal stat-utes banned priests from celebrating the mass with their offspring, it is also significant that episcopal authorities did not go out of their way to uncover and punish these clerical fathers. The episcopal registers of Barcelona and Girona contain very few letters dealing with the punishments of fathers cel-ebrating the mass with their sons.

If the visitation records indicate that many parish priests did not shy away from celebrating mass with their sons and trained their sons for a clerical career, why do these priests and their sons not appear in the diocesan or papal regis-ters? One explanation is that not every son who helped his father in church sought an ecclesiastical career. The son could have chosen another profession. Esteve, the son of the hebdomedarian Cervià de Soler of Pedret, trained as an apprentice to a carpenter in Castelló, and the cleric Francesc Cocó apprenticed his son Pere to a tailor in Castelló.[55] Of the two sons of the Franciscan monk

---

53. ASV, Registra Vaticana, no. 151, no. 155 (1342–1343). Ten registers for the years 1342–1343 exist for Pope Clemens VI. In the two registers that I surveyed, six clerics from the diocese of Girona, fifteen from the diocese of Vic, four from the diocese of Barcelona, two from the diocese of Urgell, and none from the dioceses of Tortosa and Tarragona received dispensations for illegitimate birth. I also counted sixty-one dispensations from nineteen Spanish dioceses outside the ecclesiastical prov-ince of Tarragona in these registers. The Catalan dioceses are not entirely exceptional. Kirsi Salonen has found that, in a seventy-four-year period, only twenty supplicants from the diocese of Turku in Finland sought a dispensation for illegitimate birth; "In Their Fathers' Footsteps: The Illegitimate Sons of Finnish Priests According to the Archives of the Sacred Penitentiary, 1449–1523" in *Roma magistra mundi: Itineraria culturae medievalis: Mélanges offerts au Pére L.E. Boyle à l'occasion de son 75e an-niversaire*, ed. Jacqueline Hamesse (Louvain-la-Neuve: Fédération Internationale des Instituts d'Études Médiévales. Textes et Études du Moyen Âge, 1998), 355–66.

54. Wertheimer, "Illegitimate Birth and the English Clergy," 216, 222.

55. For the document outlining the apprenticeship contract between Esteve, son of Cervià de Soler, and Pere Montiró in Castelló, see AHG, Notarials, Castelló, no. 368, XV kalendas Novembris (1325). (The folios of this register are unpaginated.) Cervià de Soler appears as a hebdomedarian in

Guillem de Roset, only one son, Pere Roset, pursued a clerical profession in Vic. The other son, Bernat de Roset, received a house, lands, and 125 sous from his father to contract a marriage with a local woman.[56] Another explanation that is suggested by these numbers is that the sons of clergymen from the ecclesiastical province of Tarragona, and probably from all of Iberia, simply did not bother to obtain a papal dispensation. Considering the distance, it seems unlikely that the sons of peasant priests could have afforded the time and cost of travel to Rome; such a luxury might have been reserved for the sons of the elite clergymen, who needed a formal dispensation to have a successful career in the Church.[57]

It was even possible for some clerics to receive a tonsure and progress through the orders without ever applying for a dispensation. In a visitation to the parish of Cubelles, parishioners mentioned in passing that a local priest, Berenguer Boschet, was the son of a priest but did not have a dispensation. In another example, the cleric Pere Joan Palay served as the rector of Cardona and previously as a cleric in Sort, but it was not until a visitation to Cardona that the episcopal visitor determined that he did not have a dispensation for *defectum natalium*. It is not improbable, then, that a number of fathers, such as the rector of Foix, who took his six-year-old son to another parish to have him tonsured, or the priest Pere Cervera, who was caught having his two sons fraudulently tonsured, found ways to promote their sons, albeit illicitly, to the minor and major orders.[58] In both of these cases, the bishop discovered the

both the notarial documents of the town of Castelló and in episcopal visitation records to the parish of Pedret. In the 1329 visitation to Pedret, the hebdomedarian Cervià de Soler is described as an old man; AHG, Notarials, Castelló, no. 43, Vidus Augustii (1324); AHG, Notarials, Castelló, no. 2137, XII kalendas Marcii (1325); ADG, Visites, quaderno no. 1, 23v. (1323); ADG, Visites, no. 4, 8v. (1329). For the apprenticeship of Pere, son of the cleric Francesc Cocó, see AHG, Notarials, no. 320, Castelló, April 6 (1372). It is likely that the cleric Francesc Cocó from Castelló was related to the sacrist menor Pere Cocó and the cleric Castelló Cocó, who were related to each other and who both served in Santa Maria de Castelló d' Empúries. I thank Josep Maria Gironella i Granés for bringing these documents to my attention and sharing his transcriptions.

56. AEV, Capitols Matrimonials, ACF 3308, 10v.–11r. (1312).

57. Kirsi Salonen has argued that almost all the men who turned to the Penitentiary for dispensations were seeking higher ecclesiastical positions and hoped to advance their careers; "In Their Fathers' Footsteps," 360.

58. ACV, Visites, Calaix 31/ 43, no. 1, 26r. [letter] (1312); ADB, Visites, no. 5, 103r. (1342). The sons of the priest Pere Cervera, Bernat and Berenguer, were not identified as the sons of a priest when they were tonsured. The bishop, after the fact, discovered that neither boy had a dispensation for illegitimate birth. Once the bishop determined that the two boys had been fraudulently tonsured, he ordered the rector of the church to chastise Bernat and Berenguer publicly before the parish during the church service and excommunicated their father, who on the same day was pardoned, presumably after paying a fine. When the bishop of Tarragona tonsured Pericó Gillida in the parish of Alcalà, he later learned that Pericó was "spurius" and ordered that he not be permitted to wear the tonsure; García Egea, *Visita pastoral*, 229. See also Martí Bonet, "Visitas pastorales," 703, 685–87. Salonen has also found examples of priests' sons who held an ecclesiastical office and were seeking

deception only after he had tonsured the boys, but we can only wonder how many others were able to do the same without getting caught. If the diocese of Barcelona is any indication—more than 7,000 escolares tonsured in 862 parish visitations over a thirty-three year period—a significant number of boys and young men sought the tonsure, and it seems plausible that among such great numbers the sons of priests could be unknowingly incorporated into the fold of newly tonsured clerics.[59] How diligent episcopal officials were in determining the legitimacy of each candidate for tonsure is open to debate, but clearly some illegitimate sons of the clergy and laity were tonsured without dispensations. Once they had been tonsured and placed in a different parish with a priest who was a family friend and could support their candidacy for ordination to any of the seven grades to the priesthood, priests' sons may not have found the lack of a dispensation for illegitimate birth much of an impediment to their seeking to join the priesthood.

Some priests' sons could operate as clerics without having received the tonsure, which can be seen in the case of the elderly rector Berenguer de Puigrubí and his sons from a 1330 visitation to the parish of Sant Esteve de Vinyoles in the diocese of Vic. The two nameless sons are not identified as clerics, but they clearly functioned as parish clergy. Both celebrated mass with their father and with the beneficed cleric Pere Effortat; their aged father was so "weak" and "impotent" that the eldest son collected the tithes that belonged to the church and the younger son composed documents, presumably wills, for his father.[60] The rector had obviously trained his sons, and they performed the duties of clerics who were at least in the minor orders even though neither one appears to have been tonsured at this time.[61] Fourteen years later, the papal registers from 1343 show a dispensation for illegitimate birth and promotion to all orders for Pere de Puigrubí from the diocese of Vic, probably one of the

---

dispensation, not only for illegitimate birth but also for illegally obtaining their office; "In Their Fathers' Footsteps," 358.

59. Joan Ademar, the son of single man and woman from the town of Peralada, was also tonsured without a dispensation for illegitimate birth; ADG, Lletres, no. 8, 18r.v. 1344. For the 7,000-plus tonsured escolares during the pontificate of the bishop Ponç de Gualba and Ferrer d'Abella, see Baucells i Reig, *Vivir en la edad media*, 1: 2281–83. See also Martí Bonet, *Historia de las diócesis españolas*, 157, 162–63.

60. AEV, Visites, no. 1200/1, 13r. (1330). The episcopal visitor fined the rector of Sant Esteve de Vinyoles but did not punish his sons or the beneficed cleric Pere Effortat. If either son had been tonsured, it seems likely that they would have been identified as clerics.

61. The rector Bernat Guad had also trained his son to "assist in the mass and in all things." In this case, the son is clearly identified as not being a cleric but a layman who was married. Martí Bonet, "Visitas pastorals," 709–10. Other examples of priests celebrating mass with their sons who are not mentioned as being tonsured in the Barcelona visitation of 1303 include the rector of Pax with his two sons, the rector of Fontrubí, the rector of Albà with his sons, and the rector of Calafell with his two sons (678, 685, 690, 696).

sons of the rector Berenguer de Puigrubí. The 1330 visitation does not indi-cate that the episcopal visitor bothered to determine whether the rector had tonsured either son illegally, which suggests that the authorities were not greatly concerned about young sons who aided their fathers.[62] Indeed, in the majority of cases in which priests' sons were identified as tonsured clerics, episcopal visitors did not require them to show a dispensation for illegitimate birth—but they did request that a cleric show a previous dispensation for con-cubinage or fathering a child. What is more, a priestly father may have waited to tonsure his son until the son was certain of his vocation. The case from Vic indicates that some priests' sons were able to serve as clerics without having received this most basic step in acquiring the status of a clergyman until they sought an ecclesiastical career and benefice. It is also possible that clerics forged licenses of tonsure and ordination and letters of provision to ben-efices—a practice that the bishops of Catalunya attempted to prevent by maintaining episcopal registers that kept track of such records in the fourteenth century.[63] Granted, the evidence presented is limited, but these few cases show that at least some priests' sons found ways to infiltrate the minor orders and priesthood without obtaining a papal dispensation.

Although a priest's celebrating mass with his son might be perceived sim-ply as a subversive act that flouted church law, there are other factors to con-sider about this practice. A number of priests who relied on the help of their young sons lived in poor parishes that could not afford to employ another cleric. For example, two priests were required to serve the impoverished church of Sant Climent de Castelltort, but the community could support only one full-time chaplain. Parishioners testified that the chaplain celebrated mass with his son and did not have an "adequate student" (scolarem sufficientem).[64] In the mountains near Jonquera, the rector of Sant Martí de la Vajol served the church with his young son and grandson, the eldest of the two not having reached the age of eight. Here, too, parishioners commented that the rector did not have an "adequate student" and, instead, celebrated with the boys, who could barely help him with the mass.[65] It is conceivable that a priest might have difficulty finding an apprentice among the peasant families, who could not

---

62. The 1314 episcopal visitations for the diocese of Tortosa similarly do not show that officials were very concerned about the young sons of priests helping in the church. In a visitation to the vil-lage of Pobla de Nules, the rector seems to have avoided any trouble with the visitor when parishio-ners testified that his young sons aided only the other priests during the mass and not their father. The rector did not receive any punishment; García Egea, Visita pastoral, 237.

63. Utterback, Pastoral Care, 16, 19.

64. ACV, Visites, Calaix 31/43, no. 3, 37v. (1314). The church of Sant Climent de Castelltort is located near Sant Llorenç de Morunys in a mountainous area.

65. ADG, Visites, no. 1, 75v.–76r. (1314).

afford to relinquish the labor potential of a son, but it is more likely that the priest preferred training his own son because it was more economical to do so. Medieval children in general received age-appropriate training from family members and contributed to the household economy from an early age. Lower-class clerical families must have employed this strategy also, especially if no benefice or church funds existed to support a doorkeeper, lector, or acolyte to help with the care of the church. The rector Pere Arnau de Pla claimed that he celebrated mass with his tonsured son Ramon because "he does not have the means or the funds from his benefice from which he could keep a scolarem." In fact, the rector asserted that out of "necessity" he was "forced" to celebrate with his own son.[66]

It is not a surprise that priests in remote and extremely impoverished villages could not afford to employ a scolar out of their own funds.[67] Even if the family of the young boy could have afforded to the pay the priest, the sum might not have covered the upkeep of the child. On the one hand, it may have simply been easier and more cost-effective for a priest to use the labor of a son; on the other hand, accepting a local boy under his tutelage would most likely have strengthened a priest's ties to the community, so there was an incentive (in addition to a financial one, if the parents could pay) to training a scolar alongside his son. Both the rector of Cabrera and the rector of Torreyles, who trained scolares together with their sons, appear to have been prosperous—the former owned a business selling bread and wine, and the latter supplemented his income with the revenue he made as bailiff.[68] The prosperity of these clerics meant not only that they could afford a scolar but that parishioners may have wanted to form an important connection with men who held positions of authority and financial influence in their village. The likeliest scenario, then, is that a parish priest mentored a scolar when it was to his benefit and financial interest to do so; otherwise, his son or nephew was the

66. ADG, Visites, no. 4, 53v.–54r. (1329). The visitor fined the rector a sizeable sum of 50 sous. It is interesting that the episcopal visitor did not ask to see the dispensation that allowed the son Ramon to be tonsured but, instead, wanted proof of the rector's claim that he had previously received a dispensation for his relationship with Ramon's mother, Brunisenda.

67. The capellan in the remote parish of Els Castells, who "frequently" celebrated mass with his son is described as living in poverty; ACV, Visites, Calaix 31/43, no. 7, 22r. (1313). The rectors in the following parishes celebrated mass with their sons and lived in very small villages that episcopal visitors did not frequently visit: Sant Fruitós de Guils del Canto, Sant Martí de Bahamal, Sant Cristòfol de Queralt, Montargull, Sant Vicenç de Fals, Ginestar; ACV, Visites, Calaix 31/43, no. 7, 24r. (1313), ACV, Visites, Calaix 31/43, no. 4, 14r. (1314); AEV, Visites, no. 1200/2, 3v., 39v., 41v. (1331); ADG, Visites, no. 4, 202r. (1330).

68. The rector of Cabrera could also afford to pay to female servants to help his concubine with the home and business; Benito i Monclús, *Parròquies del maresm*, 280–81, 284; Martí Bonet, "Visitas pastorals," 710–11.

ideal substitute. This explains why so many clerics kept their sons with them—even when they were single parents or when they housed the rest of the family in a separate home or neighboring village to avoid a fine. Although many of these cases are not reported specifically as a priest celebrating mass with his son, a significant number of sons are described as living with their father and some as "helping," which most likely entailed cleaning the church and ringing the bells during the service.[69] A son, therefore, provided company, free labor, and the ultimate proof of a cleric's virility and paternity.

The training of priests' sons leads us once again to the question of how these boys' immediate environment and the influence of their father might have affected their expectations about the priestly profession and clerical life in general. The two sons of the vicar Berenguer, who acted as his scolares while he ministered the mass, not only based their image of parish clergy on their father, who kept their mother and his three children in the rectory, but also on the rector of the parish, who had two young children with his domestic partner.[70] In another example, the son of the rector of Bahamal celebrated mass with his father, who was known for gambling, spending time in taverns, and strumming his musical instrument for women of ill repute.[71] The rector's son would have grown up seeing his father participating in the masculine lay culture of his community: flirting with women, playing dice games, and drinking with village men. The villagers may not have believed the rector to be an exemplary priest, but he nevertheless functioned as a model for his son. The deacon and four concubinary priests who served in the villages surrounding the rector and his son would have more or less confirmed the expectation that parish clergy had families and were integrated into the male community.[72] When a rector performed his duties well, the assistance of a son did not always elicit criticism. Guillem, the son of the rector of Sant Genís d'Orís, "ministered and served his father in the church and at mass" as

<hr />

69. For example, the rector of Muntmael kept both of his sons in his home, while their mother, Margarida, lived in a different village; ADB, Visites, no. 2, 70r. (1314). Also, the hebdomedarian of Vilatenim, Pere Papini, was fined 20 sous for keeping both of his sons in his home, and there is no mention of their mother; ADG, Obligacions de Penes, no. 1, 28r. (1343). Other examples of priests keeping their sons in their homes while the mother and, in some cases, younger children, especially female children, lived elsewhere can be found in ADG, Visites fragmentaris, 18r.v. (1303); ADG, Visites fragmentaris, 31r.v. (1320); ADG, Visites, no. 4, 69v., 99v.–100r. (1329); ADG, Remissions de Penes, no., 1, 7r. (1347) and 11r. (1348); ADG, Lletres, no. 8, 42r. (1344); AEV, Visites, no. 1200/2, 3v.–4r., 48v.–49r. (1331); AEV, Visites, no. 1200/3, 28v. (1331) and 50r. (1336); ADB, Visites, no. 4, 31v. (1336); ACT, Visites, 1r. (c. 1337).

70. AEV, Visites, no. 1200/2, 41v. (1331).

71. ACV, Calaix 31/43, no. 4, 14r. (1314).

72. ACV, Calaix 31/43, no. 4, 13v.–14r.v. (1314). See the visitations for Sant Vicenç de Cabdella, Sant Juià de Puig Cabdella, Astell, Oveix, and Mont-ros.

a "scolaris," but parishioners nonetheless described the rector as leading a reputable life and had no complaints to offer the episcopal visitor.[73]

Certainly, whether a priestly father took care of his church and community or did not served as an example to a son; however, the larger issue here is the underscoring of the clerical culture found in these villages. These young boys would have learned from an early age that priests could establish households, have families, and partake in the masculine culture of village life. Their gender identity was formed during the years they spent as scolares serving at the altar with their father—a father whose profession and masculine identity shaped their notions of what it meant to be a man in priestly robes.

The inquiry into the conduct of the rector Bernat Guad reveals how young boys and men acquired a professional identity as clerics that would have impacted their gender identity. During the course of a visitation, the rector confessed to the bishop that he celebrated mass with his married son Bernat and the son of an artisan. According to the rector, neither was tonsured, but, again, this may not have been unusual if ordination had been delayed for some reason. Of course, Bernat junior's marriage meant that he could officially be admitted only into minor orders. It is clear, nevertheless, that the priest's son had assisted his father for at least six years, indicating that he would have been well versed in the rites and ceremonies of the priestly office because the rector stated that Bernat "assists in the mass and in all things." The artisan's son apparently had the basics covered as well. When questioned about his knowledge, the rector answered that, "he understands the confession which takes place at mass and he knows the epistle of the dead and 'amen' and 'cum spiritu tuo' and responds 'sanctus' and 'agnus' and 'agnus dei' and 'Kirieleison.'"[74] The training of Bernat junior and the artisan's son sheds light on the extent to which clerical masculinity had incorporated the behaviors of lay masculinity. Not surprisingly, the rector had a family. His concubine Geralda had lived "for a long time in his own home" and had given birth to "many children," two of whom the rector himself had baptized. The rector was also an enterprising man. In addition to holding his priestly office, he was and had been the bailiff of the parish for seven years. Parishioners complained that as bailiff he captured men "violently" and had introduced "many evil customs and harmful practices against parishioners" based on his "authority" for the temporal lord.[75]

The complaints against the rector certainly give the impression that he was disliked and possibly feared in his community—most likely because of his

---

73. AEV, Visites, no. 1200/ 1, 12v. (1330).
74. Martí Bonet, "Visitas pastorals," 709–10.
75. Ibid., 710.

power and authority as both bailiff and rector. Parishioners reported to the bishop a list of sexual and violent misdeeds, in addition to the rector's abuse of authority and mismanagement of parish funds. The fact that, over these seven years, the rector Bernat had taken the gifts that parishioners had provided for the ornamentation of the church and kept them for himself is at least one possible explanation for the parishioners' complaints. There were other scandals as well. The rector had allegedly tried to seduce the wife of a parishioner during confession, but she had refused to be kissed or "known" in any manner. Still, the rector's promiscuous behavior was nothing new to his parishioners. Earlier, he had been absolved for having an incestuous affair with a female relative, the daughter of the Lord Magre, with whom he had also fathered a child. Clearly, the sexual misbehavior of the rector did affect his reputation. Keeping a de facto wife was permissible, but accusations that he engaged in adultery and fornication meant that the rector lacked self-governance. The rector Bernat also had a history of violence. We know that he intimidated his parishioners with his "violent" capture of men. Indeed, Bernat senior and Bernat junior must have been threatening figures in their community because, when the rector slapped the parishioner Pere Langer in the face, Bernat junior "defended his father in such a manner that the said Pere did not dare to speak." Bernat junior was not a stranger to violence either; ten years had passed since he had wounded a questor from Santa Maria de Montserrat in the head. The rector, however, had more recently taken to assaulting female relatives. Not only had he beaten and wounded his own concubine Geralda, but he had also beaten the pregnant wife of his own son so severely that she had lost the child.[76]

Can we consider the rector Bernat Guad to be a typical parish priest? Bernat's position as a bailiff was forbidden by the Church but was, nevertheless, one of status, power, and authority in his community. Bernat's post as bailiff may not have been uncommon. His concubinous relationship, the training of his son, and his violent actions were not uncommon either. Even the rector's history of domestic violence was not unusual, although perhaps extreme in that his beating caused his daughter-in-law to miscarry a child. It was after all, his right as the paterfamilias to reprimand his family and, if necessary, to inflict punishment to maintain order in his household. The family was the cornerstone of patriarchy, and many medieval writers would have been in agreement that "moderate" violence was necessary to maintain control of

76. Ibid., 711. On both occasions, Bernat was absolved, although he was fined 30 sous by the Lord Guerau de Cervilion for wounding his concubine Geralda. The sacrist Berenguer Mir of Sant Martí Vell was also fined for beating the pregnant wife of a parishioner so severely that she miscarried; ADG, Remissions de Penes, no. 1, 37r. (1352).

one's family, especially in cases in which women challenged male authority.[77] In his roles as paterfamilias, bailiff, and priest, the rector's manhood could not be questioned. The example he set no doubt influenced his young protégé and reinforced the gender identity of younger clerics.

Thus, the training and socialization of clergy who worked and lived with senior clergy strengthened and fortified the masculine ideals that clerics had learned prior to their religious vocation. Tonsured boys and adolescent clerics were prepared for their profession by men who lived and defined themselves according to many of the precepts of lay masculinity; therefore, these apprentices would not have easily embraced the Church ideological standards of celibacy, nonviolence, and passivity. Nowhere is the indoctrination of a clerical gender identity more obvious than in the examples of priests and their sons. Trained and educated in an environment in which they witnessed and lived in a family setting and household and in which their fathers carried weapons and acted according to the secular ideals of honor, strength, agency, power, and domination, the sons of priests followed in their fathers' footsteps. As Michael Kimmel has observed, "the real power of gender typing resides less in the child than in the environments in which a child finds itself."[78] The setting in which priests' sons and scolares were taught to be clergymen was filled with gendered messages and gendered activities. The examples provided in this chapter illustrate how life experience and education could reinforce gender stereotypes in young tonsured children and imprint on them the importance of these gender characteristics.

Clerical participation in the Holy Week riots further indicates that mainstream clerical culture found violence acceptable and reveals an additional connection between violence and the professional and gender identity of clergy. Throughout the Crown of Aragon in Barcelona, Girona, Valencia, Zaragoza, Vilafranca del Penedès, Camarasa, Castellón, Pina, Besalú, Daroca, Alcoletge, Burriana, Apiera, and Teruel, Holy Week riots that attacked the Jewish community (*aljama*) of town were a long-held tradition and practice, dating from

---

77. Philippa Maddern, "Interpreting Silence: Domestic Violence in the King's Courts in East Anglia, 1422–1442," in *Domestic Violence in Medieval Texts*, ed. Eve Salisbury, Georgiana Danavin, and Merral Llewelyn Price (Gainesville: University Press of Florida, 2002), 31–56. See also the Eve Salisbury, Georgiana Danavin, and Merral Llewelyn Price, "Introduction," in *Domestic Violence in Medieval Texts*, ed. Eve Salisbury, Georgiana Danavin, and Merral Llewelyn Price, 1–27; Marilyn Migiel, "Domestic Violence in the Decameron," in *Domestic Violence in Medieval Texts*, 164–79. Migiel's article underscores how women who mistreated men or questioned their husband's authority received "just retaliation" in these stories. Not surprisingly, violence was used against women when they gained any power that threatened masculinity.

78. Kimmel, *Gendered Society*, 92.

at least the mid-thirteenth century if not earlier.[79] Although deaths due to the violence were uncommon, Jewish *aljamas* prepared for the riots by hiring guards, and royal officials were frequently ordered to protect the *call* (Jewish quarter) because the destruction of property and injuries to people were not unusual. The main participants in the riots were clerics, made up primarily of tonsured youths and scolares, as well as the servants of the clerics but also included beneficed clergy and canons. In *Communities of Violence*, David Nirenberg sees the confrontation between clergy and secular officials during Holy Week as a form of ritualized aggression. Clerics demonstrated their willingness to act violently by displaying their weapons, taking aggressive postures, and taunting officials with the threat of death. He notes that such confrontations had the potential to cause severe harm or death but that participants were typically restrained so that only minor injuries resulted.[80] Thus, in addition to reinforcing the religious divisions between Christians and Jews, Holy Week riots provided an opportunity for clergy to participate in a violent sport that showcased their boldness and audacity in front of their companions and community without getting seriously hurt. In addition, taking part in the riots was also a way for young clerics to prove their bravado to their religious peers and participate in a rite of passage that condoned violence and created a bond among clerics-in-training.

The attacks on the *call* were a ritual that began with clerics causing "a great commotion" and shouting insults at Jews while stoning the Jewish quarter. In Girona, tonsured youths congregated with their weapons or slingshots before the walls and gates of the *call*. The riot of 1331 began in this way when the bailiff and *sagiones* (police officials), following the king's orders to protect

---

79. The letters of King Pere III to the bishop of Girona and his officials recall that his father Jaume I (1213–1276) had once spent Good Friday in Girona and had taken up arms to defend his Jews from clerical attacks on the Jewish Quarter. During Pedro's own reign from 1276 to1285, he complained to the bishop of Girona on several occasions about the riots, especially in 1278 when the damage that clerics had done to Jewish property was widespread. A transcription of Pere III's letter can be found in D. Enrique Claudio Girbal, *Los judíos en Gerona. Colección de noticias históricas referentes a los de esta localidad, hasta la época de su espulsion de los dominios españoles* (Gerona, 1870), 70–71. The most extensive documented example in Girona stems from an investigation into the death of a young Christian boy who died during the stoning of the *call* on Good Friday in 1302; ADG, Processos, no. 20 (1302). Witnesses testified that the custom of stoning the *call* in Girona had been observed for anywhere from twenty to thirty-five years. David Nirenberg addresses the evidence of violent Easter rituals against Jews in the Mediterranean basin and finds that as early as 1018 attacks against Jews during Holy Week had taken place in southern France. His preliminary survey of royal documents finds at least fourteen towns in the Crown of Aragon where the riots were reported (because the violence had gotten out of hand and destroyed much property) or guards had been employed during Holy Week to protect the Jewish *call*. Nirenberg notes that "unless extensive damage occurred, people were injured, or Jewish communities asked for special protection, Good Friday riots were tolerated, and their mention omitted from chancery documentation." *Communities of Violence*, 203, 202–5.

80. Nirenberg, *Communities of Violence*, 210.

the Jews, attempted to disband and disarm the scolares, who ranged in age from ten to seventeen, along with twenty male servants of the canons who were stoning the call.[81] The tradition of clerics attacking the call was so popular that few had heeded the king's warning, announced on Holy Thursday by the bailiff of Girona, that anyone who injured or insulted Jews would be fined 100 sous.

The 1331 inquest into the riot reveals that the situation escalated when a number of clerics, led by canons of the cathedral, challenged the authority of royal officials attempting to disarm them. On Holy Thursday, when many young clerics had attacked the walls of the call with stones and had set fire to a gate, royal officials had simply patrolled the area throughout the day to ensure that the attack did not get out of hand and breach the walls or injure any Jews. Previous encounters with the clerics and children had ended simply with disbanding the troublemakers; many of the young boys had run away when they saw officials. It was not until the bailiff and his men encountered a group of clerics in front of the cathedral steps that things turned violent. The group, made up of mostly scolares and the servants of the canons, contained at least three men (homines) armed with swords. Guillem, the squire (scutiffer) of the cathedral chantor, was the leader of the group and was outfitted with a sword, helmet, and shield. When the bailiff confiscated Guillem's sword, another cleric threatened him with a sword to his chest while some brandished their swords and daggers and others threw stones and shouted insults at the officials. Surrounded, outnumbered, and threatened with the weapons of more than twenty angry clerics, the bailiff and his men, bearing some minor injuries, retreated.[82] Two officials sought sanctuary in the nearby home of a cleric of the cathedral chapter but were accosted by their attackers and threatened by two canons for disturbing their Holy Week tradition. The canon Vidal de Vilanova drew his sword and promised the officials, "we will give you so many stab wounds that it will be an evil day for you," but the abbot of Sant Feliu

---

81. ADG, Processos, no. 119, 2v.–3r. (1331). King Alfons ordered an investigation of the 1331 riots on account of the attacks on his officials who were stoned with rocks and attacked with swords while carrying out their orders to protect the call. Ferrer de Lillet and Ramon de Prat, officials of the king, carried out the inquest in June of 1331. A transcript of the inquest can be found in José M. Millás Vallicrosa and Luis Batlle Prats, "Un alboroto contra el call de Gerona en el año 1331," Sefarad 12 (1952), 297–335. Reports state that groups of clerics usually assembled near the religious buildings of Girona; this may have been because the Jewish call was surrounded on its northern and eastern sides by the cathedral, the bishop's palace, the Pia Almoina, and the archdeaconry of Girona. For a map of Girona during the fourteenth century, see J. Canal i Roquet, Eduard Canal i de Diego, J. M. Nolla i Brufau, and J. Sagrera i Aradilla, La ciutat de Girona en la primera meitat del segle XIV (Girona: Ajuntament de Girona, 1998).

82. ADG, Processos, no. 119, 2v.–3rv., 5v.–6r., 8v.–9r., 14r.v. (1331).

restrained the canon and allowed the officials to withdraw.[83] Later, when the
bailiff and his officials returned with reinforcements, they found the group,
joined by the previously mentioned two canons, fighting with their swords,
daggers, and rocks against the bailiff's men and screaming "kill them, kill
them." Two police officials were injured in the head, which caused the bailiff
to retreat temporarily and gave the clerics an opportunity to flee to the cemetery next to the cathedral. The clerics then proceeded to throw stones and
bricks at the officials while the canon Vidal taunted them: "to God you will
go *bacalars* (villains) because you will die." The bailiff and his men retreated
once again, sounded the alarm of *"via fors"* throughout the city, and sought
out the archdeacon of Raons to end the conflict.[84] The following day, on Good
Friday, many of the same young clerics returned to stone the *call*.

David Nirenberg attributes the clerical violence against Jews to clergy demonstrating their contempt for royal authority and for the Jews, who received
such royal protections. I believe that, in addition, the participation of clerics
in the Holy Week riots was about young boys and adolescents performing rituals of bravado to validate their manliness. By challenging the authority of
the bailiff and his officials, these youths used violence to bond with one another and asserted their manhood in a way that was tolerated, if not implicitly condoned, by senior church leaders. As youths, scolares and young tonsured
boys began the attacks by throwing rocks against the *call*; some would advance
to more daring deeds, as did the twelve-year-old tonsured son of a local vicar
and his two tonsured friends who set fire to the gate of the *call*. The activities
of this group were considered more of a nuisance than a serious threat. Officials never arrested any of the tonsured children or young clerics in the riot
of 1331, not even when they pulled pranks such as setting the gate on fire. Two
weeks before the riots began, when young boys, encouraged by the music of
a *juglar* (jongleur), had stoned a Jewish burial procession transporting a body
to Montjuïc, the bailiff had arrested the *juglar* and not the children. And, of
the group of clerics who broke into the synagogue of Besalú on the Monday
after Pentecost in 1345, only the tonsured cleric Jaume was fined, most likely
because he personally stole the Torah from the synagogue and had led the
group who perpetrated this crime.[85] Even when the fifteen-year-old tonsured
cleric Simó accidently killed Nicolau, a youth similarly participating in the
stone throwing at Jews, it was understood that these were the actions of adolescents participating in a game.[86] Yet the clerics who behaved most ag-

83. ADG, Processos, no. 119, 11v.–12r. (1331).
84. ADG, Processos, no. 119, 4r.v., 7v., 9r.v., 12r., 14r.v., 15v., 16r.v., 19v.–20r.v. (1331).
85. ADG, Remissions de Penes, no. 1, 4r. (1346).
86. ADG, Processos, no. 20 (c. 1300).

gressively and who openly confronted officials were older and fully armed, for example, Guillem, the squire (*scutiffer*) of the cathedral chantor and his two friends, the canons En Vidal and En Mont, and the beneficed cleric En Peralta.[87] Young tonsured boys who observed the most intrepid clerics threatening officials and displaying their weapons were very likely impressed by such behavior. This image of a combative cleric might have influenced future encounters with secular authorities. And, considering the examples of clergy who violently confronted secular officials, it is apparent that clerics were more than willing to defy and engage in clashes with secular authorities.[88]

The court documents reveal that ecclesiastical leaders knew that younger clergy were participating in the stoning of the *call* and intervened only when the violence got out of hand. Many of the attacks against the *call* took place before ecclesiastical buildings such as the cathedral, the bishop's court, and the archdeacon of Raos's home. During the first encounter with the older group of clerics, two police officials sought protection in the home of a cathedral cleric and encountered the abbot of Sant Feliu, who restrained the canons En Vidal and En Mont from attacking them. Later, after officials retreated from the cemetery, the bailiff and subvicar went to the home Jaspert Folcran, a chapter cleric, to deliberate about their next move and seek counsel while the magistrate (*veguer*) sought out the archdeacon of Raos. The archdeacon brokered an agreement with officials to withdraw from the cathedral and managed to diffuse the immediate situation. The attacks on the *call*, nevertheless, continued on Good Friday, but this time, only the young tonsured boys participated in the stoning. The continuation of the attack on the Jewish quarter indicates that the archdeacon saw the participation of young clerics as nothing more than a game.

Moreover, it does not appear that episcopal officials sought to control or punish clerics, or at least very little effort went into restraining clergy because secular officials were the ones who called on ecclesiastical officials to rein in their clerics. Previous riots show that the ecclesiastical hierarchy might have been reluctant to interfere with the clerics' tradition. When the clerics of Girona destroyed Jewish vineyards, orchards, and tombs during the Holy Week riots of 1278, King Pedro III complained to the bishop of Girona and questioned his failure to punish and castigate his clerics. The king reminded

87. ADG, Processos, no. 119, 13r. (1331). The bailiff and his men encountered the canons En Mont and En Vidal on at least three different occasions. While in pursuit of the fleeing armed clerics on the way to the cemetery, officials once again come across the canons En Mont and En Vidal, who were brandishing their swords and threatening them for entering the cathedral with their weapons.
88. See, for example: ADG, Processos, no. 73 (1323); ADG, Processos, no. 125 (1333); ADG, Processos, no. 134 (1334–1335); ADG, Processos, no. 275 (1354).

the bishop that he had on several occasions warned him not to permit his clerics such behavior. Rebuking the bishop for his contempt of "nostrae dominationis," he declared that "we are amazed why the above-said has continued to occur, and it appears that instead of punishing them, you have given your permission. . . ."[89] The bishop of Girona was not alone in his tolerance of the clerical activities that took place during Holy Week. In 1335, with his "knowledge and consent," the archdeacon of Lleida permitted the clerical members of his household to dig a secret tunnel into the Jewish *call* of Barcelona. Once inside the *call*, clerics began assaulting Jews, and looting and pilfering religious objects and business documents.[90] In this case, the secular authorities failed to respond to the riots because they believed it to be too dangerous. Similarly, in 1320 the bailiff of Girona could not muster help to protect the Jews in the *call* and was so frightened of the rioters that he wanted to abandon his office because of their death threats. Although the Holy Week riots were largely limited to tonsured children and teens, the mayhem could escalate to such a level of violence that authorities feared to act against clerics and other participants.

The Holy Week riots in the Crown of Aragon illustrate how violence functioned to both prove the masculinity of young clerics and display their professional identity as clergymen. Clergy who witnessed or joined in the ritualized violence against Jews could gain prestige and status, and in the process, they greatly influenced the gendered identities of young and impressionable boys. These youthful adventures also worked to forge a group identity among clerical youths. As Alexandra Shepard has noted in her study of young men performing rituals of bravado in early modern England, the fraternal bonding that occurred during group activities "validated claims to manliness and provided a large unacknowledged source of intimacy during this most homosocial phase of the life course."[91] That the link between older and younger clerics participating in the Holy Week riots functioned to bestow a male identity on these impressionable youths should not be underestimated. Although groups of tonsured youths were known to take part in the camaraderie of drinking and running about at night armed and causing mischief,[92] these activities were not the same as the Holy Week riots. The riots included the participation of clerics of all ages and were essentially sanctioned by the ecclesiastical authorities as a ritual that was part of the profession. This means that the clerical collec-

89. Claudio Girbal, *Judíos en Gerona*, 70.

90. Nirenberg, *Communities of Violence*, 213–14. A full transcript of this account is found in Nirenberg's *Violence and the Persecution of Minorities in the Crown of Aragon: Jews, Lepers and Muslims before the Black Death* (PhD diss., Princeton University, 1992), 355–58.

91. Shepard, *Meanings of Manhood*, 95. See also Karras, *From Boys to Men*, 95–98.

92. See, for example, ADG, Processos, no. 186 (1337); ADG, Processos, no. 30 (1319).

tive incorporated into their professional identity as clergymen the violence that took place and the attendant challenges to secular authority that went hand in hand with the rioting. The zealous involvement of clerics in this ritualized violence does not mean that all clerics had an excuse or an inclination to be violent but simply that they had learned and received the message that violence could be accepted and even celebrated in their profession. The violence of Holy Week was a part of the mainstream clerical culture in Catalunya and Aragon and is a sign that clerics believed that aggression was not only a tolerated and customary behavior among their profession but also a component of their clerical identity.

Conclusion

Clerics-in-training were not immune to their environments. In their everyday lives and in their surroundings as boys and young men, they witnessed a very distinct model of clerical masculinity. As these clerics progressed in age and through the orders, they too adopted this model, which entailed carrying weapons, resorting to violence to compete with and dominate other men, and establishing relationships with women. Few clerics had access to formal education. In most cases, senior clergy trained and educated lower-ranking clerics. Priests trained their sons, uncles trained their nephews, and senior clerics mentored the scolares and clerics-in-training in their parish church. In particular, the example of priests' sons who followed in their fathers' footsteps illustrates how priestly masculinity was inculcated from father to son. Because priestly fathers found ways to promote their sons into holy orders without obtaining a papal dispensation for *defectus natalium,* it seems likely that far more sons of priests entered into the priesthood than the registers of bishops indicate. Rather than employ another scolar or cleric, priests trained their own sons because it was the more economical option and had the added benefit of advertising their virility and paternity to the community. Clerical gender identity was formed during the years scolares spent serving at the altar with their father, uncle, or senior cleric, whose profession and masculine identity shaped their notion of what it meant to be a man in priestly robes. They witnessed and participated in a clerical culture in which establishing a household and family, and taking part in masculine culture was the norm, not an aberration.

Although violence is not typically associated with the priestly profession now, the sources reveal that it was a component of the medieval clerics' professional identity. Clerics-in-training were subjected to disciplinary violence as a form of correction. Examples of senior clergy using violent correction indicate that they did so to maintain their authority. Physical discipline served to uphold the hierarchy of age and rank in the parish church and taught younger clerics that violence could be wielded to safeguard their position.

The yearly participation of clerics, particularly the clerics-in-training, in the Holy Week riots further demonstrates that violence was incorporated into the clerical profession and was viewed as a sport that demonstrated manliness to religious peers. The stoning of the *call* was a ritual and a tradition—a game essentially—that trained young clerics to view aggression as a part of their profession. As a rite of passage, challenging secular authorities and partaking in aggressive behaviors were a platform for clerics to display their bravado and functioned to forge a group identity. The ritualized aggression of the Holy Week riots involved clerics from all levels of the ecclesiastical hierarchy, but it was a more meaningful exercise for clerical youths looking to prove their masculinity. Participation in a peer group that showed off acts of bravado played an important role in conferring membership in a brotherhood of clergy as well as validating these assertions of manliness. Episcopal officials implicitly condoned the participation of clerics in the riots and stepped in to negotiate with secular authorities only when the violence escalated, but in general, they were reluctant to interfere with this clerical tradition. As an institution of men, the Church and its officials had an interest in promoting and showing off their primacy in medieval society, and the clerics who rioted and challenged secular authority proved their special status in this way.

That episcopal officials tolerated the ritualized violence of Holy Week and disregarded the wishes of the king prohibiting clerics' participation in the riots would certainly appear contrary to the default position of the Church that clerics should not perpetrate violent deeds or act in contempt of royal authority. But the clerics, like most of human society, had received contradictory messages about the expected behaviors of their gender and profession, and each individual chose which messages to follow or reject. Just as the family and training of young *scolares* laid the foundation for the acquisition of gender identity, the Church itself was a gendered institution that influenced the socialization process because it created a homosocial environment in which power and privilege were embedded in its hierarchy. Young clerics and novice priests learned their professional and gendered behavior based on the demeanor and actions of these senior role models, who had incorporated lay ideals of honor, status, and revenge into their own gender identity.

CHAPTER 6

Hierarchy, Competition, and Conflict
The Parish as a Battleground

Competition for status, authority, and funds defined the relations among parish clergymen and often led to violent conflict. Violence was an effective and powerful tool used to prove a cleric's masculinity, and it was often deemed a necessary response when his honor and authority were threatened. Because the vast majority of secular clerics learned their profession from parish clergy, the parish became a battleground in which rivalries among clerics took place and in which young clerics learned from senior clergy how to establish their position in the church hierarchy. In this chapter, I argue that the violent acts of the clergy can be connected to their professional identity as clerics and their masculine identity. Dominating socially inferior laymen in the parish village was only one component of the gender identity of parish clergymen—carving out a status and privilege in the hierarchy of parish clergy to gain prestige and greater access to economic resources was another element. The parish clergy were not wielding swords in service to God in Catalunya; they were wielding swords as a means of demonstrating their manhood to their religious colleagues. Indeed, clerics followed the gendered behaviors they had learned during their training as clergymen: resorting to violence to define themselves as men and to establish their place among the parish clergy.

One core feature of medieval manhood that Ruth Karras has identified in her study of masculinity across different segments of male society was "the need to prove oneself in competition with other men and to dominate others."[1] Knights, university students, and craftworkers were trained from an early age to obtain their share of power and authority over other men, especially their peers. Clergymen were no different. They may not have had a training field, a university lecture room, or a workshop in which to compete and perform their masculinity, but clerics did have a church and a parish where they displayed their aggression and where the violent domination of others took place. Examples of violent conflict among parish clergy suggest that clerics, like laymen, resorted to violence to prove their manhood and did so to compete with or dominate their religious coworkers. An integral part of a cleric's gender identity included proving his masculine authority through violence, which often entailed competing and fighting with his religious colleagues to establish a clerical hierarchy in the parish that could be translated into economic gain. Given that violence can "guarantee both individual and social control, while maintaining and perpetuating hierarchy and inequality," parish clergy acted aggressively to protect their standing in the parish and to show that they had power over churchmen as well as laymen.[2] The conflicts that existed among clergymen were also part of what Daniel Lord Smail has labeled the "social institution of hatred"—an inimical public relationship between two adversaries that involved reputation, honor, and vengeance that often emerged between men of a similar status who were vying for social precedence. The social language of hatred was scripted and understood widely across the social spectrum of medieval society because "it was more or less [a] permanent feature of the landscape of social relations."[3] While aristocratic warriors and the nobility had the means and resources to engage in full-scale feuds and vendettas, the lower levels of society practiced a more diluted and inexpensive form of enmity that was made public to the community by means of frequent insults, threats, and aggressive acts.

Table 5.1 shows how frequently the conflict among priests serving in these benefices was reported in the diocesan parishes of Girona. Episcopal registers for the dioceses of Girona and Barcelona often deal with the quarrels and physical attacks between parish clergy. Although a significant number of clerics in the minor orders perpetrated these violent encounters, deacons, priests, and monks also appear with some frequency. Unfortunately, many of these episcopal letters do not always provide details about the issues that caused the

---

1. Karras, *From Boys to Men*, 10–11, 151. Karras's study shows that young boys in all three of her models proved their adult masculinity by testing themselves against other men and by using women as commodities or trophies when they competed with each other.

2. Hatty, *Masculinities, Violence, and Culture*, 10–11.

3. Smail, "Hatred as a Social Institution," 110.

dispute or why authorities investigated the matter. For example, in the parish of Aro from 1326 to 1332 episcopal authorities investigated the "crimes and excesses" committed by the clerics of the parish, which had to do with the conflict between the hebdomedarian Ramon de Miert, and the sacrist and two other priests serving in the village.[4] The root cause of the dispute, or what crimes were allegedly committed, are not always explained in the documents. In other cases, letters simply mention that one cleric physically injured another; for example, the priest Guillem Merconis, who while serving in the monastery of Sant Sebastià seriously injured a monk living in the same monastery.[5] Again, no other information is given about the reason behind an attack, but it seems more likely that the violent conflict was a product of personal animosity rather than a random act of violence. Although the motives behind the conflicts among clergymen are frustratingly opaque in episcopal registers (and thus have been excluded from table 5.1), they nevertheless reveal that clerical violence aimed at colleagues was not uncommon and suggest that the conflicts reported in visitation records do not fully represent the amount of physical violence and quarreling that took place among parish clergy.

The penalty for violent acts included a fine administered by episcopal authorities to receive a letter of absolution, or a couple of months spent in the bishop's jail on a diet of bread and water if the cleric did not have the means to pay the fine, in addition to a sum of money paid to the victim. Depending on the severity of the injury, such as a simple wound or a mutilation (the most common was the loss of fingers or a hand during a sword fight), the fine could range anywhere from 20 to 200 sous. In cases of accidental death or homicide, exile, a number of years confined in the bishop's jail or a staggering fine of 500 sous or more could be administered, but such cases occurred infrequently. Throughout the fourteenth century, very few clerics traveled to the papal court to obtain a dispensation for killing or attacking a religious colleague.[6] The

4. ADG, Lletres, no. 2 bis, 12v.–13r., 25v.–26r. (1326); Lletres, no. 5, 51r. (1332).

5. See, for example, ADB, Registrum Communium, no. 3, 86v. (1316). Some examples of conflicts between clergy recorded in a survey of the Barcelona episcopal registers are ADB, Registrum Communium, no. 1, 4v. (1311); ADB, Registrum Communium, no. 2, 69v. (1315); ADB, Registrum Communium, no. 3, 23r. (1314), and 143r., 150r. (1319); ADB, Registrum Communium, no. 4, 136v., 159r. (1327); and 163v., 165v. (1328); ADB, Registrum Communium, no. 9, 14v. (1339); ADB, Registrum Communium, no. 12, 38v.–40r. (1343). See also Baucells i Reig, *Vivir en la edad media*, 3: 2430–40; Hillgarth and Silano, *Register "Notule Communium,"* 38, 46, 47, 65, 69, 95, 96, 137. For the diocese of Girona, see ADG, Notularum, no. 4, 123v. (1324); ADG, Notularum, no. 13, 179r.v. (1339); ADG, Lletres, no. 2, 84r., 98r., 166r.v. (1326); ADG, Lletres, no. 6, 30v. (1337?) and 145v., 178r. (1343); ADG, Lletres, no. 7, 58r. (1341); ADG, Lletres, no. 8, 12v.–13r., 117r. (1344).

6. See the clergymen fined and absolved in ADG, Imposicions de Penes, no. 1 (1335–1363); ADG, Obligacions de Penes, no. 1 (1336–1388); ADG, Remissions de Penes, no. 1 (1345–1367); ADG, Lletres, no. 2, 84r., 107v., 166r. (1326); ADG, Lletres, no. 6, 14v.–15r. (1335) and 52r. (1338); ADG, Lletres, no. 7, 40r.v. (1340); ADG, Notularum, no. 18, 134r. (1346). Very few papal dispensations appear in

majority of violence between religious colleagues did not result in death; it was limited to slaps and punches associated with an exchange of injurious words and sword fights that sometimes resulted in serious injuries. In most cases reported in the visitation records, the conflict between colleagues started out as verbal insults, threats, and displays of weaponry that eventually escalated to brawling and sometimes to the clashing of swords. The purpose of displaying such physical aggression and bravado, it seems, was a performative act that announced each cleric's willingness to defend his position, honor, and perceived rights to privileges associated with his benefice. As Scott Taylor has emphasized in his study of aggressive male sociability and violent confrontations among Castilian men, men chose to make their conflict a public performance to announce that they were capable of defending themselves, their family, and reputation, and equally important, they wanted to show that their opponent was weak.[7] The point of clerical aggression between colleagues, then, was to force a rival to accept a passive or subordinate role, which also worked to effeminize one's opponent.

In the parishes of late medieval Catalunya, hatred for one's colleague typically emerged among clerical peers competing for primacy and authority in the church. Consider the history of animosity between the sacrist and hebdomedarian of Sant Julià d'Ordis. For more than six years, from 1329 to 1346, the friction between the two men had resulted in frequent verbal disputes and fist fights, both "inside and outside the church and principally and especially while the divine office is celebrated . . . and in the presence of many people in the church."[8] The sacrist's actions indicate that he was intent on keeping his command of the church. On one occasion, he beat the hebdomedarian so "atrociously" that he bled inside the church because, according to the hebdomedarian, the sacrist was angry that he had allowed scolares to destroy several books that were in his possession.[9] On a separate occasion, the sacrist took the opportunity to retaliate against the hebdomedarian, who had employed a substitute to celebrate the mass during the week of Pentecost. During high mass before the community of parishioners and fellow clerics, the sacrist interrupted the priest's reading from the gospels, seized his book, and told him that "he should not read the gospel on the right side of the altar, but on the left side." Obviously, this was not a gross error on the priest's part. It

the bishop's registers for the diocese of Girona; for example, see ADG, Notularum, no. 13, 176v.–181r. (1339). See the various clerics detained in the bishop's jail in Girona for their crimes in ADG, Lletres, no. 6, 27r.v.–39r. (1337). See also Baucells i Reig, *Vivir en la edad media*, 3: 2440–44, 2455–57.

7. Taylor, *Honor and Violence*, 152–54.

8. ADG, Visites, no. 8, 47r. (1346).

9. ADG, Visites, no. 6, 25v. (1338).

was, however, an effective strategy to embarrass the substitute priest. Not only did the sacrist assert his authority in public, but his actions also implied a criticism of the hebdomedarian's choice of a substitute. Hearing what had transpired, an angry hebdomedarian confronted the sacrist for his behavior. What followed was an exchange of insults and threats that involved the family and friends of both parties, including the hebdomedarian's nephew, who subsequently wounded the sacrist.[10]

Colleagues from the parish of Ordis testified that the arguments and fights between the sacrist and hebdomedarian were so disruptive that "many times they had to abandon their recitation of the office and take off their surplices and leave the church since they were not able to say anything on account of the words and reproaches between them." Interestingly, the other clerics blamed the sacrist, stating that "the hebdomedarian always or for the greater part has words and fights with the sacrist when requesting his rights in the church which the sacrist refuses him."[11] Disputes between sacrists and hebdomedarians were common.[12] Both offices were at the top of the ecclesiastical hierarchy in small parish churches. There was little distinction between the two benefices because either benefice could hold the care of souls, and this fostered an aggressive environment because humiliating one's subordinate worked to maintain the pecking order and preserve authority. Both men had served together in the parish of Ordis for more than twenty years, which meant they were long-time rivals in the competition for influence and status in the parish church. Humiliation seems to have been a key factor in how adversaries competed to dominate and degrade their opponents. In this vein, disrupting the mass was one way in which clerics chose to embarrass their colleagues. Take, for example, the hebdomedarian Jaume Tarascó, who harassed the hebdomedarian Jaume Pastor by shouting and causing a great commotion while the hebdomedarian Pastor celebrated the mass in the church of Sant Feliu de Lledó.[13] Such behavior worked to undermine the authority of the priest who was saying mass and was a way to show disrespect for one's adversary. Because the parish church of Sant Feliu de Lledó was large enough to need two hebdomedarians and a sacrist, the hebdomedarian Jaume Tarascó was competing against his colleagues for prestige and influence in the parish, which may be the reason he was reported to ecclesiastical officials for "inciting" the people

---

10. ADG, Visites, no. 8, 47v. (1346). It is unclear how the nephew wounded the sacrist, but the visitation record states that episcopal officials were investigating the confrontation between the two parties.

11. ADG, Visites, no. 8, 49r.v. (1346).

12. See the examples in table 5.1.

13. ADG, Processos, no. 104 (1329).

of the parish against the hebdomedarian Pastor and the sacrist. Twenty years later, the competition between the two priests holding the benefice of hebdomedarian continued in the church of Sant Feliu de Lledó when hebdomedarian Jaume Gorner was fined for fighting with the hebdomedarian Berenguer Rider and the sacrist Guillem Clar.[14]

Provoking and demeaning one's coworkers was a convenient strategy in the social institution of hatred to diminish the honor and status of an enemy and rival. Hiding the key to the church, as the sacrist from the parish of Sant Vicenç de Maià did when he locked the scolares Guillem and Pere inside the church (see Chapter Five), was one popular way to goad and humble an opponent. Similarly, in the parish of Mieres in 1331, the deacon Ramon de Corbs and the hebdomedarian Guillem Báscara also fought over the key to the parish church. The deacon Ramon explained that the quarrel began when the sacrist entrusted him with the key during his absence from the parish and specified that he should protect the key "so that the said church should not be opened for anyone." When the hebdomedarian Guillem Báscara then asked the deacon Ramon for the key "to say matins and celebrate the mass," Ramon refused, claiming that, unless there was a dangerous situation in which Guillem had to baptize or perform another necessary sacrament immediately, he could not hand over the key.[15] The fact that the sacrist left the deacon Ramon in charge of the key, and not the hebdomedarian Guillem, is telling. The sacrist, who held the care of souls, had handed over control of the parish church to hebdomedarian's subordinate and created a situation in which the hebdomedarian was humiliated both by having to ask for and being denied the key. The sacrist knew very well that Ramon would have to allow the hebdomedarian Guillem access to the church if an emergency arose. The situation was meant to provoke the hebdomedarian and also worked to create tensions between the deacon and hebdomedarian.

In his testimony, the deacon Ramon admitted that the hebdomedarian Guillem resented him because "he had not brought the key when he wished it." The animosity intensified when Guillem found the deacon throwing rocks at his dog. Our understanding of this event is unfortunately one-sided because the deacon's statements are the only ones preserved in the records. In his statement, the deacon Ramon recounts the events that had led to a sword fight. Around midnight, the deacon left his home barefoot and half-clothed for the reason of "walking about and scattering water," when he saw a dog standing by the belfry of the church of Sant Pere de Mieres. He threw a rock at it and

14. ADG, Remissions de Penes, no. 1, 47r.v. (1353).
15. ADG, Processos, no. 122, 3v.–4r. (1331).

followed the dog as it fled toward the church, where he encountered the heb-domedarian Guillem, who became angry with the deacon for harassing his dog. The hebdomedarian Guillem told the deacon to leave and threatened that "an evil adventure will come your way." More harsh words were exchanged, and Guillem drew his sword. Ramon, unarmed, had started back to his own house when the hebdomedarian Guillem threw a rock at him. A fight ensued, with both men "throwing many rocks at each other," and the deacon Ramon, meanwhile, called to his young nephew, who was in his home, to bring out his sword. After both men were armed with swords, they fought until their neighbors intervened and separated them.[16]

Once again, the confrontation between the deacon Ramon and the heb-domedarian Guillem was not a lethal one and consisted mostly of threaten-ing behavior and words. The very fact that hebdomedarian waited to use his sword against the deacon Ramon until Ramon had obtained his own sword indicates that Guillem was more interested in displaying his aggression than in taking advantage of the deacon's vulnerability when he was unarmed. Per-haps Guillem was trying to take back the control he had lost when the sacrist gave his subordinate, the deacon Ramon, the key to the church. Nonetheless, episcopal officials charged the deacon Ramon, and not the hebdomedarian Guillem, with instigating the violence. That the deacon was found culpable suggests that the episcopal authorities believed the hebdomedarian should have access to the parish church at all times and had a right to defend his position.[17] Officials, however, overlooked the actions of the sacrist, who was partly responsible for creating the clash between the deacon and hebdome-darian. What is more, the fact that Ramon held the benefice of a deacon but was, in actuality, a priest who could not obtain a priestly benefice probably fueled his resentment of and competition with the hebdomedarian.[18] Both

---

16. ADG, Processos, no. 122, 2r.v (1331). This was not the first time that the hebdomedarian Guillem had been involved in violent conflict. A letter registered in the episcopal registers notes an inquest into injuries suffered by the hebdomedarian, allegedly perpetrated by the monk Arnau de Torroella; ADG, Notularum, no. 4, 123v. (1324).

17. ADG, Processos, no. 122, 1r.v (1331). The charges leveled against the deacon Ramon included drawing his sword with the intent of striking Guillem; impeding the hebdomedarian's office; refusing to bring the key to the church; having a carnal affair with the wife of en Planela; engaging in usury; being a quarrelsome man; and blaspheming God, the Virgin Mary, and the saints. It is likely that the hebdomedarian Guillem's accusations provided the added charges of concubinage, usury, and blas-phemy; it was not unusual for adversaries in legal cases to expose the unrelated transgressions of their opponents. As in most cases of clerical misconduct brought before church courts, the officials in this case tried to indict the deacon Ramon on as many charges as possible in the hopes that some of them would stand. Regrettably, the documents reveal nothing further about the added charges.

18. In 1324 and 1326, Ramon de Corbs was given permission to serve, with the responsibility of exercising the care of souls, for the sickly Bernat de Puig in the parish of Sant Martí de Campmaior; ADG, Lletres, no. 2, 107r.v. (1326); ADG, Notularum, no. 4, 124r. (1324). In 1327, however, Ramon

men were priests, but the hebdomedarian held a higher office and could exercise greater authority.

The number of priests who could not find priestly benefices in the dioceses of Barcelona and Girona appears to be significant and a phenomenon that was less present in the more rural Pyrenean dioceses such as Urgell and Vic, where it was not unusual to find only one priest assigned to remote churches.[19] The parishes in Urgell and Vic were smaller and more impoverished, and the income from these benefices was quite small, which is why many of these parishes supported only one priest, a rector, and sometimes a vicar rather than the three or more priests—the sacrist, hebdomedarian, and stabilitus—found in the more populated dioceses of Barcelona and Girona. And, particularly in the early 1330s, during the years of the famine and economic hardship, several physical conflicts are reported in the records (see table 5.1). The overabundance of priests seeking priestly benefices and competing for more lucrative benefices, status, and influence in the parish created a competitive, even aggressive, environment in which priests fought for supremacy among their religious colleagues. In Mieres, where the sacrist, who held the care of souls, was frequently absent because he continued to serve in the parish of Sant Martí de Sacosta in Girona (his appointed substitute did not last more than a year in the parish), the hebdomedarian and deacon were left to fight for primacy in the parish. In parishes where clerical infighting appears, the conflict was typically among priests who held the benefices of sacrist and hebdomedarian, but in Mieres, the absence of the sacrist resulted in the protracted rivalry between the hebdomedarian and deacon.

The competition for rank and status in the clerical hierarchy of the parish of Mieres lasted a few more years until the hebdomedarian left the parish and eventually renounced his benefice for another in 1334, because of, according

---

was prohibited from serving in Campmaior on account of certain "excesses" that episcopal officials had found him guilty of during his time in the parish; ADG, Lletres, no. 2, 72r. (1327). The letter does not specify what "excesses" the deacon had committed, but they most likely had to do with the conflict he had with the Bernat de Puig, a cleric serving in the parish of Sant Martí de Campmaior; ADG, Lletres, no. 2, 107r. (1326).

19. In her study of the Barcelona diocesan records, Kristine Utterback notes that "the large numbers of ordinations contained in the visitation and ordination registers supports the idea that there were many unbeneficed clergy in Barcelona during the fourteenth century." *Pastoral Care*, 139–40. There are also numerous examples of priestly violence against fellow tonsured clerics, priests, and monks in the Barcelona Registra Communium, but most omit the reason the clerics were fighting; examples are ADB, Registrum Communium, no. 2, 69v. (1315); Registrum Communium, no. 3, 4r., 23r. (1314), 143r. (1316), and 150r. (1319); Registrum Communium, no. 4, 123r., 136v., 153r., 159r., 163v. (1327); Registrum Communium, no. 7, 128r. (1337); Registrum Communium, no. 8, 19r. (1338); Registrum Communium, no. 8, 36r. (1338); Registrum Communium, no. 9, 14v. (1339), 126v. (1340), and 182v. (1341).

the bishop's letter, the animosity of parishioners.[20] The deacon left Mieres in 1339 because he had finally obtained the benefice of hebdomedarian in the parish of Sant Martí de Cabissó.[21] That the hebdomedarian Guillem felt it necessary to leave the parish suggests that the infighting had created tensions with parishioners to the point that he felt threatened, and he had requested a leave of absence from the parish until he could transfer to another benefice. The competition between parish clergy, however, was nothing new to the parishioners of Mieres. Prior to the assignment of the hebdomedarian Guillem and the deacon Ramon to their parish, they had lived with discord between the previous sacrist and hebdomedarian for at least ten years. Parishioners had reported in visitations to Mieres in 1315 and again in 1321 that the sacrist Joan Ferrar and the hebdomedarian Arnau Rovira fought frequently. Indeed, they complained that every single day the sacrist and hebdomedarian "say such nasty words, one towards the other, in the church and outside the church and before the people, that common women do not say such shameful things like they do." Parishioners begged the visitor to the parish, "for the love of God," to make peace between the sacrist and the hebdomedarian.[22] The people of the parish emphasized that the hebdomedarian Arnau had a temper, but they also pointed out that one of the reasons for the discord between the two men had to do with the divine office. The hebdomedarian rose very early in the morning to plough his fields and was in the habit of saying the divine office before taking care of his land. The sacrist, however, did not like to perform the divine office that early in the morning because his home was far from the church and he reportedly could not arrive in time to join the hebdomedarian.

Although personal animosity seems to have played a role in the tensions that existed between the two clerics, this example underscores how a disagreement over carrying out clerical duties could lead to conflict. Parish clergy had to work together to discharge many of their duties. The time to perform the divine office became a clash of wills because neither cleric wanted to compromise, which in the end meant that these priests no longer worked together but performed their office separately. This was the case in the church of Sant Genís de Toroella de Montgrí, where in 1329 the sacrist Guillem claimed that two stabiliti priests, Pere Pich and Pere Sagio, frequently disturbed the divine office with their antics or refused to participate with their coworkers. Twelve years later in 1341, the sacrist Guillem once again complained about the same

---

20. ADG, Lletres, no. 5, 96r. (1333) and 155r. (1334).
21. ADG, Lletres, no. 7, 10r. (1339).
22. ADG, Visites, no. 3, 46r.v. (1321). See also ADG, Visites, no. 1, 55v.–56r. (1315). The sacrist Joan Ferrer resigned his benefice in 1326 and died in 1328.

priests and their attempts to spoil the solemnity of the office.[23] Other clerics managed to carry out the divine office together but made it such a contentious affair that the office deteriorated into a battle of words. In the parish of Llanars, the verbal insults between the hebdomedarian Bernat des Puyol and the deacon Guillem de Brugada had become such a problem when the two worked together that the visitor imposed a fine of 10 sous on each cleric if they continued insulting each other.[24] Cooperation and accommodation may not have been viewed as a trait that bolstered the assertion of priestly masculinity, particularly in a context in which colleagues were vying for control of the church.

Uncooperative colleagues were also a byproduct of a competitive environment, and visitations afforded clerics an opportunity to expose the bad behavior of their fellow coworkers, in the hopes, perhaps, of causing trouble for their colleagues. It was not unusual for parish clerics to complain to a visitor that a coworker was frequently absent from the parish, did not diligently perform his duties, blasphemed and gambled, and committed any number of offenses. Others objected to the professional standards of their colleagues; for example, the sacrist of Santa Creu de Rodes told the visitor that the hebdomedarian was "thoroughly ignorant" and did not know how to manage the care of souls in the parish.[25] In the parish of Darnius, the cleric Ramon Salera reported that the sacrist was a drunk, was known to beat his mother, and was so ignorant that he did not know when to sign the cross during mass.[26] Parish clergy in the village of Cadaqués described their coworker, the chaplain Arnau Ferrer, as woefully lacking in the skills of preaching because he preached "many things that should not be said." In addition, they complained that the chaplain drank in the church, ate in the cemetery, frequently disturbed the office because he was drunk, and prohibited other clerics from singing the mass on Sundays and feast days.[27] Denouncing a coworker to the visitor could result in his punishment and could have a serious economic impact on his finances. When the hebdomedarian of Tordera reported that the sacrist failed to provide the oil for the lamps and light the lamps for the evening service, the visitor imposed a fine of 50 sous on the sacrist. The hebdomedarian Bernat of

---

23. ADG, Visites, no. 4, 20v.–21r. (1329); ADG, Visites, no. 7, 85r. (1341).

24. ADG, Visites, no. 4, 139r.v. (1329).

25. ADG, Visites, no. 4, 35v. (1329). For other examples, see ADG, Visites fragmentaris, 5v.–6r. (1323); ADG, Visites, no. 3, 5r. (1321); ADG, Visites, no. 4, 7r., 14v., 16v.–17r., 30v., 49v., 69v.–71r.v., 88r., 104r., 106r.v., 166r.v. (1329); ADG, Visites, no. 8, 88r.v. (1346).

26. ADG, Visites, no. 3, 9v.–10r.v. (1321). In the church of Toroella de Montgrí, the hebdomedarian Bartomeu Cabater described his fellow priest, Bartomeu de Toro, as "greatly ignorant"; ADG, Visites, no. 8, 79r. (1346).

27. ADG, Visites, no. 3, 17r.v.–18r.v. (1321).

Vilajuïga was fined 30 sous during a visitation when the sacrist revealed to the visitor that Bernat was frequently absent from the parish and had not celebrated Sunday mass.[28]

The many complaints made by colleagues may have been true, exaggerations, or spiteful attempts to retaliate against a fellow cleric; they reveal, nonetheless, the inherent tensions in a hierarchical system that fostered competition among parish clergy. Moreover, by criticizing their colleagues, these clerics gave the appearance that they upheld the standards of their profession and that, by comparison, their fellow priests were incompetent. Even if the conflict in these situations did not escalate to the point of physical violence, parish clerics frequently clashed, snitched on one another, and found creative ways to provoke their coworkers.

The lack of cooperation among coworkers and an attempt to sabotage a colleague can be seen in the parish of Sant Medir near Cartellà, where the sacrist Arnau de Llor and the hebdomedarian Bernat de Brugeria fought over the key to the church and a missal. The sacrist refused to hand over the key to the hebdomedarian when he failed to show up for vespers. Instead of participating in the evening service, the hebdomedarian had remained in the cemetery to speak with some women, which had angered the sacrist. The subsequent violent exchange over the key took place at the sacrist's house before his scolar and pedisseca, as well as a neighbor, and resulted in a minor injury to the sacrist. To the episcopal official, the hebdomedarian painted the sacrist's behavior as petty and unreasonable. The hebdomedarian craftily defended his decision not to join the sacrist for vespers by impugning the sacrist's character. He told the visitor that the sacrist had been in a foul mood that day because the sacrist's son had been arrested by officials of the secular court for giving false testimony and for threatening his enemy, thereby implying that neither the word of the son nor the father could be trusted. As with many of the reported conflict-ridden relationships between parish clergy, the dispute over the key was one event among many that had a created deep animosity between religious colleagues. Parishioners reported that both priests quarreled inside and outside the church, said "dishonest words" to each other, and were a "bad example" to the community. During his inquiry into the conflict between these colleagues, the episcopal visitor heard from the sacrist that, a year before, the hebdomedarian had in "contempt" of the sacrist plotted to impede the mass for and burial of a family friend. The hebdomedarian had "abstracted" and "absconded" the missal on the day the funeral mass was to be held and prevented the sacrist and various other clerics from the community from celebrating

---

28. ADG, Visites, no. 4, 85v.–86r. (1329); ADG, Visites, no. 4, 38r.v. (1329).

the mass until the book was returned.[29] Although the hebdomedarian admitted to this deed, he charged that the sacrist made money by selling candles from the wax that parishioners donated to the church. Indeed, according to parishioners, the hebdomedarian had gone out of his way to discourage parishioners from making their offerings and, to the sacrist's ire, told them the wax was not used for the church but only to enrich the sacrist. The hebdomedarian wanted to discredit the sacrist before the parishioners, perhaps in hope that they would seek out his services rather than his colleague's for baptisms, marriages, and burials. Both men held the care of souls, so the competition between the hebdomedarian and sacrist most likely stemmed from vying for prestige, authority, and influence in the parish than from their positions in the parish church hierarchy. Fighting over the key and hiding the missal were acts meant to aggravate a colleague, but the men also competed over the financial resources available to them through their ecclesiastical office.

Parish clergy regularly quarreled over the control of church affairs and acted shrewdly to protect their interests and purse. This was certainly the case with the previously mentioned sacrist in the church of Sant Julià d'Ordis, who frequently fought with the hebdomedarian over precedence in the church. His parishioners and colleagues reported to the visitor in 1346 that a public document had been drawn up that outlined the duties of the sacrist "in the church or for the 'work' of the church." It was the responsibility of the sacrist to provide the wine, candles, and hosts to his fellow clerics, but he had refused to do so for some time. The clerics complained that, "when the mass for anniversaries or other masses are celebrated in the church, the sacrist does not want to provide candles to the beneficed clerics as he should." The deacon had given the document to the sacrist at the latter's request, but the sacrist denied having any knowledge of such a document and even swore before the bishop's official that he did not have the document in his possession. Providing wine, candles, and hosts were expenses that came out of the sacrist's own purse and the motive to "lose or conceal" the document was, in part, an economic one.[30] The official, however, sided with the deacon and excommunicated the sacrist for failing to produce it. Without a document, parishioners would have had a hard time proving what exactly the sacrist was responsible for supplying. Parishioners protested to the visitor that, although the sacrist was required to do so, he no longer provided candles at the altars for the important liturgical

---

29. ADG, Visites, no. 8, 61v. (1346).

30. ADG, Visites, no. 8, 49v.–50r.v. (1346). Parishioners even testified that the document "fuit perditum seu absconditum per sacrista." For another example of a dispute about what clerics were responsible for providing items based on the benefice they held, see Hillgarth and Silano, *Register "Notule Communium,"* no. 49, 38.

feasts such as Christmas, Easter, Pentecost, and All Saints.[31] Conflicts over supplying wine, candles, oil, and hosts affected not only the relationship among parish clergy, who complained they could not perform their duties correctly,[32] but also parishioners, who believed such negligent clerics had failed to serve their parish church properly.

The bad harvests of the early 1330s that resulted in famine and economic depression, combined with the insufficient income from benefices, clearly contributed to the clashes among parish clergy. Given that a good number of parishes in the diocese of Girona and Barcelona supported three to six clergy in the major orders, clerics competed with one another at the parish level to augment their income. Reports that parish clergy charged for the sacraments; stole from their neighbors; skimped on providing wax, oil, and wine; and neglected the maintenance of the church increased during this economic crisis. Although clergy were strictly forbidden to charge for the administration of the sacraments, they still received customary gifts from the laity when they officiated at baptisms, marriages, and funerals. These monetary gifts could range from 12 denarios for burying a child to 1 sous for burying an adult to 12 sous for performing the office of the dead to 20 sous for celebrating an anniversary mass.[33] Parish clergy vied with one another to receive the customary gifts bestowed by the laity, and they sought to undermine the authority of their competitors. The economic crisis aggravated the tensions among clerics in the hierarchy of the parish, and the clergy acted to protect what little they could gain from their office and the laity, even if it meant stinting on the religious necessities of the community.

Disputes over economic resources often involved several clerics serving in the parish church and sometimes resulted in violent confrontations. In Madremanya, parishioners reported that there were frequent fights among the hebdomedarian, sacrist, and deacon concerning how the offerings made by parishioners for baptisms and feast days were to be divided among them. The fighting had escalated to such an extent that the clerics had drawn their

---

31. In a visitation to the parish in 1338, parishioners had complained about the sacrist's failure to provide oil for the lamps, and in 1346, they complained that he also failed to provide candles for the altars in the church; ADG, Visites, no. 6, 25r. (1338). In another example, the clergy in Santa Maria de Pineda del Mar reported having issues with the sacrist Berenguer Martorell; he was supposed to provide all the priests who celebrated the mass with hosts, but the sacrist refused to give them hosts or provided them with defective ones. Due to the lack of hosts, the clerics complained that they could not celebrate the mass on a daily basis; ADG, Visites, no. 4, 83r. (1329).

32. ADG, Visites, no. 3, 26r.v. (1321); ADG, Visites fragmentaris, 22v.–25r. (1323); ADG, Visites, no. 3, 16r. (1321).

33. Baucells i Reig, *Vivir en la edad media*, 1: 59. The rector of Calders received one chicken for every burial service he performed; Martí Bonet, "Visitas pastorales," 698.

swords.[34] In another example, the sacrist of Garrigàs's decision to sell the wax that parishioners had donated to the church for his own profit contributed greatly to his animosity with the hebdomedarian and stabilitus. It did not help the situation when the sacrist refused to celebrate a mass for the dead with his colleagues because, according to parishioners, he wanted the money for the mass all to himself. The situation deteriorated to such an extent that the sacrist and hebdomedarian came to blows with their swords in the church after exchanging insults.[35] Both parishioners and lower-level priests complained of the monopoly that rectors tried to impose; for example, the rector of Sant Esteve de Vilanova prevented other priests from celebrating mass in the church chapel. According to parishioners, the rector charged 12 denarios, but the other priests charged 6 denarios.[36] In the parish of Cadaques along the Costa Brava, the chaplain Arnau Ferrar prohibited the other two clerics in his parish from singing the mass on Sundays and feast days so that he alone collected the alms, and he was also accused of pocketing other offerings made to the church. In addition, this chaplain was known to eject Dominicans from the parish, presumably because he did not want parishioners giving alms to mendicants that he could have received.[37]

The competition for alms extended to mendicant friars who traveled from parish to parish preaching and hearing confessions. Some parish priests refused to offer hospitality to traveling mendicants as a way of making it known that they were not welcome in the parish, but others were more forceful in driving them out of the village.[38] Ecclesiastical officials were aware of this tension between the parish clergy and friars. For example, the bishop of Girona granted the sacristans in the important town of Castelló d'Empúries the right to prohibit the friars of the Order of Merced from hearing confessions and receiving offerings from the laity for celebrating the mass and preaching sermons because of the "great financial loss and prejudice" to the rights of clergy

---

34. ADG, Visites, no. 8, 2r.v. (1345). See also ADG, Visites, no. 6, 96v.–97r. (1340). In another example, the priest Pere de Alda and the rector of Santa Maria de Caldes de Montbui fought over the mass and the administration of last rites. The fighting was so bad that the archdeacon had imposed a fine of 2,000 sous on the priest Pere de Alda for fighting and provoking rebellion in the parish; ADB, Registra Communium, no. 4, 161v. (1328).

35. ADG, Visites, no. 7, 143r., 147r., 148r., 150v.–151r. (1343).

36. ADB, Visites, no. 2, 27v. (1313). The rector also reportedly wanted 1 denarius for the wine to celebrate the mass for the dead.

37. ADG, Visites, no. 3, 18v.–19r.v. (1321).

38. Examples are ADG, Visites, no 3, 19r. (1321); ADG, Visites, no. 4, 88r. (1329); ADG, Visites, no. 6, 18v.–19r. (1338) and 44v.–45r.v. (1339); ADB, Visites, no. 5, 66r. (1342); Martí Bonet, "Visitas pastorales," 697; ACT, Llibres de Visites Pastorals, loose quarderno, letter (1337).

serving in the church.[39] The bishop of Barcelona also protected the clergy of Vilafranca by excommunicating parishioners of the church who sought out Franciscans for the act of confession or for offering oblations to the Franciscans.[40] Jill Webster, in her study of Franciscans in medieval Catalonia, has noted the "bitter animosity" between the friars and secular clergy, which often became violent, particularly in the fourteenth century when economic conditions deteriorated. The friars competed with the clergy for the alms given and fees due when hearing confessions, conducting marriages, and burying the dead.[41] Webster also reports attacks on friars by "incensed" secular clerics who resented the friars for the loss of income that resulted from, as the clerics claimed, the "infringement of their territory."[42]

The conflict between three clerics from the monastery of Sant Miquel de Fluviá further illustrates how clerical colleagues competed over status and economic gain. Revenge in this case motivated the attack on the priest Llorenç Lluqués by his colleagues, Nicolau Rei and en Perot Battle. During Lent in 1330, Llorenç Lluqués was promoted to the position of chanter for the monastery and also received the charge of the scolares of the monastery. His promotion came at the expense of Nicolau Rei, his colleague, who at the insistence of the archbishop's official visiting the monastery, was ordered to disband the school and send away the students under his care. Nicolau blamed Llorenç for his dismissal, believing his friend en Perot's claim that Llorenç had organized a group of parishioners and associates from the parish and monastery of Sant Miquel to plead his case before the bishop's official and steal his students.[43] Earlier that year, Llorenç had made an enemy of en Perot, too. Around Easter, several clerics and monks from the monastery traveled to Girona to the house of the cathedral canon Bernat Latu to pay their tithe to the bishop. During the course of their interaction, it was revealed that Perot Battle had not sent his portion of the payment. The canon Bernat was displeased because en Perot had also failed to pay his tithe the year before and had been excommunicated. Llorenç then informed the canon that en Perot, knowing that he had been excommunicated, had nevertheless allowed himself to be promoted to major orders and the priesthood. The canon Bernat subsequently proclaimed en Perot's ordination invalid, and it is

39. ADG, Lletres, no. 7, 45r. (1340). See also ADG, Visites, no. 7, 86v. (1343); Utterback, *Pastoral Care*, 114–15.

40. ADB, Registrum Communium, no. 13, 75v.–76r., 76r.v., 77r. (1345).

41. Webster, *Els Menorets*, 101, 150–52, 162–64, 171.

42. Ibid., 183–84.

43. ADG, Processos, no. 111, 8r.v., 17v.–18r. (1330). The chamberlain of the monastery also stated that before the attack there were hatred and injurious words between the men because Llorenç was now directing the school.

clear from the documents that en Perot held Llorenç responsible for revealing his ruse.[44]

Llorenç's actions give us an insight into the competition that occurred among religious coworkers. If Llorenç did indeed lead a delegation of monks, clerics, and parishioners to Girona to complain of Nicolau's being in charge of the school, he went to great lengths to remove a rival teacher. Llorenç's revelation meant that Nicolau lost his school and status in his community, as did en Perot because of his ordainment to the priesthood while excommunicated. More than likely, economic gain was a factor. Nicolau could have received added compensation and prestige for being in charge of the school; en Perot lost the chance to be provided a benefice and therefore a secured income, that he would have obtained if his ordination as a priest had gone unchallenged. Seen in this context, it is not surprising that both men felt they needed to retaliate, which they did one evening before their religious colleagues and the village. Shortly after compline, Nicolau and en Perot walked through the village with short swords (*gladius de mediae*) and arrived at Llorenç's house, where they battered on his door with large rocks until they discovered that Llorenç was not at home. Afterward, the men headed back to the monastery, and according to the scolaris Berenguer, who was sitting in the cemetery adjacent to the church, Nicolau and en Perot entered the church with their swords. The scolaris Berenguer ran to the church and witnessed both men fleeing when he heard Llorenç's cry for help. There he found Llorenç stabbed in the shoulder and soon surrounded by the choir monks, who assisted him to the abbot's chamber, where the treasurer and butcher tended to him.[45]

In his testimony, the twelve-year-old scolaris Berenguer admitted that his father and many others from the parish believed that the clerics Nicolau and en Perot had injured Llorenç because "they were enemies and hateful toward each other as it is said on account of the students which the said Llorenç was directing." Clearly the parish was familiar with the hostilities occurring at the monastery. Like other members of the community and monastery, the scolaris Berenguer witnessed firsthand the cycle of animosity among the three men. He had also been present that evening during compline when Nicolau had done his best to aggravate Llorenç. The altercation started when Nicolau took the lead and began singing "Hail Queen" as if "choking and strangling." Llorenç, angry with Nicolau for singing in a mocking voice and usurping his position of chanter, left the church in the midst of the singing. Nicolau also

---

44. ADG, Processos, no. 111, 10r.v., 16v.–17r. (1330). The chamberlain confirmed Llorenç's account, stating that en Perot had told him that he had been ordained knowing that he was excommunicated.

45. ADG, Processos, no. 111, 9r.v., 14r.v., 17r. (1330).

left, and then Nicolau and en Perot were seen going to their homes in the village to retrieve their weapons to seek out Llorenç.[46] The attack on Llorenç was not intended to kill him but was an act of retribution that showed strength and defiance. Nicolau and en Perot hoped to humiliate their victim, which included tearing Llorenç's clerical vestments before a number of their religious colleagues. Andrew Miller has argued that the mutilation of clerical vestments, which shamed and emasculated a cleric because defrocking meant depriving a clergyman of his spiritual authority, was also an attack on the masculinity of the cleric.[47] Physically assaulting Llorenç and mutilating his clothing were acts that allowed Nicolau and en Perot to regain some of the status they had lost in the monastery and village due to Llorenç's advancement.

As we have seen, status, hierarchy, and authority were often contested among religious colleagues. Violence was used to humiliate one's rival and reestablish the hierarchy in a limited domain, and it conferred a certain level of authority on its perpetrators. Reports that monks fought among themselves and rebelled against the authority of their prior are not uncommon.[48] Just like a rector, a prior, who functioned as a superior officer of a religious house, exercised authority over a community of religious men and the parishioners of the village that attended his church. The prior of Sant Joan de les Fonts was known for his combative nature. He ruled the priory and village with a harsh hand; he fought with the clergy, beat parishioners, and rebelled against the authority of the episcopal visitor when he disregarded the visitor's orders to expel his concubine from the monastery. As the prior, he outranked the priests and chaplains in his community and treated them as his inferiors, which these clerics resented. The prior's actions, moreover, reveal that he believed he had the authority and right to discipline his clerics and parishioners.[49] In the parish of Sant Vicenç de Besalú, a dispute over honor, prestige, and professional jealousy led to a serious clash between the prior of Santa Maria and the sacrist Pere de Caselles. It started when the bishop's official paid a visit to the par-

46. ADG, Processos, no. 111, 13v.–15r., 22r. (1330).

47. Andrew G. Miller, "To 'Frock' a Cleric: The Gendered Implications of Mutilating Ecclesiastical Vestments in Medieval England," *Gender & History* 24, no. 2 (2012): 271–91.

48. The monks of Sant Sebastià in the diocese of Barcelona were described not only as being heavily armed but also as a contentious lot who fought among themselves as well as with parishioners; Martí Bonet, "Visitas pastorales," 671. In another example, the monks Guillem Tomàs and Ponç Pagès from the monastery of Sant Miquel de Cruïlles were brought to the bishop's court for injuring and threatening the prior with their swords; ADG, Processos, no. 274, 34ff. (1343). Other examples include the violence that arose between two factions in the monastery of Sant Pere de Riudebitlles over which faction's candidate should be elected prior, and the concubinary priest in the monastery of Sant Sebastià who injured the monk Bernat Guarner; Hillgarth and Silano, *Register "Notule Communium,"* no. 244, no. 345, 105, 135; ADB, Registra Communium, no. 3, 86v. (1316).

49. ADG, Visites, no. 1, 26r. (1315).

ish, and the sacrist violated protocol by guiding the honored visitor to his home first and then to the house of the hebdomedarian. Outraged at such an insult, the prior of Santa Maria with his canons made his way to the parish church where he "beat and struck him [Pere], and also grabbed his throat with his hands and strangled him so that he [Pere] could not cry out or even breath until his father and others from the village of Besalú arrived in the said church and rescued him from the hands of the prior and prior's [clerical] family." As they were fleeing the church, the prior also attacked the cleric Arnau, strangling him and ripping his long tunic, while the canons beat Pere Blanc, injuring him in the head with a rock and striking two wounds to his hand with a dagger.[50]

In a village with a community of canons, the prior was a strong competitor for status, authority, and control with the clergy of the parish.[51] In fact, the prior's own words and assessment of his power in the community are striking. After the clash at the church, the vice-bailiff and other men from Besalú approached the prior with the injured Pere Blanc. The vice-bailiff asked, "Who injured this man and ridiculed him thus?" And before this group of men, the prior responded three times that "Sir, I do and have done as I wish."[52] The prior had enough confidence in his status and superiority to teach the village sacrist a lesson after the sacrist had challenged his position and snubbed him during the visitation. By choosing to escort the visitor within his sphere of influence and to visit his subordinates, the sacrist was asserting his own prestige and denying the prior his honor. But the prior was not about to let the insult pass; the outcome was a fight that involved the religious community with the subordinates of the sacrist and prior defending their collective

---

50. ADG, Visites, no. 4, 161r.v.–162v. (1330).

51. A similar situation can be seen in the conflict between the prior of the monastery of Sant Sebastià in the diocese of Barcelona and the parish priest Guillem Miró. The prior put the priest Guillem in his place after an angry exchange of words and grabbed Guillem "by the hairs" and "atrociously" beat and tore the priest's clothing. On a separate occasion, the prior had gone onto Guillem's land and events unfolded to the point that the prior was strangling the priest while the prior's brother (most likely a monastic brother) punched Guillem. According to parishioners, there were frequents fights between the monks of the monastery and the priests serving in the parish church. As a side note, both the prior and priest Guillem kept concubines. Also, the scolaris Pere Passada, who witnessed the violent confrontations between the priest and prior, was most likely related to Bartomeu Passada, a priest serving in the parish church; ADB, Visites, no. 2, 55r.v.–56r.v. (1314). Andrew Miller discusses a brawl between the archbishops of Canterbury and York over who was seated at the right hand of a visiting papal legate in "To 'Frock' a Cleric," 271, 276–78.

52. ADG, Visites, no. 4, 162v. (1330). It is unclear whether Pere Blanc was a cleric or a layman, but Bernat Blanc, the beneficed cleric in the church of Besalú, is most likely his brother. Probably Pere was at the church with his brother Bernat when the attack occurred, and the vice-batlle's response to the injury of his person indicates that he may have been an innocent bystander.

honor.[53] The brawling, however, escalated to the point that secular officials and lay parishioners became involved. This example also demonstrates that familial ties were an advantage to clergymen; they were a source of support, assistance, and even defense. Consider that the father of the sacrist Pere de Caselles from Besalú intervened to help his son when the prior was choking him, and think back to the nephew of the deacon from the parish of Mieres, who brought his uncle a sword during the rock fight with the hebdomedarian. Nephews and sons could help to settle scores, particularly when the family was involved in the conflict and hostilities between religious colleagues. The competition for status and hierarchy could be both a community and a family affair. Clergymen could have been all the more invested in their reputation and honor precisely because it directly affected their family. Losing face before their relatives and neighbors who had known them since childhood was more embarrassing than losing it in front of strangers. The pugnacious character of so many clergymen in Catalunya, moreover, is evidence that issues of honor, vengeance, professional rivalries, and competition for authority and influence permeated many levels of medieval society, including the village, parish, and monastery.

Conclusion

Clerics did not have to look far to see their religious colleagues displaying the markers of lay masculinity, such as participating in physical confrontations to dominate, control, and compete with their coworkers or the laity. Daniel Lord Smail has argued that adversaries commonly vied with each other and pursued enmities to gain social prestige and power in their communities.[54] It is not unusual that parish clergy participated in personal enmities; people at all levels of medieval society engaged in social hatred because it was inextricably tied to issues of honor, competition, prestige, and status. Thus, social hatred was a persistent and permanent feature of medieval society. Conflict and the violence resulting from frequent insults and threats worked in a similar fashion when religious colleagues vied for status and control in the parish church. The parish church was the one place where clergymen could compete and dominate other men in their profession, which is why the episcopal

---

53. The prior also appears to have flaunted his relationship with the wife of Pere de Beuda, who was reported to be his concubine. Witnesses reported that the prior's concubine had been conspicuously escorted into the priory, and they further revealed that the prior had in the past had a son by Na Moneta; ADG, Visites, no. 4, 162r. (1330).

54. Smail, "Hatred as a Social Institution," 90–126.

registers from the dioceses of Girona and Barcelona are peppered with cases of episcopal authorities looking into the disputes, attacks, and injuries between clergymen. Although the reason behind the violent actions of clerics is often omitted from these documents, it is likely that many of these cases followed a general cultural pattern of enmity that escalated to violence. The information that is revealed, however, points to clergymen seeking not kill their clerical enemies or rivals but to force them into a subordinate role to increase the masculine status and professional standing of the victor.

The aggressive behavior of clergymen in Catalunya was often aimed at a specific target, normally the lower-ranking cleric who was threatening or challenging the power and status of a senior colleague. These violent acts conveyed a message of power and who was subservient to that power. Therefore, the parish church was in many ways a battleground for the parish clergy. Before drawing swords, however, a cleric humiliated his adversary through acts of sabotage, such as criticizing and interrupting his performance of the mass in front of parishioners and subordinate clerics. Withholding the key to the church and hiding religious texts to prevent a rival from carrying out important sacramental duties were other tactics used to embarrass him. Such interference challenged a priest's professional ability and was meant to degrade an adversary in front of the lay and clerical community. Many clerics responded with violence, battling it out with their fists, rocks, and swords. Yet the goal was not to slay the adversary; very few of these reported conflicts ended in death. The objective was to demean him with insults and to intimidate him with a show of brute strength and force, demonstrating not only the perpetrator's masculinity but also his control of the parish church. Such behavior also taught younger clerics that violence could be used to compete and deprive their rivals of status and material wealth.

Given the violence that could ensue between religious colleagues and between parish clergy, it is little wonder that parishioners described their clerics as quarrelsome men—as *homo brichosus* or *homo ritxosus*—who inflicted havoc and discord in their communities. In theory, parish clerics at all levels of the parish church hierarchy were supposed to work together in service to the Church and the community, but accommodating personalities and rivalries, navigating differences of opinion concerning the performance of church duties, and the competition for economic gain created conflict among clerics that sometimes could not be overcome.

The characteristics of dominance and violence had become incorporated into clerical masculinity because they were so pervasive throughout medieval society and were more powerful than the Church ideological creation of clerical masculinity that eschewed physical violence. The Church version of clerical manhood, which was largely limited to a minority of elite clerics, could not compete with the masculine ideals of lay society. Although episcopal authorities condemned the violent deeds of clerics against fellow clergy and occasionally censored their behavior with fines, episcopal records suggest that authorities did not view the level of violence as extreme or believe the violence to be a pervasive problem that needed to be addressed. This is perhaps, more than anything, a sign of the violent and contentious nature of medieval society. What is more, it is clear that at the diocesan level episcopal officials did little to punish belligerent clerics; officials were actually more effective in punishing concubinage than violence. When aggressive confrontations escalated to the point at which a cleric was seriously injured, episcopal officials became involved and administered a fine; otherwise, minor and petty conflicts among parish clergy was usually addressed by a reprimand during a visitation when parishioners brought them to the attention of the episcopal visitor. The result was that episcopal visitors simply ordered the recalcitrant clerics to stop the fighting and perform their duties, or risk excommunication—a threat that seems to have had little impact. In many cases in which clerics were embroiled in a conflict-ridden relationship, documented over numerous years in several visitations to the parish, the clash did not come to an end until one of the clerics died or left the parish and obtained a benefice elsewhere. Considering that many of the altercations between religious colleagues discussed here triggered an inquest or an episcopal visitor to pursue the matter because the level of animosity had gotten out of hand, we can only wonder how many conflicts marked by a lower level of violence went unreported.

Whether in a parish or monastery, priests, priors, monks, and friars shared a similar clerical culture influenced by lay ideals of masculinity and, to some degree, countenancing violence. Notions of honor, the need for retribution, and competition among rivals penetrated the walls of the convents just as they did the parish community. Michael Vargas, in his study of fourteenth-century Dominicans in the Crown of Aragon, observes that fistfights and physical threats in Dominican convents "occurred regularly." Enforcing discipline among the rank-and-file friars, Vargas argues, was difficult because Dominican leaders "normalized their own bad behavior." In addition, he attributes the culture found in the Dominican convents to poor leadership: "at all levels of management and governance, administrators contributed to their Order's difficulties by living and acting in ways they had learned to live and act," which included not only sexual indiscretions but also the carrying, displaying, and drawing of weapons.[55] The bad-boy behavior of the friars, Vargas explains,

---

55. Vargas, *Taming a Brood of Vipers*, 143, 135–36.

was an accepted part of Dominican culture that earned them a bad reputation among the laity and clergy because of their disorderly behavior and prompted their own provincial prior of the Province of Aragon to describe his friars as a "brood of vipers" because of the unruliness that brought dishonor to the Order.[56] Jill Webster has also remarked on the violent deeds of the Franciscan friars in Catalunya, particularly the violence among the friars themselves. Webster has found that friars attacked, wounded, and sometimes even killed their fellow confreres to take revenge for past slights and, in one case, even joined together as a convent to attack and raid another convent of friars.[57] In her assessment of the friars, Webster writes, "the medieval friar differed little from his contemporaries: he shared their values and code of behavior, and often became embroiled in their concerns and quarrels."[58] Similarly, the Order of Merced, a Catalan caritative order that collected alms to ransom captive Christians, also had issues with violent brothers. Although fornication was considered a serious offense, physical violence directed at a fellow brother was punished more severely—double the penalty for illicit sex—which amounted to more than one year in confinement and weakly fasts.[59]

That regular orders and mendicant friars engaged in the very same behaviors as the secular clergy serving in parish churches attests to the fact that a clerical culture existed in Catalunya that was influenced by lay ideals concerning honor and vengeance, as well as competition among clergymen for influence, authority, and economic resources. In his study of the Barcelona episcopal visitation records and registers, Josep Baucells i Reig has also observed that violence was a regularly a product of verbal insults, vengeance among enemies, and economic motives.[60]

What is more, Yolanda Serrano Seoane's study of the ecclesiastical court records from the diocese of Barcelona reveals that violence among clerical colleagues continued into the fifteenth century. Serrano estimates that 40 percent of the cases brought before the episcopal court dealt with physical violence perpetrated by clergy, and much of this aggression between clerics had to do with vengeance and disputes over money and privileges. It is telling that even in the fifteenth century, when the economic situation had improved in Catalunya, clergy were still very aggressive in defending the rights attached to their benefice and challenging rivals for the customary dues expected to carry out

56. Ibid., 3.
57. Webster, Els Menorets, 184–85, 171; ibid., 135–38.
58. Webster, Els Menorets, 196.
59. James William Brodman, Ransoming Captives in Crusader Spain: The Order of Merced on the Christian Islamic-Frontier (Philadelphia: University of Pennsylvania Press, 1986), 65.
60. Baucells i Reig, Vivir en la edad media, 3: 2438.

their services. In one case, the monks of Sant Cugat kidnapped and imprisoned the rector of Sant Pere d'Octavià over a protracted dispute concerning
certain rents that the rector had refused to pay the monastery. In another, the
priest Pere Brinyà attempted to kill his colleague, the priest Pere Vilar, in the
parish of Millars due to quarrels over the dues charged for performing anniversary masses.[61] Surely times of economic upheaval exacerbated conflicts
over resources among parish clergy, but the persistence of masculine aggression before and after the famines and plagues of the fourteenth century suggest that tension and belligerence characterized many of the relationships
among the parish clergy. In addition, male codes of honor that sanctioned performative acts of aggression clearly influenced the conduct of clergymen.

Despite the physical attacks and sheer bellicosity evidenced in the visitation
records, episcopal registers, and court records, it is doubtful that Catalan clergymen in the late medieval period were extraordinary in their propensity for
violence. Although few studies have focused solely on physical attacks between religious colleagues, Kirsi Salonen has also found evidence of violence
between clergymen at the papal curia in Rome, an international place with
clerics from many parts of Christendom, suggesting that violent behavior
among the clergy, even in the most sacred of cities in Europe and in the midst
of the ecclesiastical leaders of the Roman Church, was not exceptional. In
her study of the Penitentiary registers for a six-year period, from 1458 to 1464,
Salonen finds that forty-eight priests, monks, and clerics requesting dispensation for their violent acts in Rome claimed that their combative behavior was
due to hatred and anger, or self-defense against an enemy—acts of interpersonal violence, therefore, that were not random.[62] My own study of the 1438
Apostolic Penitentiary register reveals twenty-three dispensations granted to
priests, clerics, and regular clergy from mostly Italy, Spain, and France for acts
of violence and bearing arms. Twelve of these clergymen had physically attacked or killed a fellow cleric, and three of these twelve petitioners were from
the Iberian Peninsula.[63] One in particular, the beneficed cleric Joan Martí de
Lorias, serving in a church in Valencia, petitioned for a dispensation for injuring his colleague, the subdeacon Pere Nieto, during a sword fight after Pere
allegedly attacked Joan and his uncle on a street near the church. This example
demonstrates that, even in the fifteenth century, truculent clerics and violent
conflict continued to exist throughout the Crown of Aragon. Moreover, dispensations granted by the Penitentiary in the fifteenth century speak more

---

61. Serrano Seoane, "Sistema penal. Primera parte," 351, 364, 372–73, 377.

62. Salonen, "Apostolic Penitentiary," 25–27.

63. ASV, Penitenzieria Apostolica, Registra matrimonialium et diversorum, no. 2, 5r., 6v., 7v., 10r.,
11r., 12r., 13r.v., 15v., 17r., 19r., 21r., 24v., 25r., 33r., 75v., 78r., 80r., 96r.v., 97r., 98r.v. (1438).

broadly to the existence of a clerical culture in which arms and violent confrontations among religious colleagues were not uncommon. It is likely that such a clerical culture existed throughout Europe, but only further studies of clerical violence will reveal if this was a widespread phenomenon. Considering the evidence of arms-bearing and physical aggression among the Catalan secular and regular clergy in parishes, monasteries, and the cathedral and papal curia, we can only conclude that the clergy in Catalunya throughout the fourteenth and fifteenth centuries frequently used violence to resolve conflicts with and enact retribution against their religious colleagues. The defense of honor and the competition for status, authority, and wealth indicates that these clergymen had incorporated violence into their professional and gender identities.

Conclusion

In May and June 2014, the two most popular newspapers in Spain, *El Mundo* and *El País*, published articles discussing the estimated 8,000 out of 27,000 Spanish priests who had left the Catholic Church to marry since the 1970s. The articles featured disgruntled former priests who were hopeful that Church policy would soon change to make celibacy a voluntary option rather than an obligation. One priest in particular blamed the "obstinacy" of the Church for reducing the priesthood to a "separate caste" whose vows of celibacy relegated them to "minorities" in society, and the wife of another former priest stated, "Being with a woman is not a sin. Priests are also men and it is natural for a priest [to be with a woman]."[1] It is quite possible that medieval priests and their partners felt the same way as their modern counterparts, but the difference between them lies in the choice that the modern men made to leave the priesthood to pursue marriage. Medieval priests did not renounce their ministry and their ecclesiastical careers to marry and have families. Rather, in fourteenth-century Catalunya, parish clergy were

---

1. Silvia R. Pontevedra, "El corazón o el púlpito," *El País*, June 1, 2014, 38–39. Andrés Muñoz is quoted as saying, "la hipocresía y la cerrazón, el empecinamiento en mantener a los curas como una casta aparte, según él, acabarán reduciéndola a algo minoritario." Pura Loureiro, the wife of the former priest Guillermo Prieto, stated that "Estar con una mujer no es pecado. Los curas también son hombres y es lo natural." See also José Manuel Vidal, "Decenas de curas católicos están casados en España," *El Mundo*, May 27, 2014.

able to meld a family and household with their profession despite the prohibition against marriage. The fact that so many clergymen were promoted through the holy orders to become parish priests and still managed to form de facto marriages, support their children, and train their sons to be clergymen indicates that, even though the standards of the medieval Church had changed since the Gregorian period, the customs of parish clergy had not. Contrary to our contemporary assumptions, celibacy and the absence of a marital union did not define the medieval Catalan priest.

For historians, our assessment of the types of sexual behaviors and relationships that the greater medieval populace found permissible has been skewed by a reliance on ecclesiastical and secular sources whose aim was to police as well as influence the sexual conduct of medieval people. Relying solely on these sources serves only to conceal the lives of a great majority of parish priests who made up the largest segment of the medieval Church. The stereotype of the randy, sexually indiscriminate priest that looms large in the history of the late medieval Church needs to be expanded to include the image of the parish priest as husband and father. Although the official position of the medieval Church condemned priests and their families, the internal documents of Catalan dioceses demonstrate a great tolerance for the ubiquitous phenomenon of clerical unions—unions that were, in essence, marriages in terms of their affection, longevity, and economic support. Throughout the High and Late Middle Ages, the Church campaign to criminalize clerical sexuality had not eliminated the social practice of marriage, nor had it succeeded in convincing these men that celibacy was the core feature of priestly identity and masculinity. In defiance of canon law, clerics openly formed unions with women and were still promoted to the priesthood and obtained benefices in spite of their punishments for maintaining a family. Countless clergymen defied official orders to expel their women and set aside their families, regardless of the threats of excommunication and repeated fines that were inconsistently applied to the clerical population. Judging from the number of priests who persisted in long-term unions, the financial burden was ultimately tolerable, not only because these clergymen were emotionally attached to their families but also because the role of paterfamilias (who ruled a household with a wife and children) was central to the masculinity of priests.

It was not merely proof of sexual activity or evidence of offspring that conferred masculine status in the parishes of late medieval Catalunya. Priests established marital households because medieval society defined adult male masculinity as taking on the roles of husband and father. Imitating the most common characteristics of secular manhood was important to the masculine identity of priests, but there were also practical reasons for having a family:

women and children contributed to the household economy through their labor. Nevertheless, clergymen were invested in their relationships beyond simply receiving and providing financial support. Priests openly recognized their families in the parish; treated their domestic partner as a "wife"; and nurtured, raised, and married off their children in the village community. Far from the Gregorian ideal of the priest separated from the laity by adopting a celibate lifestyle, these clerics were fully integrated into the social and economic aspects of parish life. And although their profession and clerical privilege set them apart from the laity, bonds of kinship incorporated priests into their community as much as their farming activities and side businesses made them important contributors to the parish economy. Priests and their partners also maintained strong connections to their natal families and forged new ties to the people of the parish when they married their children and grandchildren to fellow villagers. It was difficult, therefore, for the laity as well as the clergy to see clergymen cast only in the role of pastoral shepherd because villagers knew these men as husbands, fathers, sons, brothers, uncles, and godfathers to the people of the parish.

The solid familial and friendship ties in the village meant that parish clergy could easily become involved in the interpersonal rivalries and family feuds in their community. The conflict-ridden interactions between parishioners and their priests was a product of how fully integrated clerics were into village life, particularly when these hostile interactions were based on personal animosities and hatreds. It is not surprising, then, that parish priests were involved in personal conflicts and used violence to avenge and restore their reputations when their personal honor was in question or that they competed for social prestige and economic resources to ensure their status. The people of the parish could hardly idealize their clergy because they dealt with them as inconsiderate neighbors, as men who avenged their honor and protected the reputations of their families, and as men with enemies who carried out acts of retribution. What is more, employing violence to resolve disputes, uphold authority, and exert male privilege in the patriarchal culture of Catalunya was key for clergymen to demonstrate their masculinity in the parish community. A great number of priests were reported to be belligerent, quarrelsome men who acted violently against parish villagers. Their priestly position elevated them to a higher place in the male pecking order of the community, and sources show that priests used violence to intimidate parishioners to bolster their control over villagers and parish affairs. Indeed, parish clergy used their status and clerical authority to establish a hierarchy in the parish that allowed them to subordinate their parishioners.

Violence was also a part of mainstream clerical culture and integral to both the parish clergy's professional identity and gender identity. Parish clergymen resorted to violence to compete with or dominate their religious coworkers. In fact, displaying weapons and a willingness to act violently against their clerical opponents was a part of the professional identity of clergymen that they learned during their training and employed throughout their careers to establish a hierarchy among their religious colleagues in the parish church. The dominant form of clerical culture among secular clergy in Catalunya accepted, if not embraced, such displays of masculinity because they were an important part of the gender identity of parish clergymen. Tonsured children learned from the example of their superiors when they were receiving their education and training by living or working with senior clergy, as most did.

What is most revealing about the lives of the parish clergy are the strong connections they had with their families. Fathers trained their sons, and uncles trained their nephews. Thus, many tonsured boys and novice clerics grew up and served in the same parish where they were born or in a closely neighboring parish where villagers knew their families. This meant that they experienced firsthand that an ecclesiastical career was not at odds with forming their own family. These future clergymen were also professionalized to view violence as acceptable when it was used to discipline lower-level clergy and parishioners, and when it was aimed at Jews during Holy Week. As clerics-in-training, they witnessed senior clerics using violence to compete with their religious colleagues for prestige, authority, and economic resources. Even though Church standards deemed such conduct illicit and inappropriate for parish priests, who were supposed to serve as exemplars to the laity, the internal documents of the dioceses of Catalunya show, to the contrary, that ecclesiastical officials were tolerant of such behaviors and dealt with the sexual unions and violent tendencies of their clergy as mundane affairs.

Their public sexuality, use of violent acts in defense of honor, and participation in competition for standing in the community are evidence that clerics adopted characteristics of lay manhood in medieval society. Medieval manhood, in essence, was understood as the opposite of femininity—a trait that anthropologists have identified in societies where both the levels of violence and gendered violence are quite high. Interpersonal violence and intrasocietal violence are widespread in societies where the definitions of masculinity and femininity are highly differentiated and in which the epitome of manhood is associated with dominance over both men and women.[2] Achieving a position

2. Kimmel, *Gendered Society*, 317; Karras, *From Boys to Men*, 10–11.

of standing in the parish in addition to acquiring a woman conferred male adult status on parish clergymen, and the use of violence also enforced and maintained their position of power. The extent to which Catalan clerics conformed to secular medieval masculine behaviors illustrates the great influence of lay culture on medieval secular clergy. Local practices and expectations, as well as the idealized models of the greater medieval society at large, influenced what it meant to be man in fourteenth-century Catalunya. Parish priests were not immune to these influences and chose to follow the ideals of lay manhood, fully knowing that their choices went against the standards of the Church. The evidence shows that these secular expectations of what constituted manliness influenced parish clergy to the extent that they valued the social practice of marriage; sought the role of paterfamilias; and used arms and violence to defend their honor, status, and economic standing in the village community.

Priestly masculinity adopted many of the characteristics of secular manhood; nevertheless, priestly identity was still distinct from that of laymen. Priestly authority, influence, and power meant that these men believed they held a position in the parish community that allowed them to discipline and dominate their parishioners, social inferiors, and lower-level colleagues. The priestly profession, along with the social and economic privileges it entailed, was central to the gender identity of these clerics.

This micro-history of priestly sexuality and masculinity in Catalunya underscores the importance of regional studies to understand the persistence of clerical marriage into the late medieval period and the link between priests' manhood and their marriage-like unions. It also shows that, when assessing the sex practices of the clergy and religious masculinities in general, documents of practice allow us to present a more realistic assessment of parish priests and the impact of religious reforms. In effect, the reliance of historians on the writings of clerical elites and their ecclesiastical ideal of celibate manhood has obscured the experiences of parish priests. The exaggerated focus on canon law and synodal statutes in lieu of the diocesan records that reveal the on-the-ground realities have skewed our understanding of what was happening at the parish level. The level of education, upbringing, and social and economic backgrounds of the clergy greatly influenced their identity as men and as priests; thus, the masculine identities of elite clergymen and parish priests could differ greatly. Parish clergymen maneuvered through the secular and religious ideals of manliness and the expectations of priestly comportment in multiple ways. Taking into account factors such as the active agency of parish priests in accepting or rejecting reforms, the actual episcopal implementation of the reforming agendas, royal support (or the lack thereof), the religiosity of the populace, and regional attitudes toward premarital sex and the practice of concubinage may further distinguish the differences and similarities among the proletariat of the Church across Europe. Deciphering the particular characteristics that allowed some clerical populations to keep the custom of clerical unions longer than others is key to understanding why clerical marriage and concubinage were successfully curtailed or why they stubbornly flourished.

Reconsidering Celibacy as the Defining Characteristic of the Medieval Priesthood

My aim in this study has been to expose the divergent practices and lifestyle of Catalan clergy and is not meant to universalize the experience of parish priests throughout late medieval Europe. The example of the Catalan priesthood is germane to the study of clerical sexuality and masculinity because it illustrates that the region of Catalunya offers an alternative narrative to the effects of the Gregorian reform and the imposition of clerical celibacy. The scholarship on this reform movement and the effect of celibacy on the clergy has largely ignored Iberia, and too often it uses England and France as the standard when explaining the history of priestly celibacy, the decline of clerical marriage, and the rise of the debauched, fornicating priest.[3] Such a myopic view has the effect of presenting the history of clerical celibacy as a homogenous process; it distorts the experiences of men in the priestly profession and the social context in which they lived and worked. Indeed, the repeated claim that clerical marriage died out by the end of twelfth century, and certainly by the beginning of the thirteenth century, must be revised to account for the situation in Iberia, as well as other areas where studies have shown that clerical marriage continued because these regions were not fully integrated into the institutional framework of the Church until the High Middle Ages.[4] The standard narrative, therefore, must do more to include the diversity of

---

3. In spite of Peter Linehan's numerous works on the medieval Iberian church and the scholarship of J. N. Hillgarth, Federico Aznar Gil, José Rodríguez Molina, José Sànchez Herrero, José Martí Bonet, and Josep Baucells i Reig (and many others) that date from the 1970s to the 2010s, their work has yet to be integrated into the history of clerical celibacy in the medieval Church. For example, Iberia is rarely mentioned even in the most recent histories dealing with clerical marriage and the imposition of celibacy, such as Helen Parish's 2010 book, *Clerical Celibacy in the West.* See also the essays in Frassetto, *Medieval Purity and Piety,* which also tend to leave out the Iberian church.

4. C. N. L. Brooke first made the claim in 1956 that clerical marriage among elite clergy died out by the mid-twelfth century in "Gregorian Reform in Action," 19–21. Nearly sixty-years later in 2015, Julia Barrow and Jennifer Thibodeaux both repeated this claim, although sometimes with the caveat that it certainly died out by the early thirteenth century; Barrow, *Clergy in the Medieval World,* 135–39, 145–46; Thibodeaux, *Manly Priest,* 111, 151–54.

experiences of men in the priesthood beyond the regions directly affected by enthusiastic reformers. Iberian priests, like many of their counterparts in the Mediterranean, Scandinavia, and eastern Europe, were still getting married well into the thirteenth and fourteenth centuries.[5] Indeed, as far as the priesthood in Iberia was concerned, celibacy was not uniformly recognized as the rule for clerics in the major orders. The thirteenth-century Castilian legal code, *Las Siete Partidas*, reflects the permissible attitude toward clerical unions found in secular society, which was supported by the king of Castile, Alfonso X, who granted bishops the power to absolve priests who married virgins and allowed these men to keep their benefices.[6] Throughout the fourteenth century in the kingdom of Navarre, as well as in the kingdom of León, which housed the dioceses of Segovia, Zamora, Salamanca, Palencia, Santiago de Compostela, and Pamplona, priests were still getting married, so synods were left to repeat the ban on marriage as well as concubinage.[7] In the first half of the fourteenth century in Catalunya, evidence shows that priests entered into betrothal agreements and some continued to perform the sacrament of marriage, although in private with their families in attendance. The reality is that clerical marriage died out slowly among the proletariat of the Church; it persisted in some geographical locations into the late Middle Ages, especially in regions where clerical culture and ecclesiastical oversight were more tolerant of priests flouting canon law. It is likely, too, that clerical marriage persisted longer than the available sources reveal due to the fact that ecclesiastical officials were inclined to label these unions concubinous and not marriage. A clerical couple could have easily validated their union with the sacrament of marriage privately, with or without the help of a priestly colleague, regardless of whether the Church deemed the marriage to be valid. Considering that Church officials dealt with the very similar issue of clandestine marriage among the laity, it is not outside the realm of possibility that clerics continued to

5. Reginetta Haboucha and Roldàn Jimeno Aranguren have discussed the persistence of priestly marriage in Castile and Navarre; Haboucha, "Clerics, Their Wives, and Their Concubines," 92–93; Aranguren, "Concubinato, matrimonio y adulterio," 548–50; Sánchez Herrero, *Diocesis del reino de León*, 154–55, 164–66. Maureen Miller, in her study of clerical reform in Verona, mentions that synodal statutes continued to bann clerical marriage in the fourteenth century; *Formation of a Medieval Church*, 55n. 51. Anthony Perron has also noted that priests in thirteenth-century Scandinavia remained in their "public marriages" despite episcopal attempts to impose celibacy on the clergy; "Saxo Grammaticus's Heroic Chastity," esp. 117. For eastern Europe, see Sutt, "Uxores, ancillae and dominae"; Karbic, "Illicit Love in Medieval Salvonian Cities," 338–39.

6. Burns, *Siete Partidas*, 1: 79, 102–3 (Title V. Law LXIII. In What Way Prelates Can Grant Dispensations to the Priests of Their Bishopric). This thirteenth-century legal code had a greater impact on the law of the kingdom in the fourteenth century under Alfonso XI; O'Callaghan, *A History of Medieval Spain*, 451.

7. Aranguren, "Concubinato, matrimonio y adulterio," 549–50; Sánchez Herrero, *Diocesis del reino de León*, 155–57.

marry their "concubines" in discreet ceremonies knowing very well that their marriages were not legally recognized. Whether clergy in late medieval Catalunya were unique in their partiality for de facto marriages is hard to determine at this time, but it is likely that there is a distinction between the Mediterranean and Nordic regions, where clerical unions appear to be more common, and the more studied areas of England and France, where the practice of clerical marriage appears to have died out sooner.

Equally problematic in scholarly accounts that deal with the history of clerical celibacy are generalized statements claiming that celibacy became a normative trait of priestly masculinity by the end of the Middle Ages.[8] Such assertions overestimate the long-term effects of the Gregorian reform in changing the behavioral standards of the priesthood and often do not take into account on-the-ground evidence from the fifteenth and sixteenth centuries. We know that the enforcement of celibacy during this late medieval and early modern periods remained just as unenthusiastic as in the centuries before because diocesan officials continued to tolerate concubinage as long as priests paid a fee. In fact, James Brundage in his grand opus *Law, Sex, and Christian Society in Medieval Europe* judges that "By the end of the fifteenth century many Churchmen had concluded that further attempts to enforce celibacy were futile: the best they could do was to confine the clergy's sexual activities within tolerable limits."[9] This assessment is further corroborated in the fifteenth-century registers of the Apostolic Penitentiary in the Vatican Secret Archives.[10] From all the dioceses across Europe, concubinary priests and their illegitimate sons appear in such high numbers that, in the 37,916 recorded dispensations for illegitimate birth, 60 percent of the fathers were clergymen.[11] Moreover, such a high percentage does not truly reflect how common fatherhood was to the clergy because the registers covering a period of twenty-six years are

---

8. In his history of the medieval Church, Joseph Lynch states that, "celibacy was the distinguishing mark of the higher clergy." *The Medieval Church: A Brief History* (London: Longman, 1992), 294–95. Paul Beaudette has also argued that celibacy became a symbol by which ecclesiastical culture defined itself against the laity; '"In the World but Not of It,'" 23–46. Although this may have been true for some elite churchmen, such an argument does not take into account that the proletariat of the Church may not have defined themselves in the same way or that the laity in some regions were so accustomed to concubinary priests that they did not associate celibacy with secular clergy. More recently, Helen Parish and Jennifer Thibodeaux have both made the same argument as Beaudette, and they too have based their claim more on Church rhetoric than in actual documents of practice that show that celibacy could hardly have been associated with parish priests when, in fact, so many practiced concubinage; Parish, *Clerical Celibacy in the West*, 128; Thibodeaux, *Manly Priest*, 111, 151.

9. Brundage, *Law, Sex, and Christian Society*, 537.

10. See the one hundred sixty volumes covering the years 1409 to 1569 that include dispensations for illegitimate birth (*de defectu natalium*) in the ASV, Penitenzieria Apostolica, Registra Matrimonalium et Diversorum.

11. Salonen and Schmugge, *Sip from "Well of Grace,"* 58–59.

missing, in addition to other significant gaps in the registers, and the reported figure of 60 percent only represents the sons of clergymen who were seeking ecclesiastical careers and needed to petition the Penitentiary.[12] In Rome itself, concubinage among prelates took on a "quasi-official status" in the papal city throughout the fourteenth and fifteenth centuries; the example of Rodrigo Borgia (Pope Alexander VI) is the most famous, of course, and it underscores the existence of a clerical culture in Rome that permitted Borgia to attain such power and also allowed clerical unions at all levels of the papal court.[13] What is more, episcopal sources from the sixteenth century confirm the widespread practice of clerical concubinage in German lands. In her study of the transition of clerical concubinage to clerical marriage in the early German Reformation period, Marjorie Elizabeth Plummer draws attention to the prevalence of clerical unions during the fifteenth century prior to the reform of the 1520s and underscores the rebellious nature of German clergymen, particularly parish priests, in refusing to be separated from their "wives." Plummer argues that reform started with the lower-level clergy and their parishioners supporting clerical marriage, which was eventually adopted by ecclesiastical leaders who were in support of the Reformation and who then used the prevalence of clerical concubinage as a reason to allow clerical marriage.[14] Forty years later while the Council of Trent was deliberating the policy of mandatory celibacy, a German official declared to the council that "chaste marriage would be preferable to sullied celibacy" because a 1561 visitation to parishes in Bavaria had found that "of a hundred priests hardly three or four can be found who did not publicly live in concubinage or in a clandestine marriage, or had even got married in public."[15]

The evidence for clerical de facto marriage surviving openly in Spain after the fifteenth century is apparent at every turn; therefore, it seems highly unlikely that people considered celibacy to be the most significant trait of the priesthood in Iberia throughout the medieval and the early modern periods. Court cases from the episcopal see of Barcelona and Valencian episcopal visitation records reveal the continued custom of clerical unions in the Crown of Aragon throughout the fifteenth century.[16] A visitation to the diocese of Palencia in 1481 revealed that 30 percent of the cathedral canons lived openly

---

12. Ibid., 5–7.

13. John F. D'Amico, *Renaissance Humanism in Papal Rome: Humanists and Churchmen on the Eve of the Reformation* (Baltimore: Johns Hopkins University Press, 1983), 5–6.

14. Marjorie Elizabeth Plummer, *From Priest's Whore to Pastor's Wife: Clerical Marriage and the Process of Reform in in the Early German Reformation* (Burlington: Ashgate, 2012), 14–26, 41–42, 53, 58, 88.

15. Brundage, *Law, Sex, and Christian Society,* 568.

16. The evidence for clerical concubinage in the fifteenth century can be found in Yolanda Serrano Seoane, "El sistema penal del tribunal eclesiástico de la diócesis de Barcelona en la Baja Edad Media.

with their concubines. At the end of the fifteenth century, episcopal visitors noted the same situation among cathedral canons in Salamanca, Astorga, and Toledo, which shows that concubinage was not limited to parish priests in the rural countryside but continued among elite clergy as well.[17] In the archive of Simancas in Spain, Ricardo Córdoba de la Llave has found that the bastard children of clergymen represented the largest group of petitioners (61 percent) who purchased legitimization decrees from the Crown during the earliest years of the Registro General del Sello, from 1474 to 1495. These records not only illustrate the enduring practice of concubinage among ecclesiastical elites but also reflect the prosperity and social ambition of well-to-do clerics who could afford to provide a higher social status for their children by paying the Crown a substantial sum to legitimize their progeny, usually a son who sought a career in public office or royal service.[18] In addition, Sara Nalle has underscored the propensity of ordinary parish priests to flout their vows of celibacy in the diocese of Cuenca, the region known as La Mancha, during the first half of the sixteenth century. She notes that, contrary to the usual response, the new bishop of the diocese, Ramírez de Villaescusa, was not only greatly disturbed by the fact that ecclesiastical officials did not punish priests for concubinage but was also outraged by its acceptance, so much so that the bishop admitted that "ignorant people were not even aware that their priests could not marry." These shameless priests, according to the bishop, were so blatant in their disrespect for Church law that they publicly celebrated mass with their family present and attended their children's weddings.[19] In Catalunya during the sixteenth century, concubinage among the clergy had yet to be seriously curtailed, and as the testimony of one rural priest in 1539 reveals, he still believed that "clergy may in good conscience marry even if they are priests."[20] For the people of early modern Spain, then, the medieval tradition of clerics engaging in marriage and concubinous unions continued as a custom among the clergy on the eve of the Counter-Reformation.

Given the widespread practice of clerical unions across the clerical landscape in Europe throughout the Middle Ages, after the Council of Trent

Segunda parte. Documentos," *Clio & Crimen*, no. 3 (2006): 430–508; Cárcel Ortí y Boscá Codina, *Visitas pastorales de Valencia*.

17. Sánchez Herrero, *Diocesis del reino de León*, 165. Sánchez Herrero also lists the bishops and archibishops in the dioceses of León that were known to have children with their concubines.

18. Córdoba de la Llave, "Relaciones extraconyugales," 612–15.

19. Sara T. Nalle, *God in La Mancha: Religious Reform and the People of Cuenca, 1500–1650* (Baltimore: John Hopkins University Press, 1992), 24, 26–27.

20. Henry Kamen, *The Phoenix and the Flame: Catalonia and the Counter Reformation* (New Haven: Yale University Press, 1993), 324.

(1545–1563), and well into the seventeenth century, we must question whether the clergy or the laity truly associated celibacy with the priestly profession. Lawrence Duggan has made the point that other historians too often attribute the hostility between the clergy and the laity on the eve of the Reformation to the sexual immorality of the priesthood while ignoring the acceptance or popular indifference to clerical concubinage.[21] Marjorie Plummer's work supports this assessment; she finds that, throughout the towns and territories of Germany from the 1520s to 1540s, "most laity still considered clerical concubines in parishes neither transgressive nor problematic, and accepted these clerical concubines and their partners far more than confessional identity would suggest."[22] Plummer's research further shows that ecclesiastical officials were unsuccessful in eliminating clerical concubinage or marriage in areas where local patrons, clergy, and parishioners did not support these efforts.[23] This highlights the role of the laity in influencing the permissibility of these unions, whether concubinous or marital, among the clergy. In all parts of Europe, considerable sentiment among both churchmen and the laity in support of clerical marriage had continued unabated in every generation since the ban on legitimate clerical unions in the eleventh century. Duggan asserts that the pre-Tridentine Church had been moving toward accepting clerical marriage but that doctrinal issues of the Reformation intervened to make clerical celibacy the dividing line between Catholic supporters and evangelical leaders.[24] In her study of clerical celibacy, Helen Parish notes, "The Council of Trent, by its rejection of clerical marriage, and articulated intention to reform clerical conduct, had established clerical celibacy as a visible symbol of the distinctiveness of the Catholic priesthood and its function, and therefore the eradication of clerical concubinage as a tangible sign of the effectiveness of Catholic reform."[25] Yet the reassertion by the Council of the law of celibacy did not have an immediate effect on the practices of the clergy. Clerical concubinage was a persistent problem throughout the early modern period and remained difficult to eradicate among generations of clergy after the Council of Trent, even though the laity had now been exposed to the message that clerical celibacy was essential to Catholic belief on

---

21. Lawrence G. Duggan, "The Unresponsiveness of the Late Medieval Church: A Reconsideration," *Sixteenth Century Journal* 9, no. 1 (1978): 21.

22. Plummer, *From Priest's Whore to Pastor's Wife*, 169.

23. Ibid., 60–62, 67, 83–85, 88, 102, 178–79, 189–90, 196–98, 201–4, 207–9, 289.

24. Brundage, *Law, Sex, and Christian Society*, 538; Parish, *Clerical Celibacy in the West*, 144, 152–57; Duggan, "Unresponsiveness," 21–23; Anthony F. D'Elia, *The Renaissance of Marriage in Fifteenth-Century Italy* (Cambridge, MA: Harvard University Press, 2004), 122–34.

25. Parish, *Clerical Celibacy in the West*, 197.

an exceptional level.[26] Simone Laqua's study of clerical concubinage shows that the practice prevailed in Münster into the late 1620s.[27] And, in spite of the post-Tridentine reforms in Italy, clerical concubinage persisted in places such as Siena during the 1600s.[28] Once again, regional efforts determined the success of post-Tridentine efforts to change the customs of the clergy. Several generations after Trent, securing the general observance of celibacy among the clergy was still a challenge for the early modern Church.

In Spain, the Counter-Reformation served as turning point in the new and unprecedented effort to enforce the rule of celibacy in which reforming bishops worked in tandem with the Spanish Inquisition to change clerical culture. Starting in the sixteenth century, the Spanish Inquisition turned its inquisitorial gaze to investigating and punishing the sexual transgressions of the laity and clergy, in conjunction with its original mission of seeking out the religious deviance of Conversos, Moriscos, and heretics.[29] It is important to stress, however, that the Tridentine reforms and the impact of the Inquisition were not uniform across Spain. Although it is true that higher educational standards, a greater commitment to the enforcement of clerical discipline, and a more uniform and systematic preparation for the priesthood helped transformed attitudes toward clerical sexuality, the truth is that the effort to stamp out the tradition of clerical unions was not successful in the more remote regions of Spain. Even though there was a greater expectation that priests would adhere to their vows of chastity, celibacy did not become the norm. The once openly tolerated unions of the clergy were no longer as acceptable or as public, especially in urban religious centers, but many among the clergy refused to give up their women. Clerics simply went to greater efforts to hide their relationships from public scrutiny, as does the well-to-do archpriest of Salvador in the anonymous picaresque novel *Lazarillo de Tormes*, who marries his concubine to Lazarillo to conceal his illicit union. Others channeled their sexuality into impermanent relationships, frequented brothels, or sought out women in the secrecy of the confessional.[30] The Inquisition, moreover, was more active in

26. Merry Weisner-Hanks recognizes that the laity in some regions tolerated clerical concubinage until the nineteenth century; Weisner-Hanks, *Christianity and Sexuality in the Early Modern World: Regulating Desire, Reforming Practice* (New York: Routledge, 1999), 145–46.
27. Simone Laqua, "Concubinage and the Church in Early Modern Münster," *Past and Present* 1, suppl. 1 (2006), esp. 73.
28. Oscar Di Simplicio, "Perpetuas: The Women Who Kept Priests, Siena 1600–1800," in *History of Crime*, ed. Edward Muir and Guido Ruggiero (Baltimore: John Hopkins University Press, 1994), 32–64.
29. Henry Kamen, *The Spanish Inquisition: A Historical Revision* (London: Weidenfeld & Nicolson, 1997), 267.
30. Stephen Haliczer has shown that sexual solicitation in the confessional increased with the emphasis that the Counter-Reformation placed on confession and its greater effort to address issues

Castile-León than in the Crown of Aragon, where the Inquisition had always
been regarded as a foreign institution imposed by Castilians and thus was a
source of resentment.[31] In Catalunya, Inquisition officials had minimal contact with the people because of the inaccessibility of the countryside. In his
lifelong study of the Spanish Inquisition, Henry Kamen comments, "the fact
remains that the vast majority of Catalans never saw an inquisitor in their lives
or had any contact with the Holy Office." Indeed, neither the Inquisition nor
episcopal visitations during the sixteenth and seventeenth centuries managed
to greatly influence the social and religious mores of Catalans living outside
of Barcelona.[32]

Clerical concubinage as a custom among the clergy continued to thrive in
the rural areas of Spain in spite of Catholic Reformation efforts. Allyson Poska
has found that in the mountainous areas of seventeenth-century Galicia it was
normal for single women to form unions with parish priests, so much so that
these unions were not a secret in their communities.[33] Henry Kamen has further observed that in Counter-Reformation Catalunya the repression of clerical sexuality was a long struggle that brought about "little effective change"
because the "irrepressible tradition" of clerical concubinage "continued to persist" in the Catalan countryside. Given the tenacity of this custom among the
clergy, it is hardly surprising that during the sixteenth century the provincial
councils of Tarragona reiterated the ban on clerical concubinage a total of
twenty-four times. Even among its own officials, the Inquisition in Catalunya
disciplined thirty-eight *comisarios* (local clergy who worked for the Holy
Office) in 1613 for keeping women. Kamen, further, underscores the "con-
spiracy of silence" that protected parish priests and their partners from Church
authorities as long as the clerical couples avoided conflict with the community.[34] This reveals, once more, the importance of lay cooperation in abetting
concubinous clergy. Although post-Tridentine reforms and the efforts of the
Spanish Inquisition had an impact on the widespread practice and visibility of

---

of clerical incontinence. Yet the vast majority of clerical offenders were drawn from religious orders,
particularly the mendicants. He notes that out of the 223 clergymen accused of sexual misconduct in
the confessional, only 59 (26 percent) were secular clergy. It seems likely that the low numbers of parish priests prosecuted by the Inquisition for sexual misbehavior in the confessional had to do with the
fact that a good many managed to still form unions with women. Parish priests were less likely to
resort to indiscriminate sex and risk angering male parishioners, whereas mendicant clergy usually
traveled throughout the dioceses serving as confessors and, thus, were more likely to engage in temporary sexual indiscretions; Stephen Haliczer, *Sexuality in the Confessional: A Sacrament Profaned*
(Oxford: Oxford University Press, 1996), 86, 88, 98, 152–55.

31. Kamen, *Phoenix and the Flame*, 211–17; Kamen, *Spanish Inquisition*, 280–82.

32. Kamen, *Phoenix and the Flame*, 250–52.

33. Poska, *Women and Authority*, 83–86.

34. Kamen, *Phoenix and the Flame*, 251, 324, 326.

clerical unions, which meant that clerical couples had to be more secretive to avoid detection, it is clear that the tradition of clerical de facto marriages endured in the more agricultural and pastoral communities of Spain. Iberian priests also brought the tradition of clerical unions with them to the colonies in Latin America, where concubinage among the laity in both urban and rural settings was so common as to be "banal."[35] In this frontier environment, clerical unions flourished alongside the concubinous unions of the laity in a live-and-let-live attitude that demonstrates a tolerance for clerical couples.[36]

The evidence for the continued practice of clerical concubinage in Counter-Reformation Germany, Italy, and Spain, and in the Americas, should give us pause in accepting the claim that celibacy marked the priesthood as its single most defining characteristic. Considering the endurance of clerical unions and the association of priests with sexual activity throughout the medieval and early modern periods, it seems disingenuous to depict the premodern priest as distinct from the laity based on a vow of celibacy, particularly because a great many priests chose in practice not to make celibacy the defining feature of their lifestyle.

---

35. Susan Migden Socolow, *The Women of Colonial Latin America*, 2nd ed. (Cambridge, UK: Cambridge University Press, 2015), 77–80.

36. See Ann Twinam, *Public Lives, Private Secrets: Gender, Honor, Sexuality, and Illegitimacy in Colonial Spanish America* (Stanford: Stanford University Press, 1999), 115–17, 239, 247–51; María Emma Mannarelli, *Private Passions and Public Sins: Men and Women in Seventeenth-Century Lima* (Albuquerque: University of New Mexico Press, 2007), 42–44, 47, 53–54.

Appendix

Table 1.1   Clerical unions in the diocese of Girona, 1303–1344

	NUMBER OF CHURCHES	NUMBER CHARGED WITH INCONTINENCE, TOTAL	CHARGED WITH CONCUBINAGE		NUMBER WITH CASUAL OR SHORT-TERM AFFAIR[a]	NUMBER OF CHILDREN
			NUMBER	PERCENTAGE		
Visites, 1303–1305, fragmentaris	49	64	39: 36 major orders 2 unknown rank 1 *tonsuratus*	61	25: 21 major orders 4 unknown rank	120+
Visites, 1312–1313, fragmentaris	20	13	8: 7 major orders 1 unknown rank	62	5: 3 major orders 1 minor orders 1 unknown rank	11+
Visites, 1318, fragmentaris	7	8	4: 2 major orders 2 unknown rank	50	4: 4 major orders	8+
Visites, 1320, quaderno	25	28	14: 6 major orders 7 unknown rank 1 *tonsuratus*	50	14: 7 major orders 7 unknown rank	39+
Visites, no. 1 1314–1316	305	113	82: 48 major orders 34 unknown rank	68	31 (4)	110+
Visites, no. 2 1315	117	48	29: 22 major orders 5 unknown rank	60	19: 12 major orders 7 unknown rank	46+

Visites, no. 3 1321	76	61	50: 32 major orders 18 unknown rank	82	11: 8 major orders 3 unknown rank	109+
Visites, no. 4 1329	391	253	207: 182 major orders 25 unknown rank	82	49 (5)	287+
Visites, no. 5 1331–1332	170	37	34: 30 major orders 4 unknown rank	92	3: 3 major orders	56+
Visites, no. 6 1338–1341	91	78	61	78	19 (2)	133+
Visites, no. 7 1341–1344	43	45	34	76	11	67+
Visites, no. 8 1345–1346	26	21	11: 10 major orders 1 *tonsuratus*	52	10: 8 major orders 2 unknown rank	16+
Total	**1,391**	**787**	**591**	**75**	**212**	**1,038+**

[a]Numbers in parentheses indicate clerics who were counted for both a concubinous relationship and a short-term affair.

Table 1.2 Clerical unions in the diocese of Urgell, 1312–1316

| | NUMBER OF CHURCHES | NUMBER CHARGED WITH INCONTINENCE, TOTAL | CHARGED WITH CONCUBINAGE | | NUMBER WITH CASUAL OR SHORT-TERM AFFAIR[a] | NUMBER OF CHILDREN |
			NUMBER	PERCENTAGE		
Visites, no. 1 1312–1313	149	66	58	88	8 (2)	75+
Visites, no. 2 1313	160	53	51	96	3 (1)	15+
Visites, no. 3 1313–1315	149	64	58	90	6	35+
Visites, no. 4 1314–1315	117	87	84	96	3	36+
Visites, no. 5 1315–1316	91	73	68	93	5	27+
Visites, no. 6 1315	60	43	40	93	3	14+
Visites, no. 7 1313–1314	152	86	83	96	3	37+
Visites, no. 8 1314–1315	97	57	51	89	6	28+
Total	**975**	**528**	**492**	**93**	**37**	**267+**

[a]Numbers in parentheses indicate clerics who were counted for both a concubinous relationship and a short-term affair.

Table 1.3   Clerical unions in the diocese of Vic, 1330–1339

	NUMBER OF CHURCHES	NUMBER CHARGED WITH INCONTINENCE, TOTAL	CHARGED W/ CONCUBINAGE		NUMBER WITH CASUAL OR SHORT-TERM AFFAIR	NUMBER OF CHILDREN
			NUMBER	PERCENTAGE		
Visites, no. 1 1330	61[a]	45	33	73	12 (2)[b]	47
Visites, no. 2 1331–1332	179	149	119	80	37 (7)[c]	205+
Visites, no. 3 1332–1333	132	57	52	91	5	58+
Visites, no. 3 1334–1336	23	36	36	100	0	42+
Visites, no. 3 1339	66	44 (2)	39	88	3	33+
Total	**462**	**331**	**279**	**84**	**57**	**385**

[a]Five visitations from Visites, no. 2, were added to the fifty-six churches in Visites, no. 1, because the visitor conducted these visitations in 1330.

[b]Number in parentheses indicates clerics were counted as "incontinent" but did not fit into either category, "concubinage" or "short-term affairs." These clerics kept and provided for their children, but there was no mention of a "concubine," which means that the woman had moved on to another relationship; the woman had died; or the notary, in an oversight, left out this information.

[c]Seven clerics kept concubines and were also engaged in casual affairs. Also, out the thirty counted in this category, ten clerics were not involved with women but had a child whom they provided for or took care of in their home.

Table 2.1 Selected clerical families in the diocese of Girona

PARISH	PRINCIPALS	NOTES	SOURCE
Sant Martí de l'Armentera	Hebdomedarian Mateu Carbó + Sibil·la Martorell (daughter of Na Berengaria Martorell)	7 children—"*multos infantes magnos et parvos*"	ADG, Visites, no. 1, 85r.v. (1315); Visites, no. 3, 3r.–33r. (1321); Visites, no. 4, 22v. (1329); Imposicions de Penes, no. 1, 3r. (1335)
Aiguaviva	Stabilitus Pere Sartor + Na Marta	3 children (2 filios + filiam) / 15+-year relationship / The couple already had two children in 1320	ADG, Visites fragmentaris, 30v. (1320); Visites, no. 4, 100v.–101r. (1329); Visites, no. 5, 82r.v. (1331); Visites, no. 5, 135r.v. (1333)
Sant Valentí d'Arcs	Rector úúú Guerau + Sibil·la ça Costa de Pinoses	22+-year relationship	ADG, Visites, no. 4, 141r. (1329); Visites, no. 5, 68v. (1331); Imposicions de Penes, no. 1, 39r. (1342) and 66v. (1346)
Aro	Hebdomedarian Berenguer Cunyl + Beatriu Pagès (sister of Guillem Pagès de Calonge)	4 filios / Berenguer bought Beatriu a home for her "*opus*" / Beatriu looks after cows, pigs, and fowl	ADG, Visites, no. 4, 73r.–74r. (1329); Visites, no. 6, 1r.–4r. (1338); Imposicions de Penes, no. 1, 5r. (1336), 18r. (1338), 25v. (1339). Lletres, no. 7, 162v. (1344)
Sant Vicenç de Besalú	Beneficed cleric Bernat de Banc + Cilia	4 children (2 filios + 2 filias) / Cleric keeps family in parish of Capelada	ADG, Visites, no. 4, 161r.v. (1329)
Santa Maria de Bolós	Rector Guillem de Boix + Saurina	5 filios / Rector celebrates mass with his son Pere / Daughter, Margarida	ADG, Visites, no. 1, 43v. (1315); Visites, no. 4, 141r. (1329); Visites, no. 5, 68r.v. (1331)
Bordils	Deacon Bonanat + Na Fresca	3 children / 16+-year relationship	ADG, Processos, no. 35 (1320); Visites, no. 4, 59r. (1329); Visites, no. 6 145r.v. (1331); Imposicions de Penes, no. 1, 5r. (1336)
Sant Feliu de Calabuig	Sacrist Bernat Jover + Alamanda Valent from Lampaies	2 living children (duas filias + filium; last child died at the age of 6) / 12+-year relationship	ADG, Visites, no. 4, 46r. (1329); Visites, no. 7, 9r.v.–10r. (1341)
Calonge	Beneficed cleric Bernat Mola + Berengaria Rotlana	Proles (youngest child 15 years old) / 16+-year relationship / Berengaria is 50 years old in 1341; in 1345, Bernat and Berengaria live separately but their daughter stays with Bernat.	ADG, Visites, no. 4, 71v.–72r. (1329); Visites, no. 7, 35r. (1341); Imposicions de Penes, no. 1, 35r. (1341) and 44v. (1345); Visites, no. 8, 17v. (1345)

Santa Maria del Camp	Stabilitus Guillem de Pedrinyà + Guillema Straderie	Filios + filias; oldest son named Francesc	ADG, Visites, no. 1, 30v. (1315)
Sant Mateu de Canet	Rector Berenguer Bonet + Guillema Torreta	4 children (2 filios + 2 filias); youngest child 12 years old, oldest 20 years old. Married a daughter. Sons help with the mass. The twenty-six-year-old child was mentioned in the 1315 visitation, which means that in 1329, when the rector and Guillema still lived, their eldest child would have been 40 years old.	ADG, Visites fragmentaris, 4v. (1303); Visites, no. 1, 86v. (1315)
Sant Esteve de Cantallops	Sacrist Guillem de Vilar + Saurina	Filios. Elderly couple—considered too old to have carnal relations	ADG, Visites, no. 3, 11r. (1321); Visites, no. 4, 32v. (1329)
Sant Martí de Capsec	Rector Pere de Penocars + Mateva	4 filios. Rector bought a manse called Noguer in the village of Socarrats for his family	ADG, Visites, no. 4, 144v. (1329); Visites, no. 5, 50v.–51r. (1331); Imposicions de Penes, no. 1, 40r. (1343)
Casamor	Rector Guillem + Guillema Caubite	Elderly couple. Guillema + infantes live in parish of Sant Martí de Queixàs	ADG, Visites, no. 2, 69v., 72r.v. (1315)
Sant Genís de Cervià	Hebdomedarian Ramon Llorenç + Bernarda	5 or 6 infantes. Promised 500 sous for daughter's dowry	ADG, Visites fragmentaris, 8v. (1303)
Sant Cristòfol de Cogolls	Hebdomedarian / Stabilitus d'Hostoles Pere de Font + Maria de Prat	Infantes. 30-year relationship. Keeps family on a manse called ça Fabrega	ADG, Visites fragmentaris, 10r.v. (1305); Visites, no. 2, 34v.–35r. (1315); Visites, no. 4, 113v.–114r. (1329); Imposicions de Penes, no. 1, 55r. (1344)
	Deacon Guillem + Maria de Cigario	3 filios. 15+-year relationship	ADG, Visites, no. 1, 20v. (1314). Visites, no. 2, 34v.–35r. (1315); Visites, no. 4, 113v.–114r. (1329)
Monastir Sant Miquel de Cruïlles	Monk Bernat Miars + Anglesa	2 children (daughter 10 years old, youngest child 3 years old). Family visits Bernat at the monastery	ADG, Imposicions de Penes, no. 1, 7v. (1336); Visites, no. 7, 68r. (1343); Visites, no. 8, 12v. (1345)

(continued)

Table 2.1 Selected clerical families in the diocese of Girona (*continued*)

PARISH	PRINCIPALS	NOTES	SOURCE
Sant Iscle d'Empordà	Deacon Jaume de Prat + Andreva (daughter of Maymoni de Ultramort)	4 filias + pregnant Andreva (youngest child 4 years old)	ADG, Imposicions de Penes, no. 1, 4r. (1336) and 23v. (1339); Visites, no. 7, 20r. (1341)
Estanyol	Sacrist Pere de Pol + Berengaria Giberta	Multos infantes 30+-year relationship	ADG, Visites fragmentaris, 5r.v. (1320)
Santa Maria de Faga	Hebdomedarian Pere de Quintana + Ermesenda de Comba	7 or 8 proles (youngest 13 years old, oldest 20 years old) Young daughter watches over sheep	ADG, Visites fragmentaris, 18r. (1303); Visites fragmentaris, 11v. (1305)
Figueres	Sacrista Bernat Mata + Berengaria Caliva	4 infantes	ADG, Visites, no. 3, 23v. (1321); Visites fragmentaris, 13v.–17r. (1323)
Monastir Sant Joan de les Fonts	Prior + Ermesenda	Elderly couple; "vetula concubina" Ermesenda lives in the monastery	ADG, Visites, no. 1, 26r. (1315)
Sant Miquel de Garrigàs	Stabilitus Joan Fresc + Na Michaela	3 infantes 12+-year relationship	ADG, Visites, no. 4, 11r. (1329); Imposicions de Penes, no. 1, 5v. (1336); Visites, no. 7, 142v. (1341)
Sant Mateu de Jafre	Hebdomedarian Bernat Oliver + Elisenda Clot	1 prolem 18+-year relationship	ADG, Visites, no. 4, 189v. (1329); Imposicions de Penes, no. 1, 74v. (1347)
Llanars	Hebdomedarian Guillem de Soler + Beatriu	5 children (filios + filias)	ADG, Visites fragmentaris, 8r. (1303)
Sant Andreu de Llorona	Hebdomedarian Arnau Melera + Francesca	7 or 8 infantes Married 2 daughters and 1 son	ADG, Visites fragmentaris, 22v. (1303)
Massanes	Sacrist Guillem Pere de Frigola + Berengaria de Costa	4 infantes vel plures	ADG, Visites, no. 4, 164v.–165r. (1329)
	Hebdomedarian Joan de Apila + Na Saura	4 filios Keeps Na Saura in separate home in the parish	ADG, Visites, no. 4, 88r. (1329)

Sant Pere de Montfullà	Hebdomedarian Ramon de Lors + Ermesenda	2 children (12-year-old son, married daughter Bonanada) Capellan lives with married daughter and son-in-law; son lives with Ermesenda in separate home in parish	ADG, Visites, no. 2, 47v.–48r. (1315); Visites fragmentaris, 32r.v.–33r. (1320); Visites, no. 4, 125r.v. (1329)
Sant Joan de Palamós	Capellan Pere Rubey + Ermesenda	Infantes —married son Bernat Capellan gave the family manse to his son Bernat	ADG, Visites, no. 1, 4r. (1314); Visites, no. 2, 10v. (1315)
Sant Pere de Pals	Hebdomedarian Pere Otger + Brunisenda (daughter of Bernat Miquel)	2 living children 27+-year relationship In 1329, Brunisenda had lived with Pere for 12 years	ADG, Visites, no. 4 68r. (1329); Visites, no. 5, 148v. (1333); Imposicions de Penes, no. 1, 54r. (1344)
Sant Isidor de La Pera	Deacon Bernat Mateu + Agneta Cudina	Proles (youngest child 18 years old)	ADG, Visites, no. 4, 59v. (1329); Visites, no. 7, 19r. (1341)
Sant Climent de Peralta	Hebdomedarian Guillem Albert + Geralda (married)	3 living children (youngest child 1 year old, daughter Agnes 3 years old, one child died)	ADG, Visites, no. 6, 94v.–95r. (1340)
Sant Martí de Queixàs	Sacrist Berenguer + Berengaria de Plano	Plures infantes Live in separate homes in the parish	ADG, Visites, no. 2, 69v. (1315)
Requesens	Sacrist Guillem + Beatriu	"Multos infantes" Married a daughter and gave a farmstead as her dowry Celebrated the marriage with a banquet; the celebration of the marriage was mentioned both in the village of Requesens and Cantallops	ADG, Visites, no. 11r., 11v.–12r. (1321)
Santa Maria de Ridaura	Monk and sacrist Francesc Coquet + Astruga Suinarda	2 infantes + pregnant Astruga	ADG, Visites, no. 4, 147v. -148r. (1329)
Monastir Santa Maria del Roure	Canon and Sacrist Marc + Raimunda (married)	Infantes The couple had one child in 1315 and two or more in 1321	ADG, Visites, no. 2, 60v.–61r. (1315); Visites, no. 3, 8r.v. (1321)

(continued)

Table 2.1   Selected clerical families in the diocese of Girona (*continued*)

PARISH	PRINCIPALS	NOTES	SOURCE
Sant Sadurní	Sacrist Pere Jover + Ermesenda	3 filios "diu est quod tenuit eam" In 1315, parishioners testified that the sacrist lived with Ermesenda for "a long time"	ADG, Visites, no. 2, 8r.v. (1315); Visites, no. 4, 61r.v. (1329)
	Hebdomedarian Ramon + Maria Almora	Infantes 21+-year relationship In 1305, Maria reportedly had given birth to her last child 12 years ago in 1293	ADG, Visites fragmentaris, 25v. (1305); Visites, no. 1, 3r. (1314)
Santa Eugènia de Saldet	Rector Guillem Caragall + Berengaria (daughter of Na Ramona Hostena)	3 filios (youngest 12 years old) 23+-year relationship	ADG, Visites, no. 1, 85r. (1315); Visites, no. 3, 32r.–33r. (1321); Visites, no. 6, 9v. (1338). Visites, no. 6, 10v. (1338)
Sant Vicenç del Sallent	Rector Berenguer + Berengaria	Infantes—youngest child 25-year-old daughter, son Arnau de Puijolo	ADG, Visites, no. 3, 45r.v. (1321); Visites, no. 4 155v.–156r. (1329)
Sords	Rector Berenguer + Guillema de Sords	4 filios (youngest child 12 years old)	ADG, Visites fragmentaris, 1r.v.–2v. (1295)
	Rector Guillem Teyes + Elisenda Vergera	4 children: Guillem, Pere, Alamanda, Francesca 20+-year relationship In 1342, Guillem Teyes was serving in the parish of Sant Pere de Vilaür and already had four children with Elisenda	ADG, Imposicions de Penes, no. 1, 37r. (1342) and 108v. (1356); Visites, no. 6 (1339)

Location	Person(s)	Children / relationship	Sources
Monastir Santa Maria d'Ullà	Canon Pere Arnau + Guillema Jaffera	3 filios (youngest 8 years old)	ADG, Visites, no. 5, 31v. (1332); Visites, no. 6, 120r. (1341); Imposicions de Penes, no. 1, 39v. (1342)
	Canon Bernat Huguet + Ermesenda Juglar	5 proles	ADG, Visites, no. 5, 33r. (1332); Imposicions de Penes, no. 1, 21v. (1338); Visites, no. 6, 119r.v., 121r. (1341)
	Canon Berenguer Sartor + Geralda Peregrina	3 children (2 filios + filiam) Keeps sons in the monastery	ADG, Visites, no. 5, 122r.v.–123r.v. (1332); Imposicions de Penes, no. 1, 4r. (1336), 20v. (1338), 34r. (1341): Visites, no. 6, 121r.v.–122r. (1341)
Sant Esteve de Ullastret	Deacon Bernat de Cerrar + woman from Girona	10 infantes (youngest 11 years old)	ADG, Visites fragmentaris, 4r. (1305)
Sant Cebrià de Valalta	Rector Pere Flaquer + Sibil·la deç Castelar	"multos filias et filias" (oldest 26 years old)	ADG, Visites, no. 4, 85r. (1329); Visites, no. 6, 79v. (1340)
Santa Eulàlia de Vilanova	Sacrist Pere de Mans + Na Cerdana	2 filios 26+-year relationship	ADG, Visites, no. 1, 101v. (1315): Visites fragmentaris, 9v.–10r.v. (1323); Visites, no. 4, 6v. (1329); Visites, no. 4, 184v. (1329); Imposicions de Penes, no. 1, 2v. (1336): Visites, no. 6, 156r. (1341); Lletres, no. 7, 106v. (1341)
	Stabilitus Nicolau Sunyer + Na Esmengartz	4 filios 20+-year relationship	ADG, Visites fragmentaris, 10r. (1323); Visites, no. 4, 6v. (1329); Imposicions de Penes, no. 1, 2v. (1336) and 38v. (1343); Visites, no. 6, 156v. (1341)
Vulpellac	Hebdomedarian Guillem Mul + Na Ferrara	Elderly couple; together 35+ years Daughter lives in their home to care for them	ADG, Visites fragmentaris, 22r. (1305); Visites, no. 1, 88v. (1315)

Table 2.2 Selected clerical families in the diocese of Urgell

PARISH	PRINCIPALS	NOTES	SOURCE
Sant Martí d'Adren	Capellan + married woman	3 filios Woman and children live in Urgell	ACV, Calaix, 31/43, Visites, no. 3, 35r. (1313)
Santa Eulàlia d'Ahuri	Rector + concubine	Bought homes for his children in Santa Maria de Çavila Rector celebrates mass with son Arnau	ACV, Calaix, 31/43, Visites, no. 1, 24r. (1312)
Santa Maria d'Alareny	Capellan Pere de Barany + concubine	3 filios parvulinos	ACV, Calaix, 31/43, Visites, no. 4, 11v. (1314)
Sant Esteve d'Andorra	Rector + Guillema	20+year relationship	ACV, Calaix, 31/43, Visites, no. 1, 20r. (1312)
Sant Esteve de Das	Rector + concubine	Plures filios	ACV, Calaix, 31/43, Visites, no. 1, 41v. (1312)
Sant Feliu d'Àreu	Rector Miquel Bonfil + Na Blanca	Prolem Elderly couple: "sunt ambo adeo senes"	ACV, Calaix, 31/43, Visites, no. 5, 18r. (1315)
Santa Maria d'Argentera	Capellan + *meretrix* from Vilanova de Meya	5 filios (Capellan identified as father of all children)	ACV, Calaix, 31/43, Visites, no. 4, 38r. (1315)
Sant Andreu d'Aristot	Rector + concubine	Elderly couple; concubine is "vetula" Rector keeps married daughter in his home	ACV, Calaix, 31/43, Visites, no. 1, 34r. (1312)
Sant Esteve d'Aaros	Rector Pere Donat + concubine	Elderly couple: "sunt senes et quasi indecrepita etate"	ACV, Calaix, 31/43, Visites, no. 5, 17v. (1315)
Sant Iscle de Bexech	Capellan + Guillema	4 children (filios + filias) Couple described as elderly	ACV, Calaix, 31/43, Visites, no. 8, 12r., 25r., 26r. (1314)
Sant Sadurni de Canillo	Rector + Berengaria	4 children (filios + filias)	ACV, Calaix, 31/43, Visites, no. 1, 22v. (1312)
Sant Martí de Capolat	Capellan + concubine	Elderly couple: "sunt senes et impotentes"	ACV, Calaix, 31/43, Visites, no. 3, 22v. (1313)
Sant Martí de Caregue	Rector + concubine	Elderly couple: "non habet rem cum ipsa cum sunt senes"	ACV, Calaix, 31/43, Visites, no. 1, 13r. (1315)
Santa Maria de Castellàs	Rector + Simona	4 filios	ACV, Calaix, 31/43, Visites, no. 1, 31v. (1312)
Santa Coloma d'Andorra	Rector + Guillema	30-year relationship	ACV, Calaix 31/43, Visites, no. 1, 20r. (1312)
Sant Martí de Cost	Rector + Guillema	6 filios (youngest child 7 years old)	ACV, Calaix, 31/43, Visites, no. 1, 17v. (1312)

Place	Relationship	Notes	Source
Sant Marçal d'Estach	Rector + concubine	Plures filios Rector gave one of his children 1,000 sous	ACV, Calaix, 31/43, Visites, no. 5, 11r. (1315)
Sant Julià d'Estavar	Rector + Na Grayda	3 filios	ACV, Calaix, 31/43, Visites, no. 6, 9v. (1315); Visites, no. 7, 46r. (1313)
Santa Gràcia	Capellan + concubine	Celebrates mass with his son Bought property for his children	ACV, Calaix, 31/43, Visites, no. 4, 6r. (1314); Visites, no. 5, 4r. (1315)
Sant Iscle de Maçana	Rector + Raimunda Mireta	5 or 6 filios Rector keeps daughter and son-in-law in his home	ACV, Calaix 31/43, Visites, no. 1, 20r. (1312)
Sant Fruitós de Muçer	Rector (*senex*) + concubine	Filios Rector and woman described as "sunt quasi indecrepita etate"	ACV, Calaix, 31/43, Visites, no. 1, 34r. (1312); Visites, no. 7, 35r. (1313); Visites, no. 8, 27r. (1314)
Sant Pere de Oçeya	Rector + concubine	4 filios	ACV, Calaix, 31/43, Visites, no. 7, 44v. (1313)
Sant Vicenç de Pinós	Rector + concubine	Elderly couple: "non habet rem cum ipsa propter senectutem"	ACV, Calaix, 31/43, Visites, no. 2, 34v. (1313)
Sant Martí de Puig	Rector + Cuglesa	Elderly couple: "ambo sunt senex"	ACV, Calaix, 31/43, Visites, no. 2, 7v. (1312)
Santa Maria de Ribes	Rector + concubine	Plures filios	ACV, Calaix, 31/43, Visites, no. 7, 54r. (1313)
Urgell	Canon Bernat de Condaminis + Saurina	3 filios Canon keeps married daughter and son-in-law in his home	ACV, Calaix, 31/43, Visites, no. 1, 6r. (1312)
Santa Maria de Vardia	Rector + Berengaria de Puijolo (married)	3 filios + pregnant Berengaria	ACV, Calaix, 31/43, Visites, no. 2, 17r. (1312)

Table 2.3 Selected clerical families in the diocese of Vic

PARISH	PRINCIPALS	NOTES	SOURCE
Sant Martí de Bas	Rector Pere Gaia + Francesca	Filios + filias	AEV, Visites, no. 1200/2, 64r. (1331); Visites, no. 1200/2, 85r. (1332); Visites, no. 1200/3, 24r. (1332)
		Rector keeps family on a manse in Sant Vicenç de Torelló	
Sant Nicolau de Bellpuig	Rector Ramon Saugia + Berengona	2 filias: Elienor + Agnes	AEV, Visites, no. 1200/3, 55r. (1339)
		Married daughter Agnes	
Castelloli	Rector Pere de Reges + concubine in Igualada	4 filios	AEV, Visites, no. 1200/2, 48v.–49r. (1331)
		Rector keeps two sons in his home in Castelloli	
Cervera	Beneficed cleric in chapel Pere de Roqueta + Mereta	4 filios	AEV, Visites, no. 1200/2, 6r. (1331); Visites, no. 1200/3, 43v. (1334) and 40v. (1336)
		"tenet publice tanquam uxorem concubinam in domo"	
Sant Feliu de Estiula	Rector Ramon Arrufat + Sibil·la	3 filias + 1 filium	AEV, Visites, no. 1200/3, 21v. (1332)
		Bought a manse and placed it in Sibil·la's name	
Santa Maria de Folgaroles	Priest Berenguer Cavila + Raimunda Vessella	3 filios	AEV, Visites, no. 1200/1, 23r. (1330)
Santa Maria de Granyena	Priest Andreu Morell + Mateva	3 filios	AEV, Visites, no. 1200/2, 21v. (1331)
Granollers de la Plana	Monk + Elisenda de Correla	Provides for family "de bonis ecclesiasticis" 3 filios	AEV, Visites, no. 1200/1, 26v. (1330)
Gurb	Priest En Feliu + concubine	Plures filios	AEV, Visites, no. 1200/1, 27r. (1330)
Sant Augustí de Lluçanès	Rector Bartomeu Lobet + concubine (*decrepita*)	Filios magnos Elderly couple	AEV, Visites, no. 1200/2, 64v. (1331)
Mor	Rector Bernat Daltaraga + Na Novela	Elderly couple: so old they cannot "carnally sin"	AEV, Visits, no. 1200/3, 11r. (1332)
Santa Eulàlia de Pardines	Rector Jaume des Merdos + Elisenda	Plures filios	AEV, Visites, no. 1200/2, 66r. (1331); Visites, no. 1200/3, 9v. (1332)
		Family lives in Sant Pol de Pinos	
Sant Pedor	Beneficed cleric Bernat Mans + daughter of Na Gentil	Plures filios	AEV, Visites, no. 1200/2, 61v. (1331)

Sant Pere de Pla	Rector Pere Bernat ça Carada + Beatriu	Filium + filiam Married a daughter Keeps Beatriu on a manse, which is farmed	AEV, Visites, no. 1200/3, 24v. (1332)
Santa Maria de Prats de Rei	Deacon Pere de Corilion + Na Cuxa Priest Guillem Ferran + Na Guanarela	3 filios Filios Na Guanerela recently gave birth Married a daughter, provided 1,000 sous for dowry	AEV, Visites, no. 1200/2, 5r. (1331) AEV, Visites, no. 1200/2, 5r. (1331)
Santa Coloma de Queralt	Beneficed cleric Arnau Vidal + concubine	4 children (2 filios + 2 filias) Youngest is half a year old	AEV, Visites, no. 1200/2, 40v. (1331)
Sant Christófol de Queralt	Vicar Berenguer Osteleyla + concubine	1 filiam + 2 filios Two sons assist with the mass	AEV, Visites, no. 1200/2, 41v. (1331)
Querós	Rector + Guillema de cesFrabrages	3 filios + 3 filias Rector built a house for his family	AEV, Visites, no. 1200/2, 82v. (1332)
Sagar	Rector Ramon Gardit + Na Maniars	5 filios Three children living at home, plus son and daughter-in-law	AEV, Visites, no. 1200/2, 31r. (1331)
Santa Romà de Sau	Rector + Elisenda des Frexe	Proles Bought a plot of land and built a house for Elisenda Gave a small manse called Ça Frigola to his son Ramon des Frexe Gave pastureland to his daughter Sibil·la (wife of Bernat de Casalorenç) Married two daughters, provided 450 sous in dowry Celebrates mass with another son	AEV, Visites, no. 1200/2, 80r. (1332)
Segur	Vicar En Cases + "wife"	Filios	AEV, Visites, no. 1200/2, 51v. (1331)
Sant Bartomeu de Sesgorgues	Rector + a woman from Cagueda	Plures filios magnos Keeps concubine "multo tempore"	AEV, Visites, no. 1200/2, 1r. (1330)

(continued)

Table 2.3 Selected clerical families in the diocese of Vic (*continued*)

PARISH	PRINCIPALS	NOTES	SOURCE
Sant Martí de Sobremunt	Rector Pere de Casacamela+Guillema	7 filios Rector bought a manse called Funaya for the family Guillema pregnant Youngest child 2 years old 4 children live at home	AEV, Visites, no. 1200/2, 64v. (1331); Visites, no. 1200/3, 29v. (1333)
Sant Sadurní de Sovelles	Rector Simó de Prat+concubine (dead)	5 children (filios+filias) Married daughter Beatriu	AEV, Visites, no. 1200/1, 4r. (1330)
Uxols	Rector Jaume des Veger+Elisenda Cirada	6 children Bought a manse called Çes Pujades for Elisenda in her name 15+-year relationship	AEV, Visites, no. 1200/2, 77v. (1331)
Sant Martí de Viladrau	Rector Pere Jaume+Raimunda ça Sala	Keeps Raimunda in a separate home in the parish Married a daughter; provided a dowry Son Guillem	AEV, Visites, no. 1200/1, 20v. (1330)
Vilagrassa	Rector+Na Roqueta	5 children (duos filios+tres filias) Married a daughter Rector keeps family in Cervera	AEV, Visites, no. 1200/2, 22v. (1331)
Vilanova	Vicar Guillem Perpinyà+Blanca	Filios magnos	AEV, Visites, no. 1200/3, 15r.v. (1332)
Sant Esteve de Vilaramó	Rector Bernat de Mans+concubine	8 children Married two daughters Mother provided dowry of 350 and 300 sous	AEV, Visites, no. 1200/2, 69r. (1331)
Sant Esteve de Vinyoles	Rector Berenguer de PuigRubí+Maria de Romagaos	1 son (filius magnus) Elderly couple: "sint ambo veteres et quasi debiles" Son sometimes helps with the mass	AEV, Visites, no. 1200/1, 13r. (1330)
Sant Martí de Vinyoles	Cleric Roca de Bebores+Maria de Soler	4 filios	AEV, Visites, no. 1200/1, 4r. (1330)

Table 3.1 Diocese of Girona, family relations in the parish

PARISH	CLERIC	NOTES	SOURCE
Sant Vicenç de Besalú	Sacrist Pere de Casellis	Father lives in the village	ADG, Visites, no. 4, 161r.v. (1329)
Sant Martí de Biert	Deacon Simó de Soler	"ancilla" Ermesenda, daughter of En Perer de Camons, is the "consanguinea germana" of the deacon	ADG, Visites, no. 1, 17r. (1314)
Bestracà	Cleric Ramon	Related to concubine Mariona de Costa "in gradu consanguinitatis"	ADG, Visites fragmentaris, 11r. (1303)
Sant Feliu de Beuda	Sacrist Arnau de Quera	The sacrist sins with Agneta Pinyola from Besalú, who is related to him within four degrees of consanguinity	ADG, Remissions de Penes, no. 1, 35r. (1352)
Caça de Pelràs	Beneficed cleric Arnau Caner	Father Arnau Caner lives in the parish	ADG, Visites fragmentaris, 11v.–12r. (1320)
Santa Maria de Castelló d'Empúries	Sacrist menor Pere Cocó	Uncle Castelló Cocó founded two benefices, one obtained by his nephew Pere	ADG, Visites, no. 4, 7r. (1329)
Centenys	Stabilitus Berenguer Simó	Brother Bernat Simó lives in the same parish Both Berenguer and Bernat possibly related to the Stabilitus Pere Simó, who also serves in Centenys	ADG, Visites, no. 5, 6v. (1331)
Sant Genís de Cervià	Hebdomedarian Ramon Llorenç	Related to Ermesenda de Font in "tercio gradu consanguinis," with whom he had a child	ADG, Visites fragmentaris, 8v. (1303)
Monastir Santa Maria de Cervià	Stabilitus Pere Batlle	Father lives in the parish and is the local bailiff, and is also the patron of Pere's benefice	ADG, Visites, no. 5, 29v. (1331)
Crespià	Pere Caragoll, stabilitus in capella Sant Jaume de Garrigà	Related to Guillem de Carraria Pere kept Guillem's wife Barchiona as his concubine	ADG, Visites, no. 5, 101v. (1331)
Santa Maria de Colomers	Hebdomedarian Berenguer Feliu	Keeps Maria Costa, his "comatre" and spiritual daughter as concubine	ADG, Visites, no. 4, 13v. (1329)
Santa Maria de Darnius	Sacrist Pere de Palomer	Mother lives in parish Carnally knows his "comatre" Maria Cardona	ADG, Visites, no. 2, 82v.–83r. (1315)

(continued)

Table 3.1 Diocese of Girona, family relations in the parish (*continued*)

PARISH	CLERIC	NOTES	SOURCE
Serra de Daró	Hebdomedarian Simó Alenyà	Mother lives in the adjacent parish of Fonolleres Simó Alenyà first started out serving in the parish of Sant Juià de Corçà near the village of Fonolleres and eventually obtained the position of hebdomedarian in Serra	ADG, Visites, no. 1, 2v. (1314); Visites, no. 2, 7r.v. (1315); Visites fragmentaris, 2r. (1318); Notularum, no. 6, 125v. (1327)
Esponellà	Hebdomedarian Ramon Bartomeu	Related "in gradu parentele" to Pere Guerau; Hebdomedarian had affair with Geralda, Pere Guerau's wife Uncle Berenguer Cunyl keeps a tavern in the village Sister Sibil·la Bartomeu is married to a fellow villager	ADG, Visites, no. 5, 9v., 11v. (1331)
	Sacrist Guillem d'Anglada	Brother Berenguer d'Anglada lives in the village	ADG, Visites, no. 5, 15r. (1331)
Santa Coloma de Farners	Deacon Pere de Calico	Brother and stabilitus Guillem de Calico serves in the same parish	ADG, Visites, no. 4, 212r. (1329)
Figueres	Hebdomedarian Joan Serra	His nephew, the cleric Jaume Dalmaç, serves the office of hebdomedarian for him	ADG, Visites, no. 3, 24r. (1321)
Sant Miquel de Fluvià	Beneficed cleric Pere Batlle	Brother and saig Bernat Batlle lives in the parish	ADG, Processos, no. 125 (1333)
	Cleric Nicolau Rei in monastery of Sant Miquel	Mother and sister lives in nearby village of Vilacolum Another sister lives in the village of Vilafant	ADG, Processos, no. 111 (1330)
Foixá	Hebdomedarian Guillem Martor	Related "in gradu parentela" to concubine Saurina (daughter of Ramon Pere de Toralles)	ADG, Imposicions de Penes, no. 1, 10r. (1336)
Castell de Foixá	Rector and prior Ramon Bernat	Mother Maria, wife of Guillem Bernat, as well as his brother, the tonsured cleric Arnau, and another brother, Bernat, live in Foixá	ADG, Processos, no. 188 (1337)
Fontanilles	Deacon Bernat de Toro	Related in third or fourth degree to concubine Bertrana de Vilanó	ADG, Visites fragmentaris, 6r.v. (1305)

Fornells	Hebdomedarian Bernat de Comes	Father Vidal de Comes lives in the parish	ADG, Visites fragmentaris, 7v.–8r. (1320)
Sant Juià de Fortià	Deacon Berenguer Escuder	Brother Bernat Escuder, a married cleric, lives in the parish	ADG, Visites, no. 6, 155r. (1340)
Sant Feliu de la Garriga	Sacrist Guillem	Father Berenguer Jaume Related to Pere, son of Pere de Garrigas Second cousin to Bernat de Ferreres and Guillem de Ferreres	ADG, Processos, no. 23 (1315)
	Deacon Arnau de Basso	Brothers live in nearby village d'Armentera	ADG, Processos, no. 23 (1315); Visites, no. 1, 36r.v. (1315)
	Sacrist Pere Vidal	Keeps a home in Vilamacolum where his concubine Sibil·la and his nephew Antonio Vidal live	ADG, Visites, no. 7, 42r. (1342)
Garrigàs	Sacrist Pere Carnallera	Father Bernat Carnallera, brother Ramon Pere, sister Raimunda live in the parish	ADG, Visites, no. 7, 146r., 149v.–150r. (1341)
Sant Feliu de Girona	Cleric Arnau de Vic	Sister lives in Girona	ADG, Processos, no. 100 (1328)
Sant Gregori	Sacrist Bernat de Verdaguer	Sister Brunisenda de Verdaguer and nephews Guillem and Bernat live in the parish Sister Elisenda and husband Mateu Mir live in the parish	ADG, Notularum, no. 17, 139v.–140r. (1344)
Hostalric	Deacon Bernat de Terrades	Brother Pere de Terrades lives in nearby village of Sant Celoni	ADG, Processos, no. 197, 2r. (1338)
Hostalric	Rector Ramon Rosell	Cousin Berenguer Rosell is a cleric in Hostalric Nephew Anton de Surell is a tonsured cleric in the neighboring village of Tordera	ADG, Processos, no. 197, 2v.–3r. (1338)
Sant Cristòfol de les Planes d'Hostoles	Hebdomedarian Pere de Fabrica	Uncle Bernat de Pineda lives in parish Related to Na Pegoç "in secundo gradu parentela" with whom he carnally sinned	ADG, Visites, no. 4, 111r. (1329)
Llançà	Cleric Ponç de Roca	Father Ponç de Roca lives in the parish	ADG, Processos, no. 16 (1308)

(continued)

Table 3.1 Diocese of Girona, family relations in the parish (*continued*)

PARISH	CLERIC	NOTES	SOURCE
Maçanet	Cleric Berenguer Collel	Sister and brother-in-law live in Maçanet	ADG, Processos, no. 106 (1330)
Sant Vicenç de Maià de Montcal	Hebdomedarian Guillem Jaubert	Tonsured clerics and scolares Guillem Llorenç and Pere Fuser are Guillem's nephews and live in the parish	ADG, Visites, no. 4, 170v.–172r. (1329)
Sant Genís de Matajudaica	Deacon	Lives in neighboring village of Casavells with father	ADG, Visites, no. 4, 17r. (1329)
Mieres	Deacon Ramon de Corbs	Nephew lives in his home	ADG, Processos, no. 122, 2v. (1331)
Santa Maria de Montcal	Stabilitus Jaume	God-father to Brunisenda de Berlana (married) with whom he had an affair	ADG, Visites, no. 1, 70r. (1315)
Sant Llorenç de la Muga	Stabilitus Guillem Sala	Cousin Bernat Sala lives in parish (Guillem carnally sinned with cousin Bernat's wife)	ADG, Visites, no. 6, 58v. (1340).
Santa Eulàlia de Noves	Stabilitus Castelló Cerbols	Brother lives in the parish, testified before episcopal visitor on Castelló's behalf	ADG, Visites, no. 4, 198v. (1329)
Peralada	Stabilitus Jaume Sala	Brother Joan Sala de Peralada instituted benefice for Jaume Uncle Nicolau Ade lives in parish	ADG, Notularum, no. 6, 150r. (1327); Visites, no. 6, 47v.–48r., 49v. (1340)
Santa Maria de Palera	Stabilitus Bernat Miró	Related to concubine who is his "consobrina"	ADG, Visites, no. 6, 51r. (1340)
	Rector Bernat Roca	Related to concubine Maria (wife of Pere de Esglesia)	ADG, Visites, no. 1, 71r. (1315); Lletres, no. 2, 118r. (1326)
Sant Feliu de Pallerols	Capellan Bernat d'Anglada	Related to concubine "in gradu parentela"	ADG, Visites, no. 2, 36v.–37r. (1315)
Sant Pere Pescador	Stabilitus Ramon Perpinyà	Related in third or fourth degree to concubine Dolça Monda	ADG, Visites fragmentaris, 5v. (1303)
Sils	Sacrist Arnau de Terrades	Sister lives in his home	ADG, Visites, no. 3, 31r.v. (1321)
	Rector Berenguer de Camp	Related to concubine Oliveta "in gradu parentela"	ADG, Visites, no. 4, 81v. (1329)

Location	Role/Name	Description	Source
Taravaus	Stabilitus Joan de Font	Parents Bartomeu and Guillema de Font live in the parish of Taravaus, as have the clerics Ramon de Font and Joan de Font In 1320, Joan de Font is identified as a "scolar" who was presented to the benefice of stabilitus with the condition that he employ a substitute while he attend a singing school for two years and then attend grammar school. In 1329, Joan is identified as holding the benefice of stabilitus even though he is not yet promoted to the sacred orders	ADG, Notularum, no. 3, 12r. (1320); Visites, no. 4, 44v. (1329)
Ullastret	Sacrist Guillem Mata	Nephew Guillem Miró lives in Ullastret	ADG, Processos, no. 134 (c.1334–1335)
Verges	Sacrist Pere Vidal	Sister and brother-in-law live in the parish	ADG, Processos, no. 198 (1338)
Santa Maria de Vidreres	Stabilitus Bernat Rafard	Lives in the home of his "consobrina"	ADG, Visites, no. 4, 94v. (1329)
Sant Vicenç de Viladasens	Hebdomedarian Guillem de Vidal	Related "in gradu consanguinitatis" to Bonanata, daughter of Pere Morer Bonanata is identified as Guillem's consobrina who he "carnally knows"	ADG, Visites, no. 4, 63v–64r.v., 210v. (1329)
Vilanova	Stabilitus Joan Escuder	Joan's daughter and niece, the widow Alayda, and his brother Bernat Escuder live in Vilanova	ADG, Processos, no. 185 (1337)
Vilanova de la Muga	Cleric Ponç d'Om	Father helped Ponç cultivate lands near the village. Ponç appears as hebdomedarian of the parish in 1349	ADG, Visites, no. 6, 157r. (1341)
Vilamalla	Sacrist Ramon Rubí	Family relatives live and own a manse called Rubí in the nearby village of Saus	ADG, Lletres, no. 8, 146r.v. (1344)

Table 3.2 Diocese of Urgell, family relations in the parish

PARISH	CLERIC	NOTES	SOURCE
Sant Pere d'Alp	Rector	Brother lives in the parish	ACV, Calaix, 31/43, Visites, no. 1, 40v. (1312)
Sant Feliu d'Àreu	Rector Miquel Bonfil	Related to his concubine Na Blanca within the third or fourth degree of consanguinity	ACV, Calaix, 31/43, Visites, no. 5, 18r. (1315)
Sant Pere de Colls	Rector Ramon de Roda	Related to concubine Anglesa, daughter of Salvador d'Astruc, within the third or fourth degree of consanguinity	ACV, Calaix, 31/43, Visites, no. 5, 6r.v. (1315)
Sant Quirze et Juià de çaComa	Capellan	Related to witnesses interrogated by episcopal visitor	ACV, Calaix, 31/43, Visites, no. 3, 36r. (1314)
Sant Maria de Llivia	Cleric Ramon Grayt	Related to concubine Elisenda Ovelgra	ACV, Calaix, 31/43, Visites, no. 6, 9v. (1315)
Sant Salvador de Meya	Rector Bernat Bertran	Related to concubine Çaldua through ties of affinity	ACV, Calaix 31/43, Visites, no. 4, 37v. (1315)
Santa Maria de Montcuy	Rector	Related to parishioner Bernat de Tornafort within the second degree of consanguinity Rector keeps Bernat's wife Maria as his concubine	ACV, Calaix, 31/43, Visites, no. 5, 11v. (1315)
Sant Cebrià d'Ordino	Deacon Berenguer Joan	First cousin to capellan's concubine Keeps capellan's daughter Maria as his concubine	ACV, Calaix 31/43, Visites, no. 1, 21v. (1312)
Sant Iscle de Taltendre	Vicar	Uncle Guillem Puig lives in the parish	ACV, Calaix, 31/43, Visites, no. 7, 39v. (1313)

Table 3.3 Diocese of Vic, family relations in the parish

PARISH	CLERIC	NOTES	SOURCE
Sant Fruitós de Balenyà	Rector	Granddaughter Maria, daughter of Joan, the rector's son, lives in the parish Provided 1,000 sous for Maria's dowry	AEV, Visites, no. 1200/1, 18r. (1330); Visites, no. 1200/3, 1v. (1332)
Balenyà	Beneficed cleric Andreu de Feyra	Sister Pascal and her husband and children live in the parish	AEV, Testaments, ACF-3509 (1319–1324), 70r. (c. 1319–1324)
Cans	Rector Ramon de Sant Pere	Brother Bartomeu de Sant Pere and his wife Elisenda live in the parish	AEV, Visites, no. 1200/2, 55v. (1331)
Contabella near Cervera	Rector	Mother lives in his home with concubine and daughter	AEV, Visites, no. 1200/2, 8r. (1331)
Sant Joan de Fàbregues	Rector Pere ces Planta	En Mas de Rupit "consanguinei germani sui" Wife of en Mas de Rupit "comater"	AEV, Visites, no. 1200/2, 83r. (1332)
Santa Maria de Granyena	Priest Arnau Cota	Related to Sibil·la, his concubine, within the four degrees of consanguinity	AEV, Visites, no. 1200/2, 21v. (1331)
Millany	Rector Bernat ça Manera	Uncle lives in the parish	AEV, Visites, no. 1200/1, 22r. (1330)
Sant Andreu de Pruit	Rector Guillem ça Devesa	Had a daughter with Elisenda de Coll, his "consanguinea germana et comatre"	AEV, Visites, no. 1200/2, 84r. (1332)
Segúries	Rector	Baptized the wife of his son Berenguer de Tergurano	AEV, Visites, no. 1200/3, 48r. (1336)
Sant Martí de Sesgueioles	Priest Jaume Feliu	Related to concubine Elisenda, wife of Ramon de Puigalt	AEV, Visites, no. 1200/3, 10r. (1332)
Sant Pere de Valldeneu	Rector Berenguer de Puig	Uncle, a beneficed cleric, lives in the parish	AEV, Visites, no. 1200/1, 16r. (1330)
Vic	Cleric Bernat Hort	Brother Ferrar de Hort and nephew Berenguer live in the neighboring parish of Gurb Godson Berenguer Arnau and goddaughter live in Vic	AEV, Testaments, ACF-3509 (1319–1324), 3r. (c. 1319)

Table 4.1 "Quarrelsome" clergymen in Catalunya

PARISH	CLERIC	"QUARRELSOME" CHARGE	SOURCE	OTHER CHARGES
Agullana	Sacrist Jaume Flors	Found guilty of injuring a woman during a fight with four male parishioners	ADG, Remissions de Penes, no. 1, 32r. (1351)	
Albons	Hebdomedarian Guillem Gilabert	"Great fight and contumelious words" between the hebdomedarian and other clerics of the church	ADG, Visites, no. 7, 88v. (1343)	The priests Guillem Vals and Berenguer Caules, who fought with Guillem, were noted for their relationships with single women.
Aro	Hebdomedarian Ramon Eimeric and the claviger Ramon Joffre	Clerics are described as "brachosi et rixosi" The hebdomedarian fought with the deacon Ramon in the parish church. In 1326, Ramon Eimeric was also cited for fighting with the sacrist Guillem de Castellar, the hebdomedarian Berenguer Conil, and the stabilitus Ramon de Quintana. In 1332, Ramon Eimeric was ordered to appear before the bishop's court for his quarrel with the capellan Berenguer de Sous.	ADG, Lletres, no. 2 bis, 12v.–13r., 25v.–26r. (1326); Lletres, no. 5, 51r. (1332); Visites, no. 6, 1v.–2r. (1338); Visites, no. 8, 23v.–24r. (1345)	Both men kept concubines and had a minimum of two children each
	Sacrist Guillem de Castellar	Described as a "homo rixosus" Insults and says contumelious words against fellow clerics while in the church and performing the divine office Travels about the parish armed	ADG, Visites, no. 4, 200v.–201r. (1329)	The sacrist keeps Maria Carbonela as his concubine
Sant Vicenç de Besalú	Prior of Santa Maria	Struck and choked the sacrist Pere de Casellis in the church of Sant Vicenç Injured Pere Blancher in the head with a rock	ADG, Visites, no. 4, 161r.v.–162r. (1329); Lletres, no. 4, 87v. (1330)	The prior reportedly kept in concubinage the wife of Pere de Beuda; he also had a daughter with Na Moneta

Parish	Cleric(s)	Description	Citation	Notes
Sant Feliu de Beuda	Hebdomedarian Berenguer de Gualba, sacrist Pere Pelicer, and deacon Mateu Losa	The three clerics fight among themselves within the church and often during the divine office The hebdomedarian was also charged with injuring the deacon The sacrist Arnau Quera received a letter of remission for the injurious and shameful words against the prior of Sant Tomàs	ADG, Visites, no. 6, 71r.–72r.v. (1340); ADG, Remissions de Penes, no. 1, 6r. (1346)	The hebdomedarian was also charged with sinning with Guillema de Pont, daughter of Na de Pont
	Hebdomedarian Arnau Quitart and the sacrist Arnau Quera	Both found guilty of fighting with their swords against each other inside and outside the parish church	ADG, Remissions de Penes, no. 1, 50r.v. (1354)	
Sant Martí de Caçà de la Selva	Sacrist Bernat Mascort	Fought and was injured by Arnau Barner over a dispute concerning Arnau's sister; the sacrist is described as being in love with the sister Abandoned his benefice because he impregnated and injured the daughter of Guillem Grayt	ADG, Visites, no. 8, 25r. (1345)	
Cadaqués	Capellan Arnau Ferrar	Described as "multum rixosus" Argues and insults parishioners, reports them to the curia Causes others in the parish to fight; beat the layman Pere Gitard with a staff Prohibits the Dominicans from preaching in the parish Drinks and interrupts the divine office Prohibits other clerics from singing the mass	ADG, Visites, no. 3, 17r.v.–18r.v. (1321)	
Priory of Sant Esteve de Caneres	Prior Vicenç de Roure	Attacked the hebdomedarian Guillem Fuster of Darnius	ADG, Remissions de Penes, no. 1, 44r. (1354)	The prior was also found guilty of siring two daughters with Francesca, the widow of Pere Riera
Sant Medir de Cartellà	Hebdomedarian Bernat de Brugeria	Fights inside and outside the church with the sacrist Arnau de Laura; attacked the sacrist with a bow and arrow while wearing a dagger Took a missal from the church so that the sacrist could not perform the mass	ADG, Visites, no. 8, 60r.v. (1346)	
Sant Medir de Cartellà	Sacrist Arnau de Llor	Described as a "homo bricosus" Fights with the hebdomedarian Bernat de Brugeria	ADG, Visites, no. 8, 61v. (1346)	Has a son by the name of Guillem de Llor who lives in the parish

(continued)

Table 4.1 "Quarrelsome" clergymen in Catalunya (continued)

PARISH	CLERIC	"QUARRELSOME" CHARGE	SOURCE	OTHER CHARGES
Sant Julià de Corçà	Deacon Bernat Castelló	Carries arms through the village and at night Parishioners fear being assaulted by the deacon and call him "dishonest"	ADG, Visites, no. 1, 2v. (1314)	
Sant Iscle d'Empordà	Stabilitus Bernat Mercer	Fought and threatened sacrist over Bernat's possession of a gambling board	ADG, Visites, no. 4, 16v–17r. (1329)	The stabilitus Bernat keeps Maria as his concubine
Castelló d'Empúries	Cleric En Carbonel	Reported to have killed En Ropidel	ADG, Visites fragmentaris, 7r. (1323)	
	Cleric Ramon Cursanini	Reported to have killed Françesc Serra	ADG, Visites fragmentaris, 7r. (1323)	
	Cleric Bernat Gener	Travels with arms throughout the town Brought before the bishop's court for insulting, beating, and cutting the layman Joan Alaó with a large dagger	ADG, Visites fragmentaris, 7v.–8r.v.(1323); Processos, no. 33, 4ff (1320)	Fined 40 sous for having a child with a "defamed" woman, the daughter of Na Ponça
Sant Martí de Colonge	Hebdomedarian Pere Ferrar	Attempted rape of Elisenda, wife of Guillem Barber Fought with the husband, and during the struggle Elisenda's infant daughter was injured and died	ADG, Visites, no. 8, 17v, 18v. (1345); Remissions de Penes, no. 1, 1v. (1345)	
Santa Maria de Darnius	Sacrist Pere de Palomer	Described as a "homo rixosus" Known to beat his mother "Invades" the homes of parishioners Slapped a man from Agullana	ADG, Visites, no. 2, 82v–83r. (1315)	Also known to keep a concubine
Esponellà	Sacrist Guillem d'Anglada	Intervened on his brother's behalf in a fight with the layman Pere Sardina	ADG, Visites, no. 5, 15r.v. (1331)	
Sant Andreu d'Estanyol	Stabilitus Berenguer Pagès	Described as "homo valde rixosus" Drew his sword against the layman Pere Garangonis in a dispute Engaged in a sword fight with the layman Guillem de Sigario in the church cemetery Reported to have plotted to kill the hebdomedarian Castelló of Estanyol	ADG, Visites, no. 4, 103v–104r.v. (1330); Visites, no. 5, 135v. (1332)	Reported to have more four children from three women in the parish By 1332, Berenguer obtained the benefice of stabilitus in the parish of Rabós

Location	Persons	Description	Source	Notes
Flaçà	Rector Berenguer de Mediavilla and deacon	Contention between the rector and deacon over celebrating the morning mass during Easter and Christmas	ADG, Visites, no. 6, 89v.–90r. (1340)	
Castell de Foixà	Rector Ramon Bernat	Injured the layman Bord de Foixá in a swordfight	ADG, Processos, no. 188, 83ff. (1337)	Keeps Englentina and his two daughters, Maria and Beatriu, in the village
Fornells	Capellan Arnau Marenes	Injured and mutilated the sister of his concubine	ADG, Visites fragmentaris, 7v. (1320)	
Sant Juià de Fortià	Deacon Berenguer Scutifer and his brother Bernat Scutifer	The deacon and his brother fought and extracted their swords against Castelló Baldomar	ADG, Visites, no. 6, 155r. (1340)	
Sant Feliu de la Garriga	Deacon Arnau de Basso	Engaged in a sword fight with Guillem Agustí and Berenguer Agustí, including the sacrist who left the parish because of the fight	ADG, Processos, no. 23, 10ff. (1315); Visites, no. 1, 36r.v. (1314)	Both the deacon Arnau and the sacrist were known to have sexual relationships with two women from the parish
Sant Miquel de Garrigàs	Sacrist Pere Camaller	Performs the divine office with a sword belt. Fought with swords in the church and exchanges insults with the hebdomedarian Bernat Fortià. Exchanged insults with the layman Guillem	ADG, Visites, no. 7, 143r., 149v, 151r.v. (1343)	
Sant Feliu de Girona	Sacrist Pere Dalmau and the cleric Frances Caluet	Fought with the bailiff of Girona. Arrested for public disorder, carrying weapons, and for minor violence against secular officials	ADG, Processos, no. 275, 30ff. (1354)	
Llanars	Hebdomedarian Arnau Melera and another hebdomedarian	Both clergymen fight with each other and are frequently absent from the parish	ADG, Visites fragmentaris, 22v.-23r. (1305)	
Llanars	Hebdomedarian Bernat des Puyol and the deacon Guillem de Brugada	Exchange "injurious words" with each other. Visitor imposed a fine of 10 sous on both men and ordered that they no longer insult each other	ADG, Visites, no. 4, 139r.v. (1329)	

(continued)

Table 4.1 "Quarrelsome" clergymen in Catalunya (continued)

PARISH	CLERIC	"QUARRELSOME" CHARGE	SOURCE	OTHER CHARGES
Lledó	Rector Nicolau de Roca	Hated by parishioners and described as "valde rixosus"	ADG, Visites, no. 4, 81v. (1329)	
Sant Feliu de Lledó	Hebdomedarian Jaume Tarascó	Shouts and disrupts the mass when performed by the hebdomedarian Joan Pastor; incites the people against the hebdomedarian Joan, the sacrist, and the deacon	ADG, Processos, no. 104, 12ff. (1329)	
	Hebdomedarian Jaume Gorner	Received a letter of remission for his fight with the hebdomedarian Berenguer Rider and the sacrist Guillem Clar	ADG, Remissions de Penes, no. 1, 47r.v. (1353)	
Santa Maria de Lledó	Stabilitus Joan Oliver	Gravely beat Na Oliva and punched her mother in the face "Atrociously beat" Na Feyna and another woman from Sant Martí Vell Described as a "homo bricosus" and "homo vilis" Known to carry arms, gamble, swear, and associate with armed men to do "bad things" Reputed to be the "enemy" of the prior of Santa Maria de Lledó	ADG, Processos, no. 66, 94ff. (1323)	
	Sacrist Guillem de Serra	Described as a "homo rixosus" Travels about the parish armed Hit a parishioner with a gaming board in the face Beat another parishioner with a staff Insults parishioners and their wives	ADG, Visites, no. 5, 81r.v. (1331)	Previously kept a woman in his home for more than one year, but she left the parish
Sant Martí de Maçanet	Sacrist Berenguer Molar	Fought with the husband of Mercera, his concubine, and reported to have arranged the husband's death	ADG, Visites, no. 6, 60v. (1340)	
Matajudaica	Sacrist Francesc Alagtoz	Described as "est homo valde motus et rixosus" The parishioners twice in 1340 and 1346 complained that Francesc was combative and quarreled with parishioners	ADG, Visites, no. 6, 113r.v. (1340); no. 8, 94v. (1346); Penes, 64r. (1346)	The sacrist kept the pregnant Raimunda Rega and his son Joan in the parish and was known to have previously kept the woman Verlora as his concubine

Place	Role	Description	Source	Notes
Sant Sadurní de Medinyà	Sacrist	Verbally insults parishioners "idem sacrist pluries dicit eisdem parrochianis verba injuria et turpia et valde enormia"	ADG, Visites, no. 8, 53v. (1346)	The unnamed sacrist also kept a woman in his home
Sant Pere de Mieres	Sacrist Joan Ferrar and hebdomedarian Arnau de Rovira	Frequently fight and verbally insult each other; there is such discord between the two clerics that the sacrist rarely attends church or performs the divine office	ADG, Visites, no. 1, 55v.–56r. (1315); Visites, no. 3, 46r.v. (1321)	The sacrist Joan Ferrar has children with Elisenda de Puig Molin
Mieres	Hebdomedarian Guillem Bàscara	Created so much conflict in the parish that on account of the "animosity" of villagers, he was granted permission to serve in another parish. Quarreled with the monk Arnau de Torroella from Banyoles.	ADG, Lletres, no. 5, 96r. (1333) and 155r. (1334); Notularum, no. 4, 123v. (1324)	
Sant Vicenç de Maià de Montcal	Sacrist Guillem Ferrar	Fights with the hebdomedarian Guillem Jaubert	ADG, Visites, no. 2, 74r.v.–77r. (1315); Visites, no. 4, 192v. (1329)	The sacrist keeps Maria Rosa and his son in house next to his. Also fined 100 sous for his involvement with two married women
	Hebdomedarian Guillem Jaubert	Attends church armed with a sword, lance, shield, and crossbow. Numerous fights and insults exchanged with the sacrist Guillem Ferrar	ADG, Visites, no. 4, 170v.–172r., 192v. (1329)	
Mollet	Sacrist Berenguer de Font	Found guilty of wielding arms and injuring a cleric in the church of Força and a man in Flaçà	ADG, Remissions de Penes, no. 1, 12v. (1348)	
Sant Llorenç de la Muga	Deacon Bartomeu de Roure	In 1332, the deacon beat the butcher Berenguer Parada for pushing his son off a table. By 1352, Bartomeu held the benefice of stabilitus and was fined for taking part in a fight with parishioners that included the hebdomedarian Berenguer Salvador	ADG, Processos, no. 124, 4ff. (1332); Remissions de Penes, no. 1, 40r.v. (1352)	
	Cleric Guillem de Roure and the married cleric Guillem Geroni	Received letters of remission for their participation in the fight against four parishioners, including the breaking into and invasion of the hebdomedarian's home	ADG, Remissions de Penes, no. 1, 41r.v. (1352)	

(continued)

Table 4.1 "Quarrelsome" clergymen in Catalunya (*continued*)

PARISH	CLERIC	"QUARRELSOME" CHARGE	SOURCE	OTHER CHARGES
Sant Juià d'Ordis	Hebdomedarian Pere Jaume	In 1338, reported to the episcopal visitor that the sacrist Bernat Brasconi beat him "atrociter" in the church	ADG, Visites, no. 6, 25v. (1338)	
	Sacrist Bernat Brasconi	In 1346 reported that there has been great "discord" between the hebdomedarian Pere Jaume and the sacrist for more than six years that has resulted in beatings and injuries	ADG, Visites, no. 8, 47r. (1346)	
		Sacrist known to verbally abuse the hebdomedarian when he performs the mass		
Sant Pere de Pescador	Hebdomedarian Pere de Banc and the stabilitus Pere Fresc	Both described as "rixosus" and carrying arms	ADG, Visites fragmentaris, 5r.v. (1303)	
		The hebdomedarian reportedly beat a male parishioner in the face with his fists		
	Stabilitus Guillem Jaffer	"Violavit" a virgin girl from Armentera	ADG, Visites, no. 3, 31r., 32v. (1321)	
		Fought with Ramon Pere de Armentera and killed another man		
	Sacrist Arnau de Terrades	Fought with hebdomedarian Arnau de Cornellis over the hebdomedarian's amorous pursuit of his sister	ADG, Visites, no. 3, 31r.v. (1321)	
Peratallada	Cleric Bartomeu Roig	Stabbed a man with a hayfork	ADG, Processos, no. 244, 15ff. (1347)	
		Described as "homo brichosus et rixosus," "multum inhonesta," and "homo valde motus"		
		Accuses villagers of crimes to the local lord		
		Involved in usury and charges to remove ground meal from the local mill		
Riudellots de la Selva	Claviger Berenguer Gombau	Found guilty of fighting (*bricham*) with the priest Bernat Rufi and the sacrist of Corçà	ADG, Remissions de Penes, no. 1, 30r. (1351)	
Rupià	Hebdomedarian Bernat Ullà and the sacrist Arnau de Guardia against the stabilitus Berenguer de Puigalt	A "magna brica et rixa" between the hebdomedarian and sacrist on one side, and the stabilitus on the other concerning the allotment of oblations and gifts	ADG, Visites, no. 6, 96v.–97r. (1340)	

Location	Cleric	Description	Source	Notes
Sant Morí	Stabilitus Guillem Camallera	Parishioners reported that their stabilitus was being investigated for homicide	ADG, Visites, no. 3, 28r. (1321)	
Monastir Sant Tomàs	Príor Pere de Vic	Beat and dragged a male parishioner by the hair Beat Guillema Blanca because she was disparaging him (*vituperabat cum*)	ADG, Visites, no. 6, 37v.–38r.v. (1338)	
Santa Coloma de Siurana	Hebdomedarian Pere Messaguer	Kidnapped a "puella" and kept her in his home until the Count of Empúries' men came and forcibly took the young girl	ADG, Visites, no. 3, 25r.v. (1321)	The hebdomedarian had a child with Cilia, daughter of Castelló de Ruppa from Siurana
	Hebdomedarian Pere Bernat	Described as "multum brichosus" Performs the divine office armed Fought and threatened the stabilitus En Garrigas	ADG, Visites, no. 4, 9v.–10r. (1329)	Pere Bernat was known to keep Na Benaguda in the parish of Saus
Sant Genís de Torroella de Montgrí	Stabilitus Francesc Canet	Carries arms inside the church and choir	ADG, Visites, no. 4, 20v.–21r. (1329)	Francesc has two children with Simoneta, the daughter of Simó Sartor
Torroella de Montgrí	Hebdomedarian Bernat Rourich	Participated in the assault of Joan Pedret Described as a "homo vilis" who leads a "depraved life" (*prave vitae*) Known to carry arms, gamble, swear, and drink excessively Attempted to rape a woman in Monells	ADG, Processos, no. 259. 15ff. (c. 1350)	
	Priest Bartomeu de Tor	Excommunicated and absolved for placing violent hands on the cleric Bernat Pich, who also served in the parish.	ADG, Notularum, no. 18, 134r. (1346)	
	Beneficed cleric Guillem de Tor	Started a sword fight with Pere Terreguini over a gambling dispute Attacked the bailiff of Torroella with a sword and injured the bailiff's son Injured the son of Guillem Ponç, and beat the wife of Guillem with a staff Invaded the house of Guillem Saloni Gravely beat Francesca with a staff	ADG, Processos, no. 73, 17ff. (1323)	

(continued)

Table 4.1 "Quarrelsome" clergymen in Catalunya (*continued*)

PARISH	CLERIC	"QUARRELSOME" CHARGE	SOURCE	OTHER CHARGES
Ullastret	Sacrist Guillem Mata	Involved in a fistfight with the sheriff of the castle after an exchange of "injurious words"	ADG, Processos, no. 134, 12ff. (c. 1334–1335)	
St. Iscle de Vallalta	Deacon Joan de Puig	Described as "valde rixosus" Travels about armed with a large knife	ADG, Visites, no. 4, 84r. (1329)	The deacon also keeps in his home Sibil·la Cordera as his concubine
Valveralla	Sacrist Pere Soquert	Fought with the layman Joan de Vilafreser and was injured during the fight; both men are considered "enemies"	ADG, Visites, no. 3, 37r.v–38r. (1321)	
Verges	Sacrist Pere Vidal	Threatened, exchanged insults with, and beat his neighbor Guillem Fuxà until he was "half-dead" Also killed the neighbor's pig	ADG, Processos, no. 198, 8ff. (1338)	
Sant Vicenç de Vilamala	Sacrist Pere Ricart	Injured the layman Bernat de Santa Eulàlia with his sword	ADG, Visites fragmentaris, 5r. (1312)	The sacrist was also involved in a carnal relationship with Moneta Sartra
Vilanova	Hebdomedarian Pere Bernat	Described as "rixosus" and "bricosus," as well as dishonest	ADG, Visites, no. 6, 156r. (1341)	The hebdomedarian had a child with Garssenda when he served in the parish of Siurana
	Stabilitus Joan Escuder and the tonsured cleric Bernat Prim	Came to blows with the cleric Ponç de Tina because of Ponç's unwelcomed sexual advances against Joan's daughter and niece	ADG, Processos, no. 185, 24ff. (1337)	
Sant Joan de Vilatenim	Sacrist Pere Martí	Sacrist gambles in the cemetery with parishioners and exchanges "injurious words" Beat the layman En Marches	ADG, Visites, no. 6, 12v. (1338)	
Sant Pere de Castellfollit de Boix	Rector	Slapped Na Sorisa Fought with a cleric in the church and drew his sword; also made a disturbance while the cleric said mass Reveals the confessions of parishioners Produces false documents	AEV, Visites, no. 1200/2, 61r. (1331)	

Location	Person	Description	Source	Notes
Sant Vicenç de Espinelves	Rector	Rector does not reside in the parish on account of his enemies in the village	AEV, Visites, no. 1200/2, 81r. (1332)	
Santa Maria de Granyena	Priests Andreas Morell and Pere Bonet	Reported to "secretly plant hatred and discord between parishioners and the lord of the place or his officials"	AEV, Visites, no. 1200/2, 21v. (1331)	
Grevalosa	Rector Francesc de Coll	Reported to have associated with "murderers" but found not guilty in a certain homicide committed by these men	AEV, Visites, no. 1200/2, 51r. (1331)	
Manlleu	Sacrist	Beat a parishioner in the face with a candlestick	AEV, Visites, no. 1200/3, 3v. (1332)	
Porqueroles	Rector	Rector beat and broke the arm of the wife of Arnau Tarrat from Copons / Gravely injured a baker	AEV, Visites, no. 1200/2, 44r. (1331)	
Santa Maria de Tàrrega	Beneficed priest Pere Martí	Daily carries arms and is quarrelsome	AEV, Visites, no. 1200/2, 25r.v. (1331)	
Sant Vicenç de Torelló	Rector Berenguer Ça Carrera	Quarrels daily with neighbors and parishioners / Reports people to be captured by the secular court / Physically injured Na Pascala in a dispute / Violently removed his concubine Venguda from her husband / The vicar leaves on account of the rector	AEV, Visites, no. 1200/1, 10r.v. (1330)	
Sant Martí d'Aran	Rector Ansoler	Former rector Ansoler renounced his church to the rector Pere d'Agramont on account of a homicide he perpetrated	ACV, Calaix 31/43, Visites, no. 7, 35r. (1313)	
Beders	Pere de Riba, rector of Beders and a canon of Talló	Episcopal visitor charged Pere with being "rixosum et sediciosum" / Also found guilty of saying "verba contumeliosa" to faithful Christians	ACV, Calaix 31/43, Visites, no. 7, 37r. (1313)	The rector was also charged with keeping a concubine publicly and for fathering a son

(continued)

Table 4.1 "Quarrelsome" clergymen in Catalunya (*continued*)

PARISH	CLERIC	"QUARRELSOME" CHARGE	SOURCE	OTHER CHARGES
Cardona	Priest Berenguer de Aguilar	Causes quarrels among people and says "injurious words"	ACV, Calaix 31/43, Visites, no. 1, 28v. (1313)	
Sant Quirze de Ça Coma	Capellan	Quarrels with parishioners "over nothing"	ACV, Calaix 31/43, Visites, no. 3, 36r. (1315)	
Sant Policarp de Cortàs	Capellan	Described as "ritxosus"	ACV, Calaix 31/43, Visites, no. 7, 39v. (1313)	The chaplain reportedly kept a concubine but, according to witnesses, not publicly
Sant Sadurni de Fusteya	Capellan	Described as quarrelsome: "rixatur cum populo"	ACV, Calaix 31/43, Visites, no. 7, 53v. (1314)	
Santa Maria de Merola	Capellan Bernat	Described as "sediciosus," as a man who daily creates discord among parishioners Beat and stabbed the layman Berenguer de Puig In the same fight with Berenguer, the capellan beat Ermesenda who subsequently died from her wounds Travels about the parish armed	ACV, Calaix 31/43, Visites, no. 3, 15r. (1314)	
Santa Maria de Muntayana	Cleric Pere Borell	Described as "ritxsosus"	ACV, Calaix 31/43, Visites, no. 4, 8v. (1314)	
Sant Sadurni de Pratz	Rector	Described as "ritxosus cum suis parrochianis"	ACV, Calaix 31/43, Visites, no. 8, 32r. (1315)	The rector kept a concubine and had sons and daughters; parishioners reported that the rector's concubine revealed to people in the village what parishioners had confessed to the rector
Santa Maria de Puigcerdà	Priest Pere Gris	Hit the priests Jaume Seguerra and Pere Fabra within the church Accused of gambling and swearing	ACV, Calaix 31/43, Visites, no. 6, 16v., 18r. (1315)	The priest Pere was also known for keeping a concubine publicly

Location	Person	Description	Source	Notes
Santa Coloma de Ter	Vicar Bernat Ricart	Quarrels with parishioners concerning the food provided to him for presiding over nuptials and funeral rites	ACV, Calaix 31/43, Visites, no. 6, (1316)	Vicar keeps a married woman as concubine in the village of Urtx
Sant Cristòfol de Toses	Capellan	Described as a "homo rixosus"	ACV, Calaix 31/43, Visites, no. 6, 20v. (1316)	Unnamed capellan kept two concubines, Berengaria and a married woman
Sant Marçal de Castellet	Rector Ponç Vedell	Described as a "homo rixosus et dissolutus"	Visitatio diversarum, HMML, microfilm no. 31951, Visites, no. 1, 124v. (1310)	
Santa Coloma de Cervelló	Rector Guillem Soradel	Described as despising parishioners and disparaging them	Visitatio diversarum, HMML, microfilm no. 31951, Visites, no. 1, 57r. (1306)	
Sant Feliu de Codines	Rector Bonanat de Roca	Described as "multum mobilis et rixosus" Fought with two men and extracted his sword	Visitatio diversarum, HMML, microfilm no. 31951, Visites, no. 1, 74r. (1307)	The rector keeps Dolça Sala as his "wife" and has a seven-year-old daughter
Corró d'Amunt	Rector Guillem Bou	Described as a "homo rixosus" who causes many conflicts and fights inside and outside the church Reported to have revealed the confessions of parishioners Fought with the layman Bernat Carbó and injured him in the face when he threw a rock Injured the layman Carbonell Torrens with his sword Slapped the priest Jaume Cot in the face and caused blood to be shed within the church The rector and priest Jaume Cot were reported to have exchanged insults	Martí Bonet, "Visitas pastorals," 719–20, 728–29; Visitatio diversarum, HMML, microfilm no. 31951, Visites, no. 1, 21v. (1305)	The rector also keeps two concubines who live in different villages
Mallorca	Priest Anthonio Gilida	Presented a papal dispensation to the bishop of Barcelona for his crime of injuring a fellow priest	ADB, Registrum Communium, no. 1, 101r. (1309)	
Marata	Rector Pere de Fabrica	Ordered under penalty of 10 lliures to cease saying "illicit, vituperative, and other dishonest" words to his parishioners	Visitatio diversarum, HMML, microfilm no. 31951, Visites, no. 1, 73v. (1307)	

(continued)

Table 4.1 "Quarrelsome" clergymen in Catalunya (*continued*)

PARISH	CLERIC	"QUARRELSOME" CHARGE	SOURCE	OTHER CHARGES
Olzinelles	Rector En Costa	Described as threatening parishioners at all times	Visitatio diversarum, HMML, microfilm no. 31951, Visites, no. 1, 17v. (1305)	Parishioners also testified that the rector had previously kept a concubine in another village but that now he committed adultery with the married woman Geralda Sotzina
Sant Cugat de Segarrigues	Rector Pere	Described as spiteful and cruel in carrying out his duties	Visitatio diversarum, HMML, microfilm no. 31951, Visites, no. 1, 25v. (1303)	
Torrelles	Rector Bernat Gual	Described as a "homo rixosus" who provokes quarrels among parishioners Beat the layman Ferrer de Puig in the cemetery while exercising the office of bailiff Beat and injured a questor from the monastery of Santa Maria de Montserrat in the head Slapped the face of Pere Langer, a parishioner Severely beat his pregnant daughter-in-law who subsequently miscarried	Marti Bonet, "Visitas pastorals," 709–11, 720–27; Visitatio diversarum, HMML, microfilm no. 31951, Visites, no. 1, 92r. (1308)	The rector said mass with his son and publicly kept Geralda as his concubine
Sant Feliu de Vilamilany	Rector Pere Pedro	Described as a "homo rixosus" Parishioners abstain from attending the church service because they fear and abhor the rector's abuse	Visitatio diversarum, HMML, microfilm no. 31951, Visites, no. 1, 9v. (1303)	

Table 5.1 Clerical fathers, sons, brother, male cousins, and uncles in the diocese of Girona

PARISH	CLERIC	RELATIVES	SOURCE
Sant Pere de Albanyà	Capellan Ramon de Gordiola	Nephew Pere de Gordiola a tonsured cleric	ADG, Visites, no. 4, 166r.v. (1329)
Santa Maria de Angliès	Stabilitus Berenguer Fisque	Uncle Ramon de Fisque cleric in Bisbal	ADG, Visites, no. 1, 24r. (1315)
Sant Pol de la Bisbal	Rector Francesc Mons	Keeps his son in his home while Ortolana and daughter reside in Monells	ADG, Visites, no. 7, 82v. (1343)
La Bisbal d'Empordà	Hebdomedarian Jaume Marquès	Uncle Bernat de Lach a priest in the cathedral chapter of Girona	ADG, Notularum, no. 3, 11v.–12r. (1320)
Santa Maria de Bolós	Rector Guillem de Boix	Celebrates mass daily with his son Pere	ADG, Visites, no. 4, 141r. (1329)
Sant Joan de Borgonya	Rector Pere Arnau de Plano	Twelve-year old Son Ramon is a tonsured cleric Celebrates mass with Ramon	ADG, Visites, no. 4, 53v.–54r.v. (1329)
Cabanells	Hebdomedarian Guabert Vidal	Brother Berenguer is a cleric who serves in the parish of Espinavessa	ADG, Visites, no. 3, 4v.–5r. (1321)
Cadaques	Former rector and jureperitus Guillem de Bruguera	Established a benefice for his nephew Ramon de Bruguera	ADG, Visites, no. 7, 128r. (1343)
Sant Genís de Canavells	Sacrist Pere Pagès	Uncle Juià is a cleric in Santa Creu de Roses	ADG, Visites fragmentaris, 2v. (c. 1312–1313)
Sant Mateu de Canet	Hebdomedarian Berenguer Bonet	Celebrates mass with his son Simó	ADG, Visites fragmentaris, 5r. (1303); Visites, no. 1, 86v. (1315)
Sant Medir de Cartellà	Sacrist Arnau de Llor	His son Guillem de Llor lives in the parish	ADG, Visites, no. 8, 66v. (1346)
Centenys	Stabilitus Berenguer Simó	Family relations in parish Possibly related to stabilitus Pere Simó in Centenys	ADG, Visites, no. 5, 6v. (1331)
Caça de Pelràs	Sacrist Bernat de Caner	Possibly related to Arnau de Caner and Arnau's son Bernat, who has a benefice in Santa Margarida de Caça de Pelràs	ADG, Visites fragmentaris, 11v.–12r. (1320)
Esponellà	Sacrist Berenguer Ferrar Hebdomedarian Francesc Ferrar	Possible that sacrist and hebdomedarian are related	ADG, Visites fragmentaris, 31v.–32r. (1323)
Santa Coloma de Farners	Deacon Pere de Calico	Brother Guillem de Calico is a stabilitus in the same parish	ADG, Visites, no. 4, 211v.–212r. (1329)

(continued)

Table 5.1 Clerical fathers, sons, brother, male cousins, and uncles in the diocese of Girona (*continued*)

PARISH	CLERIC	RELATIVES	SOURCE
Figueres	Hebdomedarian Joan Serra	Nephew, Jaume Dalmaç, serves the office of hebdomedarian for him Jaume Dalmaç is identified as the hebdomedarian's "nepotem"	ADG, Visites, no. 3, 24r. (1321)
Castell de Foixá	Rector Ramon Bernat	Tonsured cleric Arnau in Foixá is his brother	ADG, Processos, no. 188 (1337)
Sant Juià de Fortià	Deacon Berenguer Escuder	Brother and "clericus conjugatus" Bernat Escuder	ADG, Visites, no. 6, 155r. (1340)
Sant Miquel de Garrigás	Sacrist Salvador Ferrar	Celebrates mass with his son The sacrist had at least five children with Cilia	ADG, Remissions de Penes, no. 1, 30v. (1351)
Ginestar	Rector Ramon de Sala	Celebrates mass with his son	ADG, Visites, no. 4, 202r. (1329)
Girona	Cleric Pere de Camp	Uncle Pere de Puig cleric in Sant Quirze de Teradello in diocese of Vic Uncle Jaume de Camp cleric in hospital de Vic	ADG, Notularum, no. 15, 108v.–109r. (1341)
	Cleric Ramon d'Estany	Nephew Pere de Bosch, cleric de la Mota Nephew Pere Olivar, scolar	ADG, Notularum, no. 15, 1v. (1340)
Hostalric	Rector Ramon Rosell	Cousin Berenguer Rosell is a cleric in Hostalric Nephew Anton de Surello is a "clericus tonsuratus" in nearby village of Tordera	ADG, Processos, no. 197, 2v. (1338)
Llambilles	Hebdomedarian Guillem Ferrar	Tonsured clerics and brothers Berenguer Ferrar and Guillem Ferrar who serve in the parish church are his sons. The hebdomedarian was fined 50 sous for keeping his two sons in his own home.	ADG, Visites, no. 4, 75v.–76r. (1330)
Monastir de Lledó	Cleric Pere Domer	Eight-year-old son helps him serve in the monastery	ADG, Imposicions de Penes, no. 1, 15v. (1337)
Mieres	Deacon Ramon de Corbs	Nephew lives in his home	ADG, Processos, no. 122, 2v (1331)
Sant Vicenç de Maià de Montcal	Hebdomedarian Guillem Jaubert	Tonsured clerics and scolares Guillem Llorenç and Pere Fuser are Guillem's nephews	ADG, Visites, no. 4, 170r.v.–171r.v. (1329)

Place	Person	Description	Source
Montfullà	Cleric Berenguer	Has "filios et filias" who ring the church bell and help in the church. The cleric Berenguer was in the major orders for the episcopal visitor to be concerned about his activities.	ADG, Visites, quaderno, 31r.v. (1320) "...quod Berengarius de Monte Foliano habet filios et filias de quadam muliere nomen cuius ignorant qui filii pulsant cimbala et faciunt multa in ecclesie pro clerico supradicto"
Olot, chapel of Sant Magdalena	Capellan Pere Quintana	Has a sixteen-year old son named Pere who lives in Olot. The chaplain was ordered not to continue sinning with the mother of his son, Sibil·la, who is the daughter of Guillem de Barbitosor from Olot.	ADG, Imposicions de Penes, no. 1, 40r. (1343)
Castell de Palafolls	Capellan Ferrar de Piraria	Has an eighteen-year-old son in the parish. The chaplain was ordered not to continue sinning with Guillema Barbera, the mother of his son, who is from the parish of Palafolls.	ADG, Imposicions de Penes, no. 1, 56r. (1345)
Peratallada	Priest Bartomeu Roig holding the benefice of deacon	Renounced his benefice of deacon so that it could be granted to Anton Roig. The tonsured cleric Bernat Roig also served in the parish.	AHG, Peratallada, no. 199, 44r.v. (1332); ADG, Notularum, no. 18, 134r. (1346)
Pontós	Stabilitus Pere Pelipari	Celebrates mass with his son	ADG, Visites, no. 7, 132r. (1343)
Sant Julià de Ramis	Sacrist Ramon Albert	Dispensation for *defectu natalium* for his son, Ramon Albert de Sant Julià de Ramis. Twelve years after the 1330 visitation that recorded the sacrist having a two-year-old son, a dispensation for a Ramon Albert from the parish of Sant Julià de Ramis can be found in the papal registers.	ADG, Visites, no. 4, 57r.v. (1330); Notularum, no. 6, 192v. (1328); Archivio Segreto Vaticano, Registra Vaticana, no. 155, 410r. (1342–1343)
Romanyà d'Empordà	Rector Berenguer de Roca	Has two sons, Pere and Guillem, in Sant Quirze de Arbúcies	ADG, Imposicions de Penes, no. 1, 78r.v. (1348)
Sant Vicenç de Rupià	Stabilitus Arnau de Guardia	Nephew Joan de Guardia serves for Arnau in his absence. Also exchanged benefices	ADG, Visites, no. 4, 15v.–16r. (1329)
Taravaus	Escolar Joan de Font	Possibly related to Ramon de Font and another Joan de Font, who previously held the benefice of stabilitus	ADG, Notularum, no. 3, 12r. (1320); Visites, no 4, 44v. (1329)

(continued)

Table 5.1 Clerical fathers, sons, brother, male cousins, and uncles in the diocese of Girona (*continued*)

PARISH	CLERIC	RELATIVES	SOURCE
Monastir Santa Maria d'Ullà	Canon Berenguer de Sartor	Keeps his two sons from Geralda Pelegrina in the monastery	ADG, Imposicions de Penes, no. 1, 20v. (1338); Visites, no. 5, 122r.v. (1331); Visites, no. 6, 119v, 120v, 122r. (1340)
Vilamalla	Sacrist Ramon Rubí	Nephew Berenguer Rubí is a cleric	ADG, Lletres, no. 8, 146r.v. (1344)
Vilanova de la Muga	Hebdomedarian Pere Bernat	Son is a cleric in Siurana; this is the son that Pere had with Garsenda Çabatera. The couple is noted as having a son in a 1329 visitation in the parish of Sant Martí de Caldes. Pere and Garsenda appear in the parish of Vilanova by 1336	ADG, Visites, no. 6, 156r. (1338); ADG, Visites, no. 4, 41r. (1329); Imposicions de Penes, no. 1, 2v. (1336)
Sant Pere de Vilars	Cleric Guillem Teyes	Prohibited from allowing his sons Guillem and Pere and two daughters from entering his home By 1356, Guillem is the rector of Sords and continued to live with Elisenda Vergera, the mother of his four children.	ADG, Imposicions de Penes, no. 1, 37r. (1342); Obligacions de Penes, no. 1, 108v. (1356)
Begur	Escolar Pere de Celrà	Dispensation for *defectu natalium*—son of a priest and unmarried woman	ADG, Lletres, no. 6, 122r. (1343)
Bellcaire	Escolar Guillem Savanera	Dispensation for *defectu natalium*—son of a priest and unmarried woman. It is likely that he is the son of Francesc Savanera, who served in the chapel of the castle of Bellcaire.	ADG, Lletres, no. 9, 7v. (1345), http://www .arxiuadg.org/recerca-per-fons-i-series [Francesc Savanera had several children with Joana and Bernardina: ADG, Penes, 21v. (1339); Visites, no. 6, 138r.v. (1340); Visites, no. 7, 86r. (1343)]
Bell·lloc	Bernat Perpinyà	Dispensation for *defectu natalium*—son of a priest and unmarried woman	ADG, Notularum, no. 3 166v. (1322)
Girona	Escolar Pere Albert	Dispensation for *defectu natalium*—son of a priest and unmarried woman	ADG, Lletres, no. 7, 166r. (1344)
Girona	Escolar Simó Galet	Received license for the tonsure with a dispensation for *defectu natalium*—son of a priest and unmarried woman	ADG, Lletres, no. 9, 86v. (1345), http:// www.arxiuadg.org/recerca-per-fons-i -series

Far	Escolar Pere de Cerdà	Dispensation for *defectu natalium*—son of a priest and unmarried woman	ADG, Lletres, no. 8, 42r. (1344)
Juvinyà	Ferrer de Vall	Dispensation for *defectu natalium*—son of a priest and unmarried woman	ADG, Notularum, no. 4, 76v. (1323)
Llers	Tonsured cleric Bernat Albert	Dispensation for *defectu natalium*—son of a priest and unmarried woman	ASV, Registra Vaticana, no. 155, 409v. (1342–1343)
Maià	Bartomeu Joan	Dispensation for *defectu natalium*—son of a priest and unmarried woman	ADG, Notularum, no. 4, 76v. (1323)
Navata	Cleric Francesc de Pont	Dispensation for *defectu natalium*—son of a priest and unmarried woman	ADG, Processos, no. 624 (1397)
Sant Andreu de Salous	Escolar Pere Fortis	Dispensation for *defectu natalium*—son of a priest and unmarried woman	ADG, Lletres, no. 14, 138r. (1349)
Saus	Escolar Ramon de Preses	Received license for the tonsure with a dispensation for *defectu natalium*—son of a priest and unmarried woman. It is likely that he is the son of Simó de Preses, hebdomedarian of Saus, and Astruga Benedicta.	ADG, Lletres, no. 9, 168r. (1345), http://www.arxiuadg.org/recerca-per-fons-i-series [The priest Simó de Preses is identified as having two sons with Astruga Benedicta, also identifed as Astruga Ramonela, in 1336; ADG, Visites, no. 6, 39v.–40r.(1338); Obligacions de Penes, no. 1, 13r. (1336)]
Terradelles	Pere de Llapart	Dispensation for *defectu natalium*—son of a priest and unmarried woman	ADG, Notularum, no. 4, 123r. (1324)
Vilamacolum	Escolar Pere Sopa	Dispensation for *defectu natalium*—son of a priest and unmarried woman. It is likely that he is the son of the sacrist Pere Sopa of Vilamacolum and Maria Silvestre	ADG, Lletres, no. 8, 2v. (1344) [For the sacrist Pere Sopa and his concubine Maria Silvestre, ADG, Obligacions de Penes, no. 1, 6r. (1336); Obligacions de Penes, no. 1, 15v. (1337)]
Not specified	Escolar Arnau Olivera	Dispensation for *defectu natalium*—son of a priest and unmarried woman	ADG, Notularum, no. 3, 217r. (1322)

(*continued*)

Table 5.1 Clerical fathers, sons, brother, male cousins, and uncles in the diocese of Girona (*continued*)

PARISH	CLERIC	RELATIVES	SOURCE
Not specified	Escolar Francesc Moresc	Dispensation for *defectu natalium*—son of a priest and unmarried woman	ADG, Notularum, no. 4, 18v. (1323)
Not specified	Escolar Bernat de Riera	Dispensation for *defectu natalium*—son of a priest and unmarried woman	ADG, Lletres, no. 9, 143v. (1345), http://www.arxiuadg.org/recerca-per-fons-i-series
Not specified	Cleric Pere Montaner	Dispensation for *defectu natalium*—son of a priest and unmarried woman	ASV, Registra Vaticana, no. 151, 195v. (1342–1343)
Not specified	Escolar Francesc Ripoll	Dispensation for *defectu natalium*—son of a priest and unmarried woman. Promotion to military orders	ASV, Registra Vaticana, no. 151, 198v. (1342–1343)
Not specified	Nicolau de Masberenguer	Dispensation for *defectu natalium*—son of a priest and unmarried woman	ADG, Lletres, no. 6, 108v. (1343)
Not specified	Cleric Pere de Llambilles	Dispensation for *defectu natalium*—son of a priest and unmarried woman	ADG, Lletres, no. 8, 146v. (1344)
Not specified	Pere Ferrar (aka Pere Sabater)	Dispensation for *defectu natalium*—son of a priest and unmarried woman	ASV, Registra Vaticana, no. 155, 417v. (1342–1343)
Not specified	Pau Gallart	Dispensation for *defectu natalium*—son of a deacon and married woman	ADG, Lletres, no. 14, 59r. (1349)

Table 5.2 Clerical fathers, sons, brother, male cousins, and uncles in the diocese of Urgell

PARISH	CLERIC	RELATIVES	SOURCE
Santa Eulàlia d'Ahuri	Rector	Celebrates mass with his son Arnau	ACV, Calaix, 31/43, Visites, no. 1, 24r. (1312)
Sant Martí de Alta Riba	Capellan	Celebrates mass with his son	ACV, Calaix 31/43, Visites, no. 5, 5v. (1315)
Sant Romà d'Arayonet	Rector	Brother Pere is a priest	ACV, Calaix 31/43, Visites, no. 2, 1r. (1313)
Sant Martí de Bahamal	Rector	Celebrates mass with his son	ACV, Calaix 31/43, Visites, no. 4, 14r. (1314)
Sant Feliu de Bruguera	Rector	Son assists with the divine office	ACV, Calaix 31/43, Visites, no. 1, 57r. (1312)
Cardona	Rector Pere Joan Palay	Does not have the appropriate dispensation (for *defectu natalium*) because he is the son of a priest	ACV, Calaix 31/43, Visites, no. 26r. (1312)
Sant Climent de Castelltort	Priest	Celebrates mass with his son	ACV, Calaix 31/43, Visites, no. 3, 37v. (1314)
Santa Maria d'Els Castells	Capellan	Celebrates mass with his son	ACV, Calaix 31/43, Visites, no. 7, 22r. (1313)
Santa Maria d'Enuey	Rector	Celebrates mass with his son	ACV, Calaix 31/43, Visites, no. 5, 11v. (1315)
Sant Marçal d'Estach	Priest Jaume Vidal	Celebrates mass with his son	ACV, Calaix 31/43, Visites, no. 4, 15v. (1314)
Santa Llogaia d'Estaviyl	Capellan	Celebrates mass with his son	ACV, Calaix 31/43, Visites, no. 5, 9v. (1315)
Sant Sadurní de Fustanya	Rector	Celebrates mass with his son	ACV, Calaix 31/43, Visites, no. 1, 54v. (1312)
Santa Gràcia	Rector	Celebrates mass with his son	ACV, Calaix 31/43, Visites, no. 5, 4r. (1315)
Sant Fruitós de Guils del Canto	Rector	Celebrates mass with his son	ACV, Calaix 31/43, Visites, no. 7, 24r. (1313)
Sant Salvador de Meya	Vicar Bartomeu Monju	Celebrates mass with his son	ACV, Calaix 31/43, Visites, no. 4, 37v. (1314)
Sant Pere de Montfalcó	Capellan	Celebrates mass with his son	ACV, Calaix 31/43, Visites, no. 3, 46r. (1315)
Santa Maria de MuntRoig	Capellan	Celebrates mass with his son	ACV, Calaix 31/43, Visites, no. 4, 40r. (1315)
Santa Maria de Muntlor	Capellan	Celebrates mass with his son	ACV, Calaix 31/43, Visites, no. 4, 2r. (1314)
Sant Vicenç de Oveç	Rector Ramon Ricart	Serves in the same parish and church where his father served as rector	ACV, Calaix 31/43, Visites, no. 4, 20v. (1314)
Sant Esteve de Sorre	Capellan	Celebrates mass with his son	ACV, Calaix 31/43, Visites, no. 5, 12v. (1315)
Not specified	Tonsured cleric Bonanat de Plan	Dispensation for *defectu natalium*—son of a priest and unmarried woman	ASV, Registra Vaticana, no. 155, 409v. (1342–1343)
Not specified	Cleric Francesc Bonfil	Dispensation for *defectu natalium*—son of a priest and unmarried woman	ASV, Registra Vaticana, no. 155, 420v. (1342–1343)

Table 5.3   Clerical fathers, sons, brothers, male cousins, and uncles in the diocese of Vic

PARISH	CLERIC	RELATIVES	SOURCE
Avello	Rector Berenguer Ninot	Nephew Pere Ninot assists with the mass	AEV, Visites, no. 1200/2, 40r. (1331)
Sant Mateu de Jovent	Rector Jaume Ça Francquea	Nephew is a cleric in Vic	AEV, Testaments, ACF-3507 (1306–1308, 1320–1330), 32r. (1307)
Santa Maria de Granyena	Rector Guillem Eimeric	Celebrates mass with his son	AEV, Visites, no. 1200/2, 22r. (1331)
Sant Vicenç de Fals	Priest Bernat de Cases	"tenet pro scolarem quendam filium suum"	AEV, Visites, no. 1200/2, 3v. (1331)
Sant Vicenç de *Medilia Groni*	Rector Ramon de Alberg	Nephews Berenguer de Guardia and Jaume de Camp are priests	AEV, Testaments, ACF-3506 (1296–1308), 49v. (1303)
Monastir Santa Maria de Manlleu	Prior Jaume ça Conamina	Nephew Bernat ça Conamina lives in the parish with his concubine and son	AEV, Visites, no. 1200/1, 26r. (1330)
Montargull	Rector	Celebrates mass with his son	AEV, Visites, no. 1200/2, 39v. (1331)
Montfred	Rector Berenguer Ninot	Celebrated mass with his nephew Pere Ninot when Pere was a scolar	AEV, Visites, no. 1200/2, 40r. (1331)
Sant Genís d'Orís	Rector	Son Guillem assists with the mass and says the epistle	AEV, Visites, no. 1200/1, 12v. (1330)
Santa Maria de Tàrrega	Cleric Bernat Ramon	Son obtained benefice in the chapel	AEV, Visites, no. 1200/3, 16r. (1332)
Vic	Rector Bernat Martí	Nephew Bernat Martí is a cleric	AEV, Testaments, ACF-3509 (1319–1324), 24r.v. (1319)
	Beneficed cleric Guillem de Noguer	Uncle Guillem de Noguer is a cleric	AEV, Testaments, ACF-3509 (1319–1324), 85r. (1323)
Sant Andreu de Tona	Cleric Olivar de Vilar	Nephew Bernat de Sala Verdider is a priest	AEV, Testaments, ACF-3507 (1306–1308, 1320–1330), 42v.-43r. (1309)
Sant Pere de Valldeneu	Rector Berenguer de Puig	Uncle is a beneficed cleric serving in the parish church	AEV, Visites, no. 1200/1, 16r. (1330)

Sant Esteve de Vinyoles	Rector Berenguer de PuigRubi	Sons assist the elderly rector with the mass Eldest son collects the tithes and the youngest composes documents for the father	AEV, Visites, no. 1200/1, 13r. (1330)
Not specified	Pere de Puigrubi	Dispensation for *defectu natalium*—son of a priest and unmarried woman; to receive the tonsure and promotion to all orders It seems likely that he is the youngest son of the rector Berenguer de PuigRubi in the parish of Sant Esteve de Vinyoles	ASV, Registra Vaticana, no. 155, 417v. (1342–1343)
Santa Maria de Tor de Ceiça	Rector Jaume Durand	Dispensation for *defectu natalium*—son of a deacon and unmarried woman	Mollat, *Lettres Communes des Papes d'Avignon. Jean XXII (1316–1334)*, Tome VII (Paris: Albert Fontemoing, 1914), 73
Not specified	Cleric Bernat de Planella	Dispensation for *defectu natalium*—son of a priest and unmarried woman	ASV, Registra Vaticana, no. 151, 195r. (1342–1343)
Not specified	Cleric Guillem Pruner	Dispensation for *defectu natalium*—son of a priest and unmarried woman	ASV, Registra Vaticana, no. 151, 196v. (1342–1343)
Not specified	Cleric Bernat de Fabrica	Dispensation for *defectu natalium*—son of a priest and unmarried woman	ASV, Registra Vaticana, no. 151, 212r. (1342–1343)
Not specified	Cleric Guillem de Prat	Dispensation for *defectu natalium*—son of a priest and unmarried woman	ASV, Registra Vaticana, no. 151, 215v. (1342–1343)
Not specified	Cleric Jaume de Vila	Dispensation for *defectu natalium*—son of a priest and unmarried woman	ASV, Registra Vaticana, no. 151, 217r. (1342–1343)
Not specified	Cleric Pere Bonel	Dispensation for *defectu natalium*—son of a priest and unmarried woman	ASV, Registra Vaticana, no. 151, 220v. (1342–1343)
Not specified	Cleric Pere de Cumba	Dispensation for *defectu natalium*—son of a priest and unmarried woman	ASV, Registra Vaticana, no. 151, 221v. (1342–1343)

(continued)

Table 5.3 Clerical fathers, sons, brothers, male cousins, and uncles in the diocese of Vic (*continued*)

PARISH	CLERIC	RELATIVES	SOURCE
Not specified	Cleric Guillem de Cumba	Dispensation for *defectu natalium*—son of a priest and unmarried woman It is possible that both Pere and Guillem de Cumba were brothers born to the same priestly father. It is odd that two males with the same last name traveled to Rome from the diocese of Vic and received a dispensation for illegitimate birth on the same date.	ASV, Registra Vaticana, no. 151, 221v. (1342–1343)
Not specified	Cleric Berenguer de Molins	Dispensation for *defectu natalium*—son of a priest and unmarried woman	ASV, Registra Vaticana, no. 155, 410r. (1342–1343)
Not specified	Tonsured cleric Berenguer Sadenesa	Dispensation for *defectu natalium*—son of a priest and unmarried woman	ASV, Registra Vaticana, no. 155, 415r. (1342–1343)
Not specified	Cleric Berenguer de Herero	Dispensation for *defectu natalium*—son of a priest and unmarried woman	ASV, Registra Vaticana, no. 155, 418r. (1342–1343)
Not specified	Cleric Ramon de Tressera	Dispensation for *defectu natalium*—son of a priest and unmarried woman	ASV, Registra Vaticana, no. 155, 418r. (1343–1343)
Not specified	Cleric Pere de Comela	Dispensation for *defectu natalium*—son of a priest and unmarried woman	ASV, Registra Vaticana, no. 155, 418v. (1343–1343)

BIBLIOGRAPHY

Published Primary Sources

Arxiu Municipal de Girona. *Catàleg de pergamins del fons de l'Ajuntament de Girona (1144–182)*. Diplomataris, 32. Vol. 1. Barcelona: Fundació Noguera, 2005.

Benito i Monclús, Pere. *Les parròquies del maresm a la baixa edat mitjana. Una aproximació des de les visites pastorals, 1305–1447*. Mataró: Caixa d'Estalvis Laietana, 1992.

Bonner, Anthony. *Doctur Illuminatus: A Ramon Llull Reader*. Princeton: Princeton University Press, 1985.

Brewer, Derek, ed. *Medieval Comic Tales*. Cambridge, UK: Boydell & Brewer, 1973.

Burns, Robert I., ed. *Las Siete Partidas*. Vols. 1–5. Trans. Samuel Parsons Scott. Philadelphia: University of Pennsylvania Press, 2001.

Caesarius of Heisterback. *The Dialogue on Miracles*. Trans. Henry von Essen Scott and C. C. Swinton Bland. London: Routledge, 1929.

Cárcel Ortí, María Milagros, and José Vicente Boscà Codina. *Visitas pastorales de Valencia, siglos XIV–XV*. Valencia, 1996.

Catalina de Erauso. *Lieutenant Nun: Memoir of a Basque Transvestite in the New World*. Trans. Michele Stepto and Gabriel Stepto. Boston: Beacon Press, 1996.

El Fuero de Teruel. Ed. José Castañé Llinás. Teruel, 1991.

García Egea, María Teresa. *La visita pastoral a la diocesis de Tortosa del Obispo Paholac, 1314*. Diputació de Castelló, 1993.

Gimeno Blay, Francisco M., and María Luz Mandingorra Llavata, eds. *Sermonario de San Vicente Ferrer*. Trans. Francisco Calero Calero. Valencia: Ajuntament de Valencia, 2002.

Gonzalo de Berceo. *Miracles of Our Lady*. Trans. Richard Terry Mount and Annette Grant Cash. Lexington: University Press of Kentucky, 1997.

Guido of Monte Rochen, *Handbook for Curates: A Late Medieval Manual on Pastoral Ministry*. Trans. Anne T. Thayer. Ed. Anne T. Thayer and Katherine J. Lualdi. Washington, DC: Catholic University of America Press, 2011.

Gyug, Richard Francis. *The Diocese of Barcelona during the Black Death. The Register Notule Communium 15 (1348–1349)*. Toronto: Pontifical Institute of Mediaeval Studies, 1994.

Higden, Ranulph. *Speculum Curatorum: A Mirror for Curates, Book I: The Commandments*. Ed. and trans. Eugene Cook and Margaret Jennings. Paris: Peeters, 2012.

Hillgarth, Jocelyn N., and Giulio Silano. "A Compilation of the Diocesan Synods of Barcelona (1354): Critical Edition and Analysis." *Medieval Studies* 46 (1984): 78–157.

———. *The Register "Notule Communium" 14 of the Diocese of Barcelona (1345–1348): A Calendar with Selected Documents*. Toronto: Pontifical Institute of Medieaval Studies Press, 1983.

Hugh of Floreffe, *The Life of Yvette of Huy*. Trans. Jo Ann McNamara. Toronto: Peregrina Publishing, 1999.

Llibre del Batlle Reial de Barcelona, Berenguer Morey (1375–1378). Ed. Josep Maria Casas Homs. Barcelona: Fundacio Salvador Vives Casajuana, 1976.

Mannyng of Bunne, Robert. *Handlyng Synne*. Ed. Idelle Sullens. Binghamton: SUNY Binghamton, Medieval and Renaissance Texts and Studies, 1983.

Martí Bonet, Josep Maria. "Las visitas pastorales y los 'communes' del primer año del pontificado del Obispo de Barcelona Ponç de Gualba (a. 1303)." *Anthologica Annua* 28–29 (1981–1982): 581–825.

Martí Bonet, José Maria, Puigvert, L. Niqui, and F. Miquel Mascort, eds. *Las Series "Visitas Pastorales," Registros "Communium" y "Gratiarum" y los "Procesos" del Archivo Diocesano de Barcelona. Aportacion Archivística a la Historia Eclesiástica de la Diócesis de Barcelona*. Barcelona: Archivo Diocesano, 1978.

Menéndez Pidal, Ramon. "Elena y María (disputa del clérigo y el caballero). Poesía leonesa inédita del siglo XIII." *Revista de Filología Española* 1 (1914): 52–96.

Mirror of Coitus. A Translation and Edition of the Fifteenth-Century Speculum al foderi. Trans. and ed. Michael Solomon. Madison: Hispanic Seminary of Medieval Studies, 1990.

Noguer i Musqueras, Tomas, and Josep M. Pons Guri. "Constitucions sinodals de Girona de La Primera Compilacio." *Anales del Instituto de Estudios Gerundenses*, no. 18 (1966–1967): 49–212. Reproduced in *Recull d'estudis d'història jurídica catalana* 2 (1989): 81–222.

Pons i Guri, Josep María, ed. "Constitucions conciliars tarraconenses (1229–1330)." *Recull d'estudis d'història jurídica catalana* 2(1989): 223–387.

Puig i Oliver, Jaume de, and Josep M. Marquès i Planagumà, eds. *Lletres del Bisbe de Girona. segle XIV*. Vol. 1. Barcelona: Corpus Scriptorum Cataloniae, 2007.

Renedo, Xavier, and David Guixeras, eds. *Francesc Eiximenis: An Anthology*. Trans. Robert D. Hughes. Barcelona: Barcino-Tamesis, 2008.

Ruiz, Juan. *The Book of Good Love*. Trans. Rigo Mignani and Mario A. di Cesare. Albany: SUNY Press, 1970.

———. *Libro de buen amor*. Trans. María Brey Mariño. Madrid: Editorial Castalia, 1995.

———. *Songs of Holy Mary of Alfonso X, the Wise*. Trans. Kathleen Kulp-Hill. Tempe: Arizona Center for Medieval and Renaissance Studies, 2000.

Tanner, Norman P., ed. *Decrees of the Ecumenical Councils*. Vol. 1. Washington, DC: Georgetown University Press, 1990.

Thomas of Chobham. *Summa confessorum*. In *Analecta mediaevalia namurcensia*, ed. F. Broomfield. Paris: Beatrice-Nauwelaerts, 1968.

Usatges of Barcelona: The Fundamental Law of Catalonia. Trans. Donald J. Kagay. Philadelphia: University of Pennsylvania Press, 1994.

Vega, Amador. *Ramon Llull and the Secret of Life*. Trans. James W. Heisig. New York: Crossroad Publishing, 2003.

Secondary Sources

Alberch i Fugueras, Ramon. *Jewry Guide of Girona*. Girona: Ayuntament de Girona, 2003.

Alexandre-Bidon, Danièl, and Didier Lett. *Children in the Middle Ages: Fifth–Fifteenth Centuries*. Trans. Jody Gladding. Notre Dame: University of Notre Dame Press, 1999.

Aranguren, Roldàn Jimeno. "Concubinato, matrimonio y adulterio de los clérigos: Notas sobre la Regulación jurídica y praxis en la Navarra medieval." *Anuario de Historia del Derecho Español* no. 71 (2011): 543–74.

Armstrong-Partida, Michelle. "Priestly Marriage: The Tradition of Clerical Concubinage in the Spanish Church." *Viator* 40, no. 2 (2009): 221–53.

——. "Priestly Wives: The Role and Acceptance of Clerics' Concubines in the Parishes of Late Medieval Catalunya." *Speculum* 88, no. 1 (2013): 166–214.

Ault, Warren O. "The Village Church and the Village Community in Medieval England." *Speculum* 45, no. 2 (1970): 197–215.

Aznar Gil, Federico R. *La institución matrimonial en la Hispania cristiana bajomedieval, 1215–1563*. Salamanca: Universidad Pontificia de Salamanca, 1989.

——. "Penas y sanciones contra los clérigos concubinarios en la Península Ibérica (ss. XIII–XVI)." *Studia Gratiana* 29 (1998): 501–20.

Bada, Joan. *Història del cristianism a Catalunya*. Lleida: Eumo Editorial, 2003.

Baldwin, John W. "A Campaign to Reduce Clerical Celibacy at the Turn of the Twelfth and Thirteenth Centuries." In *Études d'histoire du Droit canonique dédiées à Gabriel Le Bras*, Tome II, 1041–53. Paris: Sirey, 1965.

——. *The Language of Sex: Five Voices from Northern France around 1200*. Chicago: University of Chicago Press, 1994.

——. *Masters, Princes and Merchants: The Social Views of Peter the Chanter and His Circle*. Princeton: Princeton University Press, 1970.

Balzaretti, Ross. "'These Are Things That Men Do, Not Women': The Social Regulation of Female Violence in Langobard Italy." In *Violence and Society in the Early Medieval West*, ed. Guy Halsall, 175–92. Woodbridge, UK: Boydell Press, 1998.

Barrow, Julia. *The Clergy in the Medieval World: Secular Clerics, Their Families and Careers in North-Western Europe, c. 800–c.1200*. Cambridge, UK: Cambridge University Press, 2015.

——. "Hereford Bishops and Married Clergy, c. 1130–1240." *Bulletin of the Institute of Historical Research* 60, no. 141 (1987): 1–8.

Barstow, Anne Llewellyn. *Married Priests and the Reforming Papacy: The Eleventh Century Debates*. New York: Edwin Mellen Press, 1982.

Batlle Gallart, Carmen. *La crisis social y económica de Barcelona a mediados del siglo XV*. Barcelona: Consejo Superior de Investigaciones Científicas, 1973.

——. "The Growth of the Cities of the Crown of Aragon in the Later Middle Ages." In *Iberia and the Mediterranean World of the Middle Ages. Studies in Honor of Robert I. Burns*, Vol. 2, ed., Paul Chevedden, Donald Kagay, and Paul Padilla, 321–43. Leiden: Brill, 1995.

Baucells i Reig, Josep. "L'església de Catalunya a la baixa edat mitjana." *Acta Historica et Archaeologica Mediaevalia* 13 (1992): 427–42.

———. "Visitas pastorales: Siglos XIV y XV" in *Memoria ecclesiae XV: Las visitas pastorales en el ministerio del obispo y archivos de la iglesia santoral hispano-mozarabe en las diocesis de España*, ed. Agustín Hevia Ballina, 165–294. Oviedo: Actas del XIII Congreso de la Asociación celebrado en Sevilla, 1999.

———. *Vivir en la edad media: Barcelona y su entorno en los siglos XIII y XIV, 1200–1344*. Vols. 1–4. Barcelona: Consejo Superior de Investigaciones Científicas, 2004.

Baumgarten, Elisheva. *Mothers and Children: Jewish Family Life in Medieval Europe*. Princeton: Princeton University Press, 2004.

Beaudette, Paul. ' "In the World but Not of It': Clerical Celibacy as a Symbol of the Medieval Church." In *Medieval Purity and Piety: Essays on Medieval Clerical Celibacy and Religious Reform*, ed. Michael Frassetto, 23–46. New York: Garland Publishing, 1998.

Bednarski, Steven, and Andrée Courtemanche. "Learning to Be a Man: Public Schooling and Apprenticeship in Late Medieval Manosque." *Journal of Medieval History* 35 (2009): 113–35.

Benito i Monclús, Pere. "Le Clergé paroissial du Maresme (Évêché de Barcelone) d'après les visites pastorales (1305–1447): Recherches sur le thème du concubinage." In *Le Clergé rural dans l'Europe médiévale et moderne. Actes des XIIIèmes Journées Internationales d'Histoire de l'Abbaye de Flaran*, ed. Pierre Bonnassie, 187–203. Toulouse: Presses Universitaires du Mirail, 1995.

Bennett, Judith M. ' "Lesbian-Like' and the Social History of Lesbianisms." *Journal of the History of Sexuality* 9 (2000): 1–24.

———. *A Medieval Life: Cecilia Penifader of Brigstock, c. 1295–1344*. Boston: McGraw-Hill College, 1999.

Bennett, Judith M., and Amy M. Froide, eds. *Singlewomen in the European Past, 1250–1800*. Philadelphia: University of Pennsylvania Press, 1999.

Berger, Maurice, Brian Wallis, and Simon Watson, eds. *Constructing Masculinity*. New York: Routledge, 1995.

Behrend-Martínez, Edward. "Manhood and the Neutered Body in Early Modern Spain." *Journal of Social History* 38, no. 4 (2005): 1073–93.

Bishko, Charles Julian. "Fernando I and the Origins of the Leonese-Castilian Alliance with Cluny." In *Studies in Medieval Spanish Frontier History*, Pt. 2. London: Variorum Reprints, 1980.

Bisson, Thomas N. *The Medieval Crown of Aragon: A Short History*. Oxford: Clarendon Press, 1986.

———. *Tormented Voices: Power, Crisis, and Humanity in Rural Catalonia, 1140–1200*. Cambridge, MA: Harvard University Press, 1998.

Bloch, R. Howard. *Medieval Misogyny and the Invention of Western Romantic Love*. Chicago: University of Chicago Press, 1991.

Blumenthal, Debra. *Enemies and Familiars: Slavery and Mastery in Fifteenth-Century Valencia*. Ithaca: Cornell University Press, 2009.

Bornstein, Daniel. "Parish Priests in Late Medieval Cortona: The Urban and Rural Clergy." *Quaderni di Storia Religiosa* 4 (1997): 165–93.

———. "Priests and Villagers in the Diocese of Cortona." *Richerche Storiche* 27 (1997): 93–106.

Bossy, John. "Blood and Baptism: Kinship, Community, and Christianity in Western Europe from the Fourteenth to the Seventeenth Centuries." In *Sanctity and*

Secularity: The Church and the World, ed. Derek Baker, 129–43. Oxford: Basil Blackwell, 1973.

Bowker, Lee H., ed. *Masculinities and Violence*. Thousand Oaks: Sage Publications, 1998.

——. "On the Difficulty of Eradicating Masculine Violence." In *Masculinities and Violence*, ed. Lee H. Bowker, 1–14. Thousand Oaks: Sage Publications, 1998.

Boyer, Richard. "Honor among Plebeians: *Mala Sangre* and Social Reputation." In *Sex, Shame, and Violence: The Faces of Honor in Colonial Latin America*, ed. Lyman L. Johnson and Sonya Lipsett-Rivera, 152–78. Albuquerque: University of New Mexico Press, 1998.

Brackett, John K. "The Language of Violence in the Late Italian Renaissance: The Example of the Tuscan Romagna." In *The Final Argument: The Imprint of Violence on Society in Medieval and Early Modern Europe*, ed. Donald J Kagay and L. J. Andrew Villalon, 97–105. Woodbridge, UK: Boydell Press.

Brodman, James William. *Charity and Welfare: Hospitals and the Poor in Medieval Catalonia*. Philadelphia: University of Pennsylvania Press, 1998.

——. *Ransoming Captives in Crusader Spain: The Order of Merced on the Christian-Islamic Frontier*. Philadelphia: University of Pennsylvania Press, 1986.

Brooke, Christopher N. L. *Churches and Churchmen in Medieval Europe*. London: Hambledon Press, 1999.

——. "Gregorian Reform in Action: Clerical Marriage in England, 1050–1200." *Cambridge Historical Journal* 12, no. 1 (1956): 1–21.

Brown, Andrew. *Church and Society in England, 1000–1500*. New York: Palgrave Macmillan, 2003.

Brown, Peter. *The Body and Society*. New York: Columbia University Press, 1988.

Brown, Warren C. *Violence in Medieval Europe*. London: Pearson, 2011.

Brundage, James A. "Concubinage and Marriage in Medieval Canon Law." In *Sexual Practices and the Medieval Church*, ed. Vern L. Bullough and James Brundage, 118–28. Amherst: Prometheus Books, 1994.

——. *Law, Sex, and Christian Society in Medieval Europe*. Chicago: University of Chicago Press, 1987.

——. "Playing by the Rules: Sexual Behavior and Legal Norms in Medieval Europe." In *Desire and Discipline: Sex and Sexuality in the Premodern West*, ed. Jaqueline Murray and Konrad Eisenbichler, 23–41. Toronto: University of Toronto Press, 1996.

Bullough, Vern L. "On Being a Male in the Middle Ages." In *Medieval Masculinities*, ed. Clare A. Lees, 31–46. Minneapolis: University of Minnesota Press, 1994.

Bullough, Vern L., and James A. Brundage, eds. *Sexual Practices and the Medieval Church*. Buffalo: Prometheus Books, 1994.

Burns, Robert I. *Muslims, Christians, and Jews in the Crusader Kingdom of Valencia: Societies in Symbiosis*. Cambridge, UK: Cambridge University Press, 1983.

——. "The Parish as a Frontier Institution in Thirteenth-Century Valencia." *Speculum* 37, no. 2 (1962): 244–51.

——. "The Spiritual Life of James the Conqueror, King of Arago-Catalonia, 1208–1276: Portrait and Self-Portrait." *Catholic Historical Review* 62 (1976): 1–35.

Butler, Judith. *Gender Trouble: Feminism and the Subversion of Identity*. New York: Routledge, 1990.

Bynum, Caroline Walker. "Jesus as Mother, Abbot as Mother: Some Themes in Early Cistercian Writing." In *Jesus as Mother*, ed. Caroline Walker Bynum, 110–69. Berkeley: University of California Press, 1982.

Cabré, Montserrat. "Women or Healers? Household Practices and the Categories of Health Care in Late Medieval Iberia." *Bulletin of the History of Medicine* 82, no. 1 (2008): 18–51.

Cadden, Joan. *Meanings of Sex Difference in the Middle Ages: Medicine, Science, and Culture.* Cambridge, UK: Cambridge University Press, 1993.

Canal i Roquet, J., Eduard Canal i de Diego, J. M. Nolla i Brufau, and J. Sagrera i Aradilla. *La ciutat de Girona en la primera meitat del segle XIV.* Girona: Ajuntament de Girona, 1998.

Cárcel Ortí, María. Milagros. "Aproximacíon a un censo de visitas pastorales valencianas." *Memoria Ecclesiae* 9 (1996): 299–316.

Cárcel Ortí, María. Milagros, and José Trenchs Odena. "Las visitas pastorales de Cataluña, Valencia y Baleares." *Archiva Ecclesiae: Bollettino dell' Associazone Archivistica Ecclesiastica* 22–23 (1979–1980): 491–500.

Carmen Peris, M. "La prostitución valenciana en la segunda mitad del siglo XIV." In *Violencia i marginado en la societat medieval. Revista d'Història Medieval* 1(1990): 179–99.

Carpenter, Dwayne E. "Fickle Fortune: Gambling in Medieval Spain." *Studies in Philology* 85, no. 3 (1998): 267–78.

Catlos, Brian. "The de Reys (1220–1501): The Evolution of a 'Middle-Class' Muslim Family in Christian Aragon." *Viator* 40 (2009): 197–219.

Chamberlin, Cynthia L. "The 'Sainted Queen' and the 'Sin of Berenguela': Teresa Gil de Viduare and Berenguela Alfonso in the Documents of the Crown of Aragon, 1225–1272." In *Iberia and the Mediterranean World of the Middle Ages; Studies in Honor of Robert I. Burns*, ed. Larry J. Simon, 303–21. Leiden: Brill, 1995.

Chaytor, Henry J. *A History of Aragon and Catalonia.* New York: AMS Press, 1969.

Chazan, Robert. *Daggers of Faith: Thirteenth-Century Christian Missionizing and Jewish Response.* Berkeley: University of California Press, 1989.

Cheney, Christopher Robert. "The Diocese of Grenoble in the Fourteenth Century." *Speculum* 10, no. 2 (1935): 162–77.

Chojnacki, Stanley. "Subaltern Patriarchs: Patrician Bachelors in Renaissance Venice." In *Medieval Masculinities: Regarding Men in the Middle Ages*, ed. Clare A. Lees, 73–90. Minneapolis: University of Minnesota Press, 1994.

Clark, Anna. *Desire: A History of European Sexuality.* New York: Routledge, 2008.

Clarke, Peter. "The Medieval Clergy and Violence: An Historiographical Introduction." In *Violence and the Medieval Clergy*, ed. Gerhard Jaritz and Ana Marinkovic, 3–16. Budapest: Central European University Press, 2011.

Claudio Girbal, D. Enrique. *Los judíos en Gerona: Coleccion de noticias históricas.* Gerona, 1870.

Codina i Vilà, Jaume. *Contractes de matrimoni al delta del Llobregat (segles XIV a XIX).* Barcelona: Fundació Noguera, 1997.

——. "Els processos dels segles XIV i XV." In *Processos de l'arxiu diocesà de Barcelona*, ed. Josep M. Martí Bonet, Leandre Niqui i Puigvert, and F. Miquel i Mascort, 165–229. Barcelona: Department de Cultura de la Generalitat de Catalunya, 1984.

Cohen, Elizabeth S. "Honor and Gender in the Streets of Early Modern Rome." *Journal of Interdisciplinary History* 22, no. 4 (1992): 597–625.

Cohen, Jeffrey Jerome, and Bonnie Wheeler, eds. *Becoming Male in the Middle Ages.* New York: Garland Publishing, 2000.

Collins, Ross Williams. "The Parish Priest and His Flock as Depicted by the Councils of the Twelfth and Thirteenth Centuries." *Journal of Religion* 10, no. 3 (1930): 313–32.

Congost Colomer, Rosa. "La Catalunya del mas, és a dir, la Catalunya Vella." In *L'organització de l'espai rural a l'europa mediterrània*, ed. Rosa Congost Colomer, Gabriel Jover, Giuliana Biagioli, 19–36. Girona: Associació d'Història Rural de les Comarques Gironines, Centre de Recerca d'Història Rural de la Universitat de Girona, 2003.

Congost Colomer, Rosa, Gabriel Jover, and Giuliana Biagioli, eds. *L'organització de l'espai rural a l'europa mediterrània*, Girona: Associació d'Història Rural de les Comarques Gironines, Centre de Recerca d'Història Rural de la Universitat de Girona, 2003.

Connell, Robert W. *Masculinities.* 2nd ed. Berkeley: University of California Press, 2005.

Connell, Robert W., and James W. Messerschmidt. "Hegemonic Masculinity: Rethinking the Concept." *Gender & Society* 19, no. 6 (2005): 829–59.

Córdoba de la Llave, Ricardo. "A una mesa y una cama. Barraganía y amacebamiento a fines de la edad media." In *Saber y vivir: Mujer, antigüedad y medievo*, ed. Maria Isabel Calero Secall and Rosa Francia Somalo, 127–54. Málaga: Universidad de Málaga, 1996.

——. "Las relaciones extraconjugales en la sociedad castellana bajomedieval." *Anuario de Estudios Medievales* 16 (1986): 571–620.

——. "Violencia cotidiana en Castilla a fines de la edad media." In *Conflictos sociales, politicos y intellectuals en la España de los siglos XIV y XV*, ed. José Ignacio de la Iglesia Duarte, 393–444. Logroño: Instituto de Estudios Riojanos, 2004.

Cossar, Roisin. "Clerical 'Concubines' in Northern Italy during the Fourteenth Century." *Journal of Women's History* 23, no. 1 (2011): 110–31.

——. "Defining Roles in the Clerical Household in Trecento Venice." *Viator* 45, no. 2 (2014): 237–45.

Coulet, Noël. *Les visites pastorales.* Turnhout, Belgium: Brepols, 1985.

Cullum, P. H. "Boy/Man into Clerk/Priest: The Making of the Late Medieval Clergy." In *Rites of Passage: Cultures of Transition in the Fourteenth Century*, ed. Nicola F. McDonald and W. M. Ormrod, 51–64. York, UK: York Medieval Press, 2004.

——. "Clergy, Masculinity, and Transgression in Late Medieval England." In *Masculinity in Medieval Europe*, ed. Dawn M. Hadley, 178–96. New York: Longman, 1999.

——. "Learning to Be a Man, Learning to Be a Priest in Late Medieval England." In *Learning and Literacy in Medieval England and Abroad*, ed. Sarah Rees Jones, 134–53. Turnhout, Belgium: Brepols, 2003.

——. "Life Cycle and Life-Course in a Clerical and Celibate Milieu: Northern England in the Later Middle Ages." In *Time and Eternity: The Medieval Discourse*, ed. Gerhard Jaritz and Gerson Moreno-Riaño, 271–81. Turnhout, Belgium: Brepols, 2003.

Cullum, Pat H., and Katherine J. Lewis, eds. *Holiness and Masculinity in the Middle Ages*. Toronto: University of Toronto Press, 2004.

——, eds. *Religious Men and Masculine Identity in the Middle Ages*. Woodbridge, UK: Boydell Press, 2013.

D'Amico, John F. *Renaissance Humanism in Papal Rome: Humanists and Churchmen on the Eve of the Reformation*. Baltimore: Johns Hopkins University Press, 1983.

Davis, Adam J. *The Holy Bureaucrat: Eudes Rigaud and Religious Reform in the Thirteenth-Century Normandy*. Ithaca: Cornell University Press, 2006.

Dean, Trevor. *Crime in Medieval Europe, 1200–1550*. London: Longman, 2001.

——. "Gender and Insult in an Italian City: Bologna in the Later Middle Ages." *Social History* 29, no. 2 (2004): 217–31.

D'Elia, Anthony F. *The Renaissance of Marriage in Fifteenth-Century Italy*. Cambridge, MA: Harvard University Press, 2004.

Díaz Ibáñez, Jorge. *Iglesia, sociedad y poder en Castilla: El Obispado de Cuenca en la edad media, siglos XII–XV*. Cuenca: Editorial Alfonsípolis,2003.

Dillard, Heath. *Daughters of the Reconquest: Women in Castillian Town Society, 1100–1300*. Cambridge, UK: Cambridge University Press, 1984.

Di Simplicio, Oscar. "Perpetuas: The Women Who Kept Priests, Siena 1600–1800." In *History from Crime*, ed. Edward Muir and Guido Ruggiero, 32–64. Baltimore: John Hopkins University Press, 1994.

Dohar, William J. *The Black Death and Pastoral Leadership: The Diocese of Hereford in the Fourteenth Century*. Philadelphia: University of Pennsylvania Press, 1995.

Duggan, Lawrence G. *Armsbearing and the Clergy in the History and Canon Law of Western Christianity*. Woodbridge, UK: Boydell Press, 2013.

——. "The Unresponsiveness of the Late Medieval Church: A Reconsideration." *Sixteenth Century Journal* 9, no. 1 (1978): 3–26.

Dunn, Caroline. *Stolen Women in Medieval England: Rape, Abduction, and Adultery, 1100–1500*. Cambridge, UK: Cambridge University Press, 2013.

Eisenach, Emlyn. *Husbands, Wives, and Concubines: Marriage, Family, and Social Order in Sixteenth-Century Verona*. Kirksville, MO: Truman State University Press, 2004.

Elliot, Dyan. "Sex in Holy Places." In *Fallen Bodies: Pollution, Sexuality, and Demonology in the Middle Ages*, 61–80. Philadelphia: University of Pennsylvania Press, 1999.

——. "Pollution, Illusion, and Masculine Disarray." In *Constructing Medieval Sexuality*, ed. Karma Lochrie, Peggy McCracken, and James A. Schultz, 1–23. Minneapolis: University of Minnesota Press, 1997.

Engels, Odilo. "Los reyes Jaime II y Alfonso IV de Aragon y los concilios provinciales de Tarragona." In *VIII Congreso de Historia de la Corona de Aragon*, ed. Caja de Ahorros y Monte de Piedad de Valencia, Vol. 2, 253–62. Valencia, 1970.

Esteban Recio, María Asunción, and María Jesús Izquierdo García. "Pecado y marginación. Mujeres públicas en valladolid y palencia durante los siglos XV y XVI." In *La ciudad medieval: Aspectos de la vida urbana en la Castilla bajomedieval*, ed. Juan A Bonachia, 131–68. Valladolid: Universidad de Valladolid, 1996.

Falk, Oren. "Bystanders and Hearsayers First: Reassessing the Role of the Audience in Duelling." In *"A Great Effusion of Blood"?: Interpreting Medieval Violence*, ed. Mark D. Meyerson, Daniel Thiery, and Oren Falk, 98–117. Toronto: University of Toronto Press, 2004.

Farías Zurita, Víctor. *El mas i la vila a la Catalunya medieval. Els fonaments d'una societat senyorialitzada, segles XI–XIV.* València: Universitat de València, 2009.

Farmer, Sharon. "Manual Labor, Begging, and Conflicting Gender Expectations in Thirteenth-Century Paris." In *Gender and Difference in the Middle Ages*, ed. Sharon Farmer and Carol Braun Pasternack, 261–87. Minneapolis: University of Minnesota Press, 2003.

——. *Surviving Poverty in Medieval Paris: Gender, Ideology, and the Daily Lives of the Poor.* Ithaca: Cornell University Press, 2002.

Fenster, Thelma, and Daniel Lord Smail, eds. *Fama: The Politics of Talk & Reputation in Medieval Europe.* Ithaca: Cornell University Press, 2003.

Fernández Conde, Javier, ed. *Historia de la iglesia en España.* Vol. 2. Madrid: Biblioteca de Autores Cristianos, 1979.

Fernández i Trabal, Josep. *Una família catalana medieval: Els Bell·lloc de Girona, 1267–1533.* Barcelona: Pubicacions de l'Abadia de Montserrat, 1995.

Figueras, J. Romeu. "Folklore de la lluvia y de las tempestades en el Pirineo catalán." *Revista de Dialectología y Tradiciones Populares* 7 (1951): 292–326.

Finch, Andrew. "Sexual Morality and Canon Law: The Evidence of the Rochester Consistory Court." *Journal of Medieval History* 20 (1994): 261–75.

——. "Sexual Relations and Marriage in Later Medieval Normandy." *Journal of Ecclesiastical History* 47, no. 2 (1996): 236–56.

——. "Women and Violence in the Later Middle Ages: The Evidence of the Officiality of Cerisy." *Continuity and Change* 7, no. 1 (1992): 23–45.

Fletcher, Christopher. "The Whig Interpretation of Masculinity? Honour and Sexuality in Late Medieval Manhood." In *What Is Masculinity?: Historical Dynamics from Antiquity to the Contemporary World*, ed. John H. Arnold and Sean Brady, 57–75. Hampshire, UK: Palgrave Macmillan, 2011.

Fletcher, Richard. *The Episcopate in the Kingdom of León in the Twelfth Century.* London: Oxford University Press, 1987.

——. *Moorish Spain.* Berkeley: University of California Press, 1992.

Forey, Alan. *The Military Orders: From the Twelfth to the Early Fourteenth Centuries.* Toronto: University of Toronto Press, 1992.

Frassetto, Michael, ed. *Medieval Purity and Piety: Essays on Medieval Clerical Celibacy and Religious Reform.* New York: Garland Publishing, 1998.

Freedman, Paul. *The Diocese of Vic: Tradition and Regeneration in Medieval Catalonia.* New Brunswick, NJ: Rutgers University Press, 1983.

——. "Military Orders in Osona during the Twelfth and Thirteenth Centuries." In *Church, Law, and Society in Catalonia, 900–1500*, 55–69. Aldershot, UK: Variorum, 1994.

——. *The Origins of Peasant Servitude in Medieval Catalonia.* Cambridge, UK: Cambridge University Press, 1991.

Garssi, J. L. "Royal Clerks from the Archdiocese of York in the Fourteenth Century." *Northern History*, no. 5 (1970): 12–33.

Geremek, Bronislaw. *The Margins of Society in Late Medieval Paris.* Cambridge, UK: Cambridge University Press, 1987.

Gilmore, David D. *Aggression and Community: Paradoxes of Andalusian Culture.* New Haven: Yale University Press, 1987.

———. "Honor, Honesty, Shame: Male Status in Contemporary Andalusia." In *Honor and Shame and the Unity of the Mediterranean*, ed. David D. Gilmore, 90–103. Washington, DC: American Anthropological Association, 1987.

Gironella i Delgà, Anna. "L'hospital de Na Clara de Girona: Nous documents per a la història de l'assistència als pobres en època medieval." In *Miscel·lània en Honor de Josep Maria Marquès*, ed. Narcís Figueras i Pep Vila, 143–49. Montserrat: Abadia de Montserrat, 2010.

Gironella i Granés, Josep Maria. *Viure en una parròquia catalana baixmedieval: Pedret i Marzà, 1285–1348*. Girona: Ajuntament de Pedret i Marzà, 2015.

Given, James Buchanan. *Society and Homicide in Thirteenth-Century England*. Stanford: Stanford University Press, 1977.

Goldberg, Peter J. P. "Pigs and Prostitutes: Streetwalking in Comparative Perspective." In *Young Medieval Women*, ed. Katherine J. Lewis, Noel James Menuge, and Kim M. Phillips, 172–93. New York: St. Martin's Press, 1999.

———. "Women in Fifteenth-Century Town Life." In *Towns and Townspeople in the Fifteenth-Century*, ed. John A. Thomson, 107–28. Gloucester, UK: Alan Sutton Publishing, 1988.

Gransden, Antonia. "Some Late Thirteenth-Century Records of an Ecclesiastical Court in the Archdeaconry of Sudbury." *Bulletin of the Institute of Historical Research* 22 (1959): 62–69.

Guallart de Viala, Alfonso. *El derecho penal histórico de Aragón*. Zaragoza: Excma. Diputación Provincial, Institución Fernando el Católico, D.L. 1977.

Guilleré, Christian. *Diner, poder i societat a la Girona del segle XIV*. Girona: Ajuntament de Girona, 1984.

———. *Girona al segle XIV*. Vol. 1. Barcelona: Publicacions de l'Abadia de Montserrat, 1993.

———. "Les visites pastorales en Tarraconaise à la fin de moyen-âge (XIV–XV siècle). L'exemple du diocèse de Gérone." *Melanges de la Casa de Velázquez* 19 (1983): 125–67.

Haboucha, Reginetta. "Clerics, Their Wives, and Their Concubines in the 'Partidas' of Alfonso El Sabio." In *Acta*, Vol. 14: *Homo Carnalis: The Carnal Aspect of Medieval Human Life*, ed. Helen Rodite Lemay, 85–104. Binghamton: SUNY Binghamton, Center for Medieval and Early Renaissance Studies, 1990.

Hadley, Dawn M., ed. *Masculinity in Medieval Europe*. London: Longman Press, 1999.

Hale, John R. "Violence in the Late Middle Ages: A Background." In *Violence and Civil Disorder in Italian Cities, 1200–1500*, ed. Lauro Martines, 19–39. Berkeley: University of California Press, 1972.

Haliczer, Stephen. *Sexuality in the Confessional: A Sacrament Profaned*. Oxford: Oxford University Press, 1996.

Hall, Edwin. *The Arnolfini Betrothal: Medieval Marriage and the Enigma of Van Eyck's Double Portrait*. Berkeley: University of California Press.

Hammer, Carl I. "Patterns of Homicide in a Medieval University Town: Fourteenth-Century Oxford." *Past and Present* 78 (1978): 3–23.

Hanawalt, Barbara. *Crime and Conflict in English Communities, 1300–1348*. Cambridge, MA: Harvard University Press, 1979.

———. *Growing Up in Medieval London: The Experience of Childhood in History*. New York: Oxford University Press, 1993.

——. "Medievalists and the Study of Childhood." *Speculum* 77, no. 2 (2002): 440–60.

——. "Peasant Women's Contributions to the Home Economy in Late Medieval England." In *Women and Work in Pre-Industrial Europe*, ed. Barbara A. Hanawalt, 3–19. Bloomington: Indiana University Press, 1986.

——. *The Ties That Bound: Peasant Families in Medieval England*. Oxford: Oxford University Press, 1986.

——. "Violent Death in Fourteenth- and Early Fifteenth-Century England." *Comparative Studies in Society and History* 18, no. 3 (July 1976): 297–320.

Harway, Michèle, and James O'Neil, eds. *What Causes Men's Violence against Women?* Thousand Oaks: Sage Publications, 1999.

Hatty, Suzanne E. "Engendering Violence: Starting Points." In *Masculinities, Violence, and Culture*. ed. Suzanne E. Hatty, 1–22. Thousand Oaks: Sage Publications, 2000.

——, ed. *Masculinities, Violence, and Culture*. Thousand Oaks: Sage Publications, 2000.

Hayes, Dawn Marie. "Mundane Uses of Sacred Places in the Central and Later Middle Ages, with a Focus on Chartres Cathedral." *Comitatus: A Journal of Medieval and Renaissance Studies* 30 (1999): 11–37.

Heath, Peter. *The English Parish Clergy on the Eve of the Reformation*. Toronto: University of Toronto Press, 1969.

Helmholz, Richard H. "Crime, Compurgation and the Courts of the Medieval Church." *Law and History Review* 1, no. 1 (1983): 1–26.

Herlihy, David. *The Black Death and the Transformation of the West*. Ed. Samuel K. Cohn Jr. Cambridge, MA: Harvard University Press, 1997.

——. *Medieval and Renaissance Pistoia: The Social History of an Italian Town, 1200–1430*. New Haven: Yale University Press, 1967.

——. *Medieval Households*. Cambridge, MA: Harvard University Press, 1985.

Herlihy, David, and Christiane Klapisch-Zuber. *Tuscans and Their Families: A Study of the Florentine Catasto of 1427*. New Haven: Yale University Press, 1985.

Hillgarth, Jocelyn N. *The Spanish Kingdoms, 1250–1516*. Vols. 1–2. Oxford: Clarendon Press, 1976.

Huggins, Martha K., and Mika Haritos-Fatouros. "Bureaucratizing Masculinities among Brazilian Torturers and Murderers." In *Masculinities and Violence*, ed. Lee H. Bowker, 29–54. Thousand Oaks: Sage Publications, 1998.

Hyams, Paul R. *Rancor and Reconciliation in Medieval England*. Ithaca: Cornell University Press, 2003.

Jaritz, Gerhard, and Ana Marinković, eds. *Violence and the Medieval Clergy*. Budapest: Central European University Press, 2011.

Jestice, Phyllis G. "Why Celibacy? Odo of Cluny and the Development of a New Sexual Morality." In *Medieval Purity and Piety: Essays on Medieval Clerical Celibacy and Religious Reform*, ed. Michael Frasseto, 81–116. New York: Garland Publishing, 1998.

Johnson, Lyman L., and Sonya Lipsett-Rivera, eds. *Sex, Shame, and Violence: The Faces of Honor in Colonial Latin America*. Albuquerque: University of New Mexico Press, 1998.

Johnston, Mark. "Gender as Conduct in the Courtesy Guides for Aristocratic Boys and Girls of Amanieu de Sescás." *Essays in Medieval Studies* 20 (2003): 75–85.

Kamen, Henry. *The Phoenix and the Flame: Catalonia and the Counter Reformation*. New Haven: Yale University Press, 1993.

———. *The Spanish Inquisition: A Historical Revision*. London: Weidenfeld & Nicolson, 1997.

Karbic, Marija. " 'Illicit Love' in Medieval Slavonian Cities." In *Love, Marriage and Family Ties in the Later Middle Ages*, ed. Isabel Davis, Miriam Müller, and Sarah Rees Jones, 331–40. Turnhout, Belgium: Brepols, 2003.

Karras, Ruth Mazo. "The Latin Vocabulary of Illicit Sex in English Ecclesiastical Court Records." *Journal of Medieval Latin* 2 (1992): 1–17.

———. *Common Women: Prostitution and Sexuality in Medieval England*. Oxford: Oxford University Press, 1996.

———. *From Boys to Men: Formations of Masculinity in Late Medieval Europe*. Philadelphia: University of Pennsylvania Press, 2003.

———. *Sexuality in Medieval Europe: Doing unto Others*. New York: Routledge, 2005.

———. "Marriage, Concubinage, and the Law." In *Law and the Illicit in Medieval Europe*, ed. Ruth Mazo Karras, Joel Kaye, and E. Ann Matter, 117–29. Philadelphia: University of Pennsylvania Press, 2008.

———. *Unmarriages: Women, Men, and Sexual Unions in the Middle Ages*. Philadelphia: University of Pennsylvania Press, 2012.

Karras, Ruth M., and David Lorenzo Boyd. ' "Ut cum mulier': A Male Transvestite Prostitute in Fourteenth-Century London." In *Pre-Modern Sexualities*, ed. Louise Fradenburg and Carla Freccero, 101–16. New York: Routledge, 1996.

Kelleher, Marie A. ' "Like Man and Wife': Clerics' Concubines in the Diocese of Barcelona." *Journal of Medieval History* 28 (2002): 349–60.

———. *The Measure of Woman: Law and Female Identity in the Crown of Aragon*. Philadelphia: University of Pennsylvania Press, 2010.

Kelly, Henry Ansgar. *Canon Law and the Archpriest of Hita*. Binghamton: SUNY Binghamton, Medieval and Renaissance Texts and Studies, 1984.

———. "Law and Nonmarital Sex in the Middle Ages." In *Conflict in Medieval Europe: Changing Perspectives on Society and Culture*, ed. Warren C. Brown and Piotr Górecki, 175–93. Aldershot, UK: Ashgate, 2003.

Kemp, Brian. "Hereditary Benefices in the Medieval English Church: A Herefordshire Example." *Bulletin of the Institute of Historical Research* 43, no. 107 (1970): 1–15.

Kertzer, David I., and Caroline Brettell. "Advances in Italian and Iberian Family History." *Journal of Family History* 12, no. 1 (1987): 87–120.

Kimmel, Michael S. *The Gendered Society*. 3rd ed. New York: Oxford University Press, 2008.

King, James R. "The Friar Tuck Syndrome: Clerical Violence and the Barons' War." In *The Final Argument: The Imprint of Violence on Society in Medieval and Early Modern Europe*, ed. Donald J. Kagay and L. J. Andrew Villalon, 27–52. Woodbridge, UK: Boydell Press, 1998.

Kuefler, Mathew. *The Manly Eunuch: Masculinity, Gender Ambiguity, and Christian Ideology in Late Antiquity*. Chicago: University of Chicago Press, 2001.

Lacarra, María Eugenia. "La evolución de la prostitución en la Castilla del siglo XV y la mancebía de Salamanca en tiempos de Fernando de Rojas." In *Fernando de Rojas and Celestina Approaching the Fifth Century. Proceedings of an International Conference in Commemoration of the 450th Anniversary of the Death of Fernando de*

Rojas, ed. Ivy A. Corfis and Joseph T. Snow, 33–77 (Madison: Hispanic Seminary of Medieval Studies, 1993).

Lacarra Lanz, Eukene. "Changing Boundaries of Licit and Illicit Unions: Concubinage and Prostitution." In *Marriage and Sexuality in Medieval and Early Modern Iberia*, ed. Eukene Lacarra Lanz, 158–94. New York: Routledge, 2002.

Ladurie, Emmanuel Le Roy. *Montaillou: The Promised Land of Error.* Trans. Barbara Bray. New York: Vintage Books, 1979.

Lansing, Carol. "Concubines, Lovers, and Prostitutes: Infamy and Female Identity in Medieval Bologna." In *Beyond Florence: The Contours of Medieval and Early Modern Italy*, ed. Paula Findlen, Michelle M. Fontaine, and Duane J. Osheim, 85–100. Stanford: Stanford University Press, 2003.

——. "Girls in Trouble in Late Medieval Bologna." In *The Pre-Modern Teenager: Youth in Society, 1150–1650*, ed. Konrad Eisenbichler, 293–309. Toronto: Center for Reformation and Renaissance Studies, 2002.

Laqua, Simone. "Concubinage and the Church in Early Modern Münster." *Past and Present* 1, suppl. 1 (2006): 72–100.

Lawrence, C. Hugh. "The English Parish and Its Clergy in the Thirteenth Century." In *The Medieval World*, ed. Peter Linehan and Janet Nelson, 648–70. London: Routledge, 2001.

Lea, Henry Charles. *The History of Sacerdotal Celibacy in the Christian Church.* New York: Russel & Russel, 1957.

Lees, Clare A., ed. *Medieval Masculinities: Regarding Men in the Middle Ages.* Minneapolis: University of Minnesota Press, 1994.

Lesnick, Daniel R. "Insults and Threats in Medieval Todi." *Journal of Medieval History* 17 (1991): 71–89.

Lewis, Katherine J. "Male Saints and Devotional Masculinity in Late Medieval England." *Gender & History* 24, no. 1 (2012): 112–33.

Lightfoot, Dana Wessell. "The Projects of Marriage: Spousal Choice, Dowries, and Domestic Service in Early Fifteenth-Century Valencia." *Viator* 40, no. 1 (2009): 333–53.

Linage Conde, Antonio, Javier Faci Lacasta, Juan Francisco Rivera Recio, and Antoni Oliver Montserrat. "Organización eclesiástica de la España cristiana." In *Historia de la iglesia en España*, Vol. 2, Pt. 1, ed. Ricardo García-Villoslada, 141–233 (Madrid: Biblioteca de Autores Cristianos, 1982).

Linehan, Peter. "Segovia: A 'Frontier' Diocese in the Thirteenth Century." *English Historical Review* 96 (1981): 481–508.

——. *Spanish Church and Society, 1150–1300.* London: Variorum Reprints, 1983.

——. *The Spanish Church and the Papacy in the Thirteenth Century.* Cambridge, UK: Cambridge University Press, 1971.

——. "A Survey of the Diocese of Segovia (1246–47)." *Spanish Church and Society, 1150–1300*, 163–206. London: Variorum Reprints, 1983.

Lochrie, Karma, Peggy McCracken, and James A. Schultz, eds. *Constructing Medieval Sexuality.* Minneapolis: University of Minnesota Press, 1997.

Lojo Piñiero, Fernando. *A violencia na Galicia do século XV.* Santiago de Compostela: Universidad de Santiago de Compostela, 1991.

Lomax, Derek W. "The Lateran Reforms and Spanish Literature." *Iberoromania* 1 (1969): 229–313.

Lluch Bramon, Rosa. "Remences redimits: El domini de l'almoina del pa de la seu de Girona (1331–1458)." *Anuario de Estudios Medievales* 27, no. 2 (1997): 869–902.

Lluch Bramon, Rosa, and Elvis Mallorquí. "Els masos a l'època medieval. Orígens i evolució." In *L'organització de l'espai rural a l'europa mediterrània*, ed. Rosa Congost Colomer, Gabriel Jover, Giuliana Biagioli, 37–64 (Girona: Associació d'Història Rural de les Comarques Gironines, Centre de Recerca d'Història Rural de la Universitat de Girona, 2003).

Lynch, Joseph. *The Medieval Church: A Brief History*. London: Longman, 1992.

Madero, Marta. *Manos violentas, palabras vedadas: La injuria en Castilla y León, siglos XIII–XV.* Madrid: Taurus Humanidades, 1992.

Maddern, Philippa. "Between Households: Children in Blended and Transitional Households in Late-Medieval England." *Journal of the History of Childhood and Youth* 3, no. 1 (2010): 65–86.

——. "Interpreting Silence: Domestic Violence in the King's Courts in East Anglia, 1422–1442." In *Domestic Violence in Medieval Texts*, ed. Eve Salisbury, Georgiana Danavin, and Merral Llewelyn Price, 31–56. Gainesville: University Press of Florida, 2002.

Mannarelli, María Emma. *Private Passions and Public Sins: Men and Women in Seventeenth-Century Lima.* Albuquerque: University of New Mexico Press, 2007.

Manuel Vidal, José. "Decenas de curas católicos están casados en España." *El Mundo*, May 27, 2014.

Marquès, Josep M. "Apuntes históricos sobre el Palacio Episcopal de Gerona." *Anales del Instituto de Estudios Gerundeses* 14 (1960), 263–306.

——. *Arxiu diocesà de Girona: Processos medievals.* Girona: Arxiu Diocesà de Girona,1999.

——. "Fundaciones de beneficios en el obispado de Gerona, s. XII–XVIII." *Anthologica Annua* 36 (1989): 493–507.

——. "El govern de la diòcesi i de la bisbalia de Girona (1334–1362)." *Estudis del Baix Empordà* 12 (1993): 85–105.

——. *Una història de la diòcesi de Girona.* Barcelona: Abadia de Montserrat, 2007.

——. "La iglesia de Gerona." In *Historia de las diócesis españolas: Barcelona, Terrassa, Sant Feliu de Llobregat, Gerona.* Vol. 2, ed. Josep M. Martí Bonet, 463–685. Madrid: Biblioteca de Autores Cristianos, 2006.

——. "Notes històriques sobre la diòcesi de Girona i les seves parròquies." *Butlletí de l'Església de Girona* 1(1996): 91–134.

——. "Nuevas raíces en el antiguo suelo." In *Historia de las diócesis españolas: Barcelona, Terrassa, Sant Feliu de Llobregat, Gerona.* Vol. 2, ed. Josep M. Martí Bonet, 479–96. Madrid: Biblioteca de Autores Cristianos, 2006.

——. "Processos anteriors al 1500 de l'ariux diocesà de Girona." *Annals de l'Institut d'Estudis Gironins* 44 (2003): 145–77.

——. *Repertori selectiu*, Vol. 1: *Lletres: 1134–1362.* Girona: Arxiu Diocesà de Girona, 1992.

——. "Set cenobis femenins de l'empordà." In *Estudis del Baix Empordà*, no. 15 (1996): 69–100.

Márquez Villanueva, Francisco. "Juan Ruiz y el celibato eclesiástico." In *Juan Ruiz, Arcipreste de Hita, y el "Libro de Buen Amor": Congreso Internacional del Centro para la edición de los clásicos españoles*, ed. Francisco Toro Ceballos and

Bienvenido Morros, 17–33. Alcalá la Real: Centro para la Edición de los Clásicos Españoles, 2004.

Martí Bonet, Josep M., ed. *Historia de las diócesis españolas: Barcelona, Terrassa, Sant Feliu de Llobregat, Gerona.* Vol. 2. Madrid: Biblioteca de Autores Cristianos, 2006.

——. "La iglesia de Barcelona." In *Historia de las diócesis españolas: Barcelona, Terrasa, Sant Feliu de llobregat, y Gerona,* ed. Josep M. Marquès Planagumà and Josep M. Martí Bonet, 5–430. Madrid: Biblioteca de Autores Cristianos, 2006.

——. "El ministerio pastoral del Obispo Ponç de Gualba en sus visitas (a. 1303–1330)." *Memoria Ecclesiae* 4 (1993): 9–63.

Martí Bonet, Josep M., Leandre Niqui i Puigvert, and F. Miquel i Mascort, eds. *Processos de l'arxiu diocesà de Barcelona.* Barcelona: Department de Cultura de la Generalitat de Catalunya, 1984.

McCrank, Lawrence J. *Restoration and Reconquest in Medieval Catalonia: The Church and Principality of Tarragona, 971–1177.* PhD diss., University of Virginia, 1974.

McDougall, Sara. "The Prosecution of Sex in Late Medieval Troyes." In *Sexuality in the Middle Ages and Early Modern Times: New Approaches to a Fundamental Cultural-Historical and Literary-Anthropological Theme,* ed. Albrecht Classen, 691–714. New York: Walter de Gruyter, 2008.

McLaughlin, Megan. "The Bishop as Bidegroom: Marital Imagery and Clerical Celibacy in the Eleventh and Early Twelfth Centuries." In *Medieval Purity and Piety: Essays on Medieval Clerical Celibacy and Religious Reform,* ed. Michael Frassetto, 209–38. New York: Garland Publishing, 1998.

——. "The Mother of the Faithful." In *Sex, Gender, and Episcopal Authority in an Age of Reform, 1000–1122,* 123–59. Cambridge, UK: Cambridge University Press, 2010.

——. "Secular and Spiritual Fatherhood in the Eleventh Century." In *Conflicted Identities and Multiple Masculinities,* ed. Jacqueline Murray, 25–43. New York: Garland Publishing, 1999.

——. *Sex, Gender, and Episcopal Authority in an Age of Reform, 1000–1122.* Cambridge, UK: Cambridge University Press, 2010.

McNamara, Jo Ann. "Chaste Marriage and Clerical Celibacy." In *Sexual Practices and the Medieval Church,* ed. Vern L. Bullough and James Brundage, 22–33. Amherst: Prometheus Books, 1994.

——. "The Herrenfrage: The Restructuring of the Gender System, 1050–1150." In *Medieval Masculinities: Regarding Men in the Middle Ages,* ed. Clare A. Lees, 3–29. Minneapolis: University of Minnesota Press, 1994.

McSheffrey, Shannon. "Men and Masculinity in Late Medieval London Civic Culture: Governance, Patriarchy, and Reputation." In *Conflicted Identities and Multiple Masculinities,* ed. Jacqueline Murray, 243–78. New York: Garland Press, 1999.

Meyerson, Mark D. *A Jewish Renaissance in Fifteenth-Century Spain.* Princeton: Princeton University Press, 2004.

——. *The Muslims of Valencia in the Age of Fernando and Isabel: Between Coexistence and Crusade.* Berkeley: University of California Press, 1991.

Meyerson, Mark D., Daniel Thiery, and Oren Falk, eds. *"A Great Effusion of Blood"?: Interpreting Medieval Violence.* Toronto: University of Toronto Press, 2004.

——. "Introduction." In *A Great Effusion of Blood"?: Interpreting Medieval Violence*, ed. Mark D. Meyerson, Daniel Thiery, and Oren Falk, 1–17. Toronto: University of Toronto Press, 2004.

Migiel, Marilyn. "Domestic Violence in the Decameron." In *Domestic Violence in Medieval Texts*, ed. Eve Salisbury, Georgiana Danavin, and Merral Llewelyn Price, 164–79. Gainesville: University Press of Florida, 2002.

Millás Vallicrosa, José M., and Luis Battle Prats. "Un alboroto contra el call de Gerona en el año 1331," *Sefarad* 12 (1952): 297–335.

Miller, Andrew G. "To 'Frock' a Cleric: The Gendered Implications of Mutilating Ecclesiastical Vestments in Medieval England." *Gender & History* 24, no. 2 (2012): 271–91.

Miller, Maureen C. *The Formation of a Medieval Church: Ecclesiastical Change in Verona, 950–1150*. Ithaca: Cornell University, 1993.

——. "Masculinity, Reform, Clerical Culture: Narratives of Episcopal Holiness in the Gregorian Era." *Church History* 72, no. 1 (2003): 25–52.

Milton, Gregory B. *Market Power: Lordship, Society, and Economy in Medieval Catalonia, 1276–1313*. New York: Palgrave Macmillan, 2012.

Mollat, Guillaume. *Lettres Communes des Papes d'Avignon. Jean XXII (1316–1334)*. Vols. 1–4. Paris: Albert Fontemoing, 1905.

——. *Lettres Communes des Papes d'Avignon. Jean XXII (1316–1334)*. Vol. VII. Paris: Albert Fontemoing, 1914.

Monjas, Lluís. "Les visites pastorals: De l'època medieval a la vigília del Concili de Trento." In *Les visites pastorals: Dels orígens medievals a l'època contemporània*, ed. Joaquim M. Puigvert i Solà, Lluís Monjas Manso, Xavier Solà Colomer, and Eugeni Perea Simón, 45–73. Girona: La Biblioteca d'Història Rural, 2003.

Monjas, Lluís, Eugeni Perea, Joaquim M. Puigvert, and Xavier Solà. "Usos historiogràfics." In *Les visites pastorals: Dels orígens medievals a l'època contemporània*, ed. Joaquim M. Puigvert i Solà, Lluís Monjas Manso, Xavier Solà Colomer, and Eugeni Perea Simón, 19–44. Girona: La Biblioteca d'Història Rural, 2003.

Montane, Pedro Ribes. "Notas sobre la cultura eclesiástica de los reinos hispanos en los siglos XI y XII." *Anthologica Annua* 28–29 (1981–1982): 475–84.

Moore, Robert I. "Family, Community, and Cult on the Eve of the Gregorian Reform." *Transactions of the Royal Historical Society* 30 (1980): 49–69.

——. *The Formation of a Persecuting Society*. Oxford: Basil Blackwell, 1987.

Moss, Rachel E. "An Orchard, a Love Letter and Three Bastards: The Formation of Adult Male Identity in a Fifteenth-Century Family." In *What Is Masculinity?: Historical Dynamics from Antiquity to the Contemporary World*, ed. John H. Arnald and Sean Brady, 226–44. New York: Palgrave Macmillan, 2011.

Murray, Jacqueline. "Hiding behind the Universal Male: Male Sexuality in the Middle Ages." In *Handbook of Medieval Sexuality*, ed. Vern L. Bullough and James A. Brundage, 123–52. New York: Garland Publishing, 1996.

——. "Masculinizing Religious Life: Sexual Prowess, the Battle for Chastity and Monastic Identity." In *Holiness and Masculinity in the Middle Ages*, ed. Pat H. Cullum and Katherine J. Lewis, 24–42. Toronto: University of Toronto Press, 2004.

——. "Mystical Castration: Some Reflections on Peter Abelard, Hugh of Lincoln and Sexual Control." In *Conflicted Identities and Multiple Masculinities*, ed. Jacqueline Murray, 73–91. New York: Garland Publishing, 1999.

Mutgé Vives, Josefa. "L'abastament de blat a la Ciutat de Barcelona en temps d'Alfons El Benigne (1327–1336)." In *Política, urbanismo, y vida ciudadana en la Barcelona del siglo XIV*, ed. J. Mutgé Vives, 215–51. Barcelona: Consejo Superior de Investigaciones Científicas, 2004.

Nalle, Sara T. *God in La Mancha: Religious Reform and the People of Cuenca, 1500–1650*. Baltimore: John Hopkins University Press, 1992.

Narbona Vizcaíno, Rafael. *Pueblo, poder, y sexo: Valencia medieval (1306–1420)*. Valencia: Diputació de València, 1992.

Neal, Derek G. *The Masculine Self in Late Medieval England*. Chicago: University of Chicago Press, 2008.

——. "Suits Make the Man: Masculinity in Two English Law Courts, c. 1500." *Annales Canadiennes d'Histoire* 37 (2002): 1–22.

——. "What Can Historians do with Clerical Masculinity? Lessons from Medieval Europe." In *Negotiating Clerical Identities: Priests, Monks, and Masculinity in the Middle Ages*, ed. Jennifer D. Thibodeaux, 16–36. New York: Palgrave Macmillan, 2010.

Nelson, Janet L. "Monks, Secular Men, and Masculinity, c. 900." In *Masculinity in Medieval Europe*, ed. Dawn M. Hadley, 121–42. London: Longman, 1999.

Nieto Soria, José Manuel. *La época medieval: Iglesia y cultura*. Madrid: Istmo, 2002.

Nirenberg, David. *Communities of Violence: Persecution of Minorities in the Middle Ages*. Princeton: Princeton University Press, 1996.

——. "Conversion, Sex, and Segregation: Jews and Christians in Medieval Spain." *American Historical Review* 107 (2002): 1065–93.

——. *Violence and the Persecution of Minorities in the Crown of Aragon: Jews, Lepers and Muslims before the Black Death*. PhD diss., Princeton University, 1992.

O'Callaghan, Joseph F. *A History of Medieval Spain*. Ithaca: Cornell University Press, 1975.

——. "Teologos y hombres de ciencia." In *Història de la iglesia en España*, Vol. II, ed. Javier Fernandez Conde, 218–39. Madrid: Biblioteca de Autores Christianos, 1982.

Orcástegui Gros, Carmen. "Ordenanzas municipales y reglamentación local en la edad media sobre la mujer aragonesa en sus relaciones sociales y economicas." In *Las mujeres en las ciudades medievales: Actas de las III Jornadas de Investigación Interdisciplinaria*, 13–18. Madrid: Universidad Autónoma de Madrid, 1984.

Otis, Leah L. *Prostitution in Medieval Society: The History of an Urban Institution in Languedoc*. Chicago: University of Chicago Press, 1985.

Palau i Baduell, Josep M. *La moralitat dels clergues i laics als comtats de Pallars a través de les visites pastorals de 1314 i 1315*. Màster de Cultures Medievals, Universitat de Barcelona, 2009.

Parish, Helen. *Clerical Celibacy in the West: c. 1100–1700*. Farnham, UK: Ashgate, 2010.

Parker, Sandra Lee, and Lawrence R. Poos. "A Consistory Court from the Diocese of Rochester, 1363–4." *English Historical Review* 106 no. 420 (1991): 652–65.

Perron, Anthony. "Saxo Grammaticus's Heroic Chastity: A Model of Clerical Celibacy and Masculinity in Medieval Scandinavia." In *Negotiating Clerical Identities: Priests, Monks and Masculinity in the Middle Ages*, ed. Jennifer D. Thibodeaux, 113–35. New York: Palgrave Macmillan, 2010.

Perry, Mary Elizabeth. *Gender and Disorder in Early Modern Seville.* Princeton: Princeton University Press, 1990.

Phillips, Kim M. "Masculinities and the Medieval English Sumptuary Laws." *Gender & History* 19, no. 1 (2007): 22–42.

Phillips, Kim M., and Barry Reay. *Sex before Sexuality: A Premodern History.* Cambridge, UK: Polity Press, 2011.

Pladevall i Font, Antoni. "Arnau i Bertran de Mont-rodon, dos grans bisbes gironins del segle XIV." *Annals de l'Institut d'Estudis Gironins* 34 (1994): 395–425.

———. *Història de l'església a Catalunya.* Barcelona: Editorial Claret, 1989.

Platt, Colin. *The Parish Churches of Medieval England.* London: Secker & Warburg, 1981.

Plummer, Marjorie Elizabeth. *From Priest's Whore to Pastor's Wife: Clerical Marriage and the Process of Reform in in the Early German Reformation.* Burlington, UK: Ashgate, 2012.

Pobst, Phyllis E. "Visitation of Religious and Clergy by Archbishop Eudes of Rouen." In *Religion, Text, and Society in Medieval Spain and Northern Europe*, ed. Thomas E. Burman, Mark D. Meyerson, and Leah Shopkow, 223–49. Toronto: Pontifical Institute of Mediaeval Studies, 2002.

Pons i Guri, Josep María. "Nomenclatores de la Diocesis Gerundense en el Siglo XIV." *Anales del Instituto de Estudios Gerundenses* 17 (1964–1965): 5–77.

Pontevedra, Silvia R. "El corazón o el púlpito." *El País*, June 1, 2014, 38–39.

Poska, Allyson M. *Women and Authority in Early Modern Spain: The Peasants of Galicia.* Oxford: Oxford University Press, 2005.

Pounds, Norman J. G. *A History of the English Parish: The Culture of Religion from Augustine to Victoria.* Cambridge, UK: Cambridge University Press, 2000.

Puff, Helmet. "Female Sodomy: The Trial of Katherina Hetzeldorfer (1477)." *Journal of Medieval and Early Modern Studies* 30, no. 1 (2000): 41–61.

Puig i Aleu, Immaculada. "Les visites pastorals a la diòcesi de Girona, segle XV." *Annals de l'Institut d'Estudis Gironins* 28 (1985–1986): 211–41.

Puig i Puig, Sebastián. *Episcopologio de la sede barcinonense.* Barcelona, 1929.

Puigvert, Joaquim M., Lluís Monjas, Xavier Solà, and Eugeni Perea, eds. *Les visites pastorals dels orígens medievals a l'època contemporània.* Girona: Biblioteca d'Història Rural, 2003.

Ratcliffe, Marjorie. "Adulteresses, Mistresses, and Prostitutes: Extramarital Relationships in Medieval Castile." *Hispania* 67, no. 3 (1984): 346–50.

Razi, Zvi. *Life, Marriage, and Death in a Medieval Parish. Economy, Society, and Demography in Halesowen, 1270–1400.* Cambridge, UK: Cambridge University Press, 1980.

Recio, María Asunción Esteban, and María Jesús Izquierdo García. "Pecado y marginación. Mujeres públicas en valladolid y palencia durante los siglos XV y XVI." In *La ciudad medieval: Aspectos de la vida urbana en la Castilla bajomedieval*, ed. Juan A Bonachia, 155–64. Valladolid: Universidad de Valladolid, 1996.

Reilly, Bernard F. *The Kingdom of León-Castilla under King Alfonso VII, 1126–1157.* Philadelphia: University of Pennsylvania Press, 1998.

———. *The Medieval Spains.* Cambridge, UK: Cambridge University Press, 1993.

———, ed. *Santiago, Saint-Denis, and Saint Peter. The Reception of the Roman Liturgy in León-Castile in 1080.* New York: Fordham University Press, 1985.

Reilly, Kevin C. "The Conclusion of Elena y María: A Reconsideration." *Kentucky Romance Quarterly* 30, no. 3 (1983): 251–62.

Richardson, H. G. "The Parish Clergy of the Thirteenth and Fourteenth Centuries." *Transactions of the Royal Historical Society* 6 (1912): 89–128.

Richou i Llimona, Montserrat. "El baix maresme a l'època baix medieval." *Butlletí de la Societat Catalana d'Estudis Històrics* 19 (2008): 153–66.

Rocke, Michael. *Forbidden Friendships: Homosexuality and Male Culture in Renaissance Florence.* New York: Oxford University Press, 1996.

———. "Gender and Sexual Culture in Renaissance Italy." In *Gender and Society in Renaissance Italy*, ed. Judith Brown and Robert C. Davis, 150–70. New York: Longman, 1998.

Rodríguez Molina, José. "Celibato eclesiástico y discriminación de la mujer en la edad media Andaluza." *Cuadernos de Estudios Medievales y Ciencias y Técnicas Historiográficas* 18–19 (1993–1994): 37–57.

———. *El obispade Baeza-Jaén (siglos XIII–XVI): Organización y economia diocesanas.* Jaén: Diputación Provincial de Jaén, Instituto de Cultura, 1986.

Rosser, Gervase. "Conflict and Political Community in the Medieval Town: Disputes between Clergy and Laity in Hereford" In *The Church in the Medieval Town*, ed. T. R. Slater and Gervasse Rosser, 20–42. Aldershot, UK: Ashgate, 1998.

Rossiaud, Jacques. *Medieval Prostitution.* Trans. Lydia G. Cochrane. Oxford: Basil Blackwell, 1988.

Rousseau, Constance M. "Pope Innocent III and the Familial Relationships of Clergy and Religious." *Studies in Medieval and Renaissance History* 14 (1933): 107–48.

Ruggiero, Guido. "Sexual Criminality in the Early Renaissance: Venice, 1338–1358." *Journal of Social History* 8 (1974): 18–37.

Ruiz, Teofilo R. *Spanish Society, 1400–1600.* London: Pearson Education, 2001.

Ruiz Doménec, José Enrique. "Las estructuras familiares catalanas en la alta edad media." *Cuadernos de Arqueología i Història de la Ciutat* 16 (1975): 90–108.

Sabaté, Flocel. "L'esglésa secular catalana al segle XIV: La conflictive relació social." *Anuario de Estudios Medievales* 28 (1998): 757–88.

———. "Femmes et violence dans la Catalogne du XIVe siècle." *Annales du Midi* 106 (1994): 227–316.

———. *La feudalización de la sociedad Catalana.* Granada: Universidad de Granada, 2007.

Salinas, Santiago Bueno. *El derecho canónico catalán en la baja edad media: La diócesis de Gerona en los siglos XIII y XIV.* Barcelona: Facultat de Teologia de Catalunya, 2000.

Salisbury, Eve, Georgiana Danavin, and Merral Llewelyn Price, eds. *Domestic Violence in Medieval Texts.* Gainesville: University Press of Florida, 2002.

———. "Introduction," in *Domestic Violence in Medieval Texts*, ed. Eve Salisbury, Georgiana Danavin, and Merral Llewelyn Price, 1–27. Gainesville: University Press of Florida, 2002.

Salisbury, Joyce E. "Gendered Sexuality." In *Handbook of Medieval Sexuality*, ed. Vern L. Bullough and James A. Brundage, 81–102. New York: Garland Publishing, 1996.

Salonen, Kirsi. "The Apostolic Penitentiary and Violence in the Roman Curia." In *Violence and the Medieval Clergy*, ed. Gerhard Jaritz and Ana Marinković, 17–28. Budapest: Central European University Press, 2011.

——. "In Their Fathers' Footsteps: The Illegitimate Sons of Finnish Priests According to the Archives of the Sacred Penitentiary, 1449–1523." In *Roma magistra mundi: Itineraria culturae medievalis: Mélanges offerts au Pére L.E. Boyle à l'occasion de son 75e anniversaire*, ed. Jacqueline Hamesse, 355–66. Louvain-la-Neuve: Fédération Internationale des Instituts d'Études Médiévales. Textes et Études du Moyen Âge. 1998.

——. "Violence in Finland in the Middle Ages and the Sixteenth Century in the Light of Source Material from the Vatican Archives." In *Manslaughter, Fornication and Sectarianism: Norm-Breaking in Finland and the Baltic Area from Mediaeval to Modern Times*, ed. Anu Koskivirta and Sari Forsström, 100–120. Saarijärvi: Annales Academiae Scientiarum Fennicae, 2002.

Salonen, Kirsi, and Ludwig Schmugge. *A Sip from the "Well of Grace": Medieval Texts from the Apostolic Penitentiary*. Washington, DC: Catholic University of America, 2009.

Sánchez Herrero, José. *Las diócesis del Reino de León. Siglos XIV y XV*. León: Centro de Estudios e Investigación "San Isidoro,"1978,

——. "Los sínodos de la diócesis de León en los siglos XII al XV." In *León y su historia*, Vol. 3, 165–262. León: Centro de Estudios e Investigación "San Isidoro,"1975.

Saranyana, Josep-Ignasi. *La discussion medieval sobre la condición femenina, siglos VIII al XIII*. Salamanca: Universidad Pontificia Salamanca, 1997.

Scarborough, Connie L. "The Rape of Men and Other 'Lessons' about Sex in the *Libro de Buen Amor*." In *Sexuality in the Middle Ages and Early Modern Times: New Approaches to a Fundamental Cultural-Historical and Literary-Anthropological Theme*, ed. Albrecht Classen, 565–77. Berlin: Walter de Gruyer, 2008.

Schimmelpfennig, Bernhard. "'Ex fornicatione nati': Studies on the Position of Priests' Sons from the Twelfth to the Fourteenth Century." *Studies in Medieval and Renaissance History* 2 (1979): 3–50.

Schmugge, Ludwig. "'Cleansing on Consciences': Some Observations Regarding the Fifteenth–Century Registers of the Papal Penitentiary." *Viator* 29 (1998): 345–61.

Schofield, Philip R. *Peasant and Community in Medieval England, 1200–1500*. New York: Palgrave Macmillan, 2003.

Schultz, James A. "Heterosexuality as a Threat to Medieval Studies." *Journal of the History of Sexuality* 15, no. 1 (2006): 14–29.

Segura Graiño, Cristina. "La sociedad feudal." In *Historia de las mujeres en España*, ed. Elisa Garrido González, 153–84. Madrid: Editorial Síntesis, 1991.

Serra i Clota, Assumpta. *La comunitat rural a la Catalunya medieval: Collsacabra (s. XIII–XVI)*. Vic: Eumo Editorial, 1990.

Serrano Seoane, Yolanda. "El sistema penal de tribunal eclesiàstico de la diócesis de Barcelona en la baja edad media. Primera parte. Estudio." *Clio & Crimen*, no. 3 (2006): 334–429.

——. "El sistema penal del tribunal eclesiástico de la diócesis de Barcelona en la baja edad media. Segunda parte. Documentos." *Clio & Crimen*, no. 3 (2006): 430–508.

Serra Ruiz, Rafael. *Honor, honra, e injuria en el derecho medieval español*. Murcia: Sucesores de Nogués, 1969.

Shadis, Miriam. "'Received as a Woman': Rethinking the Concubinage of Aurenbi-aix of Urgell." *Journal of Medieval Iberian Studies* 8, no. 1 (2016): 38–54.

Shahar, Shulamith. *Childhood in the Middle Ages.* London: Routledge, 1990.

Sheehan, Michael M. "The Formation and Stability of Marriage in Fourteenth-Century England: Evidence of an Ely Register." In *Marriage, Family, and Law in Medieval Europe: Collected Studies.* Ed. James K. Farge, 38–76. Toronto: University of Toronto Press, 1996.

Shepard, Alexandra. *Meanings of Manhood in Early Modern England.* Oxford: Oxford University Press, 2003.

Shinners, John, and William J. Dohar. *Pastors and the Care of Souls in Medieval England.* Notre Dame: University of Notre Dame, 1998.

Silleras-Fernández, Núria. *Chariots of Ladies: Francesc Eiximenis and the Court Culture of Medieval and Early Modern Iberia.* Ithaca: Cornell University Press, 2015.

——. "Money Isn't Everything: Concubinage, Class, and the Rise and Fall of Sibil·la de Fortià, Queen of Aragon (1377–87)." In *Women, Wealth, and Power in Medieval Europe,* ed. Theresa Earenfight, 67–88. New York: Palgrave, 2010.

Simons, Patricia. *The Sex of Men in Premodern Europe: A Cultural History.* Cambridge, UK: Cambridge University Press, 2011.

Skoda, Hannah. *Medieval Violence: Physical Brutality in Northern France, 1270–1330.* Oxford: Oxford University Press, 2013.

Smail, Daniel Lord. "Common Violence: Vengeance and Inquisition in Fourteenth-Century Marseille." *Past and Present* 151 (1996): 28–59.

——. "Telling Tales in Angevin Courts." *French Historical Studies* 20, no. 2 (1997): 183–215.

——. "Telling Tales in Angevin Courts." *French Historical Studies* 20, no. 2 (1997): 183–215.

——. "Hatred as a Social Institution in Late Medieval Society." *Speculum* 76 (2001): 90–126.

——. *The Consumption of Justice: Emotions, Publicity, and Legal Culture in Marseille, 1264–1423.* Ithaca: Cornell University Press, 2003.

Smith, Damian J. *Innocent III and the Crown of Aragon: The Limits of Papal Authority.* Aldershot, UK: Ashgate, 2004.

Socolow, Susan Migden. *The Women of Colonial Latin America.* 2nd ed. Cambridge, UK: Cambridge University Press, 2015.

Soldevila i Temporal, Xavier. "Un clergue Vilatà del segle XIV. Antoni Major, de Torroella de Montgrí." In *Miscel·lània en honor de Josep Maria Marquès,* ed. Narcís Figueras i Pep Vila, 192–96. Montserrat: Abadia de Montserrat, 2010.

Solomon, Michael. *Fictions of Well-Being: Sickly Readers and Vernacular Medical Writing in Late Medieval and Early Modern Spain.* Philadelphia: University of Pennsylvania Press, 2010.

——. *The Literature of Misogyny in Medieval Spain: The Arcipreste de Talavera and the Spill.* Cambridge, UK: Cambridge University Press, 1997.

Spierenburg, Pieter. "Masculinity, Violence and Honor: An Introduction." In *Men and Violence: Gender, Honor, and Rituals in Modern Europe and America,* ed. Pieter Spierenburg, 1–29. Columbus: Ohio State University Press, 1998.

Stone, Rachel. *Morality and Masculinity in the Carolingian Empire*. Cambridge, UK: Cambridge University Press, 2012.

Strocchia, Sharon T. "Gender and the Rites of Honour in Italian Renaissance Cities." In *Gender and Society in Renaissance Italy*, ed. Judith C. Brown and Robert C. Davis, 39–60. London: Longman, 1998.

Stuard, Susan Mosher. "Burdens of Matrimony: Husbanding and Gender in Medieval Italy." In *Medieval Masculinities: Regarding Men in the Middle Ages*, ed. Clare A. Lees, 61–72. Minneapolis: University of Minnesota Press, 1994.

Sutt, Cameron. "Uxores, Ancillae and Dominae: Women in Thirteenth-Century Hungary in the Register of Várad." *Journal of Medieval History* 36 (2010): 142–55.

Swanson, Robert N. "Angels Incarnate: Clergy and Masculinity from the Gregorian Reform to Reformation." In *Masculinity in Medieval Europe*, ed. Dawn M. Hadley, 160–77. London: Longman, 1999.

——. *Church and Society in Late Medieval England*. Oxford: Basil Blackwell, 1989.

Taglia, Kathryn Ann. " 'On Account of Scandal . . .': Priests, Their Children, and the Ecclesiastical Demand for Celibacy." *Florilegium* 14 (1995–1996): 57–70.

Taylor, Scott K. *Honor and Violence in Golden Age Spain*. New Haven: Yale University Press, 2008.

Thibodeaux, Jennifer D. "From Boys to Priests." In *Negotiating Clerical Identities: Priests, Monks and Masculinity in the Middle Ages*, ed. Jennifer D. Thibodeaux, 136–58. New York: Palgrave Macmillan, 2010.

——. *The Manly Priest: Clerical Celibacy, Masculinity, and Reform in England and Normandy, 1066–1300*. Philadelphia: University of Pennsylvania Press, 2015.

——. "Man of the Church or Man of the Village?": The Conflict of Masculinities among Priests in the Thirteenth-Century Diocese of Rouen. PhD diss., University of Kansas, 2004.

——. "Man of the Church, or Man of the Village? Gender and the Parish Clergy in Medieval Normandy." *Gender & History* 18, no. 2 (2006): 380–99.

Thomson, Marilyn. "Boys Will Be Boys: Addressing the Social Construction of Gender." In *Masculinities Matter!: Men, Gender and Development*, ed. Frances Cleaver, 166–85. London: Zed Books, 2002.

To Figueras, Lluís. "La diferenciació pagesa a la diòcesi de Girona (segle XIV): Una nota metodològica." In *El feudalisme comptat i debatut. Formació i expansió del feudalisme català*, ed. Miquel Barceló, Gaspar Feliu, Antoni Furió, M. Miquel, and Jaume Sobrequés, 441–63. València: Universitat de València, 2003.

Tolan, John V. *Saracens: Islam in the Medieval European Imagination*. New York: Columbia University Press, 2002.

Townley, Simon. "Unbeneficed Clergy in the Thirteenth-Century: Two English Dioceses." In *Studies in Clergy and Ministry in Medieval England*, ed. David M Smith, 38–64. York, UK: University of York, 1991.

Tringham, Nigel J. "The Parochial Visitation of Tarvin (Chesire) in 1317." *Northern History* 38, no. 2 (2001): 197–220.

Twinam, Ann. *Public Lives, Private Secrets: Gender, Honor, Sexuality, and Illegitimacy in Colonial Spanish America*. Stanford: Stanford University Press, 1999.

Utterback, Kristine T. *Pastoral Care and Administration in Mid-Fourteenth Century Barcelona: Exercising the "Art of Arts."* Lewiston: Edwin Mellen Press, 1993.

Vargas, Michael A. *Taming a Brood of Vipers: Conflict and Change in Fourteenth-Century Dominican Convents*. Leiden: Brill, 2011.

Vela Palomares, Susanna. "Visites pastorals a la diòcesi d'Urgell. L'Example de les Valls d'Andorra (1312–1314)." *Annals* (1990): 59–103.

Viera, David J. *Medieval Catalan Literature: Prose and Drama*. Boston: Twayne Publishers, 1988.

Vinke, Johannes. "Estado e iglesia en la historia de la Corona de Aragón de los siglos XII, XIII, y XIV." In *Crónica, ponencias y comunicaciones: VII congreso de historia de la Corona de Aragón*, ed. Mercedes Costa and Federico Udina Martorell, 267–85. Barcelona: Congreso de Historia de la Corona de Aragón, 1962.

Vinyoles i Vidal, Teresa-María. *Les barcelonines a les darreries de l'edat mitjana (1370–1410)*. Barcelona: Fundació Salvador Vives Casajuana, 1976.

———. *Història de les dones a la Catalunya medieval*. Lleida: Pagès editors, 2005.

———. *La vida quotidiana a Barcelona vers 1400*. Barcelona: Fundació Salvador Vives, 1985.

———. "La violència marginal a les ciutats medievals (exemples a la Barcelona dels volts del 1400)." In *Violència i marginado en la societat medieval. Revista d'Historia Medieval* 1 (1990): 155–77.

Vinyoles i Vidal, Teresa-Maria, and Margarida González i Betlinski. "Els infants abandonats a les portes de l'hospital de Barcelona (anys 1426–1439)." In *La pobreza y la asistencia a los pobres en la Cataluña medieval*, ed. Manuel Riu, 191–285. Barcelona: C.S.I.C., 1981–1982.

Vleeschouwers-Van Melkebeek, Monique. "Mandatory Celibacy and Priestly Ministry in the Diocese of Tournai at the End of the Middle Ages," in *Peasants & Townsmen in Medieval Europe: Studia in Honorem Adriaan Verhulst*, ed. Jean Mari Duvosquel and Erik Thoen, 681–92, Leuven : Belgisch Centrum voor Landelijke Geschiedenis, 1995.

Vose, Robin. *Dominicans, Muslims and Jews in the Medieval Crown of Aragon*. Cambridge, UK: Cambridge University Press, 2009.

Webster, Jill R. *Carmel in Medieval Catalonia*. Leiden: Brill, 1999.

———. *Els Menorets: The Franciscans in the Realms of Aragon from St. Francis to the Black Death*. Toronto: Pontifical Institute of Mediaeval Studies, 1993.

Weisner-Hanks, Merry. *Christianity and Sexuality in the Early Modern World: Regulating Desire, Reforming Practice*. New York: Routledge, 1999.

Wells, Sharon. "Manners Maketh Man: Living, Dining and Becoming a Man in the Later Middle Ages." In *Rites of Passage: Cultures of Transition in the Fourteenth Century*, ed. Nicola F McDonald and William Mark Ormrod, 67–81. York, UK: York Medieval Press, 2004.

Werner, Janelle. "Promiscuous Priests and Vicarage Children: Clerical Sexuality and Masculinity in Late Medieval England." In *Negotiating Clerical Identities: Priests, Monks, and Masculinity in the Middle Ages*, ed. Jennifer D. Thibodeaux, 159–81. New York: Palgrave Macmillan, 2010.

Wertheimer, Laura. "Children of Disorder: Clerical Parentage, Illegitimacy, and Reform in the Middle Ages." *Journal of the History of Sexuality* 15, no. 3 (2006): 382–407.

———. "Illegitimate Birth and the English Clergy, 1198–1348." *Journal of Medieval History* 31 (2005): 211–29.

Whitehead, Stephen M. *Men and Masculinities.* Oxford: Blackwell, 2002.

Woodruff, C. Eveleigh. "Some Early Visitation Rolls Preserved at Canterbury." *Archaeologica Cantiana* 32 (1917): 143–80.

INDEX

affinity (ties of), 26, 126, 127, 129, 129n8, 131, 140, 157, 292
archdeacons and canons with families, 34–35, 35n17, 144, 144n61
ascetic discipline of the priesthood, 9
Apostolic Penitentiary, 167–68, 214, 215, 254, 263, 264
authority, 5, 9, 12, 26, 27, 50, 83, 162, 174, 180, 195, 203, 214, 220, 224, 232, 233, 235, 239, 243, 244, 248, 249, 250, 258, 259
  ecclesiastical, 39, 63, 78, 87, 116, 158, 170, 248
  paternal and marital (i.e. patriarchal), 2, 17, 83, 104, 111, 113, 123, 163, 185, 187, 188, 190
  priestly, 2, 4, 5, 18, 21, 24, 26, 122, 162, 163, 170, 180, 188, 190, 192, 193, 194, 213, 223, 231, 232, 235, 236, 253, 255, 258, 260
  secular, 61, 152, 176, 222, 223, 226, 227, 230
  spiritual, 19, 190, 196, 248

benefice, 27, 32, 51, 53, 57, 71, 72, 98, 132, 135, 138, 147, 154, 156, 167, 168, 196, 212, 220, 236, 238, 239, 257
  land belonging to, 91, 97, 99, 129, 137, 147
  lucrative and prestigious, 87, 142, 144, 239
  obtaining and exchanging of, 132–34, 137–38, 139, 240
  poor, 144–45, 146, 146n73, 147, 151, 239, 243, 244
  rights attached to, 27, 145, 236, 253
  worth of, 137, 144–45, 145n65, 146, 155
Black Death (plague), 7, 29n2, 38, 60, 87, 109, 157, 254
buying homes and property for families, 33, 56, 74, 89, 93–94, 97–99, 154, 155, 156, 156n108

canon law, 2, 4, 8, 9, 10, 13, 14, 27, 32, 42, 52, 55, 63, 74, 76, 82, 94, 98, 128, 166, 168, 187, 257, 260, 262
Catalan Church, 11, 13, 15, 37, 55–64, 70, 71, 72, 79–80, 268
  diocese of Barcelona, 5, 12, 25, 37–38, 41, 56, 60, 62, 63, 70, 71, 86, 109, 110, 169, 170, 203, 204, 216, 233, 239, 244
  diocese of Girona, xiv, 5, 12, 25, 37, 38, 39, 40, 41, 56, 60, 62, 63, 69, 71, 86, 108, 109, 110, 146, 153, 169, 170, 203, 204, 216, 233, 239, 244
  diocese of Tortosa, 5, 14, 38, 38n25, 54, 56, 78, 203, 216n53, 219n62, 203
  diocese of Urgell, 5, 12, 25, 37, 38, 39, 41, 56, 61, 62, 63, 108n82, 109, 110, 203, 239
  diocese of Vic, 5, 12, 25, 37, 38, 41, 48, 56, 61, 62, 63, 108, 109, 110, 146, 153, 203, 218, 239
  ecclesiastical province of Tarragona, 5, 5n8, 11, 12, 54, 203, 204n13, 203, 206, 215, 216, 217, 268
  synods and synodal legislation, 12, 52, 53, 54n68, 55–57, 59–60, 63, 79, 80, 85, 98, 99, 100, 160–61, 169, 203, 205, 206, 216, 260
Catalan peasantry, 7, 49, 49, 50, 69, 82, 83, 109, 110, 124, 129, 130, 132n17, 138, 140, 142, 151, 153, 156, 162, 163, 164, 172, 185n72, 191, 196, 219
Catalunya:
  economy, 7–8, 27, 92, 147, 151, 239, 244, 246, 253
  maritime power, 7
  population, 110
  topography, 6–7
  urban cities, 7, 14
children of clergymen, 1, 10, 16, 20, 21, 25, 33, 40, 108–10, 116, 124
  daughters caring for their priestly fathers, 118, 119, 119n122

341

CPSIA information can be obtained
at www.ICGtesting.com
Printed in the USA
LVHW011037250322
714381LV00014B/453

9 781501 748424